A Feminist Reader in Early Cinema

A Camera Obscura book

A Feminist Reader in Early Cinema

EDITED BY JENNIFER M. BEAN AND DIANE NEGRA

Duke University Press   Durham & London   2002

© 2002 Duke University Press
All rights reserved

Designed by C. H. Westmoreland
Typeset in Granjon with Bodoni display
by Tseng Information Systems, Inc.
Library of Congress Cataloging-in-Publication Data
appear on the last printed page of this book.

An earlier version of Siobhan B. Somerville's essay "The Queer Career of Jim Crow: Racial and Sexual Transformation in *A Florida Enchantment*" appeared in her book *Queering the Color Line: Race and the Invention of Homosexuality in American Culture* (2000), published by Duke University Press.

An earlier version of Sumiko Higashi's essay "The New Woman and Consumer Culture: Cecil B. DeMille's Sex Comedies" appeared in her book *Cecil B. DeMille and American Culture: The Silent Era* (1994). It appears courtesy of University of California Press.

Gaylyn Studlar retains copyright to her essay "Oh 'Doll Divine': Mary Pickford, Masquerade, and the Pedophilic Gaze."

Mary Anne Doane's essay "Technology's Body: Cinematic Vision in Modernity" originally appeared in the journal *differences*. It appears courtesy of Indiana University Press.

Catherine Russell's essay "Parallax Historiography: The Flâneuse as Cyberfeminist" originally appeared in *Scope: An Online Journal of Film Studies* [http://www.nottingham.ac.uk/film/journal/]. It appears courtesy of the Institute of Film Studies, University of Nottingham.

Essays by Diane Negra, Jennifer M. Bean, Lucy Fischer, Gaylyn Studlar, and Zhang Zhen originally appeared in the journal *Camera Obscura*, Special Issue No. 48, "Early Women Stars," published January 2002 by Duke University Press.

Contents

Acknowledgments vii

Introduction: Toward a Feminist Historiography of Early Cinema
JENNIFER M. BEAN 1

I Reflecting Film Authorship

Circuits of Memory and History: *The Memoirs of Alice Guy-Blaché*
AMELIE HASTIE 29

Nazimova's Veils: *Salome* at the Intersection of Film Histories
PATRICIA WHITE 60

Of Cabbages and Authors JANE M. GAINES 88

Reevaluating Footnotes: Women Directors of the Silent Era
RADHA VATSAL 119

II Ways of Looking

The Gender of Empire: American Modernity, Masculinity, and Edison's War Actualities KRISTEN WHISSEL 141

Making Ends Meet: "Welfare Films" and the Politics of Consumption during the Progressive Era CONSTANCE BALIDES 166

Irma Vep, Vamp in the City: Mapping the Criminal Feminine in Early French Serials KRISTINE J. BUTLER 195

The Flapper Film: Comedy, Dance, and Jazz Age Kinaesthetics
LORI LANDAY 221

III Cultural Inversions

The Queer Career of Jim Crow: Racial and Sexual Transformation in *A Florida Enchantment* SIOBHAN B. SOMERVILLE 251

Taking Precautions, or Regulating Early Birth-Control Films
SHELLEY STAMP 270

The New Woman and Consumer Culture: Cecil B. DeMille's Sex Comedies SUMIKO HIGASHI 298

"So Real as to Seem Like Life Itself": The *Photoplay* Fiction of Adela Rogers St. Johns ANNE MOREY 333

IV Performing Bodies

Oh, "Doll Divine": Mary Pickford, Masquerade, and the Pedophilic Gaze GAYLYN STUDLAR 349

Immigrant Stardom in Imperial America: Pola Negri and the Problem of Typology DIANE NEGRA 374

Technologies of Early Stardom and the Extraordinary Body
JENNIFER M. BEAN 404

Femininity in Flight: Androgyny and Gynandry in Early Silent Italian Cinema ANGELA DALLE VACCHE 444

Greta Garbo and Silent Cinema: The Actress as Art Deco Icon
LUCY FISCHER 476

V The Problem with Periodization

An Amorous History of the Silver Screen: The Actress as Vernacular Embodiment in Early Chinese Film Culture ZHANG ZHEN 501

Technology's Body: Cinematic Vision in Modernity
MARY ANN DOANE 530

Parallax Historiography: The Flâneuse as Cyberfeminist
CATHERINE RUSSELL 552

Contributors 571

Index 575

Acknowledgments

We owe immeasurable thanks to Ken Wissoker, who supported this project from the first and who responded with timely wisdom to even the most mundane of our questions at every step of the way. The invitation to edit a special issue of *Camera Obscura* on "Early Women Stars" provided both the material basis and renewed inspiration for this volume; we are indebted to the *Camera Obscura* editorial collective, especially Patricia White, for affording us this opportunity. Our exchange with the *Camera Obscura* office was facilitated in no small way by the gracious and efficient efforts of Jeanne Scheper and by the editorial assistance of Emily Davis and Christy Cannariato.

Shelley McGinnis, Manasi Sapre, and Cristobal Borges at the University of North Texas provided research assistance during the life span of this project, and Frauke Plummer at the University of Washington coordinated editorial exchange across a number of continents with grace and good cheer. A University of North Texas College of Arts and Sciences Faculty Research Grant provided funding to facilitate a meeting for the editors at an early stage of planning. Gary Handwerk and Divisional Dean Michael Halleran at the University of Washington supplied generous material and inspirational support that sustained this project's development through the past three years and made its completion possible. For Jessica Burstein's editorial savvy and guidance, shared without hesitation, we are especially grateful.

That this volume would not have been possible without the expertise of its contributors is self-evident. Less apparent is the degree to which they responded with grace under pressure and sustained an unwavering commitment to the project at every turn. We could not have asked for a more energizing community with which to develop—and debate—the ideas presented here.

JENNIFER M. BEAN

Introduction

Toward a Feminist Historiography of Early Cinema

Feminism ... must resist the impulse to reproduce only what it thinks it already knows; it must challenge the compulsion to repeat. —Robyn Wiegman[1]

Historical coherence and grand narratives are now riddled not only by holes, gaps, and omissions in our historical *knowledge* that once we might have tried to cover over or fill in, but they are also riddled by the questions and investments of past and present *desire*. —Vivian Sobchack[2]

The early years of the twenty-first century are a critical period for feminist reflection on the cinema of the early twentieth century. The access to historical materials fostered by the digital age, the increased readiness for collaboration among the members of the Fédération Internationale des Archives du Film (FIAF), and the recent escalation in the public sphere of a qualitatively new interest in silent cinema has made visible the remarkable number of roles played by early women producers, directors, stars, and writers in the formation of the young industry. The rush to distribute videos featuring "First Movie Ladies" has been matched by a spate of cable-channel documentaries on women and early cinema.[3] The monthlong celebration of "Women Film Pioneers" on Turner Classic Movies in August 2000 is a notable signpost of this initiative, not only for the bolstered visibility of previously obscure early films to the general population, but also for the prominent position allotted to feminist scholars like Jane Gaines and Alison McMahan, who were included as introductory and research commentators, on prime-time television.[4] The merger of academic and public venues also shaped the festival at the American Museum of the Moving Image in May 2000, which featured the careers of Mabel Normand, Federica Maas, Nell Shipman, and Helen Gardner, as well as two groundbreaking international conferences on "Gender and Silent Cinema"—the first organized by Annette Förster and Eva Warth at Utrecht University in October 1999; the second organized by Amelie Hastie and Shelley Stamp at the University of California, Santa Cruz, in November 2001. We are witnessing an era fueled by the energies of a feminist film archaeological project that has only just begun to explore the array of prints previously assumed lost and the cultural documents previously understood as forgotten. It is an age of discovery in which the inaugural phases of cinematic novelty and narrative development—a period predating the consolidated monopoly of the major Hollywood studios, the rise of technicians' unions restricted to men, and the fiscal quandaries associated with the coming of sound technology—increasingly appear as rich terrain for assessing women's participation in the aesthetic, industrial, and cultural shape of the cinema.[5]

For contemporary film feminism, the excitement generated by these acts of recovery is inexorably bound to a series of questions concerning the production of historical and disciplinary knowledge. How might we resist the temptation to cast a nostalgic gaze at the past, to celebrate the early period as a comforting zone of protofeminist possibility? How can we assert the presence of female film pioneers without simply amalgamating a revised set of early cinema's finest hits, of remarkable "firsts," of isolated, explanatory contributions? How might the prominent sign of "woman" in the period, her role in not only the production but also the reception of early film, be taken up in terms beyond those of a gender paradigm that has never been comprehensive enough, never able to account for the production of whiteness or blackness—indeed of race of any kind—much less ethnicity, nationality, and the distinctions of class? These questions are not new to us, but they exert a new insistence as we rush forward to recover women's roles in the early industry. This project, in turn, cannot easily be disentangled from the perceived crisis in academic feminism. Vitiated by an ongoing public and institutional backlash, contemporary feminism has experienced a dispersal that some are ready to blame as a crisis of our own making. In its worst incarnation, the scenario of feminism's intellectual decline is cast as the story of a lost (female) object, betrayed by the critical interrogation of essentialism as well as the hostile advances of poststructuralist and performance studies.[6] The disciplinary predicament of what has sometimes been called a "postfeminist" moment is compounded in film studies by the alarm sounded over other lost objects; in this case film itself, a medium struggling for survival in a digital age that seems poised to herald the end of the age of analogue.[7] Viewed across the vanishing horizon of the sign "woman" and the medium "film," the impulse to excavate the equa-

Introduction

tion linking women and early cinema may seem suspect indeed: a dubious return to past guarantees.

Rather than abandon the urgency of our preservation and recovery agendas, this reader brings together the efforts of twenty individuals whose work collectively lays the ground, in both theoretical and historical terms, for a feminist account of early cinema. The historiographies and agendas gathered under this cover are animated by a self-critical, self-reflexive scrutiny that rejects any epistemological guarantee suggested by the past in favor of embracing its complexity and, in so doing, producing new knowledge and knowledge formations. Taken together, these essays demonstrate a strong commitment to archival research, merging analyses of film form with a wide array of documents that comprise the basis of our inherited film culture: written memoirs, fan magazines, audience studies, advertisements, and screenplays. All of the essays arise from the premise that mapping a history of women's engagements with early film means being willing to fully explore the range of sites in which women produced, consumed, and performed in the growing industry. It also means being willing to engage interdisciplinary frameworks; to bring the insights of postcolonial and racial studies, dance scholarship, literary analysis, philosophies of the body, modernist, and even postmodernist, debates to bear on the variables of gender and film. What emerges is a complex array of theories on the ontology, psychology, and epistemology of cinema in its relation to identity, history, and the aesthetic realm.

It is tempting to ascribe the impact of this volume in terms of a new generation of feminist film scholarship—an era heralded by radical breaks with established methodologies as well as with the canon of key films and figures most often imbued with explanatory power. Insofar as all the essays included here were written in the final years of the twentieth century, the connotations of a millennial awakening hold true. Yet the critical project of "looking back" that the reader engages encompasses, in important ways, the generative matrix of feminism's critical legacies from the heady 1970s. Feminists' historical work from the period may not be the first to come to mind, but we would be remiss in not noting the publication of Sumiko Higashi's *Virgins, Vamps, and Flappers,* with its typology of silent-era female stars and roles, or even Marjorie Rosen's *Popcorn Venus,* which circulated the names of Lois Weber, Anita Loos, and Frances Marion, among others. By the end of the decade Anthony Slide offered us *Early Women Directors,* and Patricia Erens's edited collection, *Sexual Stratagems,* printed materials on Esfir Shub and Alice Guy-Blaché.[8] Such accounts remain rich resources for contemporary revisions of the early period, but at the time of their re-

3

lease the appeal to history went largely unnoticed in academic circles. As we know, the 1970s was more fertile ground for those dedicated to psychoanalysis and political philosophy as a means of illuminating cinema's participation in the cultural construction of women. Methodologically this entailed a shift from the categorical scrutiny of individual careers and what is often called image studies to a focus on the metapsychology of the viewing process. The resultant apparatus, or "gaze" theory, proved especially useful to feminists for pinpointing the mechanisms through which mainstream cinema perpetuates social arrangements of power. In the process of illuminating the male-oriented address of film discourse, however, and repeatedly reading the systematic exclusion of the female subject from cinematic pleasures, feminists were alarmed to discover their work was becoming complicit with the system they had set out to critique. Writing in 1990, Mary Ann Doane drew attention to the deadlock ironically brought about by theory's highly critical stance toward historicism. As she put it, in order to investigate the psychical drama of the female spectator, apparatus theory "had to posit a vast synchrony of the cinema—the cinema happens all at once (as, precisely, an apparatus)."[9] Theory thus participated in producing an ahistorical, abstracted female subject: a generalizable Woman.

The temptation to invoke history as a way out of theory's conceptual dilemmas can never be an acceptable answer for film feminism. If the momentum building throughout the 1990s has driven home the imperative of historical methodologies, then these are historiographies catalyzed by questions of spectatorship, ideological coding, and cultural interpolation that persist from earlier conversations. Several contributions to this volume, for instance, relentlessly interrogate modalities of the gaze. Drawing on sources as diverse as imperial discourse, reformers' pamphlets, discussions of flânerie, and modern kinaesthetics, essays by Kristen Whissel, Constance Balides, Kristine Butler, and Lori Landay refuse the monolithic map of a psychoanalytic paradigm in favor of emphasizing the vicissitudes of historically distinct modes of pleasurable looking. Psychoanalysis itself appears as in need of historical revision, especially the suggestion that Freud's theories may be particularly apposite to analyses of cinema given the historical coincidence of their respective births. Rather than vaunting psychoanalysis as the "key to understanding the cinematic apparatus," as Linda Williams observes, it is imperative to situate Freud's interpretive models as "simply . . . another late-nineteenth-century discourse of sexuality, another apparatus for aligning socially produced sexual desires with oedipal and familial norms."[10] The question that lingers concerns the degree to which cinema and psychoanalysis become mutually reinforcing "mechanisms of

Introduction

power and pleasure" in the modern age.[11] The response that appears in this collection—pointedly in essays by Jennifer Bean, Angela Dalle Vacche, Zhang Zhen, and Mary Ann Doane—takes shape as a rigorous remapping of early-twentieth-century scientific and popular discussions concerning the function and formation of the human psyche. It was an era witnessing a shift from pathology understood as rooted in biological or genetic traits (as inherited), to a burgeoning apprehension of the ways in which psychic and social factors are necessarily interactive. Insofar as these new aspects of psychological life were engendered by the particularities of an urban-industrial modernity, then questions concerning bodily sensation, spatial-temporal geometries, and mechanical power take priority in ways that exceed the formulations of a Freudian paradigm. As a result of this inquiry, alternative models emerge for conceiving not only the cinema's production of gender and sexual difference, but also the very basis and terms by which we account for identity.

To this reader's impact on film feminism's theoretical traditions should be added its reorientation of the methodologies and categories espoused by historical film studies. In many ways this collection brings to fruition Tom Gunning's earlier observation that "much of the exciting new work being done in film history is being done by . . . scholars [who] have undertaken a rediscovery of women's experience of cinema which has led to a fundamental questioning of the established concerns of history and its dominant methods."[12] It would of course be a regrettable mistake to claim that feminists are alone in questioning film history's concerns and methods; the conversations gathered here owe much to a broader disciplinary surge of renewed interest in the silent era and to the ongoing efforts of scholars such as Gunning, Richard Abel, Charles Musser, and Thomas Elsaesser, among others. Running parallel to the advancement of knowledge generated by earlier feminist models, revisionist approaches to early cinema also reach back to the 1970s, stemming especially from the 1978 Brighton Conference, where the excitement of viewing previously forgotten films made between 1900 and 1906 initiated the dethronement of D. W. Griffith and the institutional framework of Hollywood as the twin monarchs of cinematic invention. Over the past decade two collections in particular stand out as challenges to conventional views of early film history: Thomas Elsaesser's *Early Cinema: Space, Frame, Narrative* and Richard Abel's *Silent Cinema*.[13] Taken together, these books demonstrate a developing commitment to the urgency of early cinema's archival agendas, to the recovery of fragile and erstwhile illegitimate prints, as well as to the promotion of a sophisticated reading practice concerned with the relationship between film texts and their social and industrial contexts. These discussions have had far-reaching implications, not the least of which is the undermining of teleological models of progress whereby the history of cinema is seen as advancing from an embryonic or infantile state in the early years toward its maturation in the adulthood of a classical, narrative system.

The present volume builds on the work of the new film history, yet the focus on gender as an analytic variable augurs an unmistakable shift in praxis. In some essays this shift appears through the choice of which films are considered important; in others it appears through the choice of what counts as evidence. The editors have elected to foreground a broader shift by reconceptualizing the historical and critical category known as early cinema to be somewhat congruent with the first thirty-five years of cinema. It should be clear that the choice to do so does not imply or infer homogeneity across this three-and-a-half-decade span. A projection viewed in a Paris café, a Berlin *Kientopp,* and a New York moving-picture palace, for instance, bear little resemblance to one another at the level of either technologies, constituencies, or semiotics. Then again, the textual differences between an inaugural phase dominated by attractions and actualities and a later period of narrative integration, or, even beyond that, the differences between an emergent classical style and a European avant-garde, present a constellation of radically heterogeneous film forms and styles. Briefly, then, the choice to bracket slightly more than three decades of cinema with the term "early" has little to do with intimating resemblance and similitude and everything to do with claiming dissonance and difference as, precisely, the early period's unifying trademark.

Our use of the category "early" strategically builds from the term's current ideological and methodological associations. Generally speaking, "early cinema" has come to refer to the years between 1895 and 1917, but its semantic status is far from a neutral chronological indicator. Vigorous debates over historical periodization in the silent era have gravitated toward the fin de siècle transition, or lack thereof, from a cinema ruled by attractions to one predominantly narrative in design. The focus of interest remains insistently on the turn of the century, where the hype over attractions has accentuated a film form potentially dominated by exhibitionism rather than voyeurism, by surprise rather than suspense, and by spectacle rather than story. The concept of attractions is, admittedly, seductive for feminists, especially insofar as it removes the cinema from the totalizing terms of a controlling and gendered gaze. Yet, as Judith Mayne observes, it behooves us to remain wary of any simple opposition between exhibitionism

Introduction

and voyeurism, especially when the promotion of the former as a mode of spectatorial pleasure elides gender as a category with "signifying authority" in the early years.[14] As essays by Kristen Whissel and Mary Ann Doane in this volume demonstrate, the negotiations between attractions and narrative in fin de siècle cinema may look quite different when our inquiry privileges the articulation of sexual and racial difference. At the same time, the dynamic intertextual reading method employed in these essays shares kinship with the ongoing revisionist efforts of early film historians. Where film studies' traditional bias toward narrative economy and the universalizing efficacy of film language once marked late-nineteenth- and turn-of-the-century cinema as a "primitive" period (guttural, subverbal, barbaric, unrefined), the new orientation in historical film scholarship has found in the early years a vital source for revisiting the epistemological ground of film language as an utterance significantly shaped by meaning-making processes situated "outside" the films themselves. It is this "reassessment and reclaiming of the archive," as Vicki Callahan puts it, that has the potential to "work in concert" with feminist efforts to "question and expand the kinds of historical materials investigated in understanding spectatorship."[15]

"Early cinema" thus broadly signifies not only a historical period but also, importantly, a critical category. Current use of the term emphatically underscores the medium's intimate ties to the practices of exhibition as well as its dependency on media intertexts and shared cultural mores—especially where the formal techniques of an early cinema are positioned as consistent with the shock, stimuli, and spiraling degrees of sensation associated with modern life. Such perspectives have encouraged a shift backward in our conceptualization of the period, so that the protean composition of early cinema is increasingly traced and conceived via its tangled roots in nineteenth-century modes of entertainment and cultural expression. Leo Charney and Vanessa Schwartz's collection, *Cinema and the Invention of Modern Life,* signposts this methodological and conceptual shift by focusing on the ways in which early film can be seen as a crucible in which modern debates over perception, referentiality, and the body combine, one commensurate with a wide range of urban-cultural practices: including but not limited to amusement parks, wax museums, public morgues, shopping arcades, and department stores.[16] Such pre- and paracinematic venues inflect our conception of a transforming public sphere that catered to—and constructed—female spectators in alternative, often antagonistic ways: a multivocal field of address from which early cinema draws and responds.

This reader embraces the complexity of this period shift backward and encourages a similar shift forward. Rudely put, the question is this: when, and why, might a feminist historiography delineate the end of the "early"?

The assumption that early cinema is entirely the affair of the late nineteenth and early twentieth centuries up until the year 1917 obviates our hard-won gains over traditional biases about film history. Baldly speaking, the 1917 signpost is extrapolated—or better yet *assumed*—from projects concerned with pinpointing the longevity of a stable classical system rather than those engaged by the potent irregularities of the early.[17] Perhaps more than any other publication, David Bordwell, Kristin Thompson, and Janet Staiger's *Classical Hollywood Cinema* has ensconced 1917 as the definitive moment when a dominant mode of cinematic storytelling finally and irrevocably coalesced, giving way to the production of a seamless fictional world understood as self-sufficient, capable of organizing viewer perception through an intricate manipulation of space and time without the messy interference of extrinsic signifying systems.[18] To uncritically adopt this period marker seriously limits new film historical discourse. Moreover, to the degree that the distinctive aesthetics and effects of the classical model are conceived as concomitant with the institutionalization of patriarchal structures of looking, and to the degree that this model's flourishing is said to parallel the incursion of Hollywood's hegemonic control over international markets, it is clear that contemporary feminism has much to gain by troubling the period break between early cinema and cinematic classicism, by refusing to toe the 1917 line. The point is not to replace one date with another and shift the moment of transition from 1917 to, say, 1922, or 1927, or 1934. The paucity of celluloid documents from the silent era, especially from the years following the advent of copyright protection for moving images in the early 1910s—thus ending the practice of photographic duplication of frames that bequeathed to us the wealth of a "paper print collection" for assessing cinema's first fifteen years—must obviate attempts to specify the date and time of an allegedly wholesale shift to a systematic application of classically defined formal means. The lack of textual evidence demands that we remain agnostic about the efficacy of rigidified period breaks. More importantly we must scrutinize the hermeneutics of our critical enterprise, since choices about historical demarcations raise important ideological and methodological questions for film feminism.

By choosing to employ "early cinema" as a term more or less coextensive with silent cinema, this collection insists on the longevity of heterogeneous, aleatory modes of address and reception across the whole of cinema's silent parts. It also reinstates the imperative of advancing interpretive models

Introduction

capable of juggling the intricacies of film form relative to the plurality of its adjacent discourses. This is in keeping with Miriam Hansen's call for an alternative history of film culture that would trace the paradox of female subjectivity in its relation to dominant cinema.[19] If it is true that dominant cinema's optical field increasingly limits its address to women by the late 1910s and early 1920s, then this collection teases out a far more hapless geometry shaping audience response to the image machine. Star personae, magazine fiction, art nouveau, medical histories, legal discourse, nativist debates, international expansion, racism, youth culture, literary production, modernity, the new woman: all are seen as intersecting film's textual systems in ways that complicate the assumed parity between the so-called rise of classicism and patriarchal systems of knowledge management. Seen in light of such a methodological incursion, systems appear not so systematic after all.

A focus on methodology, however, does not satisfactorily answer the question of terminology until its effects are understood in relation to the present moment. Choosing "early cinema" over "silent cinema" is designed to ameliorate tendencies that approach the pretalkie years as a period that drops out of view following the advance of synchronized sound technologies. "Early cinema" undoes the rigid mark of a technological invention and denotes the sense of an era in transition; it also suggests that the heterogeneous and dissonant models at work in the period before film found its voice, as well as the methodologies we develop to discuss them, may bear some relation to and have some impact on our current experience of "late" cinema. I echo Annette Kuhn and Jackie Stacey (echoing Alison Butler, echoing Walter Benjamin) in reminding us that "rather than being simply 'about the past' in any straightforward way, screen histories are of necessity concerned with past-present relations with a view to the future."[20] It is possible, for instance, to see Bordwell, Thompson, and Staiger's fix on 1917 as a direct response to the constraints and concerns of film studies in the 1980s. The burden of legitimizing film studies as an academic discipline in the 1960s and 1970s was met by an ardent attempt to secure, outline, and theorize *the* unique object of our inquiry. A hegemonic model of classicism, the term itself embedded in the ethos of legitimacy, was the result, replete with formalist diagrams, theories of psychological effects, and demarcated historical boundaries. "Classical" cinema's practices and products were never as stable as its critics would suggest, but while debates linger over the efficacy of those paradigms for assessing a period potentially circumscribed by the advent of the New Deal and the onset of the cold war, no one among us can deny that the past two decades have brought an epistemic shift in the object(s) of our study. Digital imaging technologies have altered film discourse and language in direct proportion to the palpable effects of electronic media technologies on the distribution and exhibition of visual culture. Part of the terror inspired by this sea change is the thought that film per se might disappear forever; part of the excitement is the inevitable rendering of erstwhile pat critical paradigms.

Feminists in particular have found sustenance for rethinking classical models of looking, especially the construct of a transcendent spectator, by drawing parallels between what appears to be a more heterogeneous, embodied, socially configured viewer mobilized in early cinema and late cinema. Some of the most generative scholarship from the 1990s has contemplated this ground, noticeably in projects undertaken by Hansen, Anne Friedberg, and Giuliana Bruno, whose work collectively constitutes what Catherine Russell in this volume calls a "parallax historiography."[21] For these writers the parallels between early and late realms focus most clearly around modes of film consumption, and terms such as "intertextuality," "interactivity," and "mobility" have begun to jockey for prominence in the traditional lineup of more usual suspects such as mastery, fantasy, and transcendence. The risk of a parallax historiography, as Russell notes, is that of producing a seductive feminist utopia that obliterates large-scale historical differences between radically discrete poles of the twentieth century. Only through a committed, abreactive approach to the matrices of the early cinema—a need to which this volume responds—will we find ourselves able to assess the ways in which a contemporary media culture may be characterized by similar expansions and possibilities as well as by similar constraints and repressive mechanisms.

The province of early cinema found here thus insists that our studies of the past must always be determined by present concerns and written with a self-conscious sense of our contingent temporality. Yet critically connected to the resignification of an early cinema is also the way we conceptualize and make relative the geographical and cultural coordinates of historical praxis. This means taking seriously Alison Butler's caveat that revisionist historiographies must engage the "politics of location." As she observes,

> it is precise to say that history takes *place*. The corollary would seem to be that the less film historians acknowledge their place, the more their work will be invaded by its concerns. The limit case of this will be those histories which assume the universality of either their object or their approach. These histories, produced in the West, will tend strongly to imperialism of one kind or another.[22]

Introduction

Butler's reservations about the locatedness (an awkward but useful neologism, I submit) of revisionist film histories are well taken. The cry for historical specificity in film studies is too easily, too often, blithely rendered as a corrective to the universalizing metanarratives posited by earlier semiotic and psychoanalytic-based reading theories. Many of its proponents remain blind to our disciplines' ongoing replication of a governing paradigm that reiterates and confirms Hollywood's "universal" position of economic power. The 1917 cusp is, once again, a case in point. There should be little doubt that trademarks characterizing any noticeable transition in film form at that time accrue in a geographically specific space: that of the United States and, to some degree, Western Europe. What might "early cinema" signify in the context of Eastern Europe, much less of Asia or Africa?

In the Chinese context, as Zhang Zhen notes in her essay here, "the term 'early cinema' (*zaoqi dianying*) serves loosely as a common reference to the cinema before 1949, when the Communists drove the Nationalists to the island of Taiwan and founded the People's Republic of China on the mainland." Zhang joins recent Chinese scholars in making "finer periodizations within that long 'early' period," and does so by placing the Shanghai industry between the 1910s and the 1930s in conversation with issues of gender and modernity that Western scholars have brought to bear on early Euro-American products. Although Zhang's essay remains the single project on non-Western cinemas found under this cover, the inclusion of Kristine Butler's look at early French serials and Angela Dalle Vacche's work on Italian diva films, as well as the national hyphens under scrutiny in Diane Negra's study of imported stars from Eastern Europe (such as Pola Negri) and Patricia White's excavation of a European avant-garde's cross-pollination with Hollywood in the work of Alla Nazimova, all mark this reader's interest in cross-cultural research. Much more work remains to be done in order to alter the geographical and cultural biases of our periodizing categories.[23] What seems clear on all fronts is that feminists must no longer work in national isolation from one another; only then can we begin to "make good," to follow Robyn Wiegman, "on academic feminism's longtime goal of transforming . . . the institution, its organization of knowledge, and the way in which we understand both the intellectual composition and possible histories of feminism itself."[24] As we work to ensure feminism's future as a multiply situated political enterprise, it may be that the vibrancy of early cinema's international lexicon provides the very substance and ground for developing critical models that traverse and interrogate nation-bound rubrics.

For all the salutary effects promised by this reader's use of the category early cinema, the flexibility stressed here is not without its problems. It is possible, for instance, to carry expansion too far, and so lose the legibility of "early" altogether. Would we dare to imagine a history written at the end of the twenty-first or even twenty-second century that refers to twentieth-century cinema as one extended moment of the "early"? Perhaps so, though such imaginings need occupy little of our time. The excessiveness of such an extreme case simply illustrates the point that period constructions are what David Perkins calls "necessary fictions" that, themselves, have a history, and that can be rewritten in a variety of ways, depending on what it is we seek to order and classify and why.[25] The choices we make have immediately felt effects, impacting not only the texts available (and deemed worthy) for study, but also the institutionalized contours of our course offerings, hiring decisions, graduate exams, book projects, professional organizations, and so on.[26] In favor of making apparent the particularity, discontinuity, and fluctuation of the materials and dates under study, this reader avoids writing the history of early cinema under the sign of unification. If doing so leaves this volume particularly vulnerable to the charge of indeterminate expansion, then a willing vulnerability may be the necessary position from which to galvanize the very powerful ideological move that underlies this enterprise: namely, a desire to puzzle over the necessity of period questions and implications without reinforcing their hold over our thinking.

A related danger to this reader's approach is that of methodological dispersion. As mentioned above, expanding the category early cinema means expanding the types of discourses and objects deemed relevant for study. By attending to these multiple arenas some might say we risk enforcing a depreciated "cultural studies" model quite capable of eclipsing the centrality and specificity of film as the province of our discipline. As Janet Bergstrom has noted, "'cultural studies' has come to be used so broadly that it can encompass almost any approach or subject matter" and "sometimes functions as a leveling device." The attending irony of this observation is that, at the very moment in which a "critical mass of scholars finally exists in adjacent academic fields," it has become increasingly difficult to sustain detailed investigations of the "depth" of cinematic and visual media.[27] This point should give us pause. Though Bergstrom does not clarify what forms of critical scrutiny may have turned shallow, her contention conspicuously follows a recounting of "the lasting significance" of founding film semioticians, including Jean-Louis Baudry, Therry Kuntzel, and Christian Metz, and highlights projects like Raymond Bellour's 115-page study of *North by Northwest,* "Le blocage symbolique," which she describes as a "magiste-

Introduction

rial demonstration of multilayered textual analysis."[28] The assumption is that the conjoining of ideological questions with detailed textual analyses so prevalent in the 1970s constitute—to indulge the metaphor—a depth-of-our-field that has since strayed out of focus. We return to this point momentarily, but first let us underline an important caution regarding the leveling effects of cultural studies models. The interdisciplinary configurations of current work on film carry with them the potential to decimate the (carefully allocated) measures whereby cinema, or film and video, or media programs have finally gained an institutional foothold. The effects of dispersal are manifest in the diminished presence and power of film journals that no longer focus, in Bergstrom's words, on "polemics or even issues in the way that they did in the 1970s and early 1980s" and that may increasingly appear in other institutionalized loci with especially dire repercussions for feminism.[29]

In order to engage these concerns, we must scrutinize that fundamental assumption behind Bergstrom's complaint and ask what we want to mean when we talk about depth in cinema and related media studies. If we are to prepare ourselves for the battles that must be waged in the name of departmental budgets and program allocations, then a definition of cinematic "depth" is imperative. The call for doing so must loudly disclaim a return to a methodology premised on the isolation of a single film as emblematizing the textual density of cinematic language. While the disciplinary and epistemological gains of earlier critical engagements with the structural configuration of film texts remain crucial to our intellectual history and to the heuristics we pose in our introductory classrooms, the very concept of cinematic depth in such models is a severely truncated and idealized version of film space, one unable to account for the wider psychical and semiotic landscape from which film viewing draws meaning. Nowhere is the deficiency of this model more apparent than in our encounters with early cinema in which the paucity of entire film cycles, the very state of cinema's textual remnants, mandates a shift to encompass and in fact build from a topographical epistemology of film's "deep" cultural space. Giuliana Bruno's recovery of Italian film pioneer Elvira Notari's career elegantly articulates the desirable dilemmas of "working on lacunae." As she puts it, an analysis determined to explain a "lost" film exposes the degree to which "texts in general are built on 'the second degree,'" grafted onto and situated within an intertextual field of citations and meaning. Confronted with the "ruined maps" of cinema's past, we can either retreat to the safety of film's textual guarantees—essentially resting on our canonical laurels—or innovate a "kinetic analytic" that, as Bruno observes, "parallels film's own visual topography."[30] Many of the essays that follow lead us on what Bruno (trailing Umberto Eco) calls "inferential walks" through cinema's past, enacting in their methodological mobility the very modes through which women have often experienced their relationship with cinema.[31] These maps not only provide new approaches to the historical category of early cinema, but also serve as cartographic realignments for the glorious ruins of our disciplinary terrain.

A Feminist Reader in Early Cinema is divided into five parts: "Reflecting Film Authorship," "Ways of Looking," "Cultural Inversions," "Performing Bodies," and "The Problem with Periodization." These sections have been chosen to foreground cinematic categories such as authorship, spectatorship, historical topicality, stardom, and periodicity. Across these latitudes, however, other equally significant social and cultural categories provide points of connection, shared points of reference that might readily function as alternative organizing frameworks. The new woman, for instance, appears in multiple guises, alternately garbed as childish tomboy, *garçonne*, athletic star, enigmatic vamp, languid diva, working girl, kinetic flapper, and primitive exotic—all in various national, economic, and even chronological forms. A section organized around the gestalt of modern womanhood would usefully illustrate the vectors of continuity and change in early-twentieth-century constructions of identity. Similarly, a section foregrounding the fears and fantasies associated with technological modernity and urban congestion, and the results of this incursion on the representation and perception of gender, would be equally possible and equally productive. The alternative organizational structures are, if not endless, then enticingly multiple, and we leave it to future readers to provide the new dialogues by which our discipline will be sounded.

Part I, "Reflecting Film Authorship," highlights the key roles played by women directors and producers in the international field of early cinema. The historical cast alone is impressive, totaling more than 120 women whose individual creative outputs, in cases like that of Alice Guy-Blaché, often amounted to hundreds of films. Rather than approach this list in a positivist manner, however, contributors here examine women's roles in early film production as a way of questioning prevailing theories of authorship. In "Circuits of Memory and History: *The Memoirs of Alice Guy-Blaché*," Amelie Hastie explores the relation between writing and filmmaking as two interrelated authorial modes. By synthesizing the extant remnants of Guy-Blaché's directorial career with her written memoirs (themselves an attempt to reconstruct history through recollective pro-

Introduction

cesses), Hastie at once proposes and demonstrates a radically different approach to authorship, one that encompasses the multiple media forms through which a film author's "voice" is produced and disseminated.

For Patricia White, the "queer" voice that vibrates across Alla Nazimova's role as writer, producer, performer, and de facto director of *Salome* (1922) provides an instance for admonishing our nostalgic desire to pinpoint the locus of authorship in early cinema. In "Nazimova's Veils: *Salome* at the Intersection of Film Histories," White reads the 1922 film as a palimpsest of aesthetic, historical, and signature trades: a lesbian film auteur borrows the *author*ity (and notoriety) of Oscar Wilde; a mass-cultural American film product absorbs the stylistic effects of a European avant-garde; a modern film star (known for her boyish good looks) plays a biblical priestess (known for her vamplike sexuality). Here, the metaphor of "veiling" emerges as a historiographical incursion employed to emphasize how particular aspects of authorship and aesthetics "appear or disappear under different critical gazes." The critical refusal to disrobe, disclose, or "unveil" a singular authorial body is shared by Jane Gaines, who argues in "Of Cabbages and Authors" that the project of recovering a film author is predicated on the fantasy of discovering an "analyzable subject" hidden behind or within the cinematic text. Even as Gaines refuses the politics and epistemology of such a fantasy, she is concerned with resuscitating those women whose films have been undervalued and overlooked. To this end her scrutiny of Guy-Blaché's *The Cabbage Fairy* (1896) commemorates the female presence in the production of early film while highlighting the contingency of what can too easily be construed as "individual" (humanistic) vision—illuminating, in turn, how that construction so often results from the antimaterialist desire to detach film language from the very machines that produce it.

These opening essays make clear that the particularities of historical evidence—including, ironically, a lack thereof—in early cinema demand that we question what we mean by the category of director/author. In "Re-evaluating Footnotes: Women Directors of the Silent Era," Radha Vatsal turns this question into one of scholarly praxis, arguing that the project of recovering previously marginalized figures and films demands that we also recover and reconstruct the marginalized form of our research and writing: that of the "footnote." Vatsal underscores the ontological frailty of early film prints; every print has a history, she notes, often with differing credit sequences and just as often lacking credit listings per se. Then again, film prints associated with or attributed to numerous female pioneers have disappeared altogether, leaving us to trace the vestiges left in written and other visual sources that, themselves, occasion epistemological dispute. Concluding with a case study of her "preliminary research" on the elusive producer/director/writer Madeline Brandeis, Vatsal's deconstructive approach to the veracity of women film pioneers paradoxically acts as a challenge to feminist scholars to trouble the scholarly fetish for the armored argument, to make our supporting marginalia a site for tracking the vicissitudes of knowledge on which our central claims inevitably depend.

Part II of the reader, "Ways of Looking," turns from questions of authorship to questions of spectatorship. At issue in each essay gathered here are the effects of moving images on what might be called a historical spectator. Taken together, the essays map radically distinct models of looking. Even so, the vitality of this section emerges from a shared methodological approach that conjoins readings of film form with readings of adjacent textual forms. The turn toward historical accounts and materials need not deter us, these analyses show, from reflecting on broader theorizations about the effects of moving images on subjectivity.

Kristen Whissel's "The Gender of Empire: American Modernity, Masculinity, and Edison's War Actualities" opens this section with a detailed reading of an 1898 war film series produced by the Edison Manufacturing Company. Whissel demonstrates that Spanish-American War actualities were coextensive with an imperial ideology that sought to discipline and produce an especially virile form of national masculinity at the turn of the century. By reading early films alongside their accompanying catalog descriptions, Whissel argues that Edison's actualities elaborated a coherent narrative discourse, replete with a structuring point of view, that promoted spectacles of controlled white masculinity. Ironically, as Whissel points out, this optical field was constructed at the expense of "new" forms of womanhood, as well as African American masculinity, but nonetheless can be seen addressing female spectators (though specifically not black viewers) as an emergent constituent of the filmgoing public. The strategies of a disciplinary gaze similarly resonate in Constance Balides's investigation. In "Making Ends Meet: 'Welfare Films' and the Politics of Consumption during the Progressive Era," Balides argues that films like *The Cup of Life* (1915) and *Shoes* (1916) are characterized by textual strategies that place the spectator in the position of reformer in relation to the dilemma of a modern lifestyle associated with urbanization, consumerism, and heterosexual amusements. The concept of controlled consumption is crucial here. For Balides, cinema's textual strategies rearticulate reformers' studies and trade union leaders' rhetoric about consumption and working-class women, thus creating a shared perspectival field that sub-

Introduction

jected women wage earners to "normative definitions of what it meant to be a consumer." Ultimately, Balides offers both an analysis of the "narrator systems" at work in several overlooked films from the 1910s as well as a caution to feminists that broad claims about women's mobility in relation to the rise of consumerism come at the cost of locally produced meanings of terms like "consumer" and "consumption."

Recent accounts of women's visual and physical mobility in early-twentieth-century urban centers—often condensed in the figure of the alleged flâneuse—are further complicated by Kristine Butler's reading of Louis Feuillade's *Les Vampires* (1915). In "Irma Vep, Vamp in the City: Mapping the Criminal Feminine in Early French Serials," Butler underscores *Les Vampires*'s complex narrative, which obsessively circulates around the figure of the female criminal, Irma Vep, whom Butler describes as an "uncanny *tache*," a stain on the screen that motivates the detective work of the protagonist, Philippe Guérande, as well as the deciphering work of the spectator. To the degree that Irma Vep is ultimately contained or made legible, *Les Vampires* capitalizes on a conservative discourse of female deviance and fear of the moral decadence of the city. According to Butler, however, the serial's ultimate resolution of the feminine enigma is simply not comprehensive enough to undermine the visual pleasures associated with female empowerment and feminine scopophilic desire activated across the whole of the weekly episodes by Irma Vep's daring exploits. Butler's analysis, as a result, opens onto a theoretical model that articulates the female both as subject and as object. This model of possibility is also explored in Lori Landay's essay, "The Flapper Film: Comedy, Dance, and Jazz Age Kinaesthetics." Here, Landay shifts the terrain of analysis back to American film products, specifically to a group of 1920s films featuring flapper personalities Joan Crawford, Colleen Moore, and Clara Bow. It is true, Landay notes, that the construction of the flapper persona in these films can be viewed as an attempt to encourage women's self-objectification through the narcissistic mirror of the screen. The weight of Landay's analysis, however, argues for the coextensive construction of a "ludic embodiment of femininity that transcends the limited subjectivity of self-commodification, and encourages the flapper spectator to imagine and emulate a playful subjectivity that is not simply enslaved to commodity culture." The dizzying mobility that Landay attributes to flapper femininity connects to other modern forms of unrestrained bodily movement—especially the kinetic and individualistic gesticulations of the Jazz Age Charleston, the black bottom, and the turkey trot. While acknowledging the symbolic import of dance in the films under discussion, Landay's analyis centers its inquiry through close readings of the flapper girl's mobile modes of looking: her eyes that comically cross, wink, blink, or, alternately, measure in full the (male) object of her desire.

It may be a truism to claim that any attempt to account for the nascent years of narrative cinema must acknowledge the ways in which the young industry protested its respectability, countering accusations of depravity and immorality. The sense that this protest resulted in either a totalizing cooptation or an equally coherent dissidence fails to take into account historical vicissitude. As we see in part III, "Cultural Inversions," the industry's bid for greater respectability induced more rather than less complex practices and policies, particularly in the address to and representation of women. For both Shelley Stamp and Siobhan B. Somerville, the treatment of controversial subject matter such as birth control, abortion, and female "inversion" by directors whose reputations were associated with high-quality feature films and middle-class mores are indicative of the period's contradictory strategies.

In Stamp's essay, "Taking Precautions, or Regulating Early Birth-Control Films," the 1916–1917 debates surrounding films like *The Hand That Rocks the Cradle* and *Where Are My Children?* become source studies for tracing the knotty relations in which middle-class women encountered the use of film as a technology for educating the public on contraception. Stamp's analysis illustrates how newly instituted censorship policies ignited battles over cinema's status as an educational versus entertainment medium; as such, the commercial viability of birth control films altered radically depending less on what was said than how it was represented.

In "The Queer Career of Jim Crow: Racial and Sexual Transformation in *A Florida Enchantment*," Somerville's analysis of the 1914 Vitagraph film complicates matters further. In this "conventional" form of comedy (relative, that is, to slapstick antics), the titillating expansion of sexual possibilities for a white middle-class female protagonist trades on the compression and erasure of black female identity. As Somerville notes, it is unlikely that the audience that enjoyed such genteel comedies in the 1910s would have questioned the film's logic of race and racial sexuality. It is precisely that silence which Somerville takes up as a site of scrutiny, a reflection of "deep cultural anxieties" attending the "emergence of lesbian and gay identities and an increasingly racially segregated culture."

What emerges most forcefully from the essays that open part III is an understanding of the complex negotiations in which a series of ostensibly structuring binaries—old/new, modernity/tradition, female/male, white/

Introduction

black, highbrow/lowbrow — are terms of mediation rather than static positions. Sumiko Higashi thus approaches the period as a heuristic for contemporary feminists who might seize on representations of female social and sexual liberation as an unmediated fantasy of historical possibility. In "The New Woman and Consumer Culture: Cecil B. DeMille's Sex Comedies," Higashi's analysis of late 1910s and early 1920s comedies about divorce and remarriage offers, instead, a cautionary note, asking us to approach incarnations of the new woman in these films as an alluring mirage. Higashi engages DeMille's new woman as a figure increasingly open to objectification by a male gaze, a conservative momentum intimately bound up with the conventions of consumer culture that led women to gaze in narcissistic rapture at their fashion-conscious "self-made" reflections.

The section's opening survey of film representations is complemented by the work of Anne Morey, who closes part III with a focus on the textual mechanisms of the fan magazine. That the fan magazine develops in the 1920s as a prosthetic mouthpiece for the industry's project of maintaining respectability is well known. Indeed it was the policy of magazines like *Photoplay* to avoid discussions of scandal and represent Hollywood as a "sane" community. In "'So Real as to Seem Like Life Itself': The *Photoplay* Fiction of Adela Rogers St. Johns," however, Morey argues that magazine serial fiction about Hollywood — especially that of one of its main female producers during the 1920s — tells a different story. As she puts it, "serial fiction allowed the commentator a freer hand in the frank depiction of personalities and situations," precisely because it was presented as fiction. Morey usefully complicates the conventional view that fan magazines served simply as propagandistic devices for Hollywood, drawing our attention to important lapses in the discursive parity of film and film culture.

Part IV, "Performing Bodies," concentrates on the discourse and various venues that synchronically mobilized the complex semiotics of film stardom. Given Mary Pickford's long-standing position in both critical and cultural memories as an American national icon of the silent era and figure of demure and diminutive femininity, this section opens with Gaylyn Studlar's scrutiny of the Pickford persona. Drawing from advertising, publicity, fan responses, critical reviews, and Pickford films, Studlar's essay, "Oh, 'Doll Divine': Mary Pickford, Masquerade, and the Pedophilic Gaze," uncovers a youthful femininity constructed for what she calls, as her title suggests, a "pedophilic gaze." Studlar is careful to clarify that her use of this volatile term is not meant to suggest men's sexual interest in children, but rather to model a fetishistic fascination with a female figure that is safely distanced from the threatening adulthood and agency putatively granted to women in the period.

If Pickford exemplifies the most visible incarnation of the reification of girlishness, the structuring terms of femininity in the representational environment of Hollywood in the 1920s necessitated the invention of other stars associated with a deadly womanliness. Early ethnic stars were also highly functional in America's national imaginary, but in quite different ways from the canonization of Pickford. In "Immigrant Stardom in Imperial America: Pola Negri and the Problem of Typology," Diane Negra provides a case study of the probationary whiteness and troublesome femininity of the Polish-born film star who was Hollywood's first celebrated import, tracking Paramount's efforts to Americanize the ethnic "vamp" whose femininity was consistently defined as serious, sexual, and fully adult. She argues that Negri's "failure" to be Americanized became "proof" that residual anxieties about the assimilatability of new immigrants were, in fact, legitimate. Taken together, the essays by Studlar and Negra provide a sharp contrast between two very differently nationalized bodies as well as a historical sketch of Hollywood's tendency to embrace white American girls while expunging ethnic others.

The focus on the status of the body as providing a set of terms—at once enabling and inexorable—continues with the section's subsequent essays, which argue that the modalities of early stardom cannot be conceived outside the context of modernity's obsessions with the body's materiality. In "Technologies of Early Stardom and the Extraordinary Body," I place Pearl White and other action-oriented female celebrities of the 1910s at the center of an emergent star system in America. Flaunting views of potential catastrophe and narrowly avoided disaster "behind the scenes," the machinery of stardom promotes a phenomenology of performance founded on the concepts of improvisation and unpredictability—the terms of a "realness" set in opposition to the continuity and regulation increasingly afforded by cinema's mechanistic base. My interest in the "revised bodies" of American women stars intersects with Angela Dalle Vacche's work on early Italian divas like Lyda Borelli and muscle-bound "amazons of the air" such as Astrea, Linda Albertini, Emilie Samson, and Gisaliana Doria. In "Femininity in Flight: Androgyny and Gynandry in Early Silent Italian Cinema," Dalle Vacche scrutinizes Italian celebrities of the 1910s whose personae and performances enact the fantasies of a weightless, airborne, and decidedly modern physicality. The metaphoric use of the airplane and

Introduction

the curvilinear arabesque of flight patterns are well known in the iconography of art nouveau, but Dalle Vacche links this aesthetic system with a particular performative style that hinges on women's fantasies of gender and class transcendence. The rhyme between the modern and the nouveau anticipates Lucy Fischer's reading of Greta Garbo's figuration in a series of American film melodramas that employ the art deco aesthetic: *The Torrent* (1925), *Wild Orchids* (1928), *The Kiss* (1929), and *The Single Standard* (1929). In "Greta Garbo and Silent Cinema: The Actress as Art Deco Icon," Fischer shows how elements of mise-en-scène — costuming, sets, decor — as well as narrative discourse in these films, construct an isomorphic relation between Garbo's rise to stardom and cultural fascination with the glittery, glamorous, exotic surfaces of the *style moderne*. Garbo's association with the deco-style works in tandem with the iconographic significance of Garbo as an independent new woman — a female as dangerously avant-garde as the stylistic domain she inhabits.

Part V, "The Problem with Periodization," focuses directly on the issue of early cinema's boundary distinctions and how such delineations may no longer hold in the context of feminist historiographical inquiry. In one fashion or another, each of the essays tackles the most rigid of period lines: that which marks the "end" of the silent era in the late 1920s, the point at which the industry changes to technologies of producing and exhibiting synchronized sound. Zhang Zhen's "*An Amorous History of the Silver Screen:* The Actress as Vernacular Embodiment in Early Chinese Film Culture" engages textual analysis of a self-referential docudrama about the history of early Shanghai cinema. Notable as one of nine silent films produced by the Mingxing studio in 1931, *An Amorous History of the Silver Screen* is a nodal point through which the explosive transitions in the Chinese industry of the early 1930s as well as a history of Chinese women's relationship to cinema (as both performers and spectators) can be read. Significantly, Zhang's analysis promotes the specificity of what an early cinema and an early film culture might look like in the Chinese context. Her account employs a comparativist lens that alerts us to the unwitting parallels as well as the striking unevenness between the history she traces and a cinematic modernity alternately developing in the Euro-American context. At the center of this reading is the female screen actress and her counterpart — the woman in the theater — whom Zhang understands as both newly liberated and newly commodified through film technologies. Zhang's assessment of this ambivalence resonates with many of the analyses of modern femininity that appear elsewhere in this reader, but her insights into these shared points of reference reminds us that the act of unbinding one's feet, for instance, and that of shortening one's skirt remain discrete material, political, and epistemological acts.

The critical move to "look back" similarly informs Mary Ann Doane's essay, "Technology's Body: Cinematic Vision in Modernity," in which a Hollywood-produced "classical" film—*Golddiggers of 1935*—appears as an index of, and response to, cultural, philosophical, and cinematic discourses in the first two decades of the twentieth century. Doane explores the cultural anxieties induced by technological modernity, particularly those attendant on its accelerated temporality: shock, trauma, and perceptual disorientation. Within this constellation of effects early cinema functions as a compensatory prosthesis for the modern subject by increasingly distancing the (male) spectator from the aggressive impact of technology, an effect achieved through a "technically intricate manipulation of space" that takes as its "principal content" the spectacle of the female body. The literally nerve-racking effects of technologically induced sensation are, according to Doane, countered by cinema's ability to project that aggression onto the female body. She traces the development of this prosthetic apparatus from early one-shot films that fix a single stare at the female figure through the more complex spatial arrangements in Busby Berkeley's musicals, thus arguing for a visual logic that transcends the fractious transformation to sound and that offers a conceptual model capable of addressing a wide range of filmic effects.

If the two essays that open this section establish the terms by which histories of early cinema impact our assessments of later modes, the final essay, by Catherine Russell, "Parallax Historiography: The Flâneuse as Cyberfeminist," takes up the subject in earnest. Russell's work draws our attention to a dialogue that scholars such as Miriam Hansen, Anne Friedberg, and Giuliana Bruno have initiated, and that Russell terms "parallax historiography." Her useful neologism illuminates an emergent mode of historiographical reflection that recovers the radical changes that marked early cinema to better understand those that have transformed our own cinema over the past two decades. While "parallax" denotes the concept of parallelism, it also insists on perspectivism; indeed, questioning contemporary feminism's "ways of looking" at early cinema is at the heart of Russell's project. She makes clear that the "virtual, mobile" gaze increasingly attributed to female spectators in early and late forms of cinematic consumption may also reflexively function as a model for the methodologies and sight lines of contemporary feminist practice. The ability to recognize our own ideological reflections in the mirror of our analyses may be the most pro-

Introduction

ductive enactment of Laura Mulvey's call for the "passionate detachment" that film feminism has long sought to achieve.

While cognizant of the risks of representation, the reader—and this introduction—thus concludes with a call for the delicate balance between ideological investment and historical scrutiny, a balance between recognition and attachment, a project that we present to the readers as at once complete and gestural. In doing so, we trust this collection will demonstrate the imperative of continuing feminists' self-reflexive intervention in the recovery and consideration of early cinema's multiple histories—a project animated, after all, by the desire to assess and intervene in our own present "period" of critical experimental, and representational flux.

Notes

1 Robyn Wiegman, "What Ails Feminist Criticism? A Second Opinion," *Critical Inquiry* 25 (winter 1999): 371.
2 Vivian Sobchack, "What Is Film History?, or, The Riddle of the Sphinxes," in *Reinventing Film Studies,* ed. Christine Gledhill and Linda Williams (New York: Oxford University Press, 2000), 303–304.
3 I borrow the allusion from Kino International Video's collection title: "First Ladies: Early Women Filmmakers, 1915–1925." Released in September 2000, this collection makes available previously obscure copies of films by Lois Weber, Cleo Madison, Alice Guy-Blaché, Ruth Ann Baldwin, and Dorothy Davenport Reid; it is complemented by Milestone Film and Video's simultaneous release of the "Women of Cinema—The Filmmakers" series, which includes titles by Nell Shipman and Frances Marion. Of the cable-channel documentaries now available on women and early cinema, see in particular *Reel Models: The Women of Early Film* (produced by Sue and Chris Koch), which aired on American Movie Classics on 30 May 2000, and again on 1 August 2000.
4 The Turner Classic Movies series resulted largely from the efforts of the Women Film Pioneers Project, based at Duke University, directed by Jane Gaines and coordinated by Radha Vatsal (initially by Jennifer Parchesky). Throughout the August 2000 series Gaines provided introductory commentaries on the films and discussed the roles of women directors and producers in the early period. Alison McMahan appeared in the series as a research specialist on Alice Guy-Blaché in *The Lost Garden: The Life and Cinema of Alice Guy-Blaché* (originally produced as *Le jardin oublié: La vie et oeuvre d'Alice Guy-Blaché,* by Marquise Lepage for the National Film Board of Canada, 1995).
5 Kay Armatage lists a similar constellation of historical effects that might explain the drastic reduction in women's directorial efforts following the advent

of sound technologies. At the same time, Armatage usefully reminds us that "it would be foolish to argue that [silent] cinema was anything like a 'free zone' for women" but, at least, it "had not yet begun to effect the deliberate exclusion of women found in the other more established arts such as poetry, music, and painting." Armatage, "Nell Shipman: A Case of Heroic Femininity," in *Feminisms in the Cinema,* ed. Laura Pietropaolo and Ada Testaferri (Bloomington: Indiana University Press, 1995), 127.

6 By far the most vitriolic and lamentable articulation of such a perspective, one written from a position self-professed as feminism, is Susan Gubar's "What Ails Feminist Criticism?," *Critical Inquiry* 24 (summer 1998): 878–902. Robyn Wiegman's response to Gubar, cited above, should be applauded as a healthy repudiation of Gubar's complaints and ignominious concerns.

7 For a thoughtful discussion of what it may mean to talk about the "end of cinema," and how the post-analogue era forces new conceptualizations of film history, see Anne Friedberg, "The End of Cinema: Multimedia and Technological Change," in *Reinventing Film Studies,* 438–452.

8 Sumiko Higashi, *Virgins, Vamps, and Flappers: The American Silent Movie Heroine* (St. Albans, Vt.: Eden Press Women's Publications, 1978); Marjorie Rosen, *Popcorn Venus: Women, Movies, and the American Dream* (New York: Avon Books, 1973); Anthony Slide, *Early Women Directors* (New York: Da Capo Press, 1977); Patricia Erens, ed., *Sexual Stratagems: The World of Women in Film* (New York: Horizon Press, 1979). I am grateful to Jane Gaines for reminding me of this earlier work on the period.

9 Mary Ann Doane, "Remembering Women: Psychical and Historical Constructions in Film Theory," in *Psychoanalysis and Cinema,* ed. E. Ann Kaplan (New York: Routledge, 1990), 48.

10 Linda Williams, *Hard Core: Power, Pleasure, and the Frenzy of the Visible* (Berkeley: University of California Press, 1989), 46.

11 Ibid.

12 Tom Gunning, "Film History and Film Analysis: The Individual Film in the Course of Time," *Wide Angle* 12, 3 (1990): 14.

13 Thomas Elsaesser, ed., *Early Cinema: Space, Frame, Narrative* (London: British Film Institute, 1990); Richard Abel, ed., *Silent Cinema* (New Brunswick: Rutgers University Press, 1996).

14 Judith Mayne, *The Woman at the Keyhole: Feminism and Women's Cinema* (Bloomington: Indiana University Press, 1990), 166.

15 See Vicki Callahan, "Screening Musidora: Inscribing Indeterminacy in Film History," *Camera Obscura* 48 (2002): 61.

16 Leo Charney and Vanessa R. Schwartz, eds., *Cinema and the Invention of Modern Life* (Berkeley: University of California Press, 1995).

17 For Tom Gunning, whose groundbreaking work introduced the concept of attractions, cinema's emphasis on "display rather than storytelling" predominates up until or around the nickelodeon boom (1905–1909). Gunning is careful to note that "attractions," per se, "should not be taken as a monolithic definition of early cinema," but rather seen as an integral part of a complex textual

Introduction

fabric that has not yet hypostasized into a classical paradigm. Gunning is just as careful to avoid pinpointing the date of a wholesale transition, saying most simply that "early cinema" is a term that "forms a binary opposition with the narrative form of classical cinema." Nonetheless, in Thomas Elsaesser's influential volume, conspicuously titled *Early Cinema: Space, Frame, Narrative,* the life span of the period is carefully etched as the years between 1895 and 1917. See Gunning, " 'Now You See It, Now You Don't': The Temporality of the Cinema of Attractions," in *Silent Cinema,* ed. Abel, 73.

18 David Bordwell, Kristin Thompson, and Janet Staiger, *The Classical Hollywood Cinema: Film Style and Mode of Production to 1960* (London: Routledge and Kegan Paul, 1985).

19 See in particular Miriam Hansen, "Adventures of Goldilocks: Spectatorship, Consumerism, and Public Life," *Camera Obscura* 22 (1990): 51–72.

20 Annette Kuhn and Jackie Stacey, "Screen Histories: Introduction," in *Screen Histories: A Screen Reader,* ed. Kuhn and Stacey (Oxford: Clarendon Press, 1998), 9.

21 Respectively Miriam Hansen, *Babel and Babylon: Spectatorship in American Silent Film* (Cambridge: Harvard University Press, 1991); Anne Friedberg, *Window Shopping: Cinema and the Postmodern* (Berkeley: University of California Press, 1993); and Giuliana Bruno, *Streetwalking on a Ruined Map: Cultural Theory and the City Films of Elvira Notari* (Princeton: Princeton University Press, 1993).

22 Alison Butler, "New Film Histories and the Politics of Location," *Screen* 33, 4 (winter 1992): 425.

23 Feminism's future endeavors in this direction have the capacity to build from the remarkable energy of a large body of scholars, curators, and archivists whose stake in recovering and preserving silent-era cinema has mobilized a conversation of international proportions unprecedented in other areas of film studies. Though primarily devoted to the study of cinema prior to World War I, the flourishing of DOMITOR (the International Society for the Study of Early Cinema, formed in 1989) clearly marks this distinction, as do the recent activities of the FIAF, the Amsterdam Workshops held at the Nederlands Filmmuseum since 1994, and the prolific networking found at the annual Giornate del Cinema Muto. Elsewhere emergent digital media technologies have aided efforts to make erstwhile invisible or scattered national collections of early films more widely available. Yuri Tsivian's bilingual CD-ROM, *Immaterial Bodies: Cultural Anatomy of Early Russian Films* (1999), as well as Matsuda Film Productions' release of the *Masterpieces of Japanese Silent Cinema* DVD (2000), which includes scenes from forty-five films presented by benshi narrators, exemplify such advances.

24 Wiegman, "What Ails Feminist Criticism?", 376.

25 David Perkins, *Is Literary History Possible?* (Baltimore: Johns Hopkins University Press, 1992), 64. I would like to thank Marshall Brown for drawing my attention to Perkins' study, and for organizing the *Modern Language Quarterly* symposium on periodization in literary studies at the University of Washing-

ton (spring 2001). Both sources were invaluable aids for reflecting on the questions formulated in this introduction; a reminder that the issues we confront when writing film history are fruitfully thought in relation to debates taking place in surrounding disciplines. The papers presented at the spring event, including Brown's provocative introduction "Periods and Resistances," are now collected in a special issue of *Modern Language Quarterly* 62:4 (December 2001).

26 I have adapted this list from Robert J. Griffin's "A Critique of Romantic Periodization," in *The Challenge of Periodization: Old Paradigms and New Perspectives,* ed. Lawrence Besserman (New York: Garland Publishing, Inc. 1996), 143.

27 Janet Bergstrom, "Introduction: Parallel Lines," in her edited collection *Endless Night: Cinema and Psychoanalysis, Parallel Histories* (Berkeley: University of California Press, 1999), 4.

28 Ibid., 3.

29 Ibid., 4.

30 Bruno, *Streetwalking,* 4.

31 Ibid., 3.

Reflecting Film Authorship **I**

AMELIE HASTIE

Circuits of Memory and History

The Memoirs of Alice Guy-Blaché

But for all that I now knew that I was not in any of the houses of which the ignorance of the waking moment had, in a flash, if not presented me with a distinct picture, at least persuaded me of the possible presence, my memory had been set in motion; as a rule I did not attempt to go to sleep again at once, but used to spend the greater part of the night recalling our life in the old days at Combray with my great-aunt, at Balbec, Paris, Doncières, Venice, and the rest; remembering again all the places and people I had known, what I had actually seen of them, and what others had told me. —Marcel Proust

Repeating, Remembering

The majority of the work concerning the world's first woman filmmaker, Alice Guy-Blaché, has been produced under the rubric of remembering her: writings and films about her seek to recollect and retrieve her lost work and her "lost" place in history. For instance, one of the first essays to initiate some revived interest in Guy-Blaché, by film historian Francis Lacassin, is titled "Out of Oblivion: Alice Guy-Blaché." In this short piece, printed in *Sight and Sound* in 1971, Lacassin declares: "Inaugurated in the prehistoric period and over before the history of the cinema was born, Alice Guy's career on both sides of the Atlantic has been either forgotten or attributed to other people."[1] Gerald Peary's "Czarina of the Silent Screen: Solax's Alice Blaché," originally published in the *Velvet Light Trap* in 1974, opens similarly: "Look through Rotha or Jacobs or Knight or any of the standard histories of the cinema and you will not find any reference to the existence of Alice Guy-Blaché, though she directed approximately 270 films in the early silent era."[2] In fact, she was responsible for the production of more than seven hundred films, most of which have also disappeared.

Moreover, as Peary's above statement illustrates, the breadth of Guy-Blaché's cinematic output is often contrasted in those works that lament her "disappearance" from history. So, in an open statement concerning "Woman and the Formal Film," issued in 1979, a group of feminist filmmakers and scholars make the following proclamation: "Alice Guy is not represented in 'Film as Film' [a British film journal] and has scarcely been recognized anywhere. She was actively involved in film-making at the turn of the century, experimenting with narrative structures and the use of sound with film, but has long been forgotten by historians. Why are her films forgotten while those of Lumière and Méliès are used as standard texts?"[3] They then offer a general summons to women to fill such gaps in film history.[4] Other works stress the fact that no obituary appeared on Guy-Blaché's death in 1968 despite her tremendous labor.[5] Finally, a 1996 documentary about the early filmmaker, *The Lost Garden: The Life and Cinema of Alice Guy-Blaché* (dir. Marquise Lepage), comments on and corrects this lack of obituary. It ends with a printed coda that appears over an image of her gravestone in New Jersey: "Although she had been decorated by the French government and inducted into the Legion of Honour for her pioneering work in silent pictures, and went on to write, direct, and produce hundreds of films, becoming one of the most celebrated filmmakers in the early days of American cinema, Alice Guy-Blaché's contribution to the art of filmmaking was totally forgotten."

These concurrent losses — of films and position in history — are not necessarily coincidences. Indeed, I would contend that the loss of Guy-Blaché's place in history largely resulted from the loss of her films. That is, a primary reason why her contribution was "forgotten" is because most of the films she made were not preserved, or centrally archived, at the time of their production.[6] Those histories that do exist usually note this lack of availability of her films. At the same time, in their repeated emphases that Guy-Blaché's work and life have been forgotten, each of the above works attempts to correct this resultant historical amnesia: each strives to remember Guy-Blaché. They do so especially through her writings and the writings of others. In this essay, I consider the peculiarities of the construction of Guy-Blaché's history by bringing together written and cinematic forms. What, I ask, might we glean about film history and cinematic form through an analysis of words? Conversely, how might we read these words through film histories and theories of film form? These questions are particularly relevant

Circuits of Memory and History

in a study of a figure like Guy-Blaché, whose cinematic works were largely lost and whose written words sought to recollect them.

Although Guy-Blaché has begun to appear in standard histories of the cinema since 1990, and her films are now being found throughout the world, acts of remembering, recollecting, and retrieving remain significant on several levels.[7] By definition, they imply a certain repetition: to re-member is to bring to mind again; to re-collect is to gather together again or to re-member; and to re-trieve is to get back, to re-store, to re-member. We can thus deduce two important—if somewhat obvious—points concerning this work of remembrance and Alice Guy-Blaché. If we are remembering her and recollecting her work, then her work (and our memory of her) has been lost, but at one point her work (and she herself) were in mind, or known. In other words, she had to have been in mind once to be brought to mind again. Indeed, this is the assertion repeatedly made by those who have attempted to restore Guy-Blaché's history.

In their works on autobiography, both Leigh Gilmore and Paul Freeman recognize that repetition, as well as the loss—or erasure—that necessitates it, are inherent in definitions of "remember" and "recollect" (respectively).[8] In *Autobiographics: A Feminist Theory of Women's Self-Representation,* Gilmore emphasizes the repetition inherent in remembering as she scribes the word "re-member"; she then defines it as "both the act of memory and the restoration of erased persons and texts as bodies of evidence."[9] In *Rewriting the Self: History, Memory, Narrative,* Freeman similarly focuses on the inherent repetition and loss inscribed in the word "recollection": "While the 're' makes reference to the past, 'collection' makes reference to a present act, an act . . . of gathering together what might have been dispersed or lost."[10] He then goes on to consider the relationship between recollection and writing. He asserts, "Framed another way, the word recollection holds within it reference to the two distinct ways we often speak about history: as the trail of past events or 'past presents' that have culminated in now and as the act of writing, the act of gathering them together, selectively and imaginatively, into a followable story."[11] For Freeman, then, the process of remembering is essential to writing histories. These notions about memory, autobiography, and writing have much to bear on the history of Guy-Blaché, since her writings and spoken words are at the fore of all the acts of remembering her.

Recognizing herself that her work and name had been practically erased from film history and thus endeavoring to re-place herself in this history, Guy-Blaché took on the task of writing her memoirs. These memoirs (and spoken interviews with her) have now become the dominant history of Guy-Blaché; most works that treat her heavily depend on them for facts and the story of her life. So, as the generic name *memoirs* suggests, the history of Guy-Blaché is largely known through her work of remembrance and recollection.[12] This juxtaposition between memory and history is just one of many mergings between apparent oppositions in common representations of Guy-Blaché. Another such union exists between the private and public spaces of Guy-Blaché's life. Indeed, considering the fact that the process of remembering is normally a personal one, we also might recognize how Guy-Blaché's private history (necessarily) became a public one with the publication of her memoirs and their subsequent circulation in writings about her.[13]

The very title of Lepage's documentary, *The Lost Garden: The Life and Cinema of Alice Guy-Blaché,* exemplifies the common tropes in works on the filmmaker. As it rediscovers her "lost" work, it both separates and conjoins Guy-Blaché's "life" and "cinema," posing, then, an intermingling between a private and a public history, as well as the filmmaker's personal and professional status.[14] Such contrasts and connections are not uncommon in representations of women in particular, and they are certainly consistent in almost all texts on Guy-Blaché. In fact, as constructed via discursive forms ranging from her memoirs to *The Lost Garden* to her own filmic works (especially those produced with her production company, Solax), our understanding of Alice Guy-Blaché signifies a persistent merging of what might appear to be oppositional practices or spaces: public/private, professional/personal, institutional/familial,[15] history/memory, fact/fiction, and even image/word.

Moreover, the separate components of each of these sets might also be linked: history is often understood as providing a seemingly objective, institutionalized view that hence circulates in public and professional realms, whereas memory is more often understood as springing from a subjective and private position, one linked to personal and familial arenas. Tracing recent changes in the conception of these phenomena, Pierre Nora argues, "Memory and history, far from being synonymous, appear now to be in fundamental opposition."[16] He then details what positions them oppositionally, for instance, "memory is by nature multiple and yet specific; collective, plural and yet individual. History, on the other hand, belongs to everyone and to no one, whence its claim to universal authority."[17] History thus appears to have the status of fact, whereas memory—owing to its subjective and hence fallible nature—appears potentially aligned with fiction.[18] Considering, however, that such a notion as history itself guards memory, the movement between these oppositional domains becomes evident and even inevitable. At the same time, the fallibility of history, which often springs from its very institutionalization, suggests a further kinship with memory, as I later sketch. I would add, finally, that it might be her very consistent movement between these seeming oppositions that, for decades, had displaced Guy-Blaché from broader accounts of film history. As she moves between public and private, professional and personal, factual and fictional realms, we haven't known quite where or how to place her.

Although the image/word dichotomy might appear to be the most puzzling pair I have laid out here, I would like to turn to it now, as it does suggest a way to place Guy-Blaché in film history and film historiography. Indeed, it forces us to ask what happens when we seek to recreate a history of a filmmaker, the majority of whose films have been lost. One way to begin this work, as this essay shows, is through the re-collection of images in and from written forms.[19] That is, with the loss of and relative inaccessibility to her cinematic texts, I would suggest that we might read certain written works, like memoirs, not only as historical texts, but also as cinematic ones. In part, we can see the written work as an extension of the author's cinematic production. To this end, then, I am reading the memoirs as histories but also through particular theories of film form. In producing this sort of reading I do not mean to argue that the two forms (written and cinematic) are interchangeable; rather, I would like to suggest that seeing a provocative convergence of these forms can not only reveal insights into the history of the figures but can also suggest a renewed interest in the relation between writing and filmmaking. Finally, as these issues relate to the loss of images and the production of words, we can also see Guy-Blaché's memoir-writing as one authorial mode that seeks to recover another form of authorship.

Setting Memory in Motion

Because they inaugurated the re-collection of her history, I focus my subsequent examination on Guy-Blaché's memoirs, which are clearly an attempt to reconstruct the author's history through her own recollective processes. The text generally follows a chronological line, if an incomplete, or at least interrupted, one. As the memoirs narrate, Guy-Blaché was born in France in 1873, raised briefly in Chile, and returned to France as a young girl for schooling. When her father lost his publishing business in Chile, he moved with the rest of his family back to France, and died soon after.

With the death of her brother and the marriages of her sisters, Alice became the primary support for her and her mother. She took stenography lessons (unusual for a woman of the time) and found a job with Léon Gaumont. When Gaumont began producing films to market with his burgeoning camera production, Guy asked permission to try to make some films as well; soon she became the sole director for the House of Gaumont. There she experimented with a variety of genres and techniques, including the chronophone (an early mechanism to produce sound films).

In 1907 she married Herbert Blaché, an agent for Gaumont, and moved to the United States. Blaché helped set up Gaumont's American business; Guy-Blaché initially assisted him with his work, gave birth to their first child (Simone), and then began a studio of her own, the Solax Company. She had her second child around the same time that she moved Solax from Long Island to Fort Lee, New Jersey. For Solax, she supervised hundreds of films, but the company was dissolved in early 1914. Guy-Blaché then went on to work for her husband's new company, Blaché Features, as a director and Blaché's assistant. Not long after Blaché ran off to Hollywood with one of his stars, Guy-Blaché followed him in an attempt to repair their marriage. Although she made a number of films for other companies, Guy-Blaché suffered great financial loss during this period. After the clear failure of her marriage, she returned to France with her children, where she unsuccessfully sought work in the film industry. She toiled to restore her reputation in film history; she could not retrieve any of her lost films during her lifetime, but she was awarded the Legion of Honor in 1955. Having traveled with her daughter Simone throughout the latter's diplomatic career, mother and daughter retired to the United States, where Guy-Blaché was also reunited with her son's family. She died in 1968.

Even though we get this image of Guy-Blaché's life, the memoirs seem incomplete. Moreover, the often tangential stories the author tells interrupt the chronological detailing of her life. In this sense, the text seems to exemplify Walter Benjamin's definition of an (anti)autobiography; that is, the memoirs are not an autobiography but a series of reminiscences. In relation to his brief memoirs, "A Berlin Chronicle," Benjamin writes:

> Reminiscences, even extensive ones, do not always amount to an autobiography.... For autobiography has to do with time, with sequence and what makes up the continuous flow of life. Here, I am talking of a space, of moments and discontinuities. For even if months and years appear here, it is in the form they have at the moment of recollection. This strange form—it may be called fleeting or eternal—is in neither case the stuff that life is made of.[20]

Circuits of Memory and History

Guy-Blaché's *Memoirs* are made up of such "moments and discontinuities": throughout the work, one brief story or image begets another and so on, often with seemingly little connection between them. A short text, it includes a series of sketches whose individual length, in a sense, resembles many of her early short films. The sketches tell stories about her life: her upbringing, her entry into film production, her marriage, her move to the United States, and, finally, her relative disappearance from historical records.

The stories Guy-Blaché tells are, obviously, narratives of her own history and the larger history that shaped her. Although many historians did not have access to the actual volume, the memoirs managed to set the scene for much of the historical work on Guy-Blaché done in the 1970s and 1980s, as those works draw from Guy-Blaché's words (whether in the form of her memoirs, extracts from that text, or interviews with her).[21] Yet the filmmaker's memoirs set a rather different scene for texts like Lepage's *The Lost Garden:* whereas the memoirs utilize memory to produce a history, the film's structure—and the history it produces—greatly resembles processes of memory.[22] Decrying what he sees as the newly emerging distinction between history and memory and the subsumption of one into the other, Pierre Nora proclaims that "History is perpetually suspicious of memory, and its true mission is to suppress and destroy it."[23] In the case of Guy-Blaché's memoirs (as well as many texts about her), it seems that memory is instead suspicious of history.

Since they did not include her, Guy-Blaché did not recognize the histories of the periods in which she worked as completely true; hence, she attempted to reconstruct, or transform, those histories through her memories. Nora sees this sort of activity as a necessary process. Further examining phenomenological trends in the transformation of both history and memory, he claims: "The passage from memory to history has required every social group to redefine its identity through the revitalization of its own history. The task of remembering makes everyone his[/her] own historian."[24] Although this suggestion might seem a bit hyperbolic, through it Nora nicely stages the relation between history and memory that is made (and indeed reconnected) in memoirs like those of Guy-Blaché. The primary task of memoirs is often precisely to connect (or reconnect) history and memory via personal narrative. As Mark Freeman points out in consideration of the "truth" that autobiographies can tell, "the reality of living in time requires narrative reflection and that narrative reflection, in turn, opens the way toward a more comprehensive and expansive conception of truth itself."[25] While truth is often seen more as part of the purview of history rather than the more commonly fallible memory, we might see how transforming notions of what constitutes history, or histories, change our notions of the truth as well. Indeed, the inevitable narrativization of memory forms, in turn, narratives of history as well. So, considering memoirs—those narrativizations of memory and memories—as histories allows us to understand, or know, history, and the truths and nontruths that it produces, through a different lens.

Both the rediscovery and the production of alternative histories have been an important part of feminist scholarship, as this work seeks to bring to light new knowledge about women's lives that has been forgotten and/or made invisible. Still, explicitly elevating Guy-Blaché and her contemporaries to the status of historians might seem to be risky work, considering—as I discuss—the fallibility or fictionalizing function of memory. But in doing so, our knowledge of history, historiographical processes, and film culture can be valuably transformed. Not only can we again recognize the fallibility of institutionalized histories (and at this point in time, this seems common knowledge), but we can consider how active such women have always been in the production of histories.[26] Furthermore, this new form of authorship transcribes and illuminates the multiple roles as authors women have played in the film industry and in film culture more broadly. Finally, these works reveal, in sometimes unexpected and provocative ways, how narrative films—and histories of these films—always juggle and recombine fact and fiction, reality and fantasy.

The memoir and the autobiography hence constitute a sort of pivot between memory, history, and truth. Through the narrative process, they reveal the workings of the author's memory and tell an important history. While he argues against a conflation of memory and history (as I likewise would), Jacques LeGoff acknowledges that "Memory is the raw material of history. Whether mental, oral, or written, it is the living source from which historians draw."[27] He continues:

> Moreover, the discipline of history nourishes memory in turn, and enters into the great dialectical process of memory and forgetting experienced by individuals and societies. The historian must be there to render an account of these memories and of what is forgotten, to transform them into something that can be conceived, to make them knowable.[28]

Although LeGoff cautions against privileging memory over history, his remarks comment usefully on Guy-Blaché's project. Guy-Blaché would not entirely appear to be the objective historian that LeGoff insists on, yet she also acts as the historian he describes. Indeed, I would here emphasize

Circuits of Memory and History

her role as a remembering historian: her memoirs are an account of (her own) memories, which had otherwise been forgotten, and she attempts to render them into a history that might be known. As "the raw material" of her own history—and that of early cinematic production—her memories are turned into a narrative that clearly displays the dialectical relationship between history and memory in the production of knowledge.

In her memoirs, Lillian Gish directly remarks on this sort of relation between history, memory, and truth. In a sense, her claims offer a commentary both on and counter to Guy-Blaché's circumstances. Gish writes:

> [D. W. Griffith's] claim that history books falsified actual happenings struck me as most peculiar. At that time I was too naive to think that history books would attempt to falsify anything. I've lived long enough now to know that the whole truth is never told in history texts. Only the people who lived through an era, who are the real participants in the drama as it occurs, know the truth. The people of each generation, it seems to me, are the most accurate historians of their time.[29]

Certainly I would not wholeheartedly agree with her assessment; though a very strategic point to make within an autobiography, her privileging of autobiographical history belies, as Shari Benstock, Paul Eakin, and others would point out, the synchronous fictional nature of autobiographies.[30] Yet the relation between history, memory, and even autobiography that she proposes—that is, that autobiographical accounts sown from memory might correct historical ones—is important to make, especially in the case of those autobiographical subjects who have been silenced, marginalized, or otherwise misrepresented in official histories. Indeed, LeGoff insists that we be careful in how we privilege memories and histories: "Memory, on which history draws and which it nourishes in return, seeks to save the past in order to serve the present and the future. Let us act in such a way that collective memory may serve the liberation and not the enslavement of human beings."[31]

The context of Gish's statement itself directs us to the inherent problems with granting certain memories the status of historical truth over others. Quite simply, she is making a case for historical truth in regard to early film pioneer D. W. Griffith. As is well documented, Griffith utilized his familial memories to produce an extremely racist depiction of history in *Birth of a Nation*.[32] The narration of his familial memories, and then American history as the logical offshoot of these memories, attempts to erase or legitimate the injustices produced by the American institutions of racism and slavery (not to mention cinema). Guy-Blaché, in contrast, depends on her memories to illustrate (albeit, often indirectly) how institutionalized sexism has erased, or marginalized, her position in history; the writing of a new history through her memories is an attempt to make herself and her labor as a filmmaker visible and known.

These two very different cases thus point to the fact that arguments about truth are always political, ideological, and historical; because of the embedded and very complicated nature of these arguments, it is difficult to make a general case about the truth value of memoirs overall in the writing, or rewriting, of histories. While we must consider the potential veracity (or lack thereof) of these historical or remembered truths, my emphasis from here on is an investigation into how a history is constructed through memories and what various truths its facets of construction tell. To paraphrase Benjamin, I am not concerned merely with what is installed in the chamber of memory at its enigmatic center, but more with the many entrances leading into the interior.[33] Furthermore, I am interested in the way that the many entrances of memory shape the enigmatic center of history.

Technologies of Memory and Film

For Guy-Blaché, one of memory's entrances unsurprisingly lies at the entrance to the memoirs themselves. Indeed, in spite (or possibly because) of the evident recognition of seeming silenced or marginalized in history, Guy-Blaché's memoirs possess a rather humble beginning:

> In an era in which "retrospectives" are fashionable, perhaps the souvenirs of the eldest of women film directors may find some favor with the public. I have no pretense to making a work of literature, but simply to amuse, to interest the reader by anecdotes and personal memories concerning their great friend the cinema, at whose birth I assisted.[34]

This statement is significantly modest on a number of levels, and as such it opens up several important questions. First, the metaphor Guy-Blaché invokes asserts that she did not labor as the mother of the cinema but rather as an assistant: a doctor, perhaps, or a nurse or midwife.[35] Interestingly, these same metaphors—concerning the birth of the cinema as well as the assistant to its birth—circulate in other prominent writings on film, but perhaps most peculiarly in Christian Metz's *Imaginary Signifier*.[36] His particular innovation of birthing metaphors have a provocative bearing on both Guy-Blaché's wielding of the terms and her position in film studies. In "Story/Discourse: A Note on Two Kinds of Voyeurism," Metz writes:

Circuits of Memory and History

> I'm at the cinema. I am present at the screening of the film. *I am present.* Like the midwife attending a birth who, simply by her presence, assists the woman in labour, I am present for the film in a double capacity (though they are really one and the same) as witness and as assistant: I watch, and I help. By watching the film I help it to be born, I help it to live, since only in me will it live, and since it is made for that purpose: to be watched, in other words to be brought into being by nothing other than the look.[37]

His misunderstanding of the labor of a midwife notwithstanding, the "double capacity" Metz describes here—which goes beyond the singular one Guy-Blaché takes for herself—is important to note, especially because he genders both the originator of film and the subsequent spectators of film as female. In so doing, he also takes up the position of woman himself.[38] While Guy-Blaché refuses the position of birth-mother of film itself—and takes only the position as assistant/witness—the double capacity Metz describes might instead characterize Guy-Blaché's role as historian. Telling the story of her labor as a filmmaker, Guy-Blaché is a creator of and a witness to history at once. Taking a cue from Metz, we might also see subsequent historians and theorists—a special brand of film "spectators"—also as witnesses. Most, though, as Guy-Blaché suggests, and as film history has until recently borne out, have *mis*recognized her work in the history of film production. In her memoirs, however modestly, she thus produces a new image, or story, that readers can themselves also "bring into being."

Oddly, though, in so doing, she also denies her labor as a writer, for she refuses the position of a "great" author; rather, she will "simply ... amuse" her readers ("if I have any," she even notes later).[39] As she claims in the prologue, the memoirs are only an "anecdotal history."[40] Designating the memoirs as "souvenirs," moreover, also trivializes the work, for souvenirs are often considered to be mere trinkets. But more specifically, a souvenir is an object to help one remember travel through time and space. This travel is like that plotted for Guy-Blaché in *The Lost Garden,* and it also characterizes, of course, the movement and form of cinema in general. Hence, even as Guy-Blaché attempts to humbly belittle her work, her language inevitably connects—and makes visible—her authorship as a writer (an autobiographer, a historian) and a filmmaker.

Both this modest posture and a tension around the author's visibility are fairly typical within nineteenth-century traditions of women's writings, from which Guy-Blaché's work in part springs.[41] In *Private Woman, Public Stage: Literary Domesticity in Nineteenth-Century America,* Mary Kelley sketches how attempts to separate the private from the public sphere created a complicated situation for nineteenth-century women writers. Describing the scene that necessitated female authors' humble poses, Kelley writes:

> Unlike a male, a female's person was to be shielded from public scrutiny. Neither her ego nor her intellect was cultivated for future public vocation. After all, her proper sphere was the home. She was to stand in the background, out of the way. Even her exercise of moral, social, or personal influence was to be indirect, subtle, and symbolic. Her voice was to be soft, subdued, and soothing. In essence, hers was to remain an invisible presence.[42]

One way to remain "invisible," even as they were becoming published writers, Kelley documents, was for women to remain "secret writers," anonymous authors. Though not so invisible (at least in the sense Kelley invokes), the "voice" that opens Guy-Blaché's memoirs is just such a "soft, subdued, and soothing" one, unlikely to insist on her importance in the public field of history.

Continuing to draw on metaphors of visibility and the visual, Kelley goes on to acknowledge that even attempts at secrecy or anonymity could not hide women's entrance into the public sphere. As she notes, entering the public realm "suggested a new assertion of a woman's being, for, simply stated, to be a published writer was to have a visible influence, a public role beyond the home. It was to leave woman's private domestic sphere for man's, to meddle in the public affairs of men."[43] Clearly, then, such women were in a paradoxical position: they resisted the denial of their activity in the public sphere by entering the literary marketplace, but they often did so in secret: via anonymity or even in disguise as men. In fact, these acts of secrecy, paradoxically, unveiled the women's complicated and contradictory social positions. Kelley writes: "And it was ironic that to be a secret writer was also to announce that resistance, to call attention to it. To screen themselves, their being, in public, was inadvertently to dramatize in public the private subjugation of their lives."[44] Judith Fetterley also recognizes these inherent contradictions. In fact, she underscores how women writers themselves directly played with these contradictions. Contrary to Ann Douglas's claims that the tone adapted by nineteenth-century writers was one of "authorial innocence," Fetterley asserts that many women writers were "in conscious tension with the posture of 'innocence.'"[45] Surely aware of the complexities involved in being the first woman filmmaker, Guy-Blaché displays a similar "conscious tension" with "authorial innocence" in her memoirs. Thus, as the memoirs move forward, Guy-Blaché subverts the image she paints early on, that the memoirs are purely anecdotal, written only for her readers' amusement.

Kelley's metaphors might direct us to the complex layers of Guy-Blaché's (visible) authorship. First, as I note above, we can see Guy-Blaché as an author in a dual sense: she is both a filmmaker and a writer. The issues of visibility and invisibility that Kelley raises certainly have bearing on both roles. As a director, Guy-Blaché was in some ways an "invisible" presence, for she almost always worked behind the scenes. At the same time, because she directed and produced these constructions of images, she was clearly not invisible in the sense Kelley describes. (As the trade journals of the day document, she was fairly well known in the filmmaking community.) In fact, Guy-Blaché's rather prominent position within an evolving technological industry producing the newly emerging visual culture might influence and alter the ways we know, or see, her in film history. Furthermore, the history she authored in her older age was precisely that of her authorship as a filmmaker. In other words, her literary authorship was an attempt by her to return to visibility after her film authorship had been made invisible. Her work in film production thus highlights the very particular and complex tension between visibility and invisibility that she experienced and that she describes, in part through a guise of "innocent" modesty.

Indeed, after their humble beginning, her memoirs attempt to illuminate not only her visible influence on and in film history but, more specifically, her influence on the visible: the world of cinematic production. We might thus consider another definition of "screening" oneself than that which Kelley offers above. Surely a screen does not just hide what is behind it; it also acts, as does a movie screen, to unveil images before it. Whereas nineteenth-century women writers had to screen themselves *from* the public, after her initial modesty (which is only a screen anyway—and an ephemeral one at that), Guy-Blaché tries to screen her history *in* public. That is, she tries to make it visible rather than hide it.

Her modesty is indeed undermined throughout the book by her repeated insistence on her presence in film history: many of the anecdotes and personal memories she offers illustrate her important role in history-making. Even though she later claims that "I make no pretense to undertake the history of cinema in the United States. I confine myself to reporting what I have seen and heard," what Guy-Blaché did see and hear was highly significant, especially since what she "saw" defined precisely her role as film author.[46] Moreover, she was not only an onlooker or eavesdropper to cinematic inventions in the United States or in France. She tells of her participation in the discovery of filmic "tricks" such as double exposures, fade-outs, the turning of films in reverse, and others, and of her use of "science" to produce effects of realism.[47] Guy-Blaché also asserts that she imported this same sort of technical and cinematic invention to her films made in the United States, where, she claims, she received "critical praise" for such ingenuity.[48]

Along with these declarations concerning the specifics of her technical work, Guy-Blaché records how she fought for her position at Gaumont:

> I had been left to work out alone the difficulties at the beginning, to break new ground, but when the affair became interesting, *doubtless lucrative,* my directorship was bitterly disputed. However, I was combative and thanks to president [Gustave] Eiffel, who always encouraged me with kindness, the whole Board of Directors, recognizing my efforts, decided to leave me at the head of the service.[49]

Guy-Blaché's battle for her position at Gaumont in one sense parallels her battle for recognition in film history. In fact, she refers directly to her attempts to retrieve her position in film history throughout the volume. For instance, she notes her contact with French historian Georges Sadoul over her relative absence in his work on French film history. She writes, "Sadoul..., misled, and doubtless in all good faith (he says himself that he is ignorant of that epoch and speaks only from hearsay), has attributed my first films to people who probably worked for the Gaumont studios only as actors, whose names I don't even know."[50] She emphasizes that, after meeting with her and seeing documents to prove that "the films in question" were her work, Sadoul agreed to make some changes to his text, though "his numbering still contains errors."[51] In the final chapter of her memoirs, Guy-Blaché also registers that for many decades her work was not even recorded in Gaumont's own company history. From what she says, she attempted to rectify this mistake early on, but Léon Gaumont died before he made the proper corrections to the history.

Thus, Guy-Blaché's initial modesty, and her tone throughout the book (which seems to derive from a refusal to assign culpability to particular persons), camouflages her attempt to intervene in a history that had, at the time, excluded her. But of course this intervention is still apparent, clearly countering Guy-Blaché's initial claims that the memoirs are meant "simply to amuse."[52] We see the seriousness of her venture not only in the passages in which she explicitly takes credit for discovering or utilizing certain cinematic inventions or in those in which she engages with the histories that had excluded her. In fact, we see the sincerity of her critical project even in the anecdotes she tells. Many of these—which one would hardly call amusing—might serve to comment both on the recording of Guy-Blaché's history and on the impact of reading memoirs themselves as a form of history. In part they do so by revealing themselves as screen memories.

In Freud's essay "Screen Memories"—a work that, as editor James Strachey suggests, might itself be considered "autobiographical material only thinly disguised"—Freud maps out the workings of memory through his own self-analysis. That is, he includes a dialogue between patient and doctor, yet he occupies each role himself. He creates this discussion between his two divided selves in order to discover what is fictional about a particular remembered experience and what is real. His divided selves in effect enact the process of understanding a screen memory: since a screen memory is an amalgamation of two different fantasies (or, possibly, one real memory and one fictional one), it must be divided in order to be fully understood. In initially describing the memory in question, he thus tells himself, "You projected the two phantasies on to one another and made a childhood memory of them.... I can assure you that people often construct such things unconsciously—almost like works of fiction."[53] In attempting to explain what is nonetheless "genuine" about those fantasies, he goes on to define screen memory:

> There is in general no guarantee of the data produced by our memory. But I am ready to agree with you that the scene is genuine. If so, you selected it from innumerable others of a similar or another kind because, on account of its content (which in itself was indifferent) it was well adapted to represent the two phantasies, which were important enough to you. A recollection of this kind, whose value lies in the fact that it represents in the memory impressions and thoughts of a later date whose content is connected with its own by symbolic or similar links, may appropriately be called a *"screen memory."*[54]

Thus, as he says later, the screen memory is "one which owes its value as a memory not to its own content but to the relations existing between that content and some other, that has been suppressed."[55] As he implies in these definitions and states directly elsewhere in this essay (as well as in other works, including "A Disturbance of Memory on the Acropolis," a somewhat similar autobiographical sketch), Freud understands the workings of memory to be inherently transformative. In remembering, we may construct a "remembered" experience that is in part fictional, but memories also reveal—if not an actual experience—our ideas of an experience.[56]

Certainly, considering the concept of the screen memory, like those visual metaphors that Kelley uses, can again highlight the fact that Guy-Blaché's memories were, of course, of her work around the movie screen. Many of the stories in the volume are thus screen memories in this double sense: at once they hide and reveal an aspect of her history, and they narrate stories of the cinema. Yet the concept of the screen memory is not useful merely for its metaphorical possibilities for film historians and theorists. It also allows us to ponder how we might utilize memoirs in the production of history, for it at once admits to the fallibility of memory and asserts memory's reliability, often through its very complicated form. As a project of historical recovery, or what Gilmore might term "re-membering," many of Guy-Blaché's anecdotes and claims function as possible screen memories; that is, the director's genuine assertion that her place in film history was revoked seems to be projected onto stories of her film work throughout the text. Although it is impossible to prove the veracity of some of these claims or stories, their inclusion is telling. For instance, at the end of the volume, when Guy-Blaché describes the final straw that led her to leave the United States and return to France, she comments, "America, they say, always takes back everything she gives you."[57] And she ends the work with a recollection of a remark by Roosevelt: "It is hard to have failed, it is worse to have never tried."[58] These remarks serve to grant the autobiography a certain tone—both melancholic and angry—that we can see projected onto recollections of earlier times.

The melancholic and angry tone we see above is even more prominently projected in an apocalyptic story of the cinema—that is, an apocalyptic screen memory—that she tells early in the memoirs. At the end of chapter 2, which precedes the chapter in which she recalls her entrance into filmmaking and the "birth" of her first film, she recounts an early "disaster begun by the cinema" in which many people, including most members of an acquaintance's family (the Dillayes), were killed in a fire presumably started in a projection booth.

> Seventeen persons in this family which had never known sorrow perished in that terrible catastrophe. . . . Also, a year later, the eldest daughter of Dillaye, who had been separated from her mother, died of a kind of consumption. Dillaye had to wait long before he could return to his usual occupations.[59]

Aside from the memory of this family's tragedy, what other narratives does this story tell? For one, it seems possible that with this catastrophic story of the cinema, Guy-Blaché foreshadows the way in which her image will be extinguished from the cinematic record. To borrow a cliché, for Guy-Blaché, work in the film industry was both a blessing and a curse: she loved the labor but rightfully despised the fact that her work and her memory

Circuits of Memory and History

seemed lost to film history. As a literal and figurative screen memory, the above recollection appears to foretell Guy-Blaché's (metaphorical) death in the discourse of film history. Moreover, it tells of two kinds of separations: the separation, or loss, that family members endured (and that the daughter in part died from) and the father's separation from his family and his career. This sort of story—devastating in its vision of work, family, history, and the loss thereof—seems to play out in various histories of Guy-Blaché.

Other seemingly disparate stories that Guy-Blaché tells might bear even clearer associations in their close proximity to each other. That is, the moments and discontinuities that make up the memoirs might be woven together in suggestive ways. In the memoirs, Guy-Blaché offers a series of reminiscences that, read in relation to one another, offer enlightening angles from which to view certain connections between her work, her personal life, and her place in film history. Such connections are precisely what define screen memories, whose value lies not in their own content but, as Freud states, in "the relations existing between that content and some other, that has been suppressed." Other theorists also suggest that memory both is structured and creates meaning through links between images and/or ideas. An especially provocative series of linked images and ideas appears in chapter 7 of the memoirs, where Guy-Blaché tells a number of stories about the research into various social institutions that she performed in order to provide effects of realism in her films. She follows these sketches with information about changes in the control of Solax, a brief mention of actress and director Lois Weber, a short story about the discovery of the North Pole, and other tales of early film production. The content of each of these stories is interesting in itself, but the meaning becomes even more provocative when we read the stories in terms of one another, as I attempt to do in what follows.

Guy-Blaché declares at the end of chapter 6: "The trade of the cinematographer is not always a happy one. Concern for the truth obliges one to see and document sources which are sometimes tragic."[60] Chapter 7 then bears out this observation, beginning with the detailing of numerous visits Guy-Blaché took for film research: to an orphans' "asylum," a "hospital for the incurable," a "madhouse," a night court session, and a prison. Most of the stories expose broken and divided families, and some imply a culpability on the part of men. For instance, at the night court session, Guy-Blaché witnessed a fourteen-year-old girl, with no family or friends, found guilty of prostitution. After the girl was sentenced to a reformatory, Guy-Blaché reports, "A jailer came to take her; she followed quietly. Someone beside me murmured, 'What about the men?'"[61] Next she recounts the case of a young mother of an infant sentenced to six months of detention because she was "afflicted with an acute case of venereal disease": "When her baby was taken from her arms, she cried out piercingly 'Leave me my baby, I beg you. Leave me my baby.' "[62] The next brief tale concerns a "poor idiot," a man incarcerated in Sing Sing for attempting to "kiss a woman against her will." While Guy-Blaché does not seem unsympathetic to this man's plight, her sympathies — as registered in part by comments she attributes to others — primarily lie with the women's experiences. These short narratives clearly reflect Guy-Blaché's recognition of women's disadvantaged social position in public and private spaces. And all of the (unamusing) anecdotes document and bemoan the plights of broken families; such a point of view is consistent with the rest of the memoirs, though it remains relatively tacit in relation to Guy-Blaché's own family and marriage.

The two sketches that follow the above are quite telling. The first concerns Guy-Blaché's visit to a prison, culminating in her stop at the electric chair. She describes this stay as such:

> The director was so kind as to invite me to sit in it. I did so. They put the manacles on me and the director said "now, there is nothing to do but make contact. . . ." I asked if death were instantaneous. "Around eleven seconds," he answered, "some resist longer." He even invited me to attend an execution which would take place the next day. I refused. I have kept a photograph which I never see without a shudder.[63]

Immediately following this story is first Guy-Blaché's recounting of significant changes at Solax and then her mention of Lois Weber's work. I reproduce both short passages in full here:

> My husband, having finished his contract with Gaumont, had taken the presidency of Solax. I abandoned the reins to him with pleasure. I never attended any of the conferences where the Sales Co. composed the programs; I would have embarrassed the men, said Herbert, who wanted to smoke their cigars and to spit at their ease while discussing business.[64]
>
> Herbert Blaché had directed, in the little Gaumont studio at Fort Lee, a singer named Lois Weber who recorded several songs for the chronophone. She had watched me direct the first little films and doubtless thought it was not difficult. She got a directing job and certain Americans pretend that she was the first woman director. My first film, of which I speak in the first part of these memoirs, dated from 1896.[65]

Next she describes an "imposter" who attempted to take credit for the discovery of the North Pole. After he filmed a recreation of the adventure,

Circuits of Memory and History

"America swallowed it," Guy-Blaché contends, until "Peary arrived in his turn and took the crown." The sequence of these tales, and the relations inevitably intimated between them, is really rather astounding.

We might better understand these relations through philosophies of memory and film, particularly since the two phenomena structure Guy-Blaché's history in many ways. Indeed, as Sigmund Freud, Walter Benjamin, Frances Yates, Henri Bergson, and others have shown, memory flows through associations between images and ideas. For Benjamin, for instance, memory might be imagined as the streets of Berlin, so that one path leads to another; to Yates, the "art" of memory also has a spatial quality, in that in remembering we might move from one image to the next as from one room of a house to another.[66] Bergson offers a different sort of spatial metaphor to explain the workings of memory, as he imagines it operating as a series of electrical currents. Offering an image of embedded circles to illustrate the relation between memory and perception, Bergson writes: "We maintain, on the contrary, that reflective perception is a *circuit,* in which all the elements, including the perceived object itself, hold each other in a mutual state of tension as in an electrical circuit."[67] He continues:

> It is the whole of memory, as we shall see, that passes over into each of these circuits, since memory is always present; but that memory, capable, by reason of its elasticity, of expanding more and more, reflects upon the object a growing number of suggested images—sometimes the details of the object itself, sometimes concomitant details which may throw light upon it.[68]

Focusing on the embedded relationship between these circles and hence the way in which memory expands, Bergson's description here is quite like Benjamin's contention that acts of memory produce "endless interpolations into what has been."[69] Moreover, understanding memory as a kind of electrical current, Bergson illustrates here how memory itself might forge connections between images and ideas.

Film form inevitably shapes such links as well. Indeed, connected by Guy-Blaché's acts of remembering, each story has the effect of an afterimage on that which follows it, so that it is difficult to read the recollections in isolation from one another. Stressing that the mind itself creates an afterimage, Hugo Munsterberg discusses how precinematic games and devices help provoke visually and mentally the semblance of depth and movement. The "positive afterimage," he says, is "a real continuation of the first impression" in the second.[70] Such continuity is produced, for instance, by the thaumatrope, a nineteenth-century optical device that rapidly spins a two-sided card in order to merge the images on each side. Notes Munsterberg,

"As soon as the card is quickly revolved about a central axis, the two pictures fuse into one. If a horse is on one side and a rider on the other, or a cage is on one and a bird on the other, we see the rider on the horse and the bird in the cage."[71] In part what allows us to fuse the images is the "circuitry" of memory itself.

Certainly such contraptions like the thaumatrope, or the later zootrope, presaged the invention of film. Indeed, then, a more complex "fusion" takes place through cinematic montage, the welding together of images on film. For theorists like Sergei Eisenstein, montage defines the aesthetic, intellectual, and even political possibilities of film form. As Eisenstein declares, "Montage is an idea that arises from the collision of independent shots — shots even opposite to one another."[72] Thus the collision of two shots (or, in some cases, two images within a shot) creates a new idea. According to Eisenstein, montage can have an optical, emotional, or intellectual aim. (Of the three, he privileges the intellectual, for he believes it can lead to political change.) Through montage — and through the intellectual response of the spectator to the montage — film form can stimulate relations and associations between images and ideas.

Laid out next to each other on the page, Guy-Blaché's reminiscences suggest such a spatial and cinematic, as well as an intellectual or associative, relation to one another, so that one echoes in the next, and the next after that. Hence we might see how the description of sitting in the electric chair resonates — as an electrical current, like memory itself — in the filmmaker's comment that she "abandoned the reins" of Solax to her husband "with pleasure."[73] Indeed, through the collision of these two notions is borne the suggestion that Guy-Blaché lost control not only of her company, but also of her place in history. Again, the image of the electric chair, along with her husband's insistence that she would "embarrass the men" at business meetings, also resounds in her mention of Lois Weber, who, as Guy-Blaché claims here, received her start in her business through Herbert Blaché. Guy-Blaché thus emphasizes how recognition of another woman's work has displaced recognition of her own role as the first woman filmmaker in history. Moreover, following the mention of Weber with the story of the imposter who tried to credit himself with the discovery of the North Pole (indeed, through a cinematic reenactment of the event!) is also a significant rhetorical gesture. For Guy-Blaché, then, it seems even that Weber is an "imposter" who attempted to take her own rightful position. History has been reconstructed — much like many early "actualities" that merely "reenacted" historical events — to put Weber in Guy-Blaché's place. These memoirs, then, represent Guy-Blaché's attempt, not unlike that of Peary, to "take the crown" for her achievements.

Similar to her modestly proclaiming that her memoirs are merely an attempt to amuse her readers, Guy-Blaché reveals a certain humility: at least she does not overtly cast blame regarding the end of her career. But like the early proclamation, the "modesty" inherent in this indirect approach is belied in the connections that readers themselves might make between colliding anecdotes, this montage of memories. Like an afterimage produced by optical devices or the more complicated process of cinematic form, the flow of memory, narrative, and even of thought demands forging at least some links between the stories she tells. It seems, too, that although the above passages are not cited in any historical works on Guy-Blaché, their tenor resounds in works that emphasize Guy-Blaché's loss (one might even say "death") from history and that also blame her husband—directly or indirectly—for the end of her career.[74] Thus the memoirs, structured in great part as memory itself is structured, influence subsequent written and filmic histories of Guy-Blaché in myriad ways: in their form, their tenor, and their recollection of her history.

Strange Fictions

Both memory and autobiography—a genre essentially based on the telling of memories—manifest rather precarious relations between fact and fiction. One defining characteristic of screen memories, for Freud, is that they are constructed "almost like works of fiction." In more general parlance, memory is frequently defined as "elusive"; part of its elusive nature is the often impossible task of determining its "truth." Yet critics of autobiography also focus on the genre's association with fact, or truth, as well as fiction. As Leigh Gilmore suggests, "Authority in autobiography springs from its proximity to the truth claim of the confession, a discourse that insists upon the possibility of telling the whole truth while paradoxically frustrating that goal through the structural demands placed on how one confesses."[75] A complex relationship between fact and fiction thus defines memory and autobiography; because of this condition, it is nearly impossible to unravel the intertwining of these elements. Surely the above examples from Guy-Blaché's memoirs illustrate a very complicated knot of such discursive parts, and they are especially provocative in light of the field they illuminate: the history of the production of visual images. I would, then, like to conclude with a final example that is indeed "fictional," but that also comments on the inextricability of seemingly opposing categories—whether public and private, history and memory, or fact and fiction—in regard to Guy-Blaché's life and history.

In an early 1912 issue of *Moving Picture World,* fictional film narrative and the story of Guy-Blaché's life and work literally come together. In a section titled "Manufacturer's Advance Notes" is a parody of a film summary.[76] Called "A Solax Celebration," this parody tells the tale of a New Year's party at Solax. Listed as featured players in this drama are Madame Alice Blaché as "The Cause" and Herbert Blaché as "A Relative—but an outsider." The "Synopsis" is as follows:

> The good people living in the Solax community, realizing that they have cause to make merry and celebrate before the advent of a New Year, because the Almighty had been so fortunate as to guide their bread-winning footsteps in the direction of the happy atmosphere of the Solax Studio, banked together, like the big happy family which they are, and gave expression to their happiness in the form of a gift to the immediate cause of their good fortune and sunshine.... The plot is not a thick one, but the execution progresses smoothly and with "spirit." The events took the leading figure entirely by surprise, and her emotion and her gratitude brought forth a lump in her throat.[77]

The first two scenes describe the party, but in the third, titled "Jealousy," the plot thickens. It is narrated as follows: "A near relative to The Cause [Herbert Blaché] and a neighbor to us all was jealous of the aforesaid tribute paid to his kin, so, in order that he may not be outshone in hospitality, invited the mob to invade the sanctified quarters of the Gaumont Company, where he showed some wonderful Gaumont productions."[78] Though this parody hints at the way Herbert Blaché attempted to displace his wife within the production of film narratives and film history, parceling out what is historically accurate and what is fabricated about this story is an impossible task.

This example offers a movement between fact and fiction that enables us to read each in a different light: the plot summary reveals both the sometimes fictional character of history and the truthful nature of fiction.[79] In "A Solax Celebration," a seemingly factual event masquerades as fiction: at least, one narrative masquerades as another. This type of guise—which seems consistent with the narratives of many of Guy-Blaché's Solax films—brings together several elements concerning histories of Guy-Blaché (including, of course, her own). First of all, the very opposition between fact and fiction is one that often informs thinking about the relation between history and memory; the line between the former two is here blurred much like that between the latter coupling. Moreover, while "A Solax Celebration" entwines fact and fiction, it also clearly intermixes Guy-Blaché's public and private spheres. It demonstrates Guy-Blaché's independence from her husband and at the same time suggests tension, or at least competition, between the two. More importantly, the narrative points to Guy-Blaché's abilities to manage a business — yet a business in the form of a family. As such, it attests to Guy-Blaché's skills at moving between public and private spheres, professional and personal life.

Finally, since "A Solax Celebration" is a fiction of a fictional film in written — rather than purely visual — form, this example brings us back to yet another set of distinct categories, or media, that also form our understanding of Guy-Blaché. Guy-Blaché was indeed a filmmaker and a writer. As such a dual author, she produced both cinematic narratives and a written history. But, of course, these textual forms are forever conjoined. Most obviously, the memoirs link these media because, in written form, they tell the history of her authorship as a filmmaker. Additionally, the filmmaker's writings have provoked historians to seek out her films so that her place in history is further secured. And finally, the memoirs, with her films, have helped in the construction of a (cinematic) documentary about her life and work. In this sense, Guy-Blaché's work has come full circle, a route whose nonlinearity is inevitable when one's history is structured through acts of remembering.

Notes

I wish to thank Lynne Joyrich, Pat Mellencamp, Gretchen Papazian, Patrice Petro, and Kathleen Woodward for their thoughtful responses to and support of this essay. Thanks also to Diane Negra and Jennifer Bean for their suggestions for improvement, and to Alison McMahan for making her manuscript on Guy-Blaché available to me. My special appreciation goes also to Jessamyn Blau for her help with the translation of Guy-Blaché's memoirs.

1. Francis Lacassin, "Out of Oblivion: Alice Guy-Blaché," *Sight and Sound* 40, 3 (summer 1971): 151.
2. Gerald Peary, "Czarina of the Silent Screen: Solax's Alice Blaché," *Velvet Light Trap* 6 (1974): 35.
3. Annabel Nicholson, Felicity Sparrow, Jane Clarke, Jeanette Iljon, Lis Rhodes, Mary Pat Leece, Pat Murphy, and Susan Stein, "Woman and the Formal Film," in *Films for Women,* ed. Charlotte Brunsdon (London: British Film Institute, 1986), 187.

4   Peary makes a similar call in the postscript to "Czarina of the Silent Screen": "I am glad of introducing film readers to this most unusual and interesting woman, and hope that there will be more articles building on this one, just as I am indebted to the pioneering essay by Francis Lacassin."
5   See note 21.
6   Of course, Guy-Blaché's case was hardly exceptional. As we know, most films made during this period were not automatically preserved at the time. Nonetheless, I would also agree with the implication of the writers of "Women and the Formal Film" that it is not mere coincidence that loss of Guy-Blaché's films was a loss of a woman's work.
7   As *The Lost Garden* also proclaims: "Lately, however, there is a renewed interest in her work and people are rediscovering the perennial treasures of this Lost Garden." The most significant work to do so is Alison McMahan's *Alice Guy-Blaché: Lost Visionary of the Cinema* (New York: Continuum, 2002). Indeed, McMahan's detailed study is largely an exegesis on many of Guy-Blaché's films that she has labored to rediscover and make more accessible for future scholars. In general, the trend of recovery, or trope of loss, essentially ends in the early 1990s, when Guy-Blaché was written into two major studies of early French cinema: Richard Abel, *The Ciné Goes to Town: French Cinema, 1896–1914* (Berkeley: University of California Press, 1994), and Alan Williams, *The Republic of Images: A History of French Filmmaking* (Cambridge: Harvard University Press, 1992).
8   Patrick Hutton distinguishes between "repetition" and "recollection" in *History as an Art of Memory* (Hanover, N.H.: University Press of New England, 1993). I return to this distinction in a longer version of this essay.
9   Leigh Gilmore, *Autobiographies: A Feminist Theory of Women's Self-Representation* (Ithaca: Cornell University Press, 1994), 27.
10 Paul Freeman, *Rewriting the Self: History, Memory, Narrative* (New York: Routledge, 1993), 47.
11 Ibid.
12 The word "memoir" (usually pluralized) springs from the French *mémoire,* the Old French *memoire,* and the Latin *memoria,* all of which mean "memory."
13 However, her memoirs were published posthumously. She died in 1968, and the memoirs were originally published in France in 1976. They were then translated by her daughter, Simone Blaché, and published in the United States in 1986. A subsequent paperback edition came out in 1996.
14 The documentary itself also represents such interminglings through various strategies. For instance, Guy-Blaché's daughter-in-law and granddaughter appear as the primary historians of her personal and professional life stories. At times, Guy-Blaché's fictional films stand in for her real life; and at others, contemporary experts are garbed as characters from the films. In general, the film itself (and the subsequent history it tells) is greatly structured like a personal act of remembering.
15 Certainly the family itself can function as an institution. In his seminal work

on ideological theories and practices, Louis Althusser categorizes the family as an ideological state apparatus, in spite of his admission that it also "obviously has other 'functions' than that of an ISA." Althusser, "Ideology and Ideological State Apparatuses," in *Lenin and Philosophy and Other Essays,* trans. Ben Brewster (New York: Monthly Review Press, 1971), 143. Moreover, he notes that the distinction between the public and the private—an opposition that helps define the family—is one "internal to bourgeois law, and valid in the (subordinate) domains in which bourgeois law exercises its 'authority'" (144). He goes on to note that "It is unimportant whether the institutions in which [ISAs] are realized are 'public' or 'private'. What matters is how they function. Private institutions can perfectly well 'function' as Ideological State Apparatuses. A reasonably thorough analysis of any one of the ISAs proves this." The function of the family as part of an ideological discourse, if not an ideological state apparatus, has been closely analyzed in the field of television studies. See, for instance, Lynne Joyrich, *Re-viewing Reception: Television, Gender, and Postmodern Culture,* especially "Tube Tied: Television, Reproductive Politics, and *Moonlighting*'s Family Practice" (Bloomington: Indiana University Press, 1996); Dave Morley, *Family Television: Cultural Power and Domestic Leisure* (London: Routledge, 1988); and Lynn Spigel, *Make Room for TV: Television and the Family Ideal in Postwar America* (Chicago: University of Chicago Press, 1992).

16 Pierre Nora, "Between Memory and History: *Les lieux de mémoire,*" *Representations* 26 (spring 1989): 8.

17 Ibid., 8–9. Some works in film and television studies make similar distinctions to Nora's. For instance, in his essay "Third cinema as Guardian of Popular Memory: Towards a Third Aesthetic," Teshome Gabriel distinguishes between official history and popular memory: "Official history tends to arrest the future by means of the past.... [The written word of history] claims a 'centre' which continuously marginalises others. In this way its ideology inhibits people from constructing their own history or histories"; popular memory "orders the past not only as a reference point but also as a theme of struggle. For popular memory, there are no longer any 'centres' or 'margins', since the very designations imply that something has been conveniently left out.... [I]t is a 'look back to the future', necessarily dissident and partisan, wedded to constant change" (in *Questions of Third Cinema,* ed. Jim Pines and Paul Willemen [London: British Film Institute, 1989], 54). In her essay "From the Dark Ages to the Golden Age: Women's Memories and Television Reruns," Lynn Spigel similarly draws a distinction between official history and popular memory (*Screen* 36, 1 [spring 1995] 16–33). (Although she does not cite Gabriel's work, both seem influenced by Michel Foucault, who discusses popular memory in an interview in *Cahiers du Cinéma* [251–252 (1974): 5–15].) Spigel writes: "Popular memory is history for the present; it is a mode of historical consciousness that speaks to the concerns and needs of contemporary life. Popular memory is a form of storytelling through which people make sense of their

own lives and culture. In this regard, it diverges from official, professional history (by which I mean those histories deemed legitimate by schools, museums, textbook publishers and other arbiters of social knowledge)" (21). Although I do not pursue the notion of popular memory, I find Gabriel's and Spigel's approach here useful, especially as Spigel begins to work through the hybrids that form between these categories.

18 Jacques LeGoff might argue with this distinction. At least he contends, "Recent, naive trends seem virtually to identify history with memory, and even to give preference in some sense to memory, on the ground that it is more authentic, 'truer' than history, which is presumed to be artificial and, above all, manipulative of memory." LeGoff, *History and Memory,* trans. Steven Rendall and Elizabeth Claman (New York: Columbia University Press, 1992), xi.

19 An inspired response to this kind of situation is displayed brilliantly in Giuliana Bruno's *Streetwalking on a Ruined Map: Cultural Theory and the City Films of Elvira Notari* (Princeton: Princeton University Press, 1993). In this work, Bruno recreates readings of Notari's films—and a historiography of the filmmaker—through exhaustive research of other extant materials: film summaries in contemporary trade magazines, posters, film stills, production notes, and the like.

20 Walter Benjamin, "A Berlin Chronicle," in *Reflections: Essays: Aphorisms, Autobiographical Writings,* ed. Peter Demetz (New York: Harcourt Brace Jovanovich, 1978), 28.

21 The body of criticism from this time period roughly falls into two categories: those foundational texts that centered only or largely on Guy-Blaché and, hence, influenced the work that appeared after them; and reference texts that include a chapter or entry on Guy-Blaché. Into the first group would fall Lacassin's "Out of Oblivion," Peary's "Czarina of the Silent Screen," and Anthony Slide's 1986 edited volume of Guy-Blaché's memoirs, as well as his discussion of her in the 1977 *Early Women Directors: Their Role in the Development of the Silent Cinema* (revised and republished in 1996 as *The Silent Feminists: America's First Women Directors* [Lanham, Md.: Scarecrow Press, 1996]). Aside from the above works, as well as Calvin Thomas Beck's *Scream Queens: Heroines of the Horrors* (New York: Macmillan, 1978), and an essay by Lis Rhodes and Felicity Sparrow ("Her Image Fades as Her Voice Rises," in *Multiple Voices in Feminist Film Criticism,* ed. Diane Carson, Linda Dittmar, and Janice R. Welsch [Minneapolis: University of Minnesota Press, 1994]— both of which include relatively lengthy discussions of Guy-Blaché's films— the remaining work on Guy-Blaché in the United States during this period appears in historical and biographical reference texts (and, in fact, Beck's is also a reference text of sorts). Two of these texts include full chapters on Guy-Blaché: Sharon Smith's *Women Who Make Movies* (New York: Hopkinson and Blake, 1975), and Louise Heck-Rabi's *Women Filmmakers: A Critical Reception* (Metuchen, N.J.: Scarecrow Press 1984). A third, Barbara Koenig Quart's *Women Directors: The Emergence of a New Cinema* (New York: Praeger, 1988),

discusses Guy-Blaché along with Lois Weber and Germaine Dulac in a chapter called "Antecedents." Each of these works exemplifies the reliance on Guy-Blaché's own writings, or at least the transmission of her words, usually via Lacassin's inaugural essay.

22 It does so through its reliance on actual acts of remembering (by Guy-Blaché's family members and, through the inclusion of clips from an archival television interview, by Guy-Blaché herself); its nonlinear movement between temporal periods and various spaces; and even its usage of footage from fictional films to illustrate facets of the filmmaker's real life.

23 Nora, "Between Memory and History," 9. For Nora, the rise of historiography and changes in national thinking (and ideas about national histories) have "dissociated" history and memory; see pages 11–12.

24 Ibid., 15.

25 Freeman, *Rewriting the Self*, 32.

26 Memoirs by many women who worked in the silent-film industry have circulated in other histories as well. I examine the appearance of Louise Brooks's autobiographical essays elsewhere, but similar investigations could take place concerning the memoirs of Lillian Gish and Linda Arvidson, especially, who are often quoted in historical and theoretical works about D. W. Griffith. Many other women in the film industry of this period produced their memoirs, some of which have also circulated in scholarly discourse. This group of authors includes stars, directors, and screenwriters such as Marion Davies, Anita Loos, Frances Marion, Colleen Moore, Mary Pickford, Leni Riefenstahl, Nell Shipman, Gloria Swanson, and others. Most of the works listed here are authored solely by the women named, though works by Gish and Davies list a second author or editor. Many of these writings nicely expand the women's images in written form, some, for instance, by taking up tropes that were prominent in their films and others by drawing on popular knowledge about them. Certainly these facts point to a fictionalizing function inherent in the memoirs, but we might see this aspect of them not merely as troubling (and therefore of no use to "real" historians). Rather, we could recognize how a movement between reality and fantasy is perhaps unavoidable in histories of narrative filmmaking and thus opens up provocative links between these categories. Indeed, such works draw attention not only to the cinematic productions as mere fantasies; they also point to the reality involved in such work. This recognition might just be one way of seeing the memoirs among many possible readings.

27 LeGoff, *History and Memory*, xi.

28 Ibid., xi–xii.

29 Lillian Gish with Ann Pinchot, *The Movies, Mr. Griffith, and Me* (New York: Prentice Hall, 1969), 133.

30 See Shari Benstock, "Authorizing the Autobiographical," in *The Private Self: Theory and Practice of Women's Autobiographical Writings*, ed. Benstock (Chapel Hill: University of North Carolina Press, 1988); and Paul John Eakin,

"Fiction in Autobiography: Ask Mary McCarthy No Questions," in *Fictions in Autobiography: Studies in the Art of Self-Invention* (Princeton: Princeton University Press, 1985).
31 LeGoff, *History and Memory*, 99.
32 See especially Donald Bogle, *Toms, Coons, Mulattoes, Mammies, and Bucks* (1973; reprint, New York: Continuum, 1989); Thomas Cripps, *Slow Fade to Black: The Negro in American Film, 1900–1942* (1977; reprint, New York: Oxford University Press, 1993); and Ed Guerrero, *Framing Blackness: The African American Image in Film* (Philadelphia: Temple University Press, 1993).
33 As Benjamin writes, "I am not concerned with what is installed in the chamber at its enigmatic center, ego or fate, but all the more with the many entrances leading into the interior" (A Berlin Chronicle, 31).
34 Alice Guy-Blaché, *The Memoirs of Alice Guy-Blaché*, ed. Anthony Slide (Metuchen, N.J.: Scarecrow Press, 1996), 1. I work here with the English translation of Guy-Blaché's memoirs. Most of the changes in translation to the passages I am focusing on are quite subtle; I point out the significant alterations.
35 This is also an important distinction to make, though not necessarily one that has been heeded by those writers who came after Guy-Blaché. Indeed, labeling Guy-Blaché as the mother of the cinema, or even as a foremother of feminist film theory and history potentially poses certain limitations on how we perceive the filmmaker and her position in history. There are ways in which Guy-Blaché's very literal position as a mother helped in the eventual circulation of her history, especially through her daughter Simone's and daughter-in-law Roberta's efforts to translate and publish the *Memoirs*. However, labeling any woman as the mother of an institution has the potential to shut down consideration of her ongoing importance in the field; she may be seen as merely the originator whose duty has already been accomplished. In Guy-Blaché's case, other connections between her motherhood and her work in film have produced provocative, but sometimes limiting, views of her. For instance, several writers link the birth of her second child and the completion of her new Solax studio. Although this connection might suggest ways in which the public arena could be structured as a woman's field (i.e., like a family or a home), it might trap our reading of her work as connected only to familial, private life. It would be interesting to extend this analysis of Guy-Blaché's maternal position in film production and film history and of the role of foremothers in a more general sense through psychoanalytic theories of mother-daughter relations. Doing so might illuminate other reasons for Guy-Blaché's dual loss and recovery in film studies. For an insightful reading of a foremother in film history, see Rebecca Egger, "Deaf Ears and Dark Continents: Dorothy Richardson's Cinematic Epistemology," *Camera Obscura* 30 (May 1992): 4–33.
36 For instance, we can see this trope in works from André Bazin's *What Is Cinema?* volume 1, when he draws on metaphors of birth and death to describe early and later film production; to Maya Deren's writings; to Laura Mulvey's "Visual Pleasure and Narrative Cinema," *Screen 16*:3 (1975): 6–18. In such

Circuits of Memory and History

cases, as in Christian Metz's work, film is lent an anthropomorphic quality, which may partially account for the burgeoning theories of identification and spectatorship that have sprung from the work of Metz and others.

37 Christian Metz, "Story/Discourse: A Note on Two Kinds of Voyeurism," in *The Imaginary Signifier: Psychoanalysis and the Cinema,* trans. Celia Britton et al. (Bloomington: Indiana University Press, 1982), 93.
38 These two details might partly account for why Metz has been such an important figure for feminist film theorists: he suggests he has a built-in empathy for women as well as a desire to masquerade as a woman.
39 Guy-Blaché, *Memoirs,* 28.
40 Ibid., ix.
41 As McMahan claims, Guy-Blaché remained a "Victorian" throughout her life, in many senses.
42 Mary Kelley, *Private Woman, Public Stage: Literary Domesticity in Nineteenth-Century America* (New York: Oxford University Press, 1984), 111.
43 Ibid., 125.
44 Ibid., 128.
45 Judith Fetterley, *Provisions: A Reader from Nineteenth-Century American Women* (Bloomington: Indiana University Press, 1985), 5.
46 Guy-Blaché, *Memoirs,* 67.
47 Ibid., 29, 42, 76 ff. In fact, in discussing her aid in scientific experiments to display the utility of X-rays, for which she "often lent [her] hands," she declares: "I still have a little burn scar from this" (42). The evidence of her work is thus also written on her body.
48 Ibid., 69.
49 Ibid., 33, emphasis in original.
50 Ibid., 35–36.
51 Ibid., 36.
52 Moreover, the apparent insistence on her place in history seems more consistent with a short essay that is inevitably quoted by all who write about her. In this piece, Alice Guy-Blaché declares: "It has long been a source of wonder to me that many women have not seized upon the wonderful opportunities offered to them by the motion-picture art to make their way to fame and fortune as producers of photodramas. Of all the arts there is probably none in which they can make such splendid use of talents so much more natural to a woman than to a man and so necessary to its perfection" ("Woman's Place in Photoplay Production," *Moving Picture World,* 11 July 1914, 195). That particular summons, as well, noted that film production was precisely made for women: "The technique of the drama has been mastered by so many women that it is considered as much her field as a man's and its adaptation to picture work in no way removes it from her sphere. The technique of motion-picture photography, like the technique of the drama, is fitted to women's activities" (129). Such a claim was impossible without Guy-Blaché's precursors in the nineteenth-century fiction industry.

53. Sigmund Freud, "Screen Memories," in *The Standard Edition of the Complete Psychological Works of Sigmund Freud,* trans. James Strachey, vol. 3 (London: Hogarth Press and the Institute of Psychoanalysis, 1893–1899), 315.
54. Ibid., 315–316.
55. Ibid., 320.
56. In the case above, his screen memory reveals the feelings of hunger and love as attached to a further experience.
57. Guy-Blaché, *Memoirs,* 95.
58. Ibid., 96.
59. Ibid., 20.
60. Ibid., 76.
61. Ibid., 78.
62. Ibid.
63. Ibid., 79. The original French reads: "Le directeur poussa la complaisance jusqu'a m'inviter à m'y asseoir, ce que je fis" (124). This line would be literally translated as: "The director pushed his hospitality to the point of having me sit down, which I did." Guy-Blaché's original statement is, thus, more critical than the translation of her claim.
64. Guy-Blaché originally wrote that the men wanted to smoke their cigars "en paix" (in peace). See Alice Guy, *Autobiographie d'une pionnière du cinéma, 1873–1968,* présentée par l'Association Musidora, préfaces de Nicole-Lise Bernheim et Claire Clouzot, notes de Claire Clouzot, filmographie de Francis Lacassin (Paris: Denoël/Gonthier, 1976).
65. Ibid., 79.
66. Yates writes, "The artificial memory is established from places and images..., the stock definition to be forever repeated down the ages. A *locus* is a place easily grasped by the memory, such as a house, an intercolumnar space, a corner, an arch, or the like. Images are forms, marks or simulacra... of what we wish to remember. For instance if we wish to recall the genus of a horse, of a lion, of an eagle, we must place their images on definite *loci.*" See Frances Yates, *The Art of Memory* (Chicago: University of Chicago Press, 1966), 6.
67. Henri Bergson, *Matter and Memory,* trans. Nancy Margaret Paul and W. Scott Palmer (New York: Zone Books, 1991), 104.
68. Ibid., 104–105.
69. Benjamin, "A Berlin Chronicle," 16.
70. Hugo Munsterberg, *The Film: A Psychological Study* (New York: Dover, 1970), 25.
71. Ibid.
72. Sergei Eisenstein, *Film Form and Film Sense* (New York: Harcourt, Brace and Company, 1949), 49.
73. Perhaps she even takes some of the blame here for the loss of her company; after all, given the invitation, she sat in the chair herself.
74. As I noted earlier, for instance, many works emphasize that no obituary appeared on Guy-Blaché's death. Furthermore, several histories of her repeat-

edly connect the end of the filmmaker's career with the end of her marriage. Sharon Smith writes: "It was a time of great personal stress. Just when her company went into a decline, her marriage to Herbert Blaché, who had worked closely with her since the Gaumont days, came to an end" (*Women Who Make Movies,* 3). Louise Heck-Rabi similarly remarks: "Sadly, the marital partnership of the Blachés disintegrated with the collapse of their business and careers" (*Women Filmmakers,* 16). Barbara Quart notes: "After the film dissolved, the marriage did as well" (*Women Directors,* 19). And Ally Acker claims, "A time of great personal strife ensued. Her company fell into decline and so did her marriage" (in *Pioneers of the Cinema, 1896 to the Present* [New York: Continuum, 1991], 10).

75 Gilmore, *Autobiographies,* 107.
76 Gerald Peary discusses "A Solax Celebration" as if it were an actual film, but I have found no evidence to indicate it was a real production.
77 *Moving Picture World* (13 January 1912), 130.
78 Ibid.
79 In this case, the summary rather resembles the rendering of fictional films as historical evidence in Lepage's *The Lost Garden.*

PATRICIA WHITE

Nazimova's Veils

Salome at the Intersection
of Film Histories

With its early date and esoteric aura, Alla Nazimova's 1922 *Salome* seems to "guarantee" the historical presence of lesbians in film. Yet the film's iconic status itself deserves further interpretation. In his authoritative biography *Nazimova,* Gavin Lambert acknowledges a spate of 1990s studies of famous theatrical and Hollywood lesbians; the implication is that an actress like Nazimova owes any widespread contemporary interest in her story to this sudden chic. The phenomenon represents a welcome lifting of the gag order that has distorted the historical record of lesbian and gay lives, but it makes asking methodological questions about writing the history of sexuality and culture all the more necessary. The "outing" of *Salome* tends to pop the film out of historical context. This essay approaches questions of lesbian representability through Nazimova's film and argues that while *Salome*'s avant-garde pretensions have preserved its cult value and sexual cachet, interesting historical dimensions of gender, sexuality, and ethnicity, as well as of authorship, art, and entertainment have remained obscured. In what follows, I hope to indicate how current film scholarship might recontextualize the film; however, I also want to maintain the importance of *Salome*'s notoriety as a starting point for a queer historiography that could illuminate Nazimova's contribution as a lesbian auteur.

This once-celebrated stage and screen star made herself visible in her own time through one of late-nineteenth- and early-twentieth-century Western high culture's most overexposed icons of sexualized femininity, Salome, the biblical princess who danced for the head of John the Baptist. Nazimova's film adaptation of Oscar Wilde's 1893 play turned out to be ill timed and financially and professionally disastrous, but her tribute to the gay 1890s resonates in this later turn-of-the-century moment. Recent studies of the cinema of the 1910s and 1920s bring out the important role of women filmmakers in the period and stress the receptivity of female audiences emerging into the modern.[1] Particular star personae and story choices expressed female sexuality and social aspirations and at the same time "contained" and dictated the limits of female transgression—the era's popular vamp type illustrates this paradox well.² Nazimova, in taking on the role of Salome, participated in this wider solicitation of female audiences and paid tribute to notorious stage actresses and dancers before her who had made Salome their own. As writer, producer, and, evidence suggests, de facto director of the film, Nazimova also affiliated herself with Oscar Wilde—with his *author*ity as well as with his notoriety. Hers was a twentieth-century, decadent, American, cinematic, woman-made Salome. If lesbianism signifies here, it is at the intersection of these discourses, or veils. My metaphor is meant to emphasize both the lack of transparency in interpretive acts and the aesthetic dimensions of historical performances.

Salome can be illuminated by current film research in a number of ways. These include the centrality of the star system and its articulation of female sexuality with the cinema as alternative public sphere (in Miriam Hansen's phrase); women's economic and creative power as filmmakers in early cinematic production; Hollywood orientalism as thematic and aesthetic and as discourse operating in the construction of American ethnicities; the intertextuality of silent cinema; and new periodizations of the American avant-garde and of Hollywood modernism. These are shorthand designations and I will not be able to pursue all of them in this context. What I hope to emphasize is how particular aspects of the film appear or disappear under different critical gazes, suggesting ways that strategies of veiling and unveiling characterize lesbian authorship and historical interpretation alike. Available, mostly cinephilic accounts of her film—as "cult" or camp favorite, Wildean tribute, or protounderground film—can be destabilized by feminist work on silent-film history, and perhaps some of the premises of that new historiographic work tested in turn. In the next section, I offer an overview of the film and its place in Nazimova's career. Then I go on to introduce several approaches to *Salome,* starting with its latter-day reception and then turning to contextualizing theories. I argue that the Salome intertext should be seen in relation both to women-oriented film culture and to Wilde as an authorial precedent. Nazimova's film is an effort toward, a unique event in, female movie modernism.

Alla Nazimova's *Salome* sometimes seems like a hallucination of film history. The independent film's release was delayed by United Artists for nearly a year. Finally, the film premiered in New York on New Year's Eve 1922; there was a second midnight screening. On an art nouveau set "with silver cherries bobbing in her hair, the face of a petulant imp and a pertly

1. Portrait of Nazimova

boyish frame"[3] the forty-two-year-old star portrays Oscar Wilde's heroine as a fourteen-year-old, dancing the dance of the seven veils in what the *New York Times* reviewer perhaps uncharitably characterized as "an exceedingly tame and not remarkably graceful performance that Herod wouldn't have given standing room in his kingdom for."[4] Nazimova, hitherto a popular box-office draw, though one threatening to become too powerful or too "temperamental" for mainstream tastes, lost most of her financial resources and a great deal of her professional standing with the film's box-office failure. She left Hollywood and returned to the stage; her later film appearances were infrequent.

Salome was not without defenders. The *New York Times* itself applauded it as an "unusual and . . . visually satisfying spectacle" and Robert E. Sherwood called it "exceptional in every noteworthy sense," continuing, "The persons responsible for 'Salome' deserve the whole-souled gratitude of everyone who believes in the possibilities of the movies as an art."[5] But *Photoplay* and other mass-market publications warned audiences that the film was "bizarre." In a time of increasing censorship, some of this negative sentiment was generated by the source material.

Salome follows Wilde's text closely, emphasizing the play's stylization and repetitions, its air of doom and decadence. The well-known story is this: The heroine's desire is ignited by the ascetic Jokanaan (John the Baptist, played by Nigel de Brulier), who has been imprisoned by King Herod (Mitchell Lewis). The king, though married to Salome's mother, Herodias (Rose Dione), cannot stop leering at the young princess. When the prophet refuses Salome's advances, she agrees to Herod's lustful entreaties that she dance for him—at a price. After the dance of the seven veils, she names her fee, demanding the prophet's head. Her mother applauds her; Herod is appalled. He keeps his oath, but when Salome satisfies herself by kissing the severed head, he orders her death. In three remarkable costume changes, Nazimova shifts from pert and boyish dancer to a diva of the grand gesture who, drawing her peacock cloak over the head, ducks under for the kiss with a shudder of orgasmic pleasure.

Alla Nazimova was a legend of American silent cinema of the outsized style and stature that *Sunset Boulevard*'s (dir. Billy Wilder, 1950) Norma Desmond memorializes. Indeed the faded star's planned comeback in that film is what could only turn out to be a monumentally outdated treatment of the Salome story. A Russian Jew who apprenticed with Stanislavsky at the Moscow Art Theatre (an episode she embellished later), Nazimova (born Mariam Edez Adelaida Leventon in 1879) arrived in New York in 1905 with the early Zionist play *The Chosen People*. She rapidly learned English and became the American stage's foremost interpreter of the great female roles of Ibsen and Chekov. In 1917 the *Philadelphia Telegraph* reminisced: "It soon became 'the thing' to see Nazimova in a matinee performance of Ibsen.... Her Hedda and Nora became the talk of the town and were discussed in great detail by fair young critics, who raved about symbolism, universality and dramatic influence."[6] In the 1910s Nazimova became one of the first Broadway actresses to match and even surpass her stage success when she became a screen star, reportedly drawing the highest salary in Hollywood from Metro, and creating the type of European exotic with which Pola Negri and, in a different way, Garbo and Dietrich would later become identified. Her fan base, like that of most female stars, was female, whether she performed on stage or screen. The *Washington Star* reported in 1917: "Ten years ago Alla Nazimova played to an audience of Smith College girls and went to their dormitory after the play. Sitting before the fire, she answered their ... questions about the stage. She has had deep interest in college girls."[7] Later *Motion Picture Magazine* referred to her "seemingly overwhelming appeal for the feminine sex."[8] She produced her own films at Metro, and although her persona differed considerably from contemporaries such as Lois Weber and Mary Pickford, it is worth considering these women producers as part of a common phenomenon of the period. Nazimova was also well known for her extravagant entertainments at her Sunset Boulevard estate, the Garden of Alla, which in 1927 became the hotel Garden of Allah. At a period when the movie colony was becoming established as the "dream factory," Nazimova helped define the components of its lifestyle—a heady mix of opulence and orientalism, Eurocentric high-culture pretensions and California "new thought"—everything from spiritualism to diet fads. Fan magazines reported that her swimming pool—supposedly designed in the shape of the Black Sea—was "crowded with Hollywood ingenues."[9]

If her Hedda and Nora are now forgotten, Nazimova is remembered for those ingenues. In 1916, in what Lambert calls "her first known lesbian affair—which is not to say that it was her first," she met and was briefly involved with Mercedes de Acosta, who in her 1960 memoir *Here Lies the Heart* notoriously, if obliquely, details her relationships with Garbo and Dietrich, as well as her alliances with Nazimova and many others.[10] Nazimova was also involved with Eva le Gallienne (who was to have a more lasting liaison with de Acosta) and later, in 1928, joined le Gallienne's influential (and famously sapphic) New York theatrical company, the Civic Repertory. Nazimova's highly publicized artistic collaboration—rumored affair—with flamboyant designer-choreographer Natacha Rambova (née Winifred Shaughnessey) culminated in the pair's work on *Salome*. There are a few important relationships with men; most notable and enduring is what was publicly understood as a marriage to her leading man and business manager, minor English actor and *Salome*'s credited director Charles Bryant (Nazimova had never divorced an otherwise inconsequential Russian husband). Nazimova spent the last sixteen years of her life with another protegée, Glesca Marshall. As Elaine Marks asserts in her study of lesbianism and French literature: "Name-dropping in this instance is an essential preliminary activity, for if Gomorrah, as Colette observed in a criticism of Proust, is not nearly as vast or as well organized as Sodom, it is nonetheless a small, cohesive world in which connections between bed and text are numerous."[11]

Perhaps it was Nazimova's outrageous behavior, or perhaps it was the threat of her power or desire for artistic autonomy, that eventually led to her parting of ways with Metro. She formed her own production company, initially with the idea of combining several shorts in one "repertoire" film.[12] Ultimately Nazimova spent $400,000 of her own money on two projects with personal significance. Unfortunately only tantalizing production stills remain of Nazimova's 1922 film of Ibsen's *A Doll's House*, her signature stage vehicle. The film was generally well reviewed, with some criticism of the star's attempts at acting girlish at the beginning of the film that anticipates certain assessments of her Salome. For both films she enlisted the design and choreography talents of Rambova, who had designed strikingly antirealist sets for Nazimova's 1921 production of *Camille* at Metro, the star's last film at the studio. *Camille* had helped launch Rambova's husband-to-be, Rudolph Valentino, as Armand opposite Nazimova. (Nazimova's association with Valentino ensures her place in Hollywood legend; not only Rambova but another of Nazimova's lovers, Jean Acker, married Valentino, and there are sex scandals attached to both alliances.) Nazimova employed a talented professional, Charles Van Enger, as cinematographer. She used the pseudonym Peter M. Winters for her scenarios. Although Bryant, the man known as Nazimova's husband, is credited with both films' direction, he appears to have been director in name only. Perhaps Nazimova wished to defuse criticism that she had received at the end of her Metro years for overreaching, but the star clearly had full authority on her independent productions.[13]

Oscar Wilde characterized the subject of his play as "a woman dancing with her bare feet in the blood of a man she has craved for and slain,"[14] and the grande dame Nazimova turned in a stunningly stylized portrayal of the teenage femme fatale. Her choice of subject matter was not obscure, but the production's loyalty to the play was notable. Rambova's art direction and costume design were directly inspired by Aubrey Beardsley's famous illustrations of the play's first English edition. The film used only two, defiantly antirealist sets. Beardsley's black-and-white color scheme and circular motifs were picked up in visual excesses such as African American court slaves in Marie Antoinette wigs. But if Beardsley had upstaged or mocked the play's author in his graphic rendition of *Salome,* as many have argued, Rambova's visual design amounts to full collaboration in the film's aesthetic—and in its unmistakable homoeroticism.[15] The film's faithfulness in depicting the desire of Wilde's Page (Arthur Jasmina) for the Young Syrian (Earl Schenck), and Nazimova's casting decisions—although Lambert was not able to confirm the rumor of an all-gay cast, he suggests that several principles and extras were gay men and lesbians[16]—were matched by visual ambiance such as the painted nipples on the Syrian, the Executioner's (Frederick Peters) bold S/M look, Jokanaan's uncanny asceticism, and Nazimova's gamine minitunics. The film was at least as much designed as directed; who can say which of the two women had the idea to feature drag queens at Herod's court? Though a striking visuality was quite appropriate for and common in films of the period, *Salome*'s artiness made it an oddity. Possibly because of the film's excesses and fear of censorship, or possibly because of a dispute with Nazimova arising from their need to exercise control over an independent production, United Artists delayed and finally mishandled its limited release. The result was financial disaster and mixed critical reception. Nazimova never produced again.[17]

Salome is early 1920s Hollywood decadence self-consciously rendered. The ambitions a pair of female modernists had for cinema as an art form are pinned on a notorious text written by the very type of the modern homosexual. While it was certainly a star vehicle, even a vanity production, its design and staging emulated European art cinema, which had recently made its mark in the United States with the release of *The Cabinet of Dr. Caligari* (dir. Robert Wiene, 1919), as well as experimental theatrical and dance sources. Such Hollywood avant-gardism would have few successors. Certainly, the film's pervasive aesthetic of gender-bending wouldn't be seen again in American film for decades. In the very year of the film's production, Will Hays came to Hollywood to establish industry self-censorship. Henceforth stars' contracts included a moral turpitude clause to distance film production from a wave of major drug, sex, and murder scandals, most notoriously the trials of Fatty Arbuckle. Indeed, much of *Salome*'s promotion and reception struggled to emphasize its tastefulness and lack of offense to censors. This historical juncture proved to be a turning point for women directors, scenarists, and producers in Hollywood, whose power declined precipitously after the war and, ironically, coincidentally with the achievement of women's suffrage. Undoubtedly the failure of Nazimova's film and her subsequent eclipse add to its myth.

"Nazimova's Veils" is not a phrase meant to suggest merely that the actress's achievement has remained shrouded in the cinematic past and is in need of uncovering. Although the magnitude of her stardom on both stage and screen does make her subsequent obscurity notable, she is present in all the standard Hollywood histories. Certainly the vicissitudes of her career were documented extensively in the contemporary press. Even the identities that were not proclaimed aloud in such sources—lesbian, Jew, writer-director—have not precisely been hidden from subsequent generations who cared to look for them. Rather I invoke the veil as an epistemological figure something like the closet; the way Nazimova is remembered has meaning that resonates beyond the simple act of exposing her sexual and affective affinities. The veil has specifically feminine and orientalist connotations that make it a more apt trope for *Salome* than the closet would be. The homosexual secret the closet figures is veiled in this text by the public

Nazimova's Veils

sexualization of the female body. The acts of revelation and silence clustering around *Salome* and its star are multiply and unpredictably bound up with changing historical constructions of homosexuality and gender, ethnicity and agency. Nazimova's "veils" trace the contours of these contradictions.

Nazimova's outing was a standard, though not an unambiguously queer-positive, gesture before the phenomenon had a name—the word "lesbian" is almost always coupled with mentions of Nazimova in contemporary accounts. She is gratuitously though accurately referred to as "Nancy Reagan's lesbian godmother" in biographies and video guides. Perhaps Nazimova's exoticized persona allowed for the production and othering of lesbianism that kept other female Hollywood stars safe from the appellation and recuperable for wholesome heterosexuality. Kenneth Anger makes the following comparison: "[Dietrich's] passel of girlfriends was dubbed Marlene's Sewing Circle. They were not lesbians, like Nazimova's gang, but good-time Charlenes who, like Marlene, swung both ways."[18] Dietrich here is rendered nearly as American as apple pie. Nazimova's vaguely orientalized persona also veiled her identity as a Jew—though she did not advertise this ethnicity, she was always identified as of Russian nationality and could not be assimilated within nativist codes of white femininity. Nazimova's veils allure us today as her challenge to notions of core identity and transparent meaning; but we can also consider how her identities informed her film's difference in ways that have not previously been addressed. Perhaps the accoutrements of aestheticism hid in plain view a more subversive project to claim the right to public authority. Performing as a signature role Salome, the Jewish princess who died for her perverse desire, could be construed as a layered act of coming out. After discussing how contemporary and cult impressions of the film veil—that is, suggest but also obscure—this authorial act, I turn to discourses that informed the film's historical emergence.

Notably, Nazimova has been veiled as an author through the latter-day reception of her film and through the relationship to Oscar Wilde, for camp and aestheticism both enhance and undermine the lesbian specificity of her authorial performance. Lesbianism is too easily assimilated to the more defined gay male aesthetic in this case, and Wilde as a presence overwhelms the precarious authorial position of a powerful female performer-turned-producer in the Hollywood of the 1910s and early 1920s. Nazimova's film has been to a large extent preserved and put into circulation in the last several decades via its revival in the late 1960s. The *New York Times* advertised a presentation of a forty-five-minute version in 1967. The screening was presented by silent-film collector Raymond Rohauer in conjunction with an exhibition of Beardsley's drawings. It provided the occasion for a U.S. visit from Wilde's son Vyvyan Holland, whose translation of the play the program credits as the basis for the print's titles. In his program notes, Rohauer recounts gaining interest in the film, locating the original camera negative, and obtaining the exhibition rights from Nazimova's executrix.[19]

The contemporary perception of the film has been shaped by the aesthetic and social evaluations of that time and cultural context. Some sources, such as this pronouncement on the occasion of a London screening around the same time, believe that "*Salome* stands forth from the welter of ephemeral productions of the past as one of the few American pictures made with the sincere purpose of creating a work of art,"[20] whereas others echo Bosley Crowther, who, reviewing the film in 1967, called *Salome*, "One of the silent movies' more notorious Tiffany lamps, relic of a style of artsy acting that blazes as present day camp."[21] Arguably it is exactly the film's sincerity of artistic purpose that makes it camp. In her 1964 "Notes on 'Camp,'" Susan Sontag defines the sensibility in part as "failed seriousness."[22] Crowther's comparison of the film to a Tiffany lamp—a notorious one at that—betrays the influence of Sontag's definition: Tiffany lamps and the drawings of Aubrey Beardsley are featured in her sampling of "the canon of Camp."[23]

Saying the film is campy is not exactly the same thing as saying it is gay. Sontag herself is circumspect about this issue. "The peculiar relation between Camp taste and homosexuality has to be explained," she writes, but since she concedes this point in number fifty-one of her fifty-eight notes, the only appropriate response is, "Indeed." Perhaps her essay's dedication to Oscar Wilde stands in for such an explanation. However, it seems evident that the mid-to-late-1960s revival of *Salome* established the film's gay reputation. Crowther may describe Nazimova's film without reference to homosexuality. But I detect an implicit avowal of the connection in his very disdain for the film. His review continues: "Don't take this old film too seriously.... It's a preposterous bit of pretense—in its day regarded by serious critics as a limp piece of studio fashioned Art." What is connoted in an attack on a woman's work as "limp"? The "gayness" of a camp film like *Salome*—like the "gayness" of Wilde—may go without saying, but this very "obviousness," carried in the male-oriented homophobic epithet "limp," renders the meaning of Nazimova's lesbianism, and how she used the film to configure it, less historically legible.

We would do better to look to Kenneth Anger than to the *New York Times* for insight into camp sensibility and for a fuller appreciation of *Salome*'s artistry. The gay avant-garde filmmaker and "magick" practitioner all but defines cinematic camp in his scandal compendium *Hollywood Babylon,* the French publication of which shortly preceded *Salome*'s revival and Sontag's essay. Anger's work made a kind of gay-inflected excess characteristic of Hollywood—of "studio fashioned Art"—as a whole. The gay male affiliation Crowther hinted at is marshaled explicitly in Anger's canonization of Nazimova's film. He reports that she "employed only homosexual actors as 'homage' to Wilde," and his pronouncement has become central to the lore of the film.[24] It is in part in homage to Wilde that the extravagantly stylized *Salome* has maintained a steady gay cult following in recent decades. Yet if it is unintentional camp that is produced by what might be called the failed seriousness of Nazimova's interpretation of Wilde's highly self-conscious, literate work, then an attribution of conscious authorship to Nazimova becomes somewhat compromised. Nazimova is certainly not ignored in this cult celebration; she is honored as a diva, of course, and her own deviant sexual identity seems to earn her bonus points in Anger's reception. But, I argue, her agency is veiled by her gender. As a woman, she is a spectacle, or at best she is seen as paying homage to Wilde rather than as making her own contribution.

Andrew Ross understands camp as a response to aesthetic forms that correspond to an earlier mode of cultural production; these "become available, in the present, for redefinition according to contemporary codes of taste."[25] Thus a typical assessment from a recent screening: "In the annals of film history, . . . Salome stands out like a shriek at an afternoon tea. . . . As the wicked Salome the great dancer [*sic*]/actress Alla Nazimova often looks and acts like the Bride of Frankenstein, moving stiffly and dreamily under the madly stylized coiffure erupting from her head."[26] If camp evaluations since the film's 1960s revival have the virtue of celebrating Nazimova's excess—keeping her daring before us—they fall short of illuminating the situation of women and Hollywood, sex and power in 1922. In the context of this essay, I can do little more than point to new directions in film historiography that might help us reconstruct and analyze these conditions of production and reception. My aim is to begin to restore the film's historicity while preserving its strangeness.

Salome's status in film history as a curio might be modified by placing it among attempts to define an early American avant-garde. Whereas France and Germany developed distinct art cinemas in the 1910s and 1920s, it is generally accepted that in the United States the rapid establishment of an industrial model eliminated experimentation. But Jan-Christopher Horak's anthology *Lovers of Cinema: The First American Film Avant-Garde,*

1919–1945 draws more meaningful connections between the United States and Europe and begins to map historical precedents to the acknowledged avant-garde that emerged with the work of Maya Deren and others in the 1940s.[27] *Salome* is thus an important touchstone; what reviewers saw as bizarre about Rambova's designs, or strange about the film's acting style and pace, can be reevaluated as part of a genuinely avant-garde experiment. C. A. Lejeune describes Nazimova's difference from her peers in a 1931 profile:

> Her face was always a fine mask.... It was her body that was her language, and a body trained and persuaded to the limits of the camera. Her gestures had been shaped in the flat, not in the round, and always with a sense of pattern; she knew every pose and poise of expression in two dimensions—how to use limbs and throat and tilted head to strengthen and complete the design on the screen.[28]

The pictorial qualities Lejeune highlights were fundamental elements not only of Nazimova's work but of Rambova's modernist designs.

Locating *Salome* in terms of its aesthetic difference certainly makes sense in light of the "artiste" image Nazimova herself cultivated. A characteristic profile shortly after her arrival in Hollywood tells us: "Nazimova doesn't speak of her venture into picture work as the 'movies'; she calls it photodrama. Neither does she think she has sacrificed her ideals; but rather, she talks of creative principles as serious as does the sculptor, painter or composer. She actually calls it an art."[29] Rambova's pretensions went even further. In her contribution to *Lovers of Cinema* on the limits of experimentation within the classical Hollywood paradigm, Kristin Thompson cites *Salome* as a fairly "extreme" example of the "mild modernism" that was incorporated into the industry in the 1920s, particularly through set and costume design. Thompson concedes that the film "shifts the usual classical emphasis on the primacy of the narrative system," which here is subordinated to the spectacular sets and to an overall emphasis on design. Yet in Thompson's functionalist terms, the film's "innovations are motivated largely by the simple and familiar story" and its "sets and stylized acting seek to create an overall tone of decadence appropriate to the play."[30] Concepts such as "motivated" innovation and "appropriate" decadent tone neutralize the film's transgressiveness—and that of its literary source—and awkwardly press the film into the service of a teleological narrative of Hollywood's aesthetic norms. Its difference is recontained.

Yet we should be wary of encouraging *Salome*'s simple introduction into a newly expanded formal "avant-garde" canon, not least because this recognition too could come at the expense of queer visibility. Formalist and romantic models of avant-garde practice and authorship, and strict typologies and criteria of admittance to the alternative canon, have often downplayed the gayness and mutual influence of films from James Watson and Melville Webber's *Lot in Sodom* (1930) to the work of Anger, Warhol, and other contributors to underground cinema. Even popular magazine coverage hints that Rambova and Nazimova's collaboration is responsible for the "bizarre" elements of *Camille* and *Salome,* and this coding of sexual deviance as artistic flamboyance deserves attention.

Morever, I agree with Thompson that the film cannot be set in direct opposition to Hollywood product. Most importantly, it is crucial to acknowledge that the film's search for a filmic language to express female desire had affinities with the goals of more commercial Hollywood production of the 1910s; far from losing its avant-garde stamp through such a repositioning, *Salome* could be seen as linking up artistic modernism with mass-media solicitation of female desire, making the female artist persona visible in/as the spectacularized, performing female body. Feminist film scholars, among them Miriam Hansen and Shelley Stamp, have documented the importance of female audiences to the emerging narrative, visual, institutional, and broad cultural forms of the cinema of the silent era. The stress Thompson places on the "assimilable" modernisms of set and costume design (and one might extend this, as Gaylyn Studlar does in her work discussed below, to dance) ought to be considered in terms of these discourses' privileged relationship to women (and indeed to gay men). Once again we are faced with a paradox of interpretation: is *Salome* considered a "milder" attempt at avant-gardism because it is trivialized by the association of design and dance with women and the masses; or might the film's ambitions indicate that the particular kind of modernism so integral to the movies was emblematically female?

The work of Miriam Hansen provides background for these questions. In *Babel and Babylon,* Hansen argues that during the transition to what we call the classical period, the cinema functioned as an alternative public sphere—a unique experience of modernity—for women. The discourse of consumerism "cater[ed] to aspects of female experience that hitherto had been denied any public dimension," Hansen argues. Commercialized leisure provided a newly gender-integrated public space that built on consumer culture's transformation of the female private sphere.[31] "More than any other entertainment form, the cinema opened up a space—a social space as well as a perceptual, experiential horizon—in women's lives," Hansen writes.[32] Having outlined cinema's "chameleon" response, in the transitional period, to a modernity in which the social reorganization of gender was crucial, Hansen has turned to questioning the status of classical cinema itself. In recent work on the movies as vernacular or popular modernism, she argues that too heavy a stress on the "classical" in Hollywood cinema ignores the fact that its very medium and mode of expression belong irrevocably to modernity.[33] Hollywood's "mass production of the senses" can be taken to express a cultural logic of modernity that takes new relations of production and consumption into account in ways high modernism could not. The challenging of the modernist canon through questions of consumerism and mass culture has been an important direction in feminist studies; Hansen's thesis, though not emphasizing gender at this juncture, provides crucial support for such work.

The artistic and literary modernism with which *Salome* allies itself would seem to be distinct from vernacular modernism, however; the film's fin de siècle homage was dated even in 1922. A common criticism is that the film is hardly a *movie;* its aesthetic is one of stasis and pantomime (and the repetitions in the play's language, which are incorporated, although to a lesser extent, in the more condensed film's titles, seem to reiterate this). Yet Wilde's symbolist ambitions in the play could be seen as fitting with the cinema's "synesthetic" capacities—here mobilized in ways that attempt to speak to the embodied experience of women in this period. Nazimova was a star of sensational films; she was marketing her independent productions to the audience she had already attracted (even in the theater she played to the masses, touring with a repertory in vaudeville). Rambova and Nazimova were enthusiastic about turning the film medium to artistic purposes; but they must also have been interested in turning art into an experience well rendered by Hansen's phrase "mass production of the senses."

Salome's debt to Beardsley's erotic and stylized drawings might have departed from Hollywood practice of its era, but attempts were made to integrate the film with the consumerism that drove Hollywood's fascination with design.[34] The very same "Salome hat" described above, in the 1991 review from the *L.A. Weekly,* as a "madly stylized coiffure erupting from [Nazimova's] head" was heralded in a London press release during the film's first run in this fashion: "The Salome headdress, with its myriad tiny, white pearls that in the light seem moon-silvered and stand upright on flexible stems, is apparently to be long with us."[35] High modernism and mass culture are bridged in this self-conscious promotion of European influence: "There is the best of reasons to believe Nazimova's 'Salome,' which made its mark on students of motion pictures when it had its premiere in this country will, in the roundabout way of passage through London

Nazimova's Veils

2. Nazimova in her distinctive *Salome* headdress (1922).

and French appearances, imperatively influence fashions in America at an early date." The reference to "students of motion pictures" injects a note of serious culture without compromising the film's populism. Similarly, Lejeune's tribute to Nazimova opens with a memory of encountering both her charwoman and "a certain learned professor . . . engrossed in a book on philology" waiting outside a cinema for the premiere of a new Nazimova film.[36] The intertextual figure of Salome herself may be one of the most productive intersections of a high-culture fascination coded male and a vernacular, sensory, consumerist modernism coded female. I first explore this figure and then turn to the related and similarly intertextual discourse of stardom.

73

If today we recognize the figure of Salome as aestheticism's touchstone—Wilde's interest followed that of Moreau, Huysmann, and Flaubert among others, and Strauss's widely produced opera based on Wilde's play brought the obsession into the twentieth century—the female tradition of appropriating Salome is now almost forgotten. In her essay, " 'Out-Salomeing Salome': Dance, the New Woman, and Fan Magazine Orientalism," Gaylyn Studlar writes compellingly of the prominent cultural role of dance in the reconfiguration of gender in the early twentieth century. Specifically, she explores dance iconography in the movies and in fan magazines addressed to female audiences, noting the emphasis on the sensuality of movement, costume, and the body. Dance's high-art connotations were also crucial in the appeal to women. Studlar points out: "Dance as a 'classic' art stood as an ideal symbolic merger between traditional middle-class female gentility and contemporary ideals of feminine freedom from bodily and imaginative restraints."[37] Nazimova is often misremembered as a dancer in contemporary tributes, and Rambova, as Studlar puts it, "became the ultimate High-Art Dance Vamp" in the popular press.[38]

Salome dancers were a craze in the first decades of the twentieth century, and the figure "became [one of] the representational foundations for Hollywood's proliferation of vamps in the late 1910s and 1920s," according to Studlar.[39] Canadian dancer Maud Allan caused a sensation in 1905–1907 with her much emulated "Vision of Salome" dance, and "Salomania" spread: "By the summer of 1908," dance historian Elizabeth Kendall writes, "Mlle. Dazie [of the Ziegfeld Follies], was [training and . . .] sending approximately 150 Salomes every month into the nation's vaudeville circuits, each armed with the same routine—an incoherent mix of gestures and undulations addressed to a papier-mache head."[40] The year 1908 saw a Vitagraph production of *Salome,* and additional film versions followed. Female vaudeville and early film audiences watched sensational renditions of the dance of the seven veils that signified and embodied female desire and expressiveness, and they imitated the dance in private theatricals. By producing her own version of *Salome,* Nazimova added another dimension of agency to spectators' active viewing and dancers' making the role their own through performance. Coming late in the cycle, her film inevitably made use of earlier versions—those of male modernists as well as those of modern women.

The Salome story revolves around the gaze—Salome arrests the circuit of gazes objectifying her (Herod's, the Young Syrian's) and uses her to-be-looked-at-ness to get her will in the dance of the seven veils. She looks at Jokanaan and desires him; her nature is transformed by the admission of desire her look entails; she enumerates his body parts in a reversal of the fragmentation so often visited on the female body; her punishment for appropriating the gaze is absolute. The male artist, Linda Saladin argues, often found his substitute in the "mythologization of femininity," and this took on favored form in "the myth of Salome, used to obsessive lengths in the late nineteenth century."[41] The femme fatale was a way of symbolizing the mysteries of the artist's own act of creation; her perversion of procreative power was sublimated in his art. In Nazimova's production, both the character's and the artist's transgressive acts are present; the appropriation of the gaze is their common mode. One striking sequence encapsulates the film's thematizing of the gaze, extending to that of the narrational role of the gaze behind the camera. A petulant Salome looks across the terrace toward the cage over the cistern where the prophet is incarcerated, and her gaze is followed by an extreme close-up of the lock on the gate. She next looks over at the Young Syrian, who is huddling with the Page who loves him, the men depicted in a two-shot that appears frequently in the film (fig. 3). This gaze is followed by a close-up of the key tucked in the sash at the Syrian's waist (fig. 4). Next Salome, in profile and on point, exaggeratedly bends her head forward, staring with great concentration at her target, and the next shot is a remarkable frontal extreme close-up of her eyes, the frame masked so they appear, heavily outlined with makeup, in a bar across the center of the screen (fig. 5).

In a film featuring mainly long-shot tableaux on a dominating set, the use of point-of-view editing and extreme close-ups—particularly the shot of Nazimova's eyes—underscores the transgressive looking and desire that drive the film. Her gaze is castrating; the Young Syrian will kill himself after surrendering the key. The scene's stylized posing also shows that the influence of dance is not restricted to the choreographed set piece, the dance of the seven veils. Nazimova is the object of the gaze, certainly; yet her small, lithe figure in a straight, short sheath offers a different version of the spectacle of the female body. And although we look with her at Jokanaan, neither he nor the other men are coded as conventional objects of female desire. *Variety* complained that "the heroic figures were given a decided appearance of effeminacy and the slaves of color were beefy instead of muscular."[42] The film's circuit of looks demands a powerful and unusual alliance among filmmaker, heroine, and female spectator.

Thus despite the Salome figure's association with a male literary tradition, portraying the role in a star vehicle was also an attempt to solicit the historical female film audiences who, Studlar emphasizes, were passionately involved in female stars' fandoms and in the popularity of dance

3. The Young Syrian and the Page who is devoted to him shrink from Salome's desire.

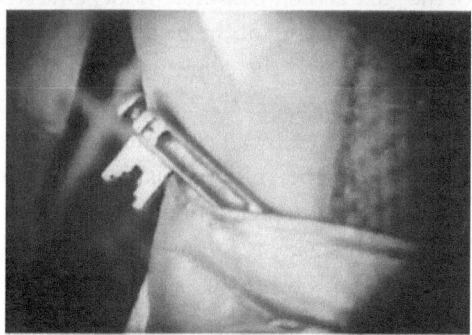

4. The key that Salome needs in order to release Jokanaan, singled out by her gaze.

5. Salome's gaze stands in for the gaze of Nazimova as filmmaker.

and orientalism in the period. The "fit" between Nazimova's star persona and the role of Salome can help us read her significance, for, as Richard Dyer and others have argued, stars powerfully express cultural contradictions around gender, sexuality, race, and ethnicity.[43] The transgressiveness of Salome's desire is consonant with Nazimova's "foreign" persona.[44] Such connotations are evident in an item appearing well before Nazimova went to Hollywood: "there are critics who contend that . . . the art of the actress has been seriously handicapped by an apparently studious avoidance of roles that are entirely free from a note of morbidness."[45] The morbidness

6. Nazimova dances the dance of the seven veils (*Salome*, 1922).

of Ibsen's new woman (the term was also associated with lesbianism in the period) would soon be transferred to that of the screen's avatar of the femme fatale, the vamp. Yet as much as Nazimova's exoticness and inscrutability overlap with the vamp persona, she also departs from the type. Her Russianness is played up in almost all accounts; her national identity facilitated high-art connotations more easily than did the Arabic trappings of vamps such as Theda Bara, although I would argue that Nazimova's Jewishness, veiled behind her Russianness, provided an orientalist link. Nazimova's publicity insists on calling her Madame; "unusual" and "temperamental" are frequent epithets. She is above all an artist, and the press surrounding her independent productions gave this aspect of her persona even more emphasis. *Motion Picture World* felicitously describes *Salome* as "One of the most artistic screen portrayals along the line of what is popularly termed 'high art.'"[46] In keeping with this notion, Salome's deal with Herod — whom she tricks with her dance so that she can call the shots — might be seen as allegorizing Nazimova's transition from performer to filmmaker.[47]

At the crucial turning point of her film career, on the release of *Camille* and her announcement of her intention to produce *A Doll's House* and

Salome independently (the period of her partnership with Rambova), Nazimova was interviewed by Gladys Hall and Adele Whitely Fletcher for *Motion Picture Magazine*. The encounter is interestingly framed by Hall's refusal to allow what one might call the Norma Desmond aspects of Nazimova's persona to be dispelled. At the premiere of *Camille* she stares at Madame in the audience: "I'm not looking at a celebrity so much as at an esthete... a tragedienne... a Woman of Sorrows," and she is shocked when the next day "Nazimova steps briskly into the room... in a blue tailored suit, mannishly tailored. Her feet are shod in low-heeled oxfords... her hair is parted on the side, sleek, boyish."[48] The star informs the interviewers that it is only on set that she is addressed as Madame; her friends call her Peter, and sometimes Mimi. The interviewers "feel at a loss. This is not the Nazimova they had prematurely visualized. No incense wreathes in serpentines about her definite, boyish head. She wears no chiffons, no morbidities, she thinks, succinctly, as a man thinks." Other profiles note Nazimova's originality in dress, but few type her new-woman persona through such masculine iconography. Despite Nazimova's having concluded the interview with a "Peterish handshake," Hall goes off still muttering "sphinx of the marble mien... empress of hate... you turn men's blood to ice."[49] Thus just before *Salome* went into production, Nazimova's star image was defined in terms of its contradictions; the aesthete qua femme fatale meets the new woman qua lesbian. Sexology's characterization of the "mannish" woman as invert was an accessible discourse during this period—Nazimova even tells her interviewers that her favorite reading is medical books.[50] At this juncture, such contradictions were still manageable, but with the film's failure came increasingly critical press coverage of the star, and the connotations of mannishness and of what a *Photoplay* profile called "bizarrerie" or "diablerie" were likely to have become more legibly lesbian.[51] The *Variety* review of the film brings issues of form, sexuality, and lack of popular acceptance together: "*Salome* as a picture is going to please a few who are Nazimova devotees, a few that like higher art in all its form perversions, and then its box office value will end."[52] Claiming this constellation of connotations in her own way, Nazimova as artist and as unconventional, even deviant, woman met in the *Salome* project.

To take on the role of this particular femme fatale is also to take on the legacy of the stars who had previously been identified with the figure and thus to ally oneself with women artists as well as female audiences. Especially when performed by a Jewish celebrity, the Jewish princess became a powerful vehicle for articulating a modern sexual identity. First among stars associated with the role is an actress who never played it: Sarah Bernhardt, who was in rehearsal with Wilde in 1892 when the production was shut down by England's examiner of plays. Sander Gilman notes that the star "was represented as the quintessential 'modern' woman in the stereotypical discourse of the late nineteenth century."[53] Through readings of the anti-Semitic elements of discourse on Bernhardt, he concludes that "La Divine Sarah is the embodiment of the sexuality of the Jew and, therefore, of the modernity which this sexuality comes to represent."[54] Nazimova's selection of Wilde's heroine is a way of affiliating with and reinterpreting from a female position the styles of European decadence and its figures *belle juive* and lesbian, specific incarnations of the femme fatale. By virtue of her own stage reputation, Nazimova exploits the high-art imprimatur of the role as associated with Bernhardt and later with Ida Rubinstein, the Ballets Russes star who was widely celebrated for dancing Salome.[55] Peter Wollen details the importance of the Ballets Russes at the intersection of modernism and mass culture (particularly fashion), and Michael Moon builds on this work to bring out the queer dimensions of the ballet's legacy, including that of Rubinstein's lesbian fandom.[56] Finally, Studlar stresses that the Ballets Russes decisively influenced early-twentieth-century women's popular culture. Thus Nazimova's movie version of *Salome* exploited an emerging mass-cultural topos—a sexualized, crypto-Semitic, and cryptofeminist other. Even the Hollywood Salome whose performance immediately preceded Nazimova's could be considered as figuring her own Jewishness as well as her sexual agency through the exotic, erotic persona. In 1918, quintessential vamp Theda Bara included a large-budget version of Salome among the vehicles for her wildly popular femme fatale persona. While a range of male authors, painters, and composers each had his Salome in the fin de siècle period, powerful women performers intervened in their construction of a female, Jewish other when embodying the role themselves.

Nazimova's performance must be situated in relation to other interpreters of the role, but her direction/production of her film distinguished her *Salome* through a particularly canny affiliation to Wilde. I argued above that Wilde tends to overshadow Nazimova in contemporary interpretations of the film; at the time of the film's production, the connotations of the association were variable. Sometimes her fidelity to the play was declared unique; at other times, the overfamiliarity of the play was grounds for dismissal of the film. In my view, a cross-gender identification with Wilde lent Nazimova the discourse of aestheticism through which to make her originality and agency visible. She and Rambova are promoted in Allied's press release as "gifted young women artists"; the characterization is enabled by the aura of Wilde's "exquisite poem drama" and the reputation of Beardsley's illustrations. But of course Nazimova borrowed more than an artistic signature from Wilde; she borrowed a queer one. Putting herself in Wilde's place, as opposed to just performing in his text, she asserted her sexual difference. In this queer film artifact, authorship and performance intersect in the star's body. Wilde's name is synonymous with homosexual perversion; his heroine connotes sexual voracity. Nazimova's visibility depends on her manipulation of these veils.

The metonymic association of Salome's impersonator with the vice of the play's author had a precedent: the strange case of Maud Allan. Allan had notably less control over the association with Wilde's perversion than did Nazimova, as it took on evidentiary status in a court of law. As I noted above, the Canadian dancer's "Vision of Salome" had been a phenomenal international success, but it was her appearance in a private London production of Wilde's play in 1918 that provided one of the most bizarre episodes in Salome studies. Noel Pemberton Billing, MP, suggested in print—as part of his campaign to expose German sympathizers during the war—that those attending Allan's performance were themselves perverts, hence traitors. (He claimed to have a black book containing the names of forty-seven thousand such homosexuals/subversives.) His dark intimations appeared under the title "The Cult of the Clitoris." Allan sued for libel and lost, after some remarkable testimony that implied that if she knew what the word "clitoris" meant, she must be the initiate of dangerous and seditious sexual practices. As Jennifer Travis recounts in her article on the trial, Billing testified that Allan's performance was "designed so as to foster and encourage obscene and unnatural practices among women."[57] The "cult of the clitoris" named an audience turned lesbian by a particular interpretation of a work of art. Nazimova went into production a few years after the Billing trial; I have no doubt that she was aware of this case that had identified Wilde's play with lesbianism by way of the actress's reputation, the play's symbolism, and its content, the princess's "sadism."

Obviously it was the stigma of the play's author, the figurehead of the cult of sodomy, that set the drama in motion. (Wilde was imprisoned during his play's Paris premiere and never saw it performed.) A common reading of *Salome* sees the transgressive sexuality of the heroine as an encoding of the author's homosexuality, and a homophobic reading views the punishment with which it concludes as just. Jane Marcus, in a passionate early 1970s defense of the play's feminism, "Salome: The Jewish Princess Was a New Woman," insists that Wilde drew a "link between the suffering artist and the aspiring woman."[58] Elaine Showalter queries, "Is the woman behind Salome's veils the innermost being of the male artist?" and reproduces a widely circulating photograph that is credited as Wilde himself costumed as his heroine.⁵⁹ Nazimova's auteurist impersonation of the heroine can also be seen as a reading of Wilde's identification with Salome.

Lesbianism, not "visible" in her performance even as her costumes spectacularize her putative lover's designs, is another veil that opens on further discrepancies. Generally accepted as the first lesbian filmmaker, Nazimova, like Salome, solicits our gaze at what appears to be an obvious feminine spectacle in order to enact a duplicitous female desire and subjectivity. She further encodes and veils her lesbian authorship by appropriating the authority of Oscar Wilde and the discourse of aestheticism. Her performance of lesbian authorship is also an authorization of lesbian performativity.

William Tydeman and Steven Price's thorough study of the production history of Wilde's play includes a very insightful reading of Nazimova's film, asserting that "the return to Wilde and Beardsley . . . represents . . . the first attempt fully to integrate a common reading of the play's sexual subtext with a design concept and performance style fully informed by that subtext."⁶⁰ Their important observation nevertheless begs the question for me of how "the play's sexual subtext," if understood as male homosexuality, might signify in the hands of a lesbian auteur. I have been implying that autonomous (albeit destructive) female sexuality, male homosexual notoriety, and a bid for female authorial recognition converge to provide the conditions of lesbian representability in the film. Tydeman and Price continue their evaluation of Nazimova's effort: "That [the film] attempts this [presentation of the sexual subtext on the level of production] covertly, and in Hollywood, makes it possible to see Nazimova's *Salome* as a coded act of resistance to perhaps the most influential contemporary medium in the regulation of sexual behavior."⁶¹ I would add that it is crucially the regulation of *female* sexuality that is contested in the film, and, according to scholars such as Hansen, in the public sphere of silent cinema. Nazimova may be using Wilde to resist Hollywood, as the authors imply, to style herself as an auteur, and to make her deviant sexual identity visible, as I have argued. But importantly she is also using Hollywood, with its mass female audience in mind.

As I have reiterated, Nazimova was a star with a large female fan base—she confided to Hall and Fletcher in *Motion Picture Magazine* that "most of her friends are young girls."⁶² This attempt to exploit the popular female audience in relation to what aimed to be a new discourse on both sexuality and film art is to me what is most exciting about the film and most daring about Nazimova's aesthetic bid. Hence the disappointment of the film's failed 1923 release. Partly because her version did not manage to reach female audiences—who had a demonstrated taste for Salomes, at the time of its release—it did not reach them later, in its 1960s revival or its gay film festival afterlife. Retrospective programming requires a certain connoisseurship that has not been built into the history of lesbian spectatorship. But Nazimova seemed explicitly to be trying to fashion such taste, perhaps such an audience, among her fan base. I like to imagine an alternative history originating in a silent-film-era "cult of the clitoris"—that is, a history that recognizes the possibility of lesbian identifications forming among female film audiences.[63] Fascinatingly, *Salome* has been kept visible by its "queerness"—in both senses, strangeness and gayness. It is now possible to nuance that visibility in relation to histories of female sexualities, ethnicities, and subcultures. While there is no denying that Nazimova's attempt to queer the female mass culture of her era through an avant-garde experiment failed spectacularly, the utopian desire to exploit the modernist elements of the popular medium on behalf of marginal subjects is memorialized in the film's cult following.

Feminist scholars have identified the veil as a double-edged figure of feminine masquerade. The veil incites the desire to see, attracts the gaze and blocks its penetration, covers the woman and gives her cover to look. The set piece of *Salome* is the dance of the seven veils, a performance that so blinds Herod with lust, and binds him within a male code of honor, that he grants Salome's desires for the head of the one who refused to return her look. The woman gets what she wants through a performance of femininity; a similar play of receptivity and agency, surface and depth, is at work in Nazimova's veiling of authorial control in her visibility as star. As I have argued, Nazimova's use of stardom as a vehicle for authorship becomes a complex performance, involving appropriation of traditional male authority via Wilde as well as intertexts and collaborations through which a lesbian signature can be decoded. What remains fascinating is the ways the performance and the audience to which it was directed did and did not match up. Like Salome's, Nazimova's transgression is significant, her defeat cautionary.

There is a notable gap in Wilde's play: he provided no stage directions for the dance of the seven veils. Its performance thus functions as a kind of supplement. Sometimes in stagings of Strauss's opera, a second Salome substitutes here, adding an interesting twist to the seduction. In other contexts it is exclusively through dance that the performer makes the role her own. Reviewing Nazimova's film on its release, the *New York Times* was disappointed that her dance was so unrevealing: "But someone may reply that the real dance wouldn't be allowed, and that if it were decent people wouldn't want to look at it. Exactly. The real *Salome* is impossible on both counts."[64] Nazimova reveals the possibilities of a spectacularly fake, constructed Salome, one unconstrained by what is allowed or by what decent people might want to look at. In homage, rather than an act of stripping back successive veils, our present-day interpretation of her film's multilayered performance must consist in their artful arranging.

Notes

1. See for example, Miriam Hansen, *Babel and Babylon: Spectatorship in American Silent Film* (Cambridge: Harvard University Press, 1991); Shelley Stamp, *Movie-Struck Girls: Women and Motion Picture Culture after the Nickelodeon* (Princeton: Princeton University Press, 2000); Janet Staiger, *Bad Women: Regulating Sexuality in Early American Cinema* (Minneapolis: University of Minnesota Press, 1995); Gaylyn Studlar, *This Mad Masquerade: Stardom and Masculinity in the Jazz Age* (New York: Columbia University Press, 1996), and the essays in this volume. The Women Film Pioneers Project, based at Duke University, collects information about and coordinates events related to women producers and directors of the silent era.
2. See Gaylyn Studlar, "'Out-Salomeing Salome': Dance, the New Woman, and Fan Magazine Orientalism," in *Visions of the East: Orientalism in Film*, ed. Matthew Bernstein and Gaylyn Studlar (New Brunswick: Rutgers University Press, 1997), 116–119; Staiger, "The Vamp," in *Bad Women*, 147–162, and Sumiko Higashi, *Virgins, Vamps, and Flappers: The American Silent Movie Heroine* (St. Albans, Vt.: Eden Press Women's Publications, 1978).
3. Program, National Film Theatre (London), 1966, *Salome* clippings file, New York Public Library, Library for the Performing Arts.
4. Unsigned review, *New York Times*, 1 January 1923.
5. Scrapbook, Margaret Herrick Library, Academy of Motion Picture Arts and Sciences. Also appears in *Best Films of 1922-23* (New York: Small, Maynard, and Company, 1923), 103.
6. B. D., "Ibsen, Nazimova, and Henry Miller," *Philadelphia Telegraph*, 5 May 1917, Nazimova scrapbook, New York Public Library, Library for the Performing Arts.
7. Unsigned, *Washington Star*, 17 March 1917, Nazimova scrapbook, New York Public Library, Library for the Performing Arts.
8. Quoted in Gavin Lambert, *Nazimova: A Biography* (New York: Alfred A. Knopf, 1997), 198.
9. Quoted in Lambert, *Nazimova*, 249.
10. Ibid., 175. De Acosta was hopelessly starstruck; her introduction to the celebrated Nazimova came through New York lesbian social director Elizabeth Marbury. Their meeting is recounted in de Acosta's *Here Lies the Heart: A Tale of My Life* (New York: Reynal, 1960), 74. On de Acosta's relationships with

Dietrich and Garbo, see my essay "Black and White: Mercedes de Acosta's Glorious Enthusiasms," *Camera Obscura* 45 (2001): 225–265.

11 Elaine Marks, "Lesbian Intertextuality," in *Homosexualities in French Literature,* ed. George Stambolian and Elaine Marks (Ithaca: Cornell University Press, 1979), 355.

12 An undated press release announces that screenwriter June Mathis is joining with Nazimova for her "first 'repertoire' film." Nazimova clippings file, Museum of Modern Art Film Study Center. Nazimova uses the term "repertoire" to describe her planned project including both *A Doll's House* and *Salome,* in Gladys Hall and Adele Whitely Fletcher, "We Interview Camille," *Motion Picture Magazine,* January 1922, 24.

13 After the association with Metro terminated, *Photoplay* coverage of Nazimova turned critical. "An Open Letter to Mme. Alla Nazimova," *Photoplay,* August 1921, 31.

14 Quoted in Lambert, *Nazimova,* 255.

15 For an overview of opinions on Beardsley's contribution, see William Tydeman and Steven Price, *Wilde: Salome,* Cambridge Plays in Production (Cambridge: Cambridge University Press, 1996), 113–122.

16 Lambert, *Nazimova,* 261.

17 In his biography of Rambova, Michael Morris details positive audience and mixed critical responses to several advance screenings of *Salome.* Morris, *Madam Valentino* (New York: Abbeville, 1991), 90–92. The screenings were held to drum up interest while United Artists delayed the film's release; when *Salome* was finally released by Allied Producers and Distributors, a UA subsidiary, in February 1922, it was undermarketed. On the release history, which was probably more responsible for the film's failure than its subject matter or aesthetics, see also Lambert, *Nazimova,* 259–260.

18 Kenneth Anger, *Hollywood Babylon* (New York: Bell, 1975), 177.

19 Program, Gallery of Modern Art (New York), 1967, *Salome* clippings file, Museum of Modern Art Film Study Center. Rohauer's program notes state that Vyvyan Holland "wrote a new translation of his father's play which provided the basis for the sub-titles of the silent film"; if this means that new titles were added or other changes were made for the release, they might have been the basis of Rohauer's copyright. He presented the film with Wurlitzer accompaniment of music from Strauss's opera "just as Nazimova had used it originally." In fact, the original score did not incorporate the opera *Salome.*

The original release print of *Salome* was 5,595 feet, with its running time put at sixty-five to seventy-nine minutes by *Harrison's Reports* (13 January 1923). 16mm and video versions of *Salome* in circulation since run as short as thirty-two minutes. I have not yet been able to determine whether these are based on Rohauer's materials. In 1990 the George Eastman House restored a 35mm print at 5,032 feet, which runs approximately sixty-seven minutes.

20 Program, Motion Picture Guild, 26 June 1967, *Salome* clippings file, New York Public Library, Library for the Performing Arts.

21 Bosley Crowther, review of *Salome, New York Times* 15 February 1967.

22 Susan Sontag, "Notes on 'Camp,'" in *Against Interpretation* (New York: Farrar, Straus, 1965), 287.
23 Ibid., 277.
24 Anger, *Hollywood Babylon*, 113.
25 Andrew Ross, "Uses of Camp," in *No Respect: Intellectuals and Popular Culture* (New York: Routledge, 1989), 139.
26 Mary Beth Crain, *L.A. Weekly*, 17 May 1991.
27 Jan-Christopher Horak, ed., *Lovers of Cinema: The First American Film Avant-Garde, 1919-1945* (Madison: University of Wisconsin Press, 1995).
28 C. A. Lejeune, "Nazimova," in *Cinema* (London: Alexander Maclehose, 1931), 81.
29 Lillian Montanye, "A Half Hour with Nazimova," *PhotoPlay Classic*, July 1917, 36.
30 Kristin Thompson, "The Limits of Experimentation in Hollywood," in *Lovers of Cinema*, ed. Horak, 75-77.
31 Hansen, *Babel and Babylon*, 116.
32 Ibid., 117.
33 See Miriam Bratu Hansen, "The Mass Production of the Senses: Classical Cinema as Vernacular Modernism," in *Reinventing Film Studies*, ed. Christine Gledhill and Linda Williams (London: Arnold, 2000), 332-350.
34 Lucy Ficher's work in progress on art deco and cinema is especially relevant to these questions. See her essay on Greta Garbo, for instance, in this volume.
35 E. A. Bachelder, *Salome* clippings file, Museum of Modern Art Film Study Center. Admittedly, other commentators had less confidence in the hat: "We are not sure whether we like Madame Nazimova's idea of Salome as a petulant little princess with a Freudian complex and a headdress of glass bubbles. We rather believe such a Salome would not have stirred men so in those good old pagan days. You have our warning: this is bizarre stuff." Scrapbook, Margaret Herrick Library, Academy of Motion Picture Arts and Sciences. The source of the clipping is *Photoplay*.
36 Lejeune, "Nazimova," 78.
37 Studlar, "'Out-Salomeing Salome,'" 113.
38 Ibid., 119.
39 Ibid., 116.
40 Elizabeth Kendall, *Where She Danced* (New York: Alfred A. Knopf, 1979), 75.
41 Linda Saladin, *Fetishism and Fatal Women: Gender, Power, and Reflexive Discourse* (New York: Peter Lang, 1993), 57-58.
42 Review signed "Fred," *Variety*, 5 January 1923, 42. The reviewer expressed a common unease about Nazimova's body and presentation in the film: "the box office won't get any great draw because of any lack of dress on the part of the star."
43 Richard Dyer, *Stars* (London: British Film Institute, 1975).
44 One profile opens by noting that Nazimova's "exotic *bizarrerie*" has generally been attributed to her Russianness. Then the author finds that even in her theater work in Russia she was cast as a foreigner. "Even her pantomime has an

accent," he concludes. Herbert Howe, "A Misunderstood Woman," *Photoplay*, April 1922, 24.
45 *Philadelphia Telegraph*, 5 May 1917.
46 *Motion Picture World*, 3 January 1923. A story in the same publication cited *Salome*'s poster design for "conveying the desired idea of art rather than sensation." Museum of Modern Art memorandum dated 29 October 1959, quoting *Motion Picture World*, 24 February 1923, 783, *Salome* clippings file, Museum of Modern Art Film Study Center.
47 A colorful passage from 1913 on Nazimova's stage performance in *Belladonna* fills in the orientalist and femme fatale dimensions of her persona: "If I went somewhere beyond Egypt, off up there beyond the source of the Nile, and came upon a community that adhered strictly to customs of centuries before the Christian era, I should expect to go into the temple and find a young lady serving at the altar.... She would have a graceful, undulating figure and... she would appear to be some remarkable creature, half serpent and half woman.... I would recognize this high priestess... because I have seen her reincarnated in the year 1913. I have seen and chatted with Alla Nazimova.... I have seen her flashing eyes, heard her panther-like moans, watched her writhe and undulate like a python. She loves sin, this woman, she glories in death and destruction—for artistic purposes. The decent little critters who swarm over the earth and live out their thoroughly respectable and moral lives are to her like a pack of worms." Archie Bell, "Remarkable Little Russian Actress Who Comes to Opera House This Week," *Cleveland Plain Dealer*, 18 November 1913, scrapbook, New York Public Library, Library for the Performing Arts.
48 Hall and Fletcher, "We Interview Camille," 98.
49 Ibid., 100.
50 Ibid. For the classic debate on the relationship among the new woman, sexology, and lesbian self-definition, see Carroll Smith-Rosenberg, "The New Woman as Androgyne," in *Disorderly Conduct* (New York: Oxford University Press, 1995), 245–296, and Esther Newton, "The Mythic Mannish Lesbian: Radclyffe Hall and the New Woman," *Signs* 9, 4 (summer 1984): 557–575.
51 Howe, "A Misunderstood Woman," 24.
52 Review signed "Fred," 42.
53 Sander Gilman, "Salome, Syphilis, Sarah Bernhardt, and the Modern Jewess," in *The Jew in the Text: Modernity and the Construction of Identity*, ed. Linda Nochlin and Tamar Garb (London: Thames and Hudson, 1995), 111. His approach to *Salome* focuses on the anti-Semitic German discourse surrounding Strauss's opera.
54 Ibid., 115.
55 Elaine Showalter calls Rubinstein "one of the first of the feminist Salomes" in her genealogy of the figure, which includes a discussion of Nazimova's film. Showalter, *Sexual Anarchy: Gender and Culture at the Fin de Siècle* (New York: Viking, 1990), 159.
56 Peter Wollen, "Fashion/Orientalism/The Body," *New Formations* 1 (spring 1987): 5–33; Michael Moon, "Flaming Closets," in *Out in Culture: Gay, Les-*

bian, and Queer Essays in Popular Culture, ed. Corey K. Creekmur and Alexander Doty (Durham: Duke University Press, 1995), 285.
57 Quoted in Jennifer Travis, "Clits in Court," in *Lesbian Erotics*, ed. Karla Jay (New York: New York University Press, 1995), 151.
58 Jane Marcus, "Salome: The Jewish Princess Was a New Woman," *Bulletin of the New York Public Library* (1974): 100.
59 Showalter, *Sexual Anarchy*, 151. The photograph, which I am told depicts not Wilde but a German diva in the role, appears on page 157 of Showalter's book.
60 Tydeman and Price, *Wilde: Salome*, 165.
61 Ibid.
62 Hall and Fletcher, "We Interview Camille," 98.
63 I speculate that certain films of the 1930s fostered a similar identification in chapter 1 of *Uninvited: Classical Hollywood Cinema and Lesbian Representability* (Bloomington: Indiana University Press, 1999).
64 Unsigned review, *New York Times*, 1 January 1923.

JANE M. GAINES

Of Cabbages and Authors

I had more trouble with a title for this essay than I usually have. What I originally wanted was a title that would convey a strong challenge to the notion of authorship as well as my own resistance to using the concept. I am, I must confess, a deep skeptic, a committed anti-auteurist. What do I mean by anti-auteurist? As a teacher, I have never offered a course or even a single unit organized around an auteur director, consistently attempting to emphasize (over the director) the authorial force of stars and other creative personnel. As a scholar the only two directors whose work I have seriously studied have been "overlooked" auteurs: the great lesbian filmmaker Dorothy Arzner and the prolific African American filmmaker Oscar Micheaux.[1] In these cases, my motive has been an interest in rectifying the historical record as well as in rethinking the prevailing approach to authorship—the approach that "lost" and subsequently "found" these two extremely interesting figures in the history of cinema. Given my dissidence, then, I originally wanted a title that would signal my position and I called the article "Disbelieving in Authors." Some will recognize my debt to Richard Dyer, who once wondered if he really "believed in authors." It occurs to Dyer that there is something similar about his use of not one but two problematic constructs: the author and the homosexual. One is as fraught as the other. In "Believing in Fairies: The Author and the Homosexual," Dyer says that he probably never believed in either the author or the homosexual in the conventional sense. As he explains his reservations, "If believing in authorship (in film) means believing that only one person makes a film, that that person is the director, that the film expresses his/her inner personality, that this can be understood apart from the industrial circumstances and semiotic codes within which it is made, then I have never believed in authorship."[2] In my ambivalence I take inspiration from Dyer, the reluctant auteurist who nevertheless completed a major research project from the premise of gay male and lesbian authorship. It is not only that the critical category has exhausted its usefulness, that the culture produces *us* far more than we produce it, and that the legal category (as I show) has been historically and continues to be slippery. It is also that authorship is humanism's grip on the age of the machine and that this grip is unyieldingly

Of Cabbages and Authors

tight. While the mechanical age allowed the intervention of humanism's creative subject, it is becoming increasingly clear that the digital age will not allow it as easily.[3] Yet here we are in the digital age, many of us newly interested in the lives and the work of early women in the film industry and any approach that we take would seem to be unavoidably informed by authorship, the broader concept that is meant here to encompass the auteur "theory" that contemporary critics agree was never exactly a theory.

Authorship as an approach has been stubbornly resilient. Stephen Crofts, in a recent reconsideration, titles a subsection of his essay "The Persistence of Authorship."[4] Despite significant critiques in the 1960s that pronounced the "death" of authors, the authorial approach to literary history, music history, and particularly art history has apparently suffered no real setback.[5] For the time being, the most sophisticated contemporary film criticism, in order to sidestep the politics of romantic individualism, is quite comfortable with authorship as a critical construct, asserting that if we treat authorship as nothing more than an abstract structure we avoid the political pitfalls of dealing with real historical authors, impossible-to-determine intentions, and the unchecked authority of the dead author over the live text.[6] This widespread critical use of authorship-as-structure, however, has meant that the concept of authorship is still available for every new wave of undergraduates to rediscover it and to reclaim not the structuralist construct but the old individualist and authoritarian notion. Although we might be teaching Howard Hawks as a structure, our students are understanding the film director as an author.[7]

Feminism has been in a somewhat awkward position in relation to these historical developments. Some have lamented the coincidence of the death of authorship and the discovery of new works by women. A case could also be made that the male auteur director as a figure has eclipsed the contributions of women who worked as screenwriters and editors and even actresses.[8] Since 1950s and 1960s auteurism in France as well as the United States overlooked women directors, it could be argued that these women should now receive their due, but no major initiative has been mounted within the academy to achieve this—although the women's film festivals of the 1970s must now be appreciated for their initiative on behalf of so many "lost" pioneers.[9] Some efforts were made by feminists, beginning in the 1970s, to restore to critical importance the work of such silent-film directors as Alice Guy-Blaché and Germaine Dulac and such sound-era pioneers as Ida Lupino and Dorothy Arzner.[10] Then the pipeline of discoveries seemed to dry up and, like other feminist scholars, I assumed that there had been only a handful of women working in the U.S. and European film industries—a few in the silent era before 1927 and a few more in the sound era.[11]

In the early 1990s, around the time of the publication of Anthony Slide's *The Silent Feminists* and his updated edition of *The Memoirs of Alice Guy-Blaché,* the academy began to think about these forgotten women.[12] Important new encyclopedias and books by feminists on early women in the industry began to appear—about twenty years after the first signs of scholarship.[13] It was then that the fact of the sheer productivity of Alice Guy-Blaché, the first woman filmmaker, hit me dramatically. Clearly, she had produced hundreds upon hundreds of films. One source refers to about seven hundred films—four hundred one-reelers at the Gaumont Studio in France between 1896 and 1907 and another three hundred in the United States between 1910 and late 1913, although she would continue until the 1920s.[14] More recently, however, Alison McMahan has suggested that we consider that as a producer Alice Guy-Blaché oversaw more than one thousand features and shorts over the course of her career beginning at Gaumont and continuing in the United States, where she headed her own studio, the Solax Company, in New Jersey.[15] Considering this remarkable record, we might be tempted to conclude that this woman is an exception. But if we thought that Alice Guy-Blaché was alone as an example of a woman who headed her own company, we were again wrong about the role of women in early cinema. Between 1912 and around 1925 there were many production companies in Hollywood and elsewhere in the United States controlled by women in the industry. To list only a few: the Mandarin Film Company in Oakland, California; Lois Weber Productions; Lule Warrenton's "first all-woman film company" at Universal; Gene Gauntier's Feature Players; the Nell Shipman Company; the Cleo Madison Stock Company; the Mabel Normand Feature Film Company; Alla Nazimova's Nazimova Productions; and companies owned by Florence Turner, Helen Gardner, Gale Henry, and Dorothy Davenport Reid.[16] The existence of so many companies points, if nothing else, to the numerical importance of women at this stage and yet this knowledge has yet to have its influence on the film history we have been teaching. Anthony Slide is often quoted as saying that "There were more women directors at work in the American film industry prior to 1920 than during any period of its history."[17] To me, the evidence of this work speaks volumes about the political economy of gender and even more significantly gives us a clue that there might have been different notions of "maker" preexisting the classic directorial role that would be worth our while to study as feminists. In short, there is much at stake for both film history and feminism. Does interest in

Of Cabbages and Authors

7. The Nell Shipman Company. Lionhead Lodge, 1923.

this topic imply that I am advocating a return to authorship? No. I need to step back from my own account and confess that it was not until I had become intrigued by this project that I realized that I had become involved in what appeared to be a classical authorship project—and here I was, a confirmed anti-auteurist.[18]

The Analyzable Arzner

I remain a confirmed anti-auteurist, and the following is thus an attempt to begin to explore theoretical options for examining the contributions of early women in the industry, for suggesting a better foundation that could have its significant impact on the rest of the field. Clearly a fuller critique is called for, particularly in view of the fact that so many films by early women have come to light and been exhibited recently.[19] I have not been entirely alone in my stand against authorship. Some of my objections to female auteurism would echo those made by others, notably, Giuliana Bruno on the

Italian Elvira Notari (to whom I return) and, more recently, Kay Armatage on the Canadian Nell Shipman, both critics writing in the context of book-length studies on these early film pioneers.[20] Most of these objections have also been raised in Judith Mayne's seminal discussion in *The Woman at the Keyhole,* a consideration that rehearses the approach she takes in her study of Dorothy Arzner.[21] Neither pure biography nor straight industry study, neither pure critical analysis nor unabashed empirical history, this book presents us with a new model of how creatively to mix sources and approaches to the lives of women in the industry. Mayne's reconsideration would seem to stand as a critique of 1950s auteurism as well as an earlier feminist position, both of which became associated with a denial of female agency but for significantly different reasons.[22] While the patriarchial assumptions of auteur theory excluded women, feminism theorized the exclusion. So the challenge for Mayne was to open up a serious new consideration of Arzner's work without falling back on auteur methodologies.[23] It is logical that Mayne would turn to the evidence of the text as support for her argument that Arzner is not a traditional auteur. However, there is no easy way out of the authorship bind. As we will see, the evidence of the text is used both to deny that Arzner is an auteur and to prove that she is a female author. Against seeing the director as a classical auteur Mayne argues, "there is little of the flourish of mise-en-scène that auteurists attributed to other directors, for instance, and the preoccupations visible from film to film that might identify a particular signature do not reflect the life-and-death, civilization-versus-the-wilderness struggles that tended to define the range of more 'properly' auteurist themes."[24] Dorothy Arzner, then, is not an auteur's auteur. Still, Mayne needs to reserve some notion of authorship in order to discuss how it is that Arzner's work diverges from that of male directors. The very rationale for her project is at stake here since the argument that Arzner is worth studying not just as a woman in the industry but also as a pioneering lesbian filmmaker is based on the assumption that, once analyzed, the films that she directed within the classical Hollywood system reveal themselves to be markedly different from those directed by men.

Few would dispute that Arzner's films are recognizably different. However, we still need to ask about the route Mayne takes to get to the textual Arzner. While her perhaps most dramatically successful move away from conventional auteurism is her argument for understanding the function of what might be called lesbian feminist irony, Mayne still needs to consider Arzner's ironic perspective on patriarchy within some of the terms of traditional auteur criticism, as in the reference to "preoccupations,"

Of Cabbages and Authors

8. Dorothy Arzner

"signature," and other signs of authorial presence. And although Arzner's "preoccupations"—most notably, a concern with heterosexual initiation and female communities—are hardly those of the old auteur, the irony Mayne finds is new content in old terms: a female "signature," even a "sign of female authorship."[25] Arzner's work is still framed in auteur vocabulary, Mayne's exercise confirming Dyer's suspicion that there is no easy way around the stubborn methodology of authorship.

In what follows, however, I want to begin to explore ways that we might sidestep, all the while critiquing authorship. Clearly it is easier to critique than to circumvent. My first inclination is to ask about the term "preoccupation," a starting point that allows me to wonder about the vocabulary we use in reference to the operation of the unconscious. Perhaps my objection is related to the way the authorial unconscious is taken for granted in cultural criticism. To be more precise, what gives me pause is the way that the unconscious always automatically implies an author who is thought to have fantasies, dreams, and "preoccupations." (And I am completely aware of the prevalence of this assumption.) I want to remind us, however, that it is not that the text and author belong to one another in any integral way but that they have become interlocked and are sometimes seen as interchangeable, even indistinguishable. (Note the way it might be said in reference to the film *Stagecoach,* "It is Ford."). Strangely, however, this interchangeability is never discussed in terms of the text/author synonymity (although this may be assumed) but is usually seen in terms of other metaphors—the authorial mark, hand, or sign. One of my objections, then, has to do with the mixed metaphors of authorship: the hand of, the mark of, the body of. My question also has to do with the difficulty of finding as well as attributing marks, with identifying signs said to have been left in the text by an author, signs that critics have read as "signatures."[26] As we know, directors and producers themselves have also been convinced that they leave something of themselves in the work. In our case, the question of the existence of a female signature hearkens back to some of the earliest attempts to articulate what it was that women directors actually contributed to the motion picture industry as well as to the film itself. Interestingly, some of these early articulations come from the writings of the women pioneers themselves.

Something or Nothing in the Text

The question as to whether or not the contribution of the female artist (whether director, screenwriter, or editor) can be "read" off from the text immediately confronts us when we encounter the rare examples of literary output from early women in cinema. Familiar to us through years of reading literary criticism is the move that assumes that something of the author can be perceived, discovered, found in the text. Volume upon volume has been written based on the assumption that there is something there. Note, however, that this sign of the author that has been so often referenced in aesthetic discourse is so illusive and undefinable as to be nothing more than "something." And not surprisingly, this would be the very something that is referred to in the various writings by early women in cinema who attempt to describe whatever it is that women in particular contribute to the film. These women directors are convinced that women make a distinctive contribution but they are at a loss when it comes to explaining what this could conceivably entail. For Alice Guy-Blaché (who in her essay "Woman's Place in Photoplay Production" sees woman as an "authority on the emotions"), it would appear that just being a woman is a guarantee.[27] And a guarantee of what? Following from the fact that she is a woman, says Guy-Blaché, she will produce photodramas that "will contain that inexplicable something."[28] This mysterious something cannot be explained! Somewhat later, Ida May Park, who worked in the industry between 1909 and 1920, becoming the most important woman director at Universal after Lois Weber, wrote a similar essay appearing in the book *Careers for Woman*. Here Park also refers to what she believes to be the existence of female particularity. This particularity, too, turns out to be nothing more than something. It is, Park says, woman's "sense of dramatic value" that contributes to the photoplay an "indefinable something."[29] Now consider the gendering of the something, the thing that eludes explanation and definition. The old something that was once the sign of the hand of the male literary author is now gendered to produce whatever it is that women add to the work. Feminist critics should experience some déjà vu here. Like Alice Guy-Blaché and Ida May Park, feminists once expected that the hand of the woman would guarantee its own legibility. We now wonder.

It is perhaps more than the metaphor of the "hand of" that does the ideological work here. Really, it is the personhood (always gendered) of the author, the body, the life of a historical person, that guarantees. In both male and female cases, something is assumed to be there in the work because of the existence of the author, not, however, because anything is systematically discerned in the work. To put this differently, it is the presumption of an author (or a woman) that produces the expectation of the something. In the case of Alice Guy-Blaché and Ida May Park, the presumption that a woman produced is even more remarkable for another reason. The presumption of female authorship negates agency. Both women, looking back at their careers in these particular essays, attempting to explain their creative product, would seem to defer to a mysterious authorial process rather than to assert a prior agency.[30] Rather than using an active, first-person voice in these advice essays (all the better to claim "I did this"), these women write in the third person in a way that suggests an incredulity about women's filmmaking process. As I have said, feminism has been here before; we have debated the existence of the feminine aesthetic as well as the creation of a feminist aesthetic, and argued for female agency. It even would seem that this female somethingness smacks of the problematic essentialism that feminist theory has so thoroughly critiqued.[31]

But I want to go somewhere else with this. I am immediately reminded of legal theory. The fact that so much is made of the something that is so mysterious (inexplicable) and incomprehensible (indefinable), that is so large and yet so small, so important and so inconsequential, so said and so inarticulable is reminiscent for me of turn-of-the-century approaches to legal authorship in the work. My own research on the question dates from an earlier attempt to look at the legal discourse around the problem of the historical establishment of authorship as the basis for copyright ownership. In nineteenth-century case law, the key cultural object in dispute was neither the humanly wrought literary work nor the fine art work. It was the machine-made work—the photograph. The argument prevailing at the turn of the last century was that photographed works of art were not copyrightable because the machine that produced them had no human soul. Although a human creator might well have been behind the camera, that subject was understood as finally negated. But copyright law stipulated human labor as the basis for protection. In the photographic process, the creative subject, the subject requisite to the establishment of authorship in the work, was said to "disappear" into the soulless machine, the camera. Nothing of the photographer made its way into the photographic work. The machine was not a creator and certainly was no author.

Eloquent arguments were made against this position, the position that, as we know, finally won out. These arguments, now forgotten, were made on behalf of the machine as author, the sunlight as author, the object before the camera as author, and even the face of the photographic subject as author. But the argument that the machine alone was not a creator prevailed, opening the way for the position that the creative subject, in this case the photographer, could "invest" something of himself in the photographic work, a position that eventually led to modern copyright in the work.[32] My interest in this argument, as one may imagine, was originally in the history of the creation of value in conjunction with the rise of commodity capitalism. Here one could recognize the capitalist opportunism of the argument that the soul in the work, that special something, was supplied by the creative subject. The creative subject, inserted between the machine and the work, just previous to the work, made rights in the work possible, and ultimately, of course, rights made value possible and value exchange, and so on. Perhaps then it is because of this historical background that I have never been impressed with any arguments for the existence of a something in the work. That something is nothing more than the figment of the creative subject, an empty construct that turns the work so quickly into protectable property.

The Analyzable Subject and Something to Analyze

It would seem to be a leap from the hard-as-tacks realm of copyright law to the soft, membranous realm of psychoanalytic theory. Yet I find some structural parallels. The legal subject that (*that,* not who) stands before the work, the subject that is said to insert itself in the work, is surprisingly like that other subject, the psychoanalyzable subject whose unconscious makes it possible for there to be something to analyze in the work. Raising questions about the subject and the unconscious will signal to many readers that this essay is written under the sign of 1970s film theory, especially as I now want to turn to a rather overlooked essay by Jean-Louis Baudry, a key figure who helped define that moment. In answer to concerns that I am advocating a return, I should say that this is more of a transition piece intended to probe the assumptions that have for so long informed our criticism, but also to gesture, briefly, toward a critical future without authorship as we have known it. In "Author and Analyzable Subject," Baudry seems to actually perform a critique of authorship as well as of the notion of the unconscious in an essay that challenges traditional assumptions about authorship while verging on traditionalism. As Baudry has theorized what he calls the "analyzable subject," this is the individual subject who "intervenes" in the production of the work or good.[33] It is the analyzable, really psychoanalyzable, subject that produces the difference between the manufactured good such as an automobile and a manufactured motion picture. The former is unanalyzable, gives us nothing to analyze, and the latter ostensibly gives us the dense unconscious of a subject to analyze.

In a nutshell: because there is an analyzable subject, there is something to analyze; without the analyzable subject, there would be nothing to analyze. A "work," says Baudry, will always "point back to" a subject. This is the subject who we assume has an unconscious, and, in a typical 1970s formulation, because there is an unconscious, this subject can be, according to Baudry, "subjected to analysis."[34] So the psychoanalytic system requires something in the work to analyze and the legal system requires something that can be the basis of rights. In both cases, it is not, however, finally the something in the work that really matters. We know what matters in the legal system and why. What matters in the psychoanalytic system? What matters is the "producer subject" to whom the something owes its existence, the "producer subject" to whom it points back, the "producer subject" that is Baudry's term here for author.[35] What matters is *someone* to analyze. Someone to analyze gets conflated with something to analyze, and thus we have an analyzable signifier. Following this reasoning, and implicating centuries of authorship criticism, this would suggest that there is nothing in the work, really, and that everything is in the author, the producer subject whose unconscious it is that gets analyzed. It is not only that something is in the work by virtue of the author, another old authorship theory premise. Actually what we have here is more of a back and forth between the author and the work, the hypothetical analogy between the two, and even the confusion between one and the other. The objection is not only to the theoretical sleight of hand. With others, I object to the way authorship has historically eclipsed something as important as audience. However, what also gets short shrift is genre, that is, other texts—other texts as sources of meaning. To put it even more dramatically and to situate this question in relation to the development of critical theory: the author has stood in the way of realizing the possibilities of one of the most important philosophical insights of the last twenty-five years, that is, the way in which we are constituted through language. Stephen Heath once put it succinctly: "the author is constituted *at the expense of language.*"[36]

So it is finally this obfuscation of the way that culture is actually produced as well as the structural confusion between author and work that confirms my disbelief and causes my political objection to authorship. And yet. To agree with Richard Dyer, again, it does matter, it does "make a difference who makes a film."[37] Here is an apparent paradox: The author may not put anything into the work that can be found there, but it does finally matter, after all, who it was who worked on the film. Let us consider, as an illustration of this paradox, a film that has been exhibited in at least one gay and lesbian film festival because it has been asserted that Dorothy Arzner photographed some of the sequences in it. The surprising example is Paramount's 1922 *Blood and Sand,* well known because it was such an important vehicle for Rudolph Valentino. Arzner was supposed to have filmed some of the bullfight sequences.[38] Not for a minute would I want to argue against screening and studying films that Arzner was connected with in any way. Elsewhere I concluded that one way around the attribution question is homage.[39] But even the most well-intended tribute "for Arzner" runs the risk of extending an invitation to authorial scrutiny. We look at *Blood and Sand* to try to find Arzner in it and behind this looking is a set of dubious assumptions. Consider, for instance: Is the operative assumption that because Arzner was who she was that she would have filmed these sequences differently? Would her authorial contribution have been discernible in the text? Would her lesbianism have made a difference? Would she have positioned the camera in a way that subverted the masculine ritual? My guess is that since the basic premises of authorship inform the most well-intended tributes, the short answer to all these unanswerable questions is "yes."

There is another set of questions familiar to film scholars, and I ask them again because it is my contention that we still have no satisfactory answers. These are the questions we have historically answered with a gesture toward the nature of industrial production and the collaboratively produced work. So what do we do with the contribution to *Blood and Sand* of director Fred Niblo, who also directed such silent action films as *Ben-Hur* (1926) and Douglas Fairbanks's *The Mark of Zorro* (1920), as well as the silent melodrama *Camille* (1927)? More problematically, seeing *Blood and Sand* as Arzner may cause us to forget the lesser-known June Mathis, who not only wrote the script for the film but wrote *Camille* for Alla Nazimova and was, like Arzner, an editor as well as a screenwriter.[40] Do we overlook the fact that this was a Rudolph Valentino vehicle when we focus on Dorothy Arzner or do we relish the apparent contradiction in her role in the production of heterosexual excess, in the creation of a matinee idol for female fans?[41] To focus on *Blood and Sand* because Dorothy Arzner shot footage may also be to overlook the entirety of her own labor on the film as an industrial product. Arzner may have shot sequences but she is also credited as the editor of *Blood and Sand* (as well as *The Covered Wagon* [1923], *Ruggles of Red Gap* [1923], *Merton of the Movies* [1924], and *Old Ironsides* [1926]). We have not even begun to discuss editing and agency and neither have film scholars thought much about editing as authorship. We would need to ask: does Arzner's editing contribution mix and mingle with Niblo's direction? Do two contradictory contributions contradict one another? Does something of one cancel out something of another? The phenomenon of contradictory signifiers is not only a feature of the many-authored text. As Baudry comments, "analyzable signifiers" can "accumulate, confront, and contradict one another . . . [and] transform the proclaimed intentions of a single author."[42] Psychosemiotics thus dismisses intentionality.

What of authorial style? Baudry gets at the question of authorial style in relation to the unconscious with a strangely suggestive metaphor. Style, he says, is the "manner in which a system of signs wrinkles repeatedly under the insistence of an unconscious." The assumption here would of course be that the signs would show signs of wrinkling. Yes, says Baudry, there would be "hidden clues (not readily apparent)" for "the artist like the criminal leaves his trace."[43] Again, generations of critics have dedicated their careers to searching for authorial clues. Here is where Baudry buys into the same system he has critiqued, showing himself to be somewhat traditional in his conviction that something can be found in the work. We are here (again) asked to assume that because there was an author, a producer subject, there will be, must be, something of her or from her in the work. Remember the problem of the mixed metaphor: the author has left something in the text and the author is the same as the text. Which is it? The author/text analogy especially breaks down when one considers the many-authored, industrially produced motion picture. In the case of motion picture "author," there is no perfect equivalency (analyzable subject/analyzable text) as one might find in the literary author/literary work equation. Recall what it is, following Baudry, that authorship really assumes: "There is something to analyze in the work because the work was produced by an analyzable subject." Why can't we recognize this for the tautology it is? Given the tautological structure of authorship, why would anyone "believe in authors?"

And yet, there have to be ways around the fraught concept, ways that would allow us to speak about women pioneers and their creative work in the formative years of the film industry. There must be a way to speak about them without diminishing their contribution by refusing to see them as auteurs. What follows is, hopefully, only one of many attempts to think our way creatively around the political drawbacks of authorship. One new model is afforded by Giuliana Bruno in her study of Italian silent-film director Elvira Notari. Bruno takes a unique approach to the problem of a retrograde auteurism, doing so in the spirit of feminist inquiry. If Elvira Notari must be an author, then her authorship, in Bruno's words, becomes a "pure function of feminist criticism."[44] Carefully, Bruno constructs a case in which, as she uncovers the work of this forgotten director, she sets up a mutually reinforcing authorial function in which her own authorship is "mirrored" by that of Elvira Notari. In fact, Bruno's own authorship is completely contingent on that of Notari: "In a way, I *desire* the author: I need her figure . . . as she needs mine."[45] Desire. In film studies, the concept of desire is everywhere, its centrality evidenced in the titles of recent books, if nothing else.[46] So I hesitate to reintroduce it again. And yet, something in Baudry's discussion of the creator's desire suggests a somewhat more oblique approach to the author/work conundrum. Baudry arrives at this formulation by beginning with the labor theory of value, embellishing Marx in his suggestion that it is not labor alone that goes into the production of the commodity-object. In particular "quality" objects, he says, in certain modes of production, in this process, the producer's desire is also manifest.[47] So to take the photographic aspect of motion picture production, "desire" is mixed with the machine, not sexual desire so much as the desire to create, to produce. Although this sounds suspiciously similar to

Of Cabbages and Authors

the human something, requisite for authorship and property, the theorization has another, different feature. It is not that this desire becomes evident on the face of the work; it is that the desire of the maker is validated by a purchaser who "recognizes the legitimate desire" in the selection of the object.[48] A different symmetry is produced: Baudry's "desire to make movies" is balanced by the "desire to see movies" (the spectator).

The Fantasy of Producing Fantasies

The desire to create is elevated over any number of other desires, other wantings. Here is the theorization of the desire to make movies, a wanting-to-produce-fantasies, that is, to produce them in the plural and to produce them for others. This desire to make movies could be seen as opposed to the more familiar psychoanalytic understanding of one's own wanting that requires satisfaction via an object that sometimes involves a singular fantasy and returns us to the analyzable subject. Whether or not it goes in another direction will depend on our own theoretical ingenuity. To get at this "movie-making desire," Baudry asks an interesting question, almost a riddle, whose answer could produce a circularity: "to what kind of representation or fantasy does the desire to make movies refer?"[49]

Rather than answer this question with an analysis of an analyzable authorial subject, we could answer it with history. The answer might be found in the lives and work of the women who made hundreds of fantasies for others before the advent of sound, and I want to start there. One would imagine that this intriguing question could be answered through a study of the history of Alice Guy-Blaché, first woman filmmaker and producer of probably as many as a thousand moving-picture fantasies. But in order to get at these fantasies we need to take an unusual route. We need to go through her own fantasy account of the production of what might or might not be her first film and might or might not be the first fantasy film produced by anyone—ever. This account can be found in her memoir where she describes the conditions of the production of a film she recalls having made in 1896—*La fée aux choux,* or *The Cabbage Fairy.*[50] The major sources in English on French film history are a different matter. One suggests that Alice Guy was assigned the job of producing short films to promote the "chronographe" and asked to work with her cameraman, Anatole Thiberville, on the production of comic films based on illustrated postcards, but not until 1897. No mention is made of *La fée au choux.*[51] Another gives Alice Guy credit for being the first "producer/director" to scout for locations and

9. Alice Guy-Blaché

commends her for her resourcefulness, but also does not refer to *La fée au choux*.[52] We are indebted to Alison McMahan for meticulously researching the claim made in the memoir, for discovering that Guy-Blaché has probably simplified what is actually a complicated history of the life of a Gaumont print.[53]

As Amelie Hastie discusses regarding Alice Guy-Blaché's memoirs in this collection, the filmmaker is writing from an unusual position: that of having been lost along with the prints of her films. It is as though the very disappearance of so many works produced the erasure of the producer herself. Thus it is that, looking back at her career, this important pioneer is placed in the position of "having to write herself back into history," as Hastie says. And it is clear that she wants to write herself in as a woman director, the first, even, as suggested by her quarrel with accounts that would award the honor to Lois Weber. Despite the modesty that contradicts the insistence on her place in the history of cinema, as Hastie notes, Madame

Of Cabbages and Authors

Blaché attempts to produce herself as a director. Whether or not she is beginning to see herself as an auteur director is an interesting question since, given that she wrote the memoirs between 1941 and 1953, it would seem that the concept, as first developed by the *Cahiers du Cinéma* editors in the 1950s in France, might not have been available to her as yet. But it is safe to say that she is looking back at the history of the motion picture industry after the first histories have been written; she is writing after the celebration of the careers of D. W. Griffith, Edwin S. Porter, Georges Méliès, Emil Cohl, and Ferdinand Zecca. Perhaps she was influenced by the "great men" histories of Georges Sadoul and others.

And yet, if we are to take the history of the cinema seriously, we would protest that in early cinema, certainly in 1896 and later, there were no directors as they were later known, and thus certainly there were no directors who were thought of as authors in the sense that they later came to be understood. So this retrospective attribution of authorship takes on enormous significance: to elevate Alice Guy-Blaché may be to honor her achievements, but to make her a director of the first or even one of the very earliest fiction films is to seriously misread the production history of the moving picture—that is, its industrial production.

Already we know from Hastie that Alice Guy-Blaché was modest about her role, perhaps reluctant to give herself credit for having done what might never have been attempted before. And yet, there is an eagerness to say "I did it!" I find a curious tension in the key passages in the memoir where Guy-Blaché describes the making of *The Cabbage Fairy*. She plays it down as she plays it up. I have referred to this as a fantasy account because of its retrospective nature, its evident yearning to set the scene of the first scene as a proper one. So much is riding on this account for Guy-Blaché as well as for us, we now discover, a little too late. Thus, because the memoir is so fortuitous, there is a danger in seeing it as "nothing more than" a fantasy about the production of (what might be) the first movie fantasy. We have much invested in seeing the memoir as the evidence that she *actually* produced this first. This is crucial, for the memoir stands where there is current confusion about the date as well as the identity of a recently located extant print. As McMahan tells us, for years *La fée aux choux* has been confused with *Sage-femme de première classe* (1902), a confusion confounded by the misidentification of a widely published still from this remake (fig. 10).[54] So the memoir especially stands where there is a question mark about the extant film. Although we might have an analyzable subject (Madame Blaché), we have only now an analyzable film text that may or may not be the text in question.

10. Still from Alice Guy-Blaché's *Sage-femme de première classe* (1902), not the earlier *La fée aux choux (The Cabbage Fairy)*, with which it is often confused.

Given the difficulty of matching up an extant film with the account in the memoir, I propose to see Alice Guy-Blaché's memoir as both a history and a fantasy, contradictory though this may seem. We need it to do a lot of work: first, to see if the memoir can help us answer the question "To what kind of representation or fantasy does the desire to make movies refer?" and second, to help us fill in the history of industry practices. Properly, we need to ask about the industrial production of fantasies, another interesting tension in both the history of the moving picture and this early account in which an office secretary solves an industrial problem with a story. As an avid reader as well as an amateur performer, Alice uses something she knows and understands (entertainment) to derive a strategy for rectifying what she perceives to be a problem for the business. Her relationship to her first job is a key factor here, for it appears to tell us much about how women pioneers in the industry went beyond the job as they made their mark on that industry. This is a history of how women started at the bottom.

Young Alice Guy (later Blaché) had trained as a secretary in order to support her widowed mother after the exhaustion of the family fortune. Her first job was with the Gaumont company in Paris and it was only after she had proven herself in the office to Léon Gaumont that she dared to ap-

Of Cabbages and Authors

proach the producer with an idea, a plan in which she went beyond the catalog of "shots" that the company was then producing. She refers to these as "demonstration films," or moving pictures that "demonstrated" mechanical problems and solutions. As Madame Blaché describes her start in the memoir:

> Daughter of an editor, I had read a good deal and retained quite a bit. I had done a little amateur theatricals and I thought that one might do better than these demonstration films. Gathering my courage, I timidly proposed to Gaumont that I might write one or two little scenes and have a few friends perform in them. If the future development of motion pictures had been foreseen at this time, I should never have obtained his consent.[55]

Clearly "I might write one or two little scenes and have a few friends perform in them" is an amazing understatement of her historical role, especially if it is her first film, or, as we are thinking, possibly *the* first fiction film.[56] Immediately, the almost apologetic tone and the reduction of significance, however, is countered by a shift that indicates a knowledge of the enormity of the occasion: "If the future development of motion pictures had been foreseen at this time, I should never have obtained his consent." Many today ask why there were so many more women in important creative positions in the industry in the silent era than at any time since. Contained in this sentence is a concise explanation of the reason women were able to work in the motion picture industry in Europe and the United States: no one knew that motion pictures would become big business. This was not yet a significant industry and with so little at stake (so little power, so little capital), much more could be entrusted to women. The field was empty and they stepped in with relative ease. Madame Blaché stepped in because there was no industry at all. In her discussion of Elvira Notari as a director, Giuliana Bruno notes the interesting twist in the fact that Notari's authorship was created out of this void. As she puts it, "Yet it is precisely because silent cinema had not yet constructed and focused upon authorship, or devised a rigid hierarchy of production roles, that Elvira Notari's authorship was able to occur."[57] Thus, it would seem, a paradox: women could become authors because there were no authors! And yet, were they authors?

Let us look further at Madame Blaché's description of this (possibly first) industrially produced fantasy film. Initially, she had to promise Gaumont that her experiment would not compete with her secretarial work for him. Then, having gained his consent, she proceeded to put together a small shoot, a miniature version of the ones she would organize so many times in her future and an industry prototype that is with us today. But in this account of industry practice, more than one creative agent steps in to fill the void where no fiction film author had stood before. First, she mentions Anatole Thiberville, her cameraman, then, the fact that there were no unions in 1896. The implication here is that everyone worked overtime—Gaumont even requesting that she serve as a moving subject, running around her garden, while he tested camera speeds on a Sunday.[58] So perhaps we are to assume that both she and Anatole continued this play-work on that day that might have been the one on which the first fiction film was shot. This first shoot might have been play-work, but as she describes it, some of the basic aspects of fiction film production are there: the studio, the scenery, the props, the costumes, the actors, and the camera.

> At Belleville, next to the photographic laboratories, I was given an unused terrace with an asphalt floor (which made it impossible to set up a real scene) and a shaky glass ceiling, overlooking a vacant lot.... A backdrop painted by a fan-painter (and fantasist) from the neighborhood made a vague decor, with rows of wooden cabbages cut out by a carpenter, costumes rented here and there around the Port Saint-martin. As actors: my friends, a screaming baby, an anxious mother leaping to and fro into the camera focus, and my first film *La Fée Aux choux* was born.[59]

A floor with a glass ceiling (existing and essential light), a backdrop or scenery, wooden props, rented costumes, actors, and a camera focused on the scene—these are the building blocks. But although I am saying that some of the aspects are familiar and therefore could be seen as testimony to the outline of a structure on which an industry would grow, it could be argued that this short (recollected) account gives evidence of a moment innocent of the possibility of either authorship or directorial role. This is the industry before either specialization and the elaborate division of labor or the studio system with its multiple directors. The several versions of the making of *The Cabbage Fairy* complicate the question: Was there a functioning author at the scene of the first fiction film shoot? Simone Blaché's version is that her mother "filmed the fairy-tale of how children are born in cabbages" after Gaumont agreed to let her use the camera because he thought of it as like a child's toy.[60] Yet this version does not match the memoir, which doesn't exactly say who shot the film. The impossibility of attribution, however, helps us think through the vicissitudes of authorship. If, on one hand, Alice Guy shot *The Cabbage Fairy* herself, film historians might consider it an example of the early "cameraman system of production." If, on the other hand, Anatole Thiberville worked with Alice Guy on that day, this would *not* be considered the cameraman system of production thought to define the industry in the United States between 1896 and 1907. More importantly, given the memoir account, neither does the shoot seem to conform to the practices of the director system of production that describes the few years before studios established the hierarchy and division of labor that emerged after 1909. It should be noted here that even this terminology of "cameraman" versus "director" system is in dispute and comparisons between American and French systems are only now beginning to be made.[61] Certainly Blaché's memoir should not automatically confirm the existence of the director system of production in which there is a role for a person who, as Janet Staiger describes it, would stage the action that another photographed and who would "manage" craftsmen on the model of the theater director.[62] Look again at the account that makes a single reference to "I," a reference made only in relation to the arrangement that Alice Guy had with Léon Gaumont—a permission that denotes that she was in charge yet in no way confirms that she directed, managed, or even staged the events before the camera. On the contrary, the passive voice—"and my first film *La Fée Aux choux* was born"—suggests that the film produced itself, that no one individually created it.

The point of this exercise is to say, "what if we turned back the clock?" What if we were to imagine the cinema as more the industrial mass-produced object and less the individually produced work, the product of an analyzable subject? This is a suggestion for checking the expansion of authorship and its mistaken approximation of the cinema to earlier modes of creative production, most notably the writing of literary texts. To some degree, Charles Musser's use of the term "collaborative system" to suggest the nonhierarchical cooperation of stage manager and cameraman puts us on the right track.[63] However, it stops short of what I am asking for: an approach that takes account of not only the contributions of cocreators but the role of other industrial elements that contribute to the function of the apparatus. Most productive here is Baudry's discussion of the "constraints" and "limitations" of the materiality of cinema as well as "intermediaries" that and who intervene between the artist and work.[64] His discussion reminds us how many intervening factors in motion picture–making, present from the very beginning, are partially or purely industrial: chemical processes and chemically based products (film stock, processing, and printing), mechanical processes and products (cameras and their internal functioning devices such as the focusing lens), illumination from electrical or natural processes (mechanical or natural light) and, most important for my argument, industrially or manually produced material props. Although the cameraman might or might not have been at the filming of *La fée aux choux,* the camera was there. A "fan-painter" and/or a "fantasist" (it is not clear from the reference) painted the backdrop and rented costumes contributed to the scene, and a carpenter "cut out" the "rows of wooden cabbages." Actors also contributed to the scene, apparently, following this account, moving of their own volition, the mother "leaping to and fro," the baby screaming, and friends playing other parts. Francis Lacassin, who interviewed Alice Guy-Blaché in later life, says that her friend Yvonne Mugnier-Serand was also there at the shoot.[65] Note the way authorship intervenes in accounts of creation. Almost immediately, as early as Lacassin's article published three years after Blaché's death, her experiment becomes evidence of singular authorship: "In a picture postcard vein of humor, it tells the story of a woman who grows children in a cabbage patch. This first effort was well received, and as she'd enjoyed the experience its author decided to continue her new career."[66] Its author? It is this easy and automatic assumption of authorship that must be challenged.

There are several ways to mount this challenge, the first being to accentuate the difficulty presented by the possible copresence of what Baudry would call the "unanalyzable collective subject" and the more authorial "analyzable subject," a recipe for, as we discussed, contradicting signifiers and the subversion of intentionality.[67] But even the plurality and heterogeneity of the analyzable subject cannot accommodate either the problem of the industrial machines that make their mechanical, unanalyzable contribution, or the problem presented by the totally unanalyzable industrial object within the film: the wooden cabbages. Some may say, following Lacassin, that *La fée aux choux* is a fantasy about where babies come from. Even Alice Guy-Blaché herself, in a rare television interview, talks about a couple who are unable to have a child until a fairy finds one for them in the cabbage patch.[68] To my mind, however, the naïveté about where babies come from can be likened to more than half a century of "not knowing" where films actually come from. Babies do not come from cabbages and films do not spring fully formed from the minds of authors. To bring home the importance of the materially and industrially produced aspect of the moving picture itself, we need to insist that although an individual creator or creators in collaboration may have conceived a story featuring cabbages and babies, the wooden cabbages themselves, essential to the visualization of the industrially produced fantasy, were crafted by a carpenter. Although one might attempt to analyze the carpenter, the wooden cabbage, having no unconscious, is as resistant to analysis as anything in the physical world. And what would be the point in psychoanalyzing the person who sawed, hammered, and painted the cabbages?

Of Cabbages and Authors

A second way to mount the challenge to authorship is to ask "whose fantasy?" Where do films come from anyway? Whose fantasy are we talking about? This set of questions is important as we research and write the stories of other female pioneers whose contributions to the film industry have been overlooked and forgotten. Nearly lost in the infancy of cinema, in this primal scene, would be the contributions of the other women involved in that first shoot. While we easily attribute an authorial contribution to Alice Guy without even knowing the circumstances behind the production, we have at our disposal no fully developed theory that will accommodate other creative agents at the scene, that will easily allow more than one analyzable subject.[69] If the friend Yvonne Mugnier-Serand was there and presumably acted in *La fée aux choux,* why wouldn't the story about babies found in the garden be *her* fantasy? Couldn't it have been her story that was played out rather than a story we may too quickly credit to the psyche of Alice Guy, who would later direct so many fantasies? Did Mugnier-Serand play the part of the anxious mother who lept back and forth in front of the camera ostensibly on her own volition and without direction? Surely the baby screamed without direction. And as it is quite likely that no one was directing anyone, why wouldn't it be logical to see all the actors, the friends playing the mother, perhaps a father, and a fairy, as enacting their own fantasies rather than the fantasy-story of someone else, that of the director-author, the someone Baudry calls the producer subject?[70]

The presumption of an individual author is a convention that dies hard. In film theory, authorship has gone hand and hand with the presumption of directorial control. Thus when we asked the question "to what kind of representation or fantasy does the desire to make movies refer," the reader may have assumed, too quickly, that the desire to make movies was the wish of the author-director, producer-subject alone. Contrary to this assumption, we might more productively consider the group of friends who shared the desire to make movies, who were captivated by a fairy tale about growing babies in the garden. Wouldn't all the actors have to agree on this fantasy and thus share in the fantasy in order to enact it together? And would they not have likewise shared the fantasy of producing fantasies? Would they have envisioned the making of the movie before they staged it? We are helped in this line of thinking by Elizabeth Cowie's clarification of the psychoanalytic theory of fantasy, which, as it turns out, is less about a story than about staging. As Cowie writes, "Fantasy involves, is characterized by, not the achievement of desired objects, but the arranging of, a setting out of, desire; a veritable mise en scene of desire." In this theory of fantasy, it is all in the planning, the orchestration; the pleasure lies in the "setting out, not the having of the objects."[71] While we have considered cinema as an institution that defers desire in the very structure of the image, we have yet to seriously consider that the creative process here, unlike the intimate processes in the other arts, is also a deferral of another kind. Entirely a team arrangement, making movies is not the thing itself, it entails the making of the things made up, a distancing from things themselves as well as the things made up about them. In the industrial fabrication that is the production of cinema the focus on staging puts emphasis on practices rather than on the unconscious. Here, then, the desire to make movies, the fantasy of producing fantasies, refers not to something else, does not necessarily stand in for a wish for something other than itself. The desire to make movies may just represent the desire to make movies.

Conclusion

Within the next decade we will most certainly become increasingly interested in the lives and the work of women who pioneered the film industry in the United States, Europe, and in developing nations around the world. Inevitably, this project will involve a reassessment of the very tools we have used to try to understand what it is that creative subjects do to, with, and around texts. Understandably, the tools and approaches devised by critics to elucidate literature and the fine arts have been adapted to the emerging arts and technologies. Humanism and even romanticism have been held over. The practice of locating and attributing authorial marks in the text and the speculation about the something that elevates the work is certainly the residue of an outmoded humanism. Furthermore, as I have suggested, a blind presumption of authorship can have the effect of negating whatever agency we would want to assert on behalf of early film industry workers. For agency in this context means credit for the women who imagined, scripted, arranged, shot, cut, and conformed the first moving pictures. Credit means recovery of the lost and languishing and reconstitution of the historical record. Giving credit to women missing and eclipsed means rewriting the cultural history of the century of the industrially produced fantasy.

Returning to the history of film from another vantage point also provides the opportunity to consider creative practices both imagined and, as yet, unimaginable. If we do not yet know what roles women stepped into in the years of invention and development, how can we know how cre-

Of Cabbages and Authors

ative personnel worked together? Surely the pioneers imagined themselves working in cooperation with one another in their shared desire to make movies.[72] Asking who did what opens the door to considering a range of contributors and alternative authors, among them the camera itself, light, the chemical base of the film, the body of the subject, and the objects before the camera that made their imprint on the celluloid. What should still be troubling the concept of authorship is the obviously industrial base of motion picture production, that base that insists on analogies between manufactured goods—motion pictures and automobiles—to return to one of Jean-Louis Baudry's original concerns. It is, as he has shown us, the mixture of the analyzable and the unanalyzable aspects and elements that defines the moving-picture industrial product. If we insist that Alice Guy-Blaché is analyzable, what do we do with the relatively unanalyzable wooden cabbages so essential in her account of the production of *The Cabbage Fairy?* What do we do with the carpenter who cut them out? With the lens that produced the cabbages as well as the cavorting friends on which the camera focused? Instead of looking exclusively for and to (psycho)analyzable subjects, we need to figure in the machines, the industrial practices, and the materiality of the mise-en-scène. More interesting than the equation between author and text is their inequivalency, or, rather, the impossibility of equivalency produced by the layers of intervention and entwinement, both human and mechanical.

Notes

Thanks to Jennifer Bean and Alison McMahan, who both generously shared their research, as well as to Amelie Hastie, with whom I discussed some of these issues.

1 In "Dorothy Arzner's Trousers" I argue that we can read the group of films "in the name of Dorothy Arzner" or "for Arzner" as homage to her without lapsing into the retrograde politics of the auteurist approach. Gaines, *Jump Cut* 37 (1992): 80. See also *Fire and Desire: Mixed Race Movies in the Silent Era* (Chicago: University of Chicago Press, 2001), in which I explain my reluctance to treat Micheaux as an auteur while understanding the inevitability that such claims would be made for him.

2 Richard Dyer, "Believing in Fairies: The Author and the Homosexual," in *Inside/Out: Lesbian Theories, Gay Theories,* ed. Diana Fuss (New York: Routledge, 1991), 187, 188. Dyer's main argument in this article is that there is an important analogy between authorship and being gay because "both are a kind of performance." But his provocative idea that authorship is as "performed" or as "put on" as one's fluid gay or lesbian identity has never really been taken up.

One might take him further to suggest that authorship has suffered from the same finality of "isness" that has characterized essentialist approaches to gay and lesbian creative production as well as selfhood. For further theorization of the "impossible identities" of "lesbian" and "gay men," see Judith Butler's "Imitation and Gender Subordination," in *Inside/Out*, ed. Fuss, 13–31.

3 See Catherine Grant's important update of authorship in the digital age in which she refers to "contemporary commercial-auteurist practices," among which is the marketing of film authors. "www.auteur.com?" *Screen* 41, 1 (spring 2000): 105.

4 Stephen Crofts, "Authorship and Hollywood," in *The Oxford Guide to Film Studies*, ed. John Hill and Pamela Church-Gibson (London: Oxford University Press, 1998), 322.

5 The relevant texts are Roland Barthes, "The Death of the Author," in *Image/Music/Text*, trans. Stephen Heath (New York: Hill and Wang, 1977), and Michel Foucault, "What Is an Author?," first translated into English in *Screen* 20, 1 (spring 1979): 13–23. See Kaja Silverman, *The Acoustic Mirror: The Female Voice in Psychoanalysis and Cinema* (Bloomington: Indiana University Press, 1988), chapter 6, for a comprehensive discussion of the theoretical implications of Barthes's proclamation of the death of the author for film theory and especially for feminism. In Silverman's view, the death of the male author does not necessarily imply the silencing of the female authorial voice.

6 See Jim Naremore, "Authorship and the Cultural Politics of Film Criticism," *Film Quarterly* 44, 1 (fall 1990): 14–22, on the romanticism of Godard and the *Cahiers du Cinéma* auteurists. In his recent reevaluation, Dudley Andrew also gives auteurism a mixed review, citing contradictory evidence of the status of the author in contemporary Japan, where "neon and simulacra" have replaced texts and authors, and in France, where the comparison between cinema and art history is ascendant. Andrew himself seems able to articulate both positions, as, for instance: "Cinema is part of the media economy that has reduced the auteur to a sign, indeed precisely to a signature." And "The signature moors the film image to a submerged reef of values by means of the slender line drawn by camera or pen." See Andrew, "The Unauthorized Auteur Today," in *Film Theory Goes to the Movies*, ed. Jim Collins, Hilary Radner, and Ava Preacher Colllins (New York: Routledge, 1993), 82, 83.

7 The reference is to the discussion of authorship in Peter Wollen's *Signs and Meaning in the Cinema* (London: Secker and Warburg, 1972). In his update of auteur theory, Andrew reassesses Wollen's structuralism; "The Unauthorized Auteur," 77–79.

8 As Judith Mayne notes: "Particularly insofar as the classical Hollywood is concerned, the conventional equation of authorship with the role of the film director can repress or negate the significant ways in which female signatures *do* appear on film. For instance, consideration of the role of the often-forgotten, often-female screenwriter might suggest more of a female imprint on the film text; and the role of the actress does not always conform to common feminist wisdom about the controlling male gaze located in the person of the male

Of Cabbages and Authors

director—witness Bette Davis as a case in point." See Mayne, *The Woman at the Keyhole: Feminism and Women's Cinema* (Bloomington: Indiana University Press, 1990), 93.

9   Women's film festivals in the 1970s, however, were significant as they combined retrospectives of work on early women with more contemporary films. Ruby Rich provides an important account of "Films by Women," the 1974 festival held at the Chicago Art Institute, in *Chick Flicks: Theories and Memories of the Feminist Film Movement* (Durham: Duke University Press, 1998), 29–39.

10 See, for instance, Karyn Kay and Gerald Peary, eds., *Women and the Cinema* (New York: E. P. Dutton, 1977); Sharon Smith, "Women Who Make Movies," *Women and Film* 1, 3-4 (1973): 77 – 91; and Marjorie Rosen, *Popcorn Venus* (New York: Coward, McCann, and Geoghegan, 1973). It is important to note that although Anthony Slide's *Early Women Directors* (New York: A. S. Barnes, 1977) appeared the same year as Kay and Peary's collection, feminist film scholars virtually ignored it.

11 The question of why we experienced a twenty-year lull in interest in women in the early industry may have to do with the great success of feminist film theory. I take up this question of the relationship between the new apparently empirical work and the prohibition against empiricism during the deeply theoretical 1970s and 1980s in "The Fantasy of Producing Fantasies," forthcoming.

12 Anthony Slide, *The Silent Feminists: America's First Women Directors (Metuchen, N.J.: Scarecrow Press, 1996); and Alice Guy-Blaché, The Memoirs of Alice Guy-Blaché*, ed. Anthony Slide (Metuchen, N.J.: Scarecrow Press, 1996).

13 See, for instance, Ally Acker, *Pioneers of the Cinema, 1896 to the Present* (New York: Continuum, 1991); Cari Beauchamp, *Without Lying Down: Frances Marion and the Powerful Women of Early Hollywood* (New York: Scribner, 1997); Giuliana Bruno, *Streetwalking on a Ruined Map: Cultural Theory and the City Films of Elvira Notari* (Princeton: Princeton University Press, 1993); Gwendolyn Audrey Foster, *Women Film Directors: An International Biocritical Dictionary* (Westport, Conn.: Greenwood Press, 1995); Annette Kuhn, ed., *Women in Film: An International Guide* (New York: Fawcett, 1990); Annette Kuhn, ed., *Queen of the "B"s: Ida Lupino behind the Camera* (Westport, Conn.: Praeger, 1994); Judith Mayne, *Directed by Dorothy Arzner* (Bloomington: Indiana University Press, 1994).

14 Kuhn, ed., *Women in Film,* 185.

15 Alison McMahan, *Alice Guy-Blaché: Lost Visionary of the Cinema* (New York: Continuum, 2002), xxvii.

16 Jennifer Bean has made some important additions to this list: Clara Kimball Young's Clara Kimball Young Film Corporation; Marie Dressler's Dressler Studios; the Danish star Valkyrien's Valkyrien Films; Madame Olga Petrova's Petrova Picture Company; Vitagraph comedian Flora Finch's Flora Finch Comedy Company.

17 Slide, *Early Women Directors,* 9.

18 Jim Naremore lets us off the hook, asking many of these same questions: "How is it possible that so many sophisticated critics, exploring quite differ-

ent problems, can continue to be interested in individual artists? The answer is that the decision to write about specific directors, producers, and writers, or actors doesn't *in itself* involve a commitment to a theory, a method, a formal taxonomy, or even a politics." He goes on to confirm my assessment: "the discourse on authorship, of which auteurism *per se* is only a small part, is full of contradictions." See Naremore, "Authorship and the Cultural Politics," 21.

19 Examples include the Museum of Modern Art's Elvira Notari and "Frances Marion and Her Circle" retrospectives and the American Museum of the Moving Image programs in April 1998 and May 2000.

20 Bruno, *Streetwalking;* and Kay Armatage, *Back to Nell Shipman* (unpublished manuscript).

21 Mayne's *Woman at the Keyhole,* chapter 3, "Female Authorship Reconsidered," lays the theoretical groundwork for her later study *Directed by Dorothy Arzner* (1994), which goes far beyond the kind of study of a director that we have been accustomed to reading by film scholars.

22 Mayne, *Woman at the Keyhole,* 93–94.

23 Important here is also Mayne's engagement with Claire Johnston's earlier work on Dorothy Arzner, which was crucial in the formative years of feminist film theory for the opening it provided for a female voice within the patriarchal text based on a reading of Arzner's *Dance, Girl, Dance.* See Johnston, "Dorothy Arzner: Critical Strategies," in *The Work of Dorothy Arzner: Towards a Feminist Cinema* (London: British Film Institute, 1975), 6. Mayne also references Johnston's earlier argument for the viability of auteur theory within feminism, noting that its mode of classification stood as the antithesis of more established ways of understanding cinema. It is clear, however, that Mayne understands Johnston as advocating something more like the structuralist auteurism that was in vogue in the early 1970s. See Mayne, *Woman at the Keyhole,* 95; and Johnston, "Women's Cinema as Counter-Cinema," in *Notes on Women's Cinema,* ed. Claire Johnston (London: British Film Institute, 1973), 26.

24 Mayne, *Woman at the Keyhole,* 99.

25 Ibid., 114.

26 In a theoretically sophisticated new consideration of Fritz Lang as an auteur, Tom Gunning still needs to use these metaphors even while going beyond them: "I see the author as precisely poised on the threshold of the work, evident in the film itself, but also standing outside it, absent except in the imprint left behind." Gunning, *The Films of Fritz Lang: Allegories of Vision and Modernity* (London: British Film Institute, 2000), 5.

27 Alice Guy-Blaché, "Woman's Place in Photoplay Production," in *Memoirs,* 140–141.

28 Ibid.

29 Quoted in Slide, *Early Women Directors,* 55.

30 Alice Guy-Blaché's "Woman's Place in Photoplay Production" is from *Moving Picture World,* 9 July 1914, 195, appearing toward the end of her career.

Of Cabbages and Authors

31 But see Naomi Schor for a comprehensive and clearheaded discussion of the feminist debates around essentialism, as well as the relationship between antiessentialism and deconstruction and the conclusion that the conflict has played itself out. Schor, "This Essentialism Which Is Not One: Coming to Grips with Irigaray," in *Engaging with Irigaray: Feminist Philosophy and Modern European Thought,* ed. Carolyn Burke, Naomi Schor, and Margaret Whitford (New York: Columbia University Press, 1994), 59–62.
32 Jane M. Gaines, *Contested Culture: The Image, the Voice, and the Law* (Chapel Hill: University of North Carolina Press, 1991), chapter 1.
33 Jean-Louis Baudry, "Author and Analyzable Subject," in *Cinematographic Apparatus: Selected Writings,* ed. Theresa Hak Kyung Cha (New York: Tanham Press, 1980), 72.
34 Ibid., 71.
35 Ibid., 68.
36 Stephen Heath, "Comment on 'The Idea of Authorship,'" *Screen* 14, 3 (autumn 1973): 88. But Gunning takes this problem into account in his new theorization of the auteur's relation to film language: "The film-maker functions less as a *scriptor* than a fashioner of palimpsests, texts written over other texts creating new meanings from the superimpositions of old ones." See Gunning, *Films of Fritz Lang,* 6.
37 Dyer, "Believing in Fairies," 185.
38 Slide, *Early Women Directors,* 107.
39 Gaines, "Dorothy Arzner's Trousers."
40 See Richard Kozarski, *An Evening's Entertainment: The Age of the Silent Feature Picture, 1915–1928* (New York: Charles Scribner's Sons, 1990), 240.
41 See Miriam Hansen, *Babel and Babylon: Spectatorship in American Silent Film* (Cambridge: Harvard University Press, 1991), chapters 11 and 12, for the most important theorization of Valentino and his appeal to female fans.
42 Baudry, "Author and Analyzable Subject," 78.
43 Ibid., 76.
44 Bruno, *Streetwalking,* 235.
45 Ibid., 240.
46 I refer to Joan Copjec, *Read My Desire: Lacan against the Historicists* (Boston: MIT Press, 1995); Mary Ann Doane, *The Desire to Desire: The Woman's Film of the 1940s* (Bloomington: Indiana University Press, 1987); and Sandy Flitterman-Lewis, *To Desire Differently: Feminism and the French Cinema* (Urbana: University of Illinois Press, 1990). See also Gaines, *Fire and Desire,* chapter 2, for more on the philosophical concept of desire and its utilization in film theory.
47 Baudry, "Author and Analyzable Subject," 75.
48 Ibid.
49 Ibid., 68.
50 The new feminist encyclopedias would seem committed to this: Gwendolyn Foster says that *La fée aux choux* was "probably the world's first film with

a plot." Annette Kuhn says, "The first one (and, according to some sources, the first scripted fiction film ever), *La fée aux choux/The Cabbage Fairy* (1896), was a joky fairytale about children born in cabbages." See Foster, *Women Film Directors,* 161; Kuhn, ed., *Women in Film,* 184.

51   Richard Abel, *The Ciné Goes to Town: French Cinema, 1896-1914* (Berkeley: University of California, 1998), 11.

52   Alan Williams, *Republic of Images: A History of French Filmmaking* (Cambridge: Harvard University Press, 1992), 56–57.

53   McMahan, 20–22, suggests that *La fée aux choux* may or may not have been as early as 1896. Although she positively identified a film in the Sieurin French Collection in the Swedish Film Institute in Stockholm, this print appears to have been shot between 1897 and 1900 and in 35mm. Since the Gaumont company would have been using not 35mm but a 60mm Demenÿ camera in 1896, the speculation is that *La fée aux choux,* a popular title, would have been copied or remade. The history of the title is further complicated by the production of a remake, *Sage-femme de première classe* in 1902, using one of the same actors and probably the same props and set.

54   See note 15.

55   Guy-Blaché, *Memoirs,* 27.

56   My case for seeing *La fée aux choux* as the first fiction film as opposed to Louis Lumière's *L'arroseur arrosé (The Waterer Watered)*, would be based on the definition of "fiction" in conjunction with the detail in Guy-Blaché's own account, which goes beyond any left by Lumière, brief though it clearly is. McMahan, 11, says that Guy-Blaché herself would have deferred to the Lumière comedy. However, to my knowledge, the extant print of what is now thought to be perhaps a copy of *La fée aux choux* has never been compared with *L'arroseur arrosé.*

57   Bruno, *Streetwalking,* 234.

58   Guy-Blaché, *Memoirs,* 28.

59   Ibid., 28.

60   As quoted in Louise Heck-Rabi, *Women Filmmakers: A Critical Reception* (Metuchen, N.J.: Scarecrow Press, 1984). The reference in Heck-Rabi is to Calvin Thomas Beck, *Scream Queens: Heroines of the Horrors* (New York: Macmillan, 1978), 34–35. I did not have time to check this last source before going to press. Heck-Rabi also quotes Ephraim Katz, *The Film Encyclopedia* (New York: Crowell, 1979), 319, to the effect that Alice Guy-Blaché was "the world's first woman director and possibly the first director of either sex to bring a story-film to the screen." Barbara Quart, referencing Heck-Rabi, says that she is "arguably the inventor of the film that tells a story," and repeats the dubious quote Heck-Rabi has from Katz. Quart, *Women Directors: The Emergence of a New Cinema* (New York: Praeger, 1988), 18.

61   Abel, *The Ciné Goes to Town,* 467, references Staiger and Musser's work on U.S. silent film in his classification of the French development of film production. Whereas Staiger sees four phases—cameraman (1896-1907), director (1907-1909), director-unit (1909-1914), and central producer (1914-1931)—

Musser thinks that between 1907 and 1909 there was a much more rapid move away from the stage manager–director working arrangement, what he calls "collaboration," to the central producer system that defines the hierarchical arrangements that characterized mass production in the emerging studio. See Janet Staiger, "The Hollywood Mode of Production to 1930," in *The Classical Hollywood Cinema: Film Style and Mode of Production to 1960*, ed. David Bordwell, Janet Staiger, and Kristin Thompson (New York: Columbia University Press, 1985); and Charles Musser, "Pre-Classical American Cinema: Its Changing Modes of Production," in *Silent Film*, ed. Richard Abel (New Brunswick: Rutgers University Press, 1996). In contrast with Lumière, Méliès, and Pathé, where either the cameraman or the director, more or less, was ascendant, Gaumont, according to Abel, was more "collaborative." Earlier, Abel notes that Gaumont assigned Alice Guy to work with her cameraman, Anatole Thiberville, on comic films. This would be similar to what Staiger defines as the director system in which responsibility was divided between the director and others such as the cameraman and other craftsmen (118). But note that Musser uses the term "collaboration" to define a similar creative arrangement. It should be noted that Alice Guy would later, probably as Gaumont evolved into something more like the U.S. director-unit system, be given responsibility for the "house style" (Abel, *The Ciné Goes to Town*, 19). My concern here is not to go too deeply into the history of the evolution of Alice Guy's own career, which has been carefully detailed in McMahan's recent *Alice Guy-Blaché*; nor is it to attempt to resolve questions of the role of early women that only further research can answer. Rather, my concern is to give some context to this short passage in the memoir.

62   Staiger, "The Hollywood Mode of Production," 117.
63   Musser, "Pre-Classical American Cinema," 86.
64   Baudry, "Author and Analyzable Subject," 70.
65   Slide (*Silent Feminists*, 16) says that Yvonne Serand was Alice Guy's "sister secretary," and that Guy "wrote, directed, and photographed" this "short subject" with her friend's help. Heck-Rabi, citing Lacassin, says that two friends—sisters—Yvonne and Germaine Mugnier-Serand, were "pressed into service" (*Women Filmmakers*, 3). See McMahan, 22, for a fuller explanation of the reference to two sisters.
66   Francis Lacassin, "Out of Oblivion: Alice Guy-Blaché," *Sight and Sound* 40, 3 (summer 1971): 151. Slide (*Silent Feminists*, 28) gives the date of her death as 24 March 1968, and the place as New Jersey. Lacassin says that *La fée aux choux* was "later retitled *Sage-femme de première classe*" (169).
67   Baudry, "Author and Analyzable Subject," 78.
68   See the footage within the Canadian documentary *The Lost Garden: The Life and Cinema of Alice Guy-Blaché*, distributed on video from Women Make Movies.
69   In reference to the problem facing the theorist looking for the author in the cinematic text, Baudry says that the difficulty is exacerbated by the "way in which the conditions of production often dictate a division of labor which

makes it difficult to determine what to attribute to whom: script writer, dialoguist, adaptor, director, but also cameraman, stage designer or lightman." See Baudry, "Author and Analyzable Subject," 70.

70 Gunning touches on this set of issues when he says, "The possibility of the modern author dedicated not to self-expression but to the play of discourse, particularly relevant in a medium like film where the *'auteur'* rarely speaks directly in 'his own voice,' but rather indirectly through sounds and images assembled, performed and in some ways produced by collaborators, remains largely unexplored." See *Films of Fritz Lang*, 5.

71 Elizabeth Cowie, *Representing the Woman* (Minneapolis: University of Minnesota Press, 1997), 133.

72 It would be interesting to consider what I call the heterosexual couples mode of creation, much of which would look at the rise of the career of the woman over the man, wives over husbands, females over their male lovers. For instance, Alice Terry, less well known than her husband, Rex Ingham, was said to have taken over for him on the set when he did not feel up to working. (See Slide, *Silent Feminists,* 130). Mr. and Mrs. Sidney Drew (the former Lucille McVey) were a directing team, as were Lillian Chester and George Randolph Chester, Helen Gardner and Charles Gaskill, Ida May Park and Joseph de Grasse, Ruth Ann Baldwin and Leo O. Pierson, Elsie Jane Wilson and Rupert Julian, and Nell Shipman and Bert Van Tuyle.

Note: Just as this essay was going to press I was able to study a copy of the film Alison McMahan identified as *La fée aux choux* from the Sieurin French Collection, the 33mm original of which is in the Swedish Film Institute in Stockholm. My discussion allows for the possibility that this is a later (McMahan says between 1898 and 1900) copy of an earlier film that might have been made in 1896. However, the questions I ask about the production of the film raise all of the issues about the various versions (possibly three) as well as the reliability of Alice Guy's memoir.

My questions, based on the memoir excerpt, refer to the creative personnel at the first shoot as "friends" and "an anxious mother leaping to and fro into the camera focus." However, the Sieurin collection version of *La Fée aux choux* features a single fairy who lifts first two babies and then a doll out of the cardboard cabbages. The memoir, it would seem, describes not *La fée aux choux* but the action of *Sage-femme de première classe* (probably 1902) in which a mother character appears on screen moving about enough to cause concern about the camera focus. Readers are referred to articles by Alison McMahan and Sabine Lenk "À la recherche d'objets filmiques non identifiés: Autour de l' oeuvre d' Alice Guy-Blaché," *Archives,* 81: août 1999. Much of this discussion is also repeated in McMahan's recently published and very rich study, *Alice Guy Blaché: Lost Visionary of the Cinema,* especially Chapter 1, 13–23.

RADHA VATSAL

Reevaluating Footnotes

Women Directors of the Silent Era

Although feminist studies of early cinema have often taken the form of readings or textual analysis, we are now witnessing an era of academic film feminism actively engaged with historiographic materials and methods. As this volume demonstrates, there are several dynamic new subfields for future feminist research in early cinema, including the study of silent-era women directors (see Hastie's, White's, and Gaines's essays here). These heretofore marginalized filmmakers are being excavated from the footnotes of film history, and their contributions to the development of the medium are now being recognized. The focus of this essay, however, is just as much on footnotes as it is on early women directors. Footnotes, both metaphorically and literally, are the undervalued, overlooked, but indispensable by-products of any body of knowledge. In the case of academic writing on early cinema, the footnote is the sidelined text and/or the research assistant's job where sources, citations, and, if we're lucky, search histories with all their attendant contradictions and equivocations get dumped. It is not only appropriate but necessary that as feminist historiographers reevaluate previously marginalized or even forgotten figures and films, we also reevaluate this systematically marginalized form of our research and writing.

Writing or reading footnotes is often the least compelling part of any essay because, frequently, footnotes simply cite sources. However, especially in the study of early cinema, these sources are never simple; they are fraught with uncertainties and complications. This is not just incidental to the discipline. The uncertainties and complications in early cinema sources reflect, and result from, the fundamental instability of motion picture production during the period. Pre-studio-era filmmaking functioned like a cottage industry: it consisted of unregulated and fluid practices, materials, and terms in every aspect of the production and consumption process. For instance, when we refer to a contemporary film, say *Blade Runner,* we can safely assume that we are referring to a stable, standardized product (though even here there are differences between the director's cut and the regular release, which in turn might be different from broadcast versions that alter the film's aspect ratio, or shorten its length in order to make time for commercials). Yet we cannot assume the same about *Mabel's Married Life* (1914), for example. Shot for shot, there are different versions of this film that exist in archives around the world. Furthermore, during the 1910s, films did not remain constant even from screening to screening. "The same film" varied according to factors such as projection speed, musical accompaniment, local censors' or exhibitors' cuts and/or rearrangements, rewriting of dialogue cards, and title/s under which the film might be reissued. It is this fluidity and lack of industrial systematization that makes studying the period so rewarding. It is also, arguably, what allowed for the possibility of so many women directors.

As the often-quoted story goes: had he realized that moving pictures were going to spawn their own lasting industry, Léon Gaumont would never have allowed his female secretary, Alice Guy (later Alice Guy-Blaché, or Mrs. Blaché), to make films. Like Guy, most women filmmakers, and other independents, flourished before the establishment of the big studios. They worked at a time when the future of the medium was still undecided, when experimentation, innovation, rapid change, and entrepreneurship were the norm. Not surprisingly, their films are difficult to come by, and textual documentation is extremely idiosyncratic. I am proposing that we develop research practices that consistently foreground this; if we do not, we risk glossing over the specifics of the period itself — most importantly, its lack of regimentation, which opened a space for the women film directors we are now engaging.

Many currently available secondary sources take a different approach. Einar Lauritzen and Gunnar Lundquist's classic and indispensable *American Film-Index, 1908–1915* is one example.[1] The index is an unannotated compilation of titles, release dates, cast and crew credits, and lengths for several thousand American films made between 1908 and 1915. Its entries are presented as a straightforward listing of data. However, in their one-page preface, the authors mention problems they encountered during the course of their research that suggest that these data are not as clear-cut as they might seem. The preface refers to the confusion generated by the common practice of reissuing old films under new titles, and by the multiple ways in which cast and crew names were spelled. However, the reader is not told how these difficulties were resolved. The authors also acknowledge that certain categories and terms used in the index do not accurately describe production methods during the 1910s. So, for instance, in reference

Reevaluating Footnotes

to the attribution of cast and crew credits for individual titles, the preface states:

> The difference between the functions of producers, supervisors, and directors [in this period] did not always exist. The difference between authors, scenarists and scriptwriters was often uncertain. Great efforts have been made to clarify these distinctions, but we are aware that they do not always correspond to actual production methods.[2]

The consequence of this type of effort is that it retroactively imposes a clarity that is incompatible with the world of spelling discrepancies, hazy division of labor, and exhibitors' modifications of prints that is early cinema. It seems that each "fact" presented in the volume is the result of decisions and judgment calls made by the authors on a case-by-case basis. In order for future researchers to get the most out of the authors' labor, additional documentation concerning sources, research histories, and authorial decisions would be required.

Perhaps what I am requesting is unfeasible: how can one expect research notes for thousands of titles? The work would never get done. But before we come to that conclusion, it is worth asking why reference sources that offer vast amounts of "factual" information with no, or very little, documentation are more the norm than those that would offer less "hard data," but include detailed notes for each entry. As described above, I think the films of the period are best understood as clusters of possibilities and practices, in relation to which any "fact" (such as cast and crew credits, length, date, etc.) is meaningful only if contextualized, and (in the case of silent cinema) therefore problematized. This is all to suggest that an early cinema reference source that consistently highlights the ambiguities generated by each entry and therefore makes it difficult to say anything simplistically about an early film or filmmaker would be a more accurate representation of the period than a source that does not. I discuss the *American Film-Index* in this regard not because it is an aberration in the field, but because both its content and omissions point to generally held values and priorities whose usefulness needs to be questioned.

This essay draws on my experience as coordinator of the Women Film Pioneers Project (henceforth WFPP) to provide an instance of the engagement of feminist film studies with historiographic and archival film research.[3] The WFPP is a collaborative and interdisciplinary project based at Duke University. Its efforts have been spearheaded by Jane Gaines and Jennifer Parchesky; its contributors include academics, archivists, curators, preservationists, and filmmakers from the United States, and abroad. The WFPP undertakes the research, restoration, and public exhibition of films made by the many women around the world who directed or produced during the silent era. Their works span a variety of genres and styles: from shorts to features, melodramas to comedies, westerns to documentaries, newsreels to serials, and animated to avant-garde. A central goal of the project is to create a reference filmography for these long-forgotten filmmakers. I situate my reevaluation of the footnote in the context of constructing this filmography. I discuss how working on the filmography (which is still in progress) prompted me to rethink its format, and then describe features that would be useful in this, as well as future, reference works. The essay concludes with an illustration of some of the ideas proposed here, in the form of a research case study on the filmmaker Madeline Brandeis. In obvious ways, my approach is a methodologically self-conscious one, and there doubtless will be readers for whom some of the basic issues raised here are redundant. It is my hope, however, that the information and ideas that follow will not only encourage awareness of research procedures for nonspecialists, but also precipitate further discussion about the direction and goals of future feminist historiographic research and writing.

One of the most pressing issues we face in creating a WFPP filmography is the tension between the filmographic tendency to categorize and standardize, and the fact that the material we are dealing with strongly resists such handling. How do we bring together the varied figures proposed as candidates for inclusion in this project? For instance, Alice Guy, Lois Weber, and Germaine Dulac directed several films in which they did not appear; Mary Pickford, in contrast, was well known to have supervised her own starring productions down to the minutest detail, and even directed specific scenes whenever she saw necessary, but never took the director credit; Esfir Shub, although she did not "direct," edited what today we would call "found footage" films. Then there are the early star-producers with eponymous production companies that produced only films featuring the star in question, such as Gene Gauntier and her Gene Gauntier Feature Players (with the direction of her films credited to Sidney Olcott); or figures like Grace Cunard, who directed some shorts but more often holds the writer and actress credit, while her partner, Francis Ford, is credited with direction. To uniformly use the term "director" to describe the activities of all these women would be misleading as well as anachronistic. A contemporary term like "filmmaker"—which might serve as a useful shorthand—would still need to be unpacked when used in a scholarly reference source.

Resolving the issue by trying to determine how the women chose to credit themselves presents its own set of difficulties. Early film credits are extremely difficult to pin down. Few films from the period still exist. When the films are extant, onscreen credits, perhaps the most obvious place to look for crew designations, are often missing. Over the years, it is precisely this section of silent films that has been dismembered, modified, or lost; and when onscreen credits do survive, they provide only the information that the producer or distributor considered important. For early, pre-1910s, films, this might be just copyright information, and/or production company name, and/or film title. Many of Alice Guy's American shorts for instance, carry only the name of her production company, Solax, and the film title. Although onscreen credits for later silent-era films do provide more detailed cast and crew information, these are also problematic. *A Bear, A Boy, and A Dog* (1921) is widely considered by scholars to be a Nell Shipman film. However, the first title card on the Idaho Film Collection 16mm print reads: "W. H. Clune presents Sunny Howard in *A Bear, A Boy and A Dog*. Story by Nell Shipman, Directed by Bert Van Tuyle, Photography by J. B. Walker." The second card reads: "Copyrighted by W. H. Clune, Released by B. Warren Corporation, Passed by the National Board of Review." There could be many reasons why scholars consider this a Shipman-directed film (one of which might be that this is a rereleased version of a 1920 title that may or may not have had different title cards; another could be that Shipman overcredited her partner Van Tuyle while she did most of the directorial work). Whatever the case, we need to create a form of filmography that, as a matter of course, provides an explanation for this discrepancy and can handle the amount of information required to account for the filmographer's decision. If not, we devalue the contributions we are making to the field, because a historiographic text that glosses over the history of its decision-making process quickly loses credibility when its claims are researched in any detail.

Since the films themselves are an incomplete resource, like Lauritzen and Lundquist we turn to print sources—filmographies; catalogs or research done by other scholars; period publications such as trade journals, fan magazines, film reviews in newspapers, etcetera; or business letters and records, for example. And here the problem just gets deferred. The 13 December 1913 issue of *Moving Picture World* famously announced that "Mabel Normand, leading woman of the Keystone Co. since its inception, is in the future to direct every picture she acts in."[4] However, we are unable to come up with a comprehensive listing of Normand-directed films without getting involved in the question of the coherence of a single director/author's works and the subsequent recognizability of her style.[5] There are numerous reasons for this: the fact that there is not enough detailed information available to make the judgment calls necessary; that Normand's films have been received by generations of viewers and scholars through the powerful filter of Charles Chaplin, with whom she costarred; that Chaplin could never admit that he ever was anything other than self-directed; that the films were so popular they went through many hands, and along the way were recut and retitled, so the same title exists in many different versions; and finally, as the films as well as interviews with Normand and other members of the Keystone gang suggest, these shorts were rapidly put together in a freewheeling and improvisational manner that doesn't leave much room for a "director" in the conventional sense. This set of issues is specific to Normand, but we face similar complications in the case of every silent-era director (male or female). Although it certainly carries more weight to be able to name unequivocally, for instance, ten films Normand directed, a far more accurate Normand filmography would be one that reflects both the fluidity of the term "director" as it pertains to Normand, and the unstandardized product that constitutes a film in this period. Such a filmography would not only sharpen our understanding of Normand's contributions and the ways in which she worked; it might also modify the way we think about Chaplin, and prompt us to characterize his early work with the same amount of rigor as we do hers.

Not surprisingly, this type of filmography would not look like the orderly, data-driven texts to which we have grown accustomed. In the introduction to his *Edison Motion Pictures, 1890–1900: An Annotated Filmography*, Charles Musser writes, "filmographies are one of the crucial underpinnings of any serious scholarship in film."[6] As such, they influence the research and theory emerging from the field. Sacrificing orderliness seems to be a small price to pay for reference sources in which seemingly simple, but in fact vexed, claims such as the attribution of directorship for silent-era titles are presented to the reader with all their attendant ambiguities and contradictions brought into the open. Such "nonauthoritative" filmographies would function not as repositories of incontrovertible fact, but rather as texts that prompt the reader to reach her own conclusions. Instead of being part of an entrenched mechanism underwriting claims of authorship, the filmography would then ironically destabilize that tradition.

A reference source of this type would veer away from categorization and uniformity. Instead of slotting information into standardized fields, the type and amount of information available for each filmmaker would dictate the way in which her entries are handled. The filmography would include an explanation and analysis of the criteria by which the featured

Reevaluating Footnotes

filmmakers have been selected; it would also describe the sources used, the biases or idiosyncrasies of each, and any concerns the researcher might have about them. Entries on individual filmmakers would note the basis on which and sources from which the "directorship" of each title has been determined. Titles would be accompanied by (sourced) synopses, information on whether—and if so where—prints exist, as well as notes on the sources from which release dates, and cast and crew credits were obtained. Finally, the filmography would give an account of the research undertaken for each filmmaker. Which archives or print sources were searched? What types of searches were performed? These are vital questions: with older materials, cross-referencing is not always a given, so the type of search directly influences the kind of information retrieved. For instance, the result of a name search depends on the way in which an archive or other source has chosen to credit a particular film. More obviously, it also depends on having the right name or set of names to search with—knowing that Lucille McVey was also called Mrs. Sidney Drew or Jane Morrow, for example. This is not an uncommon problem. Multiple names for the same figure are frequently encountered in silent-era research for several reasons:

> Firstly, filmmakers frequently changed their names, secondly, the proper recording of the name of every person who worked on a film was not as important in the teens as it is today, and thirdly, mistakes in or variations in trade reviews were common. In addition, it was a common practice in the teens to abbreviate names, for example, "Edw.," which could mean either "Edward" or "Edwin," or to use surnames only, that is "Mr. Smith" or "Miss Browne."[7]

Searching under company names is also not a straightforward procedure: "The numerous corporate mergers and takeovers which occurred between 1911 and 1920 resulted in seemingly conflicting information about company names. Often, after a merger or takeover a company name became a 'brand' or 'series' name of another company or newly formed corporation."[8] Knowing the specific forms in which personal and corporate name searches were undertaken would help other scholars determine whether or not the search needs to be redone. The same applies to title searches. Here results vary according to factors such as the existence of the film under multiple titles (including foreign translations and archival retranslations back into English). Outcomes are also influenced by the sources from which the initial search list of titles is compiled. These could be period sources such as the *New York Dramatic Mirror* or *Moving Picture World,* a general reference source like Alan Goble's *International Film Index, 1895-1990,* or perhaps more specialized works like Anthony Slide's *The Silent Feminists: America's*

First Women Directors, or Gwendolyn Audrey Foster's *Women Film Directors: An International Biocritical Dictionary.*[9] It is also helpful to list sources that were searched, but in which no references to the filmmaker or her films were found. Highlighting these absences would provide a clearer picture of the filmmaker's reception and the status of our knowledge about her. This general approach would enable us to negotiate what Musser describes as "an almost insurmountable task for historians," that is, the overcoming of "biases built into scholarly aids."[10] A filmography of the type I have described above would help ensure that other researchers are not faced with the unhappy choice of reproducing built-in biases, dismissing the respective text out of hand, or duplicating the research that went into its compilation in an effort to understand or contextualize its entries.

At this point, it might be helpful to look briefly at two texts that expand on the filmography genre: one is Musser's work on Edison, the other is Christel Schmidt's work on Mary Pickford. The meticulous and thought-provoking *Edison Motion Pictures* filmography contains fields for information including "original release" title and alternate titles, a reprint of a period description of the film with its corresponding citation (and if two significantly descriptions exist, both are reprinted), archival locations for surviving films, citations for other documents that provide information relevant to the film, and a notes section for pertinent information that does not appear in any of the other fields. The introduction provides a detailed explanation of what and why, for the purposes of the filmography, constitutes an Edison film, as well as an in-depth account of the considerations that informed the types of entries in each field. While Musser's filmography focuses more on situating the Edison films as part of a larger cultural discourse, Christel Schmidt's forthcoming survival filmography for Mary Pickford deals with silent films as sets of material bodies in different states of arrangement and deterioration.[11] Working with 35-, 28-, and 16-mm acetate and nitrate prints, Schmidt's unusually thorough approach includes comparative studies of all the surviving film elements of Pickford's 1909–1933 works. Schmidt's study has important consequences. It can be used by scholars not only to determine the locations of different versions of the same title, but also to begin to understand the many kinds of variations between the elements that constitute each print. Furthermore the assessment of the elements for condition and quality will provide invaluable information for restoration and preservation projects, as well as for programmers and others who need to find the best quality prints for projection and viewing.

Reevaluating Footnotes

Many of the ideas proposed here are long-term goals, and the objectives necessarily differ depending on the source in progress. A database like the one developing at the WFPP, as well as CD-ROM and other multimedia forums, certainly provide room for innovation unavailable in printed materials. Then again, the filmographic appendices possible in the production of a monograph on the period afford more leeway than essays circumscribed by the citation style and page lengths dictated by academic journals. Nonetheless, certain changes could be implemented relatively easily, and in most any publication form. For instance, writings on early cinema could always, as a matter of course, state whether the films in question were seen on film or video, and note the archival location — and condition — of the print. (Lois Weber's *Shoes* in the Nederlands Filmmuseum is a very different print from that in the Library of Congress. A Grapevine Video release of an early film could be very different from a Kino release of the same title.)

Every filmography, whether or not it makes this explicit, summarizes both the history of a film, as material and textual object, and the preoccupations of those who researched it. As we know from the many catalogs, compilations, and histories in which early women filmmakers are barely mentioned, filmographies do not tell us as much about films and filmmakers as they do about the status of our knowledge on the subject. Unlike more conventional resources that shut down conversation by presenting their findings as a fait accompli, a filmography that foregrounds its research procedures, thereby highlighting the contingency and limits of its knowledge, encourages further investigations and welcomes multiple conclusions.

The following case study on Madeline Brandeis offers an instance of this style of writing. It is intentionally presented in an essayistic form, designed to outline the procedures followed — and the blind spots experienced — in tracking this figure's elusive history. At this stage of my research on Brandeis I think an account of the search is more informative than any listing of her credits. Furthermore, such a text would be premature — more research would be necessary before I could meaningfully decide how to reconcile the variations between the sources consulted. This descriptive study is of course longer than would be necessary for a filmography since I have used it as an opportunity to illustrate some of the methodological issues raised above. At the same time, the texts used here are preliminary ones. A more detailed search would include other sources, primary as well as secondary, and would also follow up on the bibliographic references contained in the information below.

Madeline Brandeis: Research Case Study

My research on Brandeis was prompted by the following entries that I came across while browsing through Grapevine Video's online catalog:

> From http://grapevinevideo.com/Silent_M.htm
> MADELINE BRANDEIS PRODUCTIONS Two films from the famous producer. "THE SHINING ADVENTURE" (1925) Directed by Hugo Ballin. Cast: Percy Marmont, Mabel Ballin, Ben Alexander, B. Wayne Lamont, Mary June Irving and Stella De Lanti. Based on the 1916 book. A woman's child is removed from her care and she spends the rest of her life searching for him. 67 min. "CHILDREN OF ALL LANDS" (1927) 14 minutes. The Story of Bah, the little Indian Weaver.
> From http://grapevinevideo.com/Silent_S.htm
> THE STAR PRINCE (1918) Directed by Madeline Brandeis. Cast: Zoe Rae, Dorphia Brown, John Dorland, Edith Rothschild, Marjorie Claire Bowden. The Star Prince falls to earth on a star and is found and reared by a woodcutter. The Prince sets out to find his real mother and survives several adventures involving the wicked witch and the little princess. This film is enacted entirely by children of The Little Players' Film Co. of Chicago.

I could not recall ever having heard of Brandeis, her production company, or the films mentioned in the catalog. A phone conversation with Grapevine's staff revealed that they did not know any more about Brandeis than what appeared in their entry, that the prints (16mm) of the films were obtained from private collectors whose identities they would not disclose, and that they were not aware of any Brandeis specialists.

The print of *The Star Prince* on which the Grapevine video is based does not include "original" onscreen credits. The prints of *The Shining Adventure* and *Children of All Lands* do have credits that appear to be part of the original production. The credits for *The Shining Adventure* read "Madeline Brandeis presents, *The Star Prince,* based on the story by Dana Burnett, with Percy Marmont, Mabel Ballin, Ben Alexander. Directed by Hugo Ballin. Assisted by Robert M. Brown, Photographed by James R. Diamond, Adapted by Lawrence Trimble, Edited by Irene Morra, Titles by Malcolm Stuart Boylan, Produced by Madeline Brandeis Productions." The credit sequence of the short reads "*Children of All Lands,* Produced by Madeline Brandeis, Copyright Pathé Exchange Inc., MCMXXVII, Passed by the National Board of Review." This is followed by a dedication to "every child of every land." And then: "From the book, The Little Indian Weaver,

Reevaluating Footnotes

by Madeline Brandeis." (Note the absence of director, other crew, or cast credits.)

An Internet search with the name Madeline Brandeis produced results at various secondhand and rare book-dealer Web sites. These listed children's books by Brandeis published during the 1920s and 1930s. I was unable, however, to find any biographical information on her, despite looking through various children's-book, female-author, and other literary Web sites. A Library of Congress online catalog subject and keyword search did not yield any literature on Brandeis, though, again, she did appear as author of several children's books, including *The Little Indian Weaver, The Wee Scotch Piper,* and a novel, *Adventure in Hollywood*. None of these were available in *Books in Print,* and Brandeis's name did not produce any results in keyword searches of Lexis-Nexis and Pro Quest.

The Internet Movie Database (www.imdb.com), which has the reputation of being unreliable in its entries on silent-era film, revealed that

Her Birth name was: Madeline Frank
Date of birth (location): 18 December 1897 (San Francisco, CA)
Date of death (details): 27 June 1937
Los Angeles, California, USA (road accident)
Spouse: E. John Brandeis (28 January 1918, until her death)

It credited Brandeis with only one film: *The Star Prince*. The biographical information was unsourced and suggested no other references. So, using the Grapevine material as a starting point, I then turned to more conventional film reference sources. Unless otherwise mentioned, the categories I searched under were name: Madeline Brandeis; title: *The Star Prince, The Shining Adventure, Children of All Lands;* production company: Madeline Brandeis Productions. The following is a list of sources that I checked in which Brandeis does *not* appear:

— Paul Spehr's index to Lauritzen and Lundquist.
American Film Personnel and Company Credits, 1908-1920: Filmographies Recorded by Authoritative Organizational and Personal Names from Lauritzen and Lundquist's American Film-Index, with Gunnar Lundquist (Jefferson, N.C.: McFarland, 1996).
Search Type: name, title, and production company.
— Anthony Slide's *The American Film Industry: A Historical Dictionary* (New York: Greenwood Press, 1986).
Search: Little Players Film Co., Madeline Brandeis Productions.

— *The New York Times Film Reviews, 1913–1968* (New York: New York Times and Arno Press, 1970), appendix.
Search Type: title.
— The British Film Institute Database.
Search Type: name and title.
— Gwendolyn Audrey Foster, *Women Film Directors: An International Bio-critical Dictionary* (Westport, Conn.: Greenwood Press, 1995).
Search Type: name.
— Ally Acker, *Reel Women: Pioneers of the Cinema 1896 to the Present* (New York: Continuum, 1993).
Search Type: name.

Finally, however, I was rewarded with an entry for *The Star Prince*, in Robert Klepper's *Silent Films, 1877–1996: A Critical Guide to 646 Movies*.[12]

> Little Players' Film Company of Chicago; Directed by Madeline Brandeis; Running Time: 61 minutes; Cast: Zoe Rae; Dorphia Brown; John Dorland; Edith Rothschild; Marjorie Claire Bowden.
>
> As far as can be determined, this is the only surviving work of the Little Players' Film Company of Chicago, as well as the only surviving work of the female director, Madeline Brandeis (1898–1937), who was 19 at the time of production. She did a few more films in the early 1920s for the Hodkinson Company, none of which are known to exist. Ms. Brandeis was only 39 when she was killed in a tragic car accident in Hollywood, California, in 1937. Unfortunately, no further information could be found on any of the cast members.

This is followed by a review of the film that mentions that a sequence involving a squirrel was filmed using stop-motion techniques, and that all the parts in the movie are played by children. No bibliographic information is given. The lack of references combined with the writer's authoritative tone (which I already knew to be making somewhat inaccurate pronouncements) made this entry particularly problematic to negotiate.

Anthony Slide's *The Silent Feminists* contains a paragraph on Brandeis. Unlike Klepper, Slide cites all his sources and highlights areas of uncertainty. Although *Silent Feminists* does not mention the Grapevine titles, it did add another film and period articles to my search. Slide claims that

> Madeline Brandeis was another female director working in the American heartland. According to *The Film Mercury* (May 15, 1925), she made at least three independent feature films in Omaha, Nebraska. Whether Brandeis was primarily a producer, a director, or both is not known. The title of only one

Reevaluating Footnotes

of the features is on record, and that is *Which Shall It Be?* also known as *Not One to Spare,* released by the W. W. Hodkinson Corporation in June 1924. Madeline Brandeis is credited as producer and Renaud Hoffman as director of the feature, a domestic drama set in Vermont. "One of those tear-compelling little pictures that is going to be a money maker for producer, distributor and the exhibitor," was the opinion of *Variety* (April 9, 1924).[13]

Importantly, although *Silent Feminists* does not contain "filmographies" in the traditional sense, it remains one of the most useful, informative, and consistently accurate reference works on the subject of early women filmmakers. Perhaps this is in part owing to its prosaic style, and not in spite of it. Slide is consistently scrupulous: he opts for accuracy over rhetoric, and carefully qualifies his facts, avoids reaching grand conclusions, and resists the temptation of generating filmographies for the many obscure women included in his text.

A title and name search in the monumental *American Film Institute Catalog of Motion Pictures Produced in the United States: Feature Films, 1911–1920* yielded an entry for *The Star Prince.* The introduction to the catalog states that its entries were compiled from corporate records, trade publications such as *Moving Picture World, Variety,* and the *New York Dramatic Mirror,* copyright records, a collection of scrapbook pages known as "the Foster Files," other newspapers, editions of the *Motion Picture Studio Directory and Trade Annual* (published in the 1910s and early 1920s by *Motion Picture News*), *Wid's Film Daily Yearbook,* and issues of *American Cinematographer.* Each entry concludes with a bibliography of period articles for the title in question.

The Star Prince

Little Players Film Co. Dist States Rights. June? 1918. 5 reels.
Supv Courtland J. Van Deusen. Dir Madeline Brandeis. Scen Madeline Brandeis.
Cast: Zoe Rae (Star Prince), Dorphia Brown (Princess), John Dorland (Dwarf), Edith Rothschild (Beggar Woman), Marjorie Claire Bowden (Witch), Gulnar Kheiralla (Fairy Godmother).
Fantasy. The Star Prince falls to earth on a star and is found and reared by a woodcutter. Because the haughty prince is cruel to the beggar who claims to be his mother, a fairy transforms him into an ugly pauper. Ashamed, the prince sets out to find his mother. On his quest, he survives several adventures involving the wicked witch and the little princess, who falls in love with him. When the evil dwarf tries to force the princess to marry him, the Star Prince rescues her, whereupon he is changed back into his origi-

nal form. The dwarf, however, is turned into a pig, while the Star Prince marries the beautiful Princess. [A list of subject headings follows.]
Note: The film was enacted entirely by children according to a review. The Little Players Film Co. was located in Chicago.
ETR [Exhibitor's Trade Review] 15 June 1918, p. 121, ETR 22 June 1918, p. 198.[14]

In the creation of a Brandeis filmography, we would have to note that although *The Star Prince* is the only film for which Brandeis appears to have a director credit, this film also provides a credit for supervisor. Not only would we need to determine from where these credits have been obtained, we would also need to investigate the distinction between these positions in terms of production methods at the time.

Which One Shall It Be? as well as *The Shining Adventure* are included in the *American Film Institute Catalog of Motion Pictures Produced in the United States: Feature Films, 1921–1930,* under the year 1924. Searching by Brandeis's name produced no further feature film entries. *Children of All Lands* and any other short with which she might have been involved would not be included.

The Shining Adventure

Madeline Brandeis Productions. Dist Astor Pictures. 7 August 1925 (New York State License). si. b&w. 35mm. 6 reels, 5148 feet.
Dir Hugo Ballin. Adapt Lawrence Trimble. Photog James Diamond.
Cast: Percy Marmont (Dr. Hugo McLean), Mabel Ballin (Mary), Ben Alexander (Benny), B. Wayne Lamont (Franklin Tribbit), Mary Jane Irving ("Lamey"), Stella De Lanti.
Society melodrama. Source: Dana Burnett, The Shining Adventure (New York, 1916). Money intended for charitable purposes is misappropriated.[15]

Again, the sources for the credits are unclear here, and we must note that the Grapevine print has a more extensive list of credits than those listed above.

Which One Shall It Be?

Renaud Hoffman Poductions. Dist W. W. Hodkinson Corp. 15 Jun 1924 [c] 2 June 1924; LP 20300]. Si; b&w. 35mm. 5 reels, 4600 feet.
Madeline Brandeis Production. Dir-Adapt Renaud Hoffman. Photog Renaud Hoffman.
Cast: Willis Marks (John Moore), Ethel Wales (Mrs. Moore), Paul Weigel (music master), Mary McLane, Billy Bondwin, Newton House, Miriam Ballah, Dick Winslow, Buck Black, Thayer Strain (The Children).

Reevaluating Footnotes

Domestic Drama. Source: Ethel Lynn Beers, "Not One to Spare," or "Which Shall It Be?" (publication undetermined). A Vermont family with seven children is presented with an offer from a wealthy relative of an estate and an allowance in return for one child, which he wishes to adopt to brighten his lonely life. After much speculation, they decide on the oldest girl, whose musical interests cannot be furthered by their limited means. She no sooner leaves than the mother suffers remorse, and the father, equally unable to surrender his child, brings her back to the farm.
[A list of subject headings follows.]
Also released under its copyright title, *Not One to Spare*.[16]

In this case, I would like to point out that the credits vary slightly from Slide's account, and also that two production companies are listed here.

A title search of the FIAF Treasures from the Archives database produced only one result: Thanhouser's *Which Shall It Be?* (1915), which seems to have no connection to Brandeis's later film of the same title. Searching by Brandeis's name did, however, produce a lone entry:

The Wee Scotch Piper (1928), United States.
Children of All Lands (series), Madeline Brandeis Productions.
Dir: Madeline Brandeis [no other credits given].
Also available in its Dutch title: *De Kleine Schoste Fluitist*. Copies available at the Library of Congress, and the Nederlands Filmmuseum.

From where these credits derive is, again, unclear. The Grapevine print of another title from this series does not mention a director.

Finally, an email query to the WFPP listserve generated the following response (thanks to scholar Ingrid Periz): "She worked with Elizabeth Richey (?) Dessez of Pathé. I know of one article on her: Ruth M. Tildesley, "Filming Children for Children," *National Board of Review Magazine*, December 1929: 5–7."

I was able to find copies of some of Brandeis's books at the New York Public Library. *Adventures in Hollywood*, which I had hoped would be an autobiography, turned out to be a novel for teens.[17] The editions of Brandeis's children's books seem to have been published as a series through the 1920s and 1930s by the New York publishing house Grosset and Dunlap (copyrighted by A. Flanagan Company). Although none of the books includes an author biography, or a list of other titles by this author, or even a series title, some of the books, such as *The Wee Scotch Piper* (1929), note on the inside title page: "By Madeline Brandeis, Producer of the Motion Pictures *The Little Indian Weaver, The Wee Scotch Piper, The Little Dutch*

Tulip Girl, The Little Swiss Wood-Carver, Distributed by Pathé Exchange, Inc., New York City."

Details on Brandeis's literary career seem to be as hard to find as those on her film career. She does not figure in most standard literary biography compilations or source books, even one titled *American Writers for Children, 1900-1960*. In fact, a search through the Gale Group's online "Biography and Genealogy Index" produced only two results. The first is *Who Was Whom among North American Authors, 1921-1939*, which in turn is compiled from *Who's Who among North American Authors, 1921-1939.* (The foreword states that of the 11,900 authors appearing here at least 8,900 are not listed in other standard reference guides.)

> Brandeis, Madeline (Frank): writer; b. San Francisco, Calif., Dec. 18, 1897; d. Albert and Mattie (Ehrman) Frank; educ. Miss Burke's Sch. (San Francisco); m. E. John Brandeis, Jan 28, 1918; daughter Marie Madeline Brandeis. AUTHOR (juveniles): Little Indian Weaver, 1928; Wee Scotch Piper, 1929; Little Dutch Tulip Girl, 1929; Little Swiss Woodcarver, 1929; Little Jeanne of France, 1929; Shaun O'Day of Ireland, 1929; Little Phillipe of Belgium, 1930; Little Anne of Canada, 1931; Little Mexican Donkey Boy, 1931; Jack of the Circus, 1931; Mitz and Fritz of Germany, 1933; Little Tony of Italy [no more dates given for the following]; Little Tom of England; The Little Spanish Dancer; Little Carmen of the Golden Coast; Little Rosa of the Mesa; Little John of New England; Little Farmer of the Middle West; Adventures in Hollywood for Adolescents; Six Face the World (novel), 1938. *Has produced about eight Juvenile Motion Pictures and directed three travel films in European countries for Pathé Films.* Illustrated books with own photographs. (died June 28, 1937). [My emphasis.][18]

The second is *A Dictionary of American Authors Deceased before 1950*, compiled by W. Stewart Wallace.[19] This contains a one-line entry that lists Brandeis's birth year as 1890, and gives the same birthplace and death-date information mentioned above. Luckily, it also includes a bibliographic key for each of its entries; for Brandeis, the source used is *American Women 1935-1940: A Composite Biographical Dictionary,* edited by Durwood Howes. Besides the same information on her birth and parentage as contained in *Who Was Whom,* this source states

> *Hus. Occ,* merchant. *Clubs:* The Writers, Hollywood (bd. duts., 1930–1935). *Hobby:* photography. *Fav. rec. or sport:* horseback riding. *Author:* The Children of All Lands (14 titles pub.); The Children of America (4 titles pub.); Jack of the Circus, 1931; All Wring Book; Yankee Doodle's Adventures; Adventure

in Hollywood, 1937. *Producer of several motion pictures for children, and radio program Children of All Lands.* Address: 30 W. 54 St., NYC. [My emphasis.][20]

Clearly this is a woman who lead an active professional life: she authored children's books that were illustrated with her own photographs, produced (meaning unclear) children's films written by other writers, as well as children's shorts based on her own writing. She also seems to have "made" travel films for adults, and produced (meaning unclear) a radio program based on her own books. Why the few historical records that focus on her film career seem to be unaware of her print career bears further investigation.

The only autobiographical quote I was able to find suggests that Brandeis herself might have enjoyed thwarting contemporary or future researchers. Some of the Grosset and Dunlap editions of her children's books contain this preface:

> When I began to write these stories about children of all lands I had just returned from Europe whither I journeyed with Marie and Ref. Maybe you don't know Marie and Ref. I'll introduce them. Please meet Marie, my very little daughter, and Ref, my very big reflex camera.
>
> These two are my helpers. Marie helps by being a little girl who knows what other little girls like and by telling me; and Ref helps by snapping pictures of everything interesting that Marie and I see on our travels. I couldn't get along without them.
>
> Several years have gone by since we started our work together and Marie is a bigger girl but Ref hasn't changed one bit. Ref hasn't changed any more than my interest in writing these books for you. And I hope that *you* hope that I never change, because I want to keep on writing until we'll have no more countries to write about unless of course, some one discovers a new country.
>
> Even if a new country isn't discovered, we'll find foreign children to talk about—maybe the children in Mars! Who knows? Nobody. Not even Marie and Marie usually knows about most things. That's the reason why, you see, though I sign myself
>
> Madeline Brandeis
I am really only
Marie's Mother.

To be "only" a mother: the phrasing demands our attention by the force of its denial. Insofar as the disclaimer—"only" a mother—conceals the ideological, physical, and emotional labor demanded of motherhood, it also eclipses and contains the burdens demanded of an authorial subject. As such, Brandeis's signature—or what could be construed as its opposite, a veritable signing-off—seems to be diametrically opposed to that of her contemporaries. In her article "The Motion Picture Director," published in *Careers for Women* (1920), actress, scenario writer, and director Ida May Park insistently voices the many daunting qualities that a successful film director must possess. "Unless you are hardy and determined," she cautions, "the director's role is not for you. Wait until the profession has emerged from its embryonic state and a system has been evolved by which the terrific weight of responsibility can be lifted from one pair of shoulders. When that time comes I believe that women will find no finer calling."[21]

Yet perhaps Brandeis's and Park's perspectives on women's relationship to the early film industry are not so different after all. Indeed, Park's "terrific weight" seems to refer to two distinct burdens: that of being responsible for actual productions tasks and that of claiming authorship. Eighty years later, although filmmaking has emerged from its embryonic state, directing is still not an obvious career choice for women. Perhaps this is because, more than ever, the burden of authorship has become synonymous with the lone figure of the director. While Ida May Park was able to cope with the "terrific nervous and physical strain" of the job ("[f]or the first time in six years I am taking a ten-day vacation, and even now the tentacles of the great cinema octopus threaten . . . to drag me back), she may have been less willing to take on the traditionally male provenance of authority.[22] Marie's mother certainly seems to wish to avoid that position. In her preface, Madeline Brandeis puts the responsibility of creating and photographing stories in foreign lands (with a little girl in tow), on Ref and Marie's shoulders. In fact, since it is Ref who takes the pictures, and Marie who knows what pictures to take, Brandeis hardly seems necessary in the production or authorization process.

It may be that so many women flourished as filmmakers during the silent era precisely because it was a time when individuals were able to undertake intensive production tasks without having to name themselves or their positions through a fixed system of credits. Yet film history has, understandably, taken more notice of those who boldly aggrandized their own authority, most famously by trumpeting themselves to be, in D. W. Griffith's words, "revolutionizing the Motion Picture Drama and founding the modern technique of the art."[23] These two very different approaches toward authorship cannot be accommodated by the same filmographic techniques. And so, creating filmographies for Marie's mother, or Mrs. Blaché, or Anonymous becomes a process of analysis and close reading and, also, an opportunity to rethink early film history and the modes through which historiographic and filmographic knowledge are transmitted.

Notes

I would like to thank Jennifer Bean, Diane Negra, Jane Gaines, and Daniel Welt for their help on this essay. The information included here draws on my own research as well as the collaborative efforts of the contributors to the WFPP. Zoran Sinobad and Madeline Matz from the Library of Congress, as well as Christel Schmidt, have been especially generous with their expertise and advice. At Duke University, Lisa Poteet, Michael Quinn, Amy Spaulding, and Nicole Walker have helped support the project.

1. Einar Lauritzen and Gunnar Lundquist, *American Film-Index, 1908-1915* (Huddinge, Sweden: Tonnheims, 1984).
2. Ibid., ix.
3. For more information on the project and its work, please see www.duke.edu/web/film/pioneers.html.
4. In Anthony Slide, *The Silent Feminists: America's First Women Directors* (Lanham, Md.: Scarecrow Press, 1996), 119.
5. This is a project that Christina Mugno is currently undertaking.
6. Charles Musser, *Edison Motion Pictures, 1890-1900: An Annotated Filmography* (Smithsonian Institution Press, and Le Giornate del Cinema Muto, 1997), 14.
7. Credit and subject index to *The American Film Institute Catalog of Motion Pictures Produced in the United States: Feature Films, 1911-1920*, exec. ed. Patricia King Hanson (Berkeley: University of California Press, 1988), 19.
8. *AFI Catalog, 1911-1920*, 225.
9. Alan Goble, *International Film Index, 1895-1990* (London: Bowker-Saur, 1991); Gwendolyn Audrey Foster, *Women Film Directors: An International Biocritical Dictionary* (Westport, Conn.: Greenwood Press, 1995).
10. Musser, *Edison Motion Pictures*, 53.
11. No further publication details are available for Schmidt's work at this time.
12. Robert Klepper, *Silent Films, 1877-1996: A Critical Guide to 646 Movies* (Jefferson, N.C.: McFarland, 1999), 141–142. Also available at www.classicimages.com/reviews/starprince.htm.
13. Slide, *Silent Feminists*, 133.
14. *AFI Catalog, 1911-1920*, 884.
15. *American Film Institute Catalog of Motion Pictures Produced in the United States: Feature Films, 1921-1930*, exec. ed. Kenneth W. Munden (New York: R. R. Bowker, 1971), 709.
16. Ibid., 888.
17. Madeline Brandeis, *Adventures in Hollywood* (London: W and R Chambers, 1937).
18. *Who Was Whom among North American Authors, 1921-1939* (Detroit: Gale Research, 1976), 198.
19. *A Dictionary of American Authors Deceased before 1950*, comp. W. Stewart Wallace (Toronto: Ryerson Press, 1951).

20 *American Women, 1935-1940: A Composite Biographical Dictionary,* ed. Durwood Howes (Detroit: Gale Research, 1981), 1097.
21 Reprinted in Slide, *Silent Feminists,* 146. Originally printed in *Careers for Women,* ed. Catherine Filene (Boston: Houghton Mifflin, 1920), 335-337.
22 In Slide, *Silent Feminists,* 145.
23 Advertisement placed by D. W. Griffith in the *New York Dramatic Mirror,* 13 Dec. 1913. Quoted in Tom Gunning, *D. W. Griffith and the Origins of American Narrative Film: The Early Years at Biograph* (Urbana: University of Illinois Press, 1991), 32.

Ways of Looking **II**

KRISTEN WHISSEL

The Gender of Empire

American Modernity, Masculinity, and Edison's War Actualities

In August 1898, the *Century* magazine published accounts of naval battles fought during the Spanish-American War in which the United States defeated Spain to establish U.S. military, political, and economic dominance in the Western Hemisphere. After detailing the courage, efficiency, and technological mastery of his crew in battle, Captain John W. Philip of the *Texas* lamented, "I shall ever regret that the snap shot of the crew of the boat ... proved to be a failure, the films being ruined by sulphur. The crew was muscular and well developed, stripped to the waist and their bodies were besmeared with perspiration and the refuse of burnt powder. They were a mild and well-disposed set of men, but they looked angry."[1] Although Captain Philip lamented the destruction of this particular photograph, the increasingly popular phenomenon of moving pictures more than compensated for this loss. In 1898, the Edison Manufacturing Company's war actualities provided civilians with life-size moving images of military men (at times "muscular and developed" and "stripped to the waist") who promised to deliver the United States from the ills of technological modernity and industrial capitalism at the end of the nineteenth century.

The image of the white male body harnessed to military technology became a signifier for a newly forged national-imperial identity based on an amalgamation of social Darwinism, the imperatives of industrial capitalism, the myth of the frontier, and the ideology of manifest destiny.[2] The outbreak of war in 1898 saw a resurgence of claims to an Anglo-Saxon virility that had led the "English-speaking race" to conquer and civilize vast areas and populations around the world. At the same time, the image of an enervated male body, exhausted and effeminized by the demands of industrial capitalism and technological modernity, circulated throughout popular American culture. In turn, increased participation of the new woman in suffrage, reform, and anti-imperialist movements, and the increased presence of women and immigrants in the workplace and the spheres of commercialized leisure appeared to loosen native white masculinity's privileged grip on political legitimacy, cultural authority, and social control.[3] Alarmists warned that if native white American masculinity declined thanks to the exigencies and excesses of modern life, so, too, would American "civilization."[4] Such concerns brought American masculinity under the scrutiny of an older generation of male scientists, adventurers, psychologists, reformers, military veterans, and educators who described this younger generation as "unnatural," "degenerate," "effeminate," "overcivilized," "neurasthenic," and therefore in need of correction, reform, and regeneration. As Gaylyn Studlar has shown, this group of specialists promoted a range of semicompulsory activities (scouting, school sports, hunting trips, etc.) that would revitalize and strengthen individual character.[5] As part of this trend, the discipline of military life was promoted as a corrective for the modern ills that plagued the male body and the national body. Hence, war with Spain was welcomed in newspapers, magazines, and vaudeville houses as an opportunity to build male bodies and, consequently, national character.[6]

The Edison Manufacturing Company's "War Extra" actualities give insight into how early cinema's encounter with empire helped reformulate the relationship between modern technology and masculinity in late-nineteenth-century American culture. This article analyzes Edison's Spanish-American War actualities as part of a broader cultural project that subjected American masculinity to a scrutinizing, disciplinary gaze. War actualities brought into focus a type of American masculinity based on conceptions of discipline, control, whiteness, and power — a set of abstractions that would prove to be particularly profitable to the Edison company and peculiarly tenacious throughout the history of American cinema.[7] Analyzed alongside their catalog descriptions (which exhibitors might use in their accompanying lectures), these films reveal that by 1898 the cinema was, in many ways, elaborating a protonarrative discourse orchestrated around a coherent point of view that promoted spectacles of an ideologically powerful and visually compelling imperial masculinity.[8] Feminist scholars cannot afford to overlook these films, for, as I show, the war actuality played a significant role in shaping the early cinema's representation of gender and race. Importantly, the war actuality did more than simply document turn-of-century struggles over gender, race, and nation taking place during the war. Instead, it participated in the discursive construction of a rejuvenated white masculinity that was manufactured in response to, and at the expense of, African American masculinity, the new woman, and newly conquered overseas populations.

Overseas Empire, Modernity, and American Masculinity

Amy Kaplan has argued that following the closing of the American frontier "national power" was increasingly measured by "the extension of vaster yet less tangible networks of international markets and political influence" beyond the nation's self-contained borders.[9] Such changes led the naval officer and theorist Captain Alfred Thayer Mahan to urge Americans to turn their "eyes outward, instead of inward only, to seek the welfare of the country," for, he noted, "there is a restlessness in the world which is deeply significant if not ominous."[10] To protect the United States from foreign restlessness, and, moreover, to take advantage of distant markets that might provide an outlet for overproduction, Mahan argued that the United States needed to build up its naval power and establish "points of support" and "means of influence" on islands peppering the Caribbean and the Pacific.[11] To justify such endeavors, Mahan invoked what he called a "fundamental truth": "that the control of the seas, and especially along the great lines drawn by national interest or national commerce, is the chief among the material elements in the power and prosperity of nations. It is so because the sea is the world's great medium of circulation."[12] For Mahan, the strength and integrity of the nation's core depended on the circulation of modern American power and commodities throughout a strategically mapped network of naval bases, markets, annexes, and protectorates linked by the supporting technologies of the steamship, railway, and telegraph.

This bid for an overseas empire entailed a shift in the technology of American expansionism. In proimperial discourse, the railway lost its status as the primary mechanical icon for expansion, functioning less to expand the nation's continental boundaries than to bind the nation into a coherent commercial whole. Comparing the railway to the steamship following the close of the continental frontier, Commodore G. W. Melville argued in the *North American Review* that although the railway could "conquer time and distance" it could only offer an inflexible, "fixed, permanent way. The sea, on the contrary, gives a track—fluid, mobile, universal—which turns wherever swift prows may point, and on which massive hulls, much too huge for any form of land transit, may pass with ease from port to port."[13] Following a "fluid, mobile, universal" track, the steamship emerged in the 1890s as the primary technology for imagining and acquiring a new commercial and territorial overseas empire. Yet new naval technology alone could not fulfill this desire, for overseas empire demanded the production of a specific type of masculinity. Kaplan notes that as "politicians, intellectuals and businessmen ... were redefining national power as disembodied—that is, divorced from contiguous territorial expansion ... masculine identity was reconceived as embodied—that is, cultivated in the muscular robust physique."[14] Overseas imperialism demanded a martial masculinity that could master simultaneously the physical demands of "frontier life" and new military technology. As a result, the military recruit came to embody a newly idealized modern American masculinity.

This revised masculinity must be placed in the context of a broader shift in the construction of American masculinity in the 1890s.[15] According to Gail Bederman and Anthony Rotundo, the Victorian ideal of "manly" self-restraint lost some of its purchase in a survival-of-the-fittest social and economic milieu marked by economic depressions, labor unrest, and challenges to the native white claim to political authority by immigrant groups and suffragettes.[16] Even worse, such self-restraint was diagnosed as one of the causes of neurasthenia, a nervous affliction that resulted from an unhealthy privileging of "the labor of the brain over that of the muscles" demanded by industrial capitalism.[17] According to George Miller Beard, the accelerated pace of American capitalism combined with the rapid circulation of information via the telegraph, pneumatic tube, and press to drain "civilized" men of their "reserve of nervous energy and life force," leaving them "as weak and useless as a worn out battery."[18] Symptoms of this illness included fatigue, listlessness, and a lack of will and seemed to support claims coming from various corners of American culture, particularly those aligned with jingoism, that American men had become overcivilized. The professor of pedagogy and psychology G. Stanley Hall argued that overcivilization could be cured by recovering a latent "masculine primitive" that had been submerged beneath the veneer of civilization by allowing boys and young men to engage in what Hall's friend Teddy Roosevelt called "the strenuous life."[19]

The project of cultivating native white masculinity was inseparable from efforts to prevent what Roosevelt and others referred to as race degeneration:[20] in the 1890s, reformers argued that if native white masculinity declined, so too would the "American race."[21] As reformers scrutinized native white boys and men, anthropologists and eugenicists measured, quantified, described, and photographed populations around the world and placed them into racial categories. These categories were then arranged into hierarchies of civilization.[22] By placing the Anglo-American race at the apex of such hierarchies, these discursive projects justified U.S. cultural, military, and economic domination of those placed lower on the scale. According to imperial discourse, the fact that American and British culture had reached a high degree of technological development and civilization gave these English-speaking cultures the responsibility and even the "duty" to embark on so-called civilizing missions.[23] Thus, as Bederman stresses, the "masculine primitive" was valued most when combined with a good measure of the "virtues" of Anglo-American civilization. But it was the racially inherited bodily strength and Anglo-Saxon virility that gave "the English-speaking race" the power to prevail in physical battles that were understood to be part of an evolutionary struggle between nations and races.[24] Thus the ostensible need to reclaim masculine primitivity in Anglo-American men dovetailed with proimperialist discourse that promoted the therapeutic benefits of empire for both colonizer and colonized.

Events taking place on 15 February 1898 offer insight into this particular moment in American modernity when new relationships were being forged in popular culture between nation, gender, technology, and empire. That night, a mysterious explosion sunk the U.S. battleship *Maine* in Havana Harbor, marking the inception of U.S. overseas imperialism with an extraordinary example of modern technology's capacity for catastrophic breakdown.[25] An assertion of American military power, the *Maine* had been sent to Havana Harbor to protect American commercial interests in Cuba threatened by the conflict between Cuban freedom fighters and Spanish colonial rule.[26] The 260 men killed in the explosion represented a type of masculinity increasingly defined as the perfect embodiment of a culturally powerful "martial spirit."[27] Thus the explosion challenged the sense of historical and evolutionary inevitability on which narratives of national-racial destiny and progress were based. Crucially, the cause of the explosion was never decisively determined (it derived either from an internal technological failure or from a mine, planted by the Spanish). This indeterminacy, along with descriptions and images of the wreck, cast suspicion on the new military technology. Even the description of the explosion published by the ship's captain, Charles Sigsbee, reads like a technological apocalypse:

> To me, in my position, well aft, and within the superstructure, it was a bursting, rending, and crashing sound or roar of immense volume, largely metallic in character. It was followed by a succession of heavy, ominous, metallic sounds, probably caused by the overturning of the central superstructure and by falling debris. There was a trembling and a lurching motion of the vessel, a list to port, and a movement of subsidence. The electric lights ... went out. Then there was intense blackness and smoke.[28]

Here, the mysterious explosion appears as nothing less than a ferocious and lethal surprise attack launched by the ship against its own crew. Sigsbee's description of what he saw on inspection of the ship might have confirmed technophobic suspicions that new military technology was, at best, an unreliable ally in the quest for a disembodied empire and, at worst, a treacherous foe of American civilization. Explaining that the ship's central superstructure had been torn away, Sigsbee continues:

> The broad surface that was uppermost was the ceiling of the berth-deck, where many men had swung from beam to beam in their hammocks the night before. On the white paint of the ceiling was the impression of two human bodies—mere dust—so I was told afterward. The great piece was so torn, twisted and confused with structural details that the identification of visible parts was only possible after careful study.[29]

Reducing the bodies of two sailors to charcoal imprints on the berth-deck ceiling and twisting the battleship to an unrecognizable mass of wreckage, the explosion that sunk the *Maine* had the hallmarks of technological modernity's deadliest assault on American military masculinity.[30]

A June 1898 article in the *Atlantic Monthly* sought to ameliorate the public's anxiety over the modern battleship, lamenting that

> in the mind of the non-technical citizen, the battleship has become almost the synonym for disaster. This huge machine is considered uncertain, unwieldy, and unsafe. . . . The newspapers have contained many illustrations of terrific conflicts, in which ships have been drawn crashing into one another, and plunging into the depths, carrying men and guns down with them. One of the pictorial weeklies has gone so far as to represent the battle ship as a huge sphinx.[31]

Ultimately, though, the explosion that sunk the *Maine* acted as a catalyst for transforming this notorious example of chance, peril, and violent shock back into a narrative of national continuity and self-controlled destiny. The idea that the explosion was caused by a Spanish mine was broadly promoted by the press, allowing blame to be displaced from new American technology to Old World treachery.[32] Whatever the cause of the explosion, the sunken battleship seemed to demand a counterdisplay of technological military power that would compensate for this spectacle of catastrophic breakdown and shore up narratives on naval power, masculinity, and imperial expansion that had been written around increasingly complex U.S. involvement in the Spanish-Cuban conflict.

War Actualities and the Promotion of Fascinated Inspection

With the ability mechanically to reproduce bodies in motion and provide views of disparate and distant points around the globe, moving pictures were particularly well suited to give new and compelling visibility to an emergent imperial masculinity. Edison's *"War Extra" Catalogue* promises exhibitors films that "are sure to satisfy the craving of the general public for absolutely true and accurate details regarding the movements of the United States Army getting ready for the invasion of Cuba."[33] Focusing on short bursts of "purposeful" movement, actualities shot at the military camp in Tampa make visible the kinetic movement and circulation of the male body-in-motion preparing for the conquest of the new disembodied empire. In turn, naval views exhibit battleships adorned with "bustling" activity and the flag, thereby displaying in a single image the synthesis of militarized masculinity, powerful technology, and patriotism. For example, Edison's *"War Extra" Catalogue* promises that the film *U.S. Battleship "Iowa"* (1898)

> shows the US Battleship "Iowa" at anchor at the rendezvous near the Dry Tortugas. The camera was placed on the small yacht, which approaches and passes the battleship, thus giving a complete view of one side of this mammoth war machine. The picture was taken on the sailors' wash day, and on the line stretched along the fore part of the vessel is hung their apparel. The picture is exceedingly sharp and the cannon are plainly shown as they project from the different turrets and portholes. The American flag is flying from the mast and waves in the breeze. Some distance from the stern of the vessel are two targets, and a number of sailors are seen rowing in small boats. This is a most excellent picture of the vessel and is exceptionally good from a photographic standpoint.[34]

As part of a fleet of ships that Captain Philip described as "majestic in their suggestion of irresistible power,"[35] this view of the "mammoth war machine" was meant to inspire awe rather than the anxiety provoked by the sphinxlike mystery of naval technology only several months earlier. War actualities such as this one offered a glimpse into the everyday disciplined routine of the men that had inoculated them against the physical and sensory shocks of modern warfare and transformed them into the embodiment of what Captain Philip called "mechanical precision fortified by intelligent patriotism."[36] Moreover, the formal qualities of these films position the viewer as the subject of a disciplinary gaze. The noncentered quality of the image allows the eye to roam across and inspect a range of activities (from laundry to target practice) that characterized the disciplined routine of military life. And while the camera's distance allows the viewer to watch without being seen, it would be inappropriate to characterize this look as voyeuristic, or to classify as exhibitionist films in which soldiers acknowledge the camera's presence. For the proper functioning of the disciplinary gaze in a military setting depends on the soldier's knowledge of the fact that he exists in a state of perpetual visibility and surveillance, whether or not the subjects of the disciplinary gaze are visible to him.[37] Hence in some of these war actualities the camera is acknowledged, whereas in others it is not. In either case, the war actuality aligns the viewer with the disciplinary gaze of the imperial apparatus via the camera's look of fascinated inspection, and thereby charges this mode of viewing with a historically specific visual power and pleasure.

The film *U.S. Battleship "Indiana"* (1898) provides a similar sort of view. Shot from a moving vessel, the camera pans along the starboard length of the ship to reveal a gradually unfolding view of the battleship, manufacturing a visual tension between the sight of the massive battleship and the various activities taking place on deck. Lecturers at venues such as the Eden Musée could reveal to audiences that the spectacle before them was

> taken at the Dry Tortugas and shows the most powerful fighting machine in the world today as she lies at anchor taking on coal. The decks are covered with marines and sailors. An immense barge lies along side, from which a large gang of negroes are hustling "King coal" into the battleship, on whose decks the coal passers run to and fro. The view is taken from a moving yacht and gives the effect of the vessel itself passing through the water. As the yacht passed the starboard quarter, the powerful 13-inch, 8-inch and 6-inch guns bristle from their turrets. She looks every inch of her great length, 348 feet. The photograph is excellent.[38]

As the camera slowly peruses the length of the ship, it allows audiences to observe the coaling process taking place on board, displaying a pleasurable spectacle of the disciplined activity and energetic "hustle" that naval experts argued provided seamless continuity between peacetime and wartime activity on board the battleship. For example, Captain Henry Taylor's description of action on board the *Indiana* leading up to the Battle of Santiago emphasized the physical strength and endless energy required to sustain a battleship:

The Gender of Empire

The morning of July 3, 1898, found the battleship "Indiana" holding the eastern end of the line of battleships and armored cruisers off Santiago. For two days and two nights the labor of the officers and crew had been intense: they had coaled ship at Guantanamo until midnight of July 1, and had then hastened to the fleet off Santiago to take part in the spirited engagement of July 2.... Signaling our arrival to the flagship before day break, the answering signal flashed back, "Take position between flagship and 'Oregon' and clear ship for action." The coal dust was still thick on the deck and on the faces of officers and crew, and most of them had not had more than an hour or two of sleep, caught hurriedly and without undressing; but at this stirring and welcome signal, fatigue of body and mind vanished, and all sprang to their stations with a cool exultation of spirit characteristic of our ship's company.[39]

This article and Edison's actuality present the fantasy of continuous action carried out by men and machines propelled by endless energy and a capacity for limitless mobility: the energetic men coal the ship to fuel its "fluid, universal" mobility and in turn the ship mobilizes the men to the new frontier. Moreover, the temporal nonclosure of the actuality provides a (perhaps fortuitous) formal support to the idea of the endless imperial energy: while the inspection itself is limited to the length of the film, the fact that the camera captures activity in medias res allows it to be perceived as ongoing and continuous, without beginning or end. So great is the impulse to display the kinetic energy of the imperial machine that even "at anchor," the catalog assures, the ship seems to be in motion, thanks to the moving point of view from which the film was shot. In turn, by making available scenes of everyday military life, the war actualities circulating through civilian life undoubtedly helped normalize the type of military masculinity on display.

Actualities representing the preparations for the ground invasion of Cuba also display a visual orchestration of bodies and machines harnessed to the war effort. The description for *U.S. Cavalry Supplies Unloading at Tampa, Florida* (1898) explains

Here is a freight train of thirty cars loaded with baggage and ambulance supplies for the 9th US Cavalry. In the foreground a score of troopers are pulling, lifting and hauling an ambulance from a flat car. It slides down the inclined planks with a sudden rush that makes men "hustle" to keep it from falling off. Drill engine on the next track darts past with sharp quick puffs of smoke. A very brisk scene.[40]

In this scenario, a newly embodied and militarized masculinity masters and prevails over technology, and seems to be animated with as much energy as the drill engine that "darts past with sharp quick puffs of smoke." The arrival of the freight train occasions the display of bodily strength and the activities of pulling, lifting, and hauling. Even the contingency of an unpredictable event (the ambulance makes a sudden rush) is converted into military purposefulness and mastery, as the men "hustle" and regain control. Aided by the catalog description, this film establishes the space of war preparation as one where the male body prevails over machines now harnessed to the purposeful pace and hustle of the military endeavor. Such scenes provided audiences with the illusion of operating, if only briefly, as a functional relay in the scopic regime responsible for the production of this martial ideal.

Given their emphasis on mastery and control and scenarios of physical power and military hustle, these films seem to offer a counterdiscourse to the shock and surprise film scholars link to the modes of looking and articulation of modernity in early cinema. Lynne Kirby has persuasively shown how preclassical films featuring modern technologies (including the cinema) also feature male hysterics traumatized by the violent physical and visual shocks characteristic of technological modernity in general and the "cinema of attractions" in particular.[41] Kirby links preclassical spectatorship and modes of representation to an "undoing" of gendered identity that reduces men to traumatized hysterics and mobilizes fantasies of submission as well as pleasure in the machine-made thrill. Kirby suggests that the emergence and institutionalization of classical narration brought with it a reassertion of gendered codes and a containment of the visual assaults associated with the early cinema. Yet I would argue that Edison's war actualities offer an earlier, antihysterical mode of representation and spectatorship. If preclassical fictional films offer images of machine-made hysterics and fantasies of assault and shock—if only to generate a stimulus shield for the beleaguered modern subject—war actualities seem to offer up images of an ideal machine-made military masculinity already immune to the pathologies of modern life. At the same time that urban technological modernity created the condition of existence for hysterical, traumatized masculinity, the (highly mythologized) space of imperial warfare emerged as the territory on which American masculinity could reassert authority and control over technology, industry, and the racial/ethnic other and thrive. Moreover, by placing the spectator in a position of "fascinated inspection," these actualities invested viewers with an imaginary power simultaneously to scrutinize and delight in the image of a type of masculinity that mastered technological modernity.

The Gender of Empire

Ninth Infantry Boys Morning Wash (1898) offers a striking example of this visual pleasure. The catalog asks exhibitors and audiences to

> Imagine forty or fifty soldier boys each with a pail of water on the ground before him, sousing and spattering and scrubbing away for dear life. Soap and towels too. Every man jack of them looks as if he were enjoying the wash immensely, and also the novelty of having his picture taken. The big fellow in the center of the picture is laughing heartily. All the figures are clearly outlined, and the whole group is true to life.[42]

Here, soldiers collude with the camera to display the male body immersed in an idealized homosocial space at the perimeter of the nation, insulated from the overcivilizing effects of domestic culture and the enervating effects of big-city life. The camera displays a rejuvenated male body (no sign of neurasthenia here) that popular discourse identified as both the cause and the effect of empire. Although a common feature of such catalogs, the promise of "clearly outlined" figures is significant here, for by making highly visible the details of these strapping, soapy, laughing bodies, the camera allowed audiences to see, examine, and inspect this body in detail. Here the turn-of-the-century "cult of the body" charges imperial ideology with pleasure by making available life-size moving images of the militarized male body in a state of partial undress. Moreover, the catalog's attention to "the big fellow in the center of the picture" who is "laughing heartily" promotes, in a sense, the ontological pleasure—even joy—of embodying a type of masculinity based on physical discipline and power. Indeed, jingoes promoted the war, in part, as an opportunity to develop and display a type of masculinity that would be perceived by the nation and the rest of the world as a sign of the United States's strength, health, and progress.[43] Thus the camera captures and exhibits the cinematic signifier for the nation's newly reformed imperial identity, made visible in the spectacle of the powerful militarized male body-in-motion.

Catalog descriptions for these films reveal the degree to which the production of this body relied on a military mise-en-scène. The description for the film *Battery B Arriving at Camp* (1898), for example, focuses on the material world of the military camp:

> When Battery B of the 4th US Artillery came to Tampa, Fla. it meant business and the picture shows it. One by one the big artillery men pass by in front and reappear in the background, dismounting, unloosing saddle girths and bridles and leading away their mounts. Limbers, gun carriages and caissons

in the distance. The sweating horses and the vigorous switching of tails tell a mute story of hot weather and fly time.⁴⁴

This description evidences a fascination with the soldier's body undertaking any task at all within a military mise-en-scène. Surrounded by horses, gun carriages, and caissons, every movement and gesture, down to the smallest detail of loosening a bridle, is observed and incorporated into the purposefulness of military "business" and the broader project of expansion. The rather banal activities represented here certainly fall short of the romantic tales of imperial adventure found in yellow journalism and the historical novel circulating through popular culture at this time.⁴⁵ Yet the very absence of anything other than the more mundane activities of military preparation allows the camera to focus and linger over the image of native white masculinity as it made itself into a new embodiment of national-imperial identity. Such focus on the details of the material mise-en-scène and bodily rhetoric of soldiery suggests that rather than simply documenting war activities, these actualities participated in the active discursive construction of a martial masculine ideal. Indeed mise-en-scène and a focus on everyday routine is as important to the militarization of the white male body as it is to the eroticization of the female body in the protocinematic motion studies and early films. Linda Williams has brilliantly argued that in Eadweard Muybridge's motion studies, female subjects are surrounded by decorative objects—cigarettes, transparent veils, vases, bed linen—which create incipient narrative diegeses that aestheticize and fetishize their bodies. Here, surplus mise-en-scène has the effect of implanting the female form with sexuality, which in turn appears to be the "truth" of femininity.⁴⁶ Similarly, Constance Balides has persuasively shown how preclassical films use the objects and activities of everyday life—trying on shoes in *The Gay Shoe Clerk* (Edison, 1903), hanging laundry in a *Windy Day on the Roof* (AM & B, 1904), walking down the street in *What Happened on Twenty-third Street, New York City* (Edison, 1901)—to stage exposures of the female body that normalize the eroticization of women's bodies in everyday life.⁴⁷ At the same time that Williams and Balides note that a particular deployment of setting, looks, and fictional mise-en-scène is fundamental to the eroticization of femininity, they also note an absence of superfluous gestures and props in presentations of the male body. Thus Williams observes that in Muybridge's motion studies, "Naked and seminaked men, for example walk, run, jump, throw, catch, box, wrestle, and perform simple trades such as carpentry," and that when the male movements require props, "these props are always simple, such as a saw and some wood for carpentry."[48] In turn, Balides notes, for example, that in *Al Treloar in Muscle Exercises* (AM & B, 1905), the bodybuilder Treloar wears trunks and appears on a stage decorated only by a stand with cards that indicate the type of exercise on display, giving the mise-en-scène a didactic rather than erotic function.[49] Yet if in such films and motion studies "Men's naked bodies appear natural in action: they act and do,"[50] it is only thanks to the amount of discursive and cultural labor that went into naturalizing ostensibly "male" activities precisely at a time when other activities—brain work, office work, novel reading, tea sipping—were being identified by specialists as unnatural, unhealthy, effeminizing. Indeed, films featuring Al Treloar were part of the broader promotion by "specialists" of the strenuous life as essential to the cultivation of "healthy" American masculinity, as were the activities of boxing, running, jumping, and wrestling executed by the university "athletes" Muybridge employed as models of normative male movement. Without disagreeing with these scholars, I would simply add that the selection and display of the bodily rhetoric of specific activities (running, wrestling, jumping, boxing, sawing wood, bodybuilding) in "functional" settings in proto- and early-cinematic images was an integral part of the turn-of-the-century production and naturalization of a "strenuous" masculinity that was meant to be perceived as the opposite of (an equally manufactured) fetishized femininity.

Thus in war actualities, there is an acute attention paid to the details of bodily rhetoric and costume so necessary to the construction of the martial ideal. For example, the description for the film *Tenth U.S. Infantry Disembarking from Cars* (1898) promises

> A stirring scene; full of martial energy. No ordinary dress parade this, but a picture full of soldiers—men with a high purpose. They march up the platform in fours, and left wheel just in front of the camera, passing out of sight in a cloud of dust. The customary small boy is in evidence in great numbers, while the rear guard, the train pulls out of the station. Literally "out of sight."[51]

The catalog describes a similar film, *Tenth U.S. Infantry, Second Battalion, Leaving Cars* (1898), with a

> Hurrah here they come! Hot, dusty, grim and determined! Real soldiers, every inch of them! No gold lace and chalked belts and shoulder straps, but fully equipped in full marching order: blankets, guns, knapsacks, canteens. Trains in the background.[52]

Both of these descriptions contrast the bodies onscreen with the ornamented body of symbolic military display that might signify precisely the

"Old World" decadence and effeminacy that had increasingly been linked to Spain.[53] Thus *Tenth U.S. Infantry, Second Battalion, Leaving Cars* focuses attention on the accoutrements of imperial conquest ("blankets, guns, knapsacks, canteens") as the props needed to charge the militarized body-in-motion with power. This list again seems to promote a disciplinary gaze, one that inspects and peruses the bodies for guns, knapsacks, and canteens even as such a sight is offered up to audiences for the first time. Yet it also suggests the importance of the enclosed setting and material mise-en-scène of the imperial adventure to the construction of martial masculinity. Settings featuring either dusty landscapes filled with horses, trains, military equipment, and uniformed bodies, or seascapes dotted with battleships increasingly appear as the condition of existence for this idealized form of masculinity. Both films endow the spectator with a privileged look at an exceptional form of American masculinity propelled by "martial energy" and "high purpose" through an emergent imperial network that already extends far beyond the edges of the frame, "literally out of sight."

Just as the disciplinary gaze of the camera undertook a fascinated inspection of ideal military masculinity, it also sought out and subjected to scrutiny masculine types who apparently fell short of this ideal and were deemed in need of further discipline and training. The rest of the description for the *Tenth U.S. Infantry, Second Battalion, Leaving Cars* makes it clear that the idealization of native white masculinity depended on the production of a range of racialized male bodies that might be compared, contrasted, and ranked in relation to one another. Thus these films create what Mark Cooper and, elsewhere, Richard Dyer have respectively referred to as a visual differential system of racialized and gendered bodies, without which an idealized whiteness cannot exist.[54] The catalog goes on to describe

> crowds of curious bystanders, comical looking "nigger dude" with sun umbrella strolls languidly in the foreground and you can almost hear that yaller dog bark. Small boys in abundance. The column marches in fours and passes through the front of the picture. More small boys of all colors. The picture is excellent and full of vigorous life.[55]

This description seems to suggest that the visibility of the Tenth Infantry's "vigorous life" required the presence of the "comical looking" African American "dude" marked out as precisely the kind of ornamented, over-civilized masculinity the catalog argues the Tenth Infantry do not themselves embody. In this film the particular attraction of the African American dude's racial difference derives from the way in which his body is made

The Gender of Empire

to contrast with the "martial energy" and "high purpose" of the Tenth Cavalry. While they march, he strolls languidly. While the accoutrements of imperial masculinity—canteens, guns, knapsacks—are disavowed as decoration and made to signify the strenuous life of imperial conquest, his sun umbrella is made to signify a sharply contrasting ornamentation and delicate effeminacy. Indeed, the catalog positions him as a diegetic spectator of the newly embodied masculine ideal and makes an attraction of his failure to be incorporated into this spectacle of national-imperial unity. Moreover, the language used to describe this figure was part of a racist pro-imperial discourse that sought to consolidate definitions of the new empire around a newly unified whiteness that smoothed over the sectional and economic differences between whites while exacerbating racial divisions between whites and blacks. According to Kristin Hoganson, the "dude" was a "stereotypically effeminate wealthy man, usually from the Northeast," often depicted as a symbol "of the corrupting power of money" and the tendency to privilege class comfort over national honor.[56] Highly publicized participation in the Cuban campaign allowed many upper-class white men to refashion their "dudish" image by demonstrating their courage and patriotism on the warfront and thus their right to claim a share in the political legitimacy attached to war veterans. For example, the well-publicized exploits of Roosevelt's Rough Riders in the Battle of San Juan Hill gave Senator William Sewell (R.-N.J.) the opportunity to affirm the dude's right to political and social power:

> The darling of the parlor, the athlete at Yale, Harvard, or Princeton are lined up today on the picket line before Santiago with the farmer and the mechanic, each equal, each claiming no more right as an American citizen, and each anxious and eager for the fray. It is the most sublime spectacle, I say to the Senate of the United States, that ever has been witnessed that our very best blood, our brightest young men claim the right of citizenship to the extent that they go to the front line of battle and die with anybody and everybody, no matter from what rank of society.[57]

Such sentiments represented a broader tendency in American culture to regard the war with Spain as an opportunity not just to reunite white men of the upper classes with white men of the lower classes, but also to unite the "Blue" with the "Grey" and the city dweller with the farmer in common effort under the same flag.[58] Edison's actualities participated in a broader mass-mediated process that transformed troops such as Roosevelt's Rough Riders into "walking advertisements" for what Bederman calls "a collective imperial manhood for the white American race."[59] Thus it is quite important that the catalog description for this film marks out—even manufactures—the racial and class difference of the African American dude, for in doing so it reveals the discursive strategies used to position black Americans outside new imperial constructions of the nation.

While mustering in was promoted as a magical process that erased perceivable class, ethnic, and regional differences between white Americans, the resulting spectacle of this newly unified martial ideal intensified racial and class differences between black Americans and whites.[60] Another Edison actuality reveals the processes through which cinematic discourse participated in the positioning of African Americans outside the newly forged national-imperial identity by manufacturing interpretive frameworks that define the black soldier as in need of further discipline.[61] *Colored Troops Disembarking* (1898) shows the Second Battalion of the Twenty-fourth Colored Infantry disembarking from a transport (fig. 11) and is no different than those featuring whites: it simply projects an image of soldiers, outfitted in the accoutrements of military life, arriving in Cuba, and thus appears to inscribe the Second Battalion of the Twenty-fourth into the circuits of overseas American imperialism. Yet the catalog encourages exhibitors and audiences to perceive the black body as one that is comically at odds with the martial energy and serious high purpose embodied by, for example, the white Tenth U.S. Cavalry:

> The steamer "Mascotte" has reached her dock at Port Tampa, and the 2nd Battalion of colored infantry is going ashore. Tide is very high, and the gangplank is extra steep; and it is laughable to see the extreme caution displayed by the soldiers clambering down. The commanding officer struts on the wharf, urging them to hurry. Two boat stewards in glistening white duck coats are interested watchers—looking for tips perhaps. The picture is full of fine light and shadow effects.[62]

The catalog description intervenes to act as an early example of what Daniel Bernardi calls "the voice of whiteness" and encourages exhibitors and audiences to perceive this film as a contrast between black and white.[63] Unlike descriptions that define white soldiers in terms of an orderly purposefulness, this description defines the black body-in-motion as a comedic spectacle, as overly cautious and timid. In turn, the catalog's interpretation of the image of the white officer who, we are told, urges the Twenty-fourth to "hurry" makes the black troops appear out of sync with the accelerated pace of the new imperialism. In contrast to the bodies appearing in *Tenth U.S. Infantry, Second Battalion,* whose movements, the catalog suggests, demonstrate that they "meant business" and thereby provoke hurrahs, the bodies

The Gender of Empire

11. *Colored Troops Disembarking* (Edison Manufacturing Co., 1898). Courtesy of the Library of Congress Motion Picture Reading Room.

12. *Cuban Refugees Waiting for Rations* (Edison Manufacturing Co., 1898). Courtesy of the Library of Congress Motion Picture Reading Room.

on display in *Colored Troops Disembarking* are transformed into a type of vaudevillian masculinity meant to provoke laughter. By inscribing African Americans as either spectators-in-the-text or as military subjects in need of further discipline, the war actuality participated in the broader discursive and political marginalization of blacks from the newly forged conceptions of national unity coming out of the war and helped consolidate a dominant whiteness at the expense of newly colonized and African American populations. In this way, the war actuality worked in tandem with a range of late-nineteenth-century visual forms—chronophotography, the museum exhibit, world's fairs and exhibitions, zoos, travelogues, and early ethnographic films—to classify difference according to what Fatimah Rony calls "the narrative of evolution which slots humans into a hierarchy of color-coded categories and places the white race at the apex."[64]

To conclude I return to Captain Philip's regret over the loss of the post-battle photograph of his crew, which seems to stem in part from the ensuing loss of the audience that would have accompanied this image's mass-mediated display. Philip's desire for spectators was more than fulfilled by the audiences—women and men—who packed the Eden Musée and vaudeville houses to see war pictures in 1898.[65] Charles Musser notes that soldiers returning from the war front flocked to the Eden Musée to see war pictures.[66] And while the latter might present an early example of the narcissistic identification feminist scholars link to the masculinized spectatorship of the classical era, one suspects that these soldiers found added pleasure in watching female audiences consume and cheer life-size moving images of themselves and their comrades. The cultivation of a female audience at war programs was part of a broader process also at work in the historical novel and popular press, which, as Kaplan argues, "sought to enlist women in the traditional male realm of what Edward Said has called the pleasures of imperialism."[67] Part of this pleasure derived from the inscription of women into fantasies of rescue and protection so characteristic of imperial culture. The film *Cuban Refugees Waiting for Rations* (1898) (fig. 12) suggests how the presence of native white female spectators in war films and at moving-picture programs contributed to the broader cultural inscription of U.S. overseas imperialism as a chivalric rescue mission. The catalog description for the film describes

> A group of escaped reconcentrados, saved from the fate of starvation imposed by the Butcher, Weyler. They stand in line waiting, each man with his tin dish and cup. One expects to see just such men as these, after the centuries of Spanish oppression and tyranny. As they come forward, their walk, even, is listless and lifeless. The picture affords an exceedingly interesting racial character study. At one side stands a group of officers from the camp near by, accompanying several ladies who are seeing the sights.[68]

The apparent chivalry of the officers "accompanying several ladies seeing the sights" on one hand, and the rather ethnographically oriented spectacle of the Cuban refugees receiving relief from Spanish tyranny on the other, have the effect of promoting a perception of the military camp as a space that is outside the spheres of colonial oppression. Put differently, the description encourages spectators to perceive U.S. imperialism as the opposite of Spain's brutal colonial regime, rather than a mere replacement of it. The

The Gender of Empire

exchange of looks and distribution of bodies in this film reveals once again how the production of a native white masculine ideal depended on the production of a range of differently gendered and racialized bodies. The presence of native white "ladies" confers chivalry on their military chaperones. In turn, the protective glances of both the officers and the ladies "seeing the sights," combined with the catalog description, mark the ostensibly "listless and lifeless" Cubans as in need of U.S. protection and further intervention, discipline, reform, and rejuvenation. Enclosing and protecting its new and not-so-new dependents, the military camp emerges in this film as a space capable of producing virile native white masculinity and as a bastion of racial and patriarchal chivalric protection. Women who saw this film would have seen projected before them the position meant to be occupied by "proper" native white women in the new empire: dependent on and subordinate to a militarized masculine ideal, occupying the margins of political life as mere spectators in awe of imperial masculinity. Missing from this particular picture are the forces of resistance to U.S. imperialism, such as American anti-imperialists who protested expansion and the colonial subjects who resisted U.S. imperialism in the new colonies. While the former were disparaged in the new imperial culture in gendered terms (anti-imperialist women were represented in articles and cartoons as grotesquely masculinized while men were represented as effeminate and old), the latter were deemed savage, ungrateful, and in need of civilization.

Thus, whether we classify the Spanish-American War actuality as part of either what Tom Gunning calls "the cinema of attractions" or what Charles Musser calls "the cinema of reassurance," we cannot understand on what terms these films thrilled and/or reassured audiences without considering how the moving pictures participated in the rearticulation of gender, race, nation, and empire at the end of the nineteenth century.[69] War actualities displayed a high-tech, complex, hierarchical formation in which physically developed bodies and powerful machines worked efficiently to extend the nation's political and commercial power around the globe. These films offered a vision of unity and order that allowed white, middle-class audiences to indulge in fantasies of power, mastery, and control over the conditions of technological modernity and over the populations (women, African Americans, and "native" colonials) who were increasingly defined by dominant white culture as "problems" in the century to come. Such fantasies relied on the position of looking provided by these films, the spectacles they display, and the catalog descriptions that accompanied them. In 1898, imperial ideology intersected with moving-picture technology to make maximally visible the new figure through which American masculinity and national identity was to be imagined as the United States transformed itself into an overseas empire.

Notes

I would like to thank Lee Grieveson, Bambi Haggins, Isaac Hager, and the editors of this anthology for their patient and insightful readings of various drafts of this essay.

1. Captain John W. Philip, "The 'Texas' at Santiago," *Century*, August 1898, 99.
2. For an excellent analysis of the link between overseas imperialism, the discourse of manifest destiny, and the myth of the frontier, see Richard Slotkin's *Gunfighter Nation: The Myth of the Frontier in Twentieth-Century America* (New York: Atheneum, 1992). For primary examples of such discourse, see Theodore Roosevelt's *The Rough Riders* (New York: G. P. Putnam's Sons, 1900) and *The Winning of the West* 4 vols. (New York: G. P. Putnam's Sons, 1889–1896).
3. For analyses of the increased presence of women in the public sphere, see Kathy Peiss's *Cheap Amusements: Working Women and Leisure in Turn-of-the-Century New York* (Philadelphia: Temple University Press, 1986); Lauren Rabinovitz's *For the Love of Pleasure: Women, Movies, and Culture in Turn-of-the-Century Chicago* (New Brunswick: Rutgers University Press, 1998); and Shelley Stamp's *Movie-Struck Girls: Women and Motion Picture Culture after the Nickelodeon* (Princeton: Princeton University Press, 2000). For an analysis of the racial politics of immigrant participation and presence in public life, see Matthew Frye Jacobson's *Whiteness of a Different Color: European Immigrants and the Alchemy of Race* (Cambridge: Harvard University Press, 1998).
4. For further discussion of the link between discourses on American masculinity, "civilization," and racial theories of the late nineteenth century, see especially Gail Bederman's *Manliness and Civilization: A Cultural History of Gender and Race in the United States, 1880–1917* (Chicago: Chicago University Press, 1995).
5. Studlar details the late-nineteenth- and early-twentieth-century discourse on reforming masculinity in *This Mad Masquerade: Stardom and Masculinity in the Jazz Age* (New York: Columbia University Press, 1996).
6. See Kristin Hoganson, *Fighting for American Manhood: How Gender Politics Provoked the Spanish-American and Philippine American Wars* (New Haven: Yale University Press, 1998), and T. J. Jackson Lears, *No Place of Grace: Antimodernism and the Transformation of American Culture, 1880–1920* (Chicago: University of Chicago Press, 1983), 100.
7. Charles Musser, *Before the Nickelodeon: Edwin S. Porter and the Edison Manufacturing Company* (Berkeley: University of California Press, 1991), 126–127.

8 Catalog descriptions would have helped moving-picture exhibitors to arrange Spanish-American War actualities into thematically coherent programs at venues such as the Eden Musée. Such programs often created intertextual relationships between individual films, lantern slides, musical accompaniment, and the exhibitor's lecture or narration. For a more detailed description of such programs, see Musser, "Rethinking Early Cinema: Cinema of Attractions and Narrativity," *Yale Journal of Criticism* 7:2 (1994): 215.

9 Amy Kaplan, "Romancing the Empire: The Embodiment of Masculinity in the Popular Historical Novel of the 1890s," *American Literary History* 2 (winter 1990): 662.

10 Alfred Thayer Mahan, "The United States Looking Outward," in *The Interest of America in Sea Power, Present and Future* (London: Sampson Low, Marston and Company, 1898), 6–7. First published in *Atlantic Monthly,* December 1890.

11 Mahan, "Hawaii and Our Future Sea Power," in *The Interest of America in Sea Power,* 21. First published in *Forum,* March 1893.

12 Mahan, "The Isthmus and Sea Power," in *The Interest of America in Sea Power,* 52. First published in *Atlantic Monthly,* September 1893.

13 Commodore George W. Melville, U.S.N., "Our Future in the Pacific — What We Have to Hold and Win," *North American Review,* March 1898, 282.

14 Kaplan, "Romancing the Empire," 662.

15 Bederman, *Manliness and Civilization,* E. Anthony Rotundo, *American Manhood: Transformations in Masculinity from the Revolution to the Modern Era* (New York: Basic Books, 1993).

16 Bederman, *Manliness and Civilization,* 1–44.

17 George Miller Beard, *American Nervousness: Its Causes and Consequences* (New York: G. P. Putnam's Sons, 1881), 26.

18 Ibid., 11.

19 Bederman, *Manliness and Civilization,* 77–120.

20 See Theodore Roosevelt, "Kidd's Social Evolution," *North American Review,* July 1895, 97, 109; and, *The Winning of the West.* For an analysis of Roosevelt's writings on race suicide, see Thomas G. Dyer, *Theodore Roosevelt and the Idea of Race* (Baton Rouge: Louisiana State University Press, 1980).

21 For a discussion of the link between the "health" of native white masculinity and the "health" of what was called "the American race" in the 1890s, see Bederman, *Manliness and Civilization,* 192–206.

22 George W. Stocking Jr.'s book *Race, Culture, and Evolution: Essays in the History of Anthropology* (Chicago: University of Chicago Press, 1983) remains the most thorough and engaging analysis of the production of racial categories by scientists and pseudoscientists in the late nineteenth and early twentieth centuries. For a concise analysis of the meanings of "race" at the turn of the century, see his article "The Turn-of-the-Century Concept of Race," *Modernism/Modernity* 1, 1 (1993): 4–16.

23 See Slotkin, *Gunfighter Nation.*

24 Ibid., 186–188.

25 For an analysis of the effects of technological breakdown on the modern

individual, see Wolfgang Schivelbusch's *The Railway Journey: The Industrialization of Space and Time in the Nineteenth Century* (Berkeley: University of California Press, 1977, 1986). For analyses of representations of mechanical breakdown in early cinema and its link to developments in spectatorship and film form, see Lynne Kirby, *Parallel Tracks: The Railroad and Silent Cinema* (Durham: Duke University Press, 1997); and Tom Gunning, "Heard over the Phone: The de Lorde Tradition of the Terrors of Technology," *Screen* 32, 2 (summer 1991): 184–196.

26 For discussion of the explosion, its investigation, and the role it played in provoking hostilities between the United States and Spain, see Walter Millis, *The Martial Spirit: A Study of Our War with Spain* (New York: Houghton Mifflin, 1931), 82–139.

27 I borrow this phrase from the title of Millis's work cited above. Mary Ann Doane has argued that technological "catastrophe is at some level always about the body, about the encounter with death" so that "catastrophe might finally be defined as the conjuncture of the failure of technology and the resulting confrontation with death." See "Information, Crisis, Catastrophe" in *Logics of Television,* ed. Patricia Mellencamp (London: British Film Institute, 1990), 223.

28 Captain Charles Dwight Sigsbee, U.S.N., "Personal Narrative of the 'Maine': Second Paper," *Century,* December 1898, 242.

29 Ibid., 252.

30 Such accounts would have fed into an already burgeoning trade in sensational representations of technological accidents in illustrated weeklies that, Ben Singer argues, represented modern life as "defined by chance, peril, and shocking impressions rather than by any traditional conception of safety, continuity, and self-controlled destiny." Singer, "Modernity, Hyperstimulus, and the Rise of Popular Sensationalism," in *Cinema and the Invention of Modern Life,* ed. Leo Charney and Vanessa R. Schwartz (Berkeley: University of California Press, 1995), 79–80.

31 Ira Nelson Hollis, "The Uncertain Factors in Naval Conflicts," *Atlantic Monthly,* June 1898, 728.

32 See Charles Brown's *The Correspondents' War: Journalists in the Spanish American War* (New York: Scribner's, 1967).

33 Edison Manufacturing Company, *"War Extra" Catalogue,* 20 May 1898, 2.

34 Ibid., 7.

35 Philip, "The 'Texas' at Santiago," 90.

36 Ibid., 92.

37 Foucault offers two analyses of the disciplinary gaze relevant to the mode of looking offered by the war actuality. In his discussion of disciplinary institutions such as the military, Foucault argues that "Disciplinary power ... is exercised through its invisibility; at the same time that it imposes on those whom it subjects a principle of compulsory visibility. In discipline, it is the subjects who have to be seen. Their visibility assures the hold of the power that is exercised over them. It is the fact of being constantly seen, of being always able

to be seen, that maintains the disciplined individual in his subjection." Later, when discussing Bentham's panopticon, Foucault notes that "Bentham laid down the principle that power should be visible and unverifiable: the inmate will constantly have before his eyes the tall outline of the central tower from which he is spied upon. Unverifiable: the inmate must never know whether he is being looked at at any one moment; but he must be sure that he may always be so." See Foucault, *Discipline and Punish: The Birth of the Prison*, trans. Alan Sheridan (London: Penguin, 1991), 187, 201.

38 Edison Co., *"War Extra" Catalogue*, 9.
39 Captain Henry C. Taylor, "The 'Indiana' at Santiago," *Century*, August 1898, 63.
40 Edison Co., *"War Extra" Catalogue*, 2.
41 Lynne Kirby, "Male Hysteria and Early Cinema," *Camera Obscura* 17 (May 1988): 113–131. The term "cinema of attractions" is, of course, Tom Gunning's and is theorized in "The Cinema of Attractions: Early Film, Its Spectator, and the Avant-Garde," *Wide Angle* 8, 3–4 (1986): 63–70, and in "An Aesthetic of Astonishment: Early Film and the (In)Credulous Spectator," *Art and Text* 34 (spring 1989): 31–45.
42 Edison Co., *"War Extra" Catalogue*, 3.
43 Hoganson, *Fighting for American Manhood*, 50–75.
44 Edison Co., *"War Extra" Catalogue*, 2.
45 See Kaplan, "Romancing the Empire," and Richard Harding Davis, *The Cuban and Porto Rico Campaigns* (New York: Charles Scribner's Sons, 1898).
46 Linda Williams, *Hard Core: Power, Pleasure, and the Frenzy of the Visible* (Berkeley: University of California Press, 1991), 34–57.
47 Constance Balides, "Scenarios of Exposure in the Practice of Everyday Life: Women in the Cinema of Attractions," *Screen* 34, 1 (spring 1993): 19–37.
48 Williams, *Hard Core*, 40.
49 Balides, "Scenarios," 24.
50 Williams, *Hard Core*, 43.
51 Edison Co., *"War Extra" Catalogue*, 3. The emphasis on vitality and purposeful activity in the films shot at the military camp in Tampa is particularly interesting once we consider the broader representation of the preparations for the Cuban campaigns reported in newspapers. Most historians agree that the period of preparation intervening between the U.S. declaration of war on Spain on 20 April 1898 and the landing of the first troops in Cuba on 22 June 1898 was extremely disorganized, even chaotic. The task of trafficking volunteers, supplies, and weapons by railway proved overwhelming as cars transporting supplies and weapons were separated from cars carrying troops, while others simply went astray. This period of waiting was dubbed by the journalist Richard Harding Davis as "the rocking-chair period," a phrase that did little to bolster the sense of transformation in American masculinity and national character the prospect of war seemed to promise. The war actuality helped reinscribe this phase of the war back into narratives of national progress and imperial purpose, by selective framings that extracted the purposeful male

body from the surrounding disorder. See especially Brown, *The Correspondents' War*.
52   Edison Co., *"War Extra" Catalogue*, 3-4.
53   Hoganson, *Fighting for American Manhood*, 51-60.
54   Mark Garret Cooper, "Love, Danger, and the Professional Ideology of Hollywood Cinema," *Cultural Critique* 39 (spring 1998): 85-117; Richard Dyer, "White," *Screen* 29, 4 (spring 1988): 44-65.
55   Edison Co., *"War Extra" Catalogue*, 3-4.
56   Hoganson, *Fighting for American Manhood*, 118.
57   Quoted in ibid., 122.
58   Ibid., 124. In June 1898, an editorial in the *Atlantic Monthly* titled "The End of the War, and After" argued that as a result of the war, "We have recovered our own national feeling. Four months ago, we were a great mass of people rather than a compact nation conscious of national strength and unity. By forgetting even for this brief time our local differences, we have welded ourselves into a conscious unity such as the Republic has not felt since its early days. Not only have the North and South forgotten that they were ever at war—for time and industry had already wellnigh brought this result—but the Pacific states are nearer to the rest of the Union than they ever were before, and the great middle West is no longer estranged from the seaboard. We can work out our own problems and build our own future with a steadier purpose" (432).
59   Bederman, *Manliness and Civilization*, 44.
60   Although African American soldiers fought heroically in battle, they were nevertheless denied the same measure of honor lavished on the Rough Riders. In fact, although Roosevelt initially praised the heroism of the black soldiers who fought in the Battle of San Juan Hill, he later portrayed them as behaving cowardly in his war memoir, *The Rough Riders*. For an excellent analysis of Roosevelt's representation of black participation in the Cuban campaign, see Amy Kaplan's "Black and Blue on San Juan Hill," in *Cultures of United States Imperialism*, ed. Amy Kaplan and Donald E. Pease (Durham: Duke University Press, 1993), 219-236.
61   The acceptance of black regulars and volunteers into the campaign was based in part on the assumptions of scientific racism, which reasoned that blacks would make up a contingent of "immune troops" whose genetic constitution would act as a prophylactic against tropical diseases. These troops were forced to fight under white officers, and were subject to segregation, Jim Crow laws, and racial violence once they reached camp in the South. Significantly, the question over black participation in the Spanish-American and Philippine-American Wars was a matter of debate in the black community. For a detailed discussion of this debate, see Willard B. Gatewood, *Black Americans and the White Man's Burden, 1898-1903* (Chicago: University of Illinois Press, 1975). See also Kevin Gaines, *Uplifting the Race: Black Leadership, Politics, and Culture in the Twentieth Century* (Chapel Hill: University of North Carolina Press, 1996).
62   Edison Co., *"War Extra" Catalogue*, 6.

63 Daniel Bernardi uses this phrase to describe the racial specificity of the narrator system at work in D. W. Griffith's Biograph films in "The Voice of Whiteness: D. W. Griffith's Biograph Films (1908–1913)," in *The Birth of Whiteness: Race and the Emergence of U.S. Cinema,* ed. Bernardi (New Brunswick: Rutgers University Press, 1996), 112.
64 Fatimah Tobing Rony, *The Third Eye: Race, Cinema, and Ethnographic Spectacle* (Durham: Duke University Press, 1996), 41.
65 Amy Kaplan has located and described this longing for spectators for imperial masculinity in her analysis of the historical novel and journalistic representations of the war in "Romancing the Empire." Musser gives an account of audience enthusiasm for war programs and the Eden Musée in *Before the Nickelodeon,* 126–142.
66 Musser, *Before the Nickelodeon,* 135.
67 Kaplan, "Romancing the Empire," 661.
68 Edison Co., *"War Extra" Catalogue,* 4.
69 Musser uses the term "cinema of reassurance" to describe the mode of address and appeal of Lyman Howe's traveling exhibition moving-picture shows and war programs to "respectable" audiences. Charles Musser, *High-Class Moving Pictures: Lyman Howe and the Forgotten Era of Traveling Exhibition, 1880–1920* (Princeton: Princeton University Press, 1991).

CONSTANCE BALIDES

Making Ends Meet

"Welfare Films" and the Politics of Consumption during the Progressive Era

> The New York of the workers is not the New York best known to the country at large. The New York of Broadway, the New York of Fifth Avenue, of Central Park, of Wall Street, of Tammany Hall— these are by-words of common reference; and when two years ago the daily press printed the news of the strike of thirty thousand shirt-waist makers in the metropolis, many persons realized, perhaps for the first time, the presence of a new and different New York— the New York of the city's great working population. . . .
>
> [*Making Both Ends Meet*] is composed of the economic records of self-supporting women living away from home in [this new and different] New York . . . [and it offers] an accurate kinetoscope view of the yearly lives of chance passing workers in [the] trades. — Sue Ainslie Clark and Edith Wyatt, *Making Both Ends Meet* (1911)

The behavior of women wage earners, frequently construed as controversial in vice reports, urban commentaries, and popular journalism during the late nineteenth and early twentieth centuries, was also scrutinized through the mechanism of Progressive reformers' social surveys.[1] *Making Both Ends Meet: The Income and Outlay of New York Working Girls,* a budget study conducted for the National Consumers League and serialized in *McClure's Magazine,* details the difficult conditions working women faced in factories, laundries, and department stores as well as the exacting calculations associated with workers' consumer spending habits. Like a "kinetoscope view," *Making Both Ends Meet* gives a particular visibility to a "new and different New York—the New York of the city's great working population."[2]

The Cup of Life (Mutual, dir. West and Ince, 1915) and *Shoes* (Bluebird Photoplays, dir. Weber, 1916) are social-problem or message films in which working women's aspirations for consumer goods and upward mobility similarly fall on the terrain of harsh negotiations. Both films offer a critique of the social and economic circumstances informing the dilemma of a modern urban lifestyle for their female protagonists and, like Clark and Wyatt's study, delineate right and wrong ways of participating in consumer culture. In this essay, I historicize the question of a politics of consumption during the Progressive period by pursuing a series of connections between *Making Both Ends Meet* as a representative reformers' text, writings on consumption by organized labor, and the representation of the problem of working-class women as consumers in *The Cup of Life* and in *Shoes*. The continuities across these texts suggest a key question: how did consumption become a site for public debate about working women's character? The choice of middle-class reformers and male trade unionists foregrounds the interrelationship of class and gender interests in this debate.

The implications of mass consumer culture and commercialized entertainments for a historical understanding of the conditions that made female spectatorship meaningful are addressed in a number of feminist studies of the "silent" period of cinema.[3] Emerging heterosocial spaces such as department stores, world's fairs, and cinema theaters enabled new kinds of public experience for working and middle-class women, and an increasing body of work sensitive to this historical shift focuses on flânerie as a mode of spectatorship involving a mobile gaze. By pursuing the connections between shopping in department stores, participating in tourist activities, and cinema spectating, this work rightly points to new possibilities for women through modes of perception and experience associated with movement.[4] Giuliana Bruno, for example, argues that cinema spectating "triggered a liberation of the woman's gaze," and through flânerie opened up "a new geography" involving "women's conquest of the sphere of spatial mobility as pleasure." More generally, her approach to spectatorial fascination as a "kinetic affair" suggests a theory of spectatorship attentive to "motion, the public sphere, and historicity."[5]

This essay has a similar concern with questions of women's agency, the public sphere, and historicity.[6] It takes a different route, however, to producing the historical visibility of the female consumer in order to suggest other parameters of self-definition for women in a specific period and particular national context, namely, the Progressive era in the United States.[7] I argue that mass consumer culture and the activity of women's consumption during this period came to be meaningful as objects of knowledge in reformers' surveys, trade union tracts, and social problem films. In other words, "consumer" and "consumption" are discursively produced. In particular, the status of women as consuming subjects was implicated in a public debate about working conditions.

By focusing on specific historical discourses, I am not invoking a superiority of "history" over "theory." Rather, I adopt a theoretical approach to history writing that views history as a pluralized field of discourses and practices involving the formation of subjects of various kinds. This sense of the historical field draws on Michel Foucault's view of discontinuity as "a play of specific transformations different from one another (each one having its conditions, its rules, its level) and linked among themselves according to schemes of dependence." This view of the woman wage earner/consumer, extrapolating from Foucault's work, invokes a sense of the subject as being "subject to someone else by control and dependence, and [being] tied to his [that is, her] own identity by a conscience or self-knowledge."[8] This dual characterization does not only suggest a subject determined by regimes of power and knowledge, a critique sometimes leveled against the usefulness of Foucault's work in film studies and a view implicit in the opposition between flânerie and the panopticon as paradigms of vision.[9] Foucault also suggests the effectivity of discourses and practices in establishing the terms through which subjects inhabit the positions they occupy. The woman wage earner, then, was "subject to" normative definitions of what it meant to be a consumer and was a "subject of" consumption through various constructions of consumer agency.

Feminist work in film also raises the question of the status of archival work as well as the relationship between textual strategies specific to film and historical analysis. A general acknowledgment of perspectivism in feminist scholarship mitigates claims that archival material per se authorizes historical inquiry, and a focus on historical formations of spectatorship using a range of theories underscores problems in general models of textual positioning in film semiotics and psychoanalysis, especially the presumption of a universalized male spectator.[10] Turning to history also raises the question of the status and mode of analysis appropriate to the individual film, a problem exacerbated by the absence of so many films from the silent period.[11] In this essay, existing films retain a visibility as links in a series of homologous constructions of the meaning of consumption, and textual strategies in films are historicized in terms of their connections to other texts.

"Welfare" Films

The relationship between reform during the Progressive era and U.S. cinema of the transitional period (1907/8–1916) is generally conceived in terms of the clergy's and reformers' worries over morally suspect subject matter in moving pictures, the safety of early nickelodeons, and the problematic conduct of audiences. Work on censorship stresses the emergence of industry self-censorship from 1909 in response to these concerns. Distinguishing features of the transitional period such as films with internally coherent narrative structures, the use of uplifting themes and literary adaptations in films, and the move to respectable theatrical venues are seen, in part, as film-industry strategies to avoid direct censorship and to appeal to working- and middle-class audiences alike.[12] Social or message films from the 1910s drew on reformist sensibilities to produce their own construction of the life of working-class people, and the agendas of some of these films also dovetailed with the increasing concern for respectability on the part of the cinema industry during the transitional period.[13]

In this context, *The Cup of Life* and *Shoes* are interesting for a number of reasons. The films are made by directors and film companies associated with serious films, for example, Thomas Ince's "thesis plays" and psychologically oriented " 'soul fights,' " Lois Weber's "morality plays" and " 'missionary pictures,' " and Bluebird as a film company associated with quality productions.[14] In trade periodicals, *The Cup of Life* is praised for moving beyond a "preachment" to provide a "lesson" and a "moral," and *Shoes* is referred to as a "sociological" film, a term used by Louis Reeves Harrison in "What's New?" in *Moving Picture World* in 1913 to characterize a new trend in feature films involving a "strong leaning toward investigation of laws regulating human society."[15] Plot lines in both films link working-class women's aspirations for consumer goods and for upward mobility to dubious sexual attachments, thereby raising the question of character in the context of consumption. Finally, while these films can be broadly described as social-problem films of the type analyzed by Kay Sloan and by Kevin Brownlow, they depart from the explicit class critique in a film like *A Corner in Wheat* (Biograph, dir. Griffith, 1909) or the critique of middle-class reformers in *The Reformers* (Biograph, dir. Griffith,

13. The consuming subject: Eva looks at a pair of shoes in a shop window. *Shoes* (Bluebird Photoplays, dir. Weber, 1916). Frame enlargement from 16-mm print courtesy of the Nederlands Filmmuseum.

1913).[16] Instead, both films in this essay suggest the authority of a reformist understanding of social problems.[17]

In analyzing the films, especially the way textual strategies produce a commentary on the action, I draw on Tom Gunning's work on the 1908–1909 films of D. W. Griffith. Gunning focuses on the emergence of "the narrator system" in Griffith's early Biograph films such as *A Drunkard's Reformation* (1908). Compared to the earlier cinema of attractions period, in the Biograph films, "the filmic narrator shapes and defines visual meanings," producing judgments on the action and indicating "proper and improper behavior" by characters. Editing that emphasizes contrasts, the use of characters' psychology as the vehicle through which transformations and turning points are marked, and compositional devices of lighting and framing suggest the meaning of represented actions.[18] In *The Cup of Life* and in *Shoes*, commentary via a filmic discourse is similarly achieved through editing strategies that contrast characters' social circumstances and fates; through mise-en-scène strategies that focus on details suggesting characters' preoccupations and foreground the lessons on offer; and through the psychological delineation of characters' understandings of their circumstances, especially in key scenes of transformation. I tentatively call these

Making Ends Meet

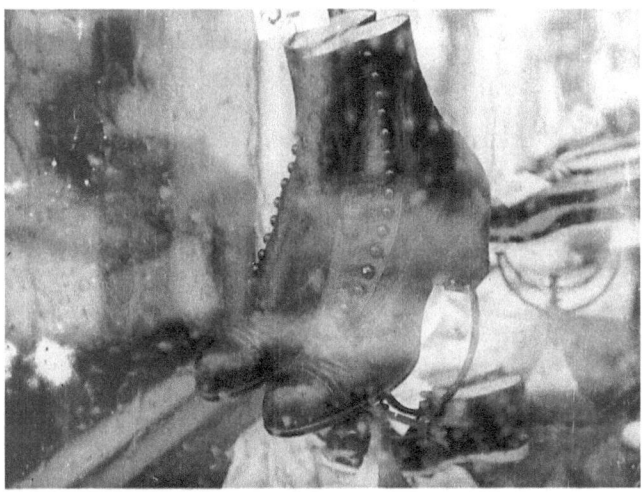

14. The object of Eva's desire. *Shoes.* Frame enlargement from 16-mm print courtesy of the Nederlands Filmmuseum.

"welfare films" to foreground the way they restage the dilemma of a modern urban lifestyle in reformist terms and invite the spectator to take up a position of reformer in relation to the social problems represented.[19]

Budgeting

Shop windows, to be sure, were enticements for flights of fancy for working-class women, who used mass-produced products to mark subcultural identities often at odds with middle-class codes of conduct, and who walked past the displays along city pavements in a mode of flânerie. Films as "living display windows" during this period also contributed to the dissemination of consumer culture by showcasing particular products as well as a consumerist lifestyle.[20] In *Shoes,* a repeated motif of a shot of Eva Meyer, a saleswoman in a five-and-ten-cent store, looking at a window display of shoes (fig. 13) followed by a reverse shot of the very pair she longs to buy in the display behind the glass (fig. 14), emphasizes the status of the commodity as an object of desire in the context of the female protagonist's active look, which also motivates the shot pattern.[21]

While both *Shoes* and *The Cup of Life* can be assessed in these terms, the representation of consumption in the films foregrounds an additional

15. A father's indolence. *Shoes.* Frame enlargement from 16-mm print courtesy of the Nederlands Filmmuseum.

register, one that emphasizes the material conditions of consumption associated with low wages, the exchange value of sex, and the sexual politics of domestic life. Unlike films of the period in which access to consumer goods and upward mobility is achieved for the female protagonist through contrived plot devices and the deus ex machina of marriage to a wealthy man,[22] both films temper the fantasy logic of consumer desire by stressing the economic pressures and emotional dilemmas consumer culture produced for women of little financial means. The films stress the disjuncture between looking and buying.[23]

In *Shoes,* a narrative dilemma over Eva's ability to buy a new pair of shoes is linked to a broader moral struggle between virtue and poverty, on one hand, and looser morals and a higher standard of living, on the other hand. Eva eventually takes the path of a female coworker, Lil, to the Blue Goose cabaret, with its association of lax behavior. The moral downfall associated with her decision to turn to treating or to casual prostitution as a way of obtaining the shoes is mitigated through plot events that suggest her psychological motivations, namely, Eva's disappointment over the broken promises of her mother to give her a portion of her own wages because money is needed for groceries, and Eva's contempt for her father, who drinks beer and smokes his pipe all day while reading dime novels in bed instead of looking for work (fig. 15).[24] In the next shot, commentary on the father's behavior is effected through the use of a high-angle shot and close framing on the details of beer pail, tobacco, and dime novel on the father's bedside table, suggesting that Eva's financial responsibilities to other family members are excessive, especially in light of the father's indolence, and that they constitute a burden.

In *The Cup of Life,* sisters, Ruth and Helen, are department store saleswomen. Ruth goes on to marry a stable working-class man and becomes a housewife and mother. Helen, who fears the poverty and drudgery associated with immigrant and tenement life, takes "the easiest path" to the rewards of consumer culture by becoming the mistress of several men until she is rejected because of her age and eventually dies in impoverished and debauched circumstances. Although the desire of a young woman for smart clothes in *The Cup of Life* is linked to a more formulaic view of moral ruin than is the case in *Shoes,* the problem of insufficient means and limited paths to upward mobility for working-class women is similarly foregrounded.

Consumption construed in terms of precise negotiations between income and expenditure necessitated by low wages is central to the representation of working-class consumer activity by middle-class reformers in budget studies.[25] Although there is some debate among feminist historians over the adequacy of amounts cited in these studies, *Making Both Ends Meet* is striking for an exactitude in the reporting of spending by department store assistants, shirtwaist makers, and laundry and factory workers. Precise amounts are quoted for lodging, food, carfare, shirtwaists, hats, shoes, occasional leisure such as nickel theaters and magazines, support of family members, and economies obtained through walking to work instead of taking the trolley or renting a sleeping space in a tenement kitchen instead of a furnished hall bedroom. In a discussion of the problem of overtime for laundry workers, for example, the expense of paying for supper is part of a difficult calculation:

> Seven cents is a fair average spent upon supper—2 cents for bread and 5 cents for sausage, cheese, or meat. If overtime is worked three nights a week, the girl is out of pocket 36 cents—not a small item in wages of $4.50 and $5 a week, where every penny counts.

The weekly budget of Miss Carr, a saleswoman in a shoe department, is another exemplary case. Her estimates of spending include "lodging, $1; board, $1.95; luncheons, $1.05; insurance, 21 cents; clothing, contributions to church, occasional carfare, and other expenses, $1.79; total $6," and only $1 annually on " 'good times' " is reported to the investigators.[26]

In addition to reports of meager spending in *Making Both Ends Meet,* reformers offer a commentary on the habits of the study's working-class subjects drawing on middle-class models of behavior, taste, and self-improvement. Clark and Wyatt applaud the educational focus of Russian immigrants, who attend evening classes and lectures, and the authors praise women whose dress sense and manner approximate a middle-class sensibility. Zetta Weyman had "quiet and grace and there was something touching, even moving in the dignity of her pure, clear English." In the case of Fanny Leysher, "everything she wore was put on carefully and with good taste," and she was also a good student. Clark and Wyatt observe that "her dress showed the quickest adaptability, and in correctness, and simplicity of line and color [this dress] might have belonged to a college freshman 'with every advantage.' "[27]

Making Both Ends Meet offers a normative model of appropriate consumption characterized in terms of restraint both in handling money and in style and manner. A similar sense of consumption is also valorized in *Shoes.* Eva's demeanor is modest; for example, she spurns the lascivious look of Charlie, a "cadet" and singer at the Blue Goose, and her desires are circumspect, especially in contrast to her "tough" friend, Lil, who introduces her to Charlie. The shoes Eva eventually exchanges for sex are sturdy if fashionable boots in contrast to the more extravagant "gift" of a new wristwatch given to Lil by Charlie and shown in an insert close-up shot. In *The Cup of Life,* the contrast between Helen, overly dressed and made-up, and Ruth, modest and plainly dressed, similarly illustrates a reformers' hierarchy.

While reformers' scrutiny over working-class women's behavior suggests a hegemonic strategy involving the imposition of middle-class mores, recent work by feminist historians suggests a more nuanced understanding of these regulatory strategies. Mary E. Odem points to different constructions of working-class women's agency by reformers. She distinguishes between purity crusades from the 1880s, especially age-of-consent campaigns, and early-twentieth-century Progressive reformers. The former group held a view of the "fallen woman," who was a sexual victim vulnerable to exploitation by men, and the latter were concerned with the "delinquent girl," whose sexually problematic behavior needed guidance and control, but whose problems stemmed from environmental factors and who, although delinquent, was a sexual agent.[28]

In a similar manner, *Making Both Ends Meet* construes the subjects of its budget analyses as consumer agents. This view is illustrated in the example of Zetta, who through watching sales and through information obtained from heads of department ... contrived to buy clothing of excellent quality, silk stockings, and well-cut suits comparatively cheaply. By waiting until the end of the season, she had paid $35, the winter before, for a suit originally costing $70. . . . She managed to have pretty and well designed hats for from $2 to $5, because a friend trimmed them.[29]

Activities of a good consumer involve foresight and management skills. This consuming subject as a consumer agent is neither someone who is victimized by the whims of fashion and advertising ploys nor someone who manipulates middle-class styles in flamboyant configurations to express a subcultural identity. Zetta's consumption is also given a wider context by Clark and Wyatt, who note:

> It must be remembered that the world in which the shop-girl follows her occupation is a world of externals. The fortunes, talents, tastes, eager human effort spent in shop-window displays on Fifth Avenue, the shimmer and sparkle of beautiful silks and jewels, the prestige of "carriage trade," ... all the worldliness of the most moneyed city of the United States here perpetually passes before the eyes of Zettas in their $1.20 muslin waists so carefully scrubbed the midnight before, and of Alices who have had breakfasts for 10 cents. Is it surprising that they should adopt the New York shop-window display ideal of the life manifested everywhere around them?[30]

The authors are describing consumer culture in the context of rising expectations associated with a society of abundance, a formulation used by economists such as Simon N. Patten in the United States at the turn of the century to positively characterize new economic developments associated with the emergence of consumer culture.[31] Consumer desires of wage-earning women are legitimate in the context of a society based on new material possibilities, and access to these goods is one expression of a democratizing impulse.[32] *Shoes* visualizes the "New York shop-window display of life" in the repeated shots of the shoes behind the display glass; it foregrounds the disparity of access to such images of abundance in the representation of Eva's dilemma; and it suggests the legitimacy of the desires of women like Eva and like the "Zettas in their $1.20 muslin waists" through contrast editing between the new shoes and Eva's old shoes, which are in an extreme state of deterioration.

In construing desire for the goods of mass consumption in a modern manner, both *Making Both Ends Meet* and *Shoes* depart from a straightforward valorization of thrift in nineteenth-century advice literature. In another repeated motif in the film, Eva attempts to extend the life of her worn-out shoes by cutting out makeshift soles from the top of a cardboard box. The status of this economizing measure is suggested by a comparison with a description of thrifty behavior in advice literature to young working women by Grace H. Dodge, founder of Working Girls Societies, in *A Bundle of Letters to Busy Girls on Practical Matters,* published in 1887. Dodge suggests that

> If we are caught out in the rain, or if it comes on while we are at work and our feet are not prepared for the wet, let us arrange paper soles. Cut out pieces of brown or newspaper the size of your feet, and slip these soles in your boots.... If shoes have holes, do the same thing.... Paper is always useful for warmth.... Buy a morning paper, read it, and keep it for a cold spell of weather, and thus make your news useful.[33]

In contrast to Dodge's paternalistic description of how to extend the life of a worn-out pair of shoes and of the multiple purposes for newspapers through thrifty, sensible behavior, the same activity in *Shoes,* twenty years later, has a different meaning. In a key scene in which Eva walks to work in a downpour, a close-up tracking shot from behind the character focuses on Eva's feet (fig. 16). Tight framing on the shoes, a low camera position, and the palpable quality of the rain suggest disintegrating cardboard and carry the implication that Eva's thrifty measure, shown in a preceding scene, is inadequate. The viewpoint and camera position distinguish this shot because they depart from a pattern of frontal and high-angle shots of Eva's old shoes and invite an editorializing comment on the harmful degradation of the working-class protagonist's spirit, reinforced by a strong suggestion of pathos. While the tracking camera movement is not a traveling point-of-view shot, it does suggest an affective alignment of the spectator's position with Eva's plight, and especially with a reformist film discourse sympathetic to Eva's rightful entitlement to the new shoes. In *Making Both Ends Meet,* thrift as a trait of good character is similarly viewed as insufficient. For Clark and Wyatt, the problem underlying women wage earners' difficulties is "the widespread precariousness in work" and in the face of this problem "no amount of thrift or industriousness or foresight can adequately provide" a solution.[34]

Constructions of consumer agency in *Making Both Ends Meet* and in *Shoes* involve both a subject under the scrutiny of the gaze of reformers and new terms for the authority of women wage earners as consuming subjects. The meaning of consuming in this context is also refigured for working-

Making Ends Meet

16. Beyond thrift: Eva's dilapidated shoes as she trudges through a heavy rain storm. *Shoes.* Frame enlargement from 16-mm print courtesy of the Nederlands Filmmuseum.

and middle-class women. *Making Both Ends Meet* was conducted under the auspices of the National Consumers League, which campaigned for minimum-wage and hours legislation and developed tactics such as the "White Label" in women's white muslin undergarments to guarantee that articles were not made in sweatshop conditions. As Kathryn Kish Sklar argues, middle-class women were enjoined to understand the political implications of their own consumer practices. In fact, knowledge of the conditions under which goods were made would help middle-class women make appropriate choices about which articles to buy, making "purchasing . . . a moral act."[35] Sklar also credits the National Consumers League with introducing the term "consumer" into public debate.

Not surprisingly, *Making Both Ends Meet* highlights problems at work for working-class women, including "low wages, casual employment, heavy required expense in laundry and dress, semidependence, uneven promotion, lack of training, absence of normal pleasure, long hours of standing, and an excess of seasonal work."[36] Even in the cases of problematic spenders, Clark and Wyatt contextualize character flaws in relation to conditions at work. Lucy Cleaver, for example, shows "weak judgement as a waist purchaser" because of her "remarkable folly of purchasing 24 waists at 98 cent," inexpensive items that fall apart on washing. This shopping strategy of "buying many articles of poor quality, instead of fewer articles of better quality," however, is "a pattern not of choice, but of necessity." More precisely:

> the cheap, hand-to-mouth buying which proves paradoxically so expensive in the end is no doubt often caused by the simple fact that the purchaser has not, at the time the purchase is made, any more money to offer.[37]

Low wages are the cause of inappropriate spending habits.

Shoes as a "sociological" film also gives visibility to working conditions in repeated close-up shots of Eva's disintegrating shoes as she stands all day behind the counter at the five-and-ten-cent store and in repeated shots of Eva soaking her feet in a bowl of hot water after work. The problem of low wages and of a lack of discretionary authority over wages is stressed in the repeated plot event of Eva's handing over her pay packet to her mother. The cost of things is emphasized by the visible price tag in shots of the new shoes behind the glass.

A normative valorization of restrained consumption suggests a politics of consumption involving a class authority over working-class women's character deriving from middle-class standards of behavior and taste. The focus on spending and earning in its minute detail, however, shifts the meaning of consumption, suggesting the necessity of a slight reformulation of the question posed earlier in this essay: how did consumption refigure a concern over women's character? The emphasis on material impediments to buying in the context of a commitment to changing working conditions suggests not only that women wage earners should be good managers, but also that an important locus of agency is the workplace. Clark and Wyatt, for example, support the strike activities of shirtwaist makers and cloak makers as well as union organizing by the Women's Trade Union League. *Shoes,* to be sure, does not offer an image of Eva as a militant worker, but to the extent that the film foregrounds the connection between her position as a consumer and as a worker, it makes consumption visible in relation to production.

The Wage and Consumption

For organized labor, especially the American Federation of Labor (AFL), the status of workers as consumers was at the center of a redefinition of the wage from the 1890s to the mid-1920s. As Lawrence Glickman argues, during most of the nineteenth century, wage labor had the connotation

Making Ends Meet

of wage slavery given that wage labor, unlike self-employment, put male workers in a dependent role in relation to employers. In the later part of the century, however, arguments for higher wages were linked to support for a higher standard of living under the banner of the "American Standard of Living," and male workers increasingly came to be defined as consumers as well as producers. For Glickman these historical transformations involve a shift from a producerist to a consumerist view of the wage. Whereas an earlier view of wage slavery was associated with theft by employers due to the "difference in value between what workers produced and what they earned in wages," the later consumerist view focused on "the inadequacy of wages that did not meet the needs of workers as family supporters, citizens, and consumers." The problem of the wage system was "its seeming inability to reward the nation's producers with a comfortable republican life style."[38] Higher wages for skilled male workers would enable greater levels of consumption, which would encourage the circulation of money and a healthy economy and, thereby, sustain higher wages. Wage slavery came to mean wages inadequate for the purposes of consumption.

Corollaries of this view in various trade union texts point to the problem both of underconsumption associated with immigrants who hoarded money or sent money out of the country to their families and improper consumption by men who spent their money on drink in saloons or in brothels. Both groups were criticized for not contributing to the stimulation of demand for consumer goods.[39] Instead, an image of appropriate consumption focused on the respectable domestic setting. John Mitchell, president of the United Mine Workers, offers the following vision in *Organized Labor*:

> In cities of from five thousand to one hundred thousand inhabitants, the American standard of living should mean, to the ordinary unskilled worker with an average family, a comfortable house of at least six rooms. It should mean bathroom, good sanitary plumbing, a parlor, dining-room, kitchen and sufficient sleeping room that decency may be preserved and a reasonable degree of comfort maintained. The American standard of living should mean, to the unskilled workman, carpets, pictures, books, and furniture with which to make home bright, comfortable, and attractive for himself and his family, an ample supply of clothing suitable for winter and summer, and above all a sufficient quantity of good, wholesome and nourishing food at all times of the year.[40]

Behind this domestically focused consumption stood the male breadwinner, and for many male trade unionists, unorganized women wage earners were often perceived as a threat. While Gompers gestures at support for unionizing activities on the part of women trade unionists in the pages of the *American Federationist,* he also expresses concern about " 'the competition of the unorganized defenseless woman worker [who] . . . tends to reduce the wages of the father and the husband.' " On the issue of married working women, he argues that "there is no necessity for the wife contributing to the support of the family by working . . . that is by wage labor . . . the wife as a wage-earner is at a disadvantage economically considered, and is socially unnecessary." Others similarly argued that the appropriate "standard of comfort" associated with a living wage for a man should include "sufficient freedom for his wife from other work to enable her to perform properly her maternal and household duties."[41]

Domestic consumption along these lines is valorized in *The Cup of Life* through contrast editing. Helen's dissatisfaction with the circumstances of her life as a saleswoman is dramatically foregrounded in a scene in which she and her sister Ruth look out their tenement window at the neighbors in the building across the street. In a shot–reverse-shot sequence, a medium shot of the two sisters looking out the window is followed by a high-angle long shot of an immigrant mother wearing a head scarf along with her two young children and an infant sleeping on a mattress on a fire-escape landing. The meaning of this shot is secured by a dialogue intertitle in which Helen says to Ruth, "You are pretty now, but wait until you've ground out your very soul for a husband who couldn't appreciate and understand you if he wanted to. For babies that will grow to hate you for bringing them into poverty."

In the extant print of this film, these shots are followed by a straight-on medium shot through a half-opened tenement window of a haggard woman doing laundry and an adolescent woman standing next to her holding a baby in the midground of the shot.[42] In the background, laundry hangs from the ceiling of the kitchen and in the extreme foreground, a man in an undershirt and suspenders and smoking a pipe walks into the shot from frame right, crosses the foreground, and exits frame left (fig. 17). The use of the window as a framing device, tight framing, and a cluttered mise-en-scène emphasize the cramped surroundings. Both the immigrant family and the tenement family shots are images of underconsumption, which is suggested through a contrast between the tenement kitchen shot and a later one of Ruth and her family.

Toward the end of the film, Helen goes to visit Ruth, who is now happily married with two children and lives in a single-family dwelling. Ruth's husband, John, returns home from work to see Ruth, who is cooking at the stove in the background of the shot, and the two children, who are playing

Making Ends Meet

17. Framing underconsumption and tenement life. *The Cup of Life* (Mutual, dir. West and Ince, 1915). Frame enlargement from 16-mm print courtesy of the Library of Congress.

in the midground in a modest but commodiously appointed home, whose details of furnishings and fitments are reminiscent of Mitchell's description of the American Standard of Living (fig. 18). John stands in the near foreground of the shot and takes in the scene. Framing devices of the kitchen doorway surrounding Ruth and of drawn curtains between the two front rooms reinforce a sense of the shot as a perfect image of domestically focused consumption. John completes the picture in his position as observer but also in his status as the breadwinner, a role secured in a preceding shot showing him working on a lathe. While there is a tenuous narrative motivation for this shot, its inclusion stresses the dignified nature of John's role as a skilled laborer and reinforces the association between the image of domesticity and John's status as a worker. His relationship to the scene sharply contrasts with the loafing husband dressed in an undershirt and suspenders in the tenement kitchen (fig. 17), which has parallels with the shot of Eva's lazy father in *Shoes*. When the man in *The Cup of Life*, moreover, walks across the foreground, his movement is jarring and disrupts the balanced composition of the shot. John, by comparison, is formally and ideologically integrated into the scene and his look draws the spectator's look into the depth of the shot.

By this point in the film, the earlier critique of domestic drudgery by

18. Framing domestic consumption. *The Cup of Life*. Frame enlargement from 16-mm print courtesy of the Library of Congress.

Helen is forgotten. In a dialogue intertitle, Helen also explicitly validates Ruth's "path" with its unassuming but long-lasting rewards in comparison with Helen's choice of the "easiest road" with greater but ephemeral rewards. Contrast editing between the two kitchen scenes further secures the implication that beyond excess (Helen) and underconsumption (immigrants) lies a third path of marriage and advancement toward a modest standard of living. The traditional division of labor between husband and wife implicated in this view is reinforced by one reviewer who invokes historical teleology as a justifying factor. Harrison in *Moving Picture World* speculates, "there may be an evolutionary reason" why women "of great beauty and light principle" are destroyed in the end, while "plain women" such as Ruth whose "simple heart goes out in natural selection" to marry "the mechanic" perseveres through hardship and achieves greater emotional rewards.[43]

Trade union texts provide another locus from which to register shifting meanings of consumption during the Progressive period. In this case, a gender privilege marks the politics of consumption, and notions of restraint are channeled into moderate upward mobility and a normative domesticity, which involves financial dependence for the former female wage earner in her capacity as a housewife. To be sure, the emotional draw of an idealized domestic scenario in *The Cup of Life* should not be underestimated for women who faced financial insecurity in urban subcultures and at work.[44] At the same time, the film's teleology toward marriage supported by the working man and his wages heightens the sense of difference between male trade unionists and reformers like Clark and Wyatt for whom the female wage earner is a legitimate figure in the workplace even while she is someone in need of the protective gaze of reformers.[45]

Moral Lessons and Kinetoscope Views

A curtailed sense of consumer agency for Ruth at home by the stove in *The Cup of Life* contrasts with the hypervisibility of sexual agency as a means toward consumption for her sister, Helen. The extent to which Helen and her story of a woman's moral descent had a hold on the popular imaginary is suggested in reviews of the film. Commenting on *The Cup of Life*, *Motography* notes, "where there is a lesson to be told, a moral to be emphasized, no vehicle proves quite so efficient or convincing as a story of which almost everyone knows some parallel or tangent."[46] Accolades for the film stressed its instructive status with regard to this common story. The *New York Dramatic Mirror* states that the film "will take its place among the classics of filmdon [sic]" because it "teaches a moral lesson" against immorality, one that is achieved through a pointed contrast between the fate of Ruth, who "sees in the love and happiness which reigns in her home the things in life that are worth living for," and Helen, who through "drink, dope, and cigarettes [ends up] draining her 'cup of life.'"[47] The *New York Dramatic Mirror* goes further and recommends that "every young girl should see it" because the film will help her in "fighting against the stings of adversity and show her the fallacy, the horrors, the misery of 'the easiest way.'"[48]

Paul Boyer distinguishes between different strands of reform during the Progressive period, especially a coercive approach associated with repressive legislation aimed at closing down brothels and vice investigations involving surveillance, and "positive environmentalism" focused on tenement reform, the development of parks and playgrounds, and lectures and concerts in settlement houses in immigrant neighborhoods. While both strands are forms of "social control," the former involved a "brittle moralism" that looked back to nineteenth-century evangelical reform, and the later, more modern, sought to "[create] the kind of city where objectionable patterns of behavior, finding no nurture, would gradually wither away."[49]

The Cup of Life in its handling of Helen's fate and in its status as a form of instruction points to a logic of coercive reform; *Shoes* in its status as "sociological" suggests an environmentalist approach. This difference is foregrounded in parallel scenes in the films in which the female characters confront their consciences by looking at their reflections in mirrors and come to a self-knowledge registered in psychological terms. Helen in *The Cup of Life* expresses horror as she looks in the mirror at her aging face and, in that moment, understands the high price she has paid for upward mobility. Her patheticized image suggests Odem's sense of the victimized "fallen woman" now abandoned, and the contrast with Ruth invokes a world of clearly delineated moral alternatives. As Eva in *Shoes* prepares to go to the Blue Goose cabaret, she registers resignation when she looks at her face in a cracked mirror. In this shot, Eva's despondent demeanor suggests she has internalized reformers' values, and the narrative discourse, through the detail of the cracked mirror, intimates that Eva's spirit has been broken by debilitating circumstances. Both the legitimacy of Eva's consumer agency and her consumer desire, which is visible through the discrepancy between money earned and money spent, shift the nature of the lesson learned toward an environmentalist analysis of social problems.

For reformers such as Jane Addams, prostitution, while deplored, was comprehensible in terms of an argument that wages insufficient to sustain a working girl would make her turn to prostitution.[50] A similar view is taken by Clark and Wyatt in their study of budgets. *Making Both Ends Meet* frequently nods in the direction of the social problem of prostitution and, like its handling of problematic spending, points to the importance of improving working conditions, even while this focus may have had the effect of denying the role of sex in working women's subcultures. Clark and Wyatt note that factory employment involving "slack and dull seasons" will "expose the women dependent in their wage-earning powers, most of them young and many of them with great beauty, to the greatest dangers and temptations." Long hours and low pay in sales work produce a "starvation in pleasure," one that "subjects the women in the stores to a temptation readily conceivable." Emily Clement, an unskilled factory worker, "had no money at all to spend for recreation" and found her future "hopeless" but because of her "natural thirst for pleasure," the authors report in a straightforward manner, "she sometimes accepted it from chance men acquaintances met on the street."[51] Reformers also criticized employers who took the view, common at the time, that low wages were justified because women were supported by their families and that they worked for "pin-money" for nonessential items. Women trade unionists as well as middle-class reformers such as Clark and Wyatt argued instead that women were

Making Ends Meet

often the breadwinners in their family and that household economies were dependent on their wages.

The importance of assessing the moral lessons in welfare films in relation to reformist agendas is also secured by formal strategies in the films that invite the spectator to take up the position of reformer in relation to the depicted events. *Shoes* explicitly does so in its opening sequence with a close-up shot of a book cover of Jane Addams's *A New Conscience and an Ancient Evil*. In this literal reference to Addams's study of the problem of prostitution, the film authorizes itself as a reformist text giving Eva's story the status of a case study illustrating the social problem assessed in the book. In drawing on a knowledge of this intertextual reference, moreover, the film invites the spectator to view subsequent events as a reformer, a vantage point that is reinforced in a medium close-up shot of a female character looking out of frame right and positioned against a plain background. While this woman turns out to be Eva, she is not yet identified as a character in the fictional world and there are no marks of the diegetic space she subsequently occupies as Eva. This quasi-diegetic status reinforces the sense of Eva as a case study under the purview of a reformist/spectatorial gaze.

The Cup of Life stages an environmentalist view in its photographing of life in the tenements, a strategy that also suggests the coexistence of different reform sensibilities in a single film. In the shots of the immigrant family on the landing and of the woman doing laundry in her tenement kitchen discussed earlier (fig. 17), subjects and settings are represented in the manner of urban reform photography, especially in terms of a staged spontaneity emphasizing the relationship between figures and their surroundings. Peter Bacon Hales describes slum photography by Jacob Riis from the 1890s in a way that aptly characterizes both shots in *The Cup of Life*, namely, "photographs usually showed slum dwellers posed in their apartments, often huddled together. . . . Outdoor slum views emphasized environmental cues suggesting overcrowded, chaotic, and unsanitary conditions."[52] The horror with which Helen and Ruth view these scenes is also akin to the shock effect associated with Riis's photographs of tenement environments. The framing of the scene by the half-opened window literalizes the view as evidence supporting Helen's assessment of the problems of impoverished marriage facing Ruth if she marries. The anonymous status of the families on the landing and in the kitchen, characters who never appear again in the film, strengthens the exemplary status of the shots. Images of problematic environments in both films link narrative strategies of uplift to visual rhetorics of reform already in circulation during the period.

The meaning of consumption and of reformism during the transitional period is less univocal and the politics of the period is more fractured along class and gender lines than is sometimes represented. There were alliances of interests between women wage earners and middle-class women on the issue of consumption even while these alliances were marked by mechanisms of class authority and class tensions.[53] Class affiliations between male and female trade unionists were also marked by gender tensions. Within the delimited field of welfare films, moreover, uplift could mean different things and the position of the spectator as reformer could involve the suggestion of various solutions to social problems.[54]

The point I want to stress is the fact of a visibility of consumer agency in terms of its connection to problematic working conditions within a context of reformers' normative agendas for working-class women. This imbrication of consumption and production (at least) foregrounds the material constraints on consumption viewed as a legitimate entitlement, but it could (at best) gesture toward an explicitly political terrain of self-definition and activism. Contextualizing consumer agency in this way, moreover, suggests the difference of the present in which discourses of consumption frequently obscure the connection between production and consumption by conflating economic and political choices.[55] The historical formation outlined here also questions the authority of a Progressive period broadly conceived as one involving a shift from a producer to a consumer society, especially when that formulation means isolating consumer practices, or when the relationship between cinema and consumption is too singularly associated with spectacle and films as display windows.[56]

Clark and Wyatt refer to the strategy of analysis in *Making Both Ends Meet* as one that offers "kinetoscope views" or snapshots of social conditions that give a new "visibility" to the New York of women wage earners. This characterization suggests an axiomatic link between vision and knowledge. The kinetoscope views in these films, and the approach to analyzing them in this paper, suggest a more mediated visibility, one through which the films are made to make sense in terms of connections across different sites. To be sure, films, budget studies, and trade union texts operate according to different rules (formal, evidentiary, persuasive), occupy different levels of existence (entertainment, social policy, workers' activism), and effect different orders of experience (entertainment, legislation, worker and employer relations). While these sites are discontinuous, however, they are also linked by "schemes of dependence" through which the discursive object, consumption, and the consumer emerge in particular ways. The historiographical logic of making connections across these sites suggests both the specificity of the historical and a historicized view of the textual. For the

Making Ends Meet

female wage earner as a consuming subject during the Progressive era, this approach foregrounds the trials and tribulations of buying.

Notes

An earlier version of this article was delivered as a paper at the Society for Cinema Studies Conference, Chicago, Illinois, March 2000. Thanks to audience members for useful questions, especially Vanessa Schwartz, and to Lee Grieveson and this volume's editors for helpful comments on earlier drafts. Thanks also to Eva Warth and Annette Förster for letting me know of the existence of a print of *Shoes*, to Madeline Matz for pointing me in the direction of *The Unshod Maiden*, and to Ronny Temme for help with obtaining stills from *Shoes*.

1   For useful discussions of the problem of women "adrift," see Joanne J. Meyerowitz, *Women Adrift: Independent Wage Earners in Chicago, 1880-1920* (Chicago: University of Chicago Press, 1988), and Timothy J. Gilfoyle, *City of Eros: New York City, Prostitution, and the Commercialization of Sex, 1790-1920* (New York: D. W. Norton and Company, 1992). Numerous vice studies focusing on prostitution and on white slavery were conducted during the Progressive era on city and state levels. For an analysis of these studies in relation to early cinema, see Constance Balides, "Scenarios of Exposure in the Practice of Everyday Life: Women in the Cinema of Attractions," *Screen* 34, 1 (spring 1993): 19–37; and Lauren Rabinovitz, *For the Love of Pleasure: Women, Movies, and Culture in Turn-of-the-Century Chicago* (New Brunswick: Rutgers University Press, 1998). White slavery was publicized by Reginald Wright Kauffman in *The House of Bondage* (1910); reprint, Upper Saddle River, N.J.: Gregg Press, 1968). For a detailed analysis of white-slavery films during the transitional period, see Shelley Stamp, *Movie-Struck Girls: Women and Motion Picture Culture after the Nickelodeon* (Princeton: Princeton University Press, 2000).

2   Sue Ainslie Clark and Edith Wyatt, *Making Both Ends Meet: The Income and Outlay of New York Working Girls* (New York: Macmillan, 1911), viii, ix. The study was serialized in *McClure's Magazine* during 1910 and 1911. Investigations into the working and living conditions of working-class and immigrant segments of society were conducted by benevolent societies, the Young Women's Christian Association, organizations devoted to improving women's working conditions such as the National Consumers League, research organizations such as the Russell Sage Foundation, and city and state government investigating committees. For an extensive list of social surveys, see Allen Eaton and Shelby M. Harrison, *A Bibliography of Social Surveys: Reports of Fact-Finding Studies Made as a Basis for Social Action; Arranged by Subjects and Localities* (New York: Russell Sage Foundation, 1930).

3   Silent cinema is something of a misnomer; however, given common usage, I use it here as a shorthand to refer to the early, transitional, and early classical periods of cinema. While it is commonly known that silent-cinema screen-

ings could include orchestral or piano accompaniment, moving images from the early period could also incorporate live sound effects, actors speaking lines from behind the screen, and commentators positioned near the screen. On this point, see Charles Musser, *The Emergence of Cinema: The American Screen to 1907* (New York: Charles Scribner's Sons, 1990).

4 For work on the implications of these new public spaces, such as department stores, see Susan Porter Benson, *Counter Cultures: Saleswomen, Managers, and Customers in American Department Stores, 1890-1940* (Urbana: University of Illinois Press, 1986), and for the connection between these new public spaces and cinema, see Kathy Peiss, *Cheap Amusements: Working Women and Leisure in Turn-of-the-Century New York* (Philadelphia: Temple University Press, 1986); Miriam Hansen, *Babel and Babylon: Spectatorship in American Silent Film* (Cambridge: Harvard University Press, 1991); Rabinovitz, *For the Love of Pleasure;* and Stamp, *Movie-Struck Girls*. For work that looks at the issue of cinema and flânerie, see Anne Friedberg, *Window Shopping: Cinema and the Postmodern* (Berkeley: University of California Press, 1993); Giuliana Bruno, *Streetwalking on a Ruined Map: Cultural Theory and the City Films of Elvira Notari* (Princeton: Princeton University Press, 1993); Vanessa R. Schwartz, *Spectacular Realities: Early Mass Culture in Fin-de-Siècle Paris* (Berkeley: University of California Press, 1998); and Vanessa R. Schwartz, "Cinematic Spectatorship before the Apparatus: The Public Taste for Reality in *Fin-de-Siècle* Paris," in *Cinema and the Invention of Modern Life,* ed. Leo Charney and Vanessa R. Schwartz (Berkeley: University of California Press, 1995), 297–319. Friedberg and Bruno focus on the implications of flânerie for female spectators. Schwartz focuses on flânerie as a mode of precinematic spectatorship, which she historicizes in the context of cultural practices that had a popular appeal for the Parisian masses with a taste for spectacularized reality. Modes of shopping such as mail-order catalogs are also assessed in terms of flânerie, for example, by Alexandra Keller in "Disseminations of Modernity: Representation and Consumer Desire in Early Mail-Order Catalogs," in *Cinema and the Invention of Modern Life,* ed. Charney and Schwartz, 156–182.

5 Bruno, *Streetwalking,* 51, 38.

6 Miriam Hansen, in particular, elaborates the theoretical implications of understanding silent cinema in terms of the public sphere. Drawing on work by Oskar Negt and by Alexander Kluge, she focuses on various instances in which silent cinema offered the structural conditions for an alternative public sphere, characterized as "an intersubjective horizon for the articulation of experience" (*Babel and Babylon,* 38). Considering cinema under this rubric foregrounds the importance of the unpredictable nature of reception when it "can gain a momentum of its own" (7).

7 There are various dates given for the Progressive period. I use the broadest periodization from the 1890s, when the National Consumers League was active and the Hull House settlement was started, to the early 1920s.

8 Michel Foucault, "History, Discourse, Discontinuity," *Salmagundi* 20 (summer-fall 1972): 233; and Foucault, "The Subject and Power," afterword to

Making Ends Meet

  Michel Foucault: Beyond Structuralism and Hermeneutics, by Hubert L. Dreyfus and Paul Rabinow, 2d ed. (Chicago: University of Chicago Press, 1983), 212.
9 For a careful characterization of the differences between the panopticon and the panorama and diorama, see Friedberg, *Window Shopping,* especially 1–38. My implication here is not that such distinctions are unhelpful, but rather that Foucault's sense of the subject goes beyond a sense of determinism. For a defense of his position, see Foucault, "History, Discourse, Discontinuity."
10 For overviews of these interventions, see Janet Bergstrom and Mary Ann Doane, eds., "The Spectatrix," *Camera Obscura* 20–21 (1989), which is a special edition devoted to female spectatorship; and Judith Mayne, *Cinema and Spectatorship* (London: Routledge, 1993).
11 Giuliana Bruno, for example, pursues an approach that explicitly acknowledges the space of this absence. See Bruno, *Streetwalking,* especially 147–160.
12 The National Board of Censorship, the first national censorship board in the United States, was formed in 1909. On early censorship, see Robert Fisher, "Film Censorship and Progressive Reform: The National Board of Censorship of Motion Pictures, 1909–1922," *Journal of Popular Film* 5, 2 (1975): 143–156; Daniel Czitrom, "The Redemption of Leisure: The National Board of Censorship and the Rise of Motion Pictures in New York City, 1900–1920," *Studies in Visual Communication* 10, 4 (fall 1984): 2–6; and Nancy J. Rosenbloom, "Between Reform and Regulation: The Struggle over Film Censorship in Progressive America, 1909–1922," *Film History* 1, 4 (1987): 307–325. For work that relates censorship issues to formal and narrative elements in films, see Tom Gunning, "From the Opium Den to the Theatre of Morality: Moral Discourse and the Film Process in Early American Cinema," *Art and Text* 30 (September–November 1988): 30–40; Eileen Bowser, *The Transformation of Cinema, 1907–1915* (Berkeley: University of California Press, 1990); Tom Gunning, *D. W. Griffith and the Origins of American Narrative Film: The Early Years at Biograph* (Urbana: University of Illinois, 1991); William Uricchio and Roberta E. Pearson, *Reframing Culture: The Case of the Vitagraph Quality Films* (Princeton: Princeton University Press, 1993); and Lee Grieveson, "Fighting Films: Race, Morality, and the Governing of Cinema, 1912–1915," *Cinema Journal* 38, 1 (fall 1998): 40–72. For a useful general overview of the period, see Roberta Pearson, "Transitional Cinema," in *The Oxford History of World Cinema: The Definitive History of Cinema Worldwide,* ed. Geoffrey Nowell-Smith (Oxford: Oxford University Press, 1996), 23–42.
13 These films are not what Steven J. Ross refers to as "partisan" films, which were made by groups such as the American Federation of Labor, the Women's Political Union, and the National Child Labor Committee. See Ross, *Working-Class Hollywood: Silent Film and the Shaping of Class in America* (Princeton: Princeton University Press, 1988). On social-problem films, see Kevin Brownlow, *Behind the Mask of Innocence* (New York: Alfred A. Knopf, 1990), and Kay Sloan, *The Loud Silents: Origins of the Social Problem Film* (Urbana: University of Illinois Press, 1988).
14 For references to Ince, see Jean Mitry, "Thomas H. Ince: His Esthetic, His

Films, His Legacy," *Cinema Journal* 22, 2 (winter 1983): 9; and Richard Koszarski, *An Evening's Entertainment: The Age of the Silent Feature Picture, 1915-1928* (New York: Charles Scribner's Sons, 1990), 217. On Weber, see Koszarski, *An Evening's Entertainment,* 223, and Brownlow, *Behind the Mask,* xxi–xxii. There is a debate over whether Ince directed *The Cup of Life* along with West. The copyright synopsis lists Thomas H. Ince as the producer, but no director credit. The film credits in the Library of Congress print also refer to a "Thomas H. Ince Feature" and give no director credit. I follow the entry for the film in the *AFI Catalog,* which lists both names. This entry points to the debate, however, and notes that contemporary sources tend to name West as sole director. See Patricia King Hanson and Alan Gevinson, eds., *The American Film Institute Catalog of Motion Pictures Produced in the United States: Feature Films, 1911-1920* (Berkeley: University of California Press, 1988). On the extent to which Ince as producer is associated with an early example of a highly organized studio structure, see Janet Staiger, "Dividing Labor for Production Control: Thomas Ince and the Rise of the Studio System," in *The American Movie Industry: The Business of Motion Pictures,* ed. Gorham Kindem (Carbondale: Southern Illinois Press, 1982), 94–103.

15 Louis Reeves Harrison, "What's New?" *Moving Picture World,* 2 November 1913, 844.

16 See Brownlow, *Behind the Mask,* and Sloan, *The Loud Silents.*

17 While sociological films and their "realism" could be valorized in the trade press, these films could also run into censorship problems, which was the case with Weber's film *The Hypocrites* (1914). According to Anthony Slide, the film, which contains an image of a nude woman as "The Naked Truth," gained notoriety when it opened in New York at the Longacre Theatre on 20 January 1915, was banned by the Ohio Board of Censors, and the mayor of Boston wanted clothes handpainted on the women on the individual frames. See Slide, *Early Women Directors* (New York: Da Capo Press, 1984), 38. On Weber and censorship, also see Shelley Stamp's essay in this volume.

18 Gunning, *D. W. Griffith,* 17, 28.

19 Other films I place in this category include *Regeneration* (Fox, dir. Walsh, 1915), *The Red Kimono* (Mrs. Wallace Reid Productions, dir. Lang, 1925), and *Linda* (Mrs. Wallace Reid/Dorothy Davenport, 1928).

20 On working-women's subculture, see Peiss, *Cheap Amusements,* and Nan Enstad, *Ladies of Labor, Girls of Adventure: Working Women, Popular Culture, and Labor Politics at the Turn of the Twentieth Century* (New York: Columbia University Press, 1999). The characterization of films as living display windows is used by Charles Eckert and is an early elaboration of this argument; in contrast to Peiss and Enstad, Eckert has a fairly disparaging view of the spectator of such displays. See Eckert, "The Carole Lombard in Macy's Window," *Quarterly Review of Film Studies* 3, 1 (winter 1978): 1–21.

21 The print of *Shoes* is held in the Nederlands Filmmuseum, Amsterdam; intertitles are in Dutch and use the name Emmy Mayer for the heroine. To my knowledge, a copy of the film with English subtitles does not exist; however,

Making Ends Meet

there is a sound film under the title *The Unshod Maiden* (Universal, [no director credit], 1932), which contains segments of the original film and was part of a short-lived series called Universal Brevities. Copyright description for the American version of *Shoes* uses the name Eva Meyer as does the description of the plot in the *AFI Catalog;* I follow these descriptions and refer to the character as Eva Meyer. See "Shoes," Copyright Descriptions, microfilm box L 8408, Department of Motion Picture, Broadcasting, and Recorded Sound Division, Library of Congress.

22 For example, the proposal of marriage to Mary Maddox by Nelson Rogers at the end of *Forbidden Fruit* (dir. DeMille, 1920) has this forced quality as does Mary's sudden rise in class position in the last scene in the film.

23 Rabinovitz in *For the Love of Pleasure,* for example, points to the disjuncture between looking and buying in relation to the issue of female flânerie in the new department stores by noting that "the equality shared among women through their looking . . . may well have been undercut by their inequality in buying" (75). Friedberg in *Window Shopping* comments on such disparities when she notes that "shopping is more than a perceptual mode involving the empowered choices of the consumer, it—quite simply, quite materially—requires money" (118). Also see Peiss, *Cheap Amusements,* and Judith Mayne, "Immigrants and Spectators," *Wide Angle* 5, 2 (1982): 32–41. An important early formulation of the theoretical implications of the relationship between the display window and the cinema screen, and of the connection between looking and buying for female spectatorship, was developed by Mary Ann Doane. See Doane, *The Desire to Desire: The Woman's Film of the 1940s* (Bloomington: Indiana University Press, 1987).

24 See Peiss, *Cheap Amusements,* on the extent to which casual prostitution as well as "treating," which involved the exchange of sex for material goods, formed a part of working-class women's dating culture. The inference as to which activity characterizes Eva's behavior is unclear in the film. In terms of the reception of *Shoes,* the film is seen as dealing with the general issue of prostitution. Within working-class women's subculture, however, it was important to distinguish treating from prostitution, which was less acceptable. See, for example, Ruth M. Alexander, *The 'Girl Problem': Female Delinquency in New York, 1900–1930* (Ithaca: Cornell University Press, 1995), especially 11–32. The ambiguities and lack of distinctions between treating, casual prostitution, and commercialized vice in *Shoes* strengthen the claim that Eva is a reformers' subject.

25 Alice Kessler-Harris points out that these studies focused on the bare necessities of living and provided for a spartan standard of living for women on their own. See Kessler-Harris, *A Woman's Wage: Historical Meanings and Social Consequences* (Lexington: University of Kentucky Press, 1990). Compared with Eva's $5 per week wage in *Shoes,* Margaret Dreier Robins of the Women's Trade Union League suggested a presumably more reasonable figure of $12 per week as an appropriate minimum in 1911. This figure in cited in Meyerowitz, *Women Adrift,* 34.

26 Clark and Wyatt, *Making Both Ends Meet*, 191, 15. I mention the reported nature of these figures to stress that the study is a representation of working-class women's experiences by middle-class reformers. The views expressed to reformers for some interviewees were probably already a censored representation of their lifestyles. At the same time, the context of this study is one of building a case for minimum-wage legislation. While these considerations do not minimize the hardships of working-class women, they are a reminder that the study is not an example of working-class women speaking for themselves.
27 Ibid., 20, 123.
28 Mary E. Odem, *Delinquent Daughters: Protecting and Policing Adolescent Female Sexuality in the United States, 1885–1920* (Chapel Hill: University of North Carolina Press, 1995).
29 Clark and Wyatt, *Making Both Ends Meet*, 21.
30 Ibid., 23.
31 For a discussion of theories by Progressive-era economists, see Daniel Horowitz, *The Morality of Spending: Attitudes toward the Consumer Society in America, 1875–1940* (Baltimore: Johns Hopkins University Press, 1985; Chicago: Ivan R. Dee, 1992).
32 On this point, also see Jane Addams, *Democracy and Social Ethics* (New York: Macmillan, 1907). This view, of course, is an optimistic version of the potential of American capitalism.
33 Grace H. Dodge, *A Bundle of Letters to Busy Girls on Practical Matters: Written to Those Girls, Who Have Not the Time or Inclination to Think and Study about the Many Important Things Which Make Up Life and Living* (New York: Funk and Wagnalls, 1887), in *Grace H. Dodge: Her Life and Work* (New York: Arno Press, 1974), 29.
34 Clark and Wyatt, *Making Both Ends Meet*, 116–117.
35 Kathryn Kish Sklar, "The Consumers' White Label Campaign of the National Consumers' League, 1898–1918," in *Getting and Spending: European and American Consumer Societies in the Twentieth Century*, ed. Susan Strasser, Charles McGovern, and Matthias Judt (Cambridge: Cambridge University Press, 1998), 28. The National Consumers League was organized in 1898, and Florence Kelley became its head in 1899. Momentum for the national organization developed from the activity of a number of local consumer leagues during the 1890s. In 1891, prior to the White Label, which was initiated by Kelley, the New York City Consumers League organized a "White List" of department stores that adhered to fair labor practices with the intent of influencing consumers to patronize those stores. After 1906, the National Consumers League was involved in lobbying efforts for protective legislation for women workers. Also see Sklar, "Two Political Cultures in the Progressive Era: The National Consumers' League and the American Association for Labor Legislation," in *U.S. History as Women's History: New Feminist Essays*, ed. Linda K. Kerber, Alice Kessler-Harris, and Kathryn Kish Sklar (Chapel Hill: University of North Carolina Press, 1995), 36–62; Sklar, *Florence Kelley*

and the Nation's Work: The Rise of Women's Political Culture, 1830–1900 (New Haven: Yale University Press, 1995); and Benson, *Counter Cultures*.

36 Clark and Wyatt, *Making Both Ends Meet*, 5.
37 Ibid., 7–9.
38 Lawrence Glickman, *A Living Wage: American Workers and the Making of Consumer Society* (Ithaca: Cornell University Press, 1997), 26, 23. Also see Glickman, "Inventing the 'American Standard of Living': Gender, Race, and Working-Class Identity, 1880–1925," *Labor History* 34, 2–3 (spring-summer 1993): 221–235.
39 On a related point, Lee Grieveson discusses the relationship between reformism and the reformation of problematic male behavior in films during this period. Grieveson, "The Feminization of Early American Cinema," conference paper delivered at the Society for Cinema Studies Conference, Chicago, Illinois, March 2000, and recently published as "'A Kind of Recreative School for the Whole Family': Making Cinema Respectable, 1907–1909," *Screen* 42, 1 (spring 2001): 64–76.
40 John Mitchell, *Organized Labor: Its Problems, Purposes, and Ideals and the Present and Future of American Wage Earners* (Philadelphia: American Book and Bible House, 1903), 116.
41 Glickman, *A Living Wage*, 47; Samuel Gompers, "Should the Wife Help to Support the Family?" *American Federationist* 13, 1 (January 1906): 36; and Professor Ira W. Howerth, "The Dignity of Labor," *American Federationist* 13, 7 (July 1906): 461.
42 In the print used from the Library of Congress, there may have been a shot of Ruth and Helen looking out the window before the shot of the tenement kitchen and/or the tenement kitchen shot may be out of order with the shot of the immigrant family on the landing. A contemporary review suggests that that tenement kitchen shot occurs before that of the immigrant family on the fire escape. Film synopsis deposited for copyright in the Library of Congress does not give a detailed breakdown of shots. For the review, see Louis Reeves Harrison, "The Cup of Life: Five-Reel New York Motion Picture Company Release of High Quality," *Moving Picture World*, 1 May 1915, 740.
43 Ibid.
44 Ruth M. Alexander points to the limited scope of agency during this period for former delinquent girls on parole after time spent in reformatories. She notes that "these young women had experienced so much grief, abuse and disappoints as rebellious adolescents that many of them eventually decided . . . freedom was to be gained through obedience to conservative cultural norms and conventions" (*The 'Girl Problem,'* 153). On expectations of financial support in marriage during this period, see Elaine Tyler May, *Great Expectations: Marriage and Divorce in Post-Victorian America* (Chicago: University of Chicago Press, 1980).
45 Organized male labor committed to a male breadwinner model could also minimize the importance of struggles around women's wage labor. On the

problematic sexual politics of trade unionism during this period, see Nancy Schrom Dye, *As Equals and as Sisters: Feminism, the Labor Movement, and the Women's Trade Union League of New York* (Columbia: University of Missouri Press, 1980).

46   Charles R. Condon, "The Cup of Life," *Motography,* 8 May 1915, 741.
47   "The Cup of Life," *New York Dramatic Mirror,* 21 April 1915, 26; and Condon, "The Cup of Life," 741.
48   "The Cup of Life," *New York Dramatic Mirror,* 26.
49   Paul Boyer, *Urban Masses and Moral Order in America, 1820-1920* (Cambridge: Harvard University Press, 1978), 179, 221.
50   See Jane Addams, *A New Conscience and an Ancient Evil* (New York: Macmillan, 1912). Similar points about prostitution were also made in studies of working conditions per se. One example is Louise De Koven Bowen, *The Department Store Girl: Based upon Interviews with 200 Girls* (n.p.: Juvenile Protection Association of Chicago, 1911).
51   Clark and Wyatt, *Making Both Ends Meet,* 109, 28, 89.
52   Peter Bacon Hales, *Silver Cities: The Photography of American Urbanization, 1839-1915* (Philadelphia: Temple University Press, 1984), 258.
53   For a revisionist assessment of the cross-class alliance in the context of urban reform during this period, see Richard Schneirov, "Rethinking the Relation of Labor to the Politics of Urban Social Reform in Late Nineteenth-Century America: The Case of Chicago," *International Labor and Working-Class History* 46 (fall 1994): 93-108. On women's cross-class alliances in the Women's Trade Union League, see Dye, *As Equals and as Sisters.* For an analysis of working-class women's popular consumer practices as a more resisting subculture, see Enstad, *Ladies of Labor.*
54   For work that looks at the complexity of address in films of this period, see Uricchio and Pearson, *Reframing Culture,* and Charlie Keil, "Reframing *The Italian:* Questions of Audience Address in Early Cinema," *Journal of Film and Video* 42, 1 (spring 1990): 36-48.
55   More recent political activism associated with antiglobalization and anticapitalism challenges this connection. See Naomi Klein, *No Logo* (Hammersmith: Flamingo, 2001).
56   The argument about a shift from producer to consumer society is associated with T. J. Jackson Lears in "From Salvation to Self-Realization: Advertising and the Therapeutic Roots of the Consumer Culture, 1880-1930," in *The Culture of Consumption: Critical Essays in American History, 1880-1980,* ed. Richard Wightman Fox and T. J. Jackson Lears (New York: Pantheon, 1983), 3-38. Also see William Leach, *Land of Desire: Merchants, Power, and the Rise of a New American Culture* (New York: Vintage Books, 1993). While I take the point that there was an increased visibility of consumption with the emergence of mass consumer culture and a move away from producerist values, the Progressive era discourses discussed here suggest a refiguration of the relationship between consumption and production.

KRISTINE J. BUTLER

Irma Vep, Vamp in the City

Mapping the Criminal Feminine

in Early French Serials

In Richard Abel's contribution to the *Velvet Light Trap*'s special issue on "Feuillade and the French Serial," he suggests two unexplored lines of inquiry for future film scholarship. One would examine the conjunction between actual criminal events occurring just prior to World War I and wartime crime serials such as Louis Feuillade's. The second would explore constructions of gender and class in Gaumont series relative to other crime films of both French and American production.[1] The *Fantômas* series, for example, directed by Feuillade and released in 1913, rigidly maintained class boundaries by "consistently represent(ing) women either as upper-class victims of criminal activity (Princess Danidoff, the Marquise de Tergell, even Lady Beltham) or as lower-class accomplices (Josephine, Nini Paulet, Rosa)."[2] Abel argues that Feuillade's series differed in this way from others of the period, such as Eclair's Protéa series, which featured a female spy, or the "American serial-queen melodramas" that "put Mary Fuller, Kathryn [sic] Williams, and Pearl White through fantasy displays of female prowess, even though graphic moments of imperilment remained a prerequisite of their 'emancipation.'"[3]

It seems, though, that Feuillade's *Les Vampires* (1915) would constitute a potential contradiction in the line that Abel is drawing between on one hand, Gaumont's supposedly rigid maintenance of class boundaries through its female characters (passive upper-class women vs. predatory but still submissive lower-class women), and on the other, series featuring female protagonists who are allowed to be active and strong without being déclassée and/or criminal (which often end up being more or less the same thing). True, *Les Vampires* does in many ways toe the Gaumont line, so to speak, in its conservative representation of the bourgeois domestic sphere and obsessive boundary maintenance. Its protagonist, Philippe Guérande, is a reporter for the *Mondial* who lives with his mother, a paragon of solid bourgeois virtue. His father, absent and presumably deceased, was a citizen of some repute. Moreover, one of the subnarratives of the late episodes of the series involves Philippe's engagement and marriage to a respectable young bourgeoise, adding a measure of patriarchal triumph to his tracking down and dismantling of the Vampires crime ring, thus restoring security and peace of mind to the Parisian upper classes in both the criminal and matrimonial spheres. However, although the lines of gender and class are in some senses very clearly drawn, the series' most recognizable villain, Irma Vep, seems nonetheless to trouble these distinctions by the complexity of her character. Although Irma is not the Grand Vampire, the official leader of the gang, she is not merely an accomplice either. Her role in the series as both the only member to figure in every episode beginning with her first appearance in episode 3, and the most recognizable member of the gang, Irma Vep could almost be said to lend an anagram of her name to the Vampires rather than the other way around. Moreover, though her gender is unmistakable, her class identity is not only a mystery but a continual space of absence within the narrative, fueled by and fueling her command of the costumes and identities she puts on. In other words, Irma is able to mask herself so well precisely because she remains classless — and she remains classless because she is able to master disguise. Finally, the question of Irma's sexuality, despite her implied promiscuity as the mistress of a succession of Grand Vampires, ultimately remains something of an enigma, as will be seen. I propose that the suggestion of Irma's sexual deviance in the discourse of *Les Vampires,* not just as a sexually promiscuous woman but as a sexual invert, is a crucial factor in her characterization as a criminal.

A figure who at once fascinates and repels, Irma is a sign to be deciphered, a captivating black mark on the moving-picture screen to be graphed into the map of Paris that Philippe translates from the secret language of the Vampire gang. Through the work of detective Philippe Guérande, the flâneur to Irma's flâneuse, whose attempts to uncover the crime ring eventually will restore order to a Paris troubled by Vampires, the spectator tracks Irma's movements through multiple episodes and witnesses multiple instances of her triumphs. Philippe and Irma offer two different models through which the spectator vicariously moves through the city. Irma eventually will be captured and brought down by the work of Guérande — but only at the end of ten episodes. Until then, she is at large in the city, which is thus offered, like Irma, for the spectator's delectation. As a woman who flies in the face of Third Republic morality and exhibits a level of independence and sexual freedom, Irma Vep is a fluid sign for criminality, and in particular female criminality, in the cinematic context of wartime France — a sign

Irma Vep, Vamp in the City

that has particular resonance in its articulation of complex visual clichés of the woman criminal in the cinematic language of the film serial.

I propose to discuss her symbolic importance in this very popular series — as a woman, as a criminal, and eventually as a public persona, Musidora, who transcends the world of the film but who is always inevitably linked back to it. Irma combines the rhetorics of criminality and female deviance that seemed to threaten the social structure of early-twentieth-century Paris with the relatively new fascination in France for screen stars. Thus *Les Vampires* capitalizes on a conservative discourse of female deviance and fear of the city's moral decadence, while simultaneously exploiting female empowerment both in the daring exploits of Irma and the developing star persona of Musidora. As such Irma/Musidora is placed as a potential object for "masculine" scopophilia, but also seems to emerge as a carrier of feminine scopophilic desire: that is, the desire for agency and liberty to move throughout Feuillade's cinematic city. The crime serial's unique rhythm of deferred resolution allows Irma to roam "at liberty" through multiple episodes, thus titillating the audience with this model of female agency, before finally bringing her down in the final episode at the hands of none other than Guérande's new wife.

Figuring Female Degeneracy

Figures of the female "degenerates," as has been shown by a number of recent scholars, had a particular resonance in the rhetorical strategies of the Third Republic, seeming to embody all manner of symptoms indicative of the general moral decay of society.[4] The Third Republic, though the longest-lived regime to date since the monarchy (1871–1940), was nonetheless fraught with social tensions and class conflict, and the rhetoric of the regime continually spun around attempts to contain the unrest that was feared irrepressible. Promotion of the nuclear family as the basis of national health and stability was a major preoccupation of the regime, and as a consequence women's position as guarantor of the domestic sphere was stressed. Progressive or feminist ideas were in general dismissed or denounced by the establishment; turn-of-the-century conservative rhetoric was suffused with conflations of feminists and female criminals, both of whom, it was implied, rejected their proper roles in society and thus contributed to the degeneration of the republic, whose stability rested solidly on that of the bourgeois family. Though it is indisputable that women's social status had improved by 1915, it is likely that most men, and quite a few women, still viewed with uneasiness the crumbling of structures that had legally assured male status and authority.[5] Conservative rhetoric in popular media, particularly cinema, tended to depoliticize this issue, couching antifeminist discourse in profamily terms, thus turning the argument away from the question of women's rights and toward the question of family (and by extension, national) harmony and strength.

Ann-Louise Shapiro has argued that turn-of-the-century authors from all positions, echoing the regime under which they lived and wrote, began to conflate the feminist and the female criminal in their narratives. Novelists, criminologists, journalists, and writers of all stripes made the connection, implied or explicit, that the two posed the same sort of challenge to the social order. As a result (or perhaps as a cause), feminists and female criminals were associated in the contemporary imagination, seeming to share a similar inversion of masculine and feminine characteristics. Moreover, lesbians, feminists, and prostitutes alike all were supposed to share an excess of "masculine" attributes; taken together, they were an indication of the depths to which their society had fallen. "In effect, the moral lassitude of the age—often described as a crisis in love and evident in various kinds of disorderly women—suggested to many a syndrome in which crime was linked, via loose and essentially affective associations, to lesbians and new women."[6]

Curiously, a seemingly contradictory discourse of the time argued that female criminality, likened to characteristic "feminine" mental illnesses such as hysteria, was the result of an excess of uncontrolled femininity, also used as a metaphor for the social ills of the era.[7] Following this line of reasoning, hysteria figures a society increasingly errant and chaotic, and in which women were more socially and sexually visible than before. Representation of female criminals in popular media picked and chose from both of these discourses; mass-circulation newspapers and popular literature, especially, capitalized on both types of characterization of female deviance.

Early cinema, which drew from both of these sources for its narratives, sought to capitalize on the popular fear of and fascination with crime in an effort to feed box-office receipts. Particularly during the war years, film narratives in France often focused on themes of urban crime and danger, perhaps as a means of channeling spectators' anxieties away from the military conflict toward subjects that gave the mundane a fantastical and enigmatic turn. The popular genre of the crime serial, as Richard Abel points out, ran on the almost superhuman power and danger of their criminal characters. These films featured masters of disguise that mocked social mobility and, we can imagine, played on the fears of the bourgeoisie while titillating audiences of more modest classes with images of class-transgressive power. Though crime films tended to eventually bring their criminals to justice, their popularity concerned many representatives of public order, mayors and prefects throughout France, which led them to call for a ban on "scandalous and demoralizing spectacles."[8] In this climate of reform and censorship, studios post-1912 did their best to sell crime films as educational and promoting morality by negative example and just punishment. Women began to appear more and more in these films, both as accomplices to the detective and as criminals to be punished, thus reifying the proper place of females at the center of the private, domestic sphere. The dangers of morally corrupt, "public" women were decried in these films, which nonetheless echoed and extended these characterizations of women, often using a condemnatory discourse to mask the fact of their capitalizing on these sensational figures.

In 1915, with French wartime studios seriously financially depleted, and competition fierce among production houses trying to maximize profit and minimize cash output, Pathé-Exchange was preparing a coup with the French release of *Les mystères de New York*. The series starred Pearl White, already well known for her role in *The Perils of Pauline,* which had been an undeniable hit in Paris. *Les mystères,* which would inevitably have called to mind Eugène Sue's popular nineteenth-century novel *Les mystères de Paris,* was predicted to be a smash hit with French audiences. Léon Gaumont, sensing the need to make a competitive move in order to keep his place as leader of the French film industry, charged Louis Feuillade to put out a series along the lines of his earlier success *Fantômas*—which he did, beating the release of *Les mystères de New York* by just three weeks.[9] The two female stars of *Les mystères* and *Les Vampires* could not have been more different: Pearl White, with her fresh, blond, innocent manner, stood in stark contrast to Musidora's dark and sensual villainess Irma Vep. Irma's smoldering eyes with their long eyelashes peered out from her formfitting black leotard as she slunk through the drawing rooms and over the rooftops of the city. To the masses of filmgoers who flocked to see the series, her unmistakable silhouette became an icon for flagrant feminine sexuality, for crime, and for the dark and unknown shadows of the Parisian night.

The general story line of *Les Vampires* is as follows. Philippe Guérande, first reporter for the *Paris Chronicle,* and eventually editor for the *Mondial,* has been assigned to cover the exploits of the famed crime ring known as the Vampires. The ring holds the elite of Paris in the throes of terror, as they use all manner of schemes — poisoned rings, kidnappings, murder —

to accomplish their thievery. Guérande and his sidekick, the scatterbrained and comic Mazamette, track the Vampires throughout the city in ten episodes, finally capturing the gang and restoring order. The Vampires' official male ringleader changes periodically through the series as each gets killed or disappears; thus it is Irma Vep, the only major female and only permanent member of the Vampires crime ring, who becomes Guérande's major rival. There is a historical reason for this constant changing of male Vampire masters: namely, the fact that in 1915 men were being mobilized in large numbers to serve in the war effort, and thus to keep one ringleader in the series proved impracticable. However, above and beyond these practical matters, Irma Vep's increasing importance in the series is part of a larger movement in Feuillade's work. As Vicki Callahan has noted, the "emphasis on eroticism through the character of Irma Vep (shifts) the weight of criminality and disruption . . . completely to the 'figure' . . . of the female."[10] Scholars of the belle epoque have argued that imagining the modern city of Paris in literature, painting, and later film, from the mid-nineteenth century onward, involved an epistemological back-and-forth movement between the city as immediately recognizable and the city as infinitely unknowable.[11] Irma Vep, in her black leotard and mask, personifies this immanently Parisian contradiction in the popular consciousness of the time, largely through her memorable but scattered appearances in a black, formfitting bodysuit complete with mask. Her sleek black form, reproduced on the publicity posters that blanketed 1915 Paris, erotically and suggestively scaled the rooftops and penetrated the private rooms of modern Paris, becoming at once its shadow and its dominatrix, emblematic of the "unknowable" quality and its criminal nether reaches of the wartime city.

Irma the Vamp(ire)

In psychoanalytic terms, the character of Irma Vep, played by the actress Musidora, might be read as figuring a disruption of the symbolic order. It is more productive for our purposes, however, to relate this disruption, this moment of the uncanny in Irma Vep's presence on the screen, to a crisis of representation foregrounded in the cinema's dynamic of perception. Since Balzac at least, the city of Paris has been (mis)understood as at once uniquely recognizable—the city is "sans égal au monde" [without equal in the world]—and ultimately unfathomable: "Paris est un océan. Jetez-y la sonde, vous n'en connaîtrez jamais la profondeur" [Paris is an ocean. Cast in the lead; you will never know its depths].[12] Literary representations of the city, especially, labored over this contradiction, and feminized the ocean of depravity and corruption. Irma might be recognized as the cinematic icon par excellence of the city, imminently recognizable and ultimately opaque. Best remembered in her black bodysuit, she is an inky fetish that simultaneously highlights the visible evidence of her gender and poses the problem of visibility. In other words, the suit that so readily identifies her curves in the light also allows her to slip into the darkness in the shadows of the city.

What Irma represented for contemporary viewers has much to do not only with the fact that she is a woman, but also with her status as a performer, both within the film (in one of her first appearances she sings in a bar that is a haunt for apaches and the criminal underworld) and in real life. Musidora, as a former Folies-Bergère dancer, took her performance as Irma Vep and later as Diana Monti in *Judex* into the everyday reality of Paris. As both film character and screen star (and later as director, writer, and all-around celebrity of the 1910s and 1920s), Musidora capitalized on her image of frank sensuality and dark, diabolic beauty. Her independence, physical prowess, and intelligence came through both in the characters she played and in her public persona. As such, her example has much to offer in terms of a feminist reading of female agency in cinema, though such is not the focus of this piece. Rather, I comment peripherally throughout the following pages on the extent to which Irma Vep/Musidora's presence in *Les Vampires* blurs the boundaries of stage/screen and "life," and the visible world and the underworld—an important element in the workings of the series.

Musidora as Irma Vep is one of the first screen actresses in France to be recognized both in her role and as a public figure. The introduction of the concept of the film "actor" occurred in France around 1908–1909, marking a sea shift in modes of reception and production geared toward legitimizing the medium. One exemplary technique that marked the transformation was the inclusion of introductory film sequences that presented the actors and the roles they played. "Following the logic of the *films d'art*, these prologues announce the importance of actors and bring to films the imprimatur and cultural capital of theater, while they instruct audiences that they should receive the film partly as a performance in which the actor's skill is appreciated beneath the role."[13] An offshoot of this new concept of the actor is the development of the star persona, which occurred in France as well as in the United States in the early and mid-1910s, as a result of the expansion of media linked to the cinema and "a marked expansion of the type of knowledge that could be produced about the player."[14] As an actor appeared in multiple roles in many films, and often roles that were similar, the question of the star's life outside the film, her or his "real life" personality, became subjects of great public interest, fed by interviews and exposés in the new popular genre of cinema magazines. Was the star similar to the roles that he or she played on the screen? The cinema industry made much of this burning question, whether or not this ended up being to the actor's advantage. Musidora, a savvy performer in her own right, already knew the benefits and dangers of typecasting, which is why she asserted so strongly the persona of her own creation, having taken her stage name from a character created by Théophile Gautier. Her fear, we might imagine, was that she would be condemned to serve as the goddess/demon Irma, the first and quintessential French "vamp." Though she certainly did manage to transcend this role and have a very prolific career as a director in her own right, as well as a writer, a lecturer, and a prominent feminist, her unforgettable image in silhouette did indeed follow her throughout, gaining her notoriety and instant visual recognition.

As Patrick Cazals acknowledges, Musidora was not the first to don the black leotard of the bat, nor the first to have a name composed of an anagram. In 1910, the American actress Theodosia Goodman took as her stage name Theda Bara, which was an anagrammatic transformation of Arab Death.[15] Her own role in the 1913 film *The Vamp* and subsequent roles transformed her in the public's eyes as the quintessential dangerous woman of the time. Janet Staiger's work on early American cinematic vamps shows these female characters to be "a foil for an extensive examination of the power of sex, women's rights in this new age, and the crumbling belief in the assertion that some nineteenth-century notions of the family's behavior were still pertinent for twentieth-century America."[16] Movies like *A Fool There Was* (1914, starring Theda Bara) portrayed the dangers for men of abnormal "bloodsucking" women, who drained the life and money out of the men they seduced, wrecking their family lives and their respected positions in society in the bargain. The vamp was portrayed as morally corrupt, though seductive; thus she played on the film audience's own susceptibility to beautiful surfaces that hid potentially poisonous depths. She is a projection of many things: masculine fear of the feminine, as well as turn-of-the-century middle- and upper-class fears of social mobility, particularly of the lower classes. The working-class vamp was dangerous for the upper-class man "because she could destroy not only a man's discipline and will by feeding off him, she could deprive him of his home, financial security, and social status."[17] And, of course, in doing so, she could destroy the security of all members of the family, and by extension the entire so-

Irma Vep, Vamp in the City

cial fabric. Diane Negra's piece in this volume addresses the unexplored issue of ethnicity in regard to the vamp, particularly in the case of "immigrant star" Pola Negri. Negra argues that the vamp type came about at "a moment of apparent U.S. prosperity but haunted by an underlying fear about the efficacy of American economic policies and the ability to maintain cultural isolation."[18] New immigrants to the United States were seen as a threat to national integrity; in popular cinema, female immigrant characters embody the fear of "spread of immigrant values into the dominant culture."[19] For Hollywood, the dark vamp, with her hazy origins in eastern or southern Europe, is a figure to be contained for what she represents sexually, economically, and ethnically. France, as well, has a similar relation to its eastern European others: Irma Vep, with her dark looks and vaguely Eastern name, contains something of this profound alterity which is "prenarrativized," as Negra puts it, by Dracula and other nineteenth-century vampire myths.

Mary Ann Doane sees early silent-era vamps as the descendants of nineteenth-century femmes fatales, who appeared with increasing frequency in late-century literature, painting, and poetry. "Her appearance marks out the confluence of modernity, urbanization, Freudian psychoanalysis and new technologies of production and reproduction (photography, the cinema) born of the Industrial Revolution."[20] The vamp, as a spiritual inheritor of these early femmes fatales, was a powerful symbol for social instability, particularly in American cinema of the early 1910s. The moral climate of films such as *A Fool There Was* contrasts with later fallen-woman films of the more restrictive atmosphere of the 1930s, in which the guilty woman in question most often meets with severe punishment in order to deter the film's female audience from following the same immoral path. Thus these early vamp films were more a "fallen man genre,"[21] in that it was the male character who ended up paying for his weakness while the vamp herself went free.

The Detective-Hero as Filmic Flâneur: Stalking the Vamp

Irma Vep, though she does exhibit many similarities to the vamp "model" identified by these scholars, does not conform in all aspects. On one hand, she certainly does represent the fears of criminal and social corruption in Third Republic France. Yet she is a paradoxical figure, at once powerfully compelling and elusive to both the cinematic audience and Philippe Guérande alike. Though she is in a sense a free-floating sexual signifier, she never truly poses a sexual risk for Guérande, who pursues her not as a man pursues a woman, but as a detective pursues a criminal. Philippe is a cinematic descendent of the nineteenth-century literary flâneur, a figure half-writer, half-detective. As Anke Gleber writes, the flâneur is

> at once a dreamer, a historian, and an artist of modernity, a character, a reader and an author who transforms his observations into literary, *or more precisely, latently filmic texts.* Collecting scenes and impressions, he then relates them through stories and histories of the city and its streets. Surrounded by visual stimuli and relying on the encompassing power of his perception, the flâneur moves freely in the streets, intent solely on pursuing this seemingly unique and individual experience of reality.[22]

The literary, and later cinematic, flâneur cannot exist textually without the barrage of visual and other stimuli surrounding him in the urban landscape. It is the process of sorting through this superabundance of sights, sounds, and smells that defines him: the act of discerning the unique or unusual from the mundane, which ultimately distinguishes the literary flâneur from the crowd. The fantasy figure of freedom that was a perennially attractive subject position, exemplified by Baudelaire's city poems, projected an image of male power that was at once completely master of, yet fundamentally apart from and superior to, modern society. Though the public image of the artist-flâneur was arguably more complex and ambivalent than Gleber suggests, the idea of a fantasy figure who could negotiate his way surefootedly through the confusing and deceptive modern city was compelling, giving rise to a number of literary and eventually cinematic genres.[23] The origins of the detective story, both in text and on screen, derive from the flâneur. For Tom Gunning, the detective and the flâneur share a similar interest in "not only mastery of observation but also a penetration of deceptive appearances."[24] The modern detective hero exposes the invisible crime of the city, making it legible and transparent, thus closing the gap between signifier and signified, at least temporarily. Like the flâneur, who benefits in his observation from his own false appearance of idleness, the detective often accomplishes this exposure of deceptive appearances by taking advantage of disguise himself. The modern detective hero is one of a new breed in cinema, "a thoroughly modern professional who acted as an independent entrepreneur with close ties to the police and whose intelligence (and skill as an actor, in disguises) repeatedly enabled him to master and control any threat from *apaches* (as well as from foreign spy networks or colonial rebels)."[25] The emergence and popularity of detective films in the prewar period, following their literary predecessors, has been linked to numerous social and cultural phenomena, among them concurrent debates on capital punishment, the labor strikes of 1906 that renewed the fear of class warfare, the upswing in violent crime, and the visibility of modern gangs of apaches that roamed Paris.[26] However, unlike the literary flâneur, the modern detective of early film and literature was not searching out enigmas and clues in order to write about them, but was rehearsing a scene of regulation. His ties to the police, yet independence from them, negotiated public suspicions of authority while still tendering a discourse of social and legal conformity. Thus Philippe Guérande, for example, as a journalist and a detective, is at once a private entrepreneur and a representative of social mores.

Perhaps the detective serves as a figure through which the filmgoer can shift her or his identity as a spectating subject away from another well-known modern type that Gunning identifies: the *badaud,* or gawker. In contrast to the flâneur, the badaud, who finds his best incarnation in Poe's "The Man of the Crowd," has lost his identity in the chaos of the city. The detective's integrity must remain intact in order for the deceptive appearances to be removed, in order for the crime to be solved, and in order for the boundaries of social class and legitimacy to be, at the last, maintained. As a model for cinematic spectatorship, the detective is in a sense a character who allows the cinema viewer to be a badaud without seeming to be: the character's pursuit and ultimate discovery of meaning (the resolution of the crime) can be counted on; until then, the spectator can enjoy the heady ambiguity of seduction without fear of "corruption."

The drawn-out thrill of *Les Vampires* capitalizes on this dynamic. In the series, it is Philippe Guérande, journalist-cum-detective, who is charged with putting order back into this system. Guérande's penetrating eye, the mastery of his pen, of vision, and of the cipher that order will be restored, is a movement that makes use of the conservative thrust identified with melodrama: the integrity of hearth and home will be assured, at least for the moment. Philippe is a sort of prophylactic eye, protecting the audience from crime. The figure of the journalist/detective, as a character whose acuity of perception is crucial to the solving of the case and attached to a medium of the visual and verbal fields, is pitted against a dark and sensorially confusing world of crime. The choice of the name Vampires for this gang is suggestive not only of the night, of shadow, and of the liminal space between life and death—of the uncanny interstices of the familiar and the unfamiliar—but also because of the common cinematic knowledge that will develop about vampires in relation to photographic technology, namely that their image cannot be photographed. Now, of course, Feuillade's Vampires are not actual vampires; yet the name of the gang reveals that the cinema houses a contradiction within it, a moment of *Unheimlich* within its very "reality principle": that at the very crux of vision there is something not seen, just as in the depths of the *Heimlich,* the familiar or canny, there is the Unheimlich.[27] The mere presence of a vampire onscreen calls attention to the contradiction in the mind of the savvy spectator at the same time as it asks her or him to accept the illusion.

Callahan has examined the uncanny as a relational signifier between the familiar and the unfamiliar in Feuillade's crime serials. She argues that the uncanny moments in these films, that is, "shifting zones of anxiety" on the level of visual style, narrative, and the figure of the star, are an index not of castration anxiety as Freud would have it, but of epistemological and ontological uncertainty.[28] I argue that in the case of Irma Vep/Musidora, Callahan's observation is particularly relevant, for she is indeed a zone of anxiety on all these levels. Narratively speaking, the rhythm of deferred resolution Callahan notes is integral to the crime series, heightens the uncertainty, and makes the elimination of this anxiety the ultimate narrative goal—but not before heightening it for ten episodes, and not without leaving the trace of this anxiety in the implied possibility for other crimes, and thus other serials. In terms of visual style, the black suits of the Vampires are just one instance of this uncertainty. Irma is the embodiment of the uncanny in *Les Vampires.* Her black suit is a visible *tache* or stain on the screen that can be read as a moment of uncertainty that the detective-cum-analyst tries to translate from textual opacity to a legible sign. The darkness of Irma's leotard (which collapses all of the Vampires into one sleek, catlike image), her dark looks, are gendered, criminalized icons of the mysteries of Paris. Irma's black silhouette is a glyph that serves many purposes. A filmic pivot on which feminine sexuality, criminality, and the modern city's hidden underworld revolve, she can be likened to the texts that Philippe must decipher in order to track down the crime ring (as seen in episode 3, "The Red Codebook"). She is also an easily recognized symbol that contributes to the success of the series through its dissemination on posters through the streets of Paris. Thus, as the sign of crime, Irma does really end up taking over the city; she is indeed everywhere, liable to turn up any place, not through crime but through advertising.

A particularly interesting example of visual style translating the uncanny occurs in episode 3. By posing as a replacement for the family maid who has been lured away by the Vampires, Irma has managed to penetrate the Guérande household as far as Philippe's bedroom, where he is working on de-

Irma Vep, Vamp in the City

coding the book. As she moves about the room Philippe, at his writing desk with his back turned to her, monitors her movements in a small table mirror. This mirror, one of those round swiveling devices, has a picture frame on the other side. In the frame is a photograph of Philippe's former girlfriend, the actress Marfa Koutiloff, who has been killed by a poisoned ring in the previous episode just as she was about to tell Guérande some information about the Vampire gang. Significantly, Guérande's picture of Marfa shows her in a bat costume she had been wearing for a ballet performance called "Les Vampires" the night she was killed. Her resemblance to Irma in the Vampire costume is striking, so much so that one might at first mistake the photo for one of Irma. As with the scrambled anagram of Vampires that composes Irma's name, the viewer needs an interpretive lens through which to read these images and construct a discourse around them. However, this time the deciphering eye is directly attached to Philippe, who, as his possession of the codebook suggests, will be in charge of decoding the visual and the verbal codes of the Vampires from here on out.

The swiveling movement of the mirror/picture suggests many things. Its pivoting movement recalls the early protocinematic inventions such as the phenakistoscope or the praxinoscope, which created the illusion of motion through experiments in persistence of vision. As a trope for the duplicity of vision, this mirror makes a conceptual link between the illusion of cinematic technology, the world of the stage, and the masking/disguise of the woman. Marfa, in episode 2, had starred in a ballet for a legitimate middle- and upper-class audience that placed her literally as a vampire bat about to bite a sleeping girl clad in white. This staged image of dangerous female sensuality, evoked through a metaphor of penetration, is referred to obliquely through the alternation of Marfa's costumed image with Irma Vep's reflection in Guérande's mirror/frame. Moreover, this slowed-down reference to persistence of vision is linked to the latency of crime in the city. Callahan has pointed out the tension in Feuillade's ouevre between the photograph and the moving-picture image, particularly the "evidentiary limits of the photographic image."[29] The crime portrait was a new and relatively unreliable genre that sought to eliminate the guesswork of police investigation, and Feuillade's play with disguise in all his films capitalizes on the unreliability of the visual. Guérande's work is all the more difficult, but all the more masterful, in light of this visual uncertainty. Thus the double surface on which both Irma and Marfa are represented, one fetishized and frozen in time and death, the other moving and always escaping the frame, becomes alternately film, world, and text—a codebook waiting to be deciphered by Guérande. The mirror through which Philippe discerns Irma's true identity sets up this pivot visually, through which the discerning eye detects and arrests, for a moment, the woman as the criminal he seeks to capture.

But there is more. Going back to what Staiger has written about the vamp, we realize that one of the ways in which *Les Vampires* differs from films like *A Fool There Was* is that Philippe (who is single, not married like *Fool*'s John Schuyler and many men who succumb to the vamp in these early films) never seems to be at serious risk of falling prey to Irma's charms. While he is from time to time put in danger by the exploits of the criminal gang, this danger never comes about directly through Irma. In fact, Irma and Philippe are almost never in the same frame together. The one notable exception to this occurs in episode 3—the first in which Irma appears—in the very scene with the pivoting mirror that I have been discussing. But significantly, this episode uses the mirror to distance Philippe from Irma's sexy, leotard-clad silhouette; the photo of Marfa inevitably suggests the Vampire costume, but displaces the sexual risk from Irma onto a dead woman. In contrast, Irma's maid costume, with its layers of figure-concealing material and restrictive bonnet, is the antithesis of the vampire costume. The film series does not bring Irma in her full sensuality into the same frame as Philippe, thereby keeping him safe from temptation. The mirror eye pivot serves as a mechanism of disguise and revelation; for the photo of Marfa in her bat costume cannot help but call to mind Irma's own black figure, at the same time reminding the spectator of Marfa's death at the hands of the gang. So the mirror/picture frame is a useful visual device by which Feuillade is able to convey to the audience that (1) Irma and the maid are one and the same, and (2) that Philippe, like the audience, knows this. But also, the two-sided image plays with the popular anxiety around the specter of dangerous feminine sexuality, playing a visual hide-and-seek game, hiding sensuality behind an image of chastity and presence (life) behind absence (death).

This is all the more true when one considers the implied relationship in *Les Vampires* between Irma Vep and the Russian dancer Marfa Koutiloff, which I suggested earlier. That these two figures are linked through the device of the mirror inevitably puts into relief the similarity of their appearances, a result primarily of the dark costumes they both wear, but also of their dark looks and foreign-sounding names. The mirror, a classic visual prop of the vamp, suggests her interest in the display and commodification of her body; the work done to enhance appearance through makeup, accessories, and hairstyle links the vamp to an unstable class system. What Negra writes about the United States is no less true of France: "In the early

Irma Vep, Vamp in the City

decades of the century, makeup was integrally tied to a cultural sense that the boundaries of class were collapsing, and the vamp iconography of pale skin and heavily made-up lips and eyes might well have connoted transformative desire to audiences of the time."[30] Darkness, either hidden or enhanced by makeup, worked to display on the screen a desire to hide one's origin: the mask exposes what it ostensibly hopes to obscure.

Deciphering the Vamp(ire)

Philippe's work to decipher the red codebook, and especially Irma (whose anagrammatic name emphasizes the need to turn uncanny tache into legible sign), emphasizes the importance of writing. His task is to decode the various ciphers and icons that constitute the Vampires' secret language of crime. One code to be cracked is contained in the graphic representations of the gang's plans to inflict their reign of terror on the city. Another is comprised of the masks and disguises that hide the criminals. Both denote a gap between signifier and signified in this urban world. Irma herself is presented as a code to be deciphered in this same episode 3, "The Red Codebook," as the spectator is introduced to the mistress of the Vampires crime ring through a publicity poster outside the café where she is performing, le Chat Huant.

A passerby stares in fascination at the poster outside the Howling Cat, motivating a close-up shot of the letters IRMA VEP, which after a moment rearrange themselves to spell the word VAMPIRE. This visual clue aligns the spectator's sudden flash of understanding with that of Philippe. The next episodes will be spent deciphering the fragmented visual clues around Irma and the gang. Anagrams recur frequently as indicators of Philippe's acuity, particularly as the main event of this episode is that referred to in the title: the discovery of a red codebook on the body of the Grand Vampire killed in episode 2. The central presence of this codebook places Philippe as a master reader, particularly as an interpreter of coded texts and false images: for it is also in this episode that Irma, in order to regain possession of the codebook, disguises herself as a maid and infiltrates the Guérande home. Though she is visually coded as a maid, Guérande sees through the disguise and is thus able to save himself and keep hold of the valuable codebook.

The textual scrambles of the codebook, the anagrams of Irma's poster, and many other Vampiric communications imply a game of verbal and visual hide-and-seek, in which the role of Philippe Guérande is to penetrate these cues and delve into the complex play of surface and depth, the visible and the hidden, that is the modern city of crime. At play as well are the numerous letters, telegrams, visiting cards (which, in this game of double identities, are just as often fictive as real), and other graphic messages that flash on the screen. Finally, of course, are the written intertitles that translate the dialogues for the audience. All of these genres point to the necessity of reading, and of reading well, in deciphering the mystery of the Vampires. The truth or falsehood of these written texts, and the degree to which both sides use coded or misleading written texts, suggests Philippe's absolutely crucial role as an interpreter.

Once again, Tom Gunning's work on early detective films and crime serials provides us with a useful lens. Gunning contextualizes the detective's position in terms of the various literary and filmic emergences of this figure in the late nineteenth and early twentieth centuries. The emerging detective genres of the nineteenth century had a number of sources, "ranging from a conservative suspicion of urban sites to more modern anxieties about alien populations crowded into new locations without shared communal values."[31] The city of Paris in particular, under the transformations of urban renewal, took on a hidden dimension in the popular imagination through "the creation of a substratum beneath the city surface which supported the circulation of energy, communication and transportation... (which) served as a metaphor for the subterranean world of urban underclasses, the city of dreadful delights which likewise excited the voyeurism of urban spectatorship in the form of explorations of the city's 'other half' by journalists and social reformers."[32] This new, hidden aspect of the underground city required a certain amount of technological prowess to navigate, and different skills of perception from those needed to go about the more aboveboard occupations of daily life. As Gunning suggests, the journalist was an appropriate figure for a detective, as it was through the popular press that the public often got their stories about criminal operations.

The crucial role of technology in this transformation must be stressed, especially where it seems to mediate a loss of perceptual acuity by effecting a loss of access to the phenomenological world. Doane's work on the femme fatale can be read alongside Gunning's to elucidate further his remarks on the detective genre. Doane suggests that the late-nineteenth-century appearance of fatal women links femininity to deception/antiknowledge or a devious and complex hidden truth. As such she is "a symptom of male fears about feminism";[33] however, in the way she emphasizes masquerades and veiling, she also personifies the mysteries of the underground city. In the case of Philippe Guérande, it is not only his role as a journalist but his mastery of the technological that will lead him to solve the mysteries of

Irma Vep, Vamp in the City

the Vampire ring that pervades the city like the complex web of unseen telephone lines and sewer mains that facilitate both daily life and unseen criminal activity.

The Vampires inhabit the underground spaces and the nighttime rooftops of the city; like bats, theirs is a different vision that surpasses that of the ordinary citizen. Philippe, to stop their destruction, must decipher the way they map out the city, as we see in episode 8, "The Master of Thunder." In this episode, the newest leader, Satanas, is planting bombs at strategic points all over Paris. Philippe, still in possession of the red codebook, must unscramble the criminal remapping of Paris. From his room, perched at the center of the city (in episode 3, we see the view from his bedroom window, with Châtelet, at the heart of Paris, in full view), he deciphers a crucial page of the red codebook, as we spectators look on. At length the page becomes a verbal map that marks out spaces of public entertainment that move all over the social map: the Blue Camelia, the Chat Huant, the Opéra. In this virtual movement of *flânerie*-cum-detective work, Philippe is able to traverse the entirety of Paris at once, a graphic echo of the series' periodic panning shots over the rooftops of Paris, "part of an investigatory gaze (the long take, the use of camera movement to follow an action) used to map urban instability."[34] This editing style traces the detective's understanding, the coordination of many viewpoints into a vast network, the mapping of "invisible paths of power and deceit (which is) *not* the known city of the flâneur."[35] When Philippe puts together the map, he is tracing the invisible spaces, graphing them, making them visible and contingent for the viewer through an act of deciphering that is ultimately an act of writing that links and makes visible the truth of the city.

Les Vampires, through its serialized play with the dangerous permeability of borders, is ultimately concerned with reifying and reestablishing the stability of the bourgeois family unit. In fact, one might consider that there are two main families in this film. The first is Philippe and his mother; the second is the "family" of the Vampires. The Guérande family is coded with all the elements of the good bourgeois household: it is a self-contained microcosm of the cherished elements of French social propriety. Conspicuously lacking, however, is a father figure, which allows a certain amount of instability that will not be resolved until the final episode. The fear of penetration, then, is present within the very structure of the Guérande household by virtue of the fact that the man of the house is unengaged in a productive "adult" union. The importance of marriage and family is signaled repeatedly, albeit in humorous fashion, by Philippe's sidekick Mazamette, who periodically takes out photographs of his children in order to explain visually instances of his buffoonery. Philippe's single status is conspicuous, and presented as one of the narrative lines to be resolved. Early in the series, he is linked to ballerina Marfa Koutiloff, though the film makes it apparent that this is not a "serious" union. Marfa, as a legitimate artist, is not completely déclassée. She represents a more benign form of costume, of feminine performance that is perceived as less threatening because Philippe is never presented as being enamored of her. Even when Marfa dies, he seems little affected by it—a stance that perhaps reifies the "correct" attitude for a bourgeois male to have vis-à-vis his actress paramour. Marfa is never a serious threat to the order, then; indeed, she is instead a victim of crime. She meets death at the hands of one of the Vampires, the evil Dr. Nox (who is in fact impersonating one of Philippe's father's friends), who gives her a poisoned ring in her dressing room. Irma is more complicated. Her physical penetrations into the Guérande home are frequent throughout the series, and both "legitimate" (as when she poses as a replacement maid) and clandestine. Her frequent entries into the private sphere of the home are a conceptual game whereby the limits of the domestic are threatened repeatedly in order to better elicit the sigh of relief at the end when order has once again been restored.

The naturalized but fragmented Guérande family unit will eventually be recomposed in episode 9, when Philippe becomes engaged to Jane Brémontier, a nice bourgeois girl worthy of him. The other main family, of course, is the unnatural alliance of the Vampires, once again with an unstable male figurehead, Le Grand Vampire, who changes a number of times throughout the series. As the only consistent representative of the gang throughout the ten episodes, Irma Vep is the embodiment of criminality, and also brings an element of uncontrolled sexuality marked by prostitution to the Vampire gang. Irma becomes the mistress of all the vampire leaders by turn, and thus is blatantly what the culture of the time would call a *fille publique*—that is, a woman for public consumption. She is, within the space of the narrative, what holds the Vampire ring together in that she most closely resembles what spectators recognize as a mother/wife figure in the ring. As unmotherly as she might be, it is precisely this element that successfully sets up the Vampires "family" in opposition to the more normative family structure figured by the Guérandes. Significantly, at the end of *Les Vampires,* it is Guérande's new wife Jane who shoots Irma, and through whom order is restored. She, then, like Philippe's mother early in the series (who is kidnapped by the Vampires but narrowly escapes when she kills her captor with a poisoned pen Philippe has given her for protection), is capable of agency, but only through association with a male figure, a sort of surrogate power. Irma, who in the first episodes is associated with and defined by the men with whom she is sexually linked, little by little becomes an agent in her own right, and in this sense moves closer to her own death as she becomes more of an active, autonomous criminal.

At this juncture, it is worth asking, why is it that Irma is never posed as a sexual threat to Philippe? Why, when her rampant promiscuity is suggested throughout the series, is he immune to her sexual presence? Or perhaps the more relevant question is, how does the series justify discursively Philippe's immunity, thus ultimately stripping Irma of her dangerous power in the face of the detective? Irma, the flâneuse to Philippe's flâneur, is paired with him in a textual cat-and-mouse game that must ultimately end in her destruction. Much theoretical work has been done on the "existence" or "nonexistence" of the flâneuse in late-nineteenth- and early-twentieth-century modernity.[36] The question, of course, is not whether there were actually women who walked in public; that there were is an incontrovertible fact. There were, for examples, middle- and upper-class women who took advantage of the new phenomenon of the department store, spending their leisure hours strolling. There were the women who worked as salesclerks, seamstresses, and floor help in these department stores, as well as women who worked as washerwomen, café servers, flower shop girls, maids, and a variety of other jobs that made them part of the public scene. There were female vagabonds; there were prostitutes; there were thieves. Women, it is undeniable, were on the streets. But what is at stake, ultimately, for theorists concerned with the existence of the flâneuse is the question of agency. In other words, when the question of the flâneuse is posed, the implication is, were flâneuses able to be active participants, agents of their own lives, in the public sphere? It is worth stating that most of these theories of the flâneuse seem to draw from a very particular notion of the flâneur: namely, the literary figure who remains master of his own domain, in control of his perceptions and separate from the general public, and *not* the embourgeoisified man of leisure nor his female counterpart, the wife out shopping for leisure. Though both of these images convey a certain sense of freedom, it is one seen as tainted by consumerism, thus ultimately constricted by capitalist ideology.

What is sought, then, is an elusive glimpse of a flâneuse as able to act independently of the constraints of patriarchal, consumerist society. Irma Vep may seem to offer the image of a powerful feminine figure. Not only a sexualized and criminalized female object, she also calls up the possibility of a privileged, mobilized female gaze of the kind that had been within the purview of male subjects. Irma is certainly a flâneuse in this sense: she knows about deceptive appearances, and knows how to use them to her advantage. She is a streetwalker; her hazy identity as a criminal, the new and disconcerting ways in which she moves through the city, her black form inevitably, irrevocably sexualizing the image, calls up and joins to it all sorts of other morally questionable nocturnal and urban pursuits. On the streets, in disguise, she could be anyone, could "become" anything, assume any identity. She crosses class lines, appearing as a socialite, a maid, a bank teller. She crosses gender lines in episode 6, when she poses as Viscount Guy, the "son" of Count Kerlor (the disguise of the Grand Vampire). At once seen and not seen, she is not possessed of a visible "real" identity yet the mobile composite of her false identities can be read as a kind of power in itself. She has the power to look, to scrutinize, usually attributed only to the male flâneur. Her extreme mobility and fluidity is at once a frightening prospect (to the extent that her black-clad figure could penetrate any public or private space) and also a potentially great source of fascination and scopophilic pleasure, particularly for women who may have felt the constraints of their own comparative immobility. Irma's easy transitions from maid to socialite to cat-(or bat-)woman called forth a fantastic, superhuman image of femininity. Her sleek black form projected an image of athleticism and placed her, for a moment, in a relationship of comparatively equal footing with other members of the gang, all the while maintaining her unmistakable femininity.

Elizabeth Wilson has argued that the lesbian is the quintessential nineteenth-century flâneuse, encapsulating the mystery of the flâneur's anonymity and distance from the modern economy that drove women out onto the streets as part of a new labor force.

> The lesbian is an inhabitant of the great cities, first glimpsed by Baudelaire in Paris, "capital of the nineteenth century." A new kind of woman emerges from the restless anonymity of the crowds, aloof from the sullen aimless excitement of the thousands that drift along the pavements and surge through the squares, a figure whose mystery and danger is that she is alone. The lesbian stands outside family, yet is not simply a worker. Her sexuality necessarily defines her. That is enough to make her lurid. She is a mirror image of the prostitute.[37]

As Wilson defines her, the mystery of the lesbian-as-flâneuse has two defining characteristics: her distance from industrial/urban economy and the

Irma Vep, Vamp in the City

family structure, and her "other" sexuality, which is always exposed yet the source of the greatest mystery.

Irma shares all the characteristics of the literary lesbian Wilson identifies: she is outside the family, yet not simply a worker. She is defined by her sexuality, which nonetheless renders her only more mysterious. Lynda Hart points out that such literary (and cinematic) representations of "aggressive 'women' . . . both underwrite and undercut the rigid dimorphism of same/opposite sex desire" and that "one ghost in the machine of heterosexual patriarchy is the lesbian who shadows the entrance into representation of women's aggression."[38] I agree with Hart in that, far from implying that Irma Vep is "really" a lesbian "in disguise," a series such as *Les Vampires* uses aspects of the lesbian stereotype as predatory and dangerous to characterize Irma the Vamp. There is not sufficient space here for a full-fledged discussion of the extent to which Irma's homosexuality is suggested, however obliquely. Nonetheless, it is worth noting that her implied sexual liaisons with all the Vampire leaders ironically works to call her heterosexuality into question. We never see any evidence of a romantic involvement onscreen, other than the intertitles that suggest as much. Onscreen, she is shown as more of a business partner, sharing the frame with the Grand Vampires and scheming with them, thus furthering her image of masculinity. Interestingly, the proliferation of her many interchangeable lovers ultimately works to negate them all, leaving her in essence with no lover. Moreover, the only point at which she succumbs onscreen to a prospective lover occurs in episode 6, "Hypnotic Eyes" in which the aspiring ringleader Moreno must hypnotize Irma in order to subdue her.

In the final episode, *Les Vampires* seems to foreclose any possibility of Irma's being an "invert," by staging her marriage to Grand Vampire Venomous. However, once again we see no onscreen evidence of romantic attachment, and the wedding and celebration that follows seem more like the raucous party at the Chat Huant from episode 3. Later in this episode, the last scene in which Irma appears has her entering the cell where Philippe's wife, Jane, and her maid are held captive. The close confines of the cell and Irma's aggressive movements toward Jane cast a strong hint of sexual threat. It is clear in this final scene that a measure of Irma's villainy is attributable to the model of the dangerous lesbian. Thus, perhaps, an additional justification for the fact that it is Jane and not Philippe who kills Irma. Perhaps Feuillade was not comfortable having a man shoot and kill a woman, and so chose to defuse the violence of this act by putting the gun in Jane's hand. However, it seems clear that in order for this potentially shocking act on the part of Philippe's wife to be sufficiently motivated to succeed narratively, Irma must be posed as a threat, however veiled, to Jane's heterosexuality and, by extension, to the sanctity of marriage and the family.

Irma/Musidora: From Screen to Street

To return to Callahan's excellent study, Irma/Musidora does indeed emerge as a zone of anxiety. This anxiety surfaces not only through visual style and narrative, but also through the figure of the star, as she suggests. With the new phenomenon of actor recognition and movie "stars" in cinema, another layer of disguise is introduced to Irma Vep/Musidora, as the film star "'returns' to the scene of the crime" in *Judex* as Diana Monti.[39] In a very important sense, Irma manages to escape death through the fascination she holds for film audiences. The play between the public desire to see phantasmagoria and crime, and desiring that it remain hidden and contained as spectacle, is well served by the popularity of the actress, as her recognition outside the film brings this world of phantasmagoria out into the "real" world, but still at a safe enough distance to be enjoyed vicariously. Musidora herself is not a criminal (one imagines), but she still carries over some of the notoriety of one, as well as the sensuality of Irma Vep, from screen to world. Irma Vep, as a woman always in disguise, is a performer — a fact made explicit in episode 3. Her first appearance onscreen is onstage, performing a song at the Chat Huant for her criminal colleagues. This scene conflates the notoriety of public performance (recall the poster with Irma's face and name outside the bar) with the notoriety of the female criminal. Significantly, Musidora's own fame was in part a direct result of this conflation. The development of the star persona is a complex discursive dance that blurs the distinction between character and actor, all the while claiming to maintain this distinction. Musidora capitalized on the blurring of these distinctions, attempting, savvy self-promoter that she was, to take advantage of the benefits of both. If Irma Vep dies at the end of the *Vampires* series, she nonetheless lived on and prospered, aiding Musidora beyond the Feuillade series into her directing career. After her famous roles as Irma Vep and Diana Monti, Musidora went on to act in more than forty films. Her debut as a filmmaker was an adaptation of Colette's *Minne ou l'ingénue libertine* (1916), with a scenario by Jacques de Baroncelli and starring Musidora herself. Her directing career comprised some ten films, including another adaptation of Colette, *La vagabonde* (1917), and a number of half-documentaries about Spain and bullfighting, in which, again,

Irma Vep, Vamp in the City

Musidora figured prominently. In addition, she wrote for several literary magazines, including *Fantasio* and *Eve;* published serial novels and poetry in the 1920s and 1930s; and was for a time the darling of the surrealists, inspiring André Breton's and Louis Aragon's play *Le trésor des jésuites*. The number of films that refer to Musidora grows even today, making her a figure of unparalleled longevity in the history of French cinema.

Contrary to what Richard Abel suggests about Gaumont's passive female figures, Irma, as an active and major female character in Feuillade's series, certainly criminalizes feminism and feminine agency in some senses, but conversely is endowed with a small measure of female empowerment. It is tempting today to read Musidora and Irma Vep from a feminist perspective, as twin figures of female agency in wartime French cinema. And it is certainly true that Musidora was a strong woman who engineered her own career as a director, a writer, and a public figure in a way that can by no means be construed as her being a mere pawn or victim of the system. However, we must also keep in mind the contradictory interests of the popular press and the cinema industry that fueled such characterizations, motivated by the contradictory goals of bringing criminals to justice and perpetuating notions of criminal rampancy as a means of generating revenue.

As I hope to have shown, it is not entirely true that Irma is a passive accomplice of the Vampire ring. Nor, however, can she be read exclusively as a model of female agency. More work needs to be done to flesh out the complexities of this ensemble of discourses that is Irma Vep. I have not, as Abel suggested, discussed Gaumont's other serial films of this period and compared them with those of other companies, and this certainly does need to be addressed. Nor have I gone at any length into issues of spectatorship beyond comments I offered on the flâneuse above. But I suggest that we continue to explore issues of the feminine in early cinema, particularly early "mainstream" cinema, while being cautious of our own potential for becoming enamored with theoretical flânerie. In other words, can we avoid moving too quickly to one end or the other of the theoretical debate that has tended to place agent and object at opposite poles? My intent in this essay has been to show how complex is the weave of the feminine in the example of this particular early French film serial, but certainly I have not exhausted the issue. More needs to be done, from a variety of different feminist perspectives, to tease out these constructions of the feminine, to complexify our flânerie through such cinematic narratives, and hence to intensify the debate on just what kind of detective work we see ourselves doing.

Notes

1. Richard Abel, "The Thrills of *Grande Peur:* Crime Series and Serials in the Belle Epoque," *Velvet Light Trap* 37 (spring 1996): 7.
2. Ibid.
3. Ibid. Williams's name was Kathlyn.
4. See especially Ann-Louise Shapiro, *Breaking the Codes: Female Criminality in Fin-de-Siècle Paris* (Stanford: Stanford University Press, 1996); Jean-Paul Aron, ed. *Misérable et glorieuse: La femme du XIXème siècle* (Paris: Fayard, 1980); James McMillan, *Housewife or Harlot: The Place of Women in French Society, 1870–1940* (New York: St. Martin's Press, 1981). The question of female malady, particularly hysteria, is also relevant here; a particularly cogent discussion of medical discourses' criminalizing of female neurosis is Janet Beizer's *Ventriloquized Bodies: Narratives of Hysteria in Nineteenth-Century France* (Ithaca: Cornell University Press, 1994).
5. See Shapiro, *Breaking the Codes,* chapter 5, for a discussion of the transformations resulting in greater legal freedoms for women.
6. Ibid., 206.
7. See Beizer, *Ventriloquized Bodies.*
8. Abel, "Thrills," 6.
9. Patrick Cazals, *Musidora: La dixième muse* (Paris: Henri Veyrier, 1978), 35.
10. Vicki Callahan, "Zones of Anxiety: Movement, Musidora, and the Crime Serials of Louis Feuillade," *Velvet Light Trap* 37 (spring 1996): 45.
11. See, for example, Christopher Prendergast, *Paris in the Nineteenth Century* (Cambridge, Mass.: Blackwell, 1992).
12. Ibid., 11.
13. Tom Gunning, "A Tale of Two Prologues: Actors and Roles, Detectives and Disguises in *Fantômas,* Film and Novel," *Velvet Light Trap* 37 (spring 1996): 33.
14. Richard deCordova, *Picture Personalities: The Emergence of the Star System in America* (Urbana: University of Illinois Press, 1990), 98.
15. Cazals, *Musidora,* 37.
16. Janet Staiger, *Bad Women: Regulating Sexuality in Early American Cinema* (Minneapolis: University of Minnesota Press, 1995), 148.
17. Ibid., 150.
18. Diane Negra, "Immigrant Stardom in Imperial America: Pola Negri and the Problem of Typology," in this volume, 379.
19. Ibid.
20. Mary Ann Doane, *Femmes Fatales: Feminism, Film Theory, Psychoanalysis* (London: Routledge, 1991), 1.
21. The term is Staiger's.
22. Anke Gleber, "Women on the Screens and Streets of Modernity: In Search of the Female Flaneur," in *The Image in Dispute: Art and Cinema in the Age of Photography,* ed. Dudley Andrew (Austin: University of Texas Press, 1997), 55 (italics mine).

23 Priscilla Ferguson suggests that by the time of the Second Empire, the flâneur had become more a figure of dispossession and disenfranchisement, more a marginalized than an enchanted figure. The ambiguous flâneur begins to connote alienation and anomie. This new figure "is neither Balzac's triumphant artist nor again the detached onlooker of the July Monarchy. He does not even attain the intermittent creativity of Baudelaire's tortured artist. He is, rather, a figure of failure, of the impossibility of placing oneself in the city so emphatically producing the space of modernity." See Ferguson, *Paris as Revolution* (Berkeley: University of California Press, 1994), 95.

24 Tom Gunning, "From the Kaleidoscope to the X-ray: Urban Spectatorship, Poe, Benjamin, and *Traffic in Souls* (1913)," *Wide Angle* 19, 4 (1997): 37.

25 Abel, "Thrills," 4.

26 On the rise of the detective genre in early cinema, see ibid. Gunning, in "From the Kaleidoscope," 25–61, discusses the evolution of the "urban spectator" in early cinema and the detective's link to the figures of the flâneur and the *badaud* ("gawker").

27 See, of course, Freud's work on the Unheimlich. See also Hélène Cixous's well-known essay "Fiction and Its Phantoms: A reading of Freud's *Das Unheimliche* (The "uncanny")," *New Literary History* 7, 3 (1976): 525–548. This apparent contradiction at the heart of the Unheimlich has served as the basis for a number of readings of the literary genre of the fantastic, particularly by Tzvetan Todorov, who sees the fantastic as defined by a moment of hesitation between two ways of reading the world, a hesitation manifested first and foremost through sensory perception. A character's (usually the protagonist's) sensory evaluation of a particular event is put into question, resulting in a feeling of dislocation produced by the clash between what the subject understands as the natural order of things and the apparent evidence of the senses. See Todorov, *Introduction à la littérature fantastique* (Paris: Seuil, 1970). Rosemary Jackson argues that the fantastic points to the basis on which cultural order rests by opening up a space for disorder, an argument that resonates with the subject of this article. See Jackson, *Fantasy: The Literature of Subversion* (New York: Methuen Press, 1981).

28 See especially Callahan, "Zones," 38–39.

29 Ibid., 40.

30 Negra, "Immigrant Stardom," 394.

31 Gunning, "From the Kaleidoscope," 39.

32 Ibid.

33 Doane, *Femmes Fatales*, 3.

34 Callahan, "Zones," 42.

35 Gunning, "From the Kaleidoscope," 52.

36 See, for example, Anne Friedberg, *Window Shopping: Cinema and the Postmodern* (Berkeley: University of California Press, 1993), especially "The Gender of the Observer: The Flâneuse," 32–37; Janet Wolff, "The Invisible *Flâneuse*: Women and the Literature of Modernity," *Theory, Culture, and Society* 2, 3 (1985): 37–46; and Gleber, "Women on the Screens," 55–86.

37 Elizabeth Wilson, "Forbidden Love," in *Lesbian Subjects,* ed. Martha Vicinus (Bloomington: Indiana University Press, 1996), 139.
38 Lynda Hart, *Fatal Women: Lesbian Sexuality and the Mark of Aggression* (Princeton: Princeton University Press, 1994), x.
39 Callahan, "Zones," 47.

LORI LANDAY

The Flapper Film

Comedy, Dance, and Jazz Age

Kinaesthetics

At the beginning of *Our Dancing Daughters* (1928), a golden art deco statue of a woman frozen middance dissolves into a pair of shoes in front of a three-way mirror (figs. 19 and 20). The next dissolve adds the woman's feet and legs, which suddenly begin to dance frenetically. "Dangerous" Diana, as our flapper heroine will call herself later in the film, is dressing before her mirror, dancing into her modern "step-in" underwear before stepping out for the evening (fig. 21). Although never static for long, the young Joan Crawford pauses to admire her reflection confidently before swooping out of her spacious boudoir, part of a kinetic—and kinaesthetic—deco design (fig. 22).[1]

An analysis of this opening scene could illustrate how female subjectivity as created out of the discourses of the culture industries is inextricably intertwined with self-commodification and self-objectification, with the split in sense of self between, to use John Berger's terms, surveyor and surveyed.[2] Diana is an incarnation of the nude deco figurine, self-absorbed in her dancing. As she dresses, she is both the surveyor and surveyed of her mirror image, a trope that has long associated women with vanity and narcissism. The female film spectator is encouraged to identify with Diana through subjective point of view, to put herself in front of the commodifying mirror of modern femininity, as if in illustration of Mary Ann Doane's explanation of the "female spectator-consumer": "The cinematic image for the woman is both shop window and mirror, the one simply a means of access to the other. The mirror/window, then, takes on the aspect of a trap whereby [the woman spectator-consumer's] subjectivity becomes synonymous with her objectification."[3]

Such links between cinema, mass consumer culture, and constructions of gender have been well established by a range of scholars.[4] In addition, there is empirical evidence, such as the comments offered by respondents to the Payne Fund Study performed by sociologist Herbert Blumer, published as

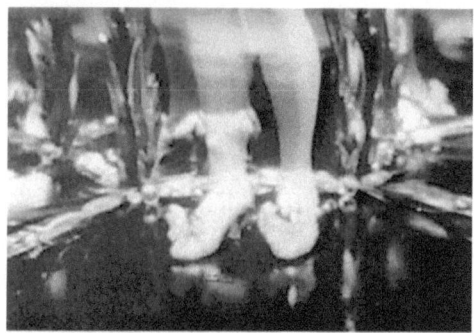

19–22. In the opening of *Our Dancing Daughters*, a series of dissolves introduces an art deco figurine (19) and empty shoes (20), which are then filled with dancing legs. The camera tilts up to reveal Joan Crawford dancing in a three-way mirror (21), then cuts to a wide shot that displays the room (22).

The Flapper Film

Movies and Conduct (1933). In the words of one respondent (female, sixteen, white high-school junior): "I remember after having seen "Our Dancing Daughters" with Joan Crawford, I wanted a dress exactly like one she had worn in a certain scene. It was a very 'flapper' type of dress, and I don't usually go in for that sort of thing."[5] Or as another respondent, a nineteen-year-old female Jewish college sophomore insightfully explained, "Certainly the movies have made me sharply aware of the fact that men place a high premium on the physical aspect of woman, that primarily a man's attention is drawn to a woman because of her beauty; that a large degree of the proverbial 'IT' may be attained by pretty clothes, risque clothes."[6]

To be sure, Joan Crawford's Diana, so riveted on the narcissistic pleasures of her expensively stylish form, might seem to be an icon of the modern femininity that required makeup and fashion for its performance in everyday life—and elsewhere I have documented that process in Jazz Age discourses of economics and erotics.[7] Clearly, commodification was (and remains) a central function of the cultural work of movie culture, but an interpretation that privileges commodification, even the active process of self-commodification that Doane advances, would not fully account for the kinetic and comic aspects of the flapper film. A more thorough look at the flapper film and the wider flapper phenomenon indicates that there is more going on in the complex relations of looking in and at the flapper films than Doane's argument would suggest. Arguing against Doane's thesis that the power of consumerism coerces women into becoming passive subjects engaged only in narcissistic or masochistic processes of self-commodification, Gaylyn Studlar makes a crucial point: "women did not go to the movies or read fan magazines merely to 'possess' the luxurious furnishings or the clothes or the stars that might be displayed. They went for an experience, one whose terms of fascination could be altered by the extratextual process. As a consequence, it is unlikely that the complex activity of the female spectator or the fan magazine reader of the 1920s can be fully explained by a model of consumerism, such as advanced by Doane, that depends on a binarism in which women can only either possess *or* comprehend."[8] Following Studlar, I would argue that the comedy in the flapper film, the kinaesthetic power of the flapper performance, and how the female spectator experienced it are undoubtedly key factors in commodification but they also exceed the processes of commodification. In other words, there is a ludic embodiment of femininity that transcends the limited subjectivity of self-commodification, and encourages the flapper spectator to imagine and emulate a playful subjectivity that is not simply enslaved to commodity culture. The modern embodied subjectivity expressed by and experienced in the lived body of both flapper actresses and flapper spectators twirled, sauntered, clowned, slid, flew, and of course danced its way into a new aesthetic—or, to use Hillel Schwartz's evocative term, a new kinaesthetic.

By considering comedy, the relations of looking in and at the film, flapper dance performance, and the construction of modern femininity, this essay seeks to open a particular vein of research in early-twentieth-century media studies to foreground how an inquiry into the flapper film can contribute to our understanding of the complexities of the relationships between the female spectator and the flapper star, and of women's experience of modern life. The opening scene of *Our Dancing Daughters* becomes the illustration of this idea: instead of the static, objectified femininity of the deco figurine, Diana appears, piece by dancing piece, delighting in the intertwined pleasures of donning her stylish clothes, performing her giddy movements, and looking at the combined impact of the two in her mirror. Although the opening image of the deco figurine is one metaphor for a dominant strain of Jazz Age femininity—the female form frozen in a moment of embodied narcissism—the dancing flapper who replaces her is another, a modern new woman who exceeds the limitations of the frame of objectification. A comic incarnation of the modern girl, she embodies and articulates the kinetic powers and pleasures—a new kinaesthetic—of the modern body in motion that develops in the early decades of the twentieth century.

The flapper film participates in the new kinaesthetics in its representation of Jazz Age femininity. The flapper film, a subgenre of silent romantic and social comedy, is characterized by its bold, "modern" heroine embodied by flapper actresses such as Colleen Moore, Clara Bow, Louise Brooks, Virginia Lee Corbin, Madge Bellamy, and Joan Crawford. Its iconography centers on the flapper, modern styles of dress and decor, jazz parties and nightlife, dancing, drinking, smoking, and the erotic possibilities of everyday life. The flapper film's plots concern the flapper's pursuit of modern life—independent from parental and other authoritarian control—and a modern romance in which her defiant actions, unruly behavior, and daring dress are either obstacles or catalysts, or both.

Throughout American culture in the post–World War I period, and with an ever-widening dissemination, the flapper phenomenon came to signify the Jazz Age. The word "flapper" was originally the British term for pre-debutantes, and became associated with young women who exhibited nontraditional clothing and behavior during and after World War I. In the late 1910s and early 1920s, the persona and image of the flapper grew out of the cultural discourses of the new woman referred to by Mencken and was

The Flapper Film

codified and disseminated by writers like F. Scott Fitzgerald (notably in his 1920 collection of Jazz Age short stories he had published in the 1910s, *Flappers and Philosophers*) and Anita Loos (who became well known as a "flapper-novelist," to quote a 1927 *Cosmopolitan* story on her), and artists such as Ralph Barton and John Held Jr., who drew humorous cartoons for magazines including *Life, College Humor,* and *Vanity Fair*. Moreover, the flapper as an icon of modern femininity was reinscribed by the interconnected parts of the Jazz Age culture industries: the film, cosmetics, fashion, advertising, retail, and magazine industries. The flapper film peaked in 1924 and faded with the end of the silent era, as the Jazz Age gave way to Depression-era America, and the flapper heroine bifurcated into the fallen woman and the screwball heroine, but this was not before the flapper film entered into a self-referential period during the transition to sound film in the late 1920s.[9]

The flapper film, and particularly the self-parodic films at the end of the genre, offer us an opportunity to revisit the oft-theorized relationship between the female film spectator and the silent-film star during the growth of the modern mass consumer society. Feminist scholarship in cinema studies and history has not fully appreciated the significance of the complex and contradictory flapper film for the study of the construction of femininity in the Jazz Age.[10] On one hand, the narrative of the flapper film explores women's liberation from Victorian restrictions, and seems to represent an emerging alternative or even oppositional culture; on the other, it contains female independence within the traditional confines of romance and marriage. According to contemporaneous studies of movie audiences (such as the Payne Fund Studies), women found "modern" models of behavior in the movies and their stars; however, recent studies have stressed how those manners, styles, and desires centered on an ethic of consumption rather than on feminist goals. The genre of flapper films was primarily comic, yet the influence that flapper films, stars, and styles had on individuals and groups of spectators and consumers attests to the ways in which the films were taken seriously. Like other Jazz Age discourses of the paradoxical new woman that juxtaposed feminist and consumerist ideals, the flapper film performed the cultural work of reflecting, shaping, and (as comedy is wont to do) mocking emerging definitions of a modern femininity.

In the flapper film, the flapper's bodily comportment, gestures, facial expressions, and actions are a central focus. The prevalence of the men characters staring, gaping, and ogling the flapper heroine led historian Mary Ryan to conclude, "The objectification of the female before male admirers was lodged deep in the scenario of the flapper film, and was depicted with entrancing finesse by movie moderns."[11] To be sure, one of the primary areas of cultural work in the early twentieth century was to objectify women and provide rhetorical strategies that encourage women to internalize their experience of being an object who is judged on the basis of appearance. Advertising, film, magazines, and radio—the Jazz Age media—worked to create the female spectator as a self-critical consumer who would turn to the products of the beauty and fashion industries. For example, facial soap ads warned, "Betty Bronson—Janet Gaynor—Clara Bow—You—Every Woman Must Pass Her Own Close-Up Test," or asked women, "What do the eyes of others see? This is a question every girl should be able to answer. Do the glances which rest on your face express admiration, or turn away with indifference? Meet yourself face to face in your mirror and pass judgement on what you see as critically as if you were another girl. Take note of every fault and learn the remedy." At the same time, though, the culture industries also posited the power of the flapper's gaze, as in a 1923 Winx mascara ad featuring flapper actress Colleen Moore. "Are you that girl— the charming person who fascinates by a mere glance? You could be, if you had long dark lashes to emphasize the depth of your eyes" (fig. 23). Or, as a 1927 Winx ad stated, "The appeal of *eyes* is Beauty's ace-of-hearts. More than any other feature, eyes that *speak* create charm and wonder." A Maybelline ad for mascara echoes this rhetoric: "Let your eyes speak the full measure of their beauty," reads the headline, and the copy embellishes, "Gay, flashing glances! Who can resist their charm? What a world of meaning the eyes can express—but not with light, scanty eyelashes!"[12]

"Eyes that *speak*"—what a provocative notion for the potential consumer in the era of silent film! What this ad and other Jazz Age discourses point to are the contradictions between commodification and modern female agency that are played out in increasingly self-conscious representations of the relations of looking.[13] Where the flapper film differs from other kinds of silent film is in its dramatization of a desiring female gaze that is indeed consumerist, but also—and here is where the dance meets the glance—embodied and productive. The kinaesthetic pleasures of watching the flapper film, with its comic, lighthearted, parodying depiction of modern femininity, may have provided a space in which a female subjectivity and idea of modern femininity exceeded the passive desire of the dominant female gaze. As the two ads discussed above and the opening sequence of *Our Dancing Daughters* suggest, in the Jazz Age culture industries the eyes become the "transfer point," to use Foucault's term, of the struggle between definitions of femininity as active or passive.[14]

The Flapper Film

23. Jazz Age cosmetics advertisements like this 1923 Winx mascara ad used photographs of flapper actresses like Colleen Moore to illustrate the power of the glance. Rhetorical strategies in the copy made mascara the essential ingredient to accessing that power.

Comedy, the Gaze, and Ludic Kinaesthetics: Colleen Moore

When Colleen Moore's "wonderful eyes" spoke, they were funny. Although she, like Bow and Crawford, first gained attention for her dancing, she soon developed into one of the silent era's best comediennes. In 1923, Moore had portrayed Patricia Fentriss in *Flaming Youth,* about which Moore said, "You see, we were coming out of the Victorian era and in my pictures I danced the Charleston, I smoked in public, and I drank cocktails. Nice girls didn't do that before." Moore's character also read a book by Freud, and forever linked the flapper's wild ways with the new pop psychology of modern sexuality. In *The Perfect Flapper* a year later, Moore played Tommie Lou Pember, a modest and old-fashioned debutante who finds herself unpopular until she resorts to the "modern" flapper behavior like dancing, drinking, and smoking. And in films such as *Ella Cinders* (1926) and *Orchids and Ermine* (1927), Moore created comic heroines who are as engaging in their failures to be glamorous as they are in their often accidental triumphs in love and career.

Moore's ludic abilities were well noted in the popular press. For example, the caption to a smiling three-quarter shot in *Vanity Fair* described her:

"Colleen Moore has, in the last three years, reached a peak of popularity in the films, due mostly to her gay portraits of the America flapper.... Miss Moore combines in her work a complete understanding of her contemporaries and a feeling for spontaneous gaiety. In a series of films the latest of which is *Naughty but Nice,* she contrives to make the younger generation laugh at itself with becoming grace. But it is more than a facile comedy style that has made Colleen Moore. She is the embodiment of the typical American girl, the everyday girl that her 'fans' admire and adore."[15]

Perhaps the greatest flapper film commentary on the power of the glance and the eyes as transfer point occurs in *Ella Cinders*. Loosely based on the Cinderella story as interpreted by the comic strip "Cinderella at the Movies," the film follows Ella, who enters a beauty contest with the prize of an acting job in Hollywood to escape her small-town life of drudgery and become a movie star. In order to help break into the movies, she reads a book titled "The Art of Motion Picture Acting" (fig. 24), which instructs: "The greatest requisite to stardom is the eyes. Master the art of expressing every emotion with the eyes." She looks over a page of pairs of eyes expressing the key acting emotions: hate, love, fear, flirtation (fig. 25). Her gaze — and ours — dwells on a pair of crossed eyes, which is then followed up with the text: "Cross-eyes — or the ability to make the eyes appear crossed have brought great fortune to certain moving picture actors." What follows is a fine piece of comic business courtesy of a split-screen trick: a close-up of Moore's face shows an extended sequence of each eye moving independently (fig. 26).

This is a freaky spectacle, one that always provokes a loud response when I show it to my students. Before the cinematic trick, along with Ella we are immersed in the acting how-to book, which frames the gag in the trappings of realism. Perhaps the buildup to the gag whets the spectator's curiosity about how eye play is achieved, and hopes to glean something from what follows. Instead, the mirror image of Ella gives us a funhouse mirror image of reality, and as Noël Carroll has argued, sight gags cause amusement by playing with the alternative interpretations offered by the image. Carroll traces one origin of the sight gag to the trick films pioneered by Georges Méliès in the first years of the twentieth century. He explains, the trick film "is a comedy that derives from exploiting the magical properties of cinema, a comedy of metaphysical release that celebrates the possibility of substituting the laws of physics with the laws of the imagination. Méliès's experiments gave rise to the early genre of the trick film, which promoted levity by animating the inanimate and by visualizing a fantastic physics."[16]

In the trick sequence in *Ella Cinders,* suddenly the power attributed to

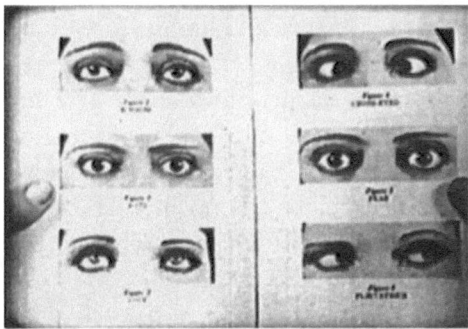

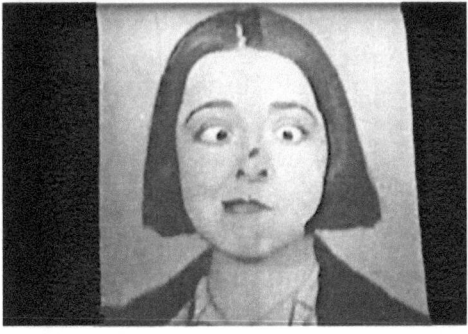

24–27. Colleen Moore parodies the centrality of the eyes for silent-film acting and the relations of looking in film culture in *Ella Cinders*. Ella sits before a mirror with a book titled *The Art of Motion Picture Acting* (24), which has pictures of the emotions communicated by different eye expressions such as fear, hate, flirtation, and crossed eyes (25). What follows is a trick sequence in which each of Moore's eyes moves independently (26). Ultimately it is the cross-eyed expression that inadvertently ends up on Ella's head shot that gets her noticed (27).

the eyes in film breaks away from the physical realities of eye movement, yet viewers are often unsure whether a comic performer might not really be able to send each eye wandering around, blinking asynchronically. Laughing equally at the possibility that Moore could and of course could not do such a thing, levity is indeed created in this surreal sequence. An optical illusion about optics in a film that is calling our attention to the importance of the eyes for movie acting, this comic sequence is a high point of self-mockery in a film that plays with ideals of stardom.

In a fine comic twist, it is Ella's cross-eyes that win her the contest. The judge explains, "Beauty means nothin'. We firemen see the best lookin wimmin at their worst. The movies needs newer and funnier faces," and shows us her head shot, which accidentally caught her looking cross-eyed at a fly (fig. 27). The comic inversion of the flapper actresses' eye play into the winning strategy of cross-eyes is an example of Moore's contribution to the development of the comic heroine. A strong antecedent of the screwball heroine who emerges in sound comedy in the early 1930s, Ella's charm stems from her vivacious personality and almost innate inability to conform.[17] The "Girl with wonderful eyes," indeed!

Moore's comic performance, especially the technological element of the trick film, exemplifies the new kinaesthetic of the Jazz Age. Her shtick both mocks and acknowledges the eyes as a transfer point of meanings and bodily practices in silent-film culture, calling attention to the convention as it subverts it. The pleasure in the cross-eyed sequence is ultimately one that fits Henri Bergson's assertion that comedy is created with "something mechanical encrusted upon the living," but there is another level of comedy at work here, what we could term a ludic kinaesthetic—a comedy that emerges from the fascination with modern motion, a kind of comedy well recognized in masculine traditions of slapstick and brought to new heights by the genius of Chaplin, Lloyd, and Keaton.[18]

To be sure, Bergson's turn-of-the-century conception of the comic arising out of the bisociation of the organic and the mechanical is itself part of the discourses that create the new kinaesthetic.[19] The dialectic of tension and elasticity central to both was played out in every aspect of American culture in the first three decades of the twentieth century. Moore's performance of a ludic kinaesthetic is only one of the many manifestations of comedy, kinaesthetics, and the construction of Jazz Age femininity; for a fuller exploration of this constellation, we turn sharply on our heel and move into the realm of the flapper's dance.

The Flapper Film

Modernism, Kinaesthetics, and Flapper Dance: Joan Crawford

Dance was one facet of the prism of the new kinaesthetics, a prism formed by the confluence of moving pictures, moving women, and modernist acceleration. From the Dress Reform movement of the late nineteenth century (which campaigned for the "bloomer" to replace the constricting corset) and the postwar cultural phenomenon that prompted women to bob their hair, to the practitioners of Delsarte (a style of dance and philosophy grounded in how movement expresses emotion), there were social currents that sought to liberate women from the physical and material confines of Victorian ladyhood. At the same time, the emergence of mass consumer culture reinforced and shaped women's entrance into the public sphere. The popular music style that exploded first as ragtime and then as jazz in the new culture industries encouraged fast dancing and flailing limbs, and prompted the national music chairman of the General Federation of Women's Clubs to wonder, "Does Jazz Put the Sin in Syncopation?"[20] Automobiles and airplanes moved people's bodies farther and faster than ever before, and the speed of communication accelerated. Amusement parks and movie palaces teemed with bodies crossing the traditional social and economic boundaries that delineated Victorian culture. If we consider the Victorian waltz—measured, coupled off, contained—and then we think of the Jazz Age Charleston, the black bottom, or the turkey trot—syncopated, individualistic, unrestrained—we can appreciate the enormity of the cultural shift represented by the flapper and acted out by dancing. If we imagine the contexts that created the dance marathon—first held in 1923 and continuing through the mid-1920s—we can appreciate a popular craze hell-bent on finding and pushing limits. With all these factors at work, we can conclude that women in the 1920s moved in ways women had never moved before, and that modern femininity is predicated on modern movement.

The new kinaesthetics were pivotal in the development of the flapper phenomenon—the mimetic and memetic spread of a new style, comportment, slang, behavior, and ideology that break with the conventions of the past. At one cornerstone of the flapper phenomenon, we find the complex connections between theatrical dance, cinematic dance, and popular dance, which contributed to the ideas and practices of modern femininity. Modern dance pioneers Martha Graham, Ruth St. Denis, and Isadora Duncan inspired the bodily expression of individual subjectivity in their schools and on the stage, flapper actresses Moore, Brooks, Bow, and others drew on their training in screen performances, and popular trendsetters like Irene Castle and her husband Vernon disseminated the new kinaesthetic.[21] Choreographers in all forms of theatrical dance were influenced by African American vernacular dances at a time when black and white music styles were blending, and much of what is considered modern popular culture was appropriated from black cultural traditions. For example, the Charleston, which still signifies the Jazz Age today, caused a stir when it was performed in the all-black Broadway revue *Shuffle Along* in 1921; like the other dances that became the rage, it was based on a black vernacular dance. The Charleston craze spread to Europe when Josephine Baker incorporated the dance into her exotic primitivist persona, and the new kinaesthetic was further disseminated in cubist-inflected theatrical posters. In a Chicago blues club, Mae West saw the shimmy performed and incorporated it into her stage act; the shimmy was one of the dances prohibited in the Production Code that was referred to by name.[22]

Like theatrical art dance, popular dance was part of the modernist revolution in style. The jolting, fragmented, and multidimensional images of modern subjectivity concocted by the futurists and cubists of the early twentieth century fused with the geometric influences on design prompted by the contents of King Tutankhamen's tomb in 1922 and the Art Deco Exhibition in Paris in 1925. The streamlined silhouette of the flapper, her clothes that were designed for movement, the images used to advertise them, the cars she drove, the skyscrapers she passed, and the interiors of restaurants and clubs she danced in: all of these were influenced by the new kinaesthetic of the fine and decorative arts expressed in new metaphors of modern freedom, fragmentation, and constraints.

Like other aspects of modern American culture, the popular dances that embodied the flapper phenomenon enacted a new relationship of the body and its parts. As Elizabeth Kendall writes in *Where She Danced*:

> Twenties dance reveled consciously and unconsciously in the general alertness about how the body looked, and its new separation into parts. The most popular vernacular dance forms of the day, the Charleston and the black bottom, were both variations on the whole person as one long stick, with hinges, and potentially flyaway arms and perhaps legs. The Charleston, to a jerky syncopation, almost tied the knees together but let the feet twist crazily against the floor and the arms either flap in opposition or make Egyptian-type designs on top. In the black bottom the backside was identified as something

The Flapper Film

that moved; the arms slapped the bobbing backside as if to push the whole person forward through the pelvis.[23]

But it was the movies that advanced dances like the Charleston so that they spread like wildfire. Like style, fashion, gesture, and expression, dancing in the movies reached more people simultaneously than any other kind of visual communication. The movies featuring dances performed by the flapper actresses were the benchmarks for popular dance, much like the television programs *American Bandstand* and *Soul Train* would be later in the century.

Not surprisingly, the flapper actresses were known at first primarily for their dancing. The notoriety that Bow, Crawford, and Brooks gained for their dancing, especially the Charleston, is suggested by a 1926 *Photoplay* article that connects Brooks's stardom and dancing: "Indeed, as the ingenue in *A Social Celebrity,* Louise was smartly beguiling. Nor should the Charleston she contributed be ignored. She was, in fact, a newcomer who demanded attention."[24] In the early flapper films from *The Girl with the Jazz Heart* (1921) to *Dancing Mothers* (1924), dancing along with drinking, smoking, and unladylike comportment were the primary signifiers of the modern femininity represented by the flapper and jazz. Joan Crawford became well known in Hollywood for her spirited dancing at clubs and parties, as were Bow and others. Several actresses had formal training with the modern dance pioneers; both Louise Brooks and Colleen Moore studied dance at Denishawn, the modern dance school run by Ruth St. Denis and her husband, Ted Shawn. There they learned the new modern dance that St. Denis and other pioneers like Isadora Duncan and Martha Graham based on popular mainstream activities for middle-class women, such as aesthetic gymnastics and Delsarteanism, that sought to express emotion through movement.

Modern dance had a huge impact on making modern femininity active and embodied. As Max Eastman eloquently wrote about Isadora Duncan's death in 1927, "All the bare-legged girls, and the poised and natural girls with strong muscles, and strong free steps wherever they go . . . they all owe more to Isadora Duncan than to any other person."[25] The new modern dance broke radically with the traditions of classical dance, and was part of the modernist movement in the arts that focused on materiality, corporeality, fragmentation, and the fracturing of conventions of form and content. According to dance scholar Janet Wolff, modern dance "totally transformed the types of movement seen on the stage, abandoning the purity of the line and denial of weight of the classical ballet and introducing angularity, pelvic movement, emphasis on the body's weight and its relationship to the ground."[26] Or, as Susan Manning summarizes, in early modern dance, "the kinesthetic dimension introduced a new image of the female body in motion that was without precedent."[27] Where ballet creates the illusion that the dancers are lighter than air, modern dance embraced gravity, effort, and the tension of the spiral around a center point, as Hillel Schwartz shows in his essay "Torque: The New Kinaesthetic of the Twentieth Century."[28] Schwartz locates a change in modern bodily experiences of movement that is created by and reflected in modern dance, exercise, the invention of the zipper in the 1920s, and both the form and practice of writing and typing. It is exactly such a documentation and dissemination of the shift that we can find in the embodied femininity of the flapper film.

The new kinaesthetics created a distinctly modern experience of spectatorship. Susan Manning contends that there was a new relationship between the female spectator and the female modern dancer: "the kinesthesia of early modern dance engaged female viewers in ways that the spectacle of late-nineteenth century ballet did not. In fact, since many female spectators had experienced the same movement techniques that the dancers transformed in performance—Delsarteanism and aesthetic gymnastics—their kinaesthetic response was particularly intense and led more than a few to identify the dancer's flow of bodily motion as reflective of their own."[29] Manning also reports that women spectators wrote enthusiastically about early modern dance in diaries, letters, and memoirs, and these sources suggest that they viewed the kinaesthetic power "as a metaphor for women's heightened social mobility and sense of possibility."[30]

We can extend the insights of the new cultural studies of dance scholarship to the film performances of the flapper stars, and suggest that women spectators may have had a particularly intense kinaesthetic response to Crawford, Moore, and Bow as well as to Duncan, St. Denis, and Graham. Therefore, instead of perceiving the flappers' performances as examples of objectification, or the narcissistic collapse of subjectivity into objectification posited by Doane, I would propose that female spectators instead experienced a particularly active subjective identification with the flapper actress because of her experiences of doing similar dances. The kinaesthetics of the frenetic Charleston, the syncopated movement that enacts the very lines, tensions, and motions of modernity—perhaps these experiences exceed the also-present frame of reference of the flapper as an objectified female body moving in ways designed to attract and please men.[31]

So, when our modern huntress Diana rips off her skirt and dances, dances, dances at a high point of *Our Dancing Daughters,* she certainly attracts the attention and appreciation of Ben, the new heir in town, as well as entertaining the male and female friends who demand that she dance for them. But the film also encourages the spectator to experience Diana's enjoyment of the dance through the close-ups, framing, editing, and camera movement as well as the performance itself (figs. 28–31). An embodiment of the kinaesthetic power of modern femininity, Diana commands the audience with her movements, and at least at this midpoint in the film, is able to enact her will. Soon, however, the deceitful Ann (played by Anita Page) seduces Ben by pretending to be conservative and traditional. Unlike the "modern" Diana, Ann is willing to lie and conform to dominant social values in order to get her man. Needless to say, Ann eventually meets with a bad end (at the bottom of a flight of stairs, drunk and dead), and eventually Diana ends up with Ben.

Our Dancing Daughters caused a sensation, and from the many comments specifically about it in Blumer's Payne Fund Study, it seems to have been to the Jazz Age what *Rebel without a Cause* (1954) was to the 1950s and *The Graduate* (1967) was to the 1960s.[32] Blumer writes, "Very frequently one can detect a distinct difference in the interpretation of the same kind of picture on the part of elders and adolescents.... An interesting example was: *Our Dancing Daughters,* featuring Joan Crawford. Many adults' conversation with the author impressed upon him their judgement that this picture was harmful and would likely lead to immoral attitudes and thoughts in high-school boys and girls... in the experience of a number of high-school boys and girls, however the picture tended to emphasize other values."[33] Blumer also commented in a footnote that *Our Dancing Daughters* was an example of how "motion pictures confound discrimination and dissolve moral judgement into a maze of ambiguous definitions" by "the sanctioning of questionable or unexpected conduct by running a moral through it."[34] Indeed, *Our Dancing Daughters* exemplifies the strategy of skirting the Hays Formula and the "Don'ts and Be Carefuls" that delineated the film industry's self-censorship: put on an ending in which the young characters either get married or pay for their infractions. At least one Payne Fund Study participant did not accept the ending's condemnation of Ann's deceptive impersonation of "good" femininity. The white female high-school senior of seventeen replied, "I have tried in many ways to adopt the mannerisms of my favorite actress, Anita Page. My first realization of this was after I had seen her picture entitled 'Our Dancing Daughters.' This picture, as well as Anita Page, thrilled me as no other picture ever has or ever will. She didn't take the part of the good and innocent girl, but she was the cheat and the gold-digger. One would think the leading man could never 'fall'

28–31. In *Our Dancing Daughters,* Diana (Joan Crawford) waits ecstatically for the music to pick up the beat (28) so she can begin her frenzied dance (29). As Diana pleases the crowd with her dance performance (and gets the admiring gaze of the new man she's met) (30), she whips off her skirt for better mobility (31). Although she is clearly presenting an enjoyable spectacle, she seems nevertheless lost in the kinaesthetics of her movements.

The Flapper Film

for that type of girl, but he certainly did. Many a time I have tried to tilt my head as she did, and wear my hair in back of my ears, and even stood in front of the mirror going through the same actions she had done."[35] Other respondents seemed more focused on Crawford and Diana, but most mentioned an exhilarated response to the film, such as one high-school sophomore who wrote, "when I go to see a modern picture like 'Our Dancing Daughters' I am thrilled."[36] A final quote from the Blumer study tells us about, in the words of a white female high-school senior, "the show that so accurately pictured the viewpoints of the younger generation—'our Dancing Daughters,' starring Joan Crawford. In Joan Crawford the true spirit of the younger generation was shown."[37] Part of that spirit was undoubtedly Crawford's dance performance as a main technique for creating the character of Diana and embodying the kinaesthetic modern spirit that hit such a nerve among young women spectators.

The Kinaesthetic Gaze: Clara Bow

If Joan Crawford's dancing highlighted the kinaesthetic pleasures of modernity, and Colleen Moore's eye play emphasized the comic potential, then Bow's active gaze accentuated the erotic possibilities of modern femininity. More than any other cultural icon of the Jazz Age, actress Clara Bow epitomized "the look"—both in the use of eye play in her acting style and in her embodiment of a "look," a term that emerged in the Jazz Age to describe a recognizable style that women tried to emulate. In her acting, Bow consciously worked to convey her emotions through the different kinds of looks she used. Clarence Badger, the director of *It*, recounted how Bow explained her changing expressions during the filming of a close-up:

> Clara, following my directions, gazed at her sweetheart with an expression of lingering, calf-like longing on her pretty face, perfectly all right if she had stopped there. But she did not. Continuing on, the camera still grinding away, her doll-like tantalizing eyes suddenly became inflamed with unwholesome passion. Then the young rascal suddenly changed her expression again, this time to one of virtuous appeal. I stopped the camera. "And what was that all about, Clara?" I demanded.
> "Well," she came back, "if you knew your onions like you're supposed to, you'd know that first expression was for the love-sick dames in the audience, and that the second expression, that passionate stuff, was for the boys and their paps, and that third expression—well, Mr. Badger, just about the time all the

old women in the audience had become shocked and scandalized by that passionate part, they'd suddenly see that third expression, become absorbed in it, and change their minds about me having naughty ideas and go home thinking how pure and innocent I was; and having got me mixed up with the character I'm playing, they'd come again when my next picture showed up."[38]

Badger's anecdote shows Bow's careful consideration of the impact of different kinds of eye play—as if she had read the same book as Ella Cinders. In the scene in *It* Badger describes and in countless other flapper films, the glance is productive, and the power of the glance plays out in the ability to enact the specifically female power that lies in the eyes—which Bow deployed to communicate emotionally with different audience constituencies, to work the same seduction on the spectator as the flapper heroine does to the object of her desire. As one of the Payne Fund Study respondents—a white female seventeen-year-old high-school junior—explained, "Yes, the movies do change my moods. Sometimes, when I feel sort of blue, and I go to see Clara Bow or some other actress I feel like flirting with everybody when I get out of the theater. I usually feel that way until the next morning, if the picture made an impression on me."[39] In *It,* Badger not only uses Bow's active gaze to propel the narrative by directing the spectator's attention to both what and how Betty Lou sees. In the scene in the Ritz dining room, which I have analyzed elsewhere as a dramatization of the triumph of the dynamic modern flapper over the composed Victorian lady, we see Betty scanning the 360 degrees of the room for Waltham's location (fig. 32).[40] At the moment of Betty's recognition, the camera cuts to her point of view, and a zoom shot that wittily conveys Betty's lock on her target (figs. 33–35). This expressionistic technique distorts time and space to show the strength of Betty's desire as a zooming, flying, speeding, and kinaesthetic gaze of modern femininity.

The zoom shot is just one of the many playful techniques Badger uses to characterize Betty Lou as a smart, independent, working girl who will not accept a "left-hand" agreement to be set up as Waltham's mistress and who supports and lives with her unfortunate, sickly friend who had a baby out of wedlock. Insulted by Waltham's reaction when he thinks the baby is hers, she quits her job and then seeks revenge on him by manipulating him into proposing marriage anyway, then rejecting him (and regretting it, and getting him back yet again). From start to finish, the film dramatizes Betty Lou's ultimately successful attempts to satisfy the acquisitive desire she articulates when Waltham first walks onto the department store floor, and the intertitle reads, "Sweet Santa Claus, give me *him*!"

32–35. In *It,* a zoom shot cleverly shows an active female gaze that locks on its object of desire. Clara Bow's Betty Lou looks around for her Mr. Waltham (32), and then from her point of view, the camera finds him and zooms in (33–35).

Bow also embodied the kinaesthetic power of dance and movement. A paragraph accompanying a 1928 *Vanity Fair* photograph of Bow in a sporty bathing suit sitting triumphantly on a pier by the sea highlights Bow's embodiment of both glance and dance: "Ladies and gentlemen (not to mention children): regard, observe, and otherwise behold—in an informal pose—the vivacious, the audacious, the orchidaceous Clara Bow! Feast your weary optics upon this super-flapper of them all—the hyper-reality and extra-ideality of a million or more film-goers. Thus, in one person, in one pose, we have the *genus* American girl refined, washed, manicured, pedicured, permanent-waved and exalted herewith. We have all watched the little lady prancing and dancing in her own entrancing way upon the silver screen. Do you wonder that for the nonce she is almost the most popular of movie stars?"[41]

Part of what made Bow the "super-flapper of them all" was her embodiment of kinaesthetics. In one of her first roles, in *Enemies of Women* (1923), Bow drew attention in a bit part by dancing on a table, and later that year provided comic relief and lively spectacle as the flapper in the drama *Black Oxen* (1923). In *The Adventurous Sex* (1925), Bow tops off a performance of a character who pursues a wild life by jumping into Niagara Falls, then climbing up a rope ladder hanging from an airplane, surely connecting the flapper heroine with the serial-adventure actresses of the silent era. One of her most physical performances is in *It* (1927); although she does not dance, Bow is hardly still for a moment—everything about her is motion and energy, from Betty Lou's animated first glance of Waltham that, like the zoom shot described above, is a desiring female gaze that is so active we can see it reach across the frame to find him.

Perhaps there is no better example of Bow's kinaesthetic power than in the scene where she and Waltham go on a date to Coney Island. In contrast to the stuffy dining room of the Ritz, where Betty Lou can scarcely sit still enough, the date on her turf celebrates the kinaesthetics of the amusement park. The scene is an example of how cinematic representations of the amusement park highlight how both were "mutual sites of pleasurable gazing doubly articulated in the cinematic process of spectatorship and the mimetic representation of the amusement park ride," as Lauren Rabinovitz explains.[42] In *It,* we have a humorous montage that shows Betty Lou and Waltham spinning on a huge inclined turntable called the "social mixer," lasting the longest in the center but finally flung to the edge by centrifugal force, and crashing into each other in boats gyrating on mechanical rough seas.[43] While careening down an enormous slide, Waltham

The Flapper Film

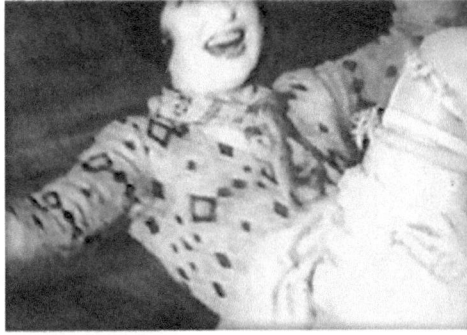

36–37. In *It*, Bow's kinetic performance exceeds the frame as she tumbles down a slide at Coney Island.

is happy to follow Betty's instruction, "Hold me tight, Mr. Waltham," and the ride is a laughing, spinning, skirt-lifting descent. Bow's legs and laughter fill the frame, much like one of John Held Jr.'s cartoons of the flapper with legs flying everywhere (figs. 36 and 37).

As Tony Bennett describes, "the amusement park addresses—indeed assaults—the body, suspending the physical laws that normally restrict its movement, breaking the social codes that normally regulate its conduct, inverting the usual relations between the body and machinery and generally inscribing the body in relations different from those in which it is caught and held in everyday life."[44] The effect of this inversion in *It* is to break down the class barriers between the working girl and her boss as they are both subject to the assault on the body; as a moment of carnivalesque topsy-turvydom, they are caught in the physical realm that includes but does not stop at the erotic. Here is the flapper as chum, as fun pal, in marked contrast to the rich, more "dignified" woman Waltham was with at the Ritz (who Betty gets to sock in the jaw so she can rescue her after they are knocked overboard at the end of the film). The ludic possibilities embodied in the

38–41. The eponymous topic of conversation in the Ritz dining room in *It* (38, 41) prompts an exchange of glances between Betty Lou and Waltham (39, 40).

tumbling couple at Coney Island are the real stars of the film: what Bow embodies in her kinetic performance, what bodies—and especially female bodies—can do in order to suspend the social laws in everyday life.

Of course *It* is a fairy tale, a fantasy story in which Betty Lou's female power is ultimately absolute, and she is a salient example of a female trickster whose social practices of romance in everyday life conflate femininity and trickery.[45] The power of the gaze that Bow commands is the result of a fantasy of modern femininity.[46] In the Ritz dining-room scene, as the elite characters discuss Elinor Glyn's latest story, "It," Betty Lou and Waltham exchange a series of flirtatious, desirous, and fascinated gazes, much to the dismay of Waltham's date (figs. 38–41).[47] Here Bow shimmers and shines with erotic energy, and we have no doubt that she tells the truth when she holds up the winning side of the wishbone, fixes that gaze on Waltham, and asserts, "I'm going to get my wish."

Conclusion

As director Cecil B. DeMille commented, modern moviegoers "don't go to the movies to be the leading characters objectively, but subjectively. They go to have their insides Janet Gaynor, insides, not outsides. They want to feel her emotions."[48] DeMille pinpoints the interior, subjective quality of the relationship between spectator and star that is at the very heart of the classical Hollywood cinema that was founded in the silent era. The flapper film offered its spectators the opportunity to identify emotionally with the stars—to have their "insides" Clara Bow, Colleen Moore, and Joan Crawford. But what this exploration of the flapper film suggests is that the connections between insides and outsides, between the emotions and the body, are in flux for women in the Jazz Age. Pondering the kinaesthetic pleasures of intertwined glances and dances gives us a more complex understanding of the cinematic and cultural discourses through which the possibilities of a ludic modern femininity are created.

Notes

This essay has benefited from insightful feedback to earlier versions at the Emerson College Graduate Division's Food for Thought Lecture Series, and at the Society for Cinema Studies, the British Association for American Studies, and the University Film and Video Association conferences. The participants of the National Endowment for the Humanities Summer Seminar on Adorno and Horkheimer's *Dialectic of Enlightenment after Fifty Years* " provided helpful comments as I began to reexamine the relationships between consumerism, modernity, and femininity in the Jazz Age. Thanks also to Brian Haffner, who collaborated on the creative documentary and the first Web version of the flapper project, and to Richard Cownie for support and encouragement.

1. The term "kinaesthetic" combines "kinetics" (the term coined in the early twentieth century for the study of movement and motion) with "aesthetics." See Hillel Schwartz's "Torque: The New Kinaesthetic of the Twentieth Century," in *Incorporations,* ed. Jonathan Crary and Sanford Kwinter (New York: Zone Books, 1992), 70–126.
2. See John Berger et al., *Ways of Seeing* (London: Penguin, 1972), 46–47.
3. Mary Ann Doane, "The Economy of Desire: The Commodity Form in/of the Cinema," in *Movies and Mass Culture,* ed. John Belton (New Brunswick: Rutgers University Press, 1996), 121, 132. Doane argues that what might seem like a contradiction between subject and object in the woman spectator-consumer is not because of the ways the female spectator actively participates in her own oppression and self-commodification. Although this argument has validity, I would like to suggest here that Doane's contention that "The feminine position has come to exemplify the roles of consumer and spectator in their embodiment of a curiously passive desiring subjectivity" does not account for the kinaesthetic power of the flapper's performance.
4. See, for instance, Miriam Hansen, *Babel in Babylon: Spectatorship in American Silent Film* (Cambridge: Harvard University Press, 1991); Lary May, *Screening Out the Past: The Birth of Mass Culture and the Motion Picture Industry* (Chicago: University of Chicago Press, 1980); Charles Eckert, "The Carole Lombard in Macy's Window," in *Movies and Mass Culture,* ed. Belton, 95–118; and Gaylyn Studlar, "The Perils of Pleasure? Fan Magazine Discourse as Women's Commodified Culture in the 1920s," in *Silent Film,* ed. Richard Abel (New Brunswick: Rutgers University Press, 1996), 263–297.
5. Herbert Blumer, *Movies and Conduct* (1933; reprint, New York: Arno Press, 1970), 32. The Payne Fund series of twelve studies of how the movies influence children and adolescents is an interesting yet problematic resource. The questions University of Chicago sociologist Blumer asked high-school and college students (who were categorized by gender, age, race, and school year) focused on how young people impersonate, imitate, daydream, fantasize about, and create "schemes of life" from what they experience in the movies. See also G. Stanley Hall, "Gesture, Mimesis, Types of Temperament, and Movie Pedagogy," *Pedagogical Seminary* 28 (1921): 171–201.
6. Blumer, *Movies and Conduct,* 154.
7. See Lori Landay, *Madcaps, Screwballs, and Con Women: The Female Trickster in American Culture* (Philadelphia: University of Pennsylvania Press, 1998).
8. Studlar, "Perils," 292.
9. A foray into the American Film Institute's catalog provides an overview of the

number of films representing either flappers or the idea of the new woman. In addition to the fifty-nine films listed under the heading "Flapper," there are forty-one titles under the heading "Flirts," twenty under "Women's Rights/Women in Public Office/Politics," thirteen under "Marriage-Companionate/Marriage-Trial," twenty-nine under "Department Stores," and sixty-four under "Jazz Life." Analyzing the per annum data for each subject illuminates a bell-curve distribution across the decade. The flapper, flirts, and jazz life categories peaked in 1924, with women's rights, marriage-companionate/marriage-trial, and department store subjects peaking a little later. The exception is 1928, which shows a resurgence of the flapper category, possibly as a result of cinema's new sound technologies. See Kenneth W. Munden, ed., *The American Film Institute Catalog of Motion Pictures Produced in the United States: Feature Films, 1921-1930* (New York: R. R. Bowker, 1971).

10 Although Mary P. Ryan and Sumiko Higashi, both writing in the 1970s, discuss, respectively, flapper films and flapper stars, neither engages questions of subjectivity in relation to film viewing. See Ryan, "The Projection of a New Womanhood: The Movie Moderns in the 1920's" (1976), reprinted in *Decades of Discontent: The Women's Movement, 1920-1940,* ed. Lois Scharf and Joan M. Jensen (Boston: Northeastern University Press, 1987), 113-130; and Higashi, *Virgins, Vamps, and Flappers: The American Silent Movie Heroine* (Montreal: Eden Press, 1978). In the past decade, feminist historical scholarship on the period has taken up issues crucial to this study, although critical attention to the flapper film per se is noticeably absent. See, for instance, Carolyn Johnston, *Sexual Power: Feminism and the Family in America* (Tuscaloosa: University of Alabama Press, 1992); Pamela S. Haag, "In Search of 'The Real Thing': Ideologies of Love, Modern Romance, and Women's Sexual Subjectivity in the United States, 1920-40," in *American Sexual Politics: Sex, Gender, and Race since the Civil War,* ed. John C. Fout and Maura Shaw Tantillo (Chicago: University of Chicago Press, 1993), 161-191; and John C. Spurlock and Cynthia A. Magistro, *New and Improved: The Transformation of American Women's Emotional Culture* (New York: New York University Press, 1998).

11 Ryan, "Projection," 117.

12 See Landay, *Madcaps, Screwballs, and Con Women,* 67-75.

13 This is the key paradox at the center of feminist discourses of the construction of female subjectivity. This dilemma is explained by Miriam Hansen in *Babel and Babylon:* "How do we account for this seeming paradox, posed by the intersection of history and theory, of, on the one hand, women's increased significance for the film industry as fans and consumer and, on the other, the systematic imposition, on the textual level, of masculine forms of subjectivity, of a patriarchal choreography of vision?" (121). Mary Ann Doane resolves the conundrum of women's agency and subjection in the female consumerist gaze by positing a "curiously passive desiring subjectivity" (Doane, "The Economy of Desire," 132) that reveals the contradiction between woman as subject and object of the commodity form as only apparently contradictory (120). Hansen both accepts and revises Doane's thesis that classical cinema creates a female

spectator who is narcissistic and masochistic, and that consumerist subjectivity is meant to turn women into commodities. By interpreting the filmic and extrafilmic discourse of silent cinema in the transitional period from early to classical cinema (which occurs between 1907 and 1917, and precedes the period of the flapper film), Hansen suggests that if cinema operates as an alternative public sphere (working off Habermas, and Negt and Kluge) then there are conditions of possibility in which people's experiences of film spectatorship would exceed the dominant subject positions and perhaps form "a variety of configurations, often ambiguous and contradictory, in which women not only experienced the misfit of the female spectator in relation to patriarchal positions of subjectivity but also developed imaginative strategies in response to it" (*Babel and Babylon,* 125). In this essay, I build on the insights of Hansen, Doane, and others to argue that in the specific subgenre of silent comedy of the flapper film, the cinema does indeed function as an alternative public sphere and that the experience (in the sense of the term used by Frankfurt School critical theorists, of experience as the ideological mediator of perception) of the female spectator's kinaesthetic response to the flapper film can be seen as what John Berger, in *Ways of Seeing,* describes as women's "ingenuity" in living within the confines of patriarchy.

14 Janet Staiger explores this idea in her essay "The Eyes Are Really the Focus: Photoplay Acting and Film Form and Style," *Wide Angle* 6, 4 (1985): 14–23, and revisits it in her book *Bad Women: Regulating Sexuality in Early American Cinema* (Minneapolis: University of Minnesota Press, 1995).
15 "A Cinema Favorite—Colleen Moore," *Vanity Fair* (September 1927), 60.
16 Noël Carroll, "Notes on the Sight Gag," in *Comedy/Cinema/Theory,* ed. Andrew Horton (Berkeley: University of California Press, 1991), 25.
17 Many of the physical hijinks central to the screwball heroine are established in the flapper films. The sound-film comediennes owe much to the unconventional flappers portrayed in silent film.
18 Henri Bergson, "Laughter" (1900), reprinted in *Comedy,* ed. Wylie Sypher (Baltimore: Johns Hopkins University Press, 1984), 84.
19 See Arthur Koestler, especially "Humor and Wit," in *Encyclopedia Britannica,* 15th ed. (1974), 5–6.
20 Anne Shaw Faulkner, "Does Jazz Put the Sin in Syncopation?" *Ladies' Home Journal,* August 1921, 16, 34.
21 See Elizabeth Kendall, *Where She Danced* (New York: Alfred A. Knopf, 1979), especially 96–98.
22 I discuss some of the connections between the dancing of Baker and West in "Dancing across the Color Line: Film Performances of Josephine Baker and Mae West" unpublished paper presented at the Society for Cinema Studies conference at West Palm Beach, Florida, April 1998.
23 Kendall, *Where She Danced,* 195.
24 Ruth Waterbury, "Manhattan Technique: Certainly It's True That a Chorus Girl Learns a Lot about Acting," *Photoplay,* April 1926, 58.
25 Max Eastman, "Obituary of Isadora Duncan," *Nation,* 28 September 1927, 12.

The Flapper Film

26 Janet Wolff, "Reinstating Corporeality: Feminism and Body Politics," in *Meaning in Motion: New Cultural Studies of Dance,* ed. Jane C. Desmond (Durham: Duke University Press, 1997), 95–96.
27 Susan Manning, "The Female Dancer and the Male Gaze: Feminist Critiques of Early Modern Dance," in *Meaning in Motion,* ed. Desmond, 164.
28 Torque is the tendency for a force to produce rotation around an axis. Schwartz sees an aesthetic based on a spiral or twisting motion around a center point that is expressed in the arc of the Wright brothers' first flight, in the fluid movement that flowed out of the torso in the choreography of Duncan and St. Denis, and in the relationship between the torso and the limbs in motion studies of typing, handwriting, and piano-playing, among other physical activities. I am using the term "kinaesthetics" to encompass some of the mechanistic, geometrical movements and designs of the deco era that I see forming an interesting dialectic with Schwartz's more specific kinaesthetic of torque.
29 Manning, "The Female Dancer," 163.
30 Ibid., 162.
31 In *Bare Knees* (1927), Virginia Lee Corbin's self-conscious—and genre-parodying—performance displayed the sexual politics of the gaze. The film opens by showing only the characters from the knees down (none of which are bare), and focuses repeatedly on former child star Corbin's knees (which indeed are bare) as flapper Billie enters her sister's birthday party in a very short dress, and proceeds to dance the Charleston in spite of (and to spite) the exaggerated disapproving stares of the guests. The musicians even stop playing to keep her from continuing her dance. In a plot device that mocks the attention given to women's legs, and the ridiculous power acsribed to them, Billie's idea for how the women's baseball team can win their game against the men is to dress them in very short shorts. *Bare Knees* is a witty comment on the flapper film. Other noteworthy dances include Louise Brooks in *Love 'Em and Leave 'Em* (1926), Clara Bow's serpentine shimmy in *My Lady of Whims* (1925), and "Laughing Legs" in the Gloria Swanson shop-girl vehicle *Manhandled* (1924).
32 *Our Dancing Daughters* is the first of three films that teamed Crawford and Anita Page (and a third actress in each film); the others are *Our Modern Maidens* (1929) and *Our Blushing Brides* (1930), a talkie.
33 Blumer, *Movies and Conduct,* 183–184.
34 Ibid., 200.
35 Ibid., 42.
36 Ibid., 152.
37 Ibid., 184.
38 Quoted in James Card, *Seductive Cinema: The Art of Silent Film* (New York: Alfred A. Knopf, 1994), 131.
39 Blumer, *Movies and Conduct,* 105.
40 See Landay, *Madcaps,* 84–88.
41 "Clara Bow en Plain Air," *Vanity Fair,* July 1928, 59.

42 Lauren Rabinovitz, "Temptations of Pleasure: Nickelodeons, Amusement Parks, and the Sights of Female Sexuality," *Camera Obscura* 23 (1990): 84.
43 Of course, Coney Island is a site of contested boundaries of class, gender, commodification, and modernization. See John F. Kasson, *Amusing the Million: Coney Island at the Turn of the Century* (New York: Hill and Wang, 1978).
44 Tony Bennett, "A Thousand and One Troubles: Blackpool Pleasure Beach," in *Formations of Pleasure,* eds. Tony Bennett, et al. (London: Routledge, 1983), 147–148.
45 See Landay, *Madcaps,* 92–93.
46 Because so many of the flapper films were written by women scenarists and/or based on women's fiction, and enacted by the flapper actresses who were auteurs of their own personae, the romance stories of *It* and the other films participate in this process of the discursive construction of a specifically female subjectivity through narrative. Both Glyn's story "It" and the film *It* are the kinds of narratives that, according to Pamela Haag, women had to create in order to own their sexuality, to think of themselves as sexual subjects, a process Haag explains is demarcated by class: "If no female naturally possessed a sexually integral self, she could earn—or lose—class status by mastering the artifice of self-invention. By appropriating love and sentiment, the authorizing ideologies of premarital sexual expression, young women cultivated sexual identities. Their self-narrations, both verbal and symbolic, strengthened the attenuated boundary between illicit and legitimate sexuality and might earn them the sexual self-ownership claimed as a general right for men." From "In Search of 'The Real Thing': Ideologies of Love, Modern Romance, and Women's Sexual Subjectivity in the United States, 1920–40," in *American Sexual Politics: Sex, Gender, and Race since the Civil War,* ed. John C. Fout and Maura Shaw Tantillo (Chicago: University of Chicago Press, 1993), 184.
47 Although *It* is based on the ideas in Glyn's *Cosmopolitan* story (February 1927), the film is not an adaptation. Instead, the characters read the magazine, the camera dwells on the cover and the text, and the characters discuss the story. Elinor Glyn makes a cameo appearance in the Ritz dining-room scene, surely a bizarre intersection of the passive, receptive femininity advocated by Glyn in her writing, and the active flapper's modernity represented by Bow. See Landay, *Madcaps,* especially 84–87.
48 Quoted in May, *Screening Out the Past,* 230.

Cultural Inversions **III**

SIOBHAN B. SOMERVILLE

The Queer Career of Jim Crow

Racial and Sexual Transformation in

A Florida Enchantment

During the last two decades, Vitagraph's 1914 film comedy *A Florida Enchantment* has gained a privileged location in critical discussions of lesbian, gay, and transgender film history and representation. The program for the 1989 San Francisco Lesbian and Gay Film Festival, for instance, buoyantly advertises *A Florida Enchantment* as an example of early gay-positive images in film. Recuperating the film for its play with gender and sexuality, the reviewer exclaims over the "many sexual reversals in the astonishing A FLORIDA ENCHANTMENT from 1914.... Its way of toying with gender-specific body gestures remains amazingly witty seventy-five years later."[1] A recent catalog of representations of gay men and lesbians in mainstream cinema lists *A Florida Enchantment* as the first film in its chronology.[2] The late Vito Russo similarly includes it in his pioneering survey of lesbian and gay images in film, *The Celluloid Closet*. His discussion lingers on the actress Edith Storey, who plays the film's central character: "Visually uncanny, especially in her scenes of dapper male attire on a visit to New York, her performance throughout is laced with an insouciance that tempers male arrogance with a secret, barely withheld sensitivity."[3]

It is easy to valorize the sexually transgressive aspects of *A Florida Enchantment,* which at least temporarily overturns the dominant narrative of heterosexual romance. Based on a novel cowritten by Archibald Clavering Gunter and Fergus Redmond, *A Florida Enchantment* depicts the comic transformation of two women into men.[4] Lillian Travers, a white heiress, arrives in Florida with her "mulatto maid" Jane to visit her elderly aunt and fiancé, Fred. During her visit, Lillian purchases a mysterious box that contains magical "sex-change seeds" that originated from a tree in Africa. After a tiff with her fiancé, Lillian swallows one of the magical seeds and begins her transformation into Lawrence (fig. 42). Realizing that, as a proper gentleman, s/he will need a valet rather than a maid, Lillian/Lawrence forces Jane to swallow a seed also. The rest of the film concerns the comedy of errors and confusion that result from the women's dual sex changes (figs. 43 and 44). Through its various levels of masquerade, *A Florida Enchantment* thus provides an unusually sustained and unambiguous display of female homoeroticism and playfully foregrounds the subversive possibilities of "gender trouble."[5] Lillian's name—Travers—itself suggests her association with transvestism and inversion: she literally traverses the boundaries of male and female.

As it receives more and more attention as a "protogay" or transgender film, critical discussions of *A Florida Enchantment* tend to replicate the film's boundless interest in sexuality and gender and to ignore questions of race.[6] Thomas Cripps and Daniel Leab have voiced the only exceptions to this tendency: both have briefly noted *A Florida Enchantment* as an example of early films that portray African Americans through humiliating stereotypes.[7] The "mulatto maid" Jane, for instance, is played in blackface by white actress Ethel Lloyd, performing a racist caricature drawn directly from the minstrel stage. Cripps's and Leab's brief comments point to the importance of thinking about race in *A Florida Enchantment,* yet there is much more to say about the film's processes of racialization. As Stuart Hall has noted, "the play of identity and difference which constructs racism is powered not only by the positioning of blacks as the inferior species but also, and at the same time, by an inexpressible envy and desire."[8] Once we consider the possibility that the film's representation of race might have something to do with its figurations of gender, sexuality, and desire, different questions and readings of *A Florida Enchantment* emerge. As I argue, although *A Florida Enchantment* itself draws little attention to its own systems of racialization, it is important to interrogate its racial logic in order to reveal how the emerging discourse of homosexuality was linked to ideologies of race in the early film industry and American popular culture at large.

In approaching these questions, my analysis moves between textual readings of *A Florida Enchantment* and analyses of its relationship to the early cinema industry, as well as the conflicting cultural meanings of race and sexuality during this period. The translation of *A Florida Enchantment* from novel to film occurred at a crucial moment of transition for the film industry as a whole, as it confronted new questions about its own cultural status. Through the example of *A Florida Enchantment* it is possible to see how questions of race and sexuality were being negotiated and inscribed not only in film images and narratives, but also in the structures of the film industry and in moviegoing practices. Within the historical context of the

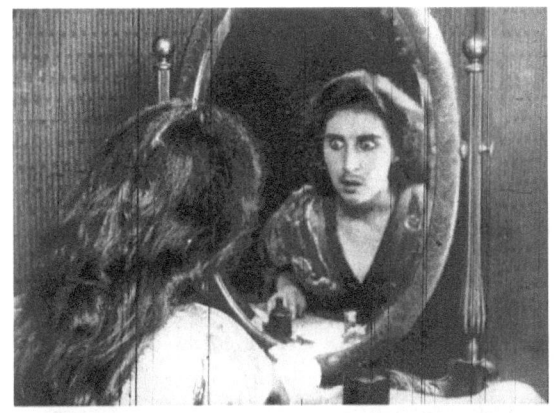

42–44. Top: Lillian Travers (Edith Storey) begins her physical transformation after swallowing a magical sex-change seed. Middle: Lillian (Edith Storey) gazes at herself as Lawrence Talbot, with the approval of Jane (Ethel Lloyd). Bottom: Jane (Ethel Lloyd) is transformed into Jack, much to Lillian's amusement. All from *A Florida Enchantment,* courtesy of the Library of Congress.

emergence of lesbian and gay identities and an increasingly racially segregated culture, the vertiginous comedy of Vitagraph's *A Florida Enchantment* reflected deep cultural anxieties about the slippage of bodies out of their conventional systems of visual representation, both on screen and off.

Vitagraph, Respectability, and the Transformation of Early Cinema

Vitagraph created the film adaptation of *A Florida Enchantment* in the early 1910s, the period of the studio's greatest commercial success, when the nascent film industry in the United States was undergoing a period of transition, in both organization and practice.[9] The period between 1907 and the mid-1910s saw the formation of the Motion Picture Patents Company (MPPC), a trust made up of the most powerful studios at the time, which intended to regulate and control the production, distribution, and exhibition of motion pictures. The MPPC, along with film trade journals, began to respond to increasing public criticism of the morality of the motion picture industry and to align itself with more "respectable" forms of popular entertainment. Film historian Tom Gunning points out that

> MPPC's drive to improve theatres centred on an issue now almost forgotten—fear of the dark. The darkness of the motion picture theatre blackened film's image for the respectable classes. In that darkness, anything could (and perhaps *did*) happen. Crawling with real or imagined "mashers," the darkened theatre was a place a middle-class patron hesitated to enter (unless, of course, he was a masher).[10]

Although he does not discuss the racial implications of his description of middle-class audiences' "fear of the dark" (a subject I have addressed elsewhere),[11] Gunning emphasizes the MPPC's attempts to revise associations of the theater with danger. The motion picture industry took deliberate steps during this period to reform the physical appearance of theaters and to associate them with bourgeois standards of respectability through such accoutrements as less-darkened theaters, improved ventilation, and comfortable chairs.[12]

Related to this new self-consciousness about the cultural status of the motion picture industry was a transformation in film form and content, moving away from the earlier period's exhibition of short films as part of the variety format of vaudeville to longer "feature" films, which were shown in theaters increasingly devoted to film exhibition alone. The production of feature films based on novels became part of a strategy in the movie industry's attempt to appeal to a larger audience based in the white middle class. Reflecting this shift within the movie industry as a whole, in the early 1910s Vitagraph began buying and adapting novels by a number of popular authors, including Gunter (the coauthor of *A Florida Enchantment*), as well as Richard Harding Davis, Arthur Train, and Mary Roberts Rinehart.[13] The studio and exhibitors advertised these films as familiar entertainment to middle-class audiences, capitalizing on the previous success of well-known novels or plays. Vitagraph confidently asserted that such films "will not only draw record crowds, but will bring Higher Class Patronage at Higher Prices."[14] In technical terms, the use of novels and stage drama for screenplays demanded a shift to a different format, increasing in length from one reel to three reels or more. It also required a different conception of the actor's importance to the individual film as commodity. In vaudeville, the development of a middle-class audience had depended in part on attracting "respectable" press attention. One way to receive such attention was for vaudeville shows to recruit leading stars from the legitimate theater (a practice known as the "headliner policy").[15] The motion picture industry followed this successful strategy; by the early 1910s, film companies were recruiting well-known actors from dramatic and vaudeville theaters. In fact, Sidney Drew, who directed and starred in *A Florida Enchantment,* was one such actor who had a respectable career on the legitimate stage and in vaudeville, and who carried his reputation and presumably at least part of his audience into cinema.[16]

Vitagraph's adaptation of *A Florida Enchantment* was shaped by the studio's efforts to maintain its reputation and to expand the class makeup of its audience during this period of transition in the film industry. Vitagraph's own promotional materials demonstrate the importance of unspoken but rigidly enforced sexual and racial ideologies to its public image. One of the studio's promotional profiles, "The Home of the Vitagraph," which appeared in a film-industry trade journal, provided a detailed account of the physical layout of the Vitagraph studio and its personnel. Although the article focused on architecture and furnishings, it also suggested crucial details about how sexual ideologies shaped the studio's practices. In a description of its dressing rooms, the article mentioned that one building was

> entirely for women, thus separating the sheep from the goats. Each dressing room is equipped with hot and cold water, porcelain basins and all conveniences, and there is a well-fitted bath-room, of goodly size, on each floor.

The walls, floors and ceilings are of cement, neatly finished and painted in pleasing designs.[17]

The language used to describe the fixtures emphasizes taste and respectability: the furnishings are "well-fitted," "of goodly size," "neatly finished," and "pleasing." The attention to genteel furnishings suggested that the studio as a whole deferred to respectable ideals of domesticity and femininity. Albert E. Smith, one of the founders of Vitagraph, stated more explicitly that the reputation of his studio was inseparable from that of the actresses he employed. According to historian Lary May, Smith "recalled that formality and full names were essential, for 'this was part of a plan to exert every precaution in favor of our young actresses. While it may be regarded as unusual precaution on our part, we nevertheless ordered all couches removed from the dressing rooms and make-up areas.'"[18] In Smith's view, dissociating his "young actresses" from any suggestion of sexual impropriety was essential for securing a good name for his studio.

While the actresses were safely ensconced in decorous dressing rooms, other women working at Vitagraph had important roles in shaping the representation of the studio. The job of adapting Gunter's *A Florida Enchantment* for the screen went to Marguerite Bertsch, one of the most powerful women working at Vitagraph at the time.[19] Bertsch began directing films in 1916, but was perhaps best known for her important role as head of Vitagraph's scenario department, as well as editor and screenwriter at the Famous Players Film Company. As an established scenarist and director, in 1917 Bertsch published a book titled *How to Write for Moving Pictures: A Manual of Instruction and Information,* a volume that both shaped and reflected the conventions and demands of screenwriting for feature films.[20] In the introduction, Bertsch explained that the aim of her book was to provide readers and potential scriptwriters with the skills "to judge a photoplay so capably that you yourselves could decide fairly on the acceptance or rejection of a manuscript."[21]

In the absence of documents that directly comment on the adaptation of *A Florida Enchantment* for the screen, Bertsch's manual provides some insight into the process of revising the original plot of the 1891 novel. Bertsch clearly advised, for example, that a central requirement of a screenplay was "a wholesome atmosphere" and the avoidance of "vice," crime, and "the dark, unpleasant side of life."[22] Bertsch's emphasis on a "wholesome atmosphere" may have shaped the most significant changes to the plot of *A Florida Enchantment,* including the omission of the novel's treatment of slavery and the erasure of its seeming acceptance of same-sex desire between women. Whereas the film simply explained that the seeds had been discovered as a result of a shipwreck off the coast of Africa, the original novel by Gunter and Redmond instead included an extended subplot narrating the discovery of the sex-change seeds "on an excursion after both white and black ivory" (the latter being slang for a cargo of slaves).[23] Not only does the slave trader use violence to extract the seeds from their African context, but he also undergoes a sexual transformation himself and becomes smitten with desire for one of his fellow (male) crew members. Likewise, the film avoided using the novel's ending, which invoked the conventional narrative resolution of romantic comedy—marriage—but with a twist: the novel's happy ending is the marriage of Bessie to Lawrence, the post-sex-change version of her friend Lillian. In the last scene of the novel the newlyweds set sail for their honeymoon and their future: "Lawrence Talbot, who will be a man forever, and his bride, Bessie, who will still remain to him forever a woman, and a joy."[24] Such explicit references to the slave trade and same-sex eroticism may have alarmed Bertsch, who was mindful of securing an image of genteel respectability for Vitagraph. In a chapter on the "power of mental suggestion" in *How to Write for Moving Pictures,* Bertsch wrote that

> If we really care for those we serve [the audience], it . . . would be impossible . . . to write anything that might stir up in them vulgar feelings or sexual thought, for such are conveyed by the attitude of the author toward his subject, rather than by the story itself, and a mind that thinks purely, radiates purity by mental suggestion.[25]

Through the rhetoric of moral purity and self-regulation, Bertsch aligned herself and the film industry with agents of social reform, attempting to reverse the public's previous association of cinema with corruption and sexual danger.

Although Bertsch did not mention racial conflict, race played a vital part in the construction of the studio's origins, legacy, and employment practices. Reflecting the pervasiveness of racial segregation in the culture at large, like other motion picture companies, Vitagraph seems to have hired predominantly (if not only) white employees. Its founders, J. Stuart Blackton and Albert E. Smith, seem to have been fascinated with racialized performance, having participated themselves in vaudeville acts. Some of Vitagraph's earliest films were short animated subjects that portrayed racist caricatures, including one titled *Cohen and Coon,* in which Blackton "writes Cohen and Coon on a board, then proceeds to change Cohen into a stereotype Jew and Coon into a stereotype Negro."[26] By confounding Jewishness and blackness, this routine enacted the ways in which Vitagraph would later position itself in relation to the rest of the film industry. After the studio's heyday had passed, an article detailing its history explicitly (and in disturbingly glowing terms) characterized Vitagraph's success as a product of imperialist ideals. "Small England grew into the vast British Empire because of the pioneering impulse of the Anglo-Saxon race," wrote William Basil Courtney, "and thus Vitagraph, the only one of the original motion picture companies that was founded entirely by Anglo-Saxons, has ventured first toward every farflung screen frontier."[27] Courtney's pointed references to the "Anglo-Saxon" origins of Vitagraph carry specific anti-Semitic implications: by 1925, when Courtney wrote this article, power in the Hollywood industry had been consolidated within eight major studios, with predominantly Jewish management.[28] While Courtney's characterization of the studio may have had as much to do with the writer's own racism and anti-Semitism as with the studio's actual practices, Vitagraph does seem to have been a predominantly, if not exclusively, white operation.

Cross-Dressing, Inversion, and Lesbian Identity

The twenty-three years that intervened between the novel and the film versions of *A Florida Enchantment* saw an extended and increasingly intensified struggle among competing cultural discourses over the meanings of erotic relationships between women. As a number of historians have shown, gender ambiguity became increasingly interpreted as and conflated with "abnormal" sexual practices.[29] By 1914, the figure of the invert — understood as a man's soul trapped in a woman's body or vice versa — had begun to gain a more prominent place in public consciousness. In her study of female impersonators at the turn of the century, historian Sharon Ullman has pointed out that stage performances of cross-dressing became increasingly associated with homosexuality during this period. Countering the view that the stigmatization of cross-dressing occurred later in the 1930s, Ullman's research "indicates that such stigmatization was widespread by 1913," and that it is evident as early as 1906.[30] While Ullman's research focuses on female impersonators (men performing as women), she notes that for male impersonators (women performing as men) "questions of sexual deviancy did arise, [and] other issues not present in female impersonation appear as well — most particularly concerns over public politics and the relationship between . . . male impersonation and the highly contentious suffrage movement."[31]

In *A Florida Enchantment,* Edith Storey's depiction of Lawrence, the male version of Lillian, seems to embody contemporary constructions of the sexual invert. What arouses suspicion, as well as much of the film's humor, is her masculine behavior while she is dressed as a woman.[32] After she first eats the magical seeds, she rebuffs her fiancé and instead flirts aggressively with her friend Bessie and a local young widow, while her aunt and Fred look on worriedly. Later, Lillian/Lawrence smokes cigars and flexes her biceps in front of the befuddled Fred. While the film represents Lillian's masculine performance almost indulgently, it turns much more anxious when Fred and Jane undergo their gender transformations. Toward the end of the film, Fred eats a seed and performs a grotesque caricature of a woman. Whereas Lillian/Lawrence is represented as delightful to many of the characters in the film, Fred's transformation elicits panic. A crowd chases him to the ocean and he nearly drowns. Similarly, Jane/Jack's advances toward another "black" woman become so threatening that the town constable must intervene. Clearly, cultural constructions of gender and race shaped the perceived threat of cross-dressing. A young, wealthy white female character like Lillian had more license for gender fluidity than a white male character like Fred or a (supposedly) African American maidservant like Jane.

Offscreen portrayals of actress Edith Storey in the popular press also tended to indulge her seemingly instinctive talent for male impersonation. A promotional piece for *A Florida Enchantment* asserted that "In male attire, Edith Storey is as great a male impersonator as Vesta Tilly [sic]."[33] Indeed, Storey herself apparently relished these roles. In a 1914 interview, Storey claimed that " 'When it is necessary for me to play male characters, I am always careful to make them just as masculine as possible. Your audience, really looking through the keyhole, is so often offended by the obvious disguise of many girls who try to play male parts; and it therefore sees the artificiality that pervades the whole portrayal.' "[34] Storey's success at male impersonation was reinforced by numerous profiles in which she was described as an adventurous, tough tomboy affectionately known as "Billy." She recalled playing cowboys in her early roles: "At that time my muscles were too hard to be easily bruised even from the severest bumps."[35] A few years after *A Florida Enchantment* was made, Storey revealed that she was also sympathetic to contemporary feminist challenges to gender norms. When asked if she wanted to get married, she responded,

> "Only fools say 'yes' or 'no' to that question.... I'll say this: marriage may be a pastime for men, but for a woman it's always a business if she makes a

success of it.... I have never wished to marry. I don't wish to marry now.... When I'm working I'm thinking situation, studying character, all my hours away from the studio. I might forget to get dinner, and if my husband asked me why, I'd probably bite him."³⁶

Storey's response, however tongue-in-cheek, suggested that her male impersonation was in fact linked to a refusal to adhere to normative constructions of heterosexual femininity. (Indeed, the rest of her life bore out this refusal: Storey never married.)

Given the growing pathologization of women who visibly transgressed cultural standards of proper white femininity, one might have expected the film version of *A Florida Enchantment* to meet with outrage in 1914. Yet contemporary reviews of Vitagraph's *A Florida Enchantment* were lukewarm, most registering nothing remarkable about the film, and a few responding with contempt toward the transvestite performances. Typical was a response appearing in the *New York Dramatic Mirror* that called the film "satisfactory Summer entertainment.... The direction is capable and photography good."³⁷ One of the most negative reviews appeared in *Variety*, which described the film as "a weary, dreary, listless collection of foolish things."³⁸ Some of this reviewer's irritation suggested a negative response to the lesbian possibilities of the story. "The 'fantasy' is of a young woman who [swallowed] a seed and [became] a man, and not so much a man in this instance as just mannish," the reviewer explained. "To make it 'funnier,' she gave a seed to her colored maid, and the maid became mannish.'"³⁹ The review's contemptuous invocation of "mannish" placed Lillian and Jane well within contemporary medical and popular constructions of the invert.⁴⁰

Although the critical response included such recognition of the lesbian meanings of gender play in *A Florida Enchantment,* the generally muted responses to the film were most likely the result of Vitagraph's attempts to contain such meanings within the realm of fantasy. Instead of ending with the marriage of Lawrence and Bessie, as Gunter and Redmond's novel had done, the film relied on a stock dream device to dissolve this resolution. As the narrative accelerates into a panicky chase scene, it cuts to a shot of Lillian fast asleep in her aunt's drawing room. Startled, Lillian wakes up and looks at the seeds, the note, and the box. When she sees the vial intact with the seeds inside, she sighs, relieved to discover that the whole story of her gender transformation has been only a dream. In the final shot of the film, Fred returns and embraces Lillian, diffusing the previous moments of panic with an affectionate laugh.

The Queer Career of Jim Crow

The movie's dream device resolves the story as it dissolves the sexual ambiguities: it neutralizes Lillian's sex change by relegating it to the realm of fantasy. Further, the dream device restores the characters to their original identities and seals the story with the final shot of the happily engaged "natural" female and male couple, Lillian and Fred. Thus, although most of the film gets its erotic charge from the representation of same-sex desire, the revised ending contains that eroticism within a dream. Homosexual desire and gender confusion are figured as a nightmare, albeit a giddy one, while white heterosexuality becomes the naturalized and reassuring happy ending of this comedy.

Blackface and Racialization in Early Cinema

While Vitagraph had to negotiate the emerging cultural recognition and pathologization of lesbians, it was also engaged in positioning itself in relation to ideologies of race and conventions of racialized performance, particularly blackface minstrelsy.[41] Gunter and Redmond's novel had drawn heavily on the tradition of minstrelsy with its blackface stereotypes, particularly in its portrayal of Jane. After Jane's transformation into Jack, for example, the novel invokes an unambiguously racist portrait: "[Jane] is now a headstrong, wild and harum-scarum darky boy, with that peculiar addition called down South 'nigger-brains,' at this time peculiarly dangerous to [Lillian] from its idiotic logic and extraordinary syllogisms."[42] To complete this tableau from blackface minstrelsy, the scene also included the cook Dinah, described as "a darky woman of wondrous potency" and "the nucleus of all domestic bliss."[43] Here again Gunter and Redmond borrowed the stock figures of Jim Crow and Mammy straight from the minstrel stage, perhaps in order to capitalize on stereotypes that had already been a commercial success. In a stage version of *A Florida Enchantment* performed in 1896, casting choices also made explicit the ways in which the character Jane embodied the conventions of the minstrel stage. The stage role of Jane was played by Dan Collyer, a veteran blackface actor from vaudeville.[44] This decision directly linked the play to blackface minstrelsy, in which the combination of blackface and drag was a familiar practice for white male performers, beginning in the 1840s with the low-comedy "wench" role.[45] White women rarely appeared in early blackface minstrel shows, and when all-female minstrel shows later developed, they apparently did not typically wear blackface.[46]

While the stage version of *A Florida Enchantment* drew on minstrel traditions by casting the white actor Dan Collyer to play Jane, Vitagraph took a significantly different approach in the 1914 film, by casting Ethel Lloyd, a white actress, to play this part in blackface. White actresses did perform occasionally in either blackface *or* drag, but the combination of blackface *and* drag was anomalous for white actresses during this period, according to existing conventions not only of cinema but also of the minstrel, burlesque, and vaudeville stages.[47] Although it apparently broke with convention, the film, in fact, did not draw much attention to Jane's supposed blackness (or to Lillian's whiteness, for that matter), in comparison with its self-conscious interest in both characters' sexual transformations. Nor did reviewers apparently take much notice of Ethel Lloyd's performance in blackface and drag. The apparent lack of controversy about the character Jane is, I suggest, evidence of a transformation not only in technical uses and conventions of blackface, but also in the cultural possibilities for racialized performance.

In order to understand why Lloyd's performance in *A Florida Enchantment* did not apparently draw attention to itself despite its break with conventions, it is useful to place it within a larger context of the uses of blackface in film. Some early blackface roles in film directly continued traditions developed in the nineteenth-century minstrel show. Thomas Edison, for instance, used blackface minstrel acts in *The Edison Minstrels, Minstrels Battling in a Room,* and *Sambo and Jemima* (c. 1897–1900), early test films in his experiments with synchronizing sound-on-cylinders with film.[48] These blackface performances made a spectacle of racial difference: audiences and performers alike (who for the most part were white and male, though there were occasional exceptions) played out sexual, racial, and class anxieties through theatrical exaggeration. In this way, they participated in what Tom Gunning has called "the cinema of attractions," the tendency of the earliest films to privilege theatrical display over narrative absorption.[49]

Yet slightly later, blackface began to function in an entirely different way in cinema owing to a combination of changes both within the film industry and within American culture at large. As discussed above, one effect of the film industry's transition between 1907 and 1913 was the shift toward the feature film as the dominant genre. In contrast to the earlier "cinema of attractions," as Gunning has noted, this period saw the "narrativization of the cinema, culminating in the appearance of feature films which radically revised the variety format" and realigned the cinema with the legitimate theater.[50] Importantly, this shift coincided with a revision of the conventions of blackface: blackface characters and performances now became subordinated to a narrative rather than standing alone as spectacularized attractions. Expanding on the comic and sentimentalized stereotypes developed in minstrelsy and vaudeville, the film industry now incorporated blackface characters into dramatic film roles based on literary sources. As racial segregation became increasingly institutionalized, the use of black makeup became a way to maintain all-white acting companies while still portraying African Americans on film. D. W. Griffith, the director of *The Birth of a Nation,* for instance, is reported to have forbidden "any 'black blood' among the players who might have to touch white actresses. Those actors were always whites in blackface."[51] According to Cripps, "as late as the mid-1920s major Negro roles went to white men in blackface. Not until after 1925 would a small cadre of Los Angeles Negroes replace the old white actors."[52] Although blackface minstrel performances and their counterparts in vaudeville continued to be represented directly in films such as *The Jazz Singer* with Al Jolson, ironically many dramatic films transformed "blacking up" into a standard method of portraying racial difference on film while maintaining actual practices of racial segregation.

Blackface was transformed from theatrical spectacle, then, to supposedly naturalistic makeup. The actor and the film did everything possible to make audiences forget that they were watching a racial impersonation. In effect, where minstrel performers had used blackface in order to produce exaggerated and comic stereotypes of African Americans, the goal of many white movie actors in blackface was to "pass," to act "black" in a mode believable to white audiences. The seeming authenticity of blackface performances on film depended on white audiences' and actors' assumption that race was a transparent visual sign. The naturalization of blackface on film was significantly related to the increasingly naturalized structures of racial segregation within American culture at large.[53] Ethel Lloyd's portrayal of Jane in *A Florida Enchantment* attempted to achieve in part this naturalistic effect in blackface. Based on its faith that the audience would accept Lloyd's performance as an African American character, the film constructed a division between "black" and "white" through the seemingly parallel narratives of Lillian and Jane. Lillian's manly swagger and sexual interest in Bessie is mirrored by Jane's aggressiveness and desire for Malvina, another household servant (also played in blackface by a white actress). During the scenes at the farewell ball, the film also posits a comparison between Lillian and Jane through parallel editing, in which scenes of Lillian stealing Bessie away from her date for a dance are intercut with scenes of Jane fighting over Malvina with Gus Duncan.

The parallelism between Lillian and Jane, however, ultimately breaks down. Although both women swallow the seeds and become men, Lillian does so voluntarily, whereas Jane does so under duress, both physical and economic. Lillian declares that, as a gentleman, she will need a valet instead of a maid, and, in one of the most disturbing moments in the film, she traps Jane and physically forces her to eat one of the seeds. Once the transformation is complete, the constructions of each character's masculinity are anything but parallel. While Lawrence swaggers, he nevertheless remains within genteel codes of behavior. Jack, however, immediately becomes uncontrollable on transformation; to the white characters, his behavior is so threatening that Lillian/Lawrence eventually knocks Jane/Jack unconscious with chloroform. The film thus calls on asymmetrical contemporary cultural constructions of black and white masculinity, reinforcing stereotypes of the aggressive black male and seeming to justify drastic measures to control it.[54] Racialized gender stereotypes circumscribe their subsequent pursuits of women: Lillian is successful at courtship with Bessie, whereas Jane repeatedly subjects Malvina to unwanted sexual advances.

While the film constructs an illusion of parallel stories for Lillian and Jane, it insists, too, that these narratives remain separate. Even though we see many scenes of Lillian and Jane changing clothes together and laughing over their secret, the film denies the possibility that Lillian and Jane (or "inverts," more generally) might be sexually interested in one another. They are portrayed as buddies who share a wink, but who never gaze sexually at each other. Nor does the film admit the possibility that desire might cross racialized class divisions. According to the film's logic, it seems unthinkable that the white "gentleman" Lawrence might pursue the "mulatto" servant Malvina or that Jack might desire the white Bessie. While the film seems to embrace, at least temporarily, ambiguities of gender and sexuality, it rigorously contains them within supposedly stable racial and class boundaries. If the film hints at homosexuality, it does so by denying the possibility of interracial desire.

It is possible, however, to see that the segregationist tactics of Vitagraph's *A Florida Enchantment* had the potential to backfire and could destabilize rather than fix racial difference. By including the practice of blackface in a narrative that self-consciously displayed cross-dressing and gender transformation, the film perhaps inadvertently suggested even as it repressed an analogy between race and gender. If the film displayed the pleasures and anxieties of gender transformation, perhaps race, too, could be imagined as more malleable than dominant ideologies of racial difference would suggest. Although the film attempted to construct a stable division between black and white, the very use of blackface and its proximity to drag threatened to break down that division.

Importantly, the film's farcical treatment of gender play depended on the audience's awareness of the difference between bodies on- and offscreen: the audience knew it was watching cross-dressed female actors, but admitted that they were men within the logic of the movie. Yet the film could not afford this kind of epistemological and representational play around its depiction of race and racial difference. While it pointed up and played on the discrepancies between what audiences knew about the actors' gender and their contradictory appearance onscreen, it did not engage in the same kind of play around race. Ethel Lloyd's "real" racial identity, her whiteness, was paradoxically *visible* enough, perhaps unconsciously, to assuage the racial anxieties of a segregated white audience; at the same time, the discrepancy between her "black" appearance onscreen and her "white" identity offscreen had to remain *invisible* to support the film's own insistence on racial separation.

Vitagraph's film adaptation of *A Florida Enchantment* reveals a number of pressure points in the shifting cultural understandings of race and sexuality between 1891 and 1914 in the United States. While it offered a narrative that spoke comically to cultural anxieties about white women's increasing independence and visibility in public, *A Florida Enchantment* also, perhaps inadvertently, raised the unspoken possibility of racial mutability. In order to salvage the comic plot of gender transformation, the studio used various strategies to neutralize the story's racial meanings. By downplaying race and racial narratives, the film helped white middle-class audiences to both forget and feel secure in their own positions within segregated social structures. These relations were not abstractions, of course, but were in fact played out and continually renegotiated in the very space in which a movie like *A Florida Enchantment* would be viewed. Segregated movie theaters encouraged white viewers to forget about racial difference, while reminding African American audiences with a vengeance that they had only limited access to dominant positions of spectatorship. By subordinating the racial impersonation of Ethel Lloyd to the device of sex change, the film naturalized blackface performance: it thus reaffirmed the invisibility of actual African American bodies both on screen and off, replicating and simultaneously masking the cultural architecture of racial segregation. The film reassured white audiences that the potential instability of race would remain invisible, even as it spoke to the comic possibilities of gender transformation. For moviegoers in 1914, the enchantment of this film lay in its ability to help audiences forget that the visible upheavals in cultural meanings of gender and sexuality coincided with a corresponding racial narrative, one that remained anchored in imperialism, racial violence, and segregation.

Notes

1 Scott Simon, "Sex Change and Cross-Dressing in the Early Silent Film" (program, San Francisco International Lesbian and Gay Film Festival, 16–25 June 1989), 13.
2 James Robert Parish, *Gays and Lesbians in Mainstream Cinema: Plots, Critiques, Casts, and Credits for 272 Theatrical and Made-for-Television Hollywood Releases* (Jefferson, N.C.: McFarland and Company, 1993), viii.
3 Vito Russo, *The Celluloid Closet: Homosexuality in the Movies* (New York: Harper and Row, 1981), 11–13.
4 Archibald Clavering Gunter and Fergus Redmond, *A Florida Enchantment* (New York: Hurst and Company, 1891).
5 I borrow this phrase from Judith Butler, *Gender Trouble: Feminism and the Subversion of Identity* (New York: Routledge, 1990), a key text in discussions of gender and performativity.
6 See, for example, R. Bruce Brasell, "A Seed for Change: The Engenderment of *A Florida Enchantment*," *Cinema Journal* 36, 4 (summer 1997): 3–21.
7 See Thomas Cripps, *Slow Fade to Black: The Negro in American Film, 1900–1942* (New York: Oxford University Press, 1977), 24; and Daniel J. Leab, *From Sambo to Superspade: The Black Experience in Motion Pictures* (Boston: Houghton Mifflin, 1975), 16.
8 Stuart Hall, "New Ethnicities," in *Black Film/British Cinema*, ed. Kobena Mercer (London: Institute of Contemporary Arts, 1988), 27.
9 My summary of this transition period relies on recent work by film historians, including Eileen Bowser, *The Transformation of Cinema* (New York: Scribner, 1990); David Bordwell, Janet Staiger, and Kristin Thompson, *The Classical Hollywood Cinema: Film Style and Mode of Production to 1960* (New York: Columbia University Press, 1985); and William Uricchio and Roberta E. Pearson, *Reframing Culture: The Case of the Vitagraph Quality Films* (Princeton: Princeton University Press, 1993). On Vitagraph's success, see Uricchio and Pearson, *Reframing Culture;* Anthony Slide, *The Big V: A History of the Vitagraph Company* (Metuchen, N.J.: Scarecrow Press, 1976); Henry Jenkins, *What Made Pistachio Nuts? Early Sound Comedy and the Vaudeville Aesthetic* (New York: Columbia University Press, 1992); and Peter Kramer, "Vitagraph, Slapstick, and Early Cinema," *Screen* 29, 2 (spring 1988): 9–104.
10 Tom Gunning, "Weaving a Narrative: Style and Economic Background in Griffith's Biograph Films," in *Early Cinema: Space, Frame, Narrative*, ed. Thomas Elsaesser (London: British Film Institute, 1990), 338–339. Original emphasis.

11 See Siobhan B. Somerville, *Queering the Color Line: Race and the Invention of Homosexuality in American Culture* (Durham: Duke University Press, 2000), 67–70.
12 Gunning, "Weaving a Narrative," 338–339.
13 Slide, *The Big V,* 8. One tactic in this attempt to attract middle-class audiences was Vitagraph's production of "quality films," which were based on biblical stories and literature by authors such as Shakespeare and Dante. For a full discussion of these films, see Uricchio and Pearson, *Reframing Culture.*
14 Cripps, *Slow Fade to Black,* 118.
15 Jenkins, *What Made Pistachio Nuts?,* 81.
16 See "Sidney Drew One of First Actors of Established Reputation to Quit Legitimate Stage for Vaudeville," 16 September 1912, Sidney Drew scrapbook, series 2, volume 135, Robinson Locke Collection, Billy Rose Theatre Collection, New York Public Library. A well-known instance of this practice was the formation of Famous Players in Famous Plays by Adolph Zukor, Jesse Lasky, and Cecil B. DeMille in 1914, which brought such famous stage actors as Sarah Bernhardt, Douglas Fairbanks, and Mary Pickford to film. See Lary May, *Screening Out the Past: The Birth of Mass Culture and the Motion Picture Industry* (New York: Oxford University Press, 1980), 175–176.
17 F. H. Richardson, "The Home of the Vitagraph," *Moving Picture World,* 24 January 1914, 401–402.
18 Quoted in May, *Screening Out the Past,* 186.
19 Einar Lauritzen and Gunnar Lundquist, eds., *American Film Index, 1908–1915* (Stockholm: Film-Index, 1976).
20 Marguerite Bertsch, *How to Write for Moving Pictures: A Manual of Instruction and Information* (New York: George H. Doran, 1917).
21 Ibid., 13.
22 Ibid., 20.
23 Gunter and Redmond, *A Florida Enchantment,* 51.
24 Ibid., 260.
25 Bertsch, *How to Write for Moving Pictures,* 267.
26 Slide, *The Big V,* 17. This characterization of the slippage between popular visual representations of Jews and African Americans is an early instance of a phenomenon discussed expertly and at length by Michael Rogin in *Blackface, White Noise: Jewish Immigrants and the Hollywood Melting Pot* (Berkeley: University of California Press, 1995).
27 William Basil Courtney, "History of Vitagraph," *Motion Picture News,* 7 February 1925, 342c.
28 See May, *Screening Out the Past,* 167–199, 253. In fact, 1925 was the very year in which Warner Brothers would buy out Vitagraph studios.
29 See, for example, George Chauncey, "From Sexual Inversion to Homosexuality: Medicine and the Changing Conceptualization of Female Deviance," *Salmagundi* 58–59 (1982): 114–146; and Lisa Duggan, "The Trials of Alice Mitchell: Sensationalism, Sexology, and the Lesbian Subject in Turn-of-the-Century America," *Signs* 18, 4 (summer 1993): 791–814.

30 Sharon Ullman, " 'The Twentieth Century Way': Female Impersonation and Sexual Practice in Turn-of-the-Century America," *Journal of the History of Sexuality* 5, 4 (1995): 578 n. 9, 587.
31 Ibid., 577 n. 8. On the ideological uses of a negative portrayal of lesbians, see Chauncey, "From Sexual Inversion to Homosexuality"; and Christina Simmons, "Companionate Marriage and the Lesbian Threat," *Frontiers* 4 (1979): 54–59.
32 Whether or not one sees Lillian as a lesbian, one must take into account the question of Bessie's desire: how do we make sense of this character's unambiguous delight in being courted by Lillian, whom she thinks is still a woman? Dominant cultural constructions of lesbian identity since the late nineteenth century have consistently erased the sexual desire of feminine women for other women, whether masculine or feminine. Bessie fully returns the desire that Lillian/Lawrence (while dressed as a woman) expresses toward her: she dances with her at the ball, kisses Lillian on the lips, and tries to convince Lillian that they should sleep in the same bed. While no character in the film marks Bessie's behavior as abnormal, nevertheless her desire for Lillian is unmistakable.
33 Vitagraph Company of America, *Vitagraph Bulletin of Life Portrayals* 4 (1–30 September 1914): 6.
34 Justus Dickinson, "Putting One's Best Face Forward," *Green Book Magazine,* December 1914, 1016.
35 Edith Storey, "My Theories of Physical Culture," *Physical Culture,* September 1916, 76. See also "Queen of the Wild West Films," *St. Louis Globe Democrat,* 14 December 1913, series 2 (Stevens-Stuart), Robinson Locke Collection, New York Public Library.
36 Julian Johnson, "The Story of Storey," *Photoplay,* January 1920, 114.
37 "A Florida Enchantment," *New York Dramatic Mirror,* 19 August 1914, 26.
38 Sime, "A Florida Enchantment," *Variety,* 14 August 1914, 21.
39 Ibid., 22.
40 On constructions of the "mannish" lesbian, see Esther Newton, "The Mythic Mannish Lesbian: Radclyffe Hall and the New Woman," *Signs* 9, 4 (summer 1984): 557–575.
41 In a longer version of this article, I detail how *A Florida Enchantment* makes apparent Vitagraph's negotiation of its relationship to a number of older forms of popular entertainment, including the dime museum, burlesque, and minstrelsy. See Somerville, *Queering the Color Line,* 39–76.
42 Gunter and Redmond, *A Florida Enchantment,* 151.
43 Ibid.
44 In 1885, when the famous team of Edward Harrigan and Tony Hart dissolved, Collyer replaced Hart, regularly appearing in blackface and drag roles. See William Torbert Leonard, *Masquerade in Black* (Metuchen, N.J.: Scarecrow Press, 1986), 258, 285. Robert Toll in *On with the Show: The First Century of Show Business in America* (New York: Oxford University Press, 1976) includes

an illustration of Collyer in blackface and drag as "Clara" in Edward Harrigan's *McNooney's Visit* (188).

45 For a discussion of the interplay of blackface and drag on the minstrel stage, see Eric Lott, *Love and Theft: Blackface Minstrelsy and the American Working Class* (New York: Oxford University Press, 1993), 159–168.

46 Robert C. Allen, *Horrible Prettiness: Burlesque and American Culture* (Chapel Hill: University of North Carolina Press, 1991), 165, 311 n. 10.

47 For a more complete discussion of these conventions, see Somerville, *Queering the Color Line*, 61–62.

48 Cripps, *Slow Fade to Black*, 12, 393 n. 16.

49 Tom Gunning, "The Cinema of Attractions: Early Film, Its Spectator, and the Avant-Garde," *Wide Angle* 8, 3–4 (1986): 63–70; reprinted in *Early Cinema*, ed. Elsaesser, 56–62.

50 Ibid., 60.

51 May, *Screening Out the Past*, 83. Gender seems to have circumscribed filmic conventions for the use of blackface as well. Although this area needs further research, it is suggestive that in Leonard's list of 145 white actors and actresses who appeared in blackface in film, only one of the blackface roles was also a cross-dressed performance (*Masquerade in Black*, 371). The actor was Nick Cogley, who played Aunt Mandy in *Boys Will Be Boys* (1921).

52 Cripps, *Slow Fade to Black*, 118.

53 The *Plessy v. Ferguson* Supreme Court ruling of 1896, for instance, formally and explicitly legitimated Jim Crow segregation through its logic of separate but equal accommodations.

54 For a discussion of early-twentieth-century stereotypes of black masculinity, see Jacquelyn Dowd Hall, *Revolt against Chivalry: Jessie Daniel Ames and the Women's Campaign against Chivalry* (New York: Columbia University Press, 1979).

SHELLEY STAMP

Taking Precautions, or Regulating Early Birth-Control Films

Late in 1916 commentators noticed that birth control had become a "popular subject" of feature films, eclipsing even white slavery as a fashionable theme for "weighty picture dramas."[1] *Where Are My Children?, Birth Control, The Hand That Rocks the Cradle,* and a host of lesser-known titles all tackled contraception in 1916 and 1917, just as Margaret Sanger, the era's most celebrated birth-control advocate, stepped-up her campaign for "voluntary motherhood." Released even as Sanger's legal battle was unfolding, the films drew explicitly on her headline-generating activism. *Where Are My Children?* (1916) featured the trial of a doctor accused of illegally circulating information on contraception in a story that one reviewer found "plainly indicative of the Margaret Sanger case."[2] *The Hand That Rocks the Cradle* (1917) alluded even more directly to the activist's struggle, with director and screenwriter Lois Weber playing a woman imprisoned for disseminating instructions on family planning; and Sanger herself appeared in *Birth Control* (1917), guiding viewers through a series of arguments favoring legal contraception illustrated with incidents from her own storied career. Something of cinema's newfound stature can be seen in the fact that Weber, one of the most respected filmmakers of the day, brought her reputation for high-quality feature films to this contentious issue, and that Sanger, one of the era's leading radicals, turned to motion pictures to promote her cause, like many other feminists of her generation.[3] Early birth-control films thus did much more than simply capitalize on a topical, even sensational, issue; they asserted cinema's claim to participate in national debates on an equal footing with newspapers, magazines, and other forms of political commentary. And they did so at a key historical juncture: just one year earlier the U.S. Supreme Court had denied motion pictures protection under the First Amendment, paving the way for much stricter regulation.

At a time when disseminating contraceptive advice remained a felony and when motion pictures were no longer protected by guarantees of free speech, birth-control films like *Where Are My Children?, Birth Control,* and *The Hand That Rocks the Cradle* encountered significant problems with censorship and regulation. Like the white-slave films released a few years earlier, contraceptive pictures complicated the film industry's desire for "quality" features on subjects of topical and social import by introducing sexuality into the equation, for reproductive politics engaged not only questions of female sexuality, but sexuality outside marriage and motherhood, issues that dominated and divided American popular discourse throughout these years. On what grounds might a popular medium like the cinema be permitted to depict a topic that was itself still illegal? Could the industry's desire for quality features on weighty subjects encompass questions of sexuality and reproduction? And did motion pictures have a public role comparable to print media in the wake of the Supreme Court's landmark decision?

Debates over motion picture regulation echoed larger questions in the birth-control movement, for Sanger's fight was not simply over reproductive freedom itself, but over more basic rights to disseminate family-planning advice and speak freely on the topic. Through her publication *The Woman Rebel,* Sanger actively challenged Comstock laws that prohibited the circulation of contraceptive knowledge. After several issues advocating family planning in early 1914, Sanger was indicted for violating postal obscenity laws in August. Fleeing to England to avoid prosecution, Sanger authorized her supporters to distribute one hundred thousand copies of her pamphlet on "Family Limitation," a crime for which her husband, William Sanger, was arrested and imprisoned the next year. She returned to the United States late in 1915, then embarked on a national speaking tour during most of 1916, eventually settling in New York, where she opened the nation's first contraceptive clinic in the Brownsville section of Brooklyn that October. Police raided the clinic and arrested Sanger after only nine days of operation, and the activist served a thirty-day prison sentence for illegally distributing information on contraceptive methods.[4] Even before the most well-known birth-control films appeared, commentators linked the suppression of family-planning information to contemporaneous debates about motion picture regulation, noting the inevitable complexities of censorship in a civil society. *Survey,* one of the leading Progressive journals, tied William Sanger's 1915 arrest to the controversy swirling around the National Board of Censorship's decision to pass *The Birth of a Nation* earlier that year.[5] Ironically, *Survey* noted, Progressives were calling for an end to prohibitions governing contraceptive education, while demanding the suppression of D. W. Griffith's racist film.

Indeed, in the wake of the Supreme Court decision the Board of Censorship found itself under increasing pressure to define its mandate. Formed in 1909 through an alliance between film-industry leaders and the People's Institute, the board was designed to prove that the motion picture business could regulate itself without the need for government intervention. Though its influence quickly grew—by the early 1910s it was previewing up to 85 percent of the country's film output—it had no legal authority. As a result, state and municipal agencies sought to enforce stricter forms of motion picture regulation. The city of Chicago had formed a police censorship board in 1907 and several states followed suit, explicitly challenging the authority of the national board: Pennsylvania approved motion picture censorship in 1911, followed by Ohio and Kansas in 1913, and in early 1914 legislation proposing a federal motion picture commission was introduced in the House of Representatives.[6] Legal challenges to state censorship failed in 1915 when the U.S. Supreme Court deemed motion pictures a form of commerce not covered by First Amendment guarantees of free speech and therefore subject to regulation in a suit stemming from the state of Ohio's attempt to limit exhibition of *The Birth of a Nation*.[7] As Lee Grieveson has demonstrated, many early legal decisions involving film regulation turned on epistemological definitions of the new medium, particularly arguments about whether it ought to be considered an arm of the "free press" and therefore guaranteed freedom from state-controlled censorship.[8] Early in 1916, just as it began to consider the birth-control films, the board changed its name to the National Board of Review, emphasizing its role in classifying films over its role in censoring them, all but admitting defeat.

Released during a period when activists defied prohibitions governing the distribution of contraceptive information, when the motion picture business aggressively asserted its right to participate in informed national debates on an equal footing with media outlets, and when the struggle for control over film censorship was particularly vexed, birth-control films highlight struggles over motion picture regulation in the late 1910s, when ideas about the educational and interventionist role cinema might play in society clashed with its evolving role in the entertainment sphere.

Although the battle over *Where Are My Children?* was the fiercest and longest of the early birth-control films, Weber's offering was, in fact, not the first motion picture to deal with abortion and reproduction. At least two earlier films, *The Miracle of Life* (released in October 1915) and *The Question* (released in February 1916), tackled the issue in much the same manner as Weber's would, presenting abortion (absent any discussion of contraception) as the selfish, unilateral decision of spoiled society wives unwilling to let pregnancy or motherhood curtail their social calendars. Outraged husbands abandoned these women in both stories, demonstrating, according to one critic, that "it behooves wives to allow nature to take its normal course," otherwise, as another pointed out, "those who fight against it are doomed to not only have an unhappy old age, but everlasting punishment after death."[9] Charged with regulating pictures on such highly charged topics, the National Board of Censorship requested extensive revisions to *The Question,* after first refusing to pass it altogether. Besides prohibiting any scenes showing women smoking, the board asked for a substantial reorientation of the narrative, including the removal of sequences depicting central character Grace Tudor's visit to "an illegal doctor," along with the elimination of virtually all scenes featuring her husband's mistress, Anna, and any suggestion that the infant later adopted by the reconciled Tudors was the product of that adulterous affair. A scene where Grace, explaining her refusal to get pregnant, says, "I am not willing to lose my looks and be out of society for a season," was the object of particular concern, since, according to the board, "it hints at race suicide, etc."[10] With *The Question,* the Board of Censorship exercised fairly conservative and predictable moral objections centered around the constellation of female sexuality, marriage, and reproduction, protesting any misalignment of those terms, particularly Grace's interest in sexuality outside motherhood, and Anna's practice of sexuality and reproduction outside marriage. Such objections would prove to be unusual, however, for in debates about subsequent birth-control films, the board's attempts to shape the moral tenor of story lines took a decided backseat to more fundamental arguments concerning cinema's role in heated political debates.

Released just one month after *The Question, Where Are My Children?* dealt with similar subject matter, though it received very different treatment from the board. A more high-profile offering, it was a feature film from Lois Weber, one of the era's leading director-screenwriters, whose penchant for weighty social issues was by then as well known as her brushes with censoring agencies over onscreen nudity in her earlier film *Hypocrites* (1914), and whose studio, Universal, had been known to stand up to the board in the past. Weber's script also took on the prohibitions governing contraception much more directly than previous offerings, intertwining legal battles around contraception with more intimate marital struggles over reproduction, by focusing on the character of District Attorney Richard Walton. Walton comes to favor family planning during the trial of a doctor accused of circulating contraceptive information to impoverished working-class women overburdened with large families and poor health. Yet later, while prosecuting another doctor for performing abortions, Walton's housekeeper's daughter dies following a botched procedure and the attorney discovers that his wife and her society friends have been using the doctor's services to avoid motherhood. His climatic cry, "Where Are My Children?," accuses Edith Walton and her circle of murder.

Perhaps mindful of the cuts requested in *The Question,* Universal submitted *Where Are My Children?* to the National Board of Review in New York on 16 March 1916 after a test screening at Universal City in Los Angeles. The board's Review Committee initially voted to pass the picture without requesting any changes, but, given the delicacy of the subject matter, left the final decision up to the organization's Board of Appeal.[11] Inviting members of the General Committee to assemble for a second screening of the picture the following week, executive secretary William McGuire pointed out that since contraception had been discussed "in magazines and newspapers, the question arises as to whether the National Board are to attempt to deny its discussion upon the motion picture screen."[12] Mindful of the fact that *Where Are My Children?* was the first film to "bring this subject up for public discussion on the motion picture screen" and that it was important that "the National Board reflect the best public opinion," special invitations were also issued to notable guests, including famed vice crusader George Kneeland and Dr. William F. Snow of the American Social Hygiene Association, a fairly unusual practice adopted in the past only in the case of several white-slave films, including 1913's *Traffic in Souls,* and the venereal-disease picture *Damaged Goods* in 1914.[13]

Following discussion between committee members and guests, the General Committee voted unanimously to reject *Where Are My Children?*, reversing the original Review Committee's decision to pass the film, not because of its subject matter, nor in its relatively explicit treatment of contraception and abortion, but because of what the board perceived to be incorrect, or at best, confusing information on what it termed "delicate and dangerous topics" like "the actual control of life." Chief among the board's objections was the fact that the film contained medical misinformation, by presenting surgical abortion as "a very simple matter" and by implying that Mrs. Walton was unable to conceive a child after having multiple abortions. The board was also concerned that the film confused contraception and abortion, and that it contained mixed messages about the use of both, seeming to advocate family planning "in order to protect young girls from the consequences of their misdeeds," and appearing to oppose any form of birth control in the plot involving the Waltons.[14] Cranston Brenton, chairman of the National Board, feared that the picture "so confuses the question of birth control and abortion that even a second viewing of the picture failed to make the distinction clear." In announcing the board's refusal to pass the film he stressed that it was not on account of the subject matter itself, arguing that he "would not assume that any subject in itself is unsuited for film presentation." Instead he maintained that films of this nature, while ostensibly permissible, "must have the unanimous approval of medical men rather than an emotional endorsement, however sincere, of those who may overlook scientific significance."[15] The board, in other words, was holding a dramatic film to the standards of journalistic accuracy. This, I believe, represents a significant shift in board policy in the wake of the Supreme Court's 1915 Mutual decision. Whereas three years earlier the board had insisted that moralistic narratives of punishment and redemption accompany screen portrayals of white slavery and prostitution, here they were troubled by the film's "emotional appeal," calling instead for more precise information.

The film's "confusing" conflation of contraception and abortion, so troubling to the National Board of Review, results from its moralistic plot about female sexuality. Indeed, *Where Are My Children?* appears far less contradictory if the film is seen as an argument for eugenics-based family planning rather than pregnancy prevention per se. Quite unlike birth-control advocate Margaret Sanger, who argued for the dissemination of information about and access to birth control across class lines, *Where Are My Children?* makes the case that poverty-stricken women ought to practice birth control in order to limit the size of their families, whereas women of wealth and "good breeding" were selfish if they chose to remain childless. In doing so, the film advances a eugenics argument not uncommon in birth-control movements during these years, many of which tied their appeal to racist and classist fears about "race suicide." Faced with the "double threat" that working-class and immigrant populations were reproducing at a faster rate, while wealthy, native-born white women practiced family planning, many in the eugenics movement advocated fertility control for certain classes and races, while encouraging the "threatened" white elite to propagate.

To underscore this message Weber's screenplay separates the issues of contraception and abortion: working-class women desperately need to prevent multiple pregnancies through adequate family planning, the film implies, in order to curtail the population of their communities; the supposed selfishness of bourgeois women disinterested in "bettering" the human race through reproduction is given added emphasis by their repeated use of abortion rather than contraception. This is contrary to practices at the time, as contemporary reviewers pointed out, since it would have been poorer women unable to get adequate contraception who relied on abortion, whereas their wealthier counterparts practiced safe and effective methods of preventing pregnancies with the help of the medical establishment. During the first doctor's trial, the film advances an argument for birth control within the clear context of eugenics, for the doctor's advocacy is framed within his broader goal of enabling the "race" to "conquer the evils that have brought it down." Birth control, if used properly, could eliminate crime altogether, he implies, making it clear that the primary targets of fertility control ought to be "the ignorant and the undisciplined." Abortion, in contrast, is linked to dangerous and unrestrained female sexuality, through the comparison of Edith Walton's circle of married friends and the plight of a single woman faced with an unwanted pregnancy—Lillian, the Walton's housekeeper's daughter, who dies after an unsafe abortion and whose case ultimately spurs District Attorney Walton into action. While the narrative appears to contrast the two cases, setting Lillian's sexual naïveté against Edith Walton's confident navigation of the abortion process, the two are also connected through the film's condemnation of female sexuality indulged beyond the parameters of reproduction. Lillian's seducer is Mrs. Walton's brother, a link that ties the young couple's hedonistic approach to sexuality with Mrs. Walton's own. The extravagance of Edith's other pursuits—fashion, socializing, dotting on her dogs—is associated through this link with sexual indulgence. Abortion (conceived in this context as murder) is the logical consequence of unbridled feminine desire, anathema to the bourgeois morality held over the heads of Edith and her friends. Though its harshest judgment is reserved for Mrs. Walton, the film seems firmly addressed to women of her class, for it simply reinforces views about the superiority of their own social station and the necessity of restraining forces that threaten it from "lower" classes and unrestrained (female) sexuality. Read in this manner, *Where Are My Children?* is perhaps less confusing than the Board of Review would have it, but certainly no less moralistic.

Unwilling to accept the board's condemnation of the film's potential to misinform viewers, Universal fought the board's ruling, insisting that the film carried a viable message to its audiences. Having successfully shepherded the first white-slave film, *Traffic in Souls,* through the board's dominion three years earlier and not part of the powerful Motion Picture Trust of major film production companies that had helped form the board in 1909, Universal seems to have maintained a more adversarial relation to the organization than other production outfits, even during these waning years of the board's authority. The studio's general manager, Joe Brandt, met with board executives McGuire and Brenton to discuss *Where Are My Children?* and, at Hal Reid's request, they viewed the picture together a second time to suggest possible changes that might allow the board to pass the film. However, no acceptable compromise was reached.[16] Throughout its dealings with the board, Universal operated as if the agency had censured *Where Are My Children?* solely on the basis of its controversial subject, not because of concerns about its potential to mislead viewers about the nature of contraception and abortion. A disclaimer added to the opening of the film, asking whether a "subject of serious interest" ought to be "denied careful dramatization on the motion picture screen," only played up such a perception. If the board appealed to concepts akin to responsible journalism in its refusal to pass the picture, Universal employed similar rhetoric in its rebuttal, appealing to concepts of the free press. Less than a year after the Supreme Court's Mutual decision, both sides were evidently very conscious of defining a place for serious social-problem films in contemporary media culture.

Looking to circumvent the board's restrictions, and eager for an alternative forum, Universal held two screenings of *Where Are My Children?* for invited guests, hoping to secure endorsements from the likes of noted anti-vice crusader Dr. Charles H. Parkhurst, prominent members of the clergy, and other leading figures in the reform community.[17] A second invited audience saw the film in New York's one thousand-seat Globe Theatre on Broadway at a matinee screening on Wednesday, 12 April, during the regular run of another Universal film directed by Lois Weber, *The Dumb Girl of Portici,* a highly touted picture starring famed Russian dancer Anna Pavlova. Universal evidently hoped that the cultural cachet associated with the Pavlova film, a historical drama based on a well-known opera and starring a renowned performer, would lend legitimacy to *Where Are My Children?*, despite the latter film's more polemical message.

Still unapproved by the Board of Review, *Where Are My Children?* then began a regular engagement at the Globe on Sunday, 16 April, with four daily screenings accompanied by an "augmented" symphony orchestra.[18] Large advertisements in New York's daily newspapers stressed, simultaneously, the film's endorsement by "press, public and clergy" and its spectacular appeal, with one such notice promising an entertainment that was both "dignified" *and* "sensational." Pledging "a powerful portrayal of the premeditated destruction of the un-born" and declaring the picture "society's greatest weapon against race suicide" in terms much stronger than those used within the film itself, the ads emphasized conservative elements of the film's message, while also guaranteeing titillating details on banned topics like contraception (figs. 45 and 46).[19] Press coverage only added to the sensation when one paper reported that "nervous feminine spectators" had fainted during a sequence where the housekeeper's young daughter dies after an unsafe abortion.[20] By early the following week, patrons were being turned away from sold-out screenings, the theater was doing record business, and additional daily showings were being planned.[21] Still eager to gather sufficient "public opinion" on the picture that might refute the board's protective stance, Universal circulated postcards at these initial Globe screenings inviting patrons to comment on the film. Of the more than one thousand cards collected, only four apparently voiced negative views, allowing Universal to argue that the board's decision was "not in line with public opinion."[22] Universal clearly hoped that these New York screenings could secure enough endorsements to guarantee national bookings, with or without the Board of Review's approval.[23]

Once it became clear that Universal was determined to show *Where Are My Children?* commercially, regardless of its decision, the board sent a special report on the film to the New York Department of Licenses, detailing its objections to the picture, especially its concerns that children were being admitted despite advertised proscriptions.[24] Although License Commissioner George Bell ultimately chose not to act on *Where Are My Children?*, the board's attempt to involve his agency in the controversy was not insignificant, given their divergent approach to regulation. Whereas the People's Institute that ran the National Board of Review usually took a favorable view of mass entertainment forms, Bell's agency had been far more likely to regard them with suspicion. In fact, it had been the commission's unilateral revoking of all motion picture theater licenses in December 1908 that had prompted the formation of the National Board in the first place. Clearly unsure of its status as arbiter of public opinion in the wake of the Supreme Court decision, the board increasingly relied on outside experts to justify its rulings on controversial films, and when those rulings proved unenforceable in the face of confident outfits like Universal, the board readily turned to more legally enforcible forms of regulating motion pictures.[25]

Industry trade papers chronicled the exhibition battle with great interest, for rarely, if ever, had a major production company flouted the board's condemnation with such untested subject matter: it was still illegal, after all, to disseminate contraceptive information in *any* medium, let alone one designed for such a mass audience. For this reason *Moving Picture World* predicted that *Where Are My Children?* would likely "become one of the most discussed films of the year," not simply because of its topicality, but

45–46. Advertisements from the *New York Herald*, April 1916.

also because of Universal's determination to release the film "whatever the attitude of the National Board of Review."[26] Most in the trades felt the subject had been handled with tact and defended the cinema's ability to grapple with such controversial topics. Noting that contraception was an issue being addressed by "countless numbers of very prominent persons," *Wid's* maintained that the film would generate a significant amount of discussion around the subject and, for that reason alone, was worthy of presentation. Matters of contraception and abortion had been "carefully and intelligently handled," *Wid's* claimed, "and surely [the film] should not be barred from exhibition."[27] The *New York Dramatic Mirror* congratulated the filmmakers on producing a film that dealt "boldly yet... inoffensively" with such a contentious subject.[28] *Variety* praised the film, confident it would "get money providing local censorship boards will pass some of the scenes," admitting, nonetheless, that "there isn't much that could be cut even by the most bigoted."[29] *Moving Picture World*'s Lynde Denig was the most enthusiastic, praising the filmmakers' "sincere, courageous and intelligent effort." Not simply a good picture, *Where Are My Children?* provided a model of how photoplays should advance "if they are to contribute to a better understanding of human nature and the complexities of modern society."[30]

While obviously invested in arguments endorsing the cinema's ability to tackle weighty social problems, arguments they could make via *Where Are My Children?,* trade commentators were more reluctant to endorse the film's political agenda. Many recognized the film's conflicted message, complaining, much as the Board of Review had, that its presentation of the subject was clouded by its confusion of contraception and abortion: "It starts off seemingly as an argument in favor of birth control and suddenly switches to an argument against abortions," *Variety* protested.[31] With no differentiation "between birth control, race suicide, and abortion," the *New York Dramatic Mirror* complained, the film ended up with a "confusing" message. "We cannot believe this to be the purpose of the authors."[32] Even Lynde Denig, who provided the most favorable of the trades' reviews, argued that the film "departs from the path of strict consistency" by apparently favoring family-planning instruction in its initial scenes, then focusing on a condemnation of Mrs. Walton and abortion in the second. More significantly, Denig maintained, the film contradicted arguments advanced by birth-control advocates Margaret Sanger and Emma Goldman, who were careful to stress how class differences affected women's access to knowledge about contraception. Hack abortionists of the sort portrayed in the film were not patronized by wealthy women like those in Mrs. Walton's circle, Denig insisted, since most had ready access to reliable methods of pregnancy prevention. It was impoverished women, lacking access to adequate birth-control advice, who were forced to resort to unsafe abortions.[33]

Those within the film industry were not the only ones to condemn the film's apparently contradictory logic. When *Where Are My Children?* played in Portland, Oregon, that autumn, members of the Birth Control League mounted a similar charge, protesting that the film failed to distinguish between "birth control properly speaking and abortion" and generated "misunderstanding and confusion" about their objectives. They pointed out that Sanger, who brought the term "birth control" into general usage, never intended to include abortion under that rubric, and that one of her chief reasons for advocating pregnancy prevention was to reduce the number of abortions.[34]

For her part, Weber took great issue with these objections, first blaming censors for forcing her to dilute her original intentions, but then arguing that in order to make a successful dramatic film about reproductive politics one had to follow the dictates of effective storytelling much more than rigorous propaganda. "The propagandist who recognizes the moving picture as a powerful means of putting out a creed," she claimed, "never seems to have any conception of the fact that an idea has to come to terms with the dramatic if it is to be successful screen drama."[35] Weber, in other words, defended her film on the grounds that it must serve as entertainment first and propaganda second, in effect rejecting the board's view of the medium.

Criticism of the film's political agenda or its confusing message appear to have had little effect on its popularity and did nothing to curb Universal's enthusiasm for wide distribution. In fact, the studio's strategy to force the board's hand was evidently successful, for in the face of the film's continued popular run at New York's Globe Theatre, and Commissioner Bell's refusal to take action, the National Board of Review elected to reconsider its initial opinion on *Where Are My Children?* several weeks into the film's commercial run, apparently swayed by the fact that "a number of well-known clergymen" had endorsed the film and that Universal had limited screenings at the Globe to adults only. Again, the board sought "a well-defined public opinion" on the film and hosted a private screening for members of New York's progressive community representing such institutions as the American Social Hygiene Association, the Society for Sanitary and Moral Prophylaxis, the Drama League, and the Neighborhood Workers' Association. The overwhelming majority of guests present voted to allow screenings of the film for adult audiences—close to half voted to allow children as well.[36] Obviously sensitive about their handling of the film, the board issued a self-congratulatory public statement making it seem as if they had been on top of the issue all along. In the same statement, however, one also hears the voice of a less confident board, wary of adopting national censorship standards in the face of widely varying local statutes: "Any endeavor to express or enforce one opinion for the whole United States as regards a picture of this character is impossible," the board concluded.[37]

Shortly after this announcement, the board's authority was undermined further when *Where Are My Children?* encountered problems in the borough of Brooklyn where District Attorney Harry E. Lewis made Weber's picture the starting point of his campaign to "protect the morals of youths and young girls" by battling "films that portray the sex relations, and also exhibit the hidden crimes of society for the curious mind of the young." No complaint had been filed against the film; Lewis merely took his own initiative, despite the fact that a Brooklyn magistrate, himself faced with a complaint about the picture, had ruled there was no cause to issue a summons to its producers or exhibitors.[38]

Confident nonetheless, Universal put the film into national release shortly thereafter, announcing the sale of states rights in full-page trade ads. The film's New York success was touted in the campaign, which featured a photo of crowds lined up along Broadway outside the Globe during the film's run. If the film could draw such business on "the hardest show street" and "the greatest theatre neighborhood in the world," exhibitors around the country could not go wrong.[39] In an indication of the board's diminished national stature, Universal's ad campaign for states rights did not even mention the board's approval, citing instead the approval of the Ohio Board of Censors.[40] Following these announcements, *Moving Picture Weekly*, Universal's own trade paper, claimed it had been "literally besieged and bombarded with telegrams, telephone and special delivery communications" from states rights buyers.[41] Indeed, the film did well around the country, setting box-office records in many communities, including Albany, New York, where twenty-four thousand patrons reportedly saw the picture in its first week, with nearly as many returning during the second week of the run. *Where Are My Children?* enjoyed record business at Chicago's La Salle Theater, the best owners had seen since the venue opened. And "several enthusiastic audiences" saw the film in San Francisco in August. According to National Board of Review records, the film played without incident in cities and towns in many states across the country, including those in East Coast states like Maine, Vermont, Massachusetts, and Connecticut, southern states like West Virginia, Kentucky, Arkansas, and Louisiana, and western states like Wyoming, Idaho, and Utah.[42]

Taking Precautions

State and municipal censorship agencies varied considerably in their approach to the film, and appear to have operated independent of the Board of Review's assessment of the film. Municipalities each found ways to scrutinize the film that do not seem to have been standardized—in other words, the film appears to have been given special consideration, likely because of its popularity combined with the "delicacy" of its subject matter. In many cases communities conveyed private screenings of local "authorities" to view the picture, including "business men, doctors, members of the Women's Christian Temperance Union, ministers and police inspectors" in Leominster, Massachusetts, and the postmaster, the principal of the Normal School, the newspaper's city editor, and the manager of the local Gas and Electric Company in Fitchburg, Massachusetts.[43] Even Boston's censorship commission, notorious for its strict enforcement, did not prevent *Where Are My Children?* from being shown in that city, where it proved so popular that some two thousand patrons were turned away on opening night in July and continued to generate "enormous business" during a run of several months. In fact, Boston's Mayor Churley became an unlikely advocate for Weber's film, and even lobbied Pennsylvania senators in an effort to get the picture past that state's censorship board, which had complained that the film "visualizes in revolting detail the subject of 'Birth Control.'"[44] Pennsylvania requested considerable eliminations in the film, including "all views" of the interior and exterior of Dr. Malfit's offices and "all that occurs" within, every mention of the term "birth control" in the intertitles, as well as a significant reduction in the "seduction" scene involving Mrs. Walton's brother and the housekeeper's daughter, Lillian. Even after these changes were made and the film was submitted for a second time, the board of censors refused to pass it. A Pennsylvania film exchange ultimately sued over the case, arguing that the board had condemned *Where Are My Children?* "for reasons not pertaining to the morality or propriety of said motion picture play" and that such a decision lay beyond the mandate of the board, which was charged only with regulating material that might be "sacrilegious, obscene, indecent or immoral." The appeal failed and the film was banned in the state.[45] Still, Pennsylvania's decision remained atypical and the film drew large audiences across the country in 1916, just at the time when activist Margaret Sanger was embarking on her nationwide speaking tour.

One year after the release of *Where Are My Children?*, *Photoplay* complained that the picture had spawned a "filthy host of nasty-minded imitators": evidently many in the business sought to capitalize on Weber's box-office success.⁴⁶ Indeed, several even more conservative offerings appeared shortly after the film's release, many taking an even less ambiguous stance against contraception and abortion than Weber's film had: *The Valley of Decision,* released in late 1916, portrayed a woman haunted by "the shadow land of souls unborn" after an abortion; and *Enlighten Thy Daughter,* released early the next year, showed a character dying from an abortion after her affair with a wayward playboy.⁴⁷ However, the reactionary sentiments voiced in these two relatively obscure titles were countered by much more high-profile offerings conceived in the wake of Margaret Sanger's arrest and imprisonment late in 1916: Sanger's own film, *Birth Control,* and Lois Weber's second foray into the topic, *The Hand That Rocks the Cradle.* Unlike Weber's earlier offering, these two new films encountered little difficulty with the Board of Review but faced substantial opposition from other regulatory agencies. They received much more favorable handling from the board, largely, I would argue, because each presented itself from the outset as an outgrowth of actual events and presented their narratives within the framework of reportage, not melodrama. Weber's second film was frankly and obviously drawn from recent, much publicized events in Sanger's life, a resemblance noted by most critics at the time;⁴⁸ and Sanger's own project, conceived while she was serving time in prison following the raid on her Brownsville clinic, sought to use film for explicitly propagandistic purposes. This overall conception, much more so than each film's particular rendering of still-vexed contraceptive issues, spared the two films the kind of trouble with the Board of Review endured by their more melodramatic predecessor *Where Are My Children?* Thus, in the debate surrounding these two subsequent contraceptive films, positions were reversed: while the Board of Review voted to pass both titles, other regulatory bodies intervened to curtail their circulation. Once again, competing views of cinema's role in public debates on sensitive issues remained at the forefront of these discussions.

Billed as "Margaret Sanger's Message to the Millions," *Birth Control* was the advocate's first foray into the motion picture arena, and marked the newly aggressive tenor of her campaign following her release from prison (fig. 47).⁴⁹ Sanger herself planned to speak at screenings, intending that portions of the box office proceeds would be directed toward her cause. Sanger stars in the film, and in the first part recounts through flashbacks stories of women and children living in impoverished, overcrowded conditions, demonstrating the need for widely available family-planning information. Viewers are "taken hither and thither throughout New York's teeming child streets, to the almost childless precincts of the informed

Taking Precautions

47. Advertisement from the *New York World,* May 1917.

wealthy, and shown the lesson of sex temperance." We see two sisters, one living in poverty and unable to support her large family, while the other lives in prosperity after having limited her family to two children. We see women pushed to the point of physical collapse by childbearing and the demands of child care, children weakened and incapacitated from malnutrition. And we see the story of Helen Field, a young mother who died because of inadequate information on birth control, a story drawn from one of Sanger's actual cases, but, according to her, "one martyr of hundreds and hundreds she knows of by name and of tens of thousands she knows of by deduction." The remainder of the film illustrates Sanger's own efforts to improve these circumstances, showing scenes of her working at the Brownsville clinic, and emphasizing that she dispenses contraceptive information only to unfit or financially strapped women.[50]

Although *Birth Control* traffics in many of the same class-based arguments that haunt *Where Are My Children?,* it avoids conflating contraception and abortion as the first film had done. In both films patrician commentators draw viewers through diegetic space — a doctor on trial in the earlier film, Sanger herself in the latter — each giving voice to the complaints, emotions, and memories of working-class subjects they encounter, as if they are the very instrument of cinema itself, lending these stories visibility. But unlike *Where Are My Children?,* which gives us access to women's stories only through male protagonists, and encourages sympathy with female characters only in their moments of victimization and sexual humiliation, *Birth Control* champions the deeds of its activist heroine. More didactic than *Where Are My Children?*, *Birth Control* is ultimately more concerned with advancing a rhetorical argument than presenting a compelling narrative, in marked contrast to the earlier film, which wraps its eugenics platform in the cloak of a melodramatic tale about punishment and redemption for sexual transgressions.

While Sanger appeared in *Birth Control* promoting her cause, Weber wrote, directed, and starred in *The Hand That Rocks the Cradle*, a project frankly based on Sanger's own story originally titled "Is a Woman a Person?"[51] In the film Weber plays Louise Broome, a doctor's wife charged at the outset with distributing information on family-planning methods. Striking a deal to prevent his wife's prosecution, Dr. Broome agrees to persuade her to cease her activities, an arrangement that she refuses, saying, "I am sorry, dear, but we each have our own convictions and must live up to them," and reminding him that he agreed to "limit" their own family out of concern for her health. When their friends the Grahams discuss family planning with the Broomes, Louise remembers the story of their former nursemaid, Sarah, whose story is narrated in a flashback. Trapped in poverty, Sarah and her husband John could not provide for their many children and their relationship disintegrated until Sarah received Louise's help in preventing pregnancy. The Grahams, however, remain unconvinced by Louise's story: Mr. Graham is embarrassed by the open discussion of such "indecent" matters, and his wife pleads for "self-control" rather than birth control. When she receives word from Sarah, eager to spread contraceptive information to her friends, Louise decides to defy the arrangement her husband has struck with the police, telling him she "cannot permit" him to be responsible for her good behavior and chastising her husband and the medical profession for keeping family planning away from women. Meanwhile, the Grahams' marriage has collapsed under the wife's pleas for abstinence. At the film's climax Louise addresses a group of women, including Sarah and her friends, arguing that "man" ought to control "his own powers of reproduction" in much the same manner that "he" has always "endeavored to direct the forces of nature." Arrested, tried, and imprisoned for disseminating contraceptive information, Louise rejects her husband's pleas that she "give up her public work for the sake of our children," and goes on a hunger strike instead. Pardoned at last, Louise lives to see her husband agree that physicians ought to provide patients with instructions on contraceptive use. At the film's close, newspaper headlines announce that birth control may soon be legal in the state of Illinois. "What do *you* think?," the film's final title asks, inviting audiences to talk among themselves, as the two middle-class couples can be seen doing in the last sequence.

The Hand That Rocks the Cradle strikes quite a different tone from Weber's earlier film, as *Wid's* reviewer noted at the time: "it is rather interesting to note that her big success, *Where Are My Children?*, was very much opposed to birth control, while this, in many ways, preaches for it when handled by the proper authorities."[52] Here the melodrama evolves from struggles over reproductive control in all three screen marriages, rather than the threat that female sexuality poses to bourgeois domesticity, which had been the case in *Where Are My Children?* Arguing strongly for sexuality in marriage, the story makes Mrs. Graham's desire for "self-control" seem wholly unreasonable. *The Hand That Rocks the Cradle* also does not traffic so heavily in discourses of eugenics, but instead presents a case for "intelligent childbearing" for all classes, although pregnancy prevention is rationalized differently in each instance: the mental and physical health of bourgeois women much be protected, whereas contraceptive use is promoted for working-class women in order to put an end to "murderous operations, insanity, poverty and criminal tendencies in the human race." Significantly, an educated, middle-class woman, Louise Broome, serves as the viewer's guide through this landscape, providing a female perspective (as opposed to that of her husband), an educated outlook (as opposed to that of her untutored nursemaid, Sarah), and a healthy approach to sexuality (as opposed to that of the prudish Grahams).

Despite their frank treatment of family planning, both films were passed by the Board of Review with relatively little fanfare, in stark contrast to the fight over *Where Are My Children?* the previous spring. If at first this seems counterintuitive—the two newer pictures, after all, included much more militant calls for contraceptive use than their predecessor—the absence of moralizing story lines and the insistence on a didactic rhetorical structure in both offerings may have been precisely what appealed to the board. Each title frames its presentation of reproductive politics within an educational context that assumes the perspective of a middle-class reformer, rather than circumscribing events within story lines centered around individual virtue and vice. Such a framework may have appealed to the board's broader conception of cinema's elevated role in cultural debates, and indeed, its *own* role in arbitrating them.

Birth Control was passed by the board in late March 1917, well over a month before it was slated to open in New York.[53] Though subsequently advertised as "law proof and censor proof," the film's producers were still mindful that exhibitors in various regions of the country might be subject to differing regulations, and prepared interchangeable promotional materials, one set using the title "Birth Control," another set cloaking the film's subject under the title "The New World." The film itself would remain identical.[54] *The Hand That Rocks the Cradle* also did not encounter serious difficulties with the Board of Review, in sharp contrast to the struggle Universal had mounted in support of *Where Are My Children?* less than one year earlier. One of the board's review committees screened Weber's new film on 23 April 1917 and deemed "the moral effect of the picture is good." Important to the committee was the fact that the film's treatment of birth control was "dignified and sincere," that it provided "no details" of specific contraceptive methods, and that even though the film questioned laws restricting the dissemination of contraceptive information, it still "upholds the present law."[55] Despite the review committee's positive assessment, the board arranged for a larger audience of 250 invited guests to view the film before it would officially pass *The Hand That Rocks the Cradle* for general audiences, suggesting their continued unease with the subject matter. About one hundred guests turned up for the screening at New York's Wurlitzer Fine Arts Hall and watched the film together with members of the General Committee. After a discussion, the assembled audience voted in favor of the film's public exhibition, with only five people objecting. Those in favor of the film valued its "impartial" presentation of "existing conditions" governing birth control, arguments "which have frequently appeared in the public press." "It was the apparent aim of the photoplay to leave the question entirely open for discussion by the public itself."[56]

However, it appears that the board's sentiments were increasingly at odds with views of cinema's public function circulating overtly in trade discourse and, more tacitly, among those charged with regulating commercial amusements. Even though the board appeared to favor the didactic tenor of Weber's second birth-control picture, reviewers at the time complained that *The Hand That Rocks the Cradle* was "too preachy" and chastised the filmmaker for having "taken up her club" in defense of family planning. Indeed, *Wid's* and the *New York Dramatic Mirror,* which had both praised Weber's other film just one year earlier, cautioned exhibitors to warn their patrons that the film was "a birth control preachment," that it was "frankly propaganda" and dealt with "a subject that is still under the ban of the law."[57] Others felt compelled to comment on the very suitability of using motion picture screens as a public forum. *Moving Picture World*'s Edward Weitzel was the most strident on this issue: "Persons with serious ethical questions to propound have as much right to utilize the screen as they have to hire a hall and set forth their opinions in more or less eloquent speech; but the family photoplay theater, in the opinion of the writer, is not the proper place for them." Cinemas should be reserved for "amusement and recreation," not "propaganda," he concluded.[58]

Those charged with regulating the sphere of amusement and recreation into which Weitzel so insistently placed cinema were equally alarmed by family-planning advocacy onscreen. New York License Commissioner George Bell, who had refused to interfere with screenings of *Where Are My Children?* one year earlier when the Board of Review had explicitly (and quite desperately) called for his intervention, now stood against both *The Hand That Rocks the Cradle* and *Birth Control,* defying the board's decision to pass those titles and exerting his control over motion picture exhibition in Manhattan, where both films premiered within a week of one another in the spring of 1917.

Less than twenty-four hours before *Birth Control* was scheduled to open at New York's Park Theatre on Sunday, 6 May, for a one-week engagement, Bell threatened to revoke the Park's license and screenings were cancelled pending an appeal. Crowds that had gathered in Columbus Circle that evening outside the theater, eager to see the film and to hear Sanger speak beforehand, had to be turned away.[59] Bell alleged to have received numerous complaints about *Birth Control* from organizations like the Catholic Theatre Movement and the Committee of Fourteen, although it had not yet been shown commercially anywhere in the country, and Bell admitted that he himself had not seen the film. Contraception, in his opinion, could not be classified as "theatrical entertainment" given that the subject itself remained illegal. Although Bell took refuge in this by now familiar distinction between film entertainment and print media, other comments reveal he was antagonistic to the film's arguments. He questioned the wisdom of limited birth rates during wartime, for instance, and mentioned his fear that *Birth Control* might incite class warfare since it revealed discrepancies between wealthy couples who had ready access to contraceptives (and therefore smaller families) and working couples saddled with large, impoverished families because they lacked adequate information.[60] Clearly he had been more comfortable with the antiabortion arguments advanced in *Where Are My Children?*

Unable to screen the film publicly under Bell's threat of censure, the Birth Control League arranged a private showing at the Park Theatre for two hundred reporters and invited guests on the day the film was to have opened. Those in attendance, many of them prominent New York reformers, apparently endorsed the picture without reservation. Likely aware of the successful strategy Universal had employed with "private screenings" of *Where Are My Children?* the previous year, Sanger and her supporters aimed to generate a ground swell of "genuine" public opinion that might rival Bell's professed objections. Affidavits from prominent clergy and members of the public who had attended this screening were included in an application for an injunction preventing Bell's further interference with the film's exhibition filed by the Birth Control League and the Message Photoplay Company.[61] Industry trade papers also supported the film, noting that its subject had been "handled with great care," and noting that there was "not a suggestive scene in the picture." They predicted that if allowed to go forward the film would generate enormous interest, promising exhibitors they could "clean up a quick profit" on the "stirring, varied and picturesque exposition . . . of the crusade that sent its martyr to a prison cell." *Moving Picture World* predicted "every woman in the world will demand to see it."[62]

Exactly one week later, on 13 May, *The Hand That Rocks the Cradle* was scheduled to open at the Broadway Theater several blocks south of the Park Theatre, where controversy still swirled around *Birth Control*. This time as well Commissioner Bell tried to prevent screenings of Weber's film, issuing an order late Saturday afternoon in an attempt to stop the premiere planned for Sunday, an eleventh-hour intervention similar to the one he had staged with Sanger's offering the previous weekend. Yet, unlike Sanger and her associates in the Birth Control League, relatively inexperienced in these matters, Universal contacted a judge late Saturday and received an injunction permitting the screening of *The Hand That Rocks the Cradle* to go ahead Sunday as planned.[63] Universal also mounted an aggressive publicity campaign aimed at challenging the commissioner and those who would object to cinematic presentations of reproductive politics, much as it had done the previous year with *Where Are My Children?* Once again, the studio appealed to concepts of a free press: "the newspaper and magazines have been full of it; the legitimate stage has no difficulty in presenting the topic when it wishes," the company proclaimed in large newspaper ads, noting that contraceptive use was discussed everywhere "except on the screen." Why should those who could not afford to see birth-control plays on stage, where admissions were two dollars, be prevented from forming an opinion at motion picture plays charging twenty-five cents, the studio asked.[64] Adopting much the same rhetoric as the Board of Review, Universal compared motion pictures to other forms of the popular press where family planning, absent any specific discussion of particular methods, could be presented quite legally, in contrast to Bell, who clearly circumscribed cinema within the sphere of popular entertainments he was charged with regulating in New York, where it became subject to considerations of obscenity and public decency.

The struggle for jurisdiction then was ultimately a struggle over how the cinema itself should be viewed, whether as an informational medium akin to the press and therefore subject to guarantees of free speech, or as a commercial entertainment medium entitled to regulations governing theatrical presentations. Injunctions and appeals involving both films continued throughout the summer and went all the way to the New York State Supreme Court, where Bell's original decision to curtail screenings was ultimately upheld. But even in these judicial debates, the central question remained how to classify motion pictures, and therefore how to regulate them. One justice, ruling in favor of Sanger's *Birth Control,* argued that the film was simply "an attempt to present a dramatic argument" in favor of contraception and therefore stood outside Commissioner Bell's purview. "It is a measured and decent exercise of the right of free speech guaranteed by our Constitution," he continued, evidently a jibe at the U.S. Supreme Court's Mutual decision. This minority view would ultimately be overturned and screenings of both films in New York were quickly shut down.[65]

Following their legal troubles in New York, neither film was able to generate much box-office revenue across the nation and neither attained the record-breaking attendance set by their precursor, *Where Are My Children?* When *The Hand That Rocks the Cradle* opened in Los Angeles at the end of June, Weber appeared at the premiere at Clune's Auditorium and complained bitterly to the press about the treatment the film had received in New York. "The propaganda plays that I have produced have been so unjustly criticized and censored by the rigid boards of censorship in the East that I am discontinuing the production of this type of play," she reported. This despite the fact that the film had been toned down during the production for fear of censorship: "It's too tame," she complained. "Hardly a jolt in it. I wanted to make it talk right out, only fear of the censors made my managers hold me down and divest it of 'ginger.' "[66]

For that matter, subsequent birth-control films shied away from the strong arguments for birth control advanced in *The Hand That Rocks the Cradle* and *Birth Control,* preferring, it seems, the moralistic tenor of Weber's earlier offering. Following the controversy that surrounded these films in the spring of 1917, several anti-birth-control pictures were released later that year, among them *The Curse of Eve,* "a solemn warning to neglectful mothers and unthinking daughters," and *Maternity* (or *The Cry of the Unborn*), about a woman who overcomes a morbid fear of childbirth to embrace motherhood.[67] Ultimately, discussions of contraception, and certainly abortion, would not surface on American screens for decades to follow, the subject of explicit prohibition under the Production Code.

Within the broader context of debates surrounding Comstock laws and contraceptive education, birth-control films like *Where Are My Children?, Birth Control,* and *The Hand That Rocks the Cradle* engaged substantial questions about the cinema's role in popular discourse, especially in the wake of the Supreme Court's decision to allow state and federal regulation of motion pictures. Many, including film companies and members of the legal system, openly questioned cinema's status in public discussions of topical, albeit sensitive, issues like family planning. The Board of Review clearly remained very self-conscious during these years, simultaneously concerned to reflect national opinion adequately, aware of the seriousness with which its judgments were regarded, and less confident in what that consensus might be. Its treatment of the birth-control films, like the vice films before them, demonstrates the board's attempts to look beyond its own membership to gather a broader sampling of the community to view and comment on films, especially those in contested subject areas. And the board continued to vie for control of motion picture exhibition with a host of other organizations, including state and municipal censorship bodies, as well as public officials charged with regulating theatrical venues. Throughout these debates the board promoted a conception of cinema's social role that differed substantially from these other agencies, objecting to *Where Are My Children?* not for reasons of morality or obscenity, but on the grounds that it furnished poor information on contraception and abortion for its viewers. Instead the board approved titles like *Birth Control* and *The Hand That Rocks the Cradle,* films that brought a more paternalistic, instructional voice to birth-control debates, a voice more in line with the board's own conception of itself, and ultimately the role that motion pictures might play in American life. Still, however forward-looking the board perceived itself to be, its members were championing a view of cinema that was, even then, on the wane and soon out of favor. By the early 1920s such radical views of cinema's interventionist mandate would be replaced overwhelmingly by visions of its function solely as entertainment. By studying the controversies surrounding these early birth-control films, we may catch glimpses of where the cinema might have gone during these early years of its formation. Those, like Weber and Sanger, who envisioned cinema's role as an informed public forum for radical feminist causes countered later, often demeaning, caricatures of the female movie fan obsessed primarily with

Taking Precautions

glamour and escapist entertainment, presenting instead the ideal of an intelligent, progressive female audience.

Notes

My thanks to Sirida Srisombati for her expert research assistance, and to Lee Grieveson, whose astute comments helped sharpen my argument.

1 *Motography*, 9 December 1916, 1297.
2 *Moving Picture World*, 29 April 1916, 817.
3 Other feminist causes during these years also turned to cinema, most notably the campaign for women's suffrage. For information on women's suffrage films, see Kay Sloan, *The Loud Silents: Origins of the Social Problem Film* (Urbana: University of Illinois Press, 1988), 99–123; Kevin Brownlow, *Behind the Mask of Innocence: Sex, Violence, Prejudice, Crime — Films of Social Conscience in the Silent Era* (New York: Alfred A. Knopf, 1990), 225–238; and Shelley Stamp, *Movie-Struck Girls: Women and Motion Picture Culture after the Nickelodeon* (Princeton: Princeton University Press, 2000), 154–194.
4 The best analysis of the early-twentieth-century birth-control movement remains Linda Gordon's *Woman's Body, Woman's Right: Birth Control in America*, rev. ed. (New York: Penguin, 1990), 93–242. For information on Sanger in particular, see Ellen Chesler, *Woman of Valor: Margaret Sanger and the Birth Control Movement in America* (New York: Simon and Schuster, 1992); and *Margaret Sanger: An Autobiography* (New York: W. W. Norton, 1938). Publicity surrounding the raid on the Brownsville clinic quickly garnered Sanger a cadre of wealthy supporters and legal challenges to her arrest eventually resulted in the New York State appellate court exempting medical doctors from the ban on disseminating contraceptive information, allowing Sanger to set up a legal clinic in 1923. However, anticontraceptive laws remained in effect for decades. It was not until 1965 that the U.S. Supreme Court ruled that state laws prohibiting the dissemination of family-planning information to married couples were an unconstitutional invasion of privacy. In 1972, the court broadened this constitutional protection to include the distribution of contraceptive devices to married and unmarried individuals alike. See Edward De Grazia and Roger K. Newman, *Banned Films: Movies, Censors, and the First Amendment* (New York: R. R. Bowker, 1982), 188.
5 "Films and Births and Censorship," *Survey*, 3 April 1915, 4–5.
6 On the early years of the Board of Censorship, see Robert Fisher, "Film Censorship and Progressive Reform: The National Board of Censorship of Motion Pictures, 1909–1922," *Journal of Popular Film and Television* 4, 2 (1975): 143–156; Charles Matthew Feldman, *The National Board of Censorship (Review) of Motion Pictures, 1909–1922* (New York: Arno Press, 1977), 20–87; Daniel Czitrom, "The Redemption of Leisure: The National Board of Censorship and

the Rise of Motion Pictures in New York City, 1900–1920," *Studies in Visual Communication* 10, 4 (fall 1984): 2–6; Nancy J. Rosenbloom, "Between Reform and Regulation: The Struggle over Film Censorship in Progressive America, 1909–1922," *Film History* 1, 4 (1987): 307–325; and Rosenbloom, "Progressive Reform, Censorship, and the Motion Picture Industry, 1909–1917," in *Popular Culture and Political Change in Modern America,* ed. Ronald Edsforth and Larry Bennett (Albany: State University of New York Press, 1991), 41–60.

7 Garth S. Jowett, " 'A Capacity for Evil': The 1915 Supreme Court Mutual Decision" (1989), reprinted in *Controlling Hollywood: Censorship and Regulation in the Studio Era,* ed. Matthew Bernstein (New Brunswick: Rutgers University Press, 1999), 16–40.

8 Lee Grieveson, "Fighting Films: Race, Morality, and the Governing of Cinema, 1912–1915," *Cinema Journal* 38, 1 (fall 1998): 40–72.

9 *Moving Picture World,* 4 March 1916, 1489; and *Motography,* 30 October 1915, 937. For more detail on *The Miracle of Life,* see *Variety,* 8 October 1915, 21; *Moving Picture World,* 9 October 1915, 281–282; *Motion Picture News,* 9 October 1915, 87–88; and *Motography,* 30 October 1915, 913. On *The Question,* see *New York Dramatic Mirror,* 26 February 1916, 33; and *Motion Picture News,* 11 March 1916, 1468.

10 "Censor Cuts to Be Made in 'The Question,' " box 106, National Board of Review of Motion Pictures Collection, Rare Books and Manuscripts Division, New York Public Library (hereafter NBRMPC). No records of the board's handling of *The Miracle of Life* survive.

11 "Lois Weber Molds Artistic Surprises," *Moving Picture World,* 11 March 1916, 1668; "Review Board Again Sees 'Children' Picture," *Moving Picture World,* 20 May 1916, 132; and letter from McGuire to Moree, 2 May 1916, box 107, NBRMPC. For an account of the different censorship battle the film encountered in Britain, see Annette Kuhn, *Cinema, Censorship, and Sexuality, 1909–1925* (New York: Routledge, 1988), 37–48.

12 Letter from McGuire to the General Committee, 18 March 1916, box 107, NBRMPC.

13 Letter from McGuire to invited guests, 18 March 1916, box 107, NBRMPC. On the Board of Censorship's treatment of the white-slave films, see Lee Grieveson, "Policing the Cinema: *Traffic in Souls* at Ellis Island," *Screen* 38, 2 (fall 1998): 149–171; and Shelley Stamp, "Moral Coercion, or the Board of Censorship Ponders the Vice Question," in *Controlling Hollywood,* ed. Bernstein, 41–59. Universal had extensive dealings with the board over *Traffic in Souls* in 1913, a film that was ultimately passed with revisions, so their confidence regarding *Where Are My Children?* is not surprising. The board's treatment of other sensitive issues during these years is well documented in Francis G. Couvares, "The Good Censor: Race, Sex, and Censorship in the Early Cinema," *Yale Journal of Criticism* 7, 2 (1994): 233–251; and Grieveson, "Fighting Films."

14 Letter from McGuire to Executive Committee, 11 April 1916, box 107, NBRMPC.

15 Unidentified correspondence, n.d., box 107, NBRMPC.

16 Letter from McGuire to Universal, 10 April 1916; and letter from Reid to McGuire, 17 April 1916, box 107, NBRMPC.
17 "Smalley's Picture Endorsed," *Moving Picture World,* 15 April 1916, 413.
18 *New York Tribune,* 13 April 1916, 14; "Women Faint at Photoplay of Birth Control," *New York Herald,* 13 April 1916, 9; "Birth Control in Films," *New York Tribune,* 14 April 1916, 11; *New York Tribune,* 15 April 1916, 7; *New York Tribune,* 16 April 1916, 2; and "'Rejected' Film Seen at the Globe," *New York Morning Telegraph,* 17 April 1916, n.p., box 107, NBRMPC.
19 *New York Tribune,* 13 April 1916, 14; 15 April 1916, 7; and 18 April 1916, 16.
20 "Women Faint at Photoplay of Birth Control."
21 "U. Film's Big Business," *Variety,* 21 April 1916, 25.
22 Letter from Reid to McGuire, 17 April 1916; and letter from Brandt to Brenton, 17 April 1916, box 107, NBRMPC.
23 "Birth Control Discussion with Conditions Plainly Pictured," *Wid's,* 20 April 1916, 524.
24 Letter from McGuire to Executive Committee, 11 April 1916; letter from Deputy Commissioner Kaufman to McGuire, 22 April 1916; letter from McGuire to Moree, 2 May 1916; and unidentified correspondence, n.d., box 107, NBRMPC.
25 New York State did not institute statewide motion picture censorship until 1921, so until then municipal license commissions held considerable power to control film exhibition. On the history of New York City licensing regulations and the early formation of the National Board, see Nancy J. Rosenbloom, "In Defense of Moving Pictures: The People's Institute, the National Board of Censorship, and the Problems of Leisure in Urban America," *American Studies* 33, 2 (fall 1992): 41–61; and Daniel Czitrom, "The Politics of Performance: From Theater Licensing to Movie Censorship in Turn-of-the-Century New York," *American Quarterly* 44, 4 (December 1992): 525–553.
26 "Smalley's Picture Endorsed."
27 "Birth Control Discussion."
28 *New York Dramatic Mirror,* 22 April 1916, 42.
29 *Variety,* 14 April 1916, 26.
30 *Moving Picture World,* 29 April 1916, 817.
31 *Variety,* 14 April 1916, 26.
32 *New York Dramatic Mirror,* 22 April 1916, 42.
33 *Moving Picture World,* 29 April 1916, 817–818.
34 "Control League Differs," *Portland Oregon News,* 18 November 1916, n.p., box 107, NBRMPC.
35 "Lois Weber Smalley," *Overland Monthly,* September 1916, 200.
36 "Review Board Again Sees 'Children' Picture"; letter from McGuire to Moree, 2 May 1916; and letter from McGuire to Pauling, 2 May 1916, box 107, NBRMPC.
37 The board's public statement is printed in "Review Board Again Sees 'Children' Picture."
38 "Lewis Makes War on Film," *New York Times,* 18 June 1916, sec. 8, p. 3.
39 *Moving Picture World,* 3 June 1916, 1615.

40 Ibid.
41 *Moving Picture Weekly,* 3 June 1916, 47.
42 *Albany Journal,* 7 June 1916, n.p., envelope 2518, Robinson Locke Collection, Billy Rose Theatre Archives, New York Public Library, Library for the Performing Arts (hereafter RLC); "Pictures in Chicago," *Variety,* 22 September 1916, 32; Mildred Joclyn, "Sordid Tale of Unborn Featured at La Salle," *Chicago Post,* n.d., n.p., RLC; "Where Are My Children? Is Market Street Theater Offering," *San Francisco Post,* 21 August 1916, n.p., RLC; and "Statement Regarding the Exhibition of *Where Are My Children?,*" box 107, NBRMPC.
43 "Statement Regarding the Exhibition of *Where Are My Children?*"
44 "'Children' Film in Boston," *Variety,* 7 July 1916, 22; and "Boston's Mayor Accused," *Variety,* 22 September 1916, 32.
45 Record Group 22, Pennsylvania State Board of Censors (Motion Pictures), Pennsylvania State Archives. Some of the records are undated and others date from 1921, when the film was resubmitted for consideration by the board. See also "Pennsylvania Turns Down 'Where Are My Children?,'" *Motion Picture News,* 7 October 1916, 2206, 2208.
46 "Next Needs in Anatomy," *Photoplay,* April 1917, 100.
47 "The Valley of Decision," unidentified newspaper clipping, c. 1916, RLC; and *Motography,* 9 December 1916, 1297. On *Enlighten Thy Daughter,* see *Moving Picture World,* 6 January 1917, 99; and *New York Times,* 29 January 1917, 11.
48 See *Variety,* 18 May 1917, 26; *Wid's,* 31 May 1917, 350; *Moving Picture World,* 2 June 1917, 1458; and Florence Lawrence, "'The Hand That Rocks the Cradle' Says Laws React against Race Benefits," *Los Angeles Examiner,* 24 June 1917, n.p., RLC.
49 *Variety,* 30 March 1917, 27–28.
50 No known print of *Birth Control* survives; my analysis is based solely on plot information contained in reviews. See *Variety,* 13 April 1917, 27; and *Moving Picture World,* 21 April 1917, 451.
51 No known print of *The Hand That Rocks the Cradle* survives; my analysis is based solely on the film's printed screenplay, published in "Continuity and Subtitles: 'Is a Woman a Person?,'" *Film History* 1, 4 (1987): 343–366. Though there is no way to compare this script to finished versions of the film, plot summaries printed at the time appear to confirm that the film was shot and released much as it was written. See *Moving Picture World,* 2 June 1917, 1501.
52 *Wid's,* 31 May 1917, 350.
53 "'Birth Control' Passed," *Variety,* 6 April 1917, 21.
54 *Variety,* 30 March 1917, 27–28; and *Variety,* 13 April 1917, 27.
55 Undated report by Secretary W. M. Covill, box 104, NBRMPC.
56 Affidavit prepared for McGuire, box 104, NBRMPC.
57 *Wid's,* 31 May 1917, 349; *Moving Picture World,* 2 June 1917, 1458; *Wid's,* 31 May 1917, 349; and *New York Dramatic Mirror,* 26 May 1917, 28.
58 *Moving Picture World,* 2 June 1917, 1458.
59 *New York Tribune,* 6 May 1917, sec. 4, p. 4: "Mrs. Sanger to Tour with Her Film," *New York Times,* 28 March 1917, 11. It is not surprising that the Park

Theatre refused to screen *Birth Control* in the face of Bell's threats. When the theater showed *The Inside of the White Slave Traffic* four years earlier, the theater manager and several employees were arrested by police on obscenity charges. See Shelley Stamp, "'Oil upon the Flames of Vice': The Battle over White Slave Films in New York City," *Film History* 9, 4 (1997): 351–364.

60 "Bars 'Birth Control' Film," *New York Times*, 14 July 1917, 7; and "'Birth Control' Barred from New York," *Moving Picture World*, 19 May 1917, 1908. Bell's relationship with the Board of Review was complex: though he publicly favored the board over governmental censorship agencies, he also praised legal decisions to halt screenings of white-slave films the board had approved, indicating that he preferred a toothless board that could control through the court system. See "Bell Opposes Board of Censors," *New York Times*, 28 September 1916, 7.

61 "Commissioner Forbids Mrs. Sanger's Film," *New York Tribune*, 7 May 1916, 7; "Birth Control 'Movie' Barred from Public," *New York World*, 7 May 1917, 9; "Would Restrain Commissioner Bell," *New York Tribune*, 10 May 1917, 11; "'Birth Control' Coup," *Variety*, 11 May 1917, 32; "Stop 'Birth Control,'" *New York Dramatic Mirror*, 12 May 1917, 32; "Film That Was Banned Is Shown," 12 May 1917, unidentified newspaper clipping, RLC; and "'Birth Control' Barred from New York."

62 *Moving Picture World*, 21 April 1917, 451; *Variety*, 13 April 1917, 27; *Variety*, 30 March 1917, 27–28; and *Moving Picture World*, 21 April 1917, 388–389.

63 "Film That Was Banned Is Shown"; and *New York Tribune*, 13 May 1917, sec. 4, p. 4.

64 *New York Tribune*, 17 May 1917, 11. See also *New York Tribune*, 18 May 1917, 9; and "The Theatre as a Forum," typewritten MS, box 104, NBRMPC.

65 "Upholds Mrs. Sanger's Film," *New York Times*, 7 June 1917, 10; and "Bars 'Birth Control' Film." Some of the legal arguments in cases involving both films are transcribed in De Grazia and Newman, *Banned Films*, 186–191.

66 "Lois Weber, Film Genius, Has Spectacular Rise to Fame," unidentified Los Angeles newspaper clipping, n.d., n.p, RLC; and Lawrence, "'The Hand That Rocks the Cradle.'"

67 On *Maternity*, see *New York Dramatic Mirror*, 26 May 1917, 28; *Moving Picture World*, 2 June 1917, 1458; and *Motography*, 2 June 1917, 1175–1176. On *The Curse of Eve*, see *New York Dramatic Mirror*, 20 October 1917, 18; and *Moving Picture World*, 27 October 1917, 522.

SUMIKO HIGASHI

The New Woman and Consumer Culture

Cecil B. DeMille's Sex Comedies

Just exactly how new was the new woman? A number of feminist studies about silent films assume that women signifying modernity represent a break with previous models of womanhood.[1] Admittedly, the very label "new woman" evokes the revolution in manners and morals symbolizing the Jazz Age. A decade dubbed the roaring twenties produced flappers, flagpole sitting, and fast cars signifying youthful rebellion. Although conventional values triumphed in the last reel, the new woman was unruly en route to a companionate marriage. Surely, she was liberated from the constraints of Victorian mores and sentimental culture.[2] Such assumptions, however, are based on stereotypes not only about the Jazz Age, but also about Victorianism. Subject to as many, if not more, clichés as the Prohibition era, Victorian society was full of contradictions. Genteel middle-class women were socially and politically active despite prescriptive literature enshrining the domestic sphere. And they may have enjoyed more, not less, sexual latitude in homosocial ties and Boston marriages. The new woman, in contrast, was unconventional while reinventing herself as a sexual commodity in a consumer society. So, again, just how new was she?[3] As a sign of social change that involved self-making, gender relations, and middle-class consumption, the new woman was in fact ambiguous. A study of her uncertain evolution, based on recent social and cultural history, reveals as much continuity as change.[4]

Signifying the diminished privatization of middle-class women and a remapping of separate spheres for the sexes, the term "new woman" first appeared in the 1890s in public affairs periodicals like *North American Review* and *Outlook*. At the time, she was alternately praised as a "more independent, better educated . . . companion to husband and children" and condemned for having failed "to prove that woman's mission is something higher than the bearing of children and bringing them up."[5] As a matter of fact, middle-class women had long been engaged in social reproduction essential to class identity, especially educating sons for white-collar status, which was arduous work. Among their many obligations, as Mary P. Ryan argues, was gainful employment in limited occupations to augment family income and careful expenditure of resources. Indeed, Stuart M. Blumin argues that middle-class formation—defined in terms of social and cultural experience rather than mode of production—was women's work. Alert to the needs of community as well as family and swayed by evangelical Protestantism, middle-class women joined benevolent associations and supported reforms.[6] As the practice of separate spheres eroded later in the nineteenth century, they continued to promote numerous civic causes.[7] A few sought white-collar employment out of economic necessity and converted government offices and private firms into heterosexual workplaces. And many shopped in department stores in downtown districts like the Chicago loop that were once male preserves.[8]

Although middle-class women had been active in the public sphere, the pursuit of heterosexual leisure in commercial venues had a profound effect on gender relations in the early twentieth century.[9] Indeed, the transition from same-sex relations in Victorian society to mixed-sex relations based on companionate marriage was a momentous reversal. As Carroll Smith-Rosenberg argues, nineteenth-century middle-class women had enjoyed kinship and sororital ties comprising a homosocial culture in which "men made but a shadowy appearance." Women married yet remained intimate with each other.[10] A generation of college-educated new women even chose to forgo marriage for careers and social activism in the years before World War I. Consequently, postwar concern with adolescent sexuality and companionate marriage—issues legitimated by social scientists—represented a significant new trend.[11] As summed up by F. Scott Fitzgerald, who modeled his heroines after his inimitable wife Zelda, the 1920s was an extravagant era of gin, jazz, and flappers.[12] Characterized as a rebellious schoolgirl in *The Flapper* (1919) and personified by stars like Eleanor Boardman in *Wine of Youth* (1924), Clara Bow in *The Plastic Age* (1925), and Joan Crawford in *Our Dancing Daughters* (1928), the postwar new woman, unlike the athletic but curvaceous Gibson girl, was boyish. She was, in Fitzgerald's words, "lovely and expensive and about nineteen."[13] But was the so-called revolution in manners and morals indeed revolutionary?

Any reassessment of the new woman as man's pal and companion requires a focus on issues of sexuality and marriage including reproduction. Birth control, a term coined by Margaret Sanger, was and remains controversial. When Sanger was arrested for dispensing contraception at a Brownsville, New York, clinic in 1916, she was, interestingly, addressing the plight of working-class women. As social historians argue, middle-class women had already learned to control their fertility through contraceptive devices and abortion so that conservatives expressed concern about race suicide.[14] Despite postwar discourse on sexual mores and companionate marriage, single-issue reformers, women a generation older than flappers and intent on the vote, hesitated to embrace contraception. Charlotte Perkins Gilman, unlike suffragists in the National American Woman's Suffrage Association, was a radical, but she too criticized preoccupation with sexuality and Freud because it stereotyped women.[15] She would change her stance later. Yet "the incitement to talk about sex" was suspect, as Michel Foucault argues, because it was part of the social mechanism to regulate female sexual behavior.[16] What then was the nature of the much ballyhooed sexual revolution? And why was this rebellion represented in terms of women becoming sexually precocious in their relations with men? Well before the advent of lesbian studies and queer theory, Smith-Rosenberg asserted:

> At one end of the continuum lies committed heterosexuality, at the other uncompromising homosexuality; between a wide latitude of emotions and sexual feelings. Certain cultures and environments permit individuals a great deal of latitude in moving across this spectrum. I would like to suggest that the nineteenth century was such a cultural environment. That is, the supposedly repressive and destructive Victorian sexual ethos may have been more flexible and responsive to the needs of particular individuals than those of the mid-twentieth century.[17]

The momentous eclipse of same-sex relations in middle-class female culture by companionate marriage, symbolized by the new woman as flapper, resulted in a problematic legacy as seen in the films of Cecil B. DeMille.

Cecil B. DeMille: Setting Postwar Trends

A director acclaimed for legitimating early features by exploiting the intertexuality of films replicating best-sellers, paintings, opera, theater, and historical pageantry, Cecil B. DeMille set postwar trends by showcasing the new woman. At the center of his sex comedies, specifically *Old Wives for New* (1918), *Don't Change Your Husband* (1919), and *Why Change Your Wife?* (1920), was the sentimental heroine transformed into a clotheshorse and sexual playmate. At first, DeMille was reluctant to exploit fashion in a culture of consumption accelerated by wartime restructuring of the economy.[18] But Jesse L. Lasky, vice-president of Famous Players–Lasky and a colleague dating back to the days they had founded the studio, was persuasive: "What the public demands to-day is modern stuff with plenty of clothes, rich sets, and action." Lasky advised the director and his scenarist Jeanie Macpherson to "write something typically American ... that would portray a girl in the sort of role that the feminists in the country are now interested in ... the kind of girl that dominates ... who jumps in and does a man's work." Specifically, he urged DeMille to make an adaptation of David Graham Phillips's novel *Old Wives for New* because it "is full of modern problems and conditions, and while there are a number of big acting parts, it does not require any one big star. ... It would be a wonderful money maker and make a very interesting picture." As an alternative to Adolph Zukor's costly negotiations with Mary Pickford, the studio's biggest star, Lasky proposed all-star features capitalizing on Famous Players–Lasky's stock company. After purchasing the rights to the Phillips novel for $6,500, he wrote to the director from his front office in New York: "Personally I would like to see you become commercial to the extent of agreeing to produce this novel ... on account of the subject matter and the fame of the novel." Unrelenting, Lasky wrote a few weeks later, "you should get away from the spectacle stuff for one or two pictures and try to do modern stories of great human interest. 'Old Wives for New' is a wonderful title. ... I strongly recommend your undertaking to do it."[19]

DeMille began production in March 1918 in time for a successful midyear release. Although he reverted to the past and filmed a remake of *The Squaw Man* (1918), among other films, Lasky next encouraged him to consider a variation of *Old Wives for New* titled *Don't Change Your Husband*. A film with elaborate fantasy sequences, the feature launched Gloria Swanson on the path to stardom as queen of the Paramount lot. Most likely, DeMille was also prodded to make *Why Change Your Wife?* another all-star feature with Swanson and the last film in the trilogy. Lasky argued, "It is really better that you produce this picture than William [DeMille's brother, who is credited with the story] on account of your being so strongly identified with 'Don't Change Your Husband.' "[20] Audience response to these films, which proved immensely popular, attests to Lasky's expert reading of postwar moviegoing. As he observed, there was "an entire change in the taste of the public" that manifested itself in the popularity of war pictures as well as "a decided tendency toward lighter subjects." Less than two years after the studio merged with Zukor's Famous Players to court the respectable middle class, Lasky was encouraging DeMille to appeal to a broad audience. The director thus set an important trend both in the industry and in a burgeoning consumer culture. After the success of *Old Wives for New*, countless titles hinting at marital strife, such as *Rich Men's Wives, Too Much Wife, Trust Your Wife, How to Educate a Wife,* and *His Forgotten Wife,* appeared on marquee signs.

DeMille's postwar films established a lighthearted tone about subjects like marital infidelity and divorce by updating the sentimental heroine of the Victorian era as a frivolous consumer. Such a woman, however, became further entrapped in the process of self-commodification as she acquired more clothes and jewelry to attract the opposite sex. A fashion plate with a mansion as backdrop, DeMille's new woman set trends influenced by orientalism in clothing and interior design, thematics relating consumption to illicit sexuality. As part of the rebellion against cluttered Victorian taste, women's fashion, as well as home decor, had been streamlined even before the war. After the armistice, *Theatre* announced in the flippant tone characterizing discourse on women as consumers:

> Los Angeles now fills the proud position Paris once occupied as the arbiter of fashion.
> ... More women see deMille's pictures than read fashion magazines ... five whole reels just crammed and jammed with beautiful creations ...
> And then there are the tips on interior decoration and house-furnishing wherewith the Art Director and his staff ... adorn each scene. It is within bounds to say that the taste of the masses has been developed more by Cecil B. deMille through the educational influence —
> Good Lord! The beans are spilled. Nobody will read any further than the word "Educational."[21]

Indeed, DeMille's mise-en-scène constituted an advice manual preaching against old habits of self-restraint, but one that only the middle and upper classes could afford. Goods such as fashion ensembles, home furnishings, and bathroom fixtures were represented in color and art deco design to signify modernity. A medium close-up of Swanson sleeping on a lace-trimmed, embroidered pillowcase in *Don't Change Your Husband,* for example, stressed the luxury of fine linens. Several years ahead of trends, the director had a profound influence on advertisers educating the "new" salaried, as opposed to the "old" propertied, middle class intent on self-fulfillment and upward mobility. Advice literature in periodicals increasingly valued expenditure on material goods symbolizing refinement.[22]

Signifying the uneven transition from a producer to a consumer economy, the middle-class self was now constructed in terms of personality rather than character. Self-realization, in other words, became a product of presentation and display rather than moral imperative. Advertisers exalted the acquisition of goods as the basis of personal identity by coopting the language of spiritual fulfillment. Particularly effective in sanctioning consumer behavior were dramatizations of the process of self-making inherent in liberal Protestantism. DeMille's mise-en-scène provided many such examples. A winning personality, well dressed and adept in performance, could aspire to become "somebody," as Warren Susman argues.[23] But constructing the female self in such theatrical terms had profound implications for women in a consumer culture. Admittedly, genteel middle-class women were already performers in social rituals staged in drawing rooms, and they promoted the vogue of parlor theatricals. But these performances were based on the assumption that such practices were a sign of proper breeding and good character.[24] As part of the modern cult of personality, however, the social construction of the female gender was now equivalent to a masquerade enhancing sex appeal. DeMille's new woman thus became a sexual commodity symbolizing the reification of human relations, especially marital ones, in a consumer society. A spendthrift, she was now exposed, unlike the sentimental heroine in a privatized domestic sphere, to the moral dangers inherent in narcissistic consumer behavior.

The Commodification of Marriage:
Old Wives for New, Don't Change Your Husband,
and *Why Change Your Wife?*

David Graham Phillips, a best-selling novelist whose stories appeared in "new" middle-class periodicals like the *Saturday Evening Post,* was ahead of his time in contemplating the impact of modernity on the family. Specifically, he was interested in "the bearing of the scientific revolution upon woman and the home."[25] Discord on the part of Charles and Sophy Murdock, the middle-aged couple in *Old Wives for New,* is revealed when the husband takes exception to his wife's slovenliness. An expression of her lack of personality, Sophy's disorderly and unkempt home attests to her neglect of self, husband, and two grown children. Phillips is sympathetic about her failings, attributed in part to rural origins, but DeMille mercilessly deconstructs the revered American wife and mother in favor of the new woman.

Significantly, Jeanie Macpherson rewrote Phillips's marital squabble in terms of the exchange value of characters involved in sexual relationships. She begins *Old Wives for New* with a symbolic sequence cleverly titled in the script as follows: "'Life's' Bargain Counter/Across which our destinies are bartered like/so many Sacks of Meal—to 'Fate.'/Some are sold for Dollars/Some for Ambition/Some for Love—but all—are 'Sold.'" As described in the script, "Life," costumed as Harlequin, is "constantly laughing" behind a counter with "tiny figurines of *live* people, grouped in four sections, marked . . . staples, remnants, novelties, and mark-downs. . . . Among these are the main characters of the story . . . Sophy Murdock—in "Marked Downs," Murdock and Juliet in "Staples"—Berkeley and Jessie in "Remnants," Viola in "Novelties."[26] Possibly, this sequence about the commodification of marital relations was too literal a representation of marketplace transactions invading the domestic sphere. DeMille begins *Old Wives for New* instead with a didactic intertitle that could be construed as a quote from the novel but was not even a paraphrase and, moreover, could not be attributed to any character in the film:

> It is my belief, Sophy, that we Wives are apt to take our Husbands too much for granted. We've an inclination to settle down to neglectful *dowdiness*—just because we've "landed our Fish!" It is not enough for Wives to be merely virtuous anymore, scorning all frills: We must remember to trim our "Votes for Women" with a little lace and ribbon—if we would keep our Man a "Lover" as well as a "Husband"!

Such was DeMille's advice to female spectators enjoined to embrace the delights of the consumer culture, if only to retain their marital status.

After an introduction depicting the social status of the main characters, the film opens with the first of DeMille's celebrated bathroom sequences. Although the set design is modest compared to the spacious tiled bathroom with sunken tub and silk-curtained shower in *Male and Female* (1919), the scene was surely impressive for audiences still living in homes without bathtubs.[27] A tub on the left stands opposite a door flanked by two wash basins, each with hot and cold water faucets, mirror, shelf, and pair of sconces. At right angle to the sink on the left is a stained glass window above a towel bar on the wall. Accentuating the cornice, doorway, window, and mirrors are designs in ornate molding. The flooring consists of alternate black and white tiles in a diamond-shaped pattern. Charles Murdock (Elliott Dexter), dressed in a bathrobe and assisted by a valet, opens the window so that a view of trees contrasts nature with artifice. A fastidious person, he is disgusted to find Sophy's hair clogging his basin, not to mention a messy comb and toothbrush carelessly left in his corner of the bathroom. Worse, a close-up from his point of view shows untidy toilet articles strewn haphazardly about his wife's sink and vanity. Sophy (Sylvia

The New Woman and Consumer Culture

48. Elliott Dexter is dissatisfied with his unkempt, overweight, middle-aged wife (Sylvia Ashton) in *Old Wives for New* (1918). Photo courtesy of George Eastman House.

Ashton), introduced in the credits as she is eating chocolates and reading the funnies, enters the bathroom in a grumpy mood and slams the window shut. She is wearing a loose bathrobe over her corpulent figure and has carelessly swept her hair into a knot. Deciding that a bath is not worth the effort, she seeks refuge in bed while her family breakfasts downstairs. Murdock seats himself at a table set with silverware and a glass fruit compote but is displeased to find an orange spoon in the wrong place. The maid, who is as slovenly as her mistress, serves poached eggs with broken yolks. As he rises from the table in disgust, his daughter, who is a more sympathetic character in the novel, murmurs, "I'm sorry dear — if mother would only let *me* run the house!"

Disgruntled, Murdock retreats to his study and stares at a photograph of his wife, shown in an insert, when she was a slender young woman with blonde curls (Wanda Hawley). A dissolve to a picturesque rural scene shows how he literally reeled in his bride while she was walking barefoot in the stream — a reference to fishing in the first intertitle. DeMille cleverly juxtaposes past and present as Murdock's memory of his lovely young bride is intercut with Sophy, now an obese and untidy matron, bursting in on his reverie. Appalled by her aging figure, he declares, "Sophy — it's a degradation for two people to go on living who no longer care for each other! I propose that you will take half of all we've got — and that you and I shall release each other." A display of armaments on the paneled wall of the study includes a pistol, a long blade, and a sword. Apparently, the battle of the sexes has begun. Murdock and his son, Charley, who sides with his mother in the novel's version of the marital breakup, decamp on a hunting expedition. Again, DeMille associates romance with sportsmanship as the businessman falls in love with Juliet Raeburn (Florence Vidor), the vacationing owner of a boutique aptly named Dangerfield's.

Sophy is angered to learn that she may indeed have a rival. During a marital argument photographed in low-key lighting, she tears up her picture as a young bride and exclaims, "Have all the fun you want with that younger, fresher woman — But just you remember... I'll never divorce you — never!" Who is at fault here? Sophy is self-indulgent. But Murdock, whose relationship with his daughter has incestuous overtones, is in love with a much younger woman. Dramatic lighting is thus keyed to the emotional mood of a shot rather than the articulation of moral issues, as in DeMille's earlier films like *The Cheat* (1915) or *The Heart of Nora Flynn* (1916). Characteristic of the director's postwar visual style, set decoration and costumes provide a more reliable sign of personal ethics.[28] Several weeks after the hunting trip in *Old Wives for New,* for example, Murdock shops with his daughter at Dangerfield's and meets his business partner, Tom Berkeley (Theodore Roberts), accompanied by his mistress Jessie (Julia Faye) and her friend Viola (Marcia Manon). DeMille's mise-en-scène underscores the decline of separate spheres or the interpenetration of home and marketplace in that Juliet's boutique resembles a tasteful upper-class residence. A split-level design features a checkerboard black-and-white marbled floor, walls framed with moldings and intersected with pilasters and columns, an imposing chandelier, an elegant floor lamp and sconces, dark velvety drapery with tiebacks, plush upholstered chairs, and artistic floral arrangements. Yet this well-appointed establishment, as signified by its name, is the site of questionable transactions involving the commodification of women.

Because Juliet now shuns him as a married man, Murdock joins Berkeley, Jessie, and Viola at a supper club. An exotic dancer in a sensual harem costume evokes orientalist fantasies about illicit sexuality that is the focus of the plot. Unfortunately, Berkeley has a wandering eye and transfers his attentions that evening to a flirtatious blonde named Bertha (Edna Mae Cooper). Jesse, intent on revenge, intrudes on their rendezvous with a gun and retaliates with deadly aim. A sign of lower-class origins as well as loose morals, the prostitute's boudoir becomes the scene of Berkeley's unfortunate death. Bertha has a penchant for garish furniture decorated with gilt rococo curves, ruffled drapery, shiny bedspreads, cheap art work on wainscoted walls, and kitsch memorabilia. Certainly, her garish room contrasts with Juliet's tasteful boutique.

Old Wives for New concludes when Sophy, flattered by Murdock's impecunious secretary, Melville Blagden (Gustav Seyffertitz), decides to undergo a torturous beauty regimen in order to remarry. A benign representative of a patriarchal order, Blagden educates Sophy to redefine herself as a commodity by purchasing cosmetics, gowns, and accessories. At the film's conclusion, DeMille cuts from Sophy's elegant wedding to Murdock's own second marriage in Venice. After meeting at an outdoor flower market signifying nature as opposed to artificiality, the businessman and dressmaker reconcile. Yet the film's affirmation of self-theatricalization emphasizes the importance of artifice in sexual and marital relationships. Put another way, the reification of social relations under consumer capitalism has now invaded the boudoir to redefine matrimony. A sign of the erosion of separate spheres, even the private space of respectable homes now simulates the marketplace as a site for commodified female bodies.

According to a fan magazine article, "So many wives wrote indignant letters to DeMille about 'Old Wives for New' that C. B. and his clever writer, Jeanie Macpherson, wrote a story from the wives' standpoint." The *Chicago News* described the second film of the trilogy as an attempt "to restore harmony with . . . feminine followers."[29] Although *Don't Change Your Husband* was interpreted as the wife's version of marital strife, the heroine has already been transformed into a new woman so that her next lesson is tolerating her mate's humdrum habits. DeMille begins the film with a humorous intertitle that foregrounds the battle of the sexes to contrast its more intimate scale with the tumult of World War I: "This does not deal with the tread of victorious Armies, nor defeated Huns—but is just a little sidelight on the inner life of Mr. and Mrs. Porter." Leila Porter (Gloria Swanson), an elegant and fastidious woman, finds "several dull gray years of matrimony—getting slightly on her nerves." Blind to his wife's discontent, Jim Porter (Elliott Dexter) has an expanded waistline, buries his head behind newspapers, forgets their wedding anniversary, and indulges a taste for green onions.

DeMille registers marital reversals through clever use of mise-en-scène. During a compromising flirtation at a ball with ne'er-do-well Schuyler Van Sutphen (Lew Cody), Leila, costumed as Juliet with ropes of pearls in her hair, ascends a marble staircase featuring an ornate balustrade on screen right. After declaring that she can no longer tolerate a " 'corned beef and cabbage' existence," Leila descends a marble staircase on the left in the vestibule of the house she is abandoning. While Jim, seated to her right, buries his head in the papers as the film opens, in her second marriage Leila finds Schuyler seated to her left at breakfast and equally immersed in the news. DeMille's mise-en-scène thus dramatizes the reification of marital relations: husband and wife are interchangeable parts as modern personali-

49. Gloria Swanson finds that at breakfast her second mate is as immersed in the news as the spouse she has just divorced in *Don't Change Your Husband* (1919). Photo courtesy of George Eastman House.

ties signifying the dominance of exchange value in commodity production. Such a turn of events raises disturbing moral issues about the nature of consumption as practiced by the new woman exploiting the marriage market. An art title, interestingly, shows a pyramid and sphinx symbolizing "The Eternal Feminine" to equate female self-gratification with mysterious orientalism.

Determined to win back his former spouse, Jim shaves off his mustache, adopts an exercise regimen, and acquires a swank wardrobe. Phillips observes in *Old Wives for New*, "of those external forces that combine to make us what we are, dress is one of the most potent. It determines the character of our associations, determines the influences that shall chiefly surround and press upon us. It is a covering for our ideas no less than for our bodies."[30] Macpherson's rewriting of this quote in *Don't Change Your Husband* signifies the reification of human consciousness in that people are confused with things: "Of those external forces which combine to make us what we are, DRESS is the most potent. It covers our *ideas* no less than our bodies—until we finally become the thing we look to be." Indeed, a proliferation of mirror shots in DeMille's Jazz Age films attests to the increasing importance of style over substance.[31] A medium shot shows Jim, for example, standing in front of a mirror while staring at his image in a hand mirror. Although he is a businessman who dominates financial negotiations, his pose resembles that of prostitutes, namely Viola in *Old Wives for New* and Toodles (Julia Faye), Schuyler's mistress in *Don't Change Your Husband*. During the credits of the former film, Viola, a "Painted Lady" with orientalized features, is seated in front of a dresser and applies rouge as she gazes in the mirror.[32] Similarly, Toodles is presented in the credits as she primps in front of a three-way mirror, turns around to face the camera, and kisses an image of herself in a hand mirror. Genteel preoccupation with appearances as a sign of character has deteriorated into narcissistic self-absorption. Accordingly, Jim wins back his former wife at the end of *Don't Change Your Husband* by transforming himself into a dapper dinner guest wearing a tuxedo and a fur-collared coat. He has acquired personality. As part of the exchange, Leila now instructs the servants to serve him his favorite dish, green onions.

Although the scenario of *Don't Change Your Husband* appears to be a variation of *Old Wives for New,* the moral issues raised by self-gratification fade in the midst of pleasurable pursuits. Significantly, the characters in *Old Wives for New* are still troubled by scruples or exhibit some degree of conscience in their behavior. Juliet, for example, refuses to be involved in a relationship with a man who has deceived her about his marital status. When Sophy wrongly names her as a corespondent in a libelous divorce suit, Murdock goes to extreme lengths to protect her reputation. Even Berkeley, as he lies dying from a gunshot wound in a prostitute's apartment, begs his partner to avoid a scandal that will tarnish his family name. The frivolous characters in *Don't Change Your Husband,* in contrast, pursue their pleasures without much regard for consequences. Leila engages in a flirtation with Schuyler, whom she marries after divorcing Jim, and Schuyler in turn has an affair with Toodles during his marriage to Leila. While the members of the younger set impulsively gratify their whims, their elders, personified by Schuyler's Aunt Huckney (Sylvia Ashton) and an aging bishop (Theodore Roberts), register indignation in point-of-view and reaction shots. DeMille thus comments on generational differences by representing conscience as the disapproval of middle-aged spectators rather than an internalized set of behavioral norms. But in *Why Change Your Wife?*, the last film of the trilogy, even the older generation succumbs to pleasure. Aunt Kate, who is the equivalent of Aunt Huckney (Sylvia Ashton) in the guise of a chaperon, is no longer alarmed by the flirtatious behavior of young spouses and herself falls prey to the flattery of a violinist.

Dramatizing the less inhibited nature of marital relations in *Don't Change Your Husband,* DeMille conflates exotic visions of distant lands and employs disparate orientalist motifs in set and costume design. A Middle Eastern backdrop for social entertainment, Leila's living room features ornately carved pilasters, tapestry, carpeting, and a potted palm. An Asian servant in Chinese dress provides drinks in cups carved out of precious jade. Leila, whom Schuyler addresses as "Lovely Chinese Lotus," poses as part of the decor in a turban and carries a fan of peacock feathers. Even more exotic is Schuyler's residence, a mansion that includes a loggia with matching rattan furniture and a study simulating a display window with chinoiserie. A scroll hangs on the rear wall, and to its right an oriental vase stands on a cabinet. A chair in the foreground is upholstered in fabric with a bamboo pattern, and a fringed throw in floral print is artfully tossed over a nearby sofa. On the right side of the floor, partially covered with an oriental carpet, stands an ornate table with an incense burner. Leila, responding to the pungent aroma filling the air, enters this sybaritic domain at her peril. Delighted by a beaded costume, she drapes the fabric around her body in a mannequin's pose that recalls a similar moment in *The Cheat*. A description of this scene in the script implies that consumption has its dangers: "A change comes over Leila; . . . she seems suddenly to be slipping back into Orientalism; to be taking on a real, subtle, *un-American* personality. She is no longer a laughing Society Woman merely trying on a Chinese Cloak, for fun."[33]

A cultural practice established by halftones, magic lantern slides, panoramas, stereographs, and actualities, as well as by museum and world's fair exhibits and department store displays, consumption as visual appropriation was linked to exotic sites. Orientalism signified not only luxury but also self-indulgence and depraved sensuality. Consumption was thus equivalent to sexual license, interpreted as un-American, unpatriotic, or uncivilized, even as middle-class shoppers eased their consciences and loosened their purse strings to buy goods signifying refinement. Preoccupation with bathing rituals and elegant bathrooms, as represented in DeMille's celebrated texts, belied anxiety insofar as consuming evoked the "other," including spendthrift women.[34] Commodities that signified genteel status, moreover, theatened middle-class masculinity, already beleaguered in an urban and industrial setting. Schuyler in *Don't Change Your Husband,* for example, is an effeminate voluptuary because orientalism remains at the core of his obsession with illicit sexuality. His exclamation about "Pleasure"—"Wealth"—and "Love" cues the sensational fantasy sequence of the film. A spectacle prefiguring the well-known flashback to a Babylonian court in *Male and Female,* this footage consists of three separate scenes photographed mostly in extreme long shot: Leila seated on a gigantic swing suspended over a swimming pool adorned with masses of flowers and bathing beauties in fishnet stockings; Leila worshiped by the well-oiled bodies of black male slaves at her feet in an opulent oriental court; and Leila clad in flimsy chiffon as she lounges in an Edenic paradise, with Bacchus squeezing grapes into her mouth.

A year after completion of *Don't Change Your Husband,* Lasky prevailed on DeMille to make *Why Change Your Wife?* Although the director later

The New Woman and Consumer Culture

sought to obtain credit for Macpherson, William deMille conceived the story while Olga Printzlau and Sada Cowan wrote the scenario.[35] Admittedly, the film's intertitles are much wittier, but given the similarity of the plot to the previous two films in the trilogy, Macpherson's influence was not inconsiderable. A remodeling of the Victorian sentimental heroine as the centerpiece of a consumer culture, *Why Change Your Wife?* is a variation of *Old Wives for New* and *Don't Change Your Husband* and opens with yet another bathroom scene. Robert Gordon (Thomas Meighan) is shaving in front of an oval mirror at right angle to an oval window with a scalloped and fringed valance. As his wife Beth (Gloria Swanson) constantly interrupts his toilet, a title informs us "Marriage, like genius, is an infinite capacity for taking pains." DeMille in fact dared to show Robert sitting on the toilet seat twice when Beth demands access to the medicine cabinet behind the mirror and requires help fastening her dress. Unfortunately, Beth's "virtues are her only vices" in a hedonistic era featuring flappers, gin, and jazz. She disapproves of her husband's commodious wine cellar, furnished with leather furniture, a full-size bar, and racks of bottles. When she voices concern about postwar issues such as "the starving millions in Europe," Robert replies, "Why do you insist that everything I do for *our* happiness robs someone else?" Significantly, aspects of middle-class formation that express character, especially self-restraint, child rearing, and social activism, have given way to markers of social status, including consumption, that signify personality.

Drawing on orientalist themes about consumption that equate a boutique showcasing fashion with a woman's private boudoir, DeMille shows Robert visiting a shop aptly named Maison Chic. An Asian woman in exotic dress greets him at the door. A medium long shot shows Sally Clark, an attractive model, climbing on top of a dresser with a three-way mirror to peer out an oval window in the dressing room, a decorative motif that recalls the Gordons' bathroom. DeMille deleted an intertitle in the script that characterizes Sally as a golddigger, "who buys the necessities of her life with her salary and the luxuries with her alimony," so that she is not entirely unsympathetic. Preparing to model a backless negligee with transparent sleeves and a train trimmed with fur, she removes the full-length slip beneath the flimsy skirt in a close-up revealing high-buttoned shoes. She places a heart-shaped tattoo on her left shoulder and daubs perfume from a bottle labeled "Persian Night."[36] By contrast, Beth is outraged when she later tries on the negligee and gazes at her image in the bedroom mirror. Robert insists, "My dearest, since time began dress has played it's [*sic*] role in love, and woman has worn it to delight her mate." As in *Don't Change Your Husband,* the seduction of women with expensive apparel triggers a fantasy or flashback sequence. According to the script, the scenes that follow include a "dissolve to Gloria Swanson as a wood nymph in cave man days, then an Oriental courtesan." A photograph of Swanson and Meighan in exotic costume survives, but the director evidently deleted these scenes in the final cut.[37] Still, Beth's indignation is obviously a response to the flashback: "Do you expect me to share your Oriental ideas? Do you want your *wife* to lure you like a— Oh why didn't you marry a Turk?" Robert, in a medium shot, smells Sally's perfume on the negligee and recalls her seductive image, superimposed on the screen between himself and his incensed wife.

Aside from fashion, the transformation of the Victorian woman into a sexual playmate requires an appreciation of popular as opposed to highbrow culture. Anticipating the negligee's delivery, Robert decides to play the "Hindustan Fox Trot," a postwar tune with distinct oriental overtones. Beth insists, "Try to cultivate your taste, dear!" and prefers "The Dying Poet." Bored with his wife's dowdy clothes and spectacles, Robert prefers to attend the follies rather than listen to an adagio performed by the violinist, Radinoff (Theodore Kosloff), whom he stereotypes as "a wired-haired foreigner." Still dedicated to spiritual uplift, Beth reads books with titles such as *How to Improve Your Mind*. After a marital rupture, she removes all traces of her spouse from the living room and throws in the trash can an issue of *Motion Picture Classic*—an inspired choice for DeMille—and a baseball magazine. She then announces, "I'm going to give my whole life to charity, Aunt Kate. I hate clothes—and men." A caricature of the genteel middle-class woman who values social activism and highbrow culture, Beth is instantly converted to consumer values during a shopping trip. DeMille cuts between adjacent dressing rooms in a smart boutique to show her angry reaction when she overhears two gossips attribute her divorce to her frumpy appearance. Assuming the role of a mannequin, she places ornaments in her hair, poses with a feathered fan, and drapes brocade against her body while gazing at herself in a hand mirror. She then instructs the salesclerk, "I'll take this and six more; and make them sleeveless, backless, transparent, indecent—go the limit!"

Beth's sensational debut as a new woman occurs at a fashionable resort, where Robert is vacationing with his second wife, Sally. An establishing shot shows musicians playing on a balcony and hotel guests seated at tables around a swimming pool with an island featuring an octagonal fountain. Potted plants and palms, as well as wicker and rattan furniture, signify a tropical atmosphere as the backdrop for romance. An extreme long shot reveals Beth standing in an archway that is the entrance to the pool area. She

The New Woman and Consumer Culture

50. Thomas Meighan is disconcerted to find that his dowdy former wife (Gloria Swanson) has transformed herself into a seductive fashion plate in *Why Change Your Wife?* (1920). Photo courtesy of George Eastman House.

advances to the foreground in a floral-patterned bathing suit and matching fringed cap, an eye-catching ensemble that attracts instant attention. A long shot next shows Beth conversing with several male admirers including uniformed military men. A cut to a long shot of her seated on the ledge of the fountain, but hidden under her parasol, results in an amusing scene when Robert enters from the right. A close-up of her legs, rendered alluring by stylish high-heeled shoes and an ornate garter wrapped around her left calf, represents his point of view. Unaware that he is admiring his former wife, Robert walks behind her and peers down at her from the left. An angled close-up of her peering up at him through the plastic folds of her parasol results in a shocking yet delightful recognition. When Radinoff escorts Beth away, Robert, now thoroughly enticed by his former spouse, angrily slams his cap on the ground.

DeMille orchestrates another divorce and remarriage in a complicated scenario that results in Robert, seriously injured, being nursed in Beth's home, while Sally is determined to reclaim him. An object of struggle between two determined women, Robert lies helpless as they fight over him in a brawl that ends with Sally shattering a mirror and attempting to disfigure Beth. Since she has unmasked herself as ill tempered and vindictive, the former model concedes defeat and resumes flirting with Radinoff. Beth remarries her former husband, remodels her negligee, and plays the "Hindustan Fox Trot" in the wine cellar. DeMille's didactive voice is heard in the final intertitle: "And now you know what every husband knows: that a man would rather have his wife for his sweetheart than any other woman: but Ladies: if you would be your husband's sweetheart you simply *must* learn to forget that you're his wife." Genteel middle-class women, it appears, had become spirited new women, but even in a companionate marriage they were still not equal to men.[38]

At issue in the so-called revolution in manners and morals signifying increased commodification of female sexuality was the nature of heterosexual relations. DeMille did hint at the darker aspect of relations between men and women in a disarmingly blunt intertitle in *Old Wives for New*. After Jessie shoots Berkeley, she confides to Murdock, "I killed him—he was a beast! No man ever knows what another man is with a woman!" Also revealing is a sequence in *Don't Change Your Husband* when Toodles bursts into the Van Sutphen residence to claim a share of the cash that Jim has paid Schuyler, fallen on hard times, for Leila's solitaire. Giving her husband's mistress half a wad of thick bills, Leila explains, "Don't misunderstand—he *owed* you something—and you are paid! He promised me a few things, too, such as Love and Protection—and he didn't pay! Let's only one of us be cheated!" The use of financial language is extremely apt in a film that dramatizes the increasing commodification of matrimonial life. DeMille, interestingly, cuts from a medium two-shot of Schuyler and Jim looking away from the scrutiny of the camera to a medium long shot of the two accusing women eyeing them. For a brief moment, the battle of the sexes takes precedence over class distinctions dividing wife and mistress. Although unconventional nineteenth-century feminists like Elizabeth Cady Stanton outraged genteel society by comparing marriage with prostitution in attempts to reform divorce laws, the reification of marital relations based on exchange value, as shown in DeMille's trilogy, implied no less.[39]

Industry Discourse: Old versus New Morality

Significant change in the demographics of film attendance in the 1920s was related to trends established by the production and exhibition of DeMille's early Jazz Age films. Certainly, exhibitors distinguished between middle-class patrons of first-run theaters and working-class ethnic audiences at neighborhood venues, as well as between urban centers and rural areas. During a decade of social strife signified by the Red Scare, labor strikes, immigration restriction, Prohibition, the Sacco-Vanzetti case, the Ku Klux Klan, and the Scopes trial, the search for a national market in film distribution and exhibition was essential. The exploitation of DeMille's controversial films showed that market segmentation based on class, race, ethnicity, religion, and geographical region could be superceded by an appeal to gender. Although reception of consumer culture, including commercialized amusement, was mediated by subcultures, the director's emphasis on set and costume design appealed to women. As his brother William noted about the democratization of luxury, "Paris fashion shows had been accessible only to the chosen few. C. B. revealed them to the whole country, the costumes his heroines wore being copied by hordes of women and girls throughout the land, especially by those whose contacts with centers of fashion were limited or non-existent." DeMille himself represented this obsession with style in *The Affairs of Anatol* (1921) when a farmer's wife copies a magazine illustration, shown in an insert, to trim an ordinary hat.[40] Since the director became the industry's most important trendsetter in the late 1910s and early 1920s, his emphasis on fashion was surely related to changes in the demographics of the film audience. According to Richard Koszarski, the percentage of men in motion picture audiences began to decline in the 1910s, whereas the number of women rose from 60 percent in 1920 to 83 percent in 1927.[41]

An analysis of industry discourse shows that exploitation campaigns appealing to women displaced issues in DeMille texts that might have segmented the audience. Controversy regarding social problems in *Old Wives for New*, however, was almost passé by the time *Why Change Your Wife?* was exhibited two years later. DeMille later claimed that Adolph Zukor, who "spent millions to plaster the country about the purity of Paramount Pictures," reluctantly released the first film.[42] During the same month that critics were taking note of DeMille's new trendsetting production, Zukor asserted in *Motion Picture News* that "Wholesome dramas, uplifting in character, clean comedies, comedy dramas, and plays dealing with the more cheerful aspects of life will be exclusively chosen for production."[43] Audiences were by no means completely receptive to dramatizations of social change signifying modernity. *Old Wives for New* had in fact been subject to in-house censorship before its distribution. A few weeks before the film's premiere, Lasky received a detailed memo that proposed a number of cuts. Among suggestions was deletion of the first intertitle referring to the dowdiness of married women because "it is liable to be misconstrued by the average spectator." Clearly, Famous Players–Lasky was now marketing its product in terms of a broad-based appeal rather than targeting respectable middle-class audiences. Also objectionable were close-ups of the wash basins in the bathroom and signs of Murdock's fastidiousness. Significantly, these cuts were not made in the surviving print in the director's nitrate collection at George Eastman House. But the suggestion that DeMille insert an intertitle to indicate that Murdock, contrary to the scenario, did not engage in an affair with Viola was heeded. Furthermore, risqué scenes of Berkeley's rendezvous with Bertha were cut to emphasize Jessie confronting the couple. Perhaps most interesting, given negative Catholic reception of the director's first historical epic, *Joan the Woman* (1916), was deletion of a scene in which Jessie seeks refuge in a convent. According to the New York office, this development would be "offensive to Catholics, in as much as it implies that a Catholic Institution would receive and protect a murderess."[44]

Critical discourse on *Old Wives for New* and subsequently *Don't Change Your Husband* and *Why Change Your Wife?* did focus on the impact of controversial issues on audience reception. A reminder that *Old Wives for New* was condemned by the Pennsylvania State Board because it dealt with prostitution provides today's readers with insight about past censorship issues.[45] Critics at the time disagreed about the extent to which these films violated social conventions, yet their differences reveal a lack of consensus regarding issues like divorce. R. E. Pritchard, for example, summed up his assessment of *Old Wives for New* in *Motion Picture News:* "There are some risqué situations in the story, but these have been handled delicately." Frederick James Smith, however, objected in *Motion Picture Classic* to "scenes of disgusting debauchery" and "immoral episodes." He concluded, "It is extremely difficult to build up a pleasing romance upon a foundation of divorce." Similarly, Edward Weitzel claimed in *Moving Picture World* that "hardly any of the characters command the spectator's respect. Charles Murdock . . . has but little moral stamina, and is surrounded, principally, by well-dressed men and women of no morals at all." Weitzel even suggested censoring objectionable material: "The cabaret scene is too insistent in establishing the moral laxity of its female guests, and other scenes of the same nature would stand cutting." *Variety*'s critic also referred to censorship: "There appears to have been some doubt as to the propriety of presenting the picture in total at the Rivoli in New York [a first-run theater] . . . cutting was no doubt considered." Clearly, the critics recognized that *Old Wives for New* was questionable, if not offensive, but they moved their discussion to the high ground of art to appeal to respectable middle-class patrons. Pritchard asserted that "it is the kind of picture that will convince those who doubt that the photoplay has reached the artistic plane of the spoken drama." The "Exhibitor to Exhibitor Review Service" in *Motion Picture News* agreed that the "feature will prove objectionable to some of you. Nevertheless, this picture is very artistic."[46]

Don't Change Your Husband elicited another chorus of disagreement that is revealing about exhibition practices. Smith stated in *Motion Picture Clas-*

sic, "We do not agree with Miss Macpherson's philosophy, but we admire her effort . . . in approaching the realities of things as they are." *Variety* labeled the film "clean and wholesome," but *Motion Picture News* counseled exhibitors, "It suggests the divorce element without your having to go into that, and we wouldn't do so directly, because you are likely to sacrifice some of the intensely human appeal of this picture." As for the fantasy sequence, the trade journal claimed, "There is a sensuous touch here and there in the scenes that follow. They will offend no one, but they will create a lot of talk for the picture itself." Aware of cultural differences, exhibitors found it difficult to market films about subjects like prostitution and divorce, especially in small towns and rural areas that were increasingly centers of religious fundamentalism. As a matter of fact, the Phillips novel, though published a decade before the film's release, still construes divorce as socially undesirable in contrast to the blasé manner in which DeMille's characters exchange spouses. Apparently, exhibitors engaged in a high-wire act by exploiting the sex appeal of a film but taking steps not to offend patrons.

Despite controversy, DeMille's early Jazz Age films played to large and enthusiastic audiences in first-run theaters in major cities. At Grauman's Million Dollar Theatre in downtown Los Angeles, *Don't Change Your Husband* broke all attendance records so that Sid Grauman, departing from established policy, held the picture over for another week. By the time *Why Change Your Wife?* was released in April 1920, Smith reacted to the shifting moral standards of the postwar era: "What a shock Cecil deMille's latest silken orchid drama . . . would have caused but two short years ago." But *Motion Picture News* pointed out that the feature "practically throws that which most people call part of the moral code overboard with its teaching, [and] presents its principal characters as people who have about as much regard for the sanctity of the marriage vow 'as an Arab does for a sun bath,' . . . for an exhibitor with a neighborhood or small town house it may not be an ideal attraction."[47] Constituting a parallel discourse on the evils of modernity was the trade journal's equation of sexual license with images of orientalism.

Avoiding the cultural divide between rural and urban America, the exhibition of *Why Change Your Wife?* was successful in major cities because exploitation sidestepped divorce and stressed consumption. Although these two issues were interrelated, as the film's title implies, exhibitor emphasis on fashion was a clever way to defuse public reaction to controversial issues. Sid Grauman, for example, simulated the screen by displaying paintings of movie stills in downtown Los Angeles shops, surely a reversal of constructing the frame as a plate-glass window. Such advertising resulted in a special 10:45 P.M. performance that was added to the screening schedule to accommodate crowds at Grauman's Rialto. A similar campaign based on window tie-ups in fashionable stores was orchestrated in concert with the Memphis Chamber of Commerce. A month after the film's release, Paramount ran an ad in *Motion Picture News* to boast that "'Why Change Your Wife?' has broken records in every city in which it has been shown." Constructing an elaborate showcase for the film's premiere in New York, Adolph Zukor spent $30,000 to renovate the Criterion. Indeed, Zukor's strategy of acquiring an interest in first-run theaters meant enormous publicity for Famous Players–Lasky specials shown at higher admission prices. As *Moving Picture World* noted about the record-breaking success of *The Affairs of Anatol* in the following year, "a Broadway showing is not always indicative of the attitude of the country, [but] such a run determines a great deal."[48] The exploitation of feature films at movie palaces, especially those appealing to fashion-conscious women, thus influenced nationwide trends in exhibition practices.

Although the industry still relied on small-town exhibitors and neighborhood venues in urban areas, exploitation stressing window tie-ups in department stores and movie ads in the *Saturday Evening Post, Ladies' Home Journal,* and *Collier's* was obviously aimed at middle-class women. As for working-class and ethnic women, social historians like Elizabeth Ewen and Kathy Peiss emphasize the importance of filmgoing for a younger generation preoccupied with fashion as a mode of self-representation and assimilation.[49] Appealing to female spectators was thus an industry strategy that surmounted socioeconomic and cultural barriers. As early as 1918, *Motion Picture News* suggested that exhibitors display pictures of female stars in elegant costumes to attract women and to persuade their escorts to buy admission tickets. Advertising, moreover, did not cease once the audience was seated inside the theater and began to enjoy the entertainment. As *Motion Picture News* observed about *Why Change Your Wife?* DeMille inserted close-ups of commodities such as perfume and "a certain talking machine company's records."[50] Spectacle representing the allure of consumer goods, especially the latest fashion in apparel and home decor, was surely related to the fact that the ratio of female to male spectators continued to rise throughout the decade.

Unlike trade journals counseling exhibitors to downplay controversial issues, fan magazine discourse on DeMille's trilogy focused on the relationship between fashion and divorce as a sign of the times.[51] During the early decades of the twentieth century, the rate of divorce almost doubled while expenditures for personal grooming, clothing, furniture, automobiles, and recreation tripled. Divorce was especially common in urban areas as hasty wartime unions were dissolved. Significantly, an increasing number of complaints in divorce suits involved the desire of wives for a more pleasurable lifestyle and the inability of husbands to provide income. According to the *New York Times*, "if dissatisfied wives were guided by the argument of 'Don't Change Your Husband,' the divorce courts would be more crowded than they are now." Postwar discourse on divorce as a sign of urbanization, secularization of liberal Protestantism, and changing patterns of wage earning and consumption focused on the new woman.[52] Unlike the scenario of thousands of actual divorce cases, however, consumer behavior was touted in DeMille's films as the solution rather than the cause of marital discord.

During the production of *Old Wives for New*, DeMille expressed traditional male beliefs in an interview, arguing that the film provided a "moral lesson to wives." Bluntly, he said, "Husbands leave home because their wives are no longer physically attractive. . . . It's simply the most rudimentary example of sex psychology." As for his merciless lampooning of Sophy Murdock as an obese and indolent spouse, he argued, "It is typically American to . . . idealize the wife, paint her virtues, blacken the man, and think we're standing by the bulwarks of civilization. In reality, we're making men hide their domestic bitterness and seek their comforts . . . secretly."[53] On the release of *Don't Change Your Husband,* DeMille repeated his thoughts in *Motion Picture Magazine* by claiming, "man must have mystery, and, above all, lure, and if his wife doesn't retain it herself, he'll find it elsewhere." Gloria Swanson claimed in *Motion Picture Magazine* that "divorce should be made more easy. . . . Then the wife, knowing she might lose her husband . . . would exert herself to hold him. And . . . the husband would go on paying attention to his wife, bringing her flowers and candy, taking her to theaters." A response to discourse that appeared frivolous but revealed profound changes in marital expectations, *Motion Picture Magazine* published an editorial titled "Cinema Husbands": "Let us have a screenic [sic] burial of the movie husband. . . . The average American husband is no fool. The cinema husband is not only a fool but a blind egoist as well."[54]

Perhaps the most revealing article that pointed to the contradictions of defining the new woman in conventional Victorian terms was published after the success of *Why Change Your Wife?* Acclaimed as "the film's greatest authority on matrimonial problems," DeMille claimed in *Photoplay,* "I believe I can do more to prevent divorce, that I am doing more to prevent divorce than any minister or anti-divorce league in the world." Despite the contemporary tone of his Jazz Age films, the director expressed attitudes about sexual difference and marriage that were stereotypically Victorian. For example, he asserted, "sex ... is a universal problem. It is the one thing one is never free of. If the relations between a man and woman are not right, not harmonious, every other relation of their lives is affected—their home, their children, his business, his usefulness as a citizen." Such distinctions in use of plural and masculine pronouns implied that the practice of separate spheres for the sexes, in a new era of woman's suffrage, was still an ideal arrangement. Furthermore, the filmmaker argued, "Fidelity to the marriage covenant—the most sacred of all obligations— ... is to be gained only by showing wives how men may be, if not lifted entirely above sex, at least taught to hold it within the bounds of moral law and decency." What exactly were those bounds? DeMille blithely confessed that in eighteen years of marriage, he had never spent a Saturday evening at home—a revelation that attested to the habit of respectable middle-class men visiting brothels.[55] Apparently, a man's sexual nature required a certain amount of discreet tolerance on the part of his wife. Such an arrangement would have had very different implications for Victorian women invested in a homosocial as opposed to a heterosexual culture.

Five months later, DeMille revealed in "More about Marriage" that his interview resulted in an avalanche of mail, presumably from women, that surpassed the response to any film he had produced. Fan magazine readers wished to know if Mrs. DeMille, whose photograph was featured in the follow-up article, enjoyed the same privileges on Saturday night that he did. The director asserted, "no matter how willing a man may be to accord his wife complete freedom, men and women are not 'exactly alike,'" because "the really good woman ... is the ... wise, pure, understanding woman, who ... tries to kill the beast in man ... helping him to overcome the Adam inheritance of lust and dust that eventually lead to ruin." Asserting that a "woman's love that has not much of the maternal is only passion," DeMille contradicted his own advice that the new woman be a playmate in a companionate marriage.[56]

In sum, the new woman who emerged in DeMille's films and in fan magazines was, on one hand, a sexual playmate and herself a commodity and, on the other, a sentimental heroine adhering to a Victorian legacy. Continued emphasis on self-theatricalization in both these models of womanhood served to validate consumption rather than sexual equality or freedom. Gloria Swanson, who rose to stardom in DeMille's Jazz Age films, thus became an appropriate icon for an era of increased materialism.[57] She later claimed that "working for Mr. DeMille was like playing house in the world's most expensive department store." Attracting instant attention with her appearance in *Don't Change Your Husband,* she quickly became the subject of industry discourse. Lasky rightly predicted that the feature "ought to go a long way towards establishing her as a big possibility." Critic Frederick James Smith echoed Lasky's opinion in his review when he stated, "Gloria Swanson . . . is a distinct discovery." Similarly, *Motion Picture Magazine* labeled her "one of the distinct acquisitions" of the silver screen.[58] But fan magazines focused on Swanson's personality as a fashion plate rather than on her considerable gifts as a comedienne. *Motion Picture Classic* labeled her "The Silken Gloria." *Photoplay* described the oriental look of her exotic hairdos in articles with amusing titles such as "Don't Change Your Coiffure" and "She Changed Her Coiffure." *Variety* informed readers about the details of her costume, jewelry, and hairstyle in *Don't Change Your Husband.* And *Motion Picture Magazine* declared, "Gloria believes in the psychology of clothes. Put her in short dresses and bob her hair and she wants to play around like a child. But swathed in an evening gown with her hair high and heavily ornamented—she immediately becomes the society woman . . . Gloria loves clothes, loves luxuries, loves fame."[59]

What did Swanson's glamorous personality imply about the essence of self-theatricalization as practiced by the new woman?[60] As the moral certainties of the Victorian synthesis began to dissolve in an era of modern personalities, appearances no longer provided a reliable index of character and breeding. At issue was the nature of female sexuality in relation to the practice of consumption. A serious dilemma resulted from the transformation of Victorian homosocial culture into heterosexual relations based on romance. DeMille had demonstrated in his films that companionate marriage, especially in view of trends toward a higher marital rate among youth, was childless and sexually playful. As Walter Lippman acknowledged, however, "The whole revolution in the field of sexual morals turns upon the fact that external control of the chastity of women is becoming impossible."[61] Anxiety about women's extravagant spending, represented in DeMille's texts as a prerequisite for the pursuit of pleasure, was more than a concern about household budgets; it registered suspicion about female emotions and sexuality. Discourse in fan magazines implied that stars like Swanson assumed new personalities whenever they changed gowns. As consummate performers, could women be trusted in an era of heterosexual romance? When the wife in *The Affairs of Anatol* uses church funds to indulge her desires, the rage that she inspires in her self-righteous husband, who stomps on her dress, is telling.

Angry and suspicious husbands, however, may not have truly understood the nature of female desire as manipulated in a consumer culture. Consider that DeMille's representation of marriage as spectacle was a form of commodity fetishism so that consumption of images, as well as goods, became a source of gratification for women. Such manipulation ultimately served the purposes of consumer capitalism. As Foucault argues, discourses on pleasure were linked to efforts "to constitute a sexuality that was economically useful and politically conservative."[62] Advertisers intent on instructing consumers about the value of products followed DeMille's texts with good reason. Commodity fetishism, or the displacement of human desire onto material goods, became a powerful stimulus in the growth of postwar consumption. A significant consumer durables revolution occurred during 1922–1929, as Martha Olney argues. Advertising, a fully deductible corporate expense after 1917, stimulated sales, as did installment buying, a practice that the new middle classes, unlike blue-collar workers, could indulge.[63] Armed with disposable income, the new woman marched in the forefront of avid consumers. Women's access to fashion, home furnishings, and automobiles became essential now that self-making was defined in terms of personality. Display windows, including motion picture screens, thus represented the site of female desire. Constructed as "marble palaces," department stores had already been labeled a "ladies' paradise" or "Adamless Eden."[64] Perhaps this was the ultimate irony resulting from the reification of human consciousness and social relations in consumer society. Consumption reinforced the objectification of women subject to the male gaze, but the new woman was looking in narcissistic rapture at her own reflection.

Notes

For assistance with research, I am grateful to James V. D'Arc at Brigham Young University; Jan-Christopher Horak (now in Los Angeles), Paolo Cherchi Usai, Edward E. Stratmann, and Becky Simmons at George Eastman House; Ned Comstock at the University of Southern California; and Howard H. Prouty at the Academy of Motion Picture Arts and Sciences. I owe a special debt of gratitude to the late James Card, who repeatedly showed me DeMille's films, and his colleague, the late George Pratt, for encouraging my research in silent film when there was little interest in the subject.

1 See, for example, Janet Staiger, *Bad Women: Regulating Sexuality in Early American Cinema* (Minneapolis: University of Minnesota Press, 1995); Gaylyn Studlar, "The Perils of Pleasure? Fan Magazine Discourse as Women's Com-

modified Culture in the 1920s," *Wide Angle* 13, 1 (1991): 6–33. Staiger argues in a chapter significantly titled "The Repeal of Reticence" that "the visions of . . . the New Woman are . . . multiple" (13). But she characterizes the heroine of *Traffic in Souls* as a "self-reliant, natural, caring, and public woman" in contrast to the "pious, pure, submissive, and domestic" Victorian woman (140). Similarly, Studlar writes: "Ultimately, the Victorian models of woman as sacrificing mother or passively chaste maiden were eclipsed in the 1920s as American ideals of femininity changed in profound ways" (9–10). She also characterizes the new woman as a threat to racial purity and a prey to fantasies about the dark new immigrant in "Discourses of Gender and Ethnicity: The Construction and De(con)struction of Rudolph Valentino as Other," *Film Criticism* 9 (winter 1989): 18–35. Miriam Hansen, in contrast, argues that the new woman was not so emancipated in "Pleasure, Ambivalence, Identification: Valentino and Female Spectatorship," *Cinema Journal* 25, 4 (summer 1986): 6–32. Linda Mizejewski considers the new woman a complex phenomenon in *Ziegfeld Girl: Image and Icon in Culture and Cinema* (Durham: Duke University Press, 1999). See also Lisa L. Rudman, "Marriage—The Ideal and the Reel; or, The Cinematic Marriage Manual," *Film History* 1, 4 (1987): 327–339. Rudman argues that little research has been done on the new woman, who was not very new, but she too accepts prescriptive literature about Victorian women at face value and, despite the title of her essay, stereotypes them. See also Maureen Turim, "Seduction and Elegance: The New Woman of Fashion in Silent Cinema," in *On Fashion,* ed. Shari Benstock and Suzanne Ferriss, (New Brunswick: Rutgers University Press, 1994); 140–158. Because she relies on Foucault, Turim has a more nuanced view of Victorianism, but her attempt to reinforce her argument with reference to women's history is problematic because it is sketchy (dress reform, an essential subject, is overlooked), as is her discussion of DeMille's films.

2 On sentimental culture, especially its religious dimension, see Ann Douglas, *The Feminization of American Culture* (New York: Alfred A. Knopf, 1977). See also Jane Tompkins, *Sensational Designs: The Cultural Work of American Fiction, 1790–1860* (New York: Oxford University Press, 1985), for a less acerbic view.

3 See James R. McGovern, "The American Woman's Pre-World War I Freedom in Manners and Morals," *Journal of American History* 55 (September 1968): 315–333; Kenneth A. Yellis, "Prosperity's Child: Some Thoughts on the Flapper," *American Quarterly* 21:1 (March 1969): 44–64; Estelle B. Freedman, "The New Woman: Changing Views of Women in the 1920s," *Journal of American History* 61 (March 1974): 372–393; Nancy Woloch, *Women and the American Experience* (New York: Alfred A. Knopf, 1984), chapters 12, 16; Lois W. Banner, *American Beauty* (New York: Alfred A. Knopf, 1983), chapters 12, 13; Martha Banta, *Imaging American Women: Idea and Ideals in Cultural History* (New York: Columbia University Press, 1987); Ellen Wiley Todd, *The "New Woman" Revised: Painting and Gender Politics on Fourteenth Street* (Berkeley: University of California Press, 1993), chapter 1; Carroll Smith-

Rosenberg, "The New Woman as Androgyne: Social Disorder and Gender Crisis, 1870–1936," in *Disorderly Conduct: Visions of Gender in Victorian America* (New York: Alfred A. Knopf, 1985), 245–296; Linda K. Kerber, "Separate Spheres, Female Worlds, Woman's Place: The Rhetoric of Women's History," *Journal of American History* 75 (June 1988): 9–39. Unlike Todd, Yellis and Banner do not consider the Gibson girl, who was superceded by the flapper, to exemplify an independent new woman. Smith-Rosenberg, in contrast, focuses not on the flapper but on the androgyne as a "new woman." On silent-screen flappers as a character type, a concept used in early feminist criticism, see Sumiko Higashi, *Virgins, Vamps, and Flappers: The American Silent Movie Heroine* (Montreal: Eden Press, 1978), chapter 6; Mary P. Ryan, "The Projection of a New Womanhood: The Movie Moderns in the 1920s," in *Our American Sisters,* 3d ed., ed. Jean E. Friedman and William G. Shade (Lexington: D. C. Heath and Company, 1982), 500–518. According to British usage, the flapper was associated with left-wing politics and disenfranchised working-class women. See Billie Melman, *Women and the Popular Imagination in the Twenties: Flappers and Nymphs* (New York: St. Martin's Press, 1988), chapter 1. On the American flapper as a social activist rather than as a symbol of the sexual revolution, see Stephen H. Norwood, *Labor's Flaming Youth: Telephone Operators and Worker Militancy, 1878–1923* (Urbana: University of Illinois Press, 1990), introduction. On working-class versions of the new woman, see Kathy Peiss, *Cheap Amusements: Working Women and Leisure in Turn-of-the-Century New York* (Philadelphia: Temple University Press, 1986), introduction. Somewhat problematic is Peiss's assertion that working-class women's culture influenced middle-class women.

4 At issue is the evolving methodology of film (and cultural) studies as opposed to history proper. A field indebted to psychoanalytic and semiotic theory, feminist film scholarship has evolved toward a more historical approach based on archival research, especially in relation to issues of spectatorship and reception in the silent era. Put another way, the focus on silent cinema as opposed to, say, 1940s melodrama or film noir has raised historical issues. (At some point, feminist historians may revisit 1940s films since moving backward in time to silent films is not inherently historical.) As a discipline still dominated by scholars trained as theoreticians, however, (feminist) film history is at times characterized by reification of texts, discourses, narration, apparatus, cinema, and so forth. See, for example, Tom Gunning, *D. W. Griffith and the Origins of American Film Narrative: The Early Years at Biograph* (Urbana: University of Illinois Press, 1994), titled "D. W. Griffith and the Narrator System: Narrative Structure and Industry Organization in Biograph Films, 1908–1909" as a dissertation; Annette Kuhn, *Cinema, Censorship, and Sexuality, 1909–1925* (London: Routledge, 1988); Miriam Hansen, *Babel and Babylon: Spectatorship in American Silent Film* (Cambridge: Harvard University Press, 1991). Applying Habermas's concept of the public sphere, initially descriptive of Enlightenment France, to American nickelodeons, Hansen argues that working-class audiences became spectators constructed by film as a universal language.

Similarly, in a move indebted to earlier pychoanalytic and semiotic theory, she argues that working- and middle-class women became spectators in the public sphere. As a result, the study shifts in focus from issues of the social composition of audiences to more abstract concepts of spectatorship. By contrast, Lizabeth Cohen writes a social history of working-class audiences that stresses the significance of local cultures mediating reception of mass entertainment well into the 1920s. See *Making a New Deal: Industrial Workers in Chicago, 1919-1939* (New York: Cambridge University Press, 1990), chapter 3. Another social historian who writes about reception is Roy Rosenzweig, *Eight Hours for What We Will: Workers and Leisure in an Industrial City, 1870-1920* (New York: Cambridge University Press, 1983), chapter 8.

Unlike film historians, social historians use quantitative data, especially demographics, to construct narratives privileging human agency despite the pervasiveness of social structures. Cultural historians, in contrast, are critical of positivist models of research and focus on textuality and, to some extent, on theory, but they too privilege agency. Some film historians, to be sure, have been less abstract and more specific in characterizing social actors, especially in discussions of audience reception. At times, however, such actors compete for agency in the same text with the workings of an abstract force like cinema. Lauren Rabinovitz, for example, writes in *For the Love of Pleasure: Women, Movies, and Culture in Turn-of-the-Century Chicago* (New Brunswick: Rutgers University Press, 1998): "Cinema capitalized on this historically specific kind of spectatorship...", or "Cinema benefitted from the shopper's and tourist's training to see" (181).

Still relatively unexplored in (feminist) film history are definitions of class, ethnicity, and race as these intersect with gender in social and cultural practices. An exception is Ben Singer's "Manhattan Nickelodeons: New Data on Audiences and Exhibitors, *Cinema Journal* 34:3 (spring 1995): 5-34. See also Sumiko Higashi, "Dialogue: Manhattan's Nickelodeons," Robert C. Allen, "Manhattan Myopia; or, Oh! Iowa," and Ben Singer, "New York, Just Like I Pictured It," all in *Cinema Journal* 35:3 (spring 1996): 72-128. Allen relies on Anthony Giddens's theory of structuration to expand a definition of the middle class to include movie patrons. Singer counters that the lower middle class, who did indeed attend films, should be categorized as a clerical class rather than as a lower rung of the respectable middle class. Whether this clerical class had more in common with the working class, as opposed to the middle class, is debatable. A focus on class in relation to ethnicity would, in my view, be helpful. Also significant in making distinctions are the categories "old" and "new" middle class as defined by C. Wright Mills and Harry Braverman. My conclusion is that the plural term "middle classes" is more accurate than the singular "middle class." Above all, the middle class should not be conflated with the bourgeoisie, a term that is more applicable to European, and more specifically, French class structure. See Richard Jenkyns, "The Elusiveness of the Bourgeoisie," *Times Literary Supplement,* 28 August, 1998, 9-10. Unfortunately, film scholars and even historians use "middle class" and "bourgeoisie" as interchangeable terms. Rabinovitz, for example, writes, "Middle-class social reformers and charity workers may not have understood this in precisely these terms since their beliefs... were linked to a particular bourgeois moralism" (*For the Love of Pleasure,* 182). In sum, feminist historians tend to conflate working-class and immigrant women, who were ethnically and racially different, with middle-class women, who were Protestant and native-born. See, for example, Shelley Stamp, *Movie-Struck Girls: Women and Motion Picture Culture after the Nickelodeon* (Princeton: Princeton University Press, 2000); Constance Balides, "Scenarios of Exposure in the Practice of Everyday Life: Women in the Cinema of Attractions," *Screen* 34, 1 (spring 1993): 19–37. At times both authors become vague, as does Rabinovitz, in categorizing women, especially middle-class women, partly because rigorous definitions of class and ethnicity are lacking. Kathy Peiss, a social historian, provides a model definition of such issues in the introduction to *Cheap Amusements.* Given lack of focus on social class and structure, a methodology basic to the discipline of history despite its cultural turn, (feminist) film discourse tends to be less nuanced in characterizing social change.

5   Margaret Gibbons Wilson, *The American Woman in Transition: The Urban Influence, 1870–1929* (Westport, Conn.: Greenwood Press, 1979), 8.
6   See Mary P. Ryan, *Cradle of the Middle Class: The Family in Oneida County, New York, 1790–1865* (New York: Cambridge University Press, 1981); Stuart M. Blumin, *The Emergence of the Middle Class: Social Experience in the American City, 1760–1900* (New York: Cambridge University Press, 1989); Stuart M. Blumin, "The Hypothesis of Middle-Class Formation in Nineteenth-Century America: A Critique and Some Proposals," *American Historical Review* 90 (April 1985): 299–338.
7   On separate spheres in women's history, see Kerber, "Separate Spheres."
8   See Cindy Sondik Aron, *Ladies and Gentlemen of the Civil Service: Middle-Class Workers in Victorian America* (New York: Oxford University Press, 1987); Angel Kwolek-Folland, *Engendering Business: Men and Women in the Corporate Office, 1870–1930* (Baltimore: Johns Hopkins University Press, 1994).
9   See also Karen Halttunnen, *Confidence Men and Painted Women: A Study of Middle-Class Culture in America, 1830–1870* (New Haven: Yale University Press, 1982).
10 Smith-Rosenberg, "The Female World of Love and Ritual," in *Disorderly Conduct,* 53–76. Whether same-sex relations, sometimes referred to as Boston marriages, did indeed involve sex is still being debated.
11 See Paula S. Fass, *The Damned and the Beautiful: American Youth in the 1920s* (New York: Oxford University Press, 1977).
12 See Nancy Milford, *Zelda* (New York: Harper and Row, 1970).
13 Quoted in William E. Leuchtenburg, *The Perils of Prosperity, 1914–32* (Chicago: University of Chicago Press, 1958), 172. For a more updated study, see Lynn Dumenil, *Modern Temper: American Culture and Society in the 1920s* (New York: Hill and Wang, 1995).
14 See David M. Kennedy, *Birth Control in America: The Career of Margaret*

Sanger (New Haven: Yale University Press, 1970); Linda Gordon, *Woman's Body, Woman's Right* (New York: Penguin, 1977); James C. Mohr, *Abortion in America* (New York: Oxford University Press, 1978); John D'Emilio and Estelle B. Freedman, *Intimate Matters: A History of Sexuality in America* (New York: Harper and Row, 1998); Janet Farrell Brodie, *Contraception and Abortion in Nineteenth-Century America* (Ithaca: Cornell University Press, 1994). Sanger, interestingly, though forthright on issues of sexuality and contraception, was conservative in endorsing woman's separate sphere.

15 Charlotte Perkins Gilman, *Women and Economics* (New York: Harper and Row, 1966). See especially the introduction to this edition by Carl Degler.

16 Michel Foucault, *The History of Sexuality*, vol. 1, trans. Robert Hurley (New York: Pantheon, 1978), 23.

17 Smith-Rosenberg, "The Female World of Love and Ritual," 76. See also "The New Woman as Androgyne" in the same volume.

18 *The Autobiography of Cecil B. DeMille*, ed. Donald Hayne (Englewood Cliffs: Prentice-Hall, 1959), 212-213. William deMille gives his brother more credit than he deserves for starting the cycle of sex comedies and melodramas in *Hollywood Saga* (New York: E. P. Dutton and Company, 1939), 238-243. DeMille did not list his Jazz Age films, with the exception of *Male and Female* and *Forbidden Fruit*, among his best films. See George C. Pratt, "Forty-five Years of Picture Making: An Interview with Cecil B. DeMille," *Film History* 3:2 (1989): 133-145. I am indebted to Pratt for playing the tape recording of this interview for me.

19 Lasky to DeMille, 6 January 1917; Carl H. Pierce to Lasky, memo attached to Lasky's letter; Lasky to DeMille, 5 March 1917; Lasky to DeMille, 10 August 1917; Lasky to DeMille, 27 November 1917; Lasky to DeMille, 27 December 1917; Jesse Lasky 1917 folder, Lasky Co./Famous Players-Lasky, DeMille Archives, Brigham Young University (hereafter cited as DMA).

20 Lasky to DeMille, 26 March 1918; Lasky to DeMille, 6 November 1918; DeMille to Lasky, 23 January 1919; Lasky to DeMille, 23 May 1919, Jesse Lasky 1918 and 1919 folders, Lasky Co./Famous Players-Lasky, DMA.

21 *Theatre*, February 1919, in Cecil B. DeMille scrapbook, Robinson Locke Collection, New York Public Library, Library for the Performing Arts, Lincoln Center (hereafter cited as RLC).

22 Roland Marchand, *Advertising the American Dream: Making Way for Modernity, 1920-1940* (Berkeley: University of California Press, 1985), chapter 6; Daniel Horowitz, *The Morality of Spending: Attitudes toward the Consumer Society in America, 1875-1940* (Baltimore: Johns Hopkins University Press, 1985), chapter 6. Distinctions between the old and new middle class are important. A great deal of literature exists on this subject but essential are C. Wright Mills, *White Collar: The American Middle Classes* (New York: Oxford University Press, 1951); and Harry Braverman, *Labor and Monopoly Capital: The Degradation of Work in the Twentieth Century* (New York: Monthly Review Press, 1974).

23 Warren Susman, "'Personality' and Twentieth-Century Culture," in *Culture*

as History: The Transformation of American Society in the Twentieth Century (New York: Pantheon, 1984), 271–285.
24 See Haltunnen, *Confidence Men and Painted Women.*
25 David Graham Phillips, *Old Wives for New* (New York: Grosset and Dunlap, 1908), 100.
26 Script of *Old Wives for New,* Cinema-TV Library, Special Collections, University of Southern California (hereafter cited as USC).
27 Robert S. Lynd and Helen Merrell Lynd, *Middletown: A Study in American Culture* (New York: Harcourt, Brace and World, 1929), 256. According to the Lynds, twenty-one of twenty-six families who owned a car were without bathtubs. See also Siegfried Giedion, *Mechanization Takes Command* (New York: Oxford University Press, 1948), part 7.
28 See Thomas Elsaesser, "Tales of Sound and Fury: Observations on the Family Melodrama," *Monogram* 4 (1972): 2–15; reprinted in *Home Is Where the Heart Is: Studies in Melodrama and the Woman's Film,* ed. Christine Gledhill (London: British Film Institute, 1987), 43–69.
29 Kenneth McGaffey, "The Excellent Elliott," *Motion Picture,* January 1919, 35; W. K. Hollander, untitled article, *Chicago News,* 21 January 1919, in Gloria Swanson scrapbook, RLC.
30 Phillips, *Old Wives for New,* 43.
31 See John F. Kasson, *Rudeness and Civility: Manners in Nineteenth-Century America* (New York: Hill and Wang, 1990), 166.
32 On cosmetics, prostitutes, and changing styles, see Kathy Peiss, "Making Faces: The Cosmetics Industry and the Cultural Construction of Gender, 1890–1930," *Genders* 7 (spring 1990): 143–169.
33 Script of *Don't Change Your Husband,* USC.
34 See Mary Douglas, *Purity and Danger: An Analysis of Concepts of Pollution and Taboo* (New York: Praeger, 1966), chapters 7–9.
35 DeMille to Lasky, 12 January 1924, Jesse Lasky 1924 folder, Lasky Co./Famous Players–Lasky, DMA.
36 DeMille was allegedly a foot fetishist; his vision of the consumer culture included an extraordinary number of close-ups of women's footwear.
37 *Why Change Your Wife?* stills file, Margaret Herrick Library, Academy of Motion Picture Arts and Sciences, Los Angeles (herefter cited as AMPAS).
38 Smith-Rosenberg, "The Female World of Love and Ritual," 53–76.
39 On reification, see Georg Lukács, *History and Consciousness: Studies in Marxist Dialectics,* trans. Rodney Livingstone (Cambridge: MIT Press, 1971).
40 In fact, DeMille discusses this particular film in relation to the trilogy and *Male and Female.* See Pratt, "Forty-five Years of Picture Making," 139.
41 DeMille, *Hollywood Saga* 242; Garth Jowett, *Film: The Democratic Art* (Boston: Little, Brown, 1976), 188; Richard Koszarski, *An Evening's Entertainment: The Age of the Silent Feature Picture, 1915–1928* (New York: Charles Scribner's Sons, 1990), 30.
42 *Autobiography of Cecil B. DeMille,* 214–215; the quote is from a memo by Berenice Mosk, *Northwest Mounted, Old Wives for New,* and *Plainsman* folder,

Personal: Autobiography files, DMA. DeMille claimed during a court case years later that Lasky attempted to block release of the film and to write it off as a loss. Although Lasky received in-house instructions to cut the film, I doubt that he would have prevented the release of a project that was initially his idea. See *United States Circuit Court of Appeals for the North Circuit. Commissioner of Internal Revenues, Petitioner, v. Cecil B. deMille Productions, Inc., Respondent. Transcript of the Record. In Three Volumes. Upon Petition to Review an Order of the United States Boad of Appeals* (San Francisco: Parker Printing, 1936), 319–320.

43 Adolph Zukor, "Zukor Outlines Coming Year's Policies," *Motion Picture News,* 29 June 1918, 3869.

44 *Old Wives for New,* Paramount Collection, AMPAS. On film censorship, see Francis G. Couvares, "Hollywood, Main Street, and the Church: Trying to Censor the Movies before the Production Code," *American Quarterly* 44 (December 1992): 584–616; reprinted in *Movie Censorship and American Culture,* ed. Couvares (Washington, D.C.: Smithsonian Institution Press, 1996), 129–158.

45 Memo to Al Lichtman, general manager of Famous Players–Lasky, 28 June 1918, Jesse Lasky 1918 folder, Lasky Co./ Famous Players–Lasky, DMA.

46 R. E. Pritchard, "Old Wives for New," *Motion Picture News,* 8 June 1918, 3453–3454; Frederick James Smith, *Motion Picture Classic,* August 1918, in *Northwest Mounted, Old Wives for New* and *Plainsman* folder, Personal: Autobiography files, DMA; Edward Weitzel, "Old Wives for New, *Moving Picture World,* 8 June 1918, 1470; "Old Wives for New," *Variety Film Reviews, 1907–1980* (New York: Garland, 1983), 31 May 1918; "Exhibitor to Exhibitor Review Service," *Motion Picture News,* 8 June 1918, 3400.

47 Frederick James Smith, "The Celluloid Critic," *Motion Picture Classic,* April 1919, 44; "Don't Change Your Husband," *Variety Film Reviews,* 7 February 1919; "Special Service Section on 'Don't Change Your Husband,'" *Motion Picture News,* 1 February 1919, 728; "DeMille's Film Breaks Some Records," *Motion Picture News,* 9 March 1919, 1353; Frederick James Smith, "The Celluloid Critic," *Motion Picture Classic,* April-May 1920, 50; Ad, *Motion Picture News,* 20 March 1920, 2609.

48 "Grauman's Rialto Gets Business by Use of Novelties," *Motion Picture News,* 1 May 1920, 3837; "What Brown Did for DeMille's Special," *Motion Picture News,* 10 July 1920, 403; Ad, *Motion Picture News,* 22 May 1920, 4245; Lasky to DeMille, 19 April 1920, Jesse Lasky 1920 folder, Lasky Co./Famous Players–Lasky, DMA; "Famous Players–Lasky Plans Big Campaign," *Motion Picture News,* 24 January 1920, 1083; "Getting the Woman Appeal," *Motion Picture News,* 7 December 1918, 3358; "The Affairs of Anatol," *Moving Picture World,* 24 September 1921, 446. On the cultural wars of the post–World War I decade, see Frederick Lewis Allen, *Only Yesterday* (New York: Harper & Bros., 1931); Leuchtenburg, *The Perils of Prosperity;* Dumenil, *Modern Temper;* Paul A. Carter, *Another Part of the Twenties* (New York: Columbia University Press, 1973); Stanley Coben, *Rebellion against Victorianism: The Impetus for Cultural*

Change in 1920s America (New York: Oxford University Press, 1991); Lawrence W. Levine, "Progress and Nostalgia: The Self Image of the Nineteen Twenties," in *The Unpredictable Past: Explorations in American Cultural History* (New York: Oxford University Press, 1993), 189–205. Daniel H. Borus offers a revisionist interpretation in "New Perspectives in the 1920s in the United States" (paper delivered at SUNY, Brockport, April 1991). On film exhibition during this period, see Koszarski, *An Evening's Entertainment,* chapter 2; Douglas Gomery, *Shared Pleasures: A History of Movie Presentation in the United States* (Madison: University of Wisconsin Press, 1992), chapters 3–4.

49 Elizabeth Ewen, *Immigrant Women in the Land of Dollars: Life and Culture on the Lower East Side, 1890–1925* (New York: Monthly Review Press, 1985); Peiss, *Cheap Amusements.*

50 "Why Change Your Wife," *Motion Picture News,* 8 May 1920, 4062.

51 Famous Players–Lasky ad, *Motion Picture News,* 26 June 1920, 4.

52 *Statistical Abstract of the United States* (Washington, D.C.: Government Printing Office, 1933), 90; Report of the President's Research Committee on Social Trends, *Recent Social Trends in the United States* (New York: McGraw-Hill, 1933), 694; William L. O'Neill, *Divorce in the Progressive Era* (New Haven: Yale University Press, 1967), 20; Elaine Tyler May, *Great Expectations: Marriage and Divorce in Post-Victorian America* (Chicago: University of Chicago Press, 1980), 51, 87; Glenda Riley, *Divorce: An American Tradition* (New York: Oxford University Press, 1991), 133; *Don't Change Your Husband,* in *New York Times Film Reviews* (New York: Arno Press, 1970), 3 February 1919; Lynd and Lynd, *Middletown,* chapter 10; William H. Chafe, *The American Woman: Her Changing Social, Economic, and Political Roles, 1920–1970* (New York: Oxford University Press, 1972), chapter 2.

53 Media Mistley, "Why Husbands Leave Home," *Motion Picture Classic,* July 1918, 54–56.

54 Hazel Simpson Naylor, "Master of Mystery," *Motion Picture Magazine,* November 1919, 126; Elizabeth Peltret, "Gloria Swanson Talks on Divorce," *Motion Picture Magazine,* December 1919, 74; "Editorial: Cinema Husbands," *Motion Picture Magazine,* September 1920, 29.

55 DeMille's more well-known liaisons included relationships with Jeanie Macpherson and Julia Faye. The director also owned a ranch in the San Fernando Valley that was called Paradise for reasons other than its idyllic location.

56 "What Does Marriage Mean As Told by Cecil B. deMille to Adela Rogers St. Johns," *Photoplay,* December 1920, 28–31; "More about Marriage," *Photoplay,* May 1921, 24–26, 105.

57 See Richard Dyer, *Stars* (London: British Film Institute, 1979); Richard deCordova, *Picture Personalities: The Emergence of the Star System in America* (Urbana: University of Illinois Press, 1990); Catherine E. Kerr, "Incorporating the Star: The Intersection of Business and Aesthetic Strategies in Early American Film," *Business History Review* 64 (autumn 1990): 383–410.

58 *Swanson on Swanson: An Autobiography* (New York: Random House, 1980),

chapters 7–8; Lasky to DeMille, 3 January 1919, Jesse Lasky 1919 folder, Lasky Co./Famous Players–Lasky, DMA; Smith, "The Celluloid Critic" (April 1919), 44; Hazel Simpson Naylor, "Across the Silversheet," *Motion Picture Magazine,* April 1919, 72.

59 Frederick James Smith, "The Silken Gloria," *Motion Picture Classic,* February 1920, 16; Delight Evans, "Don't Change Your Coiffure," *Photoplay,* August 1919, 73; "She Changed Her Coiffure," *Photoplay,* September 1920, 33; untitled article, *Variety,* 7 December 1919, in Gloria Swanson scrapbook, RLC; Hazel Simpson Naylor, "Piloting a Dream Craft," *Motion Picture Magazine,* April 1921, 87. Although credits for costume design for DeMille's films are difficult to ascertain, Alpharelta Hoffman is cited as the designer for *Old Wives for New* in *Northwest Mounted, Old Wives,* and *Plainsman* folder, Personal: Autobiography files, DMA. *Motion Picture News* cites Margaretta Hoffman (the first name is an error) as the designer for *Don't Change Your Husband* in "Cecil B. DeMille's New Feature Is Started," 23 November 1918, 3084. Mitchell Leisen, who began his career designing costumes for the Babylonian sequence in *Male and Female* and became DeMille's art director later in the 1920s, may also have been involved in costume design. See David Chierichetti, *Hollywood Director: The Career of Mitchell Leisen* (New York: Curtis Books, 1973), 22–28.

60 See Anne Hollander, *Seeing through Clothes* (New York: Viking Press, 1975). See also Mary Louise Roberts, "Samson and Delilah Revisited: The Politics of Women's Fashion in 1920s France," *American Historical Review* 98 (June 1993): 657–684. French reaction to changes in women's clothing and hairstyles, which were seductively but disturbingly unisexual, was comparable to consternation expressed in American society. Roberts fails to mention that fashion had become an international phenomenon partly as a result of the influence of motion pictures. Paul Iribe, who illustrated art deco fashion plates for couturier Paul Poiret, not coincidentally, became DeMille's art director in the 1920s. See also Fass, *The Damned and the Beautiful,* passim; Allen, *Only Yesterday,* chapter 5, Leuchtenburg, *The Perils of Prosperity,* chapter 9. See also F. Scott Fitzgerald, "Bernice Bobs Her Hair," in *Flappers and Philosophers* (New York: Charles Scribner's Sons, 1920), 116–140.

61 Walter Lippman, *A Preface to Morals* (New York: Macmillan, 1929), chapter 14, 288; Lynd and Lynd, *Middletown,* chapter 10; Fass, *The Damned and the Beautiful,* 69. For studies on sexuality and marriage during this period, see Gilbert Van Tassel Hamilton, *A Research in Marriage* (New York: Albert and Charles Boni, 1929), 80–82, 383; Robert L. Dickinson and Laura Beam, *The Single Woman: A Medical Study in Sex Education* (New York: Reynal and Hitchcock, 1934), 101, 145; Lewis M. Terman, *Psychological Factors in Marital Happiness* (New York: McGraw-Hill, 1938), 320–321, 367; Katherine B. Davis, *Factors in the Sex Life of Twenty-two Hundred Women* (New York: McGraw-Hill, 1938), 14, 38–39. On the history of contraception, see note 14 above.

62 Foucault, *The History of Sexuality,* 37.

63 Martha L. Olney, *Buy Now, Pay Later: Advertising, Credit, and Consumer*

Durables in the 1920s (Chapel Hill: University of North Carolina Press, 1991), 95; chapters 1–2.

64 Susan Porter Benson, *Counter Cultures: Saleswomen, Managers, and Customers in American Department Stores,* 1890–1940 (Urbana: University of Illinois Press, 1988), 76. *The Ladies' Paradise* is the translated title of Emile Zola's novel, *Au bonheur des dames.*

ANNE MOREY

"So Real as to Seem Like Life Itself"
The *Photoplay* Fiction of Adela Rogers St. Johns

Women's relationship to early cinema has been one of the most productive areas of scholarly endeavor in film studies for over fifteen years. Scholars are now generally agreed that during the silent period filmmaking and filmgoing were pursuits unusually open to women. But while older studies of women's place in early film emphasized their presence or absence from filmmaking, more recent scholarship has tended to contemplate issues of filmgoing, whether in examining the reception of particular films or genres or in examining filmgoing as a social activity. For early filmgoing depended on the presence of a significant female audience to signal its arrival as a respectable public amusement; and in exchange for giving their imprimatur to this pastime, women used filmgoing to advance their own influence, parlaying their role as consumers into a more obviously political function as the arbiters of their own and others' consumption. As scholars such as Miriam Hansen and Janet Staiger have argued, filmgoing was an important component in a reconfigured public sphere that increasingly emphasized consumer behavior.

Hansen, for instance, has focused on the physical environment of filmgoing and its relationship to film style.[1] She contends that the classical Hollywood style did not come to complete fruition until approximately 1915, when the modes of film exhibition had matured into the forms they would maintain for the next forty-five years. In Hansen's argument, a purpose-built movie theater with pretensions to middle-class respectability (more comfortable seats, ushers, bigger and better screens, more elaborate musical accompaniments for the feature, and so on) was necessary to shape the public that would attend longer, more elaborate, and more upscale films. In other words, just as filmmakers were submitting themselves to the discipline of a cadre of writers for trade papers who would suggest what did and did not work narratively, the film exhibitor was moving toward an environment in which increasingly ambitious films could be seen to better effect.[2] A film such as Cecil B. DeMille's *The Cheat* (1915), whose markers of artistic value included Rembrandt or "Lasky" lighting, a cast containing celebrity performers such as socialite Fannie Ward, and a length of more than an hour, worked better in a movie palace than in a nickelodeon, which was more hospitable to shorter and less ambitious productions.[3]

But the environment of filmgoing extended beyond the physical bounds of the theater into the more abstract realm represented by writings on film. Industry periodicals fell into two categories: the trade paper and its younger sister, the fan magazine. Of the former, *Variety, Moving Picture World, Motion Picture News,* and the *New York Dramatic Mirror,* among others that flourished during the first thirty years of the film industry, were another force in shaping standards in film manufacturing. But although Kathryn Fuller notes that devoted moviegoers read trade periodicals before the rise of fan magazines, trades typically did not address the individual whose role within the film industry was solely that of audience.[4] That publishing niche was occupied by a welter of fan magazines and magazines about hobbies related to filmgoing that began to appear around 1910. While fan magazines may not be an ideal source for determining how films actually spoke to contemporary audiences, they are nonetheless one of the most significant and readily available reservoirs of information about how viewers might have used films, and they represent a window into a complex audience-industry relationship. Scholars such as Fuller and Gaylyn Studlar have argued that fan magazines functioned both as a venue for the regulation of filmgoing and other fan behaviors and as a place where moviegoers and the film industry conducted a dialogue.[5]

Fuller contends that fan magazines gradually worked to reshape the definition (although not necessarily the composition) of the filmgoing public. In its revised form, this audience might be envisioned as less interested in the possibility of making films, whether on an amateur or a professional basis, and as increasingly female. Initially, writing for fans consisted of hobbyist discourses associated with the technology of filmmaking familiar from *Popular Mechanics* and *Scientific American,* and of synopses designed to help viewers decide which films to see, to refresh their recollection about particular narratives, or to serve as case studies in how to write scenarios. By the mid-1910s, however, these articles had gradually been replaced by articles on stars, fashion, and Hollywood culture generally, which were presumed to appeal particularly to female readers, a more lucrative target for advertisers.[6]

"So Real as to Seem Like Life Itself"

But while Fuller holds that from 1910 to 1916 the fan was being redefined away from a more active, masculine, technologically informed amateur of film into a more passive and feminine audience, Studlar suggests that the female-oriented fan magazine—*Photoplay,* for instance—nonetheless represented something more than readers' uncritical consumption of Hollywood and all its works. If the volume of fan contributions was lessening somewhat during the 1910s, it remained an important element within the editorial design of these magazines. Indeed, one of the defining characteristics of the fan magazine appears to be its readiness to allow its readers to signal and justify their preferences about the kinds of narrative, types of star, and ideas of beauty on offer from Hollywood. Fan magazines remained dependent on fan participation through a range of activities, from responding to questions about one's favorite male star (is Rudolph Valentino to be preferred to Ramon Novarro or are they both eclipsed by Lew Cody?) to contributing longer letters, stories, or poems. Here the shift in definition of the fan to an almost exclusively female figure dovetails with Hollywood's own understanding, accurate or not, of its box office.[7]

Studlar justifies an examination of *Photoplay* as representative of fan culture on the basis of its wide circulation (two million copies by 1922) and its national availability. This magazine also reveals women's attitudes in particular toward the film industry because it boasted a large staff of female editors and female writers.[8] It would, however, be a mistake to extrapolate from these facts the notion that *Photoplay* produced a univocal and straightforward presentation of issues affecting either the film industry or women's desire for greater economic and political autonomy in the 1910s and 1920s. As Studlar's article demonstrates, fan magazines were part of a complex consumer culture; writers assumed, for example, that readers would be familiar with star scandals even when the editorial policy of the magazine prohibited in-depth looks at them. A single issue might contain articles that variously endorsed and criticized the modern girl and her habits and aspirations.[9] Finally, many articles presumed and even traded on a notion of the female reader as ready to disbelieve familiar hype or the clichés of agents and fan magazine writers themselves. Indeed, *Photoplay* spoofed such clichés in a piece about fan writers that presented wholly fictional biographies of its authors in the breathless style familiar from other articles in the magazine.[10]

This acknowledgment of audience skepticism manifested itself in the 1920s in a wide range of popular fictions about the reality behind the promise of filmdom. Works such as Harry Leon Wilson's *Merton of the Movies* (1922), Samuel Merwin's *Hattie of Hollywood* (serialized in *Photoplay* in

1922), and Adela Rogers St. Johns's stories and novellas constitute part of a genre that might loosely be categorized as light exposés of the sillier sides of filmdom. Such fictions are valuable to scholars because they amplify our understanding of the film industry during this period beyond what is available from films, trade papers, and the factual reporting in fan magazines. Indeed, it is possible that fiction allowed the commentator a freer hand in the frank depiction of personalities and situations because it could sidestep some of the aspects of editorial policy that hampered writers of factual articles (who had to be more concerned about libel laws, for instance). The fiction appearing in fan magazines thus asks to be read with and against articles, advertisements, letters, and poems to create a fuller picture of the climate of fandom and the range of interactions between film industry and followers during this period.

St. Johns (1894–1988) makes an interesting subject for this project because, like a number of other *Photoplay* contributors, she wrote both factual articles and fiction. She was perhaps most familiar to her contemporaries as a woman reporter working for the Hearst newspapers, having begun her newspaper career on the San Francisco *Examiner* at age nineteen; she evidently wrote for *Photoplay* as a break from full-time reporting while raising a family in the early 1920s.[11] Besides her reporting, St. Johns produced five novels, a number of short stories, several biographies (including two autobiographies), how-to manuals and religious works, and at least eleven screenplays.

St. Johns's wide-ranging literary output was often unified by her focus on emotion; in later life she proudly referred to her reportage as that of a "sob sister," while reviewers of her novels and biographies variously characterized them as "moving," heartfelt, and sometimes overwritten.[12] This emotionalism, which sometimes infused even St. Johns's lighter writing, made her well adapted to the peculiar environment of the 1920s fan magazine. For in the 1920s in particular, Hollywood reporting faced the task of presenting a studio system and film community that might appropriately be admired by its public, while simultaneously acknowledging the existence of scandal. Instead of a faceless and monolithic big business, Hollywood had to be sold as a concatenation of appealing individuals with touching stories, but fan magazines could not seem to be condoning immorality. Presenting stars as essentially normal or as victims of their own talent often required considerable powers of sympathy.

Along these lines, one common rhetorical move was to suggest that scandal was always elsewhere, or, more profitably, the result of innocent behavior that had been misconstrued. Another was to argue that while scandal was present in Hollywood, it was not disproportionately so: only the size of the press corps (purportedly second only to the corps dedicated to Washington coverage) and the intense public attention directed at film stars made their missteps more visible than those of the inhabitants of, say, Otumwa. Both strategies required a presentation of the star as essentially a larger-than-life boy (or girl) next door, capable of the same missteps to which we are all prone but nonetheless good at heart. Under such circumstances, stars who became involved in scandal were to be viewed compassionately; they were not irresponsible monsters of egotism, but tragic victims of a demanding environment, surrounded by onlookers determined to put the worst construction possible on events.

St. Johns's reporting and fiction fit naturally into this rhetorical framework; they clearly serve the star and studio systems. More, they fit into a paradigm identified by Robert and Helen Lynd in their 1929 analysis of Muncie, Indiana. The Lynds noted that magazine readers of this era were particularly interested in "sex adventure" stories, which, as a contemporary source described them, "should embody picturesque settings for action; they should also present situations of high emotional character, rich in sentiment. A moral conclusion is essential."[13] Thus while *Photoplay* was under some pressure to emphasize Hollywood's cultural and sexual exoticism in a style that had become familiar from "true confessions" magazines, it was simultaneously moved in both its fiction and its reportage to uphold the mores of the heartland. To the extent that Hollywood was a real locale with real inhabitants and a national reputation to be guarded, stories and articles had to reassure fans even while titillating them.

An examination of St. Johns's *Photoplay* contributions suggests that her efforts to sell Hollywood as a particular kind of model community relied in large part on her own construction of a particular kind of model heroine, one who not only might be plausibly represented as desirable within Hollywood but who also was a familiar and acceptable type within society at large. In St. Johns's *Photoplay* fiction and reportage between 1922 and 1929, that heroine often emerges forcefully as the sturdy tomboy who seeks to keep up with her male companion and who does not use sex as a weapon. A typical approving description is that of Anne Bent in St. Johns's August 1922 story "The Fan-Letter Bride": Anne walks with a "quick, boyish swing," wears a "severe, tailored coat," pats her husband's shoulder with a "light, boyish touch," and in appearance is "Not a pretty girl, exactly. Tall, rather finely built, with a lithe, quick, almost boyish grace. . . . The poise of her head was free, adventurous. A woman full of life and vitality and fun—yet oddly, surprisingly shy and reserved for all that."[14] The insistence on Anne's "boyishness," which is mentioned five times in the space of two columns, is for St. Johns the hallmark of her virtue and appeal.[15]

But even as she exalts the tomboy, St. Johns condemns certain other types of femininity: the vamp, the mother angling for advancement for her child, and, above all, the attractive young woman who uses sex to entice but never delivers on her implied promises. St. Johns's texts, written in an era in which women were asserting their claims to legal and economic authority, thus suggest that feminine virtue demands second-class status. Women who invoke weapons and powers off-limits to men, such as coquetry or maternity, come in for disapproval; tomboys who show a fitting understanding of masculine superiority through their desire to emulate the male (by demonstrating athleticism or donning boyish garb, though not by swearing, smoking, or exhibiting lax sexual morals) are approved.

The tomboy is one of many cultural types that waned and waxed in the 1920s, including the so-called new woman (an artifact of the 1890s), the vamp, and the flapper. She shares with the flapper an excess of vitality and a regard, perhaps less narcissistic than the flapper's, for a sturdy and healthy body. To be sure, even the flapper may delight in her body for its own sake, rather than for what it can get her in the world of sexual exchange. As Mary Ryan notes of Joan Crawford's performance in *Our Dancing Daughters* (1928), "the camera emphasized Crawford's gusto and liveliness, rather than eroticism. When the dancing Crawford ripped off her skirt, it was as if to remove a constricting garment, to facilitate freedom of movement and release of energy, not to entice male admirers."[16] In other words, one of the ingredients of the sexual revolution of the 1920s was a new emphasis on a practical physique for women, which had the effect of maneuvering them closer to their male admirers in form.

But another such ingredient was the establishment of rules that granted women greater discretion in sexual negotiations, and arguably it is this set of rules to which St. Johns found it particularly necessary to respond. As Paula Fass observes, it was not that the youth of the 1920s lacked a sense of boundaries in sexual matters, but rather that the boundaries had recently moved in such a way as to reduce—although not to remove—the double standard. Women could increasingly imagine having sex before marriage (although typically only with the man they intended to marry) and could permit some liberties, such as petting, without losing control over their veto of intercourse.[17] These behavioral changes resulted in a more playful view of sex because experiments were deemed beneficial in establishing the compatibility considered essential within marriage. To some extent, they may also have authorized the prolongation of adolescence for young women, since participants in the new experimentation would have found it necessary or appropriate to delay marriage and thus adulthood. The tomboy, at once male-identified and presexual, embraces this up-to-the-minute cultural emphasis on youth and playfulness while simultaneously hearkening back to a Victorian stress on innocence.

Changes in sexual mores required social justification, of course. In the culture at large, some of that justification emerged from the trauma that American youth suffered during World War I, against which mild sexual rebellion was presented as a necessary release and as a reward for suffering, one not to be gainsaid by a hypocritical and self-seeking older generation. When St. Johns and Ruth Biery investigate the phenomenon of the wild modern girl for *Photoplay* in "as told to" narratives that share many of the tropes of *Photoplay*'s fiction, Clara Bow and Joan Crawford are both made to say that their desire for pleasure as adults is the result of great deprivation in childhood. St. Johns, especially, presents Bow as the victim of a series of deranged or selfish adults: her insane mother, hidebound and tightfisted relatives, and unscrupulous agent all help to explain her manic vitality and desire for the good things in life. As Bow acknowledges, "There is only one thing you can do when you are very young and not a philosopher, if life has frightened you by its cruelty and made you distrust its most glittering promises. You must make living a sort of gay curtain to throw across the abyss into which you have looked and where lie dread memories."[18]

While Bow's later roles present her as the "prototypical flapper,"[19] St. Johns insists on her status as tomboy, characterizing it as both a feature of her poverty and also her earliest and most important stock in trade as an actress. Of her childhood, Bow reports:

> I always played with the boys. I never had any use for girls and their games. I never had a doll in all my life. But I was a good runner, I could beat most of the boys and I could pitch. When they played baseball in the evening in the streets, I was always chosen first and I pitched. I don't think I had very good clothes, they were rougher and older than the other girls', and the girls used to say snippy things to me and shout "carrot-top" and things like that. Outwardly, it seemed as though I were just a rough, strong little tomboy.[20]

In St. Johns's telling, Bow's later screen persona is merely the artifact of the movies' need for a particular female type; she is not a vamp by nature. What she *is* by nature (if she is a tomboy only "outwardly") remains somewhat ambiguous, but the implication is that she embraced boyishness in order to cover up her more tender feelings, particularly chagrin over her social inferiority to the other girls. St. Johns thus allies tomboyhood with vulnerability, a linkage that carries over into her fiction.

The as-told-to narrative has also to explain Bow's three broken engagements, which it attributes to the pressures of work, the interference of demands outside the romance, and the jealousy of her partners. Moreover, St. Johns has Bow suggest that male-female friendship is possible and that sexual relationships are not the only kind she wants with men. But tomboyhood itself creates sexual difficulties for the woman who enacts it that may offer another explanation for Bow's string of failed romances. Specifically, the tomboy is a sturdy, hardworking, and loyal young woman preparing to take her place beside her man in a companionate marriage. Yet how, when she so closely resembles her man, is the tomboy to be recognized as a sexual being at all, since her outward and visible manifestations have departed significantly from former notions of femininity? Again, the answer, St. Johns suggests in her fiction, has to do with the tomboy's vulnerability and secretly tender nature, qualities that mark her as neither threat nor competition for the male.

For instance, in her 1924 serial "The Love Dodger," St. Johns explores four competing modes of femininity. Cleveland Brown, a physical comedian of the "pure boy" Harold Lloyd type, finds himself well and truly run-after by three of the four young women and is prepared to resist all of them because, as a child, he was left holding the bag by a female playmate:

> [young] Cleveland Brown examined with horrified curiosity the straight red welts made by a buggy whip in a firm and indignant hand and came to a conclusion which was eventually to shake Hollywood to its foundations. Women were terrible. They lied. They didn't know what it was to play fair. They got you into perfectly awful messes. And they left you there.[21]

A flapper, a vamp, and a mother simultaneously set their caps at Brown, and each attempts to capture him through a set of feminine wiles appropriate to her station (a breach of promise suit, a perfumed seduction, and the solicitation of pity for a fatherless child). Their competition is Brown's leading actress, Janice Reed, who gamely performs all the physical stuff that his comedies call for, and who is not yet visible as a sexual being: dancing with Janice "wasn't very different from dancing with his kid sister, Annabelle. In the course of long days of arduous work shared, he and Janice had come to know each other very well. They were as comfortable together as a couple of puppies."[22]

The flapper's charms are a sense of humor and a nice line in slangy dialogue. The vamp promises a world completely apart: "she drew him closer, until they held each other as two people might who see death just around the corner. Held him close and hard and sweet until they were wrapped in some living flame that sealed them together and away from all the world." Both women, however, are unpleasantly masculine in certain ways—they smoke, they drink, they use slang. The vamp goes further in the rights she arrogates to herself: "since she fulfilled the duties of a rich man and a prominent citizen, she assumed that she had the right to enjoy the privileges that most of them took unquestioned."[23] Yet however masculine the vamp may be, she cannot be Brown's friend because she is too likely to challenge his authority.

Devoted mothers are suspect as well. An old friend who has been deserted by her husband and who consequently must raise her son alone also has her eye on Brown. While her home seems to be an oasis of old-fashioned virtues, she too pursues Brown by proposing to him, with her child as the motive for her desire to remarry. Even Janice's mother proves similarly forceful, claiming that Brown's attentions have compromised his costar, in a characteristic St. Johns critique of stage mothers. Of all the women in the story, in short, only Janice is not aggressive when it comes to sex.

Brown cuts through the tangle by taking counsel with a worldly older woman, who advises him to marry the woman he can best please. His bride's identity is to be determined through the bestowal of four bracelets followed by the study of each woman's reactions. After her rivals are disqualified, Janice is revealed as the woman who loves her bracelet most for its associations with Brown, but she rejects his proposal of marriage when she thinks that her mother has engineered it. In other words, although in dress, energy, and interests Janice may seem like one of the boys, she has other sides redolent of something more passionate and less outdoorsy—her fondness for Tennyson's poetry, for instance, although even her interest in books is described as boyish. When Brown finally convinces Janice of his sincerity, he discovers that tomboyhood is fully compatible with "true womanhood," since it turns out that his fiancée embodies all that is most alluring in her competitors:

> he knew even with that first kiss that the passion of Leda O'Neil had been a tinsel fire that burned but did not warm, beside the passion that lay behind Janice Reed's cool young lips. That the merriment of Ray Connable had been the merest rickery of the vaudeville clown, beside the joyousness of Janice's high heart. And that the motherhood in Janice's soul need feel no shame before that of Gertie Morrison herself.[24]

Thus despite the "trim, high-laced boots" and "tight-fitting knickers" that make her resemble "a boy woodsman," Janice is eventually legible as female through her vulnerability.[25] This vulnerability is physical as well as emotional; boy woodsman notwithstanding, she must be rescued from the ice by her costar while performing a dangerous stunt for his picture. What makes her the ideal match is that Brown can please her without being devoured by her. Her boyishness is not a symbol of feminist independence but a proof of common interests and a promise that she will not make selfish demands on her husband. Significantly, she is the only woman who does not propose to Brown and is outraged when she realizes her mother has done so on her behalf.

The marriage that concludes "The Love Dodger" is rare in St. Johns's fiction (though not her reportage) in that it represents the union of two successful actors who will continue to work together after their nuptials. It is also unusual in presenting a successful working woman within the Hollywood community. St. Johns's 1927 *Photoplay* novella "The Port of Missing Girls" offers another exploration of the variety of female types in their relation to Hollywood, this time omitting the tomboy figure and focusing exclusively on the inadequacies of other varieties of women.

The novella tells the stories of six women who go out to Hollywood and meet with rejection and failure. Patty, the flapper, uses men but refuses to cooperate sexually and is eventually shunted aside. Greta, a Scandinavian earth-mother type, is abused by a plausible leading man who leaves her pregnant, although she retrieves her fortunes by getting back to the land as the wife of a California farmer. Paula, a discontented small-town wife, runs off to Hollywood with her child and is grateful when her husband reclaims her. Judy is manipulated by her grasping stage mother into accusing a director of having sexually assaulted her; she eventually finds contentment as a waitress. And Marilyn is a successful high-school actress who goes to Hollywood full of ideals but falls in love with an actor who trifles with her affections, causing her to kill herself. Of the six, only Persis makes a successful marriage in Hollywood, becoming the wife of socialite Peter Pell Loringdale after having lost her first husband, a drunken Irish script doctor. Significantly, Persis is the only woman who does not want a career as an actress—she comes to her second husband's attention when she demonstrates old-fashioned virtue as his sister's lady's maid.[26]

A number of critics have pointed out that the flapper is not an emblem of sexual revolt, and John Parris Springer observes that St. Johns was far from advocating overtly feminist ideas in her writing; indeed, he considers that she wanted to punish women for their career ambitions.[27] Marriage remains the ideal for her female characters, and it is often what they get instead of glamorous screen careers. More specifically, in punishing, or at least failing to reward, both old-time feminine wiles (the vamp, the manipulative mother, the starry-eyed innocent) and more recent modes of feminine self-assertion (the flapper), St. Johns's fiction suggests that there is something unseemly about the association between conventional femininity and filmdom.

Indeed, at least two of her stories suggest that women who pursue artistic careers must expect to abandon certain aspects of the typical feminine baggage and consign themselves to the sidelines as spectators and advisers. Cleveland Brown's counsel comes from such a woman, who is a famous artist but makes it clear that she renounces all sexual claims on him. Perhaps less expectedly, we get in "Miss Dumbbell" (April 1922) a sympathetic portrait of the ultimate tomboy, a lesbian who serves as matchmaker for the heterosexual couple in the story. She is a short-haired, chain-smoking, jodhpur-and-puttee-clad film editor whose role is to provide the heroine with a "line," a gimmick that will bring her to the attention of her ideal mate. Candace's line is merely the revelation of her unaffected, ladylike instincts, which are explicitly contrasted to the poses adopted by "scintillating vampires and intriguing temptresses."[28]

For St. Johns, in short, it is the womanly in both men and women that is associated with scandal or the openness to scandal, whether it results from feminine frailty (as evidenced by the variously abused heroines of "The Port of Missing Girls"), from the feminine willingness to manipulate (seen in the flappers and stage mothers of both novellas), or from perceived effeminacy in men. St. Johns's ideal men, in both her fiction and her reportage, are virile but innocent types whose lack of the instinct toward sexual predation makes them the male counterpart of the tomboy, even while it renders them vulnerable to unscrupulous women. She approved, for instance, of Wallace Reid, Richard Barthelmess, and Ben Lyon, but was one of the most consistent debunkers of the Valentino aura. When she did produce paragraphs sympathetic to Valentino (after his death), she cast him as yet another victim of female sexual aggression:

> Rudolph Valentino, the greatest matinee idol who ever lived, followed that same path, seeking the right woman, the one woman, who would bring him real happiness, among the thousands who worshipped him. Surrounded always by women who offered him love, he desired the happiness that only love could give, he was constantly reminded of love and of women. He died before he came to the end of his quest.[29]

Such perceptions suggest that the mobilization of female sexual desire was of considerable concern to St. Johns, a perception reinforced by her presentation of the ideal heroine as boyish and unable to articulate her desire directly. Thus a real-life actress such as comedienne Louise Fazenda may come in for praise on the grounds of her "disgrace[ful] clothes," inability to make small talk, and "indifferen[ce] to her personal appearance," even while she simultaneously displays a more conventionally feminine expertise in cooking and hat trimming—and also "remains something always of a mystery, with hidden depths, with strange reserves, unknown desires and ambitions." Fazenda's carelessness about her sexual allure (despite her "excellent" figure and "glorious" hair) serves to guarantee the essential innocence of the mystery at her core.[30] Similarly, the effect of requiring in certain stories that sexual knowledge be in the hands of the observers, to be doled out at the crucial moment, works to assure us of the purity of the heroine, who is not knowing in the ways that less desirable women are knowing.

Significantly, St. Johns is much more likely to present the stars in factual articles without critique; she finds something to praise in stars as diverse as Marion Davies, Blanche Sweet, and Alla Nazimova, just as she selects as "the ten handsomest men" in Hollywood strikingly different types (who nonetheless share, she claims, "strength, cleanness and intelligence combined with artistic symmetry of features and body").[31] While she is ready to rank stars in terms of talent and beauty in such articles as "Our One and Only Great Actress" (February 1926), she extols the virtues of the runners-up for the accolade, and even bestows the same plaudits on more than one rival, thus subverting the whole enterprise of ranking performers (an activity that fans were encouraged to perform). One is tempted therefore to suggest that the fiction offers a truer picture of St. Johns's views on gender, in that in writing about imaginary figures she presumably did not have to concern herself with presenting the properties of real studios in a positive light. The divided nature of St. Johns's writing is intrinsic to the structure of the fan magazine itself, which contains an astonishing heterogeneity of discourses in each issue, given the juxtaposition of ads, letters, editorials, reportage, fiction, poems, illustrations, and photographs. While hewing to an editorial line favorable to the film industry was clearly the bread and butter of *Photoplay* and its competitors, this forum nonetheless offered scope for the airing of individual writers' preferences and prejudices. Particularly through her fiction, St. Johns's writing stands as an example of how the fan magazine, located in Hollywood but not precisely of it, may be viewed as another venue through which women sought to exert influence over the

"So Real as to Seem Like Life Itself"

consumption and construction of film — and, indeed, the consumption and construction of womanhood itself.

Notes

1. See Miriam Hansen, *Babel and Babylon: Spectatorship in American Silent Film* (Cambridge: Harvard University Press, 1991).
2. See David Bordwell, Janet Staiger, and Kristin Thompson, *The Classical Hollywood Cinema: Film Style and Mode of Production to 1960* (New York: Columbia University Press, 1985), 194.
3. For information on lighting and cast in *The Cheat*, see Sumiko Higashi, *Cecil B. DeMille and American Culture: The Silent Era* (Berkeley: University of California Press, 1994), 103; and Lea Jacobs, "Belasco, DeMille, and the Development of Lasky Lighting," *Film History* 5:4 (December, 1993): 416.
4. Kathryn H. Fuller, *At the Picture Show: Small-Town Audiences and the Creation of Movie Fan Culture* (Washington, D.C.: Smithsonian Institution Press, 1996), 121.
5. Fuller, *At the Picture Show*, 115; Gaylyn Studlar, "The Perils of Pleasure? Fan Magazine Discourse as Women's Commodified Culture in the 1920s," *Wide Angle* 13, 1 (1991): 8.
6. Fuller, *At the Picture Show*, 135, 145.
7. Studlar, "The Perils of Pleasure," 7.
8. Ibid., 8-9.
9. Ibid., 11, 18-19.
10. "Inside Life Stories of Photoplay Staff Writers," *Photoplay*, July 1925, 56; see also Herbert Howe, "Our Adela," *Photoplay*, November 1923, 54.
11. "Adela Rogers St. Johns," in *Contemporary Authors*, ed. Hal May (Detroit: Gale, 1983), 420-423; Eric Pace, "Adela R. St. Johns, 94, Journalist, Novelist, Teacher and Screenwriter," *New York Times*, 11 August 1988, D20.
12. "Adela Rogers St. Johns," 422, 421.
13. Robert S. Lynd and Helen Merrell Lynd, *Middletown: A Study in American Culture* (1929; reprint, New York: Harcourt Brace Jovanovich, 1957), 241.
14. Adela Rogers St. Johns, "The Fan-Letter Bride," *Photoplay*, August 1922, 82.
15. St. Johns's endorsement of the tomboy may be an artifact of her upbringing in Los Angeles by her father and grandparents; she later wrote of her mother, "My memory has rejected her, eliminated her, cannot apparently bear to remember her." See Jean C. Chance, "Adela Rogers St. Johns," *Dictionary of Literary Biography*, vol. 29, American Newspaper Journalists, 1926-1950 (Detroit: Gale, 1984), 311. As Victoria Bissell Brown notes in her discussion of girls' socialization during the period when St. Johns was a child, "Golden Girls: Female Socialization among the Middle Class of Los Angeles, 1880-1910," in *Small Worlds: Children and Adolescents in America, 1850-1950*, ed.

Elliott West and Paula Petrik (Lawrence: University Press of Kansas, 1992), "girls' participation in some masculine activities could be regarded as good preparation for their later role as helpmeets." Ambitious girls, Brown observes, would naturally prefer the activities associated with boys, who were granted a great deal more physical freedom (233-234).

16 Mary P. Ryan, "The Projection of a New Womanhood: The Movie Moderns in the 1920's," in *Our American Sisters: Women in American Life and Thought*, ed. Jean Friedman and William Shade (Boston: Allyn and Bacon, 1976), 504.
17 Paula S. Fass, *The Damned and the Beautiful: American Youth in the 1920s* (Oxford: Oxford University Press, 1977), 262-267.
18 "My Life Story, by Clara Bow, as Told to Adela Rogers St. Johns," *Photoplay* February 1928, 30.
19 The phrase is Richard Koszarski's. See *An Evening's Entertainment: The Age of the Silent Feature Picture, 1915-1928* (New York: Charles Scribner's Sons, 1990), 307.
20 "My Life Story, by Clara Bow," 78, 104.
21 Adela Rogers St. Johns, "The Love Dodger," *Photoplay*, May 1924, 53.
22 Ibid., 123.
23 St. Johns, "The Love Dodger," *Photoplay*, April 1924, 54.
24 St. Johns, "The Love Dodger," *Photoplay*, July 1924, 120.
25 St. Johns, "The Love Dodger," *Photoplay*, May 1924, 36.
26 Adela Rogers St. Johns, "The Port of Missing Girls," *Photoplay*, March-August 1927.
27 John Parris Springer, "Hollywood Fictions: The Cultural Construction of Hollywood in American Literature, 1916-1939" (Ph.D. diss., University of Iowa, 1994), 227. In *Some Are Born Great* (New York: Doubleday, 1974), in contrast, St. Johns praises a long list of accomplished women, including Amelia Earhart, Margaret Mitchell, and Margaret Sanger. As Jean Chance writes, "she notes that she is not a feminist, but believes in 'the superiority of American women'" ("Adela Rogers St. Johns," 312).
28 Adela Rogers St. Johns, "Miss Dumbbell," *Photoplay*, April 1922, 32, 98.
29 Adela Rogers St. Johns, "Why Jack Gilbert Married," *Photoplay*, August 1929, 36.
30 Adela Rogers St. Johns, "The Most Versatile Girl in Hollywood," *Photoplay*, June 1925, 84, 128-129.
31 Adela Rogers St. Johns, "Ten Handsome Men of the Screen," *Photoplay*, January 1926, 32.

Performing Bodies **IV**

GAYLYN STUDLAR

Oh, "Doll Divine"

Mary Pickford, Masquerade, and the Pedophilic Gaze

Mary Pickford, doll divine,
Year by year, and every day
At the moving picture play,
You have been my valentine.
—Vachel Lindsay (1913), opening of "To Mary Pickford Moving Picture Actress (On Hearing She Was Leaving the Moving-Pictures for the Stage)"

"Oh, you beautiful doll—you great big beautiful doll," the words and strain of the old song rushed into my mind the minute I saw her, all curled up in a steamer chair covered with her mink coat and wooly scarfs [*sic*], just the toes of her tiny feet emerging from an equally tiny footstool. And at the top of this bunch of fur and wool, those golden curls known round the world, hung shiny and saucy from beneath a blue organdy cap. Mrs. Douglas Fairbanks, as the lovely Mary Pickford likes to be called now, was on the set.—Caroline Moore, "Mary Tells of Initial Experiences: Relates Incidents to Tacoma Girl in Interview for Apollo Theater"

Mary Pickford was, arguably, the most famous woman of the first quarter of the twentieth century. Inarguably, she was one of the first major stars of the Hollywood film industry, and one of the very few—female or male—able to sustain stardom for more than twenty years. Also known as Gladys Smith of Toronto, Canada, Mary Pickford became a stage actress at age six (published age five). She first appeared in film in the one-reelers of American Biograph in the spring of 1909. In the 1910s, the actress known as Our Little Mary quickly cemented her popularity through numerous films that coincided with the Hollywood film industry's shift to using the actor as a personality for drawing audiences to the box office.[1]

Pickford was promoted as "America's Sweetheart," "The World's Sweetheart," and, as poet Vachel Lindsay dubbed her, "The Queen of the Movies."[2] Her films for Famous Players in the late 1910s regularly netted more than a million dollars a year. In 1918, an article in *American Magazine* proclaimed what was by then obvious: "Our Little Mary" had become "the most popular motion picture actress in the world."[3]

What made her so popular? What exactly was the appeal of Mary Pickford and of her films? In attempting to answer these questions, it cannot escape notice that from the beginning of Pickford's film career, the actress's characters often are ambiguously inscribed with characteristics of both child and adult woman, as a "child-woman." As I show, even when she ostensibly is cast as an adult, the grown-up Mary Pickford registers as an adolescent "girl" or a child-woman ambiguously poised between childhood and womanhood. As her career moved into the feature-film era, her screen persona grew even younger, until she was, for all intents and purposes, a child impersonator.

In 1914, an industry trade magazine, the *Bioscope,* published a review of the Pickford box-office hit, *Tess of the Storm Country* (dir. Edwin S. Porter, 1914) that articulates one view of the actress's youthful appeal:

> There are many young comediennes . . . but it is only Mary Pickford . . . who can create through the silent medium . . . just that particular kind of sentiment—ineffably sweet, joyously young, and sometimes, if one may put it so, almost unbearably heartbreaking in its tender pathos—which has become identified with her name, and with which we are all familiar.[4]

As in *Tess,* in *Rags* (dir. James Kirwood, 1915), Pickford was cast as an adolescent spitfire living in poverty. In response to the film, a *Variety* review suggested that the basis of Pickford's popular appeal was rather obvious: "She and her bag of tricks are so well established . . . [that] no matter what she does in a picture they [film followers] are sure to term it 'cute,' and in the current offering are many little scenes that call for that expression."[5] In a review of *M'Liss* (dir. Marshall Neilan, 1918), *Motion Picture News* defined "the 'typical' Pickford picture" as one that "shows her in rags and curls, in situations both humorous and dramatic."[6] A newspaper review of *M'Liss* suggested that the primary strength in this tale of an adolescent stagecoach robber (Pickford) was in offering the actress as "the ragged little

Oh, *"Doll Divine"*

51. "Rags" (Mary Pickford) holding her own against the hardened miners. *Rags* (dir. Kirwood, 1915). Photo courtesy of Academy of Motion Picture Arts and Sciences.

Mary everyone first learned to know and love." The review continues in language that confirms *Variety*'s comments on the appeal of "cuteness": "All the inimitable little mannerisms which are so much her own are in evidence.... All dressed up and in a beautiful garden she is lovely, but in funny tattered little garments, with curls flying, she is—well, just 'our Mary.' "[7] Not only did Pickford regularly play adolescents, but in the late 1910s, her characters began to grow even younger. She became a child impersonator in *The Foundling* (dir. John O'Brien, 1916), *The Poor Little Rich Girl* (dir. Maurice Tourneur, 1917), *Rebecca of Sunnybrook Farm* (dir. Neilan, 1917), and *A Little Princess* (dir. Neilan, 1917). Audiences and critics responded with enthusiasm. She spawned imitators, and wrote for *Vanity Fair* about the techniques and technical problems of undertaking child roles.[8]

One might be tempted to assume that Pickford's juvenation reflected the predictable typecasting of a popular actress by an exploitative, male-dominated industry. But such an assumption is complicated by Pickford's power within that industry. By the late 1910s, the actress was already exercising a great deal of influence over her film projects made through the

52. Studio portrait of Mary Pickford in costume for *A Little Princess* (dir. Neilan, 1917). Photo courtesy of Academy of Motion Picture Arts and Sciences.

Artcraft division of Famous Players–Lasky. She briefly moved to First National, where she exercised even greater control as her own independent producer. As one of the founders of United Artists in 1919, she was on the forefront of film artists who exercised absolute creative mastery over their vehicles, from concept through distribution.

In spite of her unprecedented control over her films, the formula for Pickford's star vehicles changed relatively little. In fact, not only did she continue to play ragged adolescents, as in her 1922 remake of *Tess of the Storm Country,* but during the years in which she exercised the most creative authority over her silent film career, many of her most important and popular films present her in the role of a child. They included, at First National, *Daddy-Long-Legs* (dir. Neilan, 1919), and, at United Artists, *Pollyanna* (dir. Paul Powell, 1920), *Through the Back Door* (dir. Alfred Green and Jack Pickford, 1921), *Little Lord Fauntleroy* (dir. Green and Pickford, 1921), *Little Annie Rooney* (dir. William Beaudine, 1925), and *Sparrows* (dir. Beaudine, 1926). A commentator reacted to Pickford in *Through the Back Door:* "She stands absolutely alone in the portrayal of youthful roles, and conveys the impression of extreme youth, both through face and conduct as no other

Oh, "Doll Divine"

53. Studio portrait of Mary Pickford circa 1916. Photo courtesy of Academy of Motion Picture Arts and Sciences.

player ever has.... She appears with equal facility and conviction a child of eleven and a girl of seventeen."[9]

The notion of a grown woman playing a child and the specific techniques used to represent Our Little Mary on-and-offscreen certainly raise a host of questions about the fascination that Mary Pickford inspired in a broad range of viewers. In spite of her enormous popularity, Pickford's sustained association with child roles did not go without comment. "Why do people love Mary?" was a question often raised in the 1910s, but Mordaunt Hall's *New York Times* review of *Pollyanna* articulates the rather more nervous question that was asked especially often in the 1920s:

> People have been asking recently *why doesn't Mary Pickford grow up?* The question is answered at the Rivoli this week. It is evident that Miss Pickford doesn't grow up because she can make people laugh and cry, can win her way into more hearts and even protesting heads, as a rampant, resilient little girl than as anything else. She can no more grow up than Peter Pan.[10]

The public strongly associated Pickford with child and adolescent roles, so much so that, as early as 1921, the actress protested: "The world wants me to remain a little girl all my life.... I want to give the very best that is in me, but whenever I try to do something different, the public complains I have tucked up my curls and left off the short pinafores. To them, I am eternal youth, and they won't let me grow up."[11]

As I argue, in the prime of her career, even when she deviated from her specialty of playing children and adolescents, the public continued to perceive Pickford in juvenated terms, terms sustained in the extratextual construction of the actress as a star persona. As a key part of this pattern, a virtual collapse occurred in the public perception of the character of Our Little Mary onscreen and Mary Pickford the actress. The latter was constructed in extratextual discourse (including fan and general-interest magazine articles, publicity photographs, and interviews) in ways that disavowed her status as an adult woman.

With regard to her films, the numerous textual reiterations of the childish Mary Pickford enabled her remarkable success. If this situation frustrated the actress's attempt to widen her range of roles, it did not become the basis of any sustained attempt to remake her screen persona. She did attempt a radical departure in Frances Marion's *The Love Light* (1921), a World War I melodrama in which her Italian peasant heroine character starts out as a typical Pickford hoyden but quickly grows up when she falls in love with a German spy. The film called for Pickford's much suffering protagonist to temporarily lose her mind after she loses her husband and baby.

Pickford immediately reverted back to type in her next film, *Through the Back Door,* but she did attempt dual roles, of mother and curly-headed son, in *Little Lord Fauntleroy,* also released in 1921. Her most famous departures from type came in 1924, in the roles of coquettish teenagers in two historical costume dramas, the Ernst Lubitsch–directed *Rosita* (1924) and Marshall Neilan's *Dorothy Vernon of Hadden Hall* (1924). The career stretch embodied in these two vehicles may now appear almost humorously conservative, but Pickford regarded both as significant failures in spite of evidence to the contrary. Neither seems to have been a financial failure, and most critics were quite positive about Pickford's performances in films that were more sexually sophisticated than her usual vehicles. However, a thoughtful review in the *New York Evening Post* concluded that these ambitious new productions offered only inconsequential differences from Pickford's usual screen work:

> Our Mary herself is better and prettier than ever before. But for some unknown reason, she seems to insist on sticking to a type. . . . This, of course, tends to monotony. We believe that this is recognized by Miss Pickford, and probably gives her many uneasy moments. . . . However, it isn't exactly fair to criticize Miss Pickford for her lack of versatility. She has so firmly established herself in the affection of a large army of movie fans that, perhaps, there

would be disappointment if Mary turned out in some picture to be any one else than Mary.¹²

In the same year, Pickford articulated the limitations created by the public's perception of her: "I created a certain type, which has been worked out now. It is finished. It is possible to do another type, of course, but the public wants me only in one character, that of Mary Pickford. Now I have finished that and I think it is time to quit."¹³

Contrary to her published remarks, Pickford didn't quit, and she didn't quit her little girl roles. In a letter to a family member, she blamed others: "Everyone seemed to resent so much the two grown up parts of Rosita and Dorothy that I felt I had to return to a little girl role."¹⁴ Did her loyal public constitute "everyone"? If so, how did the public articulate this resentment? It appears that this resentment was not conclusively articulated at the box office. We do not have access to evidence that might support Pickford's claim (such as troves of angry fan letters), but in a letter to *Photoplay* in 1925, a female fan emphasizes the powerful conflation of Pickford with her child characters that no doubt influenced the star's decision to stay true to type:

> My Dear Little Mary:
> The idea that you are "just a little girl" is so firmly established in my mind that any attempt to discard it is resented. . . . Only a great actress or one who is really a child at heart, could make those little characters so natural that they become our friends, and we refuse to give them up when another "Mary Pickford" appears in the role of an older girl. We love Dorothy Vernon, too, but we never, never associate her with our own little Mary, Rebecca, and Pollyanna.¹⁵

To the letter writer, "Little Mary" is yet another character among her favorite Pickford little girl roles. In the same issue in which this letter appeared, *Photoplay* polled readers asking which roles Pickford should play. Readers' top choices were very revealing: Anne of Green Gables, Heidi, Alice in Wonderland, Cinderella, The Little Colonel, and Sara Crewe. The magazine claimed that "almost twenty thousand readers spoke with a clear majority that was overwhelmingly in favor of roles depicting childhood."¹⁶ In the next year, when Pickford was back on the screen as a feisty tenement girl leading a neighborhood gang in *Little Annie Rooney,* Mordaunt Hall's review is appreciative but aware of the intractability of the Pickford screen persona: "Viewing Miss Pickford in such a role is like turning the clock back as this charming actress has not changed perceptibly since the early days of pictures."[17]

Mary's Masquerade and Gendered Spectatorship

Mary Pickford engaged in a masquerade of childishness with very interesting implications for a gender-determined spectatorship. This notion of a masquerade of childishness bears some structural similarities to the masquerade of femininity often cited in feminist film theory. The latter is derived from Joan Riviere's psychoanalytic theory of womanliness. In her essay "Womanliness as a Masquerade," Riviere offers a psychoanalytic case history and argues that the cultural codes of womanliness or femininity are assumed rather like a masquerade to allay anxiety and deflect patriarchal criticism of the woman patient's demonstration of masculine traits such as intellectual prowess.[18]

Rather than performing the cultural codes expected to construct womanliness, Pickford assumed the signs of childishness that rendered her womanly aesthetic perfection and her erotic potential innocent and safe. Even though she often portrayed girls who were strong-minded and vigorous rather than silly and delicate, her masquerade of childishness undercut her potential for sexual subjectivity. It did not, however, undercut her potential to be a sexual object. In this respect, Pickford's masquerade of childishness reflects a nostalgic, Victorian-influenced cultural determination of femininity.

Pickford's films were often drawn from late-nineteenth- and early-twentieth-century literature about children, but not necessarily addressed to them. Adults frequently read such literature of the time. Many of the novels and plays adapted by Pickford to film were by women writers who offered the adventures and triumphs of independent little girls whose behavior rebelled against expected norms of feminine refinement and morality. Although largely adhering to expectations for the development of rambunctious girls into refined women, sometimes this literature was critical of gender inequalities.[19] These juvenated heroines may limit the subjectivity (especially sexual subjectivity) of Pickford's characters, but "the ascription of immaturity and transition [to adulthood] gives her permission to behave in ways that might not be appropriate for a woman."[20]

Certainly this is true of Pickford's title character in *Rebecca of Sunnybrook Farm,* adapted from the book by Kate Douglas Wiggin. The mother of Rebecca cannot afford to raise her daughter and so ships her off to live

Oh, *"Doll Divine"*

54. Annie leads her gang in a neighborhood "war." *Little Annie Rooney* (dir. Beaudine, 1925). Photo courtesy of Academy of Motion Picture Arts and Sciences.

with two dour aunts. Rebecca demonstrates remarkable independence and intelligence as she adapts to living with her aunts. She is a tomboy who climbs trees, uses an umbrella like a sword against a bothersome girl, and assertively manages other children in a backyard circus performance. In spite of these qualities that might suggest a nascent new woman, two familiar aspects of the Victorian model of femininity, altruism and illness, bring Rebecca/Pickford to the brink of a virtuous womanhood. It is of some interest, nevertheless, that her actual transition to a traditional model of womanhood—one in which demure sweetness will replace brazen outspokenness—is never shown by the film. Still a child, Rebecca is shipped off again—to boarding school. She returns visually transformed, a beautiful young woman (of seventeen) ready to forgive her dying Aunt Miranda (Josephine Crowell) for her occasionally harsh treatment of her. But her character retains enough spontaneity (or rebelliousness) to run away when a neighbor, Adam Ladd (Eugene O'Brien), coded throughout the film as Rebecca's future husband, attempts to kiss her.[21]

To theorize the responses elicited by Pickford's construction of childishness in a film like *Rebecca of Sunnybrook Farm* is almost unimaginable

55. Studio portrait of Mary Pickford for *Rebecca of Sunnybrook Farm* (dir. Neilan, 1917). Photo courtesy of Academy of Motion Picture Arts and Sciences.

without an acknowledgment of the complexities of gendered spectatorship in relation to the representation of femininity—of whatever age. Although United Artists exhibitors' pressbooks from Pickford's films of the 1920s suggest that children were regarded as a very important segment of her audience, they were not regarded as her exclusive one. Women were also identified as a key part of Pickford's primary fan base.[22] Pickford herself speculated that the typical customer for her films was "a tired businessman who gets home, settles down when his wife says, 'Ben, it's Mary Pickford tonight—let's take the children.'"[23] Since Our Mary cultivated her films'

Oh, "Doll Divine"

56. After the circus, Rebecca (Mary Pickford) is punished by her Aunt Miranda (Josephine Crowell) in *Rebecca of Sunnybrook Farm*. Photo courtesy of Academy of Motion Picture Arts and Sciences.

"uplifting," "wholesome" appeal across gender and generation, her account of her audience may be a savvy marketing ploy seeking to incorporate the whole spectrum of the family into her box office.[24]

Nevertheless, male critics were intrigued with Pickford. These include Mordaunt Hall, who admitted that he found her fascinating even when he did not like her film vehicles (one of his *New York Times* reviews bemoaned the fact that so many of her films were not "adult fare").[25] Such an interest speaks volumes about the unconscious sexual force of the actress's blurring of the boundaries between "womanliness" and a masquerade of childishness. Many male critics and commentators blended an admiration bordering on worship with open curiosity about the source(s) of her popularity. Among these was poet Vachel Lindsay. In *The Art of the Moving Picture,* he repeated the question that was often asked in popular discourse of the time: "Why do the people love Mary?" His answer to this question captures something of the power of the Pickford image:

> Because of a certain aspect of her face in her highest mood.... The people are hungry for this fine and spiritual thing that Botticelli painted in the faces of his muses and heavenly creatures. Because the mob catch the very glimpse of it in Mary's face, they follow her night after night in the films. They are never quite satisfied with the plays because the managers are not artists enough to know they should sometimes put her into sacred pictures and not have her always the village hoyden.... But perhaps in this argument I have but betrayed myself as Mary's infatuated partisan.[26]

Lindsay's remarks may at first strike us as a strange accounting of the reasons for Pickford's popularity, for he articulates a fascination that reaches beyond the boundaries of the star's roles; indeed, he suggests that her roles and film vehicles frustrate rather than satisfy her audience.

Lindsay's remarks—and his "infatuation" with Pickford—constitute a useful route to the notion of a pedophilic gaze in relation to the construction of Our Mary. The idea that Pickford had anything to do with pedophilia would have scandalized her admirers in the 1910s and 1920s. Yet, how often is an "aesthetic" response to an inscription of femininity, like that of Lindsay to his "doll divine," completely unconnected to a sexual one? I do not wish to argue that Pickford appealed to male admirers who were actual pedophiles. What I do wish to suggest is that Pickford appealed to and through a kind of cultural pedophilia that looked to the innocent child-woman to personify nostalgic ideals of femininity.

Pickford's popularity was related to a phenomenon located in Victorian and post-turn-of-the-century academic painting by Bram Dijkstra in *Idols of Perversity.* Dijkstra argues that the representation of young girls in academic painting of the time created a venue as much about and for the play of male sexual fantasy as it was an idealization of childhood innocence.[27] In addition, within the cultural scenario of the 1910s and 1920s, Pickford's portrayal of an old-fashioned girl, albeit one of high spirits, may have provided an erotic object more acceptable to many men than the young but overtly sexualized flapper whose desiring subjectivity was more threat than promise. Thus the articulation of Pickford as an antimodernist, Victorian-indebted model of femininity served as one antidote to a perceived crisis

Oh, "Doll Divine"

in feminine sexual behavior. It is well documented that in the 1910s and 1920s, the flapper and the new woman symbolized American women's perceived transgression of the traditional feminine sexual norms of passivity and restraint. Considered to be a radical subversion of American gender ideals, sexual agency among modern women was met with a great deal of cultural anxiety. As social historian Paula Fass has noted: "Gazing at the young women of the period, the traditionalist saw the end of American civilization as he had known it."[28]

Liminality and the Attractive Child-Woman

Coming as it does during a time in which modernism and antimodernism waged a war of words over women and their desires, Pickford's impersonation of girls and adolescents takes on sexual complexity. That complexity is illuminated by remarks made by Martha Vicinus in another context. Vicinus argues that the symbolic function of the adolescent boy in fin de siècle culture was to "absorb and reflect a variety of sexual desires and emotional needs."[29] I wish to suggest that Pickford's astonishing popularity as a cultural figure depends on a similar process. On one hand, male fantasies were easily attached to her. She represented a dangerously attractive female whose masquerade of childishness appealed to adult men raised in the late Victorian period. Those men might find her enticing innocence a comforting alternative to the models of feminine sexual subjectivity offered by the flapper and the new woman. On the other hand, Pickford's many child-woman heroines also could serve an identificatory function for women and girls who might read her as a comforting "asexual" figure of freedom whose youth released her from the demands—including the sexual demands—of adult femininity.

Pickford's films and extratextual publicity functioned as a venue for the play of male fantasy that shares much with fin de siècle high-art representations of children, but her impersonation of the little girl, her adult performance of a masquerade of childishness, adds another complication to the eroticization of female innocence. One could argue that by its overt performative status, her juvenating masquerade makes acceptable, perhaps even inevitable, the sexualization of her child-woman signification. It may have provided a mechanism of disavowal ("I watch, I desire this child, but she is really not a child") to men who sought to deny such culturally prevalent sexual fantasies. As an added bonus for the play of sexual fantasy, the viewer might have rationalized any desire for the child character through the disavowing formula: "I desire this woman who looks/acts like a child because I know that she is not a child; still, she is as all women should be — innocent and childlike."

From the start of her film career, Pickford's screen persona evidenced liminality with regard to the inscription of her age and sexuality. This is evident as early as D. W. Griffith's *The Lonely Villa* of 1909. In this "house-invasion narrative," Pickford plays the oldest child of a besieged suburban family. What is noticeable in this film is how Pickford is distinguished, visually, from the other actors. She is extraordinarily beautiful. Her expressive face and large head, topped by long, soft curls, draw the eye and impress with their perfection. The sensitivity and mature beauty of her face suggest a contradictory relationship with her small-statured body, rendered shapeless and childish by a loose, low-waisted, white dress, a typical mode of clothing for a middle-class girl of 1909. This perching of a porcelain-perfect head on top of a shapeless body makes us understand why Pickford would call up notions of a "doll divine" for Vachel Lindsay. Pickford's womanly facial beauty, combined with an inscription of physical and fashion-coded childishness, visually articulates an uncertainty as to her status as an untouchable child or marriageable, sexual woman.

That uncertainty or ambiguity underscored many of her performances — as child, adolescent, and adult — and unsettled the inscription of sexual boundaries in everything from Griffith's *The New York Hat* (1912) to *Coquette* (1929), her first sound film. In *The New York Hat,* a motherless girl becomes the target of small-town gossip when she receives an anonymous gift of an elaborate hat. The hat, displayed in a store window, has been the object of desire of most of the town's female population. "Mary" is unaware that the minister (Lionel Barrymore) bought her the hat to keep trust with a poignant request made by her mother, who, worked to death by her husband, left the clergyman with a sum of money to buy her daughter "the bits of finery she has always been denied."

Pickford spends most of the film dressed young and playing young. Although she wears the long dress of a woman, her attire is loose and obscures her figure. As if she has suddenly outgrown her clothes, her arms stick awkwardly out of her sleeves. Her attempt to look sophisticated by carrying gloves as she walks down the street makes her look even more childish. Is she a woman or a child?

Learning that the minister has bought the large, ornate hat, the church elders suspect the worst (seduction), but he shows them the letter left him by her mother. Suddenly, with the revelation of the minister's kindness, the girl is represented as being of marriageable age when, through pantomime, the minister suggests that they marry. The scene continues to register the tension between Pickford's girlishness and womanliness as her character whispers in her father's ear to ask permission. Thus the film's ending oddly confirms the possibility of sexual union that the rest of the film seemed to deny vigorously. The denial rests chiefly in the strength of Pickford's performance of the girl as just that, a girl who appears capable of an intense interest in a hat but not in a man.

The image of the eroticized child-woman is familiar throughout the work of D. W. Griffith, where it has often been associated with Victorian ideals of femininity. Pickford's figure of the hoyden shares much with that ideal and with Griffith's child-women, but her characters' physical assertiveness and determined mind-set tend to obscure these fundamental commonalities. Pickford herself sought to distinguish her heroines from Griffith's and came to articulate her artistic differences with him as revolving around the exaggerated effects he demanded in portrayals of youthful femininity. In an interview late in life, she claimed: "I would not run around like a goose with its head off, crying 'oooooh . . . the little birds! Ooooh . . . look! A little bunny!' That's what he taught his ingenues, and they all did the same thing."[30]

Even if Pickford's heroines were less vacuous and hysterical and more assertive and "realistic" than Griffith's virginally pure child-woman, they still depended on the titillating vulnerability of the female innocent whose beauty was not complicated by sexual knowledge. As a result, Pickford's many motherless or orphaned heroines typically assume a dual function in her films throughout the 1920s, including *Little Annie Rooney* and *Sparrows*. First, the character's status as an orphan ensures that a measure of pathos is attached to the beautiful hoyden who is in need of affection as well as of adventure. As one 1924 review of *Dorothy Vernon of Hadden Hall* suggested, "her beauty placed in distressing circumstances brings the mingling of sentiment and melodrama so delightful to her admirers."[31] In some sense the orphan-heroine appealed as a poignant reflection of social reality; one in ten children of the time did not live with her/his parents.[32]

Onscreen, the situation of the orphan provides an avenue for the heroine's self-expression and adventure that would normally be repressed for the girl (or woman) secured in an intact nuclear family. It followed that these culturally resonant scenarios of the girl-orphan allowed women viewers to guiltlessly rationalize the heroine's self-sufficiency, acquired at the loss of home and family. Pickford's films often use her status as an orphan to sketch out the enjoyable and humorous dimensions of her character's independence. Women spectators could enjoy and identify with the girl's freedom as a temporary precursor to womanhood, with its promise of romantic love, but they might also revel in her childhood freedom as an alternative space, a site of resistant pleasures that slip away under the pressure of woman's cultural destiny.

Of course, Pickford's films are remembered for their sentimentality, but they also are rather insistent in their emphasis on the effects of familial economics on girls. This resonated with reformist efforts of the time to improve the lot of children and, most particularly, to release them from the burdens of labor. A more uncompromising approach to this issue is especially evident in two films in which Pickford refused to follow her own formula of depicting the transition between girlhood freedom and womanly submission to love. As the plain Cockney laundress in *Suds* (dir. John Francis Dillon, 1920) and as the homely slave Unity Blake in *Stella Maris* (dir. Neilan, 1918) Pickford used character roles to depict girlhoods of drudgery and deprivation. In these films, childhood losses are not, as in so many other Pickford films, redeemed by blossoming beauty and the promise of a loving—and economically comfortable—marriage.

More typical of her films is *Daddy-Long-Legs*, which Kevin Brownlow has called "the archetypal Mary Pickford film ... [having] all the elements an audience could hope for: a baby rescued from an ashcan, an orphanage run like a penitentiary, hilarious and touching comedy, much pathos, and a lover waiting in the wings for Pickford's character to grow up."[33] The "lover waiting in the wings" certainly applies to Pickford films as early as *The New York Hat* and comes to be the expected formula for resolution in many of her feature films. In *Rebecca of Sunnybrook Farm,* Rebecca dons her Sunday best to sell soap door to door in order to secure a soap-company prize (a lamp) to give to a poor family. During this door-to-door campaign, the heretofore assertive Rebecca unexpectedly reverts to babyish confusion when Adam Ladd (whom she calls Mr. Aladdin) shows her attention. In *Little Annie Rooney,* the title character's escapades in leading her "gang" of rock-throwing children end suddenly when she runs into Joe Kelly (William Haines), a grown man. He laughs at her, which makes her angry, but, of course, he will be her ultimate mate because, as the intertitles tell us, at this first meeting of child and man, she feels something for him (that she cannot identify).

Yet the child's heterosexual "love interest" is quite marginalized, for the heroine's bonding to other children takes precedence in her emotional life. Sometimes the heroine functions both as child and as child playing mother. This reproduction of mothering occurs in *Sparrows,* with Mama Molly (Pickford) established as the oldest among the orphans at a Florida baby farm. When a baby arrives, Molly decides it "doesn't belong" because it is obviously well fed and so must be from a caring family. To keep the baby from being killed, Molly decides that all the children will escape. Though a mere adolescent in pigtails, she leads them across alligator-infested swamps to safety—and a new life. That life serves only to reinforce our confusion about her sexuality and age. In the mansion of the widowed father of the well-fed baby, Molly continues to look after the toddler. The father agrees to adopt the other children, but the millionaire's relationship to Molly remains unclear: will she be another adopted child or his new wife? Whether it was important to her audiences that Pickford's characters find romantic success in the final reel is uncertain, for often, as in *Sparrows, Rebecca of Sunnybrook Farm,* and *Pollyanna,* her maturation into marriageable womanhood remains ambiguous at best. What is of more certainty is that these rags-to-riches scenarios had plenty of "built in" appeal to women viewers, who could readily identify across class lines to embrace Pickford's familiar character as a Cinderella who manages to eke out a great deal of fun from her miserable childhood.

The Doll Divine as a New Woman

In Pickford's films, women were invited to relive the pleasures and pains of girlhood and to identify with Our Little Mary incarnated as a feisty, irrepressible tomboy and altruistic little mother. However, these characters simultaneously carried an identity as the beautiful and successful adult actress and powerful new woman known as Mary Pickford. Through star discourse, the masquerade of childhood that Pickford played out in the plots of her films was extended and served as a means of disavowing or neutralizing the revisionary or emancipatory values contained in the distinctively new woman elements of her career, including her business acumen, her immense wealth, and her childlessness.

In the early years of her stardom, signs of childishness were represented through publicity and promotion to be indicative of Pickford's "real self." The actress was depicted as an innocent adolescent girl who practiced piano and obeyed her mother. *Cosmopolitan*'s "An Actress from the 'Movies' " declared her to be an "unsophisticated believer in fairies" and the "pet of playgoers all over the country who don't even know her name."[34] In 1915, *Ladies' Home Journal*'s "The Best-Known Girl in America" offered Pickford (at age twenty-three) in dialogue with her "girlfriends" (or more exactly, fans); the actress notes that her "mother will not let [her] eat candy."[35] *Photoplay*'s

1917 article "Speaking of the Actress" declared of Pickford: "If everybody was as pureminded as she, there would be no sin in the world."[36]

Pickford's juvenated, offscreen self was situated squarely within a family discourse that linked her to the values of a working-class, female-centered family. Many articles emphasized the difficulty of her role in the Pickford family as both "child" and "breadwinner." Extensive commentaries by Pickford followed the trends of contemporary reformist discourse and used her own "miserable" childhood as a stage actress as an example of what required reform. In a story that could be taken from one of her films, her autobiography, serialized in *Ladies' Home Journal,* relates how she had to work as a child actress to keep from being given away: "I had to give up my own childhood, but it was necessary in my case—either work or be separated from my mother." She is adamant that children should not be allowed to work in films to support adults who could work.[37]

In the 1920s, as more commentary asked when she was going to "grow up," her portrayals of childhood were increasingly attributed to her personal need to experience a childhood she missed. In a newspaper article of 1923, "A Character Study of the Real Mary Pickford: Woman and Genius," the author recounts the actress's accomplishments, her intellectual power, her "genius" as an artist. Her ultimate attainment remains securely feminine; it is her "power to give happiness," which is linked to her own childhood of economic deprivation and responsibility: "You may note a somewhat wistful look in her eyes as she tells you that among other things that she has missed in life was a REAL CHILDHOOD . . . the weekly struggle to make both ends meet, gave her hardly a nodding acquaintance with childhood as most of us have known it . . . [so] she decided to weave a fictitious one for herself on screen."[38]

As the star system developed, a gap between the fictitious screen persona and the offscreen "real" star persona was acknowledged and increasingly encouraged in an era in which the offscreen antics of actors were sometimes flagrantly at odds with their onscreen personae. The juvenating publicity surrounding Pickford continued, but coexisted with and often contradicted widespread public knowledge of the more adult particulars of the actress's private life as a grown woman. By 1916, it was common knowledge that Little Mary was married (since 1911) to Owen Moore, an actor she had met at Biograph. Knowledge of her private life reached a potential crisis when she divorced Moore to marry Douglas Fairbanks, who left his socialite wife and young son in order to wed her in 1920.

Somewhat unexpectedly, the public accepted the marriage. As Richard

Oh, "Doll Divine"

deCordova has explained, Fairbanks and Pickford "were the most idealized man and woman in moving pictures, who, because of that, could easily be imagined as an ideal couple."[39] The match was even more symbolically acceptable since Little Mary was marrying the actor sometimes known as Hollywood's "first American juvenile."[40] One might speculate that the ability of Pickford fans to accept this sudden revelation about the desire of Our Little Mary for a married man and vice versa suggests an amazing wholesale disavowal of whatever might mark the doll divine as an adult or interfere with the comforting collapse/merger between the onscreen child/adolescent and the offscreen actress.

In spite of this disavowed knowledge, or perhaps because of it, divorce and remarriage continued to be displaced in Pickford publicity by the extratextual construction of her as a dutiful daughter to an adoring but financially dependent mother. In fact, her sacrifices as a dutiful daughter were used to justify her rather scandalous marriage to Fairbanks. A newspaper article in the *Los Angeles Times* remarked of the Pickford-Fairbanks union in 1921: "No one, I'm sure, speaking humanly, who sees these two together could possibly wish to take their happiness from them — Mary, especially, perhaps, with her years of conscientious, hard labor, when as a mere child, she was mother to all her family, Jack, Lottie, even her own mother."[41]

Pickford's second marriage did not mean that extratextual discourse allowed Mrs. Douglas Fairbanks to grow up. On the contrary, her masquerade of childishness continued to flourish offscreen as well as on. For example, in 1921, *Ladies' Home Journal* featured the divorced and remarried actress in a fashion feature that exemplified the continuing disavowal of her age and sexual maturity. Pickford models clothes clearly intended for an adolescent (14–20), and her poses suggest the shy demeanor of an ingenue; however, the feature copy suggests the distance between star and image in its statement that Miss Pickford "wishes to register a debutante." At the same time, the article also collapses the difference between the twenty-nine-year-old star and her "registering" of youth by noting that these clothes for adolescents have been designed specifically for her by French high-fashion designer Lanvin. Fashion choices and captions also suggest that she represents an old-fashioned "nice girl" alternative to the flapper: she appears in a modest black afternoon frock and hat.[42]

While such articles do not have Pickford chasing bunnies à la Griffith-style femininity, they do signal the "I know but nevertheless" attitude surrounding Pickford's age and her masquerade of childishness. There is acknowledgment that her extreme youth is a construction, but there is also a disavowal of its fictionality. Pickford the girl and Mary Pickford the woman became Mary Pickford, the child-woman, on and off the screen.

Conclusion

Commentary like Lindsay's on Pickford, the doll divine, suggests the sustained power of the late-nineteenth-century idealization of the child-woman as a sentimentalized object of desire. As a phenomenon, Pickford's popularity drew on powerful cultural attitudes that sentimentalized the emergent sexuality of girls and adolescents at a time when women's more assertive and self-determined sexual desire was regarded as an intrusion into the traditional male domain of sexual subjectivity and a threat to the primacy of the family. Within the context of this widespread social discourse, Pickford's textual and extratextual construction exemplifies an antimodernist rearticulation of the Victorian child-woman as a sexually controllable and idealized version of femininity with origins in fin de siècle attitudes toward the "sacred child." While we can assume that the conscious intent of Pickford's films was not to create such a sexually enticing figure, the construction of the actress's appeal still serves as a model for broader late-nineteenth- and early-twentieth-century representational trends in the sexualized representation of femininity. Here I should acknowledge that there is always a danger for film scholars working with historically remote materials of reading back into an earlier era the preoccupations of our own—including sexual preoccupations. That said, we should not forget that Western culture has frequently rendered a woman masquerading as a child or with culturally coded childlike qualities as sexually enticing in ways that a male masquerading as a child is not.

In reading textual and extratextual materials attached to the star over a number of years, it seems apparent that Pickford's juvenation as a curly-headed child of the lower class created all the required elements to permit a disguised sexual enjoyment for male viewers of the 1910s and 1920s. Nevertheless, the pedophilic aspect of male viewing should not be regarded as the only pleasure available to men in watching Pickford's moving pictures or gazing at her still photographic image. Male viewers may have shared a whole host of feelings that Pickford's films made available to women, including reform-minded concerns, nostalgia for childhood, and identification with mischievous-minded freedom. Unlike women viewers, they could not revive the nostalgic pleasure of looking back on the lost freedom of their "asexual" girlhoods, but, for heterosexual men like Lindsay, Pickford's image (onscreen and off) might offer the pleasure of finding a confirmation of aesthetic perfection and spirituality in a child-woman whose erotic promise elided the threatening sexual agency of modern women. Thus Pickford's image—both textual and extratextually figured—proved liminal enough to negotiate a wide range of sexual desires and identifications.

The multiple possibilities of how Mary Pickford was received by her historical audiences—male and female—suggest that Pickford's persona as the erotically attractive yet not quite marriageable young woman functioned culturally and psychologically for her audiences in potentially far more complex and contradictory ways than is generally acknowledged. Pickford's on- and offscreen masquerade of childishness and the slippage between eroticized adult femininity and her inscriptions of aesthetically perfected children were attached to some meanings that appear to be quite historically and culturally specific to the waning days of the "age of the child."

Other meanings may have lingered or been rearticulated in a different cinematic form in subsequent eras. After all, we should not forget the Great Depression and that other sacred child of the screen, Shirley Temple, who remade several Pickford vehicles. Temple's stardom, which emerged virtually simultaneously to Pickford's retirement in 1933, raises equally interesting (and troubling) issues about the eroticization of childhood.[43]

Pickford's stardom and its relation to sexuality also resonate with the contemporary phenomenon of shifting boundaries between child and adult. Those shifts are manifested in a pervasive fear of and campaign against sexually explicit material depicting children; simultaneously, they are manifested in ubiquitous display of images of juvenated sexuality that characterize much of our own fin de siècle media culture.[44] This provides an echo of Pickford that may not be the semiotic equivalent of her effects. But just as Little Mary was produced as ubiquitous representations intended to represent innocence but implicated in a sexual gaze fixed on the girl-child, so does current cultural practice often produce sexualization of the representation of childhood, even in discourses that ostensibly seek to prohibit it. Thus, there are issues of gender, power, and sexual identity at work in this contemporary cultural phenomenon that might lead us to conclude that the construction of Mary Pickford is more relevant to our own experience of mass media than Vachel Lindsay, adoring poet, might ever have imagined of his own "doll divine."

Notes

1. On the development of the "picture personality," see Richard deCordova, *Picture Personalities: The Emergence of the Star System in America* (Chicago: University of Illinois Press, 1990), especially 73–74; and Janet Staiger, "Seeing Stars," *Velvet Light Trap* 20 (fall 1983), reprinted in *Stardom: Industry of Desire*, ed. Christine Gledhill (New York: Routledge, 1991), 1–16. On the early publicity surrounding Pickford, see deCordova, 70–72, and Staiger, 5.
2. Vachel Lindsay, "Queen of My People," *New Republic*, 17 July 1917, 280–281.
3. Edwin Carty Ranck, "Mary Pickford — Whose Real Name is Gladys Smith," *American Magazine*, May 1918, 35.
4. "The Charm of Mary Pickford," *Bioscope*, April 1914, 753.
5. "Rags," *Variety*, 6 August 1915, 17.
6. "M'Liss," *Motion Picture News*, 11 May 1918, scrapbook 31, MS Collection U-6, Mary Pickford Collection, Academy of Motion Picture Arts and Sciences, Beverly Hills, California (hereafter cited as Pickford Collection, AMPAS).
7. Virginia Dare, "News of Filmland: Moving Pictures," *Chicago Journal*, 16 May 1918, scrapbook 31, Pickford Collection, AMPAS.
8. On other child impersonators, see "Screen Stars in Second Childhood," *Vanity Fair*, December 1917, 74; and in the same issue, Mary Pickford, "The Portrayal of Child Roles," 75.
9. Unidentified newspaper clipping, 17 May 1921, scrapbook 35, Pickford Collection, AMPAS. Her contemporary Edward Wagenknecht suggested that it was a mistake to identify Pickford "exclusively with a portrayal of children and young girls." He remarked: "It was not until after the beginning of the feature era that Miss Pickford became definitely associated with ingenue roles, and it was not until *The Poor Little Rich Girl* that she appeared all through a feature film as a child." Wagenknecht is correct insofar that Pickford did not always play children, especially in the early years when she appeared in numerous one-reelers. Wagenknecht, *The Movies in the Age of Innocence* (Norman: University of Oklahoma Press, 1962), 156.
10. Mordaunt Hall, "*Pollyanna*," *New York Times*, 19 January 1920; reprinted in *The New York Times Film Reviews*, vol. 1 (New York: New York Times, 1970), 67–68. Pickford refers to the same question in her serialized autobiography: "I seem to be leading myself voluntarily to that question which I have been asked so many times by others: 'Am I going to grow up?'" See Mary Pickford, "My Own Story," *Ladies' Home Journal*, September 1923, 128.
11. Mary Pickford quoted in Evelyn Wells, "Big Film Role, Four Babies, Pickford Wish," *San Francisco Call*, 22 March 1921, scrapbook 29, Pickford Collection, AMPAS; my emphasis. The star wanted to play Marguerite in an Ernst Lubitsch–directed version of *Faust*, but when her mother objected to her playing a woman who commits infanticide, Pickford settled on filming *Rosita* (dir. Lubitsch, 1924) instead. See Kevin Brownlow, *Mary Pickford Rediscovered* (New York: Abrams, 1999), 197–200.

Oh, "Doll Divine"

12 "Photoplays: Miss Pickford's Universality, and Pola Negri's Comeback," *New York Evening Post,* 10 May 1924, scrapbook 39, Pickford Collection, AMPAS.
13 "Mary Will Quit Movies Because Type's Worn Out," unidentified newspaper clipping, 24 April 1924, scrapbook 39, Pickford Collection, AMPAS.
14 Quoted in Brownlow, *Mary Pickford Rediscovered,* 250.
15 Avis McMakin, "The Winning Letter," *Photoplay,* October 1925, 109.
16 "Mary Pickford Awards," *Photoplay,* October 1925, 45. Pickford had already played Cinderella (in 1914), and Sara Crewe in *A Little Princess* (in 1917). Her chief screen rival in girl impersonation, Mary Miles Minter, had essayed the role of Anne of Green Gables in 1919.
17 Hall, "Mary Pickford as of Old," *New York Times,* 19 October 1925, 26; reprinted in *The New York Times Film Reviews,* vol. 1, 280.
18 Joan Riviere, "Womanliness as a Masquerade," in *Psychoanalysis and Female Sexuality,* ed. Hendrik M. Ruitenbeek (New Haven: College and University Press, 1966), 211–214.
19 See Anne Scott MacLeod, "The *Caddie Woodlawn* Syndrome: American Girlhood in the Nineteenth Century," in *A Century of Childhood, 1820–1920,* ed. Marylynn S. Heininger et al. (New York: Margaret Woodbury Strong Museum, Rochester, 1984), 97–119.
20 Sally Mitchell, *The New Girl* (New York: Columbia University Press, 1996), 25. In a scenario file from the Pickford Collection at AMPAS, there is a company memo listing literary authors who "write things that are considered Mary Pickford material." They include Kathleen Norris, Fannie Hurst, Edith Wharton, Edna Ferber, Corra Harris, Zona Gale, Willa Cather, Margaret Porter, Eleanor Gates, and Ruth Sawyer (box 177, "188 — Scenario" file, Pickford Collection, AMPAS).
21 On turn-of-the-century literature's use of illness as a vehicle to facilitate the transition to ideal womanhood, see MacLeod, "The *Caddie Woodlawn* Syndrome," 110–112. Within Pickford's oeuvre, Pollyanna's crippling and the invalidism of Stella Maris adhere most obviously to this formula. What is most intriguing about Wiggin's original story *Rebecca of Sunnybrook Farm* is that it cannot quite bear to make the seventeen-year-old heroine grow up into a sexualized adult. At its closing, the novel remarks of Adam Ladd and his desire for Rebecca: "He had looked in her eyes and they were still those of a child; there was no knowledge of the world . . . no passion, nor comprehension of it" (Wiggin, *Rebecca of Sunnybrook Farm* [Boston: Houghton, Mifflin, and Company, 1904], 320).
22 In a publicity article of 1924, it is said that "millions of young girls—to say nothing of the boys and their elders—love the Mary Pickford of pictures, indicated by the letters received requesting photographs" (Joe Mitchell Chapple, "Flashlights of Famous People," *Brooklyn New York Times,* 22 April 1924, scrapbook 39, Pickford Collection, AMPAS). In May 1924, a review of *Dorothy Vernon of Hadden Hall* in the *New York City Post* remarked: "It's a safe bet that women of every age and condition of servitude will crown the Criterion Theatre for months to come and many a man will also find himself sharing the

joy of the powder-puff brigade" ("Subtle Mary Pickford, in New Film at Criterion Theatre, Will Delight You, If—" scrapbook 39, Pickford Collection, AMPAS). Trade magazine responses from exhibitors indicate that neither film did as well as expected.
23 Pickford quoted in pressbook for *My Best Girl* (1928).
24 This approach to marketing Pickford films in the 1920s seems indebted to the marketing concept of the "family party" promoted heavily by Pickford's former studio, Famous Players–Lasky/Paramount Pictures, in the late 1910s and early 1920s in women's magazines such as *Ladies' Home Journal*.
25 Hall, "*Pollyanna.*"
26 Vachel Lindsay, *The Art of the Moving Picture* (1915; reprint, New York: Liveright, 1970). Adele Rogers St. Johns shamelessly plagiarizes Lindsay's comments on Pickford in "Why Does the World Love Mary?" *Photoplay*, December 1921, 50–51, 110–111.
27 Bram Dijkstra, *Idols of Perversity: Fantasies of Feminine Evil in Fin-de-Siècle Culture* (New York: Oxford University Press, 1986), 182–198; see also Brownlow, *Mary Pickford Rediscovered*, 67.
28 Paula S. Fass, *The Damned and the Beautiful: American Youth in the 1920s* (New York: Oxford University Press, 1977), 25. On the sexualization of girlhood in a British context, achieved through the emergence of the "first incarnation" of the flapper in the early 1910s, see Mitchell, *The New Girl*, 182–183. On U.S. women asking for "the same promiscuity that society tacitly grants to the male" in the 1910s, see "Sex O'Clock in America," *Current Opinion*, August 1913, 113–114.
29 Martha Vicinus, "The Adolescent Boy: Fin de Siècle Femme Fatale?" in *Victorian Sexual Dissidence,* ed. Richard Dellamora (Chicago: University of Chicago Press, 1999), 83.
30 Brownlow, *Mary Pickford Rediscovered,* 67.
31 William Lea, "Growth," *New Leader,* 14 June 1924, scrapbook 39, part 2, Pickford Collection, AMPAS.
32 David MacLeod details the efforts of social reformers in the 1910s to improve the lot of children in *The Age of the Child* (Boston: Twayne, 1998), 110–130.
33 Brownlow, *Mary Pickford Rediscovered,* 157.
34 "An Actress from the 'Movies,'" *Cosmopolitan,* July 1913, 265.
35 "The Best-Known Girl in America," *Ladies' Home Journal,* January 1915, 9.
36 Ellen Woods, "Speaking of the Actress," *Photoplay,* October 1917, 82.
37 Mary Pickford, "My Own Story," *Ladies' Home Journal,* September 1923, 9.
38 Roger Lewis, "A Character Study of the Real Mary Pickford: Woman and Genius," *New York City Success,* June 1923, 90. See also George C. Warren, "Douglas and Mary Talk with Critic between Telephone Calls," *San Francisco California Daily News,* 28 March 1921. In it, Mary is quoted as saying: "Think of what I missed. I've been acting since I was five years old. I'm glad I was able to help my mother. We had no man to look after us, but I missed all the sweet things of childhood that other people have to look back on. . . . It's rather a cruel life for a child."

Oh, "Doll Divine"

39 deCordova, *Picture Personalities,* 123.
40 For an extended analysis of Fairbanks as the movies' most successful representative of the ideal American man as "boy," see my "Building Mr. Pep: Boy Culture and the Construction of Douglas Fairbanks," in *This Mad Masquerade: Stardom and Masculinity in the Jazz Age* (New York: Columbia University Press, 1996), 10–89.
41 Grace Kingsley, "Europe Again Calls Star Duo," *Los Angeles Times,* 3 March 1921, scrapbook 29, Pickford Collection, AMPAS. A newspaper article related how her mother "as usual, was with her in the studio, looking after her comfort and her health, and also giving advice as to the filming of the picture" ("Mary Pickford, Daughter of Toronto," *Toronto Star Weekly,* 12 March 1921, scrapbook 29, Pickford Collection, AMPAS).
42 "Mary Pickford in New Summer Clothes Made Specially for Her by Lanvin of Paris," *Ladies' Home Journal,* June 1921, 40–43.
43 On Shirley Temple and the aestheticization of powerlessness, see Lori Merish, "Cuteness and Commodity Aesthetics: Tom Thumb and Shirley Temple," in *Freakery: Cultural Spectacles of the Extraordinary Body,* ed. Rosemarie Garland Thomson (New York: New York University Press, 1996), 185–203. Graham Greene was successfully sued by Temple and Twentieth Century Fox for libel when he remarked, in a review of *Wee Willie Winkie* (dir. John Ford, 1937), that her charms were both erotic and akin to those of Claudette Colbert. An account of this (but not the original review) is in *Graham Greene on Film: Collected Film Criticism, 1935-1940,* ed. John Russell Taylor (New York: Simon and Schuster, 1972), 276–277. In 1935, Pickford attempted to sell the talkie rights to some of her most successful films to Fox Film Corporation. The studio's response declared that her story properties were "all a bit too unsophisticated to conform to our present dramatic requirements for Janet Gaynor in addition to all being a little too mature for Shirley Temple." Unsigned letter of 10 January 1935, to N. A. McKay, box 77, Pickford Collection, AMPAS.
44 See John Hartley, " 'When Your Child Grows Up Too Fast': Juvenation and the Boundaries of the Social in the News Media," *Continuum: Journal of Media and Cultural Studies* 12, 1 (1998): 10–11.

DIANE NEGRA

Immigrant Stardom in Imperial America
Pola Negri and the Problem of Typology

> Arriving in America from Berlin in 1922, with a $3,000-per-week Paramount contract, and long famed for her coal-black hair, camellia-white complexion, and fiery temperament, she was Hollywood's first imported international star. — "Pola Negri,"
> in *Who's Who in Hollywood*

Historically positioned as she was between the passive, pure ideal woman of the late 1800s and the new woman of the 1920s, the vamp of Hollywood silent film has ties to both stereotypes. In this article I briefly consider these relationships and then examine the career of Pola Negri—one of the actresses most associated with vamping—for the evidence it may provide about the images and understandings of transgressive ethnic femininity in turn-of-the-century American culture.

Negri's American career was not congruent with what might be called the "golden era" of the vamp (1915–1919), launched when Theda Bara appeared in *A Fool There Was* (dir. Frank Powell, 1914). Although Negri was making films at that time (and principally ones in which she starred as an exotic, threatening woman), these films were made in Poland and Germany, and Negri did not come to be known to the American moviegoing public until the early 1920s. I want to consider critically the standard account that Pola Negri simply resuscitated Bara's persona, in order to argue both that it was ideologically necessary to attempt to type Negri as vamp and that her particular incarnation extended and complicated the type. Furthermore, given the failure of Negri's American career, I also want to look into the reasons why the actress was not successfully subsumed into operative Hollywood typologies of femininity and to argue that Negri's unincorporable status was largely a function of her resistant ethnicity. My assumption is that the production of Hollywood film stars (particularly in the case of "imported" stars such as Negri) has much to do with celebrating the idea of American global power.

In this article I investigate the discursive tension between Negri's extrafilmic construction as vamp (particularly in the pages of 1920s fan magazines) and the continual recuperation of that figure in her American film roles. Arguing that at a time when attempts were being made to pitch American individualism as a global manifesto, film stars played an especially important role in fantasies of American cultural and economic dominance, I consider Negri's vamp as a form of ethnic sexuality that impeded rather than facilitated that ideological agenda. Given the classificatory dilemma catalyzed by Negri's arrival in Hollywood, the anxious discourses on the credibility of and motives for her Americanization, and her final categorization as rigidly and intransigently European, the trajectory of Negri's American stardom offers a telling instance of resistant female ethnicity.

Almost all the accounts of Negri's early life contradict one another, and it was in fact this very idea of a shadowy, mysterious past that formed the cornerstone of her initial publicity in the United States. In her autobiography, *Memoirs of a Star* (1970), Negri says that she was born Apolonia Chalupec in 1899 and raised primarily in Warsaw.[1] She took as her professional name the last name of Ada Negri, an Italian poet she admired, and continued to use the diminutive form of Apolonia as a first name. After her training in the ballet was curtailed by a diagnosis of tuberculosis, Negri spent time in a sanitarium, and, when she returned to Warsaw, began acting on the stage. She was widely praised for her performance as an exotic dancer in the play *Sumurun* and shortly thereafter began making films. Negri's American stardom was initiated as a function of the fact that in the silent era foreign films could obtain national distribution in the United States simply by translating their subtitles into English. She became well-known in the United States playing Carmen, Madame DuBarry, and other roles as a woman exploiting her sexual liaisons with men for economic and political gain. Her German films, particularly those directed by Ernst Lubitsch, won her international fame, and Negri left Berlin for Hollywood in 1922 under contract to Paramount.

From 1923 to 1928, Negri made twenty-one films, none of which equaled her early successes in Europe. Negri's exotic image, while played up in her publicity, was generally tamped down in her American films. Formerly known for her femme fatale, she made films in Hollywood that often ended happily. Remembered for the vividness of her physical presence in earlier films (the actress would apply kohl underneath her eyes, whiten her face, and paint her lips dark red), Negri was given the soft-focus, atmospheric treatment in Hollywood.

In addition to these stylistic modifications in her image, Negri was cast in films that tended to deemphasize the ethnic and class dimensions found in many of her earlier films. Because she represented a problem of type, she was cast early on in vamp parts that were then undercut by the demands of "goodness morality" in 1920s Hollywood. Nevertheless, throughout her Hollywood career, press accounts of Pola Negri consistently cast her as the vamp—unassimilatable in terms of both her sexuality and her ethnicity. Yet, like other ethnic stars of the period like Nita Naldi or Natacha Rambova, Negri did not embody a single clear and distinctive ethnicity—rather, she stood for a broader pan-ethnic threat. With her Italian surname, Polish ethnicity, and connection to the German film industry, Negri remained ethnically vague in the public imagination. Indeed, in *The Twenties in Vogue* (a collection of selected writings from the magazine in that period), the actress is recalled as "the German Pola Negri, with her smoldering eyes and blackened eyelids."[2] Such confusion did not, however, in any way detract from Negri's association with alterity and exotic excess. When we consider her career in more depth, it becomes evident that Pola Negri is in many ways an ideal example of Hollywood's ambivalent relationship with continental glamour. Known for such practices as walking a tiger on a leash down Hollywood Boulevard, Negri, according to Michael Bruno, "never quite caught on with the plain folks who were going to the movies at the rate of a hundred million a week."[3] While other imported female film stars such as Greta Garbo, Marlene Dietrich, and Ingrid Bergman would enjoy successful Hollywood careers by apparently balancing the stakes of exoticism and domesticity, with Negri this balancing act somehow never worked. Instead Negri seemed to continually confound journalists, the Hollywood community, and film audiences during her American tenure. Since virtually every account of her career takes note of her strong acting skills, and her remaining films testify to the power of her onscreen presence, it seems that the reasons for her lack of success are more industrial and ideological than aesthetic.

Cultures of United States Imperialism, an anthology edited by Amy Kaplan and Donald Pease, takes as its subject "the multiple histories of continental and overseas expansion, conquest, conflict, and resistance which have shaped the cultures of the United States and the cultures of those it has

Immigrant Stardom in Imperial America

dominated within and beyond its geopolitical boundaries." The editors seek to rectify three distinct omissions in the study of American culture: "the absence of culture from the history of US imperialism; the absence of empire from the study of American culture; and the absence of the United States from the postcolonial study of imperialism."[4] The anthology offers a useful reformulation of imperialism, pointing out that any definition of empire should attend both to its international features (foreign relations, political, social, economic oppression, and so forth) and to its domestic dimensions as well. As the editors note on the flyleaf, it is essential "to examine imperialism as an internal process of cultural appropriation and as an external struggle over international power."

It should be clear that the development of a national and international culture of American film stardom has the capacity to engage both levels of this definition. However, my particular focus is on the ways that stardom has functioned in tandem with the cultivation of empire at home, for ethnic female stars like Pola Negri had the capacity to serve as significant characters in a national narrative supportive of imperialist aims. Imported stars were particularly important in this regard, for if the United States could take a so-called raw talent, package her, and turn her into a saleable commodity, then Hollywood was, in effect, enacting American ability to control the international commercial marketplace (not to mention the representational/ideological arena when these films were marketed abroad).[5] Through the packaging and selling of such international stars, U.S. culture industries were establishing something about American global reach and power.

An actress and her location in a film narrative can serve as a register for overt and implicit discourses of imperial consolidation. Toward that end, I examine in some detail Negri's 1927 film *Hotel Imperial* (dir. Mauritz Stiller), the fourteenth film of her American career, and one that both the actress and the studio seemed to regard as having the potential to restore her to her earlier fame. Set in Austria during World War I, the film features Negri in the role of Anna Sedlak, a chambermaid in the Hotel Imperial, who shelters an Austrian lieutenant during the occupation of Galicia by the Russian Imperial Army. The film's first intertitle makes plain Negri's role as the custodian of a displaced empire, reading "Thrones and empires might be tottering—but there were still floors to be swept in the Hotel Imperial." In the role of a servant, Negri is somewhat unusually situated in this film narrative—she is neither the upper-class aristocrat nor the lower-class arriviste of many of her earlier films. *Hotel Imperial* takes on the rather difficult task of camouflaging Anna's class rise within a narrative of imperial restoration. Toward this end, the film attempts to rechannel the energy in Negri's persona that is associated with class rise into the preservation of legitimate empire. Thus, in the film's conclusion, the coupling of Anna (a servant) and the Austrian aristocrat Lieutenant Almasy is subsumed into a spectacle of national consolidation, as the couple are reunited during a ceremony in which Almasy and others are being decorated for their wartime contributions. Here Negri plays a figure of passive piety and patriotism — as Almasy is commended, Anna kneels and prays. Though she notices him first, she makes no move to approach him, and it is only when he notices her and relays the story of her help to the Austrian General Sultanov that Anna is officially recognized. As Sultanov tells her, "My dear young lady, I am honored to thank you in the name of our country." The film closes with its most emphatic equation of romance and war as a close-up of a kiss between Anna and Almasy fades to images of marching troops.

Hotel Imperial is a useful film text for its ability to shed light on the typological tension that undergirds Negri's image and its relation to the question that I suggest underscores the actress's entire American career: how could her persona be made meaningful in an American context? This film suggests one possible (though failed) route for the conversion of Negri from a European exotic to an American type. Since the narrative trajectory of *Hotel Imperial* is shaped to reflect the discrediting of a complacent, aristocratic empire and reassertion of a legitimate empire in its place, the film capitalizes on the aristocratic discourse of Negri's persona and her unique status as a shifting symbol of imperial ambition. In indirect fashion, the film plays out an idealized conception of Negri's Americanization, as she is first an obscure European girl, then converted to the status of an aristocrat. (The Russian General Judschkiewitsch dresses Anna in lavish costumes and tells her, "It is not I who command here — it is you!" When she rejects him and is restored to her servant status, another worker taunts her, "So you are not the Queen around here any more.") By the film's conclusion Negri as Anna has renounced one empire for another, rejected an elevation to privileged, aristocratic status, and accepted a more subdued and passive role in a coupling relationship charged with connotations of national solidarity and empire.

Having begun with an instance of Negri's production in conformity with American imperialist ideology near the end of her career, I now want to proceed achronologically to consider how the formation of her role as an ethnic vamp more frequently troubled such representational endeavors.

Vampire Sexuality and Cultural Predation

The vamp is a particularly potent marker of the cultural transition from viewing women's sexuality as in need of regulation for its own sake to a deep investment in that process of control and regulation to bolster patriarchal norms. Variously deployed at different moments, the vamp's vitiated sexuality consistently stands as an indictment of attempts to cross class and ethnic lines. This use of the figure of the vamp as the locus for a number of different discursivities is consistent with the cinematic vamp as incarnated by actresses such as Theda Bara, Nita Naldi, Lya de Putti, and Pola Negri in the 1910s and 1920s. Promoted and publicized as culturally and sexually predatory, all of these actresses either emanated from southern and eastern European countries or were given fictional biographies to suggest such origins. For instance, Theodosia Goodman from Cincinnati was transformed by Fox studio publicity into the mysterious Theda Bara, daughter of an Arabian princess and an Italian sculptor, raised "in the shadow of the Sphinx." Appearing at a moment of apparent U.S. prosperity but haunted by an underlying fear about the efficacy of American economic policies and the ability to maintain cultural isolation, the vamp was a charged figure indeed. She personified a whole category of newly arrived immigrants who (in the eyes of some Americans) called up these economic and social anxieties. In *Terrible Honesty: Mongrel Manhattan in the 1920s,* Ann Douglas writes:

> Immigrants were now coming mainly from eastern and southern Europe rather than, as had long been the case, from northern Europe. The Germans, Scandinavians, and Irish of the older immigrant groups were being replaced by countless Poles, Italians and Jews; 2.5 million Jews arrived from Russia and eastern Europe between 1880 and 1930, and most of them settled in New York. Some of the newer immigrants were visibly different from America's older white population, and they were no longer dispersing themselves across the nation but collecting ominously in vast city enclaves fast becoming "ghettos."[6]

If new immigrants symbolized the threat of national erasure and the possibility that American cultural consensus might be irretrievably lost, female immigrants were particularly subject to attempts at ideological management. The cinematic vamp of the 1910s and 1920s was, in essence, a thinly disguised incarnation of the threat of female immigrant sexuality. This figure was multiply deployed to quell both fear of uncontrollable female desire and the spread of immigrant values into the dominant culture. Just as the sexually insatiable woman might somehow enervate seminal substance, the ambitious immigrant might drain the country's resources dry.

Positioned as the improperly (or more threateningly yet, unsuccessfully) socialized woman, the vamp reflected an intense cultural need to regulate woman's sexuality. She was an ideal figure to manage such cultural anxiety for she represented a site of intersection for the two most important reproductive resources at a time of national expansion—birth and immigration. Thus, Hollywood representations built on Victorian formulations of the death-dealing woman for a specific purpose—to lend support to the definition of appropriate femininity as life-giving. In the case of Pola Negri, whose publicity represented her as having come out of a culture marked by death, Americanization was supposed to invigorate and revitalize her. In a *Photoplay* article previewing a series of features outlining Negri's autobiography in installments, the actress recalls her childhood in suggestively apocalyptic terms:

> "Poverty and suffering in my childhood and tragedy always," she writes in the opening chapter. "Before I knew happiness I saw death. Death, imprisonment, the Black Plague and Cossacks killing, killing. Torture and oppression, war and revolution, starving children and frantic mothers and friends shot down by my side.... The Four Horsemen always riding over my country." On the screen she achieved renown as the pagan, soulless Carmen. Since coming to this country she has been termed ruthless and temperamental.[7]

Such accounts reinforced emergent American anxieties about the new character of immigration. For the first time, it seemed possible that European émigrés might have the most powerful incentive to achieve (always considered an American characteristic). In the eyes of some Americans, it seemed that immigrant women, given the freedoms afforded by their entrance into a new culture, might indeed prove to be ungovernable, even ambitious. Such fears well complemented other contemporary anxieties about what was considered the foreign character of ethnic female sexuality.

In their history of sexuality in America, John D'Emilio and Estelle Freedman have documented the numerous economic and social factors that militated against the easy continuity of the nineteenth-century cult of true womanhood into the twentieth century. Not only were the fissures in the smoothly repressive sexual decorum of the 1800s very much in evidence by the turn of the century, but by the 1920s, "erotic life was assuming a new, distinctive importance in the consciousness of some Americans."[8] D'Emilio and Freedman write that by the early twentieth century, the sexual values of the middle class were on the edge of a decisive transformation. Old and new coexisted in an uneasy balance. That tension would make the first two decades of the century a time of conflict, as defenders of the past and proponents of change contended for hegemony in sexual matters.[9]

These authors are not alone in characterizing the early twentieth century as strongly marked by shifting social and sexual norms, and they are typical in excluding the representational history of the period from their analysis. Yet popular culture tropes played a key part in shaping and sustaining cultural debates about gender roles. Just as cinema "provides an ideal vantage point from which to observe the making of the new woman," it also betrays a level of anxiety about her incipience.[10] Close study of Pola Negri's career exposes the distinct limits faced by some ethnic women in terms of their access to the freedoms of new womanhood.

Of course, the extent of such freedoms has been appropriately called into question. Lisa Rudman, for example, has observed that "rather than a radical break from Victorian perceptions of womanhood, 'modern womanhood' can be seen as a response to urbanizing and industrializing society and an adaptation of Victorian ideology so that it could exist in a new context."[11] Thus it would seem that the vamp represented a kind of outburst of sexual anxiety that still appealed to a sexual, moral, and ideological absoluteness while responding to confusion over a newer expansion of and inquiry into sexual roles.

If the female vampire is, on one hand, a figure with the capacity to disturb gendered relations of power, she is also a figure well equipped to articulate certain social tensions in early-twentieth-century American life, for she is prenarrativized in ways that resonate strongly with the condition of the female "new immigrant." *Dracula* and other vampire myths represent the vampire first and foremost as a liminal figure, caught between an old world and a new one, at first a welcomed visitor but ultimately a new arrival who comes to be seen as a menace. Vampires are superficially incorporable, yet after a period of time their profound alterity and destructive influence necessitate their extermination. The vampire's destructive power, moreover, is a function of his or her connection to a malignant homeland; though vampires may travel the world, they are fundamentally linked to their recondite origins, a connection that they regenerate and foster by sleeping in a coffin filled with their native soil. Most threateningly, rather than adjusting to their new cultural context, vampires are always engaged in a seditious campaign to convert others to become like them. As we have seen, these were exactly the qualities that some Americans feared new immigrants possessed; to nativists, these new arrivals had the capacity to insidiously infect the American body.

The vampire is almost always represented as in possession of a strange energy that seems to speak to both a sexual and a cultural threat. Furthermore, the vampire's appearance seems to be correlated to the consolidation of power. As Nina Auerbach notes in *Our Vampires, Ourselves,* "Vampires go where power is: when, in the nineteenth century, England dominated the West, British vampires ruled the popular imagination, but with the birth of film, they migrated to America in time for the American century."[12] If we can trace the proliferation of vampire representations to moments of national consolidation, one could plausibly argue that the vampire's status as a symbol of deadly energy and a threatening return of the past makes this figure a unique symbol of empire, taking shape as an expression of the fear of an insider with a different, destructive agenda who cannot be subsumed into national interests. The vamp is clearly the outsider who is able to get inside the (national) body. In this context, the multivalent implications of the vampire's deenergizing influence become evident. It is clear that the female vampire functions simultaneously as a sexual, economic, and ethnic contaminant.

The Cultivation of Negri as Type

By all accounts, hopes were very high for Pola Negri's potential cultivation as an American film star at the time of her arrival in the United States. However, the negotiations for her arrival tend to be represented as unproblematized, when in fact, they were conducted with a great deal of delicacy and sensitivity to the possible negative repercussions of importing a European star for the nascent American film industry. Examination of Paramount files reveals that both Adolph Zukor and Ben Blumenthal (Paramount's agent in Berlin) saw a need to gingerly handle Negri's contractual arrangements. While highly enthusiastic about the artistic merits of Negri and Ernst Lubitsch (whom it is clear the studio perceived as a set), Paramount cautiously proceeded to arrange for the arrival of these foreign stars, remaining attentive to a possible nativist backlash.[13] A Western Union cable from Zukor to Ralph Kohn at Paramount Berlin on 18 July 1922 advised strongly against bringing Negri and Lubitsch to America at the same time: "Would be very bad from all angles bring over more than one at a time.

Immigrant Stardom in Imperial America

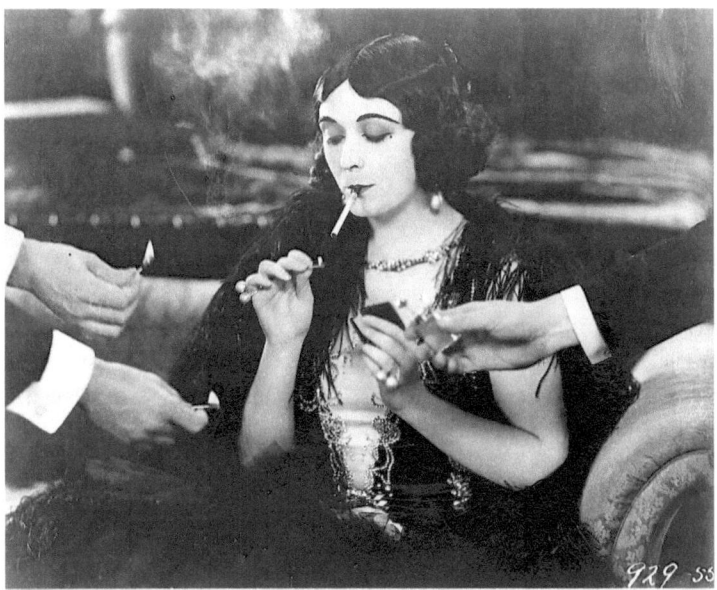

57. Arriving under contract to Paramount in 1922, Pola Negri was at first the object of effusive attention in Hollywood.

Should leave reasonable period between to avoid propagandist criticism and be sure make no promises."[14]

Thus, fears that even a small number of stars brought over from Germany in the period immediately following World War I might be perceived as an exodus provoking jingoist criticism were a crucial structuring element of the promotional efforts undertaken by Paramount on Negri's behalf. Upon Negri's arrival, her own enthusiasm and appreciation of her American sponsors is evident in a letter from Negri to Zukor dated 10 October 1922, reading in part: "California agrees with me wonderfully and since arriving in this beautiful country I have felt splendidly. After getting settled at last in my new home in a new land, I anticipate I will start in my new picture next Tuesday."[15] Despite such positive exchanges and the apparent goodwill between Negri and the studio, an immediate typological problem was becoming evident as Paramount and the American moviegoing public grappled with the question: Who is Pola Negri?[16]

When Pola Negri emerged as a star in the making in the early 1920s, she represented a problem of type for those who wrote about Hollywood culture and Hollywood stars. Fan magazine articles of the period tend to reflect this classificatory dilemma, frequently addressing (directly or obliquely) the problem of her unknowability. In the Dallas-based film magazine *Screenland,* Negri's imminent arrival was described in these terms:

> Pola Negri has the paradoxical distinction of being one of the most famous and yet at the same time one of the least known of motion picture stars. Announcement made recently that she is coming to this country in September under contract to star in a big Paramount picture has aroused curiosity as to details of her life and career. About all that is known about her over here, except that she is an actress of remarkable ability and during the last two or three years has given some of the most vivid characterizations of the screen is that she is Polish and now makes her home in Berlin.[17]

In a *Photoplay* piece titled "You Can't Hurry Pola," Joan Jordan wrote:

> Ever since Pola Negri turned her eyes upon us beneath the famous powdered wig of Madame DuBarry, we have been hearing about her. First, in the dim recesses of Continental Europe, impressionistic glimpses of the alluring, the foreign, the thrillingly different and wonderful Pola Negri.
> Then—she was coming to Hollywood to make pictures. She sailed. New York greeted her briefly—a smiling, mysterious, monosyllabic Pola. Chicago drew hardly a breath of exotic perfume as she swept her skirts through. Pasadena saw her pick a real orange from an orange tree. The American public read this and that—intriguing flashes that merely whet the appetite.[18]

Another *Photoplay* writer, Herbert Howe, described the difficulty of even meeting with Negri for a scheduled interview and devoted half of an article titled "The Real Pola Negri" to a chronicle of his attempts to actually see and speak with the star. Similarly, Rose Shlusinger framed an article on Negri in *Motion Picture Classic* as a kind of detective narrative, with the actress endlessly one step ahead of the journalist as she attempts to locate her for an interview appointment through Paris, Berlin, and Dresden.[19]

Invariably, however, Negri did become well known to the American public, apprehensible now as a vamp—the social type that most closely fit the filmic and extrafilmic information known about her. Typical of the kinds of characterizations that were made of her in the fan magazines during this period is this description: "La Negri—A tiger woman with a strange slow smile and a world-old lure in her heavy-lidded eyes. Mysterious, fascinating, an enigma."[20] Throughout her Hollywood career in the 1920s, writers would frequently employ deliberate misspellings and grammatical errors to convey Negri's foreign status through her imperfect and heavily accented English. Quotations such as "I suffer much. It is terrible," and "Miss Negri do not feel like today to work" abound in the fan magazine articles that attribute remarks to the actress.

In "She Delivered the Goods," a fan magazine piece that claimed to be "the first authoritative personality sketch of Pola Negri, the Polish Star" (and which was apparently the first American film magazine article devoted to Negri) the reasons for the actress's rise to fame were straightforwardly given: "First of all she was new; secondly she appeared in a 'vamp' part—a type of part which having been rendered ridiculous by Theda Bara and subsequently abandoned, stood in real need of resuscitation; and, most important of all, she was not camera-wise."[21] In this article, as in others, Negri is discussed in terms that obliquely suggest her status as new blood (so to speak), or as a new resource to be exploited within the Hollywood system. As one writer speculated at the time of her arrival in Hollywood:

> I wonder if other directors will understand Pola as Lubitsch does or whether they will expect fire to always be cool and a tiger cat as tame as one of the curly ingenue lambs. Will Pola escape the standardization process? Or will she have to submit to being a perfect lady, always kind to directors and always diplomatic with pestiferous interviewers who ask her all sorts of absurd questions like whether or not she is to marry [Charlie] Chaplin?[22]

It is tempting to read these kinds of questions about how this new resource (Negri) would fit into the social system (Hollywood) as pointing toward a broader cultural question for which we might interchange the terms "immigrant" for "Negri" and "America" for "Hollywood." Certainly the discourses of the fan magazines would support such a reading. For example, one early magazine piece on Negri before her arrival in the United States concluded: "So Pola steps from the Old World into the New. From the old life into the new. Let us hope that her dream of America will be realized as adequately as America's dream of her. As for me, I say, see Pola and die!"[23] Negri herself was attributed with comments that reflected a variant of "the streets are paved with gold" conception of the American Dream: "Always America has been my dream from the time I was a child in Poland. You do not know how Polish children look toward America. It is like heaven to which people go for eternal happiness. Always people return rich or send money back."[24]

But far from being able to definitively prove this kind of connection (and I am not sure that I would want to), I do want to suggest that Negri's interrelationship with immigrant identity played a substantial part in generating the huge amount of popular interest that preceded and accompanied her arrival in the United States. I also want to raise the possibility that Negri's huge publicity buildup served in some sense as an analogue to the idea of the welcome mat offered to the new immigrant and that this limited her possibilities in Hollywood by requiring her Americanization. Negri's intense professions of her own immigrant desires suggest the beginnings of an anxious discourse on the rationale for and success of her Americanization. Negri's later resistance to being Americanized—to being typed—perhaps constituted a brand of ideological transgressiveness that resonated beyond the parameters of actress/studio.

In any event, it is important to emphasize that Negri's American career (by this I mean the films she made for Paramount in the 1920s) followed the period of the popularization of the vamp.[25] Because she was seen as reviving this type, Negri's vamp is thus to be distinguished from prior incarnations in ways that prove to be extremely important. Negri's positioning as vamp is perhaps most apparent in the publicity photos circulated of her by Paramount. In these photos, the black/white mask of the characters of her German films tends to be very much in evidence. Her full-figure poses are regal and remote, or suggestively threatening. Her gaze is sometimes unsmilingly direct—more often she is shown glancing sidelong at the camera. Often she leans back in a way that facilitates the vamp's trademark heavy-lidded look. In all of her photos a certain knowing quality emerges that to some degree overshadows other representational elements.

As has been discussed, the vamp was a multivalent image, embodying not only unsupressed female desire, but (especially in the case of Negri) the potential ascendancy of a new immigrant class from southern and eastern Europe. Negri was particularly well situated to activate this latter set of meanings. As the figure who troubled the rigid regulation of sexuality, Negri was positioned as aberrantly destructive. Fan magazine articles about her from the 1920s constantly allude to her in this fashion with phrases such as: "Beneath the silken charm of Pola Negri there is the tigress-claw, with threat of instinctive cruelty."[26] In a *Photoplay* piece in which well-known actresses were asked to provide their definition of love, Negri is attributed with the comment "Love is ruthless. In pursuit of its desires it will destroy that it may achieve. That it may lavish upon one of its largesse, it will crush a thousand who stand in its way."[27]

As the figure who troubled the hegemony of white northern and western European ethnicity, Negri was certainly more potent than vamps such as Bara and Gloria Swanson. Rather than being fabricated as ethnic other in the fashion of Theda Bara, whose name was known to be an anagram for Arab Death, Negri's construction in such terms had a far greater claim to authenticity. As an actual ethnic import with a foreign accent and a well-publicized European past, Negri was well positioned to restore a seriousness to vamp characterizations that had become increasingly lampooned by stars such as Bara herself. This imagined authentic dimension of her persona, however, became increasingly problematic throughout the duration of her American career, as I later discuss. In its most benign form, the suggestion that Negri was intransigently Old World was even underscored in a May 1926 *Photoplay* article about her home, "A Bit of Europe in Hollywood," a piece that details the house's formal style and "Old World charm," and is peppered with observations such as "it is more of a Continental salon than an American living room."[28] At the time of her arrival in the United States in the fall of 1922, under contract to Paramount, Negri would have been best known to American audiences for her roles in the Ernst Lubitsch films *Gypsy Blood* (1918) and *Passion* (1919).[29] In the former film (a retelling of the *Carmen* story originally written as a novel by Prosper Merimee), Negri plays La Carmencita, a gypsy girl who enthralls soldier José Navarro (Harry Liedtke).[30] This version of *Carmen* is one that continually plays up the gypsy's role as sexual threat. When the pair first meet, it is as Navarro sits reading a letter from his sweetheart Dolores. He is accosted by La Carmencita, who mockingly tosses him a rose. The two meet again when the gypsy girl is jailed for fighting with a coworker who has snatched away an admirer's note. When she escapes, Navarro is then himself jailed for losing her. La Carmencita attempts to help him flee by smuggling in a file hidden in a loaf of bread, but Navarro resists this temptation, inspired by a vision of his virtuous sweetheart. Eventually, though, stripped of his rank and commission, he joins the gypsies. Tormented by the conflict between his passion for La Carmencita and his sense of degradation, he tries to leave her, but cannot. The gypsy becomes disgusted by his weakness and begins an affair with another soldier. Later she meets and falls in love with Escamillo (Leopold von Ledebar), a matador. The film culminates in a confrontation between Navarro and La Carmencita in an alley where he murders her, then commits suicide.

In many ways typical of the vamp narratives that seemed to best showcase Negri's talents, *Gypsy Blood* is also noteworthy for its subtext of destructive regional collaboration. When La Carmencita first meets Navarro, she comments on their shared background, "By your speech, you are from the provinces, like myself." When he visits her in jail she addresses him repeatedly as "my countryman" and "comrade of my heart." When he is imprisoned and she attempts to free him, the loaf of bread she carries takes on the status of a symbol of shared regional attributes. La Carmencita tells the guard she has brought a loaf of Alcala bread, and a remarkable intertitle footnote reports that Alcala is "a hamlet close to Seville, famous for its excellent bread." In the context of the film then, close connections based on regional affiliation tend to produce treachery.

Thus, those roles that made Negri a star in the United States, even before she had ever set foot on American soil, tended to emphasize her guile and her primitivism and to link strongly these attributes and her broad destructive influence to a vaguely ethnic and regional identity. In this respect, her pre-1922 persona represented a balance between the cosmopolitan and the regional, two terms employed by Timothy Brennan in his book on myths of nationalism. In *Salman Rushdie and the Third World,* Brennan argues that within postcolonial subjectivity the cosmopolitan is designed to replace the regional.[31] In an earlier and quite different cultural context, Negri cultivated an extradiegetic association with the cosmopolitan, becoming a symbol of European glamour and sophistication, while enacting film roles that thematized the malignancy of regionalism. This was the sort of regionalism many Americans associated with the outbreak of war in Europe, and which differed distinctly from nationalist satisfaction in noncontentious American regional diversity. In an earlier section of this analysis, I have indicated the relevance of imported stars to Hollywood as both a business and a producer of cultural representations and discourses. I am further suggesting that as the U.S. film industry (particularly Paramount) colonized Europe in the 1920s, emblematic Europeans such as Negri were expected to be cosmopolitan and not regional. This was partly because the United States was actively engaged in repressing regional difference in favor of national solidarity—to Americanize a star who connoted the fractious regionalism of Europe as opposed to the coordinated national harmony of the United States would be impossible.

However, the tension between cosmopolitanism and regionalism in Negri's persona was only one of a number of functional paradoxes she embodied. Such paradoxical constructions tend to apply at a number of levels in Negri's persona. On some occasions, they were celebrated as part of the actress's allure. Writing in her syndicated column in 1923, Gladys Hall observed:

> You know, so long as a woman remains a paradox, she is perfect. After all, she hasn't been proven imperfect. She hasn't been proven anything at all, and as gallantry still persists in a world and age that would defy it, and as it particularly persists concerning a charming woman, the woman who is the paradox is safe. Pola Negri seems to be that paradox.[32]

Framing Negri as a paradox also served as a means of acknowledging and disavowing her erotic attraction. If a commentator like Hall tended to read Negri's enigmatic persona as a positive attribute, others associated her appeal with sordidness, creating an image of Negri where her superficial cosmopolitan attractiveness was undercut by an omnipresent regional impurity. In some accounts, interestingly enough, it is suggested that Negri had not been fully "cleaned up" and that her cosmopolitan glamour always had a slight tinge of "regional dirt." Richard Griffith, for instance, writes, "She was, someone said at that time, 'sexually irresistible'—and you had the feeling that the back of her neck was dirty."[33]

The Vamp as Canny Laborer and Uncertain Commodity: Pola Negri in the Context of Industrial Production

In this section, I show how the vamp's transgressive ownership of her own labor was especially problematic at a time when imperial America wanted to codify the range of female types and channel female ethnic labor for its own use. As Negri was incorporated into an American social frame of reference, discourses of work became more prevalent in her persona. This is, on one hand, not surprising, for as Richard Dyer has noted, stardom and labor are integrally tied to one another. Not only are "stars examples of the way that people live their relation to production in capitalist society," stars are also inevitably "involved in making themselves into commodities; they are both labour and the thing that labour produces."[34] It is certainly true that the work that goes into image making and image maintenance has been the subject of ambivalent discourse throughout Hollywood history. Yet Negri's gender and ethnicity contributed to a further contradiction in that her links to immigrant ethnicities entailed that a positive value be attached to her working status, while her gender mandated that her work be invisible. The strong preoccupation with the performance of Negri's work seems indirectly to reflect the question that underscored her celebrity: How could Negri be *made* to work for American interests?

These concerns, I suggest, were really only a logical extension of anxieties about the depth and legitimacy of her Americanization. Negri's border-crossing persona implicitly raised issues in regard to the international exchange of labor that some of her film roles quite interestingly enact. Moreover, playing a courtesan, prostitute, or "kept woman," Negri also shaped a response to discomfort with women working outside the home and with a sexual activity that escaped the controlling power of the home and family. The ethnic woman's relationship to public space was particularly fraught, and it seems that the connection between the ethnic feminine and the working woman presupposed that the kind of labor she performed was inevitably sexual.

In this section, I want to contextualize a reading of the Negri film *Passion* by considering two proximate phenomena: the rapid growth in the number of women entering the workforce, and the proliferation of vamp roles in the silent films of the 1910s and 1920s. Here I argue for the vamp's significance as a complex image mobilized in part as a response to younger women's entry into the workforce in large numbers for the first time. As an incarnation of the predatory woman stereotype, the vamp has had successors as well as predecessors, and popular-culture discourses generated around the predatory female persona continue to be numerous. Nevertheless, the meanings and pleasures of the transgressive woman clearly vary in accordance with social, historical, and industrial variables. One crucial variable that has tended to remain unexamined by historians and critics is the vamp's relation to the shifting landscape of the American workforce.

Perhaps the most striking labor trend in the period under consideration here is the entrenchment of the woman worker, whose numbers increase in the late decades of the nineteenth century and continue to rise throughout the early decades of the twentieth century. In this period, the transition of women (especially young, urban women) from family workers to wage workers was increasingly normalized. For this reason, labor historian Leslie Tentler locates the period 1900–1930 as formative in establishing the labor climate for women well into the century. She argues that these years "can be seen as a first and critical chapter in the history of modern female industrial employment. In this period important precedents regarding women's work were established or confirmed."[35]

The vamp is not merely a figure who demonizes working women; rather, in an evolving consumption economy, she is too aware of her own commodity status. In personifying a mingled sexual/economic threat (we may think of the implication of the female vampire's bloodsucking as both kissing or some other kind of erotic embrace and an assertion of economic blood lust), the vamp is consistently linked to the ramifications of women's work. As will be demonstrated, Negri's vamp announces herself as manufactured in a way that foregrounds her own laboring efforts, and her appearance/sexuality is shown to be a hazardous commodity in a way that codes women's labor itself as duplicitous.

In *Passion* Negri plays Jeanne, a milliner's apprentice at the outset of the film who rises to power as Madame DuBarry, mistress of Louis XV. Although Jeanne is overtly represented as a working woman for only a brief section of the narrative, her disconnection from home and hearth and ascension to a position of power marks her with the same anxieties attached to contemporary working women. The problem at the heart of the film is the problem of the woman who works to further her own interests outside appropriate domestic channels.

Made for UFA (Universum Film Aktiengesellschaft) and directed by Ernst Lubitsch, *Passion* was, though not American-made, an enormous U.S. success in both commercial and critical terms. The film was originally produced as *Madame DuBarry* but was retitled for its U.S. release in part to disguise the circumstances of its production in Germany. When First National premiered the film in 1920, it played five times a day at the sumptuous Capitol Theatre in New York, and attendance during the first week was estimated to be about 106,000. Trade journals reported gross box-office receipts of $10,000 per day, and excitement over the film ran so high that on 19 December 1920, a reported 40,000 people tried to gain admittance to the theater and extra policemen were dispatched to "maintain order and clear traffic."[36] As a result of the enthusiasm generated around *Passion* (and to a lesser extent other collaborations between Negri and Lubitsch, such as *Gypsy Blood*) Negri was heavily recruited by the major American studios, and ultimately signed with Famous Players–Lasky (Paramount). Part of the film's success, in my view, has to do with the way in which it presents the sexually transgressive woman and the working woman as very close categories.

Briefly, the plot of *Passion* has to do with Jeanne's expanding sphere of influence in the French court, as she is first the companion of the proletarian Armand, then Spaniard Don Diego, Count DuBarry, and the French king. In the course of the film, Don Diego is killed by Armand in a duel, Louis XV dies of smallpox, and Armand is shot by his friend Paillet after attempting to defend Jeanne. As the king's consort, Jeanne shows herself to be capricious and self-indulgent, and she begins to encroach on the territory of Choiseul, the king's minister of state, who then launches a popular campaign against her. At the conclusion, she is guillotined at the hands of a bloodthirsty mob, although in its U.S. release, the film ends just before Jeanne is beheaded.

Historian Robert Smuts has written of the geographical circumstances that conditioned women's labor at the turn of the century, noting the far greater likelihood of nondomestic work for urban women.[37] Part of the vamp's connection to women's work is established through her links to city life. Jeanne Vaubernier (later DuBarry) is described in *Passion* as "freshly strayed from country lanes." From the beginning of the film, two of Jeanne's other traits are very much in evidence. She is shown to be highly aware of the value of commodities, and she understands how to transform work into pleasure. In fact, the film continually conflates work and sexuality for Jeanne. Sent out on an errand, she subordinates her work to her pleasure by stopping to visit her lover Armand on work time. On her return, the hat she carries is accidentally crushed by the Spanish envoy Don Diego's horse, and she weeps because she knows its value and anticipates her employer's anger. The encounter, however, has provoked Don Diego's interest, and he follows her to the milliner's shop and promises her that "Mademoiselle could be better employed." To conceal a liaison with Don Diego, Jeanne later tells Armand she has to work, inventing the excuse that she is visiting the residence of the Spanish envoy in order to pin his wife's gown, and he is so completely deceived that he walks her to the door.

Once under Don Diego's "protection," Jeanne finds herself still constrained by the demands of work, for Don Diego now expects her to work for him. She is barely installed as his mistress when he rouses her out of bed yelling, "Wake up, you lazy baggage, and earn your keep!" He forces her to the dressing table to work on her appearance, telling her that she must go on his behalf to attempt to collect a debt from the king of France. At the palace, the king is predictably smitten by Jeanne and sends his minister, Choiseul, to find out where she lives. When Choiseul discovers her at Don Diego's house, an exchange is quickly made, although not before the Spaniard acknowledges Jeanne's commodity value, protesting, "My broken heart—I must be paid!"

From here Jeanne ascends to the preeminent position of power in France, but through it all she undergoes a kind of development process not unlike the routines of industrial production. In fact, the entire film consists of a kind of assembly-line process of commodity production with Jeanne as the developing commodity and each of her lovers in turn playing a part in refining/honing her worth. The warning offered by the film centers on the fact that feminine duplicity ensures that Jeanne will become an excessive commodity that threatens to disturb the control of the production process. And indeed, she does this, ultimately achieving control over the agents of production who do not perceive her own self-commodification. By the time she is the consort of the king of France, Jeanne's control is such that Louis buffs her nails for her while matters of state are left waiting, behavior that the film strongly condemns.

According to the film, nondomestic female labor is seen as inevitably self-serving and the vamp's self-absorption is heavily contrasted with the unity of the family. *Passion* provides a ruptured family victimized by the actions of the predatory woman, although the significance of this family is not made clear until the revolution led by Armand near the end of the film. At this point, we are reintroduced to a minor character from early in the film, Armand's friend and an early acquaintance of Jeanne's, Paillet the tailor. When Jeanne has Paillet thrown in prison, the film emphasizes his family's deprivation, articulated through the neediness of a child—Paillet's small daughter—who inspires Armand's revolutionary spirit with the words "Monsieur Armand, I am so hungry." Thus the vamp's characteristic tendency to put her own interests before the interests of the family jeopardizes the role of the male breadwinner. If this were not already clear enough, we cut quickly to Armand crying out, "Friends, we must save Paillet!" and leading the masses with Paillet's daughter on his shoulders. In this creative reworking of historical fact, the French Revolution is fought solely on behalf of the dispossessed male breadwinner. According to this account, even Louis XVI and Marie Antoinette are represented as innocent victims of the consequences wrought by the vamp's evil—an intertitle proclaims them "waiting helplessly" as the revolutionaries descend.

It is important to consider in some depth the complex codes of the vamp body since *Passion* represents women's labor as wholly readable on and through the body. The film ties the woman whose production is solely in her own interest to bodily display and presents the vamp's making up, combing her hair, or inspecting her appearance in a mirror as actions that constitute labor in the service of the feminine form as commodity. The film emphasizes a number of instances when the vamp pauses to enhance her appearance, and these are coded as labor activity, moments of self-manufacture. Just as in the quintessential vamp film *A Fool There Was,* when Bara's vampire looks out from a porthole, watches the Schuyler family saying goodbye, and takes out her compact to check her appearance, so Jeanne Vaubernier announces her designs by performing work on her appearance. Our first glimpse of her is at work, and when her employer sends her out on an errand, she stops to powder her nose in a mirror and is looked at reprovingly. In this respect, female labor is criminalized, and it is implied that nondomestic women's work is both surface-oriented and deceptive. Women's labor outside the home is also always and inevitably sexual in *Passion*. Jeanne's work as a milliner serves only as a pretext for her efforts to snare a male protector. Thus the film codes female labor as both sexual and duplicitous, serving as a front for the only feminine concerns that the film takes to be legitimate—the search for male sponsorship.

Of course, the vamp's connection to makeup is not insignificant, as it ties her to discourses of transformation and implied class rise. In the early decades of the century, makeup was integrally tied to a cultural sense that the boundaries of class were collapsing, and the vamp iconography of pale skin and heavily made-up lips and eyes might well have connoted transformative desire to audiences of the time. Beyond the vamp's dark hair and eyes that work to imply the threat of transgressive ethnicity connecting her to devalued, "suspicious" ethnic groups, it is important to observe further that the vamp is inevitably a woman whose origins are unknown or obscure. Jeanne Vaubernier is not shown to have any family connections, and in a film that charts the dangers of a woman's rise from the working class to the nobility, it is clear that the vamp's ability to win the male provider away from his more appropriate partner is very much a threat to destabilize the boundaries of class and the hierarchy of valued ethnicities.

The vamp's tendency to posture and her inclination to wear distinctive, vivid makeup combine to render her an excessively produced body. In some sense, she threatens to be out of bounds at any moment, and her body seems always to be in danger of showing. Her laboring efforts help her carry off a kind of masquerade—a false femininity whose veneer is continually slipping. The vamp's meaning is also strongly articulated by means of costume. Heavily sexualized, her clothing tends to be dark in color or to feature aggressive prints and stripes that serve to mark her sartorial threat. The vamp draws attention to her labors through her costume, and so represents a sharp break with the patriarchal requirement that women's labor be invisible. Since we are culturally committed to effacing the female laboring body, part of the threat of the vamp is that she presents herself as the evolving site of her own laboring efforts. This potentially empowers the female body and authorizes it as a site of identity formation. This is strikingly apparent in a scene in *Passion* in which Jeanne, the milliner's apprentice, decides her fate by reading the codes of her own bodily display. As she counts off the bows on her bodice to decide between Armand and Don Diego, Jeanne interprets her own work efforts, subordinating her emotional decision-making to her own working body, and defining her identity according to her own achievement rather than to an externally defined patriarchal standard. In short, she threatens to produce herself. Moments such as this one strongly suggest that one of the vamp's most distinctive threats centers on self-production.

Immigrant Stardom in Imperial America

The vamp's problematization of women's work was coincident with the rise of female labor outside the home. As both producer and product, the vamp threatens to close the gap between labor and its results. She responds to the cultural anxiety that, if women take part in industrial production, they may learn to produce themselves in opposition to patriarchy. By presenting herself as a commodity in process, whose appearance is deceptive and whose use value in patriarchy is highly questionable, the vamp is crucially involved in the gendering of industrialized mass culture, for she demonstrates the dangers of both contemporary commodification and women's participation in the production of useful commodities. She also serves to perpetuate a superannuated discourse of women's invisibility and concealment, for the vamp's crime is that she is too much seen; she makes her labor visible. Thus, in addition to her status as a figure of ethnic threat, the vamp is also of interest for the way that she uniquely articulates a set of concerns about women's access to work and to its rewards.

Negri consistently plays the role of a woman who exploits her sexual liaisons with men for economic and political gain. She inspires death and destruction not by design, but seemingly inevitably. Onto the vamp cipher were merged two discourses—one having to do with sexuality and the other with ethnicity—both delineating the dimensions of the "problem" of woman in the 1920s. In a broad sense, Pola Negri's persona, as constituted in extrafilmic terms, connoted unenculturated femininity. As the unassimilatable woman, in both ethnic and sexual terms, she stood for a type that was in fact far more transgressive than the thoroughly American, upper-middle-class flapper who, for all her supposed flouting of social conventions, was nearly always safely married off in the end.

Negri's Unsuccessful Typological Conversion

In Pola Negri's case, as I have argued, the U.S. film narratives in which she appeared were not always coextensive with the persona being constructed. Rather, for the most part, they existed in contradictory relation to one another. Michael Bruno contends that "Hollywood did not know what to do with her, after the first flurry of excitement had abated. She was pulling in the carriage trade, but was establishing no real audience rapport, nor was she building a consistent cinematic image."[38]

While Negri's film roles failed to coalesce into a single recognizable persona, they also ran counter to the fundamental direction of her publicity. In fact, while Negri was being constructed through fan magazine articles and publicity photos as vamp, that persona was being undercut by a series of film roles that contained vamp energy. The resulting typological tension created a kind of ongoing recuperation of the vamp via the career of Pola Negri in the 1920s.

Negri's 1923 film *The Spanish Dancer* (dir. Herbert Brenon) is especially illustrative of the differences in her German screen portrayals of the late 1910s and her American films of the 1920s. In a number of interesting ways, this film "corrects" many of the more transgressive elements of *Gypsy Blood* and *Passion*. In it Negri plays Maritana, a gypsy dancer who falls in love with Don Cesar de Bazan (Antonio Moreno), a nobleman who is to be put to death for dueling. Although still the woman whose beauty and sexuality can motivate class ascension, Negri is here a savior rather than a femme fatale. When she saves the life of the queen's child, Maritana pleads for clemency for Bazan. The king (Wallace Beery), however, plots to marry Bazan to Maritana before executing him, thus giving her a legitimate place at court so that he can make her his mistress. The lovers are married, but Bazan escapes death when a friend substitutes bread pellets for the bullets of the firing squad's guns. The king follows Maritana to a hunting lodge where he plans to seduce her but is interrupted by Bazan, who begins to engage him in a duel. They are interrupted by the arrival of the queen, who is assured by Maritana that the king had only come to bless their marriage. Order is then restored at the end of the film as Bazan and Maritana are reunited with one another.

Not only does this narrative deprive the gypsy woman of the agency of her own social rise, it more generally robs her of the level of self-awareness and self-interest that made Negri's earlier roles so interesting. In *The Spanish Dancer,* Maritana must be shown to be pure-hearted despite her social and ethnic background. Here, rather than destroying her lover, she rehabilitates him, for as an intertitle claims, before their meeting, "All Spain knew Don Cesar as a reckless, carefree noble to whom gold was made for gaming, and life but a stage for rash adventure."

Even while films such as *The Spanish Dancer* were narrativizing the recuperation of the vamp, the publicity surrounding Negri ran sharply counter to any type of containment. Indeed, Negri was consistently associated with a discourse of erotic and cultural aggression that seemed to challenge American morality and American empire. One especially important source for the kinds of extrafilmic information about Negri that literalized the myth of the vamp was the publicity about her romantic relationships in Europe and America. Reports linking the actress to such beloved icons of the American cinema as Charlie Chaplin (British) and Rudolph Valentino

(Italian) seemed to inspire much disquiet in the American press. Herbert Howe's "The Loves of Pola Negri," for instance, begins: "When I facetiously asked Pola Negri in Berlin if she intended to marry Charlie Chaplin, she tossed back her head and laughed heartlessly. I felt a pang for Charlie, because even a comedian would not care to get a laugh like that."[39]

The building of a public idea of Negri as "deadly woman" was reinforced by stories of her deadliness in real life. She was widely attributed with the quote "In Poland we kill," supposedly uttered during the shooting of one of her films and directed at someone who did not share her artistic point of view. Interviewers suggested that Negri was quite capable of making good on such a threat since her allure was inevitably fatal. There were suggestions that she used men to gain social power.

> With stardom and high salary came her marriage to the Polish Count Domska. It is significant that this marriage, according to German report, was very much like that of Madame Du Barry in "Passion." You will recall that the little milliner married in order to gain a title that would permit her to move in aristocratic circles.[40]

There were also dramatic accounts of her fatal influence over the men unlucky enough to have fallen under her spell. Many such accounts described Negri's professional success as having come at a high personal price, as if her growing strength was enabled by her debilitating effects on her lovers. In one fan magazine, Negri describes her "first love," a painter whom she met just as she was beginning to attract notice for her performances on the stage:

> He was in delicate health. I knew that. It did not matter . . . I loved him. He became worse. . . . It was the dreadful quick consumption. I saw the life going from him. I thought I could save him somehow. I had overcome so much by my will, I thought I could even conquer death. Then one night he died. He died in my arms.[41]

Accounts of Negri's romantic history testified again and again to her destructive force, describing her morbid influence as inevitable, as in "The Loves of Pola Negri," which quoted the actress as saying "Always I have sought love, and always there have been disappointments. I am a fatalist. I believe in my star. It is my fate to be unhappy in love."[42] Statements such as these activated a number of different dimensions of the Negri persona; they added extratextual support to the filmic construction of Negri as fortune-telling gypsy, and they also discursively reinforced her connection to Old World values. This association of Negri with prophecy and with the past fed into her construction as the deep, eternal feminine. In terms of her vamp characterization, it also undergirded the notion that the vampire is of the East, creating a web of associations around Negri's vamp that connected her to past, rather than present, values. As Bram Dijkstra points out, in vampire mythology "to travel eastward is to travel into the past."[43] Given that the vampire is a figure of degeneration, this kind of associative web may indeed have helped craft a kind of self-fulfilling destructive prophecy around Pola Negri.

In any event, this sort of Old World fatalism that permeated press characterizations of Negri contrasted sharply with the energetic ideals of American capitalism. Interestingly, at the start of her American career, Negri was sometimes valorized in American capitalistic terms for her work ethic: "Much has been written, still more talked of, concerning Negri's life before she became celebrated. Really the details are commonplace with a record of hard work and struggle for recognition ... when the director said 'Go to it!' she went to it like one doing an honest day's job for a day's pay."[44] In "The Uncertainty of Certainty," in *Motion Picture Classic,* Shlusinger even looks forward to a conversation with Negri by observing, "Ah, one thought, there was a woman and a workman!"[45]

However, when public favor turned against Negri, she was criticized for failing to meet these same standards of diligence. The problem, according to one writer, was that "Pola came to the studio when Pola felt like it, and not one second sooner."[46] In the last years of Negri's Paramount contract (1926–1928) there was a markedly unsuccessful attempt to reverse this impression—a trend exemplified in fan magazine pieces titled "How Pola Was Tamed" and "The Transformation of Pola." This latter was a remarkable series of sketches by Malcolm St. Clair (who directed Negri in *A Woman of the World,* 1925) depicting first a disgruntled cast and crew awaiting the star's arrival on the set, and then the results of Pola's "transformation": "Then Mal showed Pola how good she'd become. He showed her a picture of herself arriving, the first star at the studio. . . . Somebody put her wise to the fact that friendliness gets you farther in Hollywood, and everywhere else, than frigidity."[47] Despite their flair, such attempts at reconfiguring Pola Negri's star persona seemed distinctly "too little, too late" to reverse a trajectory of representation that emphasized her icy European reserve and deadly effect. Negri remained a remote figure, or as one contemporary reviewer of *Loves of an Actress* suggested, an "acquired taste" too exotic for the American public at large: "Pola Negri has always been an as-you-like-her star. Even the Negri fans, however, will look askance at

58. Pola Negri's dolorousness and Old World fatalism contrasted with a Hollywood culture of energy and enthusiasm.

the stellar assignment in a role which automatically suggests a Swanson or a Talmadge rather than the severer brunet personality of the Polish star."[48]

In a remarkable conversion of the authenticity discourses of her early career, when Negri left Hollywood in 1928 to return to Europe, the failure of her American career seems to have been attributed (at least in the fan magazines) to inauthenticity. The implicit linkage here was between integrity and Americanization. In "The Passing of Pola," Leonard Hall wrote that "Pola Negri's failure was a failure of the mind and spirit." He continued:

> Stars are because film fans find in each one things to love and cherish. In Jack Gilbert is a certain irresponsible, devil-may-care charm. Buddy Rogers and Dick Barthelmess are every woman's boys . . . Mary Pickford began to fade when she grew less the dimpled hoyden and more the First Lady of Filmdom and chatelaine of the Fairbanks manor. Pola Negri just neglected to be herself.[49]

Thus, in the Hollywood of the 1920s, which prided itself on the range of its types, any unclassifiable personality was judged to be a fraud. Since every type was representable in Hollywood terms, the public's rejection of Pola Negri had to be due to her failure to represent herself truthfully. Negri's "inauthenticity" confirmed the authenticity of the star-making system — if she could be seen as lacking that authenticity associated with stardom, then Hollywood's failure to develop her talent could be explained away.

In fact, the fall of the femme fatale and the rise of the good girl were trends that went hand in hand, paralleled by the displacement of the immigrant other by American purity. Both were part of a process of cultural displacement whereby one form of femininity was replaced by another. The vamp had to be discredited in order for the good girl to come in. The iconography of the vamp was a necessary counterpoint to the iconography of female victimization coming to be popularized by filmmakers such as D. W. Griffith. In a sense, the differences between the vamp and the modern girl were posited in terms of a nature-versus-culture debate, with the kind of timeless Old World femininity embodied by Negri superseded by the tractable, modern femininity associated with such all-American actresses as Clara Bow or "convertible ethnics" like Colleen Moore.

I would be inclined to believe that Negri's career foundered for all of these reasons, but additionally and perhaps most importantly, because Hollywood had constructed two Negris, and they were fundamentally at odds with one another. The domesticated Negri was never as interesting to American audiences as her early persona of the exotic other, nor was this earlier image ever entirely put aside in favor of the rather weak discourses of transformation and containment that particularly marked the late stages of her American career. Moreover, Negri's ethnicity was presented as timeless and eternal, incapable of conversion, and so her Americanness could never be definitively established. In short, Negri's vaguely eastern European ethnicity was seen to be utterly resistant to attempts at Americanization. She could not be made to work effectively as an American cultural export, and for this reason Negri had to be excluded from rather than included in such imperial ventures.

It is widely believed that Negri was among those foreign-born stars who did not survive the transition to sound because of her heavy eastern European accent, when, in fact, she had a successful sound test for Paramount in the early 1930s. Negri's Hollywood career ended before sound came in. Such accounts are nevertheless interesting, for they are fundamentally accurate in attributing the failure of Negri's career to an ethnic impediment. When the actress returned to Germany in 1935 to make films for UFA, there were persistent rumors in the American press that her European career was advancing due in part to a romantic relationship with Hitler. Despite the unlikeliness of an association between the German leader and a non-Aryan Pole and Negri's own dismissal of the rumor in her autobiography, at the time of her death in 1987 obituary reports seized on this detail with relish, while stopping just short of confirming the affair.

The significance of Negri's failure to be successfully assimilated into Hollywood typology should not be underestimated. In the context of the culture industries' normalizing, assimilative imperatives, Hollywood's failure to recuperate Negri's sexuality and ethnicity are striking. The significance of Negri's resistant role would have been strengthened by the tremendous fanfare associated with her arrival in the United States and her status as star before she even arrived. Negri's positioning outside the Hollywood cult of personality necessitated explanation, and, at the close of her American career, many such explanations were attempted on the pages of fan magazines.

The kinds of discursive tensions that permeated the fan magazine pieces on Negri in the 1920s persist in a certain confusion about how to consider her work historically. Positioned as resource in terms of both her gender and her ethnicity, Negri was never successfully exploited by the Hollywood system, and to that extent she continues to embody a certain slippage of categories, resisting classification as an actress and as a woman in ways that, for the feminist film historian, may be entirely satisfactory.

Notes

1 See Pola Negri, *Memoirs of a Star* (Garden City, N.Y.: Doubleday, 1970).
2 Carolyn Hall, *The Twenties in Vogue* (New York: Harmony, 1983), 86.
3 Michael Bruno, "Pola Negri, or Passion's Pulsating Plaything," in *Venus in Hollywood: The Continental Enchantress from Garbo to Loren* (New York: Lyle Stuart, 1970), 29.
4 Amy Kaplan, "Left Alone with America: The Absence of Empire in the Study of American Culture," in *Cultures of United States Imperialism,* ed. Amy Kaplan and Donald E. Pease (Durham: Duke University Press, 1993), 4, 11.
5 By 1926, three-quarters of all films shown worldwide were American.
6 Ann Douglas, *Terrible Honesty: Mongrel Manhattan in the 1920s* (New York: Farrar, Straus and Giroux, 1995), 305.
7 "An Amazing Revelation: The Autobiography of Pola Negri," *Photoplay,* January 1924, 32.
8 John D'Emilio and Estelle B. Freedman, *Intimate Matters: A History of Sexuality in America* (New York: Harper and Row, 1998), 173.
9 Ibid., 201.
10 Mary P. Ryan, "The Projection of a New Womanhood: The Movie Moderns in the 1920s," in *Our American Sisters,* ed. Jean Friedman and William Shade (Boston: Allyn and Bacon, 1976), 301.

11. Lisa L. Rudman, "Marriage—The Ideal and the Reel; or, The Cinematic Marriage Manual," *Film History* 1, 4 (1987): 330.
12. Nina Auerbach, *Our Vampires, Ourselves* (Chicago: University of Chicago Press, 1995), 6.
13. See, for instance, Ben Blumenthal's letter to Adolph Zukor c/o Famous Players-Lasky Corporation, 30 June 1922, which reads "we think that with Negri and Lubitsch both working in America the financial conditions of the Hamilton will be such that they soon will be able to stand, on their own feet, the same as we know or feel that most American directors would be only too delighted to work with Negri, we are sure the great stars in America would also desire to work under Lubitsch's direction." Paramount files, Academy of Motion Picture Arts and Sciences (AMPAS), Beverly Hills, California.
14. Adolph Zukor to Ralph Kohn, 18 July 1922, Paramount files, AMPAS.
15. Pola Negri to Adolph Zukor, 10 October 1922, Paramount files, AMPAS.
16. The question had been directly posed by Harrison Haskins on page 43 of the February 1921 issue of *Motion Picture Classic*. The article "Who Is Pola Negri?" recaps the actress's stage and screen achievements, but says virtually nothing about the actress herself.
17. *Screenland*, August 1922, 4.
18. Joan Jordan, "You Can't Hurry Pola," *Photoplay*, March 1923, 63.
19. Herbert Howe, "The Real Pola Negri," *Photoplay*, November 1922, 19; Rose Shlusinger, "The Uncertainty of Certainty," *Motion Picture Classic*, October 1922, 18–19, 74, 77.
20. Herbert Howe, "The Loves of Pola Negri," *Photoplay*, November 1923, 38.
21. Maximilian Vinder, "She Delivered the Goods," *Photoplay*, May 1922, 20.
22. Herbert Howe, "The Real Pola Negri," *Photoplay*, November 1922, 38.
23. Ibid., 38.
24. Ibid., 59.
25. Negri made two other American films—*Hi Diddle Diddle* (dir. Andrew L. Stone) in 1943 and *The Moonspinners* (dir. James Nelson) in 1964. In the first film Negri plays opera singer Gegna Smetana, in a send-up of her imperious 1920s persona, and in the second film she plays a small role as a dowager.
26. Howe, "Loves," 37.
27. Pola Negri, "What Is Love?" *Photoplay*, November 1924, 30. Contrast Negri's aggressive, almost military definition of love with an altogether different kind of ethnic star, the girlish Colleen Moore, quoted in the same *Photoplay* piece, "Love is a song. It is the twittering of the birds in the treetops, an expression of sheer joy that remains muted only long enough to let the clouds of a passing shower roll away, certain of the sun behind the gloom" (29–30).
28. "A Bit of Europe in Hollywood," *Photoplay*, May 1926, 81.
29. At the same time that Negri was leaving Germany to make films in America, *The Cabinet of Dr. Caligari* (dir. Robert Wiene, 1919) was inspiring a succession of imitators in the German expressionist style, among them F. W. Murnau's *Nosferatu* (1922), starring Max Schreck as the vampire.
30. *Carmen* was a popular story in early Hollywood. Among the versions pro-

duced was one by William Fox in 1915 starring vamp prototype Theda Bara.
31 Timothy Brennan, *Salman Rushdie and the Third World: Myths of the Nation* (New York: St. Martin's, 1989).
32 Gladys Hall, "Diary of a Professional Movie Fan," 1923, unattributed clipping in the Gladys Hall Collection, AMPAS.
33 Richard Griffith, *The Movie Stars* (Garden City, N.Y.: Doubleday, 1970), 70. See also Linda Mizejewski's *Ziegfeld Girl: Image and Icon in Culture and Cinema* (Durham: Duke University Press, 1999), which profiles theatrical star import Anna Held, a woman whose combined Polish/Jewish and French/Catholic backgrounds certainly make her a comparable figure to Negri. Mizejewski's discussion of the way that elements of glamour and sordidness were held in operative tension in the Held persona equally explains Negri's appeal. She writes, "Anna Held's high-profile discourses on Parisian fashion and beauty tips were the standard entrée for the imported female celebrities at the turn of the century, offering the old world as elegant shop. But for Held, these discourses were also loosely layered strata under which the old world lurked with its damp, musky secrets. Anna Held's appeal rested within the liminal space between these two Old Worlds, fashionable and filthy" (44).
34 Richard Dyer, *Heavenly Bodies: Film Stars and Society* (New York: St. Martin's, 1986), 5-6.
35 Leslie Woodcock Tentler, *Wage-Earning Women: Industrial Work and Family Life in the United States, 1900-1930* (New York: Oxford University Press, 1979), 3.
36 Interestingly enough, in the eyes of some commentators, Negri's American career was effectively bounded by moments of such public hysteria attached to the spectacle of ethnicity. Paralleled to the pandemonium generated by *Passion* was hysteria at Rudolph Valentino's funeral in 1926, in which Negri was a significant participant.
37 Robert W. Smuts, *Women and Work in America* (New York: Schocken, 1971), 45.
38 Bruno, "Pola Negri," 36.
39 Howe, "Loves," 37.
40 Howe, "The Real Pola," 60.
41 Howe, "Loves," 38.
42 Ibid., 37.
43 Bram Dijkstra, "Metamorphoses of the Vampire: Dracula and His Daughters," in his *Idols of Perversity: Fantasies of Feminine Evil in Fin-de-Siècle Culture* (New York: Routledge, 1991), 343.
44 Vinder, "She Delivered the Goods," 20.
45 Shlusinger, "Uncertainty," 68.
46 Ivan St. Johns, "How Pola Was Tamed," *Photoplay,* January 1926, 53.
47 Malcolm St. Clair, "The Transformation of Pola," *Photoplay,* January 1926, 76.
48 Review of *Loves of an Actress, Variety,* 1 August 1928.
49 Leonard Hall, "The Passing of Pola," *Photoplay,* December 1928, 29.

JENNIFER M. BEAN

Technologies of Early Stardom and the Extraordinary Body

If everyone can agree that "why and how stars came into prominence and what purposes they served for their audiences" is a question of critical import, then exactly which stars we recover and from when remains at issue.[1] It seems logical to begin with the years between 1912 and 1922, a decade coextensive with the first flush of stardom's powerful, public appeal. What happens next is remarkably unclear. If we bracket the few familiar names—Lillian Gish, Mary Pickford—coterminous at the start with that of D. W. Griffith, and appraise the vampish Theda Bara as more notorious than illustrative (more infamous, so to speak, than famous), we are faced with a curious lacuna: the conspicuous absence of early women stars. Ineluctably linked to the crisis of the archives and to the paucity of film remnants from the period, with surviving prints in often precarious condition, elisions of all sorts haunt the historical register of early cinema. Yet whatever the outcome of battles that must be waged in the name of preservation agendas, one thing is clear: it would be a serious mistake to overlook the copious documents extant from the media system of early stardom. Here we traverse not a "ruined map" but a densely textured topos.[2] Here we encounter a pantheon of unusual female stars collectively known as "those daring misses of the movies." Agile and dauntless, ready to swim, race, fly, dangle, and fall for the sake of the screen—cinema's first en masse celebrities were anything but ordinary. Indeed, an array of quite extraordinary women typifies the onset of film stardom: extraordinary in the way that people usually are not, but in precisely the way that stars are supposed to be.

Perhaps the most adulated figure of early film fame was Pearl White. Known to her contemporaries as the "Heroine of a Thousand Stunts," White's fearless disposition and exceptional physicality became the emblematic badge of a career that catapulted to unprecedented heights following her 1914 performance as the intrepid heroine of *The Perils of Pauline* (dir. Louis J. Gasnier and Donald MacKenzie) and careened through approximately 200 films, 11 of which were action serials, totaling more than 180 episodes by 1924. Her work during those years was risky business, as the saying goes, especially if we believe accounts tallied by *Picturegoer* in 1921 that White had suffered—and emphatically survived—"3,750 attempts against her life" while performing for the camera.[3] Other figures are both breathless and lavish: in 1917 the Pathé-Frères company proclaimed that White's four serials to date had profited $24,570,000 at the box office, a lucrative bit of business for the war years.[4] While Pathé executives counted their dollars, public accolades mounted in various quarters. After defying the Clutching Hand and his dastardly death ray in *The Exploits of Elaine* (dir. Louis J. Gasnier and George B. Seitz, 1914), White became the darling of European surrealists and an icon of the Ballets Russes.[5] After defeating enemy spies in *Pearl of the Army* (dir. Edward José, 1916), she struck a pose as recruitment model for the United States Army and was elected honorary president of the American Cadets.[6] After exposing the schemes of the one-armed master criminal in *The Iron Claw* (dir. Edward José and George B. Seitz, 1916) and recovering the sacred "Violent Diamond" in *The Fatal Ring* (dir. George B. Seitz, 1917), she was ranked among viewers' most favorite players.[7] After her caper as the eponymous avenger in *The Lightening Raider* (dir. George B. Seitz, 1919) she garnered the friendship of Spanish novelist Vincent Blasco Ibáñez and the "adoration of Latin America" more broadly.[8] Such honors reveal the technologies of an emergent star system, with its circulation of paraphernalia and its inflated rhetoric, at work; but they also imply a figure in excess of that system, one whose drawing power refuted market demographics and leveled the niceties of gender, age, class, and national appeal. In what seems like nothing short of a rhetorical mirror for the wild expansion of White's fame, trade reporters turned to an enumerative structure, akin to the idiom of lists, when describing the star's ceaseless momentum. "In France French soldiers on furlough idolize her," began one commentator's litany: "In Porto Rico [sic] she crowds the theatres. In Bombay she figures frequently in the newspapers. A Scottish newspaper runs her life on its front pages. Five Australian managers make fortunes presenting her pictures. In South Africa they name babies after her, and in Tokio [sic] they give her name to theatres."[9] Inasmuch as White figured as transcultural icon and embodied a heroic new personhood freed from the laws of physics, she may be seen as the apotheosis of the metaphor of stardom—"star" understood as liminal, transcendent sphere.

Though unanimously declared the queen of courage and daring, White

JENNIFER M. BEAN

59. Pearl White

was not alone. In 1917, one commentator announced that Grace Cunard had "started after the 'Queen of the Serial' honor with Pearl White" and that "Helen Holmes is right on her trail."[10] In 1919, *Photoplay* reporter Frank Bruner numbered "Pearl White, Ruth Roland and Marie Walcamp" as stars who "have a following, extending from Oshkosh to Timbuctoo [*sic*] that surpasses with an overwhelming plurality, the vogue of any of Filmdom's feature stars."[11] To that list I would add Irene Castle, Marguerite Courtot, Grace Darmond, Marie Dressler, Helen Gibson, Texas Guinan, Juanita Hansen, Alice Joyce, Annette Kellerman, Doris Kenyon, Anita King, Mollie King, Florence LaBadie, Anna Little, Cleo Madison, Mabel Normand, Marin Sais, Nell Shipman, and Kathlyn Williams, among other daring players of lesser fame. Each of these star personae stood for a particular synthesis of femininity, athletic virility, and effortless mobility; each was shaped by a complex discursive system that produced a variety of overdetermined metaphors: the "Peerless, Fearless Girl," the "Empress of Daredevilry," the "Temptress of Chance," the "Daughter of Daring," the "Girl with Nine Lives," and, in the case of White, the "Girl with Ninety-Nine Lives." What this catalog, with its shimmer between the highly individuated and the syntactically programmatic, demonstrates, is that White's fame may have been unique in scope, but it was certainly not in type. Tracing the reducibility of White's celebrated persona to a series of principles reveals an index to the genesis of film stardom per se.

To view the birth of stardom from this perspective demands a fundamental shift in our assessment of the young industry's aesthetic and cultural dictates. Rather than a fixed galaxy of stars associated with "great" auteurs and the bid for bourgeois respectability, we find an entirely different constellation of figures associated with thrilling modern film genres and praised for their superlative physical and psychical stamina. The action serials that structure the careers of Pearl White, Ruth Roland, and Helen Holmes are obvious and crucial indices, as are mystery-crime films, western adventures, slapstick comedies, jungle safaris, deep-sea spectacles, and so on. I cannot do more than gesture toward such genres here, but their presence alerts us to the existence of a competing industrial logic in the period, one favoring the affective sensation of realistic thrills and grounded in the practice of on-location shooting. In fact, if we examine the institutional framework of the burgeoning star system, with its behind-the-scenes interviews, evidential photographs, and personal testimony, we find the contours of a larger discourse of believability built to enhance the realism of onscreen performances, particularly the difficult feats of the female players.[12] The lure of referentiality that underlies the system's epistemological endeavor makes it meaningful in the context of an industrial-urban modernity, not because it calibrates the perceptual realism associated with technological reproduction, but precisely because it does not: the technologies of early stardom, as I call them, flaunt catastrophe, disorder, and disaster rather than continuity and regulation. The successive views disclosed by the machinery of stardom thus promote a phenomenology of performance founded on the concepts of improvisation and unpredictability—the terms of a "realness" set in opposition to what is understood as the archaic, mechanical gestures of the stage.

The historical revision undertaken here also presents a challenge to contemporary feminism. This essay will not discover a historical female subject (much less a hypothetical one), nor will it recover an optical field readymade for women's viewing pleasure.[13] Rather than support an ontology of either female *or* male spectatorship, perilous stars invite a vital rethinking of viewing theories because they imperil the very constitution of subjectivity according to categories of gender, as well as those oppositions that govern many basic concepts and modes of self-definition: adult/child, mortal/immortal, nature/culture, body/mind.

The ambiguity of the word "stunt" captures this paradox neatly. Etymologically, "stunt" is traceable to the 1400s, where it refers to a state of diminution or of arrested development—the state of lack inscribed on the body of the dwarf. Yet alongside the flourishing of industrial modernity in the late nineteenth century, "stunting" would come to signify a risky endeavor, an act of exceptionalism, according to the Oxford English Dictionary. Gender conventions familiar to us from Western cultural paradigms might lead us to assign the state of being stunted and the act of stunting to, respectively, the feminine and masculine realms of signification, to the spectacle of the Bakhtinian grotesque and the experience of the Kantian sublime. The interrelated emergence of female film stars and the performance of stunting, however, allows us to see the ways in which what this body "is" and what it can "do" link together as terms of a radical and irreducible difference, the terms of a nonnormative, extraordinary, and unregulatable spectacle. This is not an impossible middle ground so much as the historical ground for a new subject—the star—whose sheer popularity testifies to the toppling of a classical humanist subject regulated by reason and sustained by self-will, in favor of a modern subject premised on corporeal spontaneity and flexibility. Early women stars reflect a heroic personhood construed as both nonknowledgeable and unknowable. This historical contrivance is not easily assimilated by contemporary feminism, but it demands understanding as an alternative to those hardened, prosthetic, metallic male bodies elsewhere populating, if not peopling, the horizon of a technologically altered world.

In the following pages, I examine the discursive strategies through which the media complex of early stardom constructed and promoted the body of its star. My analysis of these representations, however, is intended as a step toward rethinking the body in its material variety, the very stuff of the fan whose "mimetic faculty," in Walter Benjamin's sense of the term, is compelled forward and beyond itself by the technologies of stardom. At base, my interest is to widen the conceptual and historical schema used to provide a foundation or basis for accounts of identity. The technologies of early stardom invite us to ask whether the subject's relations with others, its encounter with the screen, and its position in the modern world may be better understood in corporeal rather than conscious terms. Concurrent with such a historical reorientation is my investment in altering a feminist politics that up to now has presumed the need to rescue "woman" from the intractability of the body.

The Risk of Film Realism

> Sometimes, through accidental failure of prearranged conditions of production—often in the definite determination to face conditions of danger for the sake of pictured realism—the moving picture actress faces personal peril and danger of death undreamed of by the audience.
> —*Chicago Tribune*, 21 July 1912

It is well known that comparisons between film and theater dominated the earliest writings about narrative cinema, particularly during the early to mid-1910s. One typically proceeds by noting that writing about film was often a defensive enterprise, so that differentiating film from theater was above all an effort to define film as a worthwhile form in its own right. Commentators often highlighted the rapidity of camera movements, the effect of the close-up, or the dynamic intertwining of action in different scenes as the medium's characteristic (and characteristically modern) trademarks. In addition, what Hugo Munsterberg referred to as "the use of natural settings," a practice coupled with the increase in on-location shooting and realistic dramatic enactments, became a pivotal point in such discussions.[14] "In every film that is released to-day are actualities that would have been voted impossible only a few months back," exclaimed the *Literary Digest* in 1916. In somewhat more detailed fashion, Burr C. Cook observed that "Reelism" has become "a new, big, important word in the screen vernacular." "Because of its demands," Cook explained, "movie companies travel half-way around the globe for a proper setting, or buy up a railroad, build a town, or charter a navy, for the sake of a scenario."[15]

From our contemporary perspective, cinema's capacity to dramatize and record an actual event may hardly appear to herald a revolutionary aesthetic. But for social commentators of the day, film realism—"Realism with a big R"—was deemed worthy of extended commentary.[16] "The one great advantage of the moving-picture play over the so-called 'legitimate stage' is that absolute realism is possible in it," wrote one reporter. "One can not shoot a lion at every performance of a stage-play, but a moving picture can show in a hundred places, night after night, the same lion in his authentic death-agonies."[17] Extending this logic, a pictorial insert in the August 1914 issue of *Motion Picture Magazine* displays a kind of "before and after" or "stage versus cinema" template of representational practices. On the left

60. *Motion Picture Magazine*, August 1914.

side of the page a series of images show stage hands performing elaborate behind-the-scenes special effects: they flap a curtain over the fallen hero to create raging waves in a shipwreck scene; they crack coconuts together to signify a galloping horse; they propel a papier-mâché engine across the stage for the locomotive scenes. Juxtaposed with the contrived mechanics of the stage, the other side displays a parallel series of simple, stark images: a large ship, a galloping horse, a train engine. In the center of the page a young woman clasping two reels of film and bearing a ribbon that reads "Motion Picture Industry" stands with the word "progress" inscribed like a halo above her.

It is not unnecessary to emphasize that aesthetic progress, in this context, insists on an intimacy between camera images and the objects they represent, and that efforts to heighten this referential bond stand as an important historical juncture in early cinema's turn toward a predominantly narrative form. Noticeably, the emphasis on realism in industrial publications coincides with the emergence of textual systems—incorporation of point of view and combinations of shot-matching and continuity editing—increasingly capable of supporting a film's referentiality in space and time, eventually giving way to what Jean-Louis Comolli calls "psychological realism."[18] My interest here is not to pinpoint the years in which a systematic application of formal means relocated realism to the structure of the text, but to suggest that industrial efforts to heighten the correspondence between image and object, and textual efforts to create a seamless fictional world, amount, in this period, to the same thing: both are geared toward stimulating viewer absorption and, in so doing, both take pains to obscure film's mechanical base.

This is not to say that cinema's ability to revel in (and reveal) the marvelous disappears. In fact, as we shall see, the magical properties of the moving-image machine, pronounced in turn-of-the-century trick films à la Georges Méliès and the carnivalesque thrill of cinematic "attractions," do not so much disappear as they are relocated to the phenomenology of performance.[19] The ground and support of the industry's realist imperative thus also forms the occasion of its salutary departure. But we are getting ahead of ourselves; two synchronic, if not causal, effects must be mapped. First, the difficulty of enhancing the credibility of the image was ironically compounded by the very terms on which realism made its advance. The price of realism was, in a word, fantastic. The magnitude of the Selig-Polyscope Company's zoo, purchased for the express purposes of staging "real" wild-animal dramas, for instance, not to mention the fracturing of companies into traveling branches or the founding of massive outdoor arenas in the newly settled California complexes, demonstrate how the trend toward realism paralleled an increase in the high-cost, high-return mentality of early studios that, in turn, paralleled a transformation in public perception of the industry. No longer just a mechanical toy or a cheap amusement, moving pictures were more and more perceived as commercial ventures, a logic that culminated in the U.S. Supreme Court's 1915 decision that "the exhibition of motion pictures is a business pure and simple, originated and conducted for profit."[20] Trade reporters were quick to note that the lavish expenditures necessary for realistic film enactments served, in some manifestations, to distract attention from the very aesthetic of authenticity they sought to create. One writer in the *Editor,* for instance, warned directors and screenwriters against "going to the trouble and expense of smashing a couple of trains into kindling wood." As he explained, those who have striven for such effects "expected their audiences to quake in horror. Instead every one was wondering how much it cost to stage a fake wreck... such attempts at realism merely give rise to questions not bearing on the subject at hand."[21]

The second effect of the realist hype was the cost-use-value rationalization of the player's body. If the contradictions unleashed by the paradoxical union of "realism" and "commercialism" disrupted the industry's ideological project, then the most effective means of dismantling such opposition was to rewrite the story of the high cost involved for realism's special effects as a story of the high risk involved for the player's body. By the mid-1910s it became commonplace to note, as did Albert Marple in an article titled "The Danger Element in Picture Making," that the "capable men and women" of the motion pictures are often asked to "perform 'stunts' that are indeed dangerous and in which, only too often, they are called upon even to risk their lives."[22] We thus see that the industry's promotion of realism brings with it a discursive attempt to shift attention along the axis of production from the mechanical base and financial backers of film to the people who enacted the real-life situations; it was an attempt to give a name and a face to the spectacle, to humanize the machinery of production. It is not coincidental, then, that efforts to heighten the thrilling realism of the film image and the institutional framework of the star system emerged at approximately the same moment.

To be sure, the economy of danger was part of a larger system. Even the most risk-taking player was not taxonomized exclusively with acrobatics and stunt work; the aggregate of skills demanded of most motion picture players gave way to a category of performance defined in terms of dramatic as well as physical versatility. Talk about the multidimensional nature of cinematic performance lent itself to cartoonish commentary, such as one sketch in a 1914 *Punch's Almanack* titled "Wanted, a Cinema Actor: Must Be Versatile" that listed eleven separate skills as requirements for the job. Across the top of the page, a series of captioned images addresses the importance of a protean dramatic expression: "able to portray stern relentless father . . . also romantic lovers . . . stony-hearted sheriffs . . . and 'crooks' who are not so bad as they are painted." The list proceeds by incorporating an increasingly diverse series of situations and skills—"must not mind the feel of rubber . . . should be a good boxer . . . and a long-distance swimmer"—before ending with the sketch of a slight figure dangling upside down between two steep cliffs, under which the caption reads: "and capable of remaining indefinitely in awkward positions."[23] The strenuous demands made of the film player's body explained, to many, why dramatic luminaries such as Sarah Bernhardt never quite "got over" with the filmgoing public, whereas those who succeeded in the crossover from one entertainment venue to the other were praised specifically for their physical stamina and courage. One typical review applauded Beatrice Michelena's film debut:

> The gamut of "stunts" required of Miss Michelena would test the nerve and strength of a circus performer. This versatile actress, trained for the grand-opera stage and not for pantomime, certainly not for strenuous athletic feats, has demonstrated in this one photo-play alone that she has astounding qualities of stamina and courage—for the things which she is called on to do and does without blinking.[24]

As the decade progressed, male comedians like Douglas Fairbanks and Harold Lloyd, cowboys like Tom Mix, and strongmen such as Eddie Polo would come to be known as preeminent stunt stars in their own right. Yet from the outset, public attention was riveted to the "unusual fact," as William Lord Wright described it, "that the actresses are frequently compelled to endure more in the way of unusual experiences than are the actors."[25]

This "unusual fact" impels us to investigate what light it may shed on the narrative roles available to early women players. As Ben Singer has noted, representations of female power suffuse action-packed serials of the kind that starred Pearl White and her contemporaries, suggesting that an analogue between star discourse and film discourse did, on occasion, prevail. But Singer is quick to note that such films also unfold a "representational strand" that amplifies "an extremely graphic spectacle of female distress, helplessness, and abject terror." Of the four film titles that Singer numbers as paradigmatic of this "lurid victimization" are three Pearl White vehicles — *The Perils of Pauline*, *The Exploits of Elaine*, and *The Fatal Ring* — in which an ideology of female mastery is coupled with "an equally vivid exposition of female defenselessness and weakness."[26] Although a similar organization of features — a coupling of power and pain — characterize star discourse, the radical edge and effect of the system is this: suffering on (and behind) the screen is recuperated as a sign of the "real" player's physical and psychical stamina. To survive realistic manhandling, so to speak, rated highly among female players' exceptional abilities. This framework clarifies the unmitigated inflation of Pearl White's heroic stature. It also explains why Mae Marsh would emphasize the strenuous nature of her training with Griffith;[27] why Clara Kimball Young's brush with death in filming the final scene of *Trilby* (dir. Maurice Tourneur, 1917) would circulate so prominently;[28] and why Theda Bara's attempt to amplify her star status would turn on her decidedly dangerous athletic exertions.[29]

The Catastrophe Machine

I have argued thus far that the player's body supercedes the body of the machine in the context of the industry's self-professed realist project. An impasse hence emerges: how can a real-life aesthetic take shape through a body that is necessarily absent (recorded), invariably flattened (projected), and thus dehumanized by the very technology it seeks to conceal? In the most obvious way, technologies of stardom responded to realism's call with a complex discourse designed to enhance the believability of real peril to the player's body. In order to optimize the proximity between player and character, for instance, many protagonists shared the name of the actress who portrayed her. Naming characters for stars was easy enough, with White's respective performance as Pearl Dare, Pearl Standish, and Pearl Travers, each a case in point.[30] But when Rose Gibson succeeded Helen Holmes as the athletically daring telegrapher in *The Hazards of Helen* (dir. James Davis II and J. P. McGowan, 1914–1917), the reverse was also true; Rose was soon touted as star Helen Gibson. In some cases, as with Fox's multireel spectacle *The Daughter of the Gods* (dir. Herbert Brenon, 1916), the conflation of star with character, or better yet the eclipse of character by star, carried over into trade reviews and press announcements. Headlining the fact that "Annette Kellerman Performs Almost Superhuman Feats, Braves Alligators, Fire and Water to Make Picture Realistic," *Motography*'s review of the film describes a series of "hardships" faced by the character "Anitia" while in fact experienced by Annette:

> In one scene with arms bound and absolutely helpless she is beaten against a ragged coral headland, pulled away from the rock by the undertow and hurled back again until her back from shoulders to waist was cut as if she had been beaten by a cat-o-nine tails. In another scene she swims almost with the speed of a train ahead of a shark whose fin races along the surface not ten feet behind her. She is tossed into a pool filled with savage alligators—and yet she escapes.[31]

The semantic slip between the "she" of the character and the "she" of the star is purposeful, heightening not only the scenario's realism but also enabling the system of "name-images" or "name-types" that Russian formalist Adrian Piotrovskij understood as a salient compositional device in early "cine-genres." This system flourished given that the intricacies of character psychology and development were neither possible nor necessary, as he claimed, in film. In what remains one of the most resolute exegeses on the quintessence of cinema, Piotrovskij inveighs heavily against film's absorption of literary and theatrical styles of exposition, stating that "The mere appearance on the screen of ... Pearl White, is sufficient to communicate to the spectator the film's genre and the hero's characteristic traits."[32]

The care that studios lavished on name-types tended to exceed mere rhetorical slippage, giving way to some of the earliest, and notably outlandish, "traveling star" campaigns. In one manifestation of this practice, Universal sent Grace Cunard on a transcontinental tour to promote the release of *Lucille Love, the Girl of Mystery* (dir. Francis Ford, 1914), a serial in which the heroine's desire to regain top-secret defense plans stolen from her sweetheart, Lieutenant Gibson, motivates a number of high-suspense adventures. Throughout the course of fourteen episodes Lucille chases the villain in a seaplane from Manila to a South Sea island, China, San Francisco, Mexico, and back again to the United States; throughout the course of the film's first release month, Cunard traveled across the United States and England, performing a series of "aeroplane ascents" designed to replicate the "most important scenes in the opening part of the play."[33] The logic of this new "tie-in" was twofold: by piquing viewers' curiosity about the story, it lured a broader audience into the theaters. It also granted multiple onlookers firsthand evidence of Cunard's flying skills. Though traveling star tours continued throughout the period, production companies seeking to reduce the financial outlay for their campaigns created variations in the format as multiple as the stars themselves. In 1915, Paramount shined a few fenders and sent Anita King on a "trip across the continent alone driving a six-cylinder Kissel Kar."[34] In 1916, White traveled neither far nor wide but,

61. Anita King celebrates the last leg of her transcontinental journey. Courtesy of the Museum of Modern Art Film Stills Archive.

rather more simply, up: on the morning of Saturday, 15 April, she "dangled several hundred feet in the air from the roof of the Gregory Building on Seventh Avenue, New York, and painted her initials in four-foot letters on the brick wall."[35] The tension of the drama was heightened by the antics of Pathé producer Edward José, White's current director, who "rushed out upon the parapet and begged her to desist, calling her attention to the risk she was running and stating that the success of the unfinished 'Iron Claw' depended upon her."[36]

From these descriptions it might seem that presentation—pure visual monstrance—prevails over representation in the system's evolving hierarchy of what counts as evidence. In point of fact, the worth of these spectacles was measured not by the size of the crowd that gathered to gawk, but by the scale of publicity that followed. White's skyscraper feat was acclaimed "a big success" by *Moving Picture World* since "five New York newspapers made front page stories of it, and practically all of the rest carried the story in their news columns in a prominent place."[37] Although King's trip was not linked to any particular film vehicle—that is, not initially linked—Paramount executives shortly featured her in an "automobile thriller," *The*

Race (dir. George Melford, 1916), billed as a quasi-documentary piece inspired by the star's transcontinental journey. Once spent as fodder for marketing *The Race,* King's bravado became grist for a much larger publicity mill: By August 1916, *Photoplay* magazine would announce with certitude that "if you see Miss King in a photoplay, racing an automobile ... or fighting a timber wolf, or running an airship ... there will be nothing 'phoney' or faked about it. It will be the 'sincere stuff,' as the newspaper men say. Miss King not only can but has done all these things 'off-stage.' "[38] Note as well the fan journal's allusion to "what the newspaper men say," suggesting that the relation between daily newspapers and trade publicity was one of reflection, contriving a system of mutually reinforcing media outlets. This network putatively spanned not just national but international constituencies: domestic publications such as *Moving Picture Weekly* reserved a section for translated articles from their "Japanese Correspondent, Mr. Kintaro Sakamoto," columnist for *"Katsudo No Sekai—Japanese Moving Picture Magazine,"* who avowed Universal stunt queen Grace Cunard to be the unanimous favorite in his country.[39] In India, White garnered the loudest applause, or so said *Photoplay,* recounting the opinion of "Souchet Singh, the Editor of *The Twentieth Century,* India's leading motion picture magazine."[40]

The expansive properties of stardom's institutional framework—its absorption of print and image technologies, its unequivocal *mass* circulation—is well known and need not be belabored. What warrants our attention here is the lure of referentiality that underlies the system's epistemological endeavor and, beyond that, its remarkably skeptical stance toward visual faculties as a means of establishing believability. This is not to say the conceit of vision was not ubiquitous. Star portraits, film frames, snapshots from behind the set: images were (and are) the system's ostensible guarantee. Indeed photography's condensed temporality, with its ability to isolate and index a particular moment in time, bolstered claims of empiricism by offering readers the opportunity to scrutinize and appraise daring feats at their leisure, thus compensating for film's accelerated pace. *Photoplay's* 1918 layout of an Irene Castle stunt, for instance, not only provided the image but, for good measure, assured its readers that "the magazine possesses documentary proof, in the form of statements by witnesses, that the flying figure shown in this picture is the slim form of Irene Castle, diving across death-menacing rocks, into the water, fifty feet below."[41] Trumpeting truth claims of "documentary proof," the passage overtly determines its intention. Let us look again, however, at a relatively oblique grammatical detail—the adjectival stress on those "death-menacing" rocks—that exerts an alternative, if not disruptive force on the apparent concerns of the image under scrutiny. Namely, haunting the question of identity—is the figure "really" Irene Castle?—is the far more indeterminate evaluation of scale—how dangerous is the action and, thus, how "real"?

This same detail, at once subtle and telling, surfaces more sharply in Cecilia Mount's interview with railway stunt queen Helen "Rose" Gibson. The ten-page spread is titled "The Girl with Nine Lives," but begins with a subtitle: "She Is Certain That She Has Lost Eight of Them. The Photographs Are the Evidence—What Do You Think?"[42] The question of what one *thinks* is key, since whether we interpret the gesture as an invitation to mull over the verity of Gibson's identity or, as I believe, that the degree of peril is up for deliberation, it implies that seeing is always partial and subjective. As Jonathan Crary argues, the concept of embodied vision began in the early nineteenth century when new techniques and toys of observation, of which the camera is heir, gave way to a loss of confidence in the veracity of the eye.[43] For Crary, the rationalization of vision built on the model of the camera obscura is studiously assaulted by scientific studies of such phenomena as afterimages and the persistence of vision, resulting in a dramatic defaming of vision's purchase. Understood as subjective or psychologized, as binocular rather than monocular, human sight was consigned to failure at the same moment when the amplification of visual imagery and information incited by industrial modernity began to pummel the primacy of objectivity. "It has thus been easy," Martin Jay notes, to claim that the "'glancing,' embodied, and dynamic—as opposed to 'gazing,' disembodied, static—eye of Impressionism," appears as a "repercussion of the changes that Crary details" in the early part of the nineteenth century.[44] The aesthetic variants of impressionism suggest themselves to Jay as "a withdrawal from the world of stable objects and a new preoccupation with the perceiving subject, a subject in crisis, absorbed by its own dissolution."[45] Yet more than simply reflecting a destructed and disoriented subject, modernism's antireferential impulse can be seen, from Crary's perspective, as a means of structuring subjectivity anew, of making the subject adequate to the perceptual instabilities of modernity.

As I have been suggesting, certain permutations in star discourse strain to make the limitations of vision acutely felt, to hint that seeing is not always the same as believing. The cunning of the system is its avowal of multiple epistemological models that confirm the credibility of a player's performance by quickening, rather than refusing, the contingencies of vision. In order to portend meaning unavailable to or, in fact, *occluded* by sight, reports from the players—"in her own words"—became something of a

Technologies of Early Stardom

genre itself. Witness—or rather read of—White's redaction of a particularly spectacular episode from *The Perils of Pauline* in which she agrees that the "experience looked like a double-dyed, hair's breadth peril" before emphatically confessing "it wasn't; we skimmed out over the river, back over the land and the man with me jumped out with the parachute and I volpaned [*sic*] down to earth without a jar."[46] The contradiction posed between image and experience destroys the idealism of the iconic sign in order to introduce its revision through a process of reflection and renaming that the star system alone could supply. To be sure, star testimonials heightened the dramatic tension of the referent more often than otherwise, so when White admitted that "The 'Perils' themselves don't really hurt me," she quickly added:

> What hurts though is the fact that the things that really are difficult, look so easy. For instance . . . my escape from the lighthouse in a beeches-buoy was one of the most unpleasant things I've had to do. And it looks so easy! Just get in and slide down the rope! That's how easy it looks. But the buoy itself was such an awkward thing and the distance down the rope was so far. Then, when I get [*sic*] into the water I bobbed up and bobbed down—and that buoy was not comfortable.[47]

The star's astonishment at the arduous task involved in executing her escape, a reaction ostensibly mirrored by her fans, comes up hard against the repetitive stress of the event's appearance—"it looks so easy!"

The compulsion to resignify visual referents would seem to preclude any possibility of a transparent relation to the real in film's symbolic system. This is precisely how the realist imperative articulates itself through stardom. If the lived sense of the real turns on chaos, happenstance, and chance, then the real is that which refuses the systematic control of machines, the propensity to regulate, standardize, and serialize. Born at the moment when film's narrative techniques appear increasingly routine, the star system brandishes disorder and disaster as if to unhinge the progressive, utilitarian drive of the apparatus and release it into the realm of the unpredictable real. It makes good sense, then, that the devastating whimsy of Nature made a regular appearance in those tactics that invited readers to peer behind the scenes. As early as 1911, Mary Fuller detailed her experience riding a "wild mustang" that "was new to the camera and didn't seem to like it." A self-professed "good rider," Fuller accepted the position willingly, and was pleased that the animal behaved "quite well" during rehearsals. The mustang's demeanor transformed, however, once "the camera was set up" and once the cast and crew began "shouting and working

62. Marie Walcamp in *The Red Ace* (dir. Jaccard, 1917). Courtesy of the Museum of Modern Art Film Stills Archive.

themselves up to the highest pitch in order to throw in as much realism as possible." Fuller reacted with poise, keeping the "rein steady" and her head calm—that is, until the girth slipped, at which point the "broncho maddened," gave a "wild leap," and "while going at a savage gallop it bucked again and I was thrown about twenty feet."[48]

Unbridled ponies made for newsworthy impressions, but savage beasts upped the ante. The ubiquitous presence of large cats on early studio sets presaged the "roaring lion" that became the lively centerpiece of MGM's logo by the early 1920s; and female players' notorious scraps with wild jungle creatures would showcase as parody in films like Mabel Normand's vehicle, *The Extra Girl* (dir. F. Richard Jones, 1923), in which the comedian character releases a rather testy lion that she mistakenly believes to be a costumed dog. In the 1910s, "fake" lions were anathema to stars like Kathlyn Williams, Juanita Hansen, and Marie Walcamp, whose careers were built on the backs of ungainly elephants and leveraged through climactic encounters with tigers, leopards, lions—even pumas—as well as the occasional monkey. Animals are "easily frightened," explained Williams in 1914, and will "act on impulse and strike with the speed of lightning." Though the star's training and unflappable personae were known to calm even the most nervous of beasts, accidents were inevitable. As Williams confessed: "I have

Technologies of Early Stardom

63. Marie Walcamp, posing with Kaiser Leo on the set of *The Lion's Claw* (dir. Harvey and Jaccard, 1917). Courtesy of the Museum of Modern Art Film Stills Archive.

had some hairbreadth escapes either during a combat with wild animals or while hunting them on the back of my elephant."[49] The scenario of *Lost in the Jungle* (dir. Otis Turner, 1911), for instance, called for her to lie behind a log with her face hidden until the director signaled her to rise. After waiting a period of time, remembered the star, "I thought he had forgotten and raised my head as a leopard jumped over the log. Scared at my sudden appearance, the leopard struck as he passed over me, and although I ducked, I sustained a bad scalp wound."[50] Other players sustained worse: in 1918 Marie Walcamp opted to play a female operative in a secret-service script rather than another adventure in the jungle, after surviving a "severe mauling" by an irate lion dubbed Kaiser Leo by the press.[51]

Nature's brash unpredictability permitted the ontology of a performance founded on concepts of innovation and improvisation, and of a performer faced with the imminent prospect of death: the terms of a realness structured in ostensible opposition to the anachronistic, secure, and comfortable gestures of the stage. Not unlike the capricious antics of animals, technology, too, was prone to spontaneous leaks, jams, sputters, lunges, and combustion. Best known for her work with jungle cats, Juanita Hansen's popularity trebled when she survived a dynamite explosion on the set of

Secret of the Submarine (dir. George L. Sargent, 1916): "Miss Hansen," one report clarified, "working to get the acme of realism into the scene, was standing on the veranda when the house, lifted upward by the force of the explosion, toppled over into the sea." An accompanying photo showed "the actual explosion" and a caption drew attention to the figure of "Miss Hansen" who was allegedly "hidden in the surrounding smoke."[52] Vying for prominence with dynamic explosions (and in most cases coupled with them) were staged collisions in which automobiles, locomotives, or aeroplanes (or all three) spun out of control, menacing the lives of the "brave" players as well as the larger cast and crew. It was just such a fate that befell robust comedian Marie Dressler, who was "thrown into the surf forty feet deep through the capsizing of an automobile body" while shooting the finale of *Tillie Wakes Up* (dir. Harry Davenport, 1917).[53]

The fascination with a destructive force emanating from within technology's steely body certainly exceeded (and preceded) the frame of the star system, tapping into an "imagination of disaster" that Wolfgang Schivelbusch has traced in relation to railroad travel in the nineteenth century and that Lynne Kirby has linked to a "parallel" perceptual model in fin de siècle cinema.[54] For Kirby, as for Tom Gunning, the shocking views and discontinuous moments predominant in the "cinema of attractions" — many of which, like the infamous *L'arrivée d'un train* (dir. Auguste and Louis Lumière, 1895), also take the train as subject of the image — replay the twin logic of fascination and terror that modern subjects experienced as a result of the pleasurable sensation of high speed produced by the railway, coupled with its capacity for yielding body counts on an unprecedented scale. In the shift to a predominantly narrative cinema, I am arguing, this "imagination of disaster" does not disappear; it is instead displaced onto the technologies of stardom. There are numerous examples of the elaboration of technology's destructive path behind the screen, and it is interesting to note that testimonials from figures other than stars — crew members, studio executives, innocent onlookers, and so on — invariably surface in this context. The perspective of camera operators offered an especially close view of disaster, one that could embellish sensationalism with a finer eye for technical detail. Consider, for instance, the imagery involved when Thanhouser's senior cameraman, Carl Gregory, relived for readers of *American Magazine* the day his team

> sent a White steam automobile at full speed over the steepest part of the Palisades and let her smash down. . . . There were five operators with cameras ready waiting for the smash-up, one man at the top of the Palisades to get the

car as she toppled over the precipice, and four of us down at the bottom on the shore of the Hudson River with our machines pointed up at various steep angles.... I got a picture showing the automobile shooting straight out from the rock wall, then turning a clean somersault, then with a smash of black smoke, blowing herself into a thousand pieces. One of these, a heavy chunk of steel, whizzed by my head and buried itself in the ground.[55]

Taken together, these views comprise a flurry of successive reframings within a variety of textual forms that provide readers an epistemological basis distinct from the cinematic field of vision. Notwithstanding the many voices at play, the star remained the most privileged site for exploring the effects of an unevenly regulated apparatus. By way of underscoring the hyperbole sustained by these narratives, let us witness one final example, taken from a 1918 essay in which players as diverse as Mollie King, Bessie Barriscale, Doris Kenyon, and Louise Glaum recount, as the article's title suggests, "My Most Difficult Scene." Typical of the essay's tone is Kenyon's memory of filming an episode in *The Hidden Hand* (dir. James Vincent, 1917) in which she was bound, gagged, and left alone while the villain set fire to the house. In order to make the fire surrounding her seem realistic, the director doused the set with kerosene and, the star explains:

When a match was applied to the rubbish a great sheet of flame swept round me. I could not free my hands to protect my face, and I could not scream, as the gag prevented me from being heard. My appealing look of pain and terror was misinterpreted as realistic acting. It was realistic, but it was not acting. I was in danger of being burned alive! Finally, I managed to upset the chair backward. My head struck the floor, rendering me unconscious.[56]

Here, as with prior examples, the focus on a shocking reversal—a staged event that unexpectedly turns into the real thing—reveals how star discourse assembled a semiotics of catastrophe. As Mary Ann Doane makes precise, "catastrophe" is traceable "to the Greek *kata* (over) plus *strephein* (turn)—to overturn."[57] The catastrophic flips continuity over, exposing what lies beneath: discontinuity, interruption, accident. Further, catastrophe discloses, Doane claims, the "potential collapse" of technology and the "resulting confrontation with death."[58] In the context of stardom, injury plays death's substitute. We note that Kenyon's escape from fire amounted to "a partly burned dress, several burns, the loss of an eyebrow, several strands of hair, and a big bump on the back of my head."[59] Insofar as this list catalogs, injury by specific injury, Kenyon's spectacular experience, it is peculiar that Alice Brady, who also escaped death by fire when shooting a scene from *Maternity* (dir. John B. O'Brien, 1917), reported similar mutations: "I lost a big bunch of hair from the very top of my head, together with a part of one eyebrow, the sleeve and shoulder of the waist I wore and about a third of my skirt."[60] But let us not (yet) puzzle over injury's duplication; the point is that the accident signified.

In a succinct description of accident's effect on the humanist model of an organized, cohesive, integrated subject, regulated by reason and sustained by self-will, Jean-Paul Sartre says that accident is "the negative principle par excellence: it is accident that sentences man and declares him impossible." Subjectivity as such is extirpated by accident, to the degree that being human, "or what we think it means to be human," is undone. As Sartre puts it, the encounter with accident dehumanizes "man"

> since his ends have been both stolen and restored him at the last minute by things. He can survive for a time as an object of the world but it has been demonstrated that the ideas of praxis and interiority are the dream of a dream and that the human object, an accidental assemblage that one accident conserves but another undoes, is exterior to itself.[61]

The subject emptied of volition and faced with its own dissolution, struck dumb by "maladies of agency," is the preeminent subject (if we can use that term) of industrial modernity.[62] Irony deepens the wound: the invention of new and more powerful machines embodies the promise of modernity — the thrust toward ever greater progress, civilization, and ultimate, total control over Nature. Yet the greater the machine, the greater the potential for accident on a cataclysmic scale. The predictable response — Hegel is useful here — is to perfect the machine: thesis (progress), antithesis (accident), synthesis (calibration). Thus stardom functions: forged first as an ancillary to cinematic realism, it comes to operate as its own finely calibrated technology. It is the preeminent machine of modernity, preeminent because it forestalls the devastating effects of catastrophic accident by producing, and hence containing, catastrophe. It is, in short, a "catastrophe machine," a term employed for the philosophical toy constructed in 1972 by catastrophe theorist E. D. Zeeman as a means of calculating the indeterminable: "The point of the catastrophe machine is the construction of an apparatus which is guaranteed to *not* work, to predictably produce unpredictable irregularities."[63] The cinema is often dubbed heir to the phenakistoscope and other scientific toys of the nineteenth century; technologies of stardom herald the toys of the future.

Stardom's production of catastrophe would herald a reconstituted subject — the star — a rearrangement of the classical humanist subject into an

Technologies of Early Stardom

64. Helen Holmes with director J. P. McGowan on location for *The Railroad Raiders* (1917). Holmes had driven the car for a thirty-foot leap off the docks of San Pedro. Courtesy of the Museum of Modern Art Film Stills Archive.

exceptional subject of modernity. The star not only experiences accident but, more importantly, survives and, better yet, thrives on it—her persistence in the face of ceaseless catastrophe raises the threshold of commonly held psychical, physical, and conceptual limits of human motility. Given Walter Benjamin's intimation that the screen player can show the masses how "[one's] humanity (or whatever may appear to them as such) can assert itself in the face of the apparatus," we might say that early women stars assert a stance that disarms the destructive effects of technology by fully embracing its dangers.[64] "It's all in a day's work," said Kenyon of her fiery brush with death.[65] Elsewhere Texas Guinan cavalierly described her director's request that she "jump a 15-foot ditch as an appetizer before breakfast," while Marie Dressler discussed her foray into feature-length slapstick in a tone part swagger and part sarcasm: "Yesterday I made my way carelessly through a brick wall two feet thick. The day before, I permitted an eight-cylinder automobile to pass over my defenseless body."[66] Dramatic heroines, cowgirls, comediennes, adventure queens: whatever the role, a blithe *jouissance* distinguishes the star's assessment of her work. "I'd do it even if they didn't pay me," whispered Castle to one astonished reporter. Then again, when Grace Cunard was pressed to voice her opinion on film acting following her "release from the hospital for the fourth time from injuries that resulted from one of her thrillers," the star responded with appropriate aplomb: "It's a great life — full of excitement."[67]

Nervy Movie Ladies

All children are absolute *monsters* of activity. . . . You
might say they're only conscious of all the things around
them insofar as they can act on them, or through them,
in no matter what way: the action, in fact, is all.
— Paul Valéry, *Idée fixe*

Stars trumped the threat of technological failure by mimicking the moment of catastrophic reversal and rehearsing alternatives to trauma. This much is clear. But still the question lingers: why women? We must begin by noting the rhetorical labor invested in promoting the star's femininity: "In private life Kathlyn Williams furnishes a genuine surprise," exclaimed one writer. "So closely associated has she been of late with deeds of daring and dangerous exploits that one expects to find a dashing, mannish woman arrayed in more or less masculine attire. So it is almost disconcerting to find a decidedly womanly lady."[68] As with the ruse of vision elaborated above, star discourse emphasizes the irreducibility of identity to surface features, rescripting the body's status as an arbiter of truth to the degree that virtually every description of star physiology emphasizes excessively feminine lines — petite, pretty, dainty, trim — held in striking tension with the potency of an inner, dormant prowess: "Irene Castle is a slim bit of a woman . . . slender, yet even in relaxation suggestive of tremendous vitality and strength."[69] The injunction against mannish women in the period explains, in part, attempts to mute the possibility that female stars might develop male physiological characteristics. Yet it seems more profitable to understand these personae as composite figures through which identity could be said to emanate from the inside out, rather than characterized and categorized, a priori, by the surface features of the body. The emphasis on interiority is not only a privileged view peculiar to the star system, it is also contingent, in this context, on the female form. The male body's

Technologies of Early Stardom

capacity to model invulnerability may activate, in a single glance, a specular economy; the hyperfeminine planes of the female body draw attention to something else—to a nerve-based vitality that must be acknowledged, understood, and celebrated via the intertextual framework of stardom.

The industry's promotion of "nervy movie ladies," as they were often called, must be understood in light of the alarming number of nervous disorders spanning the period of narrative cinema's ascendance and culminating in the years during and immediately following the Great War. The heirs of late-nineteenth-century railway accidents, middle-class neurasthenics, and Jean-Martin Charcot's hysterics catapulted into the twentieth century with astounding, proliferating alacrity. Diagnosed as the body's response to a culture that Ben Singer aptly terms "hyperstimulating," the nervous subject increased in direct proportion to the rising congestion of urban centers, the forward thrust of industrialization, and the increasingly high speeds typified by new inventions like the airplane, the automobile and, of course, the cinema.[70] By the mid-1910s, talk about depleted nerves saturated popular discourse, giving way to a whole host of preventive and prescriptive measures. It is of particular interest to note that nerve-strengthening solutions were prominently displayed—alongside stars—in the expanding technologies of the film industry. In 1919 the new "Body Brace" was advertised in *Photoplay* with the promise that wearing the brace will "replace internal organs" and prevent "nervousness" and weakness for "both men and women."[71] Intricate in design and yet easy to use, the body brace provided the wearer a modern shield of armor, designed to protect defenseless nerves from those nasty and devastating sensations. Elsewhere a new breed of "Nerve Culturists" crept into the pages of *Motion Picture Magazine*, offering abundant advice on how to soothe, calm, and feed the nerves.[72] Some ads, like one by self-professed "nerve doctor" Homer Davies, seemed almost to encourage anxiety, stressing it had been "definitely established that more than 99% of all humanity, past their majority, are deficient from a standpoint of nerve strength."[73]

Technologies of stardom fashioned celebrities' interiors into functional models conceived as a solution to the deadlock of a nervous modernity, but the move from outside (surface) to inside (depth) should not be read as a promotion of female agency and integrity. Among the many subjective concepts reworked in the period of narrative cinema's ascendance is the assumed link between individual interiority, the privileged space of the self, and modes of intellectuality, thought, and sentience. As early as 1903, Georg Simmel's proposed antidote to the threatening unrest of modernity takes the form of an increased intellectualism, "a sphere of mental activity

65. Ruth Roland, *Screen Acting* (1921)

which is least sensitive and which is furthest removed from the depths of personality."[74] Mature mental activity in Simmel's view skates on the surface of things and provides the individual a psychic buffer against the instability of urban environments, lending itself to a type of "blasé attitude," a critical distance not too different from the laissez-faire approach of those who are utterly, consistently, bored. The energetic star faces Simmel's metropolitan subject as stark opposite; these women inhabit a sphere of physical activity that is least mechanistic and that is furthest removed from intellectual activities. It is also one or two removes from adulthood: "She is the girl who leaps from careening automobiles into foaming chasms, the girl who plays with wild animals as tho [*sic*] they were kittens or puppies, the girl who does not hesitate, even with death staring her in the face, to perform any hazardous stunt," read one typical litany, concluding that "Marie Walcamp, the heroine of many Universal thrillers, is absolutely stupid when it comes to defining the word 'fear.'"[75]

Early women stars, in other words, ascend to the firmament of modernity by disrobing the heavy weight of adulthood and its attendant emblems of intellectual maturity: the capacity for conceptual definitions and detached understanding. "Not knowing much about fear," says Miss Williams simply, "I hardly know when I'm taking the greatest risks. They told me, though, it was a daring thing when I stepped from a motor-boat at full speed on Lake Michigan to the pontoons and then to the seat of a hydro-

Technologies of Early Stardom

aeroplane and was wheeled into the air a thousand feet." And again: "It was a task which would cause a strong man and a good swimmer to flinch, but Miss [Cleo] Madison does not know the name of fear, and it is not a question of what her director, Wilfred Lucas, can prevail upon her to do, but what he can prevail upon her not to do."[76]

The modern selfhood modeled by the star is hence a subject volatized beyond recognition and reason (for example, "not knowing much"; "absolutely stupid"; "does not know") staged in opposition to a "they" or, more often, a "he" who knows better—more simply, one who *knows*. For contemporary feminists accustomed to pinpointing and critiquing the myriad ways in which patriarchal culture slates femininity as nonrational (as body, rather than mind; as child, rather than adult), the construction of female celebrities denuded of rational thought might seem questionable. In a culture gripped by anxieties concerning a paralysis of will and the exhaustion of nerves, however, the star's ability to act without thinking—to take play seriously—registered as a sign of enviable resiliency.[77]

Insofar as the female star's body is ready-made to replace the "tiny, frail human" figure that Benjamin envisioned under attack in a modern industrial landscape, hers is a belligerent female variable in a cultural aesthetic field strewn with reimagined yet decidedly male bodies.[78] One thinks of prizefighters such as John L. Sullivan and bodybuilders like Eugene Sandow whose spectacular hard bodies revealed the metamorphoses available to men through conditioning of the physical armature. Other examples that come to mind include the disjointed mannequins and automatons that populate Dadaism, or the Taylorist-Fordist worker whose bodily movements are segmented, serialized—each matched to the efficacy of the machine. By 1916, the devastating logic of modernity culminated in horrific proportions as submarines and rolling tanks—not to mention hand grenades and pointed bullets—mutilated male bodies and psyches in incrementally novel ways on the battlefields of World War I.[79] Jessica Burstein remarks on those literary bodies unhinged and reassembled in the wake of the trenches with a succinct genealogy: "In the beginning was the 'mere body,' prewar, cloaked only in flesh, retroactively understood as fragile.... The second position, that of the armored body, is the soldier at war. The prosthetic body is the third position."[80] Rather than machines acting as naturalized prosthetics for the human laborer, the body under military industrialization begins to take on the properties of machines, begins to function prosthetically, which is to say that human body parts become reworkable, interchangeable—not only skin and limbs but character and self as well. Hence, while government committees disputed the relative merits of wooden versus metal limbs, Sigmund Freud set about revising his map of human subjectivity, proposing a mental projection of the "surface of the body," a "bodily ego" that grows onto, encases, and hardens around the subject's inner, vulnerable world.[81]

The fantasy of a body revised as compensatory is perhaps most fully pronounced in the writings of Italian impresario F. T. Marinetti, whose futurist prophesies include the construction of an entirely new subject, one "endowed with surprising organs: organs adapted to the needs of a world of ceaseless shocks."[82] Marinetti's fantasmatic projection of the superhuman prosthetic body—half man, half machine—translates the crisis of the male body blasted apart in the War to End All Wars to a body capable not only of transcending the threat of a military-industrial epoch but one that, in fact, *thrives* on it. The futurists "lust for danger," writes Marinetti: "Our nerves demand war."[83] As Hal Foster points out, Marinetti's transvaluation of the death drive, the addiction to technology as a means of incrementally steeling the self against pathology and degeneracy, may almost be seen to anticipate and intuit the greater hypothesis of *Beyond the Pleasure Principle*—"that the fundamental instinct of the organism is to return to its prior state of inanimation, to . . . its death."[84] Paradoxically, for Marinetti, to be "deader than dead," to be wholly mechanical, is the necessary premise for life in the future.[85] If we were willing to follow Marinetti back to the future, we would find the body of the male *Freikorps,* the avatar of fascism, whose signature leather garb stands in for a fully mechanized subject; the body transformed to aggressive delibidinalized weapon. As Klaus Theweleit points out, the soldiers externalize their fear of dissolution by killing what is not "them"—more specifically, by annihilating bodies associated with the antirational, with the flux and flow of the monstrous, illogical feminine. "It is, above all, the living movement of women," explains Theweleit, that forces a "defensive-aggressive stance"; these "mechanical" men exhibit the desire to reduce the female to a "bloody mass."[86]

Not coincidentally, the fascist body augments its destructive prowess through a perceptual apparatus akin to the "operation of a camera," as Theweleit explains: "When they [the soldiers] catch sight of real movement, they block out the light—the eyes narrowing to mere slits. . . . They record the living as that which is condemned to death."[87] Theweleit's terms describe perfectly the operations and effects that Mary Ann Doane attributes to early cinema's optical field. For Doane, the developing cinematic apparatus devises textual arrangements capable of dissociating the male viewer from technologically induced instability—shock, trauma, catastrophe—by projecting technology's assault onto the body of the woman or the

Technologies of Early Stardom

racial other. Such an effect, for Doane, begins in early one-shot films that fix a "rudimentary stare" at the female figure, and evolves into a "technically intricate manipulation of space" that takes as its "principal content" the spectacle of the female body.[88] Seen as a fascist, imperialist, or patriarchal harnessing of technology for the purpose of mastering an unruly feminine Nature, such analyses of the camera "eye" return us to Benjamin, specifically to the mutually reinforcing relation of "aesthetics and anaesthetics" that Susan Buck-Morss has appraised as the endpoint of the artwork essay. In this reading, cinema's unique capacity to deploy ever greater aesthetic technologies of shock and traumatic sensation—each of which admit the potential for piercing the subject's defensive, armored, conscious shield—instead aggravates the human sensorium to a degree of "self-alienation" that makes humanity "experience its own destruction as an aesthetic pleasure of the first order."[89] Trauma thrills, as Jeffrey Schnapp says elsewhere, but here it kills.[90]

The vision of a subject deadened—made mechanical by the very technology whose enablement has failed him—suffuses artistic and cultural responses to military-industrial modernity. Yet for Benjamin there was more than one way of looking at cinema's role in all this. Miriam Hansen has elucidated as much by pinpointing Benjamin's use of the term "innervation" as the key to an alternative vision of technology's reception that elsewhere dead-ends in enervation. Innervation is enervation's opposite; it turns on a two-way concept of the human sensorium's reaction to stimuli: first, the familiar route whereby mental energies are converted to motoric forms and seen to affect the somatic geography of the body (as in the shell-shocked, hysterical soldier); but second, and more importantly, that motoric stimulation (rather than, say, talking cures) can recover and reconvert repressed psychic matter. Innervation upsets the vision of a body imagined as a hardened, defensive response to stimuli by imagining a more flexible body, one that can play out the effects of alienation; one that can rehearse, perform, or mimic alternative responses to the devastating failure of technology. Technology must then encourage this form of play, and, for Benjamin, cinema remains the preeminent playground of possibility.[91]

It is telling in this regard that the figure of the female star is one who confronts technological catastrophe with an attitude at once childish and blithe. For her there is no cognitive distance, no contemplation of what might or might not be; thinking is subsumed by action, much in the way a child learns not by abstract-formal rationalization but by spontaneous mimicry—imitating through gesture and bodily performance the fantasy at hand. Benjamin's fascination with children's cognition hinges on its capacity to subvert stilted forms of bourgeois socialization by replacing mental and rule-bound cues with a tactile knowing, one linked to action. Much more could be said on early women stars as a vital *figuration* of such mimetic responses to modern trauma. Yet given the emphasis on mimetic play, it seems more profitable, in conclusion, to turn from the actor to the acted on and examine not the star, but the fan — or, rather, how the body in the seat is imaged relative to the extraordinary star on the screen.

Addendum: Mimesis

To ponder mimesis is to become sooner or later caught . . . in sticky webs of copy *and* contact, image *and* bodily involvement of the perceiver in the image, a complexity we too easily elide as nonmysterious, with our facile use of terms such as identification. — Michael Taussig, *Mimesis and Alterity: A Particular History of the Senses*

In April 1917, *Motion Picture Magazine* carried an article titled "Shell Fright vs. Screen Fright." The speaker of the piece is a soldier recently returned from the trenches who relays how his slide show and "eye-witness description of the sickening slaughter on the battle-lines" had "but a mild interest" for the movie patron, while that "same man who had yawned" would "get up on his hind legs at the spectacle of one individual, like the indestructible Helen Holmes, jumping off a bridge."[92] An illustrative sketch accompanies the essay: on the left side of the page a man slumps in his seat, eyes reduced to unseeing slits as he yawns, "Ho-Hum!" Directly opposite, the "same gent" stares wide-eyed ahead, body tensely poised, elbows, knees, and toes "curling up with excitement." A caption explains the man is "seeing Helen Holmes skin her elbow."

There are multiple ways to read this model of contrasting responses. One might appraise the difference as that between a subject so thoroughly disengaged as to be bored and only half awake on one hand, and a subject sensationally alive, alert, and hyperresponsive on the other. Spatial relations also bear remarking on: the yawning figure whose body shrinks down — shuts down — in the seat is a figure fully distanced, indeed alienated, from the image. In contrast, the figure perched on the edge of the seat watching Helen Holmes, the one with bodily limbs stretching upward and outward, is a subject whose proximity to the image is tantamount to enacting the

Technologies of Early Stardom

66. *Motion Picture Magazine,* April 1917.

image—or, more precisely, to imitating it by virtue of a reflexive process of participation. This viewer is simultaneously transfixed and transmogrified.

Perhaps the most compelling aspect of this 1917 rendering of viewer response is the way it foregrounds physiological activity as a measure of psychological affect. The emphasis placed on the body's response provides a corrective to familiar paradigms of spectatorship that unanimously confirm film viewing as a suspension of motoric activity, whether conceived as a regression to Jacques Lacan's mirror-stage, à la Christian Metz, or allegorized as Plato's cave, following Jean-Louis Baudry.[93] These latter attempts to theorize a metapsychology of spectatorship share a belief that the viewer is peculiarly susceptible to "suggestion" at the cinema, a location rife with the potential for—so goes the logic—ideological susceptibility, given the conditions of film viewing: the darkened theater, the immobility of the viewer, and the fascination with a flickering, light-filled image. The movies, that is, are literally the scene of and for hypnosis. French film theorist Raymond Bellour has been one of the main proponents for conceiving of the experience of cinema as a hypnotic and, thus, regressive one: "The subject of hypnosis gives up his/her look under the domination of the double movement which grips it tightly: regression, idealization. The subject-spectator is submitted to a similar domination in that light form of hypnosis which belongs to the spectator: the hypnosis of cinema."[94]

433

67. Pearl White, the "girl with ninety-nine lives," poses after a publicity stunt on the battleship *Mississippi*. Courtesy of the Museum of Modern Art Film Stills Archive.

Bellour elaborates the terms of "regression" and "idealization" not only to understand the "deep identification" produced by the cinema, but also to claim a historical nexus linking psychoanalysis and film as two distinct but interrelated inventions in the early twentieth century; "the filmic apparatus on the one hand, the unconscious on the other." In his opinion, both structure the ontology of a bourgeois subject who emerged between the late eighteenth and late nineteenth centuries. The fundamental link between the two inventions is their respective propensity to produce "images and words" organized around this subject's "desire for a lost object" and "welded together by the logic of the family romance."[95]

It should be clear that our figure, the body shocked upright by Helen Holmes's perilous performance, disrupts the terms joining cinema via hypnosis to the desire for lost objects. While this 1917 rendering of spectatorship does suggest hypnotic fascination, this is emphatically not hypnosis imagined as a tool for restoring the integrity of the subject and supplying his unconscious demand. Rather, it lends itself to hypnosis understood as mimesis.

More precisely, what we have is an experience of mimetic identification that occurs in a state akin to hypnosis, a theory at once formulated and consistently deferred by Freud throughout the 1920s and 1930s. In her reading of Freud's writings on trauma, Ruth Leys shows how the traumatic "event"—such as the determinate, localized event of warfare—is redefined in Freud's thinking as that which triggers the "trauma" of emotional identification, in particular a mimetic experience that precedes the Oedipus complex. In other words, the external event's ability to breach the ego's protective mechanisms, to shatter or split the constitution of the subject, is only traumatic insofar as it impels a far more definitive trauma: "the archetrauma of birth, defined . . . as a primary identification or hypnotic repetition that occurs prior to any conscious perception *or any repression.*"[96] Mimesis is significant because it lays bare, in its at once originary and imitative force, the ways in which the organism's relation to its environment, the victim's relation to the aggressor, or the individual's relation to the other, is blurred and confused. Significantly, the mimetic postulate is inassimilable to Freud's established theories of childhood psychosexual desire as the origins of the neuroses. Mimesis turns the relation between identification and desire on its head: identification emerges not as the result of the subject's unconscious desire for a loved object, but rather as an imitation by one "self" of an "other" that to all intents and purposes is indistinguishable from a primordial identification in which the organism first acts like, and only later desires, the outside or other.

The mimetic paradigm imagines the suspension of the self or, more accurately, the vertiginous openness of an entity that does not properly constitute a self. Hence, if trauma is understood in terms of a paradigm of mimetic identification, rather than an event that a pregiven ego can ultimately signal and confront, then trauma refuses representation and narration. Taking this one step further, it precludes the possibility of the diegesis on which the psychoanalytic task depends. Not surprisingly, the logical extension of trauma as mimesis troubled Freud, "haunting," Leys says, his postwar writings; but it was precisely the refusal of signification implied by mimesis, its location as an experience outside and beyond bourgeois forms of socialization, that commanded Benjamin's attention as a utopian or, at least, innervating experience most readily supplied by the cinema.

"It hit the spectator like a bullet, it happened to him, thus acquiring a tactile quality," said Benjamin with respect to Dada artworks, which he also considered as promoting a demand for film, "the distracting element of which is primarily tactile."[97] Cinema's physiological affect is borne out by its capacity for augmenting the modern subject's "mimetic faculty," that is, the ability of rehearsing or playing or "producing similarities."[98] Significantly, for Benjamin, the mimetic prowess enhanced by the cinema forged an outlet through which the individual might not only defend itself against the trauma of industrialization, but could also reconstruct the capacity for experience that had been shattered by the process. This possibility depends on the fact that the mimetic faculty is diametrically opposed to the movement of signification. Mimesis stresses the reflexive, rather than reflection; it brings the subject into intimate contact with the object, or other, in a tactile, performative, and sensuous form of perception, the result of which is an experience that transcends the traditional subject-object dichotomy. Through mimesis the subject is not stabilized or rigidified by means of its identifications. Indeed, mimesis redefines identification as process, a contagious movement that renders indeterminate, fluid, or porous the boundaries between inside and outside. "Indeterminacy does not preclude activity in terms of identity," Vicki Callahan argues with respect to the undermining of language and concept in the work of French film star/director Musidora, "although it is important here to remember that identity cannot be reduced to a fixed entity or essence."[99] Indeterminacy—mimesis as such—leaves no room for armored bodies.

Read in relation to the mimetic paradigm, the hypnotized viewer in the 1917 sketch can be seen imitating the traumatic peril Holmes enacts, rather than desiring the star as either mirrored or mastered image. The reader may object here that I am speculating, wildly, on a single rendering of spectatorial response. My hope is that this provocation will fuel the work that remains to be done, including the excavation of alternative images of early spectators, as well as the scrutiny of textual address in the early period's commercially successful, but critically obscure, "thrilling" modern film genres.

The crucial point is this: at the juncture of traumatic-mimetic postulates and the flourishing of early stardom, we find historical support for conceiving viewers' relation to the screen in terms other than those grounded in the shackled gaze, in Renaissance perspective, and in narcissistic identification. We find the apotheosis of cinema's engagement with modernity, its refusal of Cartesian mental privacy in favor of a model that privileges the "thickness," the "carnal density" of the observer's body.[100] To the extent that mimesis sidesteps oedipality, we lose a model predicated on sexual difference and sexual desire. This is a critical risk worth taking. Only then may we begin to fully consider the ways in which film spectators, as Lynne Kirby puts it, are "undone," subjects "whose sexual orientation vis-à-vis spectatorship is broken down, put into crisis"—in short, traumatized.[101] If there is desire to be had in the "nerve-racking" genres of early action, adventure, crime, and comedy films, perhaps it is best formulated as the desire not to desire; that is, the yearning to catapult forward and beyond oneself, to stunt fearlessly and without hesitation. Seen this way, it is the body of the fan that becomes extraordinary—the material on which the cinematic "real" acquires its most palpable, historical register.

Notes

This essay demands a dedication—to Madeline Matz at the Library of Congress, whose generous counsel and good cheer was offered from the start. Jessica Burstein provided inspiration, advice, and knowledge of the rarest sort. For their careful and caring reading of this essay, I am indebted to Shelley Eversley, Dianah Jackson, and Diane Negra. A special thanks to my research assistant, John McGowan-Hartmann, and to Terry Geesekin at the Museum of Modern Art, who found the stills when I most needed them. Support from the Royalty Research Fund and from the Walter Chapin Simpson Center for the Humanities at the University of Washington provided me with the time to make this writing possible.

1 Gaylyn Studlar, *This Mad Masquerade: Stardom and Masculinity in the Jazz Age* (New York: Columbia University Press, 1996), 3.
2 The quoted phrase is borrowed from Giuliana Bruno, whose apt neologism for our celluloid past figures in the title of her book, *Streetwalking on a Ruined Map: Cultural Theory and the City Films of Elvira Notari* (Princeton: Princeton University Press, 1993).
3 Alice Hall, "The Ninety-Nine Lives of Pearl White," *Picturegoer,* February 1921, 31.
4 "Pathé Claims Pearl White Greatest Drawing Card," *Motion Picture News,* 28 April 1917, 2655.
5 With regard to White's impression on surrealist artists, see Phillipe Soupault, "Cinema, U.S.A." (1923), reprinted in *The Shadow and Its Shadow: Surrealist Writings on Cinema,* ed. Paul Hammond (London: British Film Institute, 1978), 32. Leonide Massine describes the impact of White's film performances on his choreography for the Ballets Russes in *My Life in Ballet,* ed. Phyllis Haskell and Robert Rubens (New York: Macmillan, 1968), 104.
6 For a description of "Pearl's" army recruitment poster, which featured the star seated on a white horse, dressed in army fatigues, and holding a large U.S. flag—under which was written "Do You Think *I'd* Stay at Home?"—see *Motion Picture Magazine,* August 1917, 38. On White's election to the American Cadets and her interactions with other U.S. clubs, see Frank V. Bruner, "The Real Pearl White," *Motion Picture Magazine,* July 1917, 32–34, 102.
7 In 1918, *Motion Picture Magazine* published the "Motion Picture Hall of Fame," a list of the era's most popular stars based on the "greatest motion picture contest ever conducted." In this instance, White finished third with

114,206 votes, placing her just beneath winner Mary Pickford (159,199) and runner-up Marguerite Clark (138,852). See *Motion Picture Magazine,* December 1918, 12–13.
8 For one account of Ibáñez's outspoken admiration of White, see Julian Johnson, "The Girl on the Cover," *Photoplay,* April 1920, 104.
9 John Ten Eyck, "Speaking of Pearls," *Photoplay,* September 1917, 26.
10 Alfred Cohn, "Harvesting the Serial," *Photoplay,* February 1917, 25.
11 Frank Bruner, "The Modern Dime Novel," *Photoplay,* June 1919, 118.
12 It will be obvious that my argument deviates from current conceptions of the genesis of stardom, especially Richard deCordova's groundbreaking analysis of the textual elaboration that first defined the "star" in the early 1910s. Where deCordova sees a discourse of domesticity designed to separate film players from the scandalous notoriety associated with theater, I see a discourse of physicality designed to separate authentic film performance and film personae from the anachronistic mechanics of the stage. One approach does not cancel out the other, but taken together they cast the mold for a more complex genealogy of mainstream cinema: an industry tapping the safety of traditional mores while risking the pleasures of the truly modern. See Richard deCordova, *Picture Personalities: The Emergence of the Star System in America* (Urbana: University of Illinois Press, 1990), especially chapter 3.
13 Although I do not want to be understood as saying that female stunt stars repudiated cultural polemics associated with women's social emancipation and suffragette politics, let alone that their personae did not appeal to women viewers, we cannot afford to ignore the viewing pleasure suggested by their cross-market appeal. On women's specific relation to the action genre starring Pearl White and her contemporaries, see Ben Singer's groundbreaking essay, "Female Power in the Serial-Queen Melodrama: The Etiology of an Anomaly," in *Silent Film,* ed. Richard Abel (New Brunswick: Rutgers University Press, 1996), 163–193; and Shelley Stamp, *Movie-Struck Girls: Women and Motion Picture Culture after the Nickelodeon* (Princeton: Princeton University Press, 2000), chapter 3.
14 Hugo Munsterberg, *The Film: A Psychological Study — The Silent Photoplay in 1916* (1916; reprint, New York: Dover, 1970).
15 "The Search for Realism in Movie-Land," *Illustrated World,* August 1916, 802–804; reprinted in "Stagy 'Realism' in the Movies," *Literary Digest,* 19 August 1916, 1147; Burr C. Cook, " 'Reelism': The New Word in the Movies," *Motion Picture Magazine,* July 1916, 49–54.
16 Cook, " 'Reelism,' " 49.
17 "Stagy 'Realism' in the Movies," 1147.
18 Comolli argues that turn-of-the-century films assert the indexical reality of a photographic moment, which he calls "optical realism," and that later films articulate a "psychological realism" built on and through a textual system. This style was certainly asserting aesthetic logic on most every narrative film in the early 1910s but, as Miriam Hansen has stressed, the systematization of

such textual conventions, much less their coalescence in the paradigm often dubbed "classical Hollywood narrative," remained in uneasy flux throughout the decade and, potentially, well into the 1920s. See Jean-Louis Comolli, "Machines of the Visible," in *The Cinematic Apparatus*, ed. Stephen Heath and Theresa De Lauretis (New York: St. Martin's, 1980), 130; and Miriam Hansen, *Babel and Babylon: Spectatorship in American Silent Film* (Cambridge: Harvard University Press, 1991), especially chapters 1 and 2.

19 Tom Gunning has argued that the earliest projections, which he conceives as a system of "attractions," did not fascinate audiences with the indexicality of a particular moving image (Comolli's "optical realism," as noted above), so much as they enthralled by promoting the power of the moving-image machine (the cinema). See Gunning, "The Cinema of Attractions: Early Film, Its Spectator, and the Avant-Garde," in *Early Cinema: Space, Frame, Narrative*, ed. Thomas Elsaesser (London: British Film Institute, 1990), 56–67.

20 Quoted in Thomas Schatz, *Hollywood Genres: Formulas, Filmmaking, and the Studio System* (New York: McGraw-Hill, 1981), 4.

21 Reinhold E. Becker, "The Principle of Suggestion in Art as Applied to the Photoplay," *Editor*, 12 September 1917, 323–325; quoted in Ben Singer, "Machine-Made Melodrama: Social Contexts of Popular Sensationalism and American Cinema before 1920" (Ph.D. diss., New York University, 1996), 149–50.

22 Albert Marple, "The Danger Element in Picture Making," *Motion Picture Magazine*, March 1915, 87.

23 "Wanted, a Cinema Actor: Must Be Versatile," in *New York Dramatic Mirror*, 14 January 1914, 66.

24 "Earns Her Salary," *Motography*, 21 November 1914, 698.

25 William Lord Wright, "Perils of the Motion Picture," *Motion Picture Magazine*, April 1915, 95.

26 Singer, "Machine-Made Melodrama," 184.

27 Mae Marsh, *Screen Acting* (New York: Frederick A. Stokes, 1921), 39–41.

28 See "My Most Difficult Scene," *Motion Picture Magazine*, May 1918, where Young describes the pressure of working herself into the "emotional pitch" required for the final scene of *Trilby*, in which her character spies the picture of the hypnotist Svengali, falls under its haunting influence, and faints into a deathlike swoon. Significantly, the "most difficult" aspect of the performance, according to the star, was not the demands of dramatic intensity but the unforeseen physical danger: "when I fell backward over the table, to all intents and purposes dead, the table upset and my hair caught fire from the lighted candle ... only the immediate action of the members of the company saved me from being seriously burned" (75–76).

29 In 1916, Bara starred in a "Six-Reel Fox Drama," titled *Under Two Flags* (dir. J. Gordon Edwards). Publicity for the film claimed that "the story gives Theda Bara ample opportunity to display the fact that her powers do not all lie in the direction of the vampire role." Here the "far-famed dramatic actress ... pro-

vides us with a thrill when she jumps from a cliff into a body of water below, and numerous other thrills in riding horseback, falling from her mount, etc." (*Motography*, 12 August 1916, 398).

30 The listing is of White's roles, respectively, in *Pearl of the Army* (1916), *The Fatal Ring* (1917), and *Plunder* (dir. George B. Seitz, 1923).

31 "1,000,000 Film Thrills," *Motography*, 24 June 1916, 1447.

32 Adrian Piotrovskij, "Toward a Theory of Cine-Genres," in *Russian Formalist Film Theory*, ed. Herbert Eagle (Ann Arbor: University of Michigan Press, 1981), 137; the article was first published in *Poètika kino*, 1927.

33 Pressbook for *Lucille Love, the Girl of Mystery*, Film Research and Reference Room, Library of Congress, Washington, D.C.

34 For reports on King's vacation, see *New York Dramatic Mirror*, 30 October 1915, 25; and *Picture News*, 15 April 1916, 4.

35 "Pearl White in Press Stunt," *Moving Picture World*, 6 May 1916, 948. White performed a similar stunt in 1918, when she dangled from a tall building in New York to distribute pamphlets on U.S. bonds. See "News Notes from Movie Land," *Toledo Times*, 4 May 1918, Pearl White folder, Billy Rose Theatre Collection, New York Public Library.

36 "Pearl White in Press Stunt," 948.

37 Ibid.

38 Grace Kingsley, "All-Around Anita: Auto or Aviation Stuff, No One Needs to Double for Anita King," *Photoplay*, August 1916, 143.

39 See, for instance, *Moving Picture Weekly*, 2 December 1916, Grace Cunard scrapbook, Billy Rose Theatre Collection, New York Public Library.

40 Bruner, "The Modern Dime Novel," 118.

41 "She Earns Every Penny," *Photoplay*, January 1918, 70. This image of Castle's "death-defying" dive appeared in numerous publications. Elsewhere the star's personal testimony supported the truth of her physical feat. As she describes it: "In a recent picture, I had to make a high dive off a bridge, across some rocks. If I didn't jump far enough I would probably dash my brains out on the rocks, and it was a long jump. I knew it was dangerous, but it all depended upon myself and I had no hesitation." Randolph Bartlett, "Our Irene Was the Village Queen," *Photoplay*, November 1917, 46.

42 Cecilia Mount, "The Girl with Nine Lives," *Motion Picture Magazine*, February 1916, 121–125.

43 Jonathan Crary, *Techniques of the Observer: On Vision and Modernity in the Nineteenth Century* (Cambridge: MIT Press, 1995).

44 Martin Jay, "Modernism and the Specter of Psychologism," *Modernism/Modernity* 3, 2 (1996): 100.

45 Ibid.

46 Mabel Condon, "The Real Perils of Pauline," *Photoplay*, October 1914, 62.

47 Ibid., 60–61.

48 Mary Fuller, "My Adventures as a Motion-Picture Heroine," *Colliers Weekly*, 30 December 1911, 16.

49 Kathlyn Williams, "Kathlyn's Own Story," *Photoplay*, April 1914, 40; Albert

Levin Roat, "Wild Animals in Drama," *Motion Picture Magazine*, April 1915, 75.
50 Williams, "Kathlyn's Own Story," 41.
51 "Cheating the Animals," *Motion Picture Magazine*, June 1918, 61.
52 "Actress Made Unconscious by Explosion," *Motography*, 10 June 1916, 1345.
53 "Comedienne Advises Screen-Struck Girls: All Is Not Roses and Honey When Working before Camera," January 1917, source unknown, Marie Dressler scrapbook, Billy Rose Theatre Collection, New York Public Library.
54 See Wolfgang Schivelbusch, *The Railway Journey: Trains and Travel in the Nineteenth Century*, trans. Anselm Hollo (New York: Urizen, 1979); and Lynne Kirby, *Parallel Tracks: The Railroad and Silent Cinema* (Durham: Duke University Press, 1997).
55 Cleveland Moffett, "Deeds of Daring in the Movies," *American Magazine*, May 1915, 34–35.
56 "My Most Difficult Scene," 78.
57 Mary Ann Doane, "Information, Crisis, Catastrophe," in *The Historical Film: History and Memory in Media*, ed. Marcia Landy (New Brunswick: Rutgers University Press, 2001), 275.
58 Ibid., 276.
59 "My Most Difficult Scene," 77.
60 "Alice Brady Has Narrow Escape," *Moving Picture World*, 10 March 1917, 1545.
61 Jean-Paul Sartre, *L'idiot de la famille: Gustave Flaubert de 1821 à 1857*, vol. 2 (Paris: Gallimard, 1971), 1439; quoted in Dana Polan, "The Light Side of Genius: Hitchcock's *Mr. and Mrs. Smith* in the Screwball Tradition," *Comedy/Cinema/Theory*, ed. Andrew Horton (Berkeley: University of California Press, 1991), 131.
62 The phrase in quotes is drawn from Mark Seltzer's "Serial Killers (I)," *differences* 5, 1 (1993): 92–128.
63 This description, and my understanding of Zeeman's toy, are borrowed from Doane's superb essay on the televisual, "Information, Crisis, Catastrophe," 280.
64 Walter Benjamin, *Gesammelte Schriften*, ed. Rolf Tiedemann and Hermann Schweppenhauser (Frankfurt: Suhrkamp, 1989); quoted in Miriam Hansen, "Of Mice and Ducks: Benjamin and Adorno on Disney," *South Atlantic Quarterly* 92, 1 (1993): 44.
65 "My Most Difficult Scene," 77.
66 Adela Rogers St. Johns, "Guinan of the Guns," *Photoplay*, August 1919, 60. "'Why Did We Develop from Monkeys?' Asks Miss Marie," *Cleveland Leader*, 26 July 1915, Marie Dressler scrapbook, Billy Rose Theatre Collection, New York Public Library.
67 See, respectively, Bartlett, "Our Irene Was the Village Queen," 46; and *Picture Play* (1916), page and issue unknown, Grace Cunard scrapbook, Billy Rose Theatre Collection, New York Public Library.
68 Richard Willis, "Kathlyn the Intrepid," *Photoplay*, April 1914, 43.
69 Barlett, "Our Irene Was the Village Queen," 43.

70. Ben Singer, "Modernity, Hyperstimulus, and the Rise of Popular Sensationalism," in *Cinema and the Invention of Modern Life*, ed. Leo Charney and Vanessa R. Schwartz (Berkeley: University of California Press, 1995), 72–99.
71. *Photoplay*, June 1919, 118.
72. See, for instance, *Motion Picture Magazine*, December 1914, 147–148, and December 1918, 5.
73. Homer Davies, "How to Be Well and Strong without Diet, Drugs, or Appliances," *Motion Picture Magazine*, December 1914, 147.
74. Georg Simmel, "The Metropolis and Mental Life," in *The Sociology of Georg Simmel*, ed. and trans. Kurt H. Wolff (New York: Macmillan, 1950), 409–424.
75. Elizabeth Petersen, "The Serial Girl—Marie Walcamp," *Motion Picture Magazine*, September 1919, 82–83.
76. See B. H. Smith, "Nervy Movie Lady: Kathlyn Williams," *Sunset*, June 1914, 1325; and "Actress Risks Life," *Motography*, 1 August 1914, 172.
77. As Amelie Hastie remarks on the evocation of childhood in Colleen Moore's star persona in the 1920s, it may be that early film culture's insistent construction of childlike women is built to sustain a fantasy of historical possibility: the fantasy of a "new generation, represented symbolically by the child," one able to discover fresh meaning in a world grown weary of the empty promises and failed machinations of industrial modernity. See Hastie's "History in Miniature: Colleen Moore's Dollhouse and Historical Recollection," *Camera Obscura* 48 (2002): 128.
78. Walter Benjamin, "The Storyteller," in *Illuminations: Essays and Reflections*, trans. Harry Zohn, ed. Hannah Arendt (New York: Schocken, 1968), 84.
79. For a useful summary of the war's effect on male bodies and psyches, see Elaine Showalter, *The Female Malady: Women, Madness, and English Culture, 1830–1980* (New York: Penguin, 1985), chapter 7.
80. Jessica Burstein, "Waspish Segments: Lewis, Prosthesis, Fascism," *Modernism/Modernity* 4, 2 (1997): 142.
81. For an account of these disputes, see Burstein, "Waspish Segments," 142. See also Sigmund Freud, *The Ego and the Id*, trans. James Strachey (New York: Norton, 1960), 16.
82. F. T. Marinetti, *Selected Writings*, ed. R. W. Flint (New York: Farrar, Straus, and Giroux, 1972), 91.
83. Ibid., 67, 46.
84. Hal Foster, "Prosthetic Gods," *Modernism/Modernity* 4, 2 (1997): 15.
85. Ibid.
86. Klaus Theweleit, *Male Fantasies: Women, Floods, Bodies, History*, vol. 1, trans. Stephen Conway (Minneapolis: University of Minnesota Press, 1987), 215, 217.
87. Ibid., 216–217.
88. Mary Ann Doane, "Technology's Body: Cinematic Vision in Modernity," in this volume, 543–544.
89. Susan Buck-Morss, "Aesthetics and Anaesthetics: Walter Benjamin's Artwork Essay Reconsidered," *October* 62 (1992): 3–41.

90 Jeffrey Schnapp, "Crash: Speed as Engine of Individuation," *Modernism/Modernity* 6, 1 (1999): 1–49.
91 Miriam Hansen usefully excavates and clarifies Benjamin's concept of innervation in "Benjamin and Cinema: Not a One-Way Street," *Critical Inquiry* 25 (winter 1999): 306–343. See also her "Of Mice and Ducks," 27–59.
92 Hi Sibley, "Shell Fright vs. Screen Fright," *Motion Picture Magazine*, April 1917, 65.
93 See, respectively, Christian Metz's classical study, *The Imaginary Signifier: Psychoanalysis and the Cinema*, trans. Celia Britton et al. (Bloomington: Indiana University Press, 1982); and Jean-Louis Baudry, "The Apparatus: Metapsychological Approaches to the Impression of Reality in Cinema," in *Film Theory and Criticism*, 5th ed., ed. Leo Braudy and Marshall Cohen (1977; reprint, New York: Oxford University Press, 1999), 760–777.
94 Raymond Bellour, "Believing in the Cinema," in *Psychoanalysis and Cinema*, ed. E. Ann Kaplan (New York: Routledge, 1990), 107.
95 Janet Bergstrom, "Alternation, Segmentation, Hypnosis: Interview with Raymond Bellour, *Camera Obscura* 3–4 (summer 1979): 101, 102.
96 Ruth Leys, *Trauma: A Genealogy* (Chicago: University of Chicago Press, 2000), 33, my emphasis. Leys's reading of Freud draws from the work of Mikkel Borch-Jacobsen, whose elaboration of mimetic processes of identification—in which mimesis is seen to precede and hence displace the primacy of desire in the processes of identification—has shaped my formulations in this essay. See *The Freudian Subject*, trans. Catherine Porter (Stanford: Stanford University Press, 1988).
97 Walter Benjamin, "The Work of Art in the Age of Mechanical Reproduction," in *Illuminations*, 238.
98 Walter Benjamin, "On the Mimetic Faculty," in *Reflections: Essays, Aphorisms, Autobiographical Writings*, trans. Edmund Jephcott (New York: Schocken, 1978), 333.
99 See Vicki Callahan, "Screening Musidora: Inscribing Indeterminacy in Film History," *Camera Obscura* 48 (2002): 76. My thoughts on the primacy of tactility in the film-viewing experience have been influenced by Steve Shaviro's scintillating book, *The Cinematic Body* (Minneapolis: University of Minnesota Press, 1993), especially chapter 1. His work provides an important background for my closing speculations in this essay, and I wish to thank him for the conversations and collegial support that continue to enhance my conception of these issues.
100 The quoted material is borrowed from Jonathan Crary's discussion of the role played by the body in vision in "Modernizing Vision," in *Viewing Positions: Ways of Seeing Film*, ed. Linda Williams (New Brunswick: Rutgers University Press, 1995), 34.
101 Lynne Kirby, "Male Hysteria and Early Spectators," in *Male Trouble*, ed. Constance Penley and Sharon Willis (Minneapolis: University of Minnesota Press, 1993), 82.

ANGELA DALLE VACCHE

Femininity in Flight

Androgyny and Gynandry in Early Silent Italian Cinema

The Airplane and the Cinema:
Marinetti and D'Annunzio

The first Italian airplane flew in 1908, when the cinema had just taken off; together the airplane and the cinema redefined the boundaries of vision and, consequently, of subjectivity.[1] Both media—one for transportation, the other for communication—accommodated the possibility of living beyond one's body, in defiance of gravity and history. Italy excelled in the design of airplanes, just as it did in race cars. The famous brand names, Ferrari and Fiat, found their aerial counterparts in the Savoia-Marchetti, the Macchi, the Monfalconi.[2] The analogy, however, between earthbound and airbound vehicles stops at the cult of elegant design. The perceptual model conjured by the airplane was even more unsettling than the one involved in terrestrial transportation. To be sure, the train, like the cinema, is about time passing and movement through space, but the airplane and the cinema together showed the possibility of twisting time and space into beautiful arabesques of smoke set against the clouds' vapor.

The convolutions of the arabesque are part of the iconography of art nouveau.[3] By twisting the corporeal shape into a floral motif, the arabesque made the human form look more abstract and free-floating. Thus it implied that the body could transform itself and that such reshaping might also affect the perception of gender roles. In other words, this airborne redesigning of the body, through the mobilization of the eye and the defiance of weight, was not only a theme of the art nouveau style, but also an agenda consonant with the reshaping of the self sought by men and women at the beginning of a new century.

By taking humans into the heavens, the airplane enabled male pilots to feel God-like, but it also showed women what it could be like to drop the "man" of hu*man* below, onto the earth. This essay describes the impact on

Femininity in Flight

gender roles of such arabesque gyrations as they weave themselves around the star icons of feminine divas and amazon athletes of the period, figures such as Lyda Borelli and Astrea. Yet any discussion of aerial motifs in turn-of-the-century Italy must begin with two self-made, precinematic stars, F. T. Marinetti, the leader of the futurist avant-garde, and Gabriele D'Annunzio, the major figure of Italian literary decadentismo. Shortly before the outbreak of World War I, the airplane found in Marinetti and D'Annunzio two major advocates, who wielded immense influence in both Italian intellectual life and the popular media. If stardom can be said to have existed before its establishment in the cinema, Marinetti and D'Annunzio held the monopoly on it. Everything they said or did was always an event, a scandal, a statement.

The airplane fad was only one among many passionate interests cultivated by these two eclectic personalities. Indeed, they were eclectic to the point of self-contradiction. To begin with, the linear optimism of some of Marinetti's futurist statements was in keeping with automobile races, and at odds with the airplane's graceful arabesques; furthermore, the airplane, tied as it was to modern technology, clashed with D'Annunzio's love of monuments and ruins. Yet both cinema and the airplane were too new and too exciting to be ignored.

Marinetti's and D'Annunzio's early support of the airplane not only showed their eagerness to be ahead of the very latest trend but heightened their public image as men of action. Thus they flew or wrote about flying even before the outbreak of the Libyan Campaign of 1911–1912, Italy's first colonial adventure in North Africa. It was this conflict that made the rest of the world realize that the airplane was here to stay as a weapon of war. Even before the Libyan Campaign, Marinetti had linked aviation to masculinity. The protagonist of his *Mafarka the Futurist: An African Novel* (1909) is a pilot who rapes the wind and feels a terrible hate for the earth below. This hostility toward the earth and Mother Nature was also a key theme of Marinetti's manifesto *Mepris de la femme* (1909).[4] Inasmuch as woman was despised by futurism, she was deeply envied. Mafarka's behavior, for instance, exemplifies the ultimate procreative male fantasy: after landing, he copulates with a chair, and fathers a mechanical son.

Instead of taking the aggressive sexual stance of Marinetti's aerofuturism, Gabriele D'Annunzio held on to moonlight, seduction, intrigue, and love letters. The chief aesthete of the late-nineteenth-century "decadent" movement, D'Annunzio peopled his novels with languid, androgynous women and effete, male aristocrats. But he was also a daring aviator. On 16 January 1916, during World War I, the poet was flying toward the Italian city of Tri-

68. Gabriele D'Annunzio. From the author's collection.

este, which was being fought over by the Austrians and the Italians. All of a sudden he was forced to make a dangerous sea landing near the beaches of Grado. Such a traumatic experience did not keep him away from airplanes. In 1918, with the experienced pilot Locatelli, D'Annunzio climbed into the cockpit once more. He flew from Venice to Vienna, the capital of the Austro-Hungarian empire, dropping thousands of leaflets along the way that called for the liberation of Trieste.

While Marinetti achieved a strange mixture of disembodiment into vision and hypermasculinization of military technology, D'Annunzio managed to combine the amorous Don Giovanni with the intrepid hero, the modern Icarus with the patriot, the aristocratic dandy with the tough leader of a commando action. In 1919 D'Annunzio went up into the sky again and conquered Fiume, a city near Trieste that is now in Slovenia. Following this success, D'Annunzio drafted a new legislation for the area, the Carta del Carnaro; one of his major initiatives had to do with allowing women to vote. A few years later, in 1923, the Duce, Benito Mussolini, was so impressed by D'Annunzio's two aerial feats that he gave the poet a hydroplane as a gift.[5]

D'Annunzio's favorite pseudonym was Ariel, from the character in Shakespeare's *The Tempest;* and he was obsessed with flying beings in general. When the poet in a clumsy moment fell from a window at the Vittoriale, he humorously labeled the episode "volo d'arcangelo."[6] Flying for D'Annunzio involved quite a bit of military heroism, but it was also, and perhaps above all, a poetic enterprise. After losing one eye in 1916, during his forced landing, the poet started to speak of his third eye, as if the physical injury had opened the door to a sixth sense. D'Annunzio's fascination with the irrational, his love of perfumes, and his experimentation with drugs could not be farther from Mafarka's high-tech, monolithic machismo.[7]

But what is most important about these two writers' love for the airplane is that this new invention was made of death and exhilaration. Perhaps they put on wings, believing that self-destruction was the first step toward rebirth. Their allegiance to the airplane suggests a rewriting of the Icarus myth. This ancient Greek tale is about a father, the inventor, and his son, the explorer. The story is well known, except for the ending that concerns Daedalus: after Icarus crashes into the sea because he flew too close to the sun, the architect of the labyrinth for the Minotaur flies safely to Sicily on his own set of wings and is received kindly by the king.[8] While Icarus's wings are easily comparable to the airplane, his death hardly fits the fantasy of rebirth behind Marinetti's all-seeing futurist flier and D'Annunzio's dissolution of visual language into cosmic sound effects. This is why these two writers' passion for the airplane makes sense only if Icarus does not really die and Daedalus who lands in Sicily is not the father, but a "new" Icarus—a mechanical futurist man, in Marinetti's case, and a refined aesthete, in D'Annunzio's. In fact, the poet's longing for all sorts of male alter egos was expressed through the androgynous female heroines of his novels.

Femininity in Flight: A History of Visual Forms

In the wake of Marinetti's and D'Annunzio's highly publicized experiences with the airplane, Italian men and women got involved in different degrees with both aspects of the airplane's appeal: the airplane as a weapon for military action, and as a fantasy of imaginative freedom and sensual upheaval. More specifically, in the days of the Libyan Campaign, shortly before World War I broke out in Italy in 1915, Marinetti and D'Annunzio were not flying alone. In an issue of *La Donna,* a women's magazine published in Turin, dated 5 February 1911, the theater actress Lyda Borelli appears as Salome on a lavish front-page spread. On a subsequent page, in a little photograph, she is also shown as the only woman passenger inside a hot-air balloon. The caption below the image reads: "In love with strong emotions, after the flights of fancy, Lyda Borelli has decided to try the fantasy of flight, and she came back most enthusiastic from her nocturnal ascension."[9] This "nocturnal ascension" happened two years before Borelli was launched as a major film diva in Mario Caserini's *Love Everlasting* (1913).

The photograph of Borelli in a hot-air balloon from *La Donna* makes it clear that the theater actress is the catalyst that puts to work the ten gentlemen standing around her. To a much greater extent than the hot-air balloon, the airplane could twist and turn and thus revolutionize time and space, making what had been perceived as linear into a series of jagged angles and unpredictable curves. What is most significant about the airplane fad, however, is not its cinematic mobilization of the point of view, but rather the secret it hides beneath its wings. In fact, the silent-film diva can be said to live according to this new invention's extremes: she may crash, killing the enemy at the cost of killing herself; or she can fly beyond the constraints of her own body into a utopian realm. The airplane's ability to move between ground and sky as well as the diva's oscillation between historical change and personal ruin suggest that a newly born technology can house an older cultural type.

The term "diva," an Italian word from the operatic stage meaning "goddess" or "prima donna," refers to the female stars of silent Italian cinema immediately before and after World War I. A combination of the nineteenth-century femme fatale and of the twentieth-century new woman, divas mostly starred in melodrama, playing not only the seductress, but also the unhappy wife, the abandoned lover, and the rejected daughter. No matter which female characters they played—fallen women or wealthy socialites—the Italian divas' excessive but also curvilinear acting style (it involved graceful arm movements and sinuous body movements) was reminiscent of the art nouveau serpentine line and of the arabesques performed by the airplane in the sky. It is as if the discontinuous but also elastic body of the diva began to model an unknown entity in the attempt to signal the birth of a new way of being, a new psychological outfit to be worn—so to speak—by the "modern" women of Italian society.[10] And, of course, the new woman accessorized that outfit when she wore short hair, smoked cigarettes, flew up into the sky, and drove her own car.

It is the curve that interests me in the construction of the film diva as a cultural type. In fact, her acting is so protean that it looks like a metamorphosis in progress. The curve also combines the revolving trajectory of the flying and moving eye with the trademark of art nouveau, an international style known for its overlapping organic and inorganic forms, human and animal shapes, hieroglyphic and esoteric elements. Most important, the curve is a special kind of line that travels neither backward with the canon nor forward with the avant-garde. The curve is the mixed form par excellence; and thus it also echoes cinema's blurring of the boundaries between high culture and popular entertainment. This mixing of directions and levels can be assessed through two complementary processes at work in art nouveau itself: on one hand, the raising of minor arts to aesthetic ranking; on the other, the serializations and consequent lowering of icons from high culture into clichés for popular consumption. In this essay the sky-borne gyrations of the diva's airplane are contrasted with the aerial acrobatics of female performers in the circus and in the cinema, in such a way as to throw light on how the arabesque-like body of the diva and the grotesque figure of the amazon star rely on similar iconographies. Furthermore, the diva and the stunt woman cite different class origins. Through the diva's body, flight turns into disappearance, abstraction, and sexual sublimation, whereas the woman acrobat balloons into a phallic mother, one forever bouncing from one adventure to the next, but also bound to the earth.

Despite the serpentine line connecting the film diva as art nouveau icon and the airplane as the symbol of space and time intertwined, outside the movie theater the role of revived, successful Icarus remained a male prerogative. Women could not fit into the Icarus myth with the same degree of satisfaction because its oedipal genealogy goes from father to son, not from mother to daughter. Furthermore, the problem was not just with storytelling, but with history itself. With the convulsions of hysteria keeping women on the margins of history, mothers and daughters could hardly find a good place for themselves within a linear and teleological view of the historical process.[11] As a result of this double difficulty with the temporality of both history and storytelling, women, or at least some of them, were dreaming of bending the rules into a new way of living when they looked at aerial twists onscreen. They were seeking a redefinition of femininity beyond the gender-biased structures of the Icarus myth. They longed for the mobility of the aerial arabesque, the empty openness of the sky, and the freedom of flight.

By reporting different examples from silent films starring divas and by illustrating flying stunts in the circus, I show how, for Italian women, the airplane was not an easily accessible vehicle. Men, who flew more frequently, could more readily turn this new invention into their own flag of modernity and courage. Thus, like the flight of Icarus and Daedalus, the twentieth-century airplane took its place within a male genealogical narrative and a metonymic, oedipal trajectory. In response to this discrepancy between men and women in their use of the airplane, the aerial iconography scattered through diva films and women's fashion suggests a metaphorical, poetic view of aviation. It also expresses a utopian longing, a desire to fly beyond the body and history. Besides a metaphorical approach, the key components of these women's lyrical association with flight are androgyny, the arabesque, and a nonfigurative mode.

The transformation of flight into reverie, however, applies to the airplane fad as a pastime for the upper classes, and to the register of melodrama in film, a genre in Italian silent cinema lower in status than the historical film, but certainly more literary and highbrow than comedy where gynandry and the grotesque prevail.[12] In other words, the flip side of the diva's leaning toward abstraction can be found in another female star hidden at the very bottom of the airplane frenzy: Astrea, the woman athlete of a few action-adventure films. Her presence on the screen is explained by the popularity of airborne female acrobats in the circus of the times. Astrea embodies the disfigurative side of flying: grotesque and gynandrous, her oversize body balloons over enemies and dangers. Both Borelli and Astrea are transgressive women, but whereas the former's flight is an aesthetic gesture, the latter's is a dehumanizing activity.

This essay is concerned with the description of visual forms in relation to flying and femininity.[13] I argue that androgyny and the arabesque, gynandry and the grotesque, differ at the level of social class. Yet these two visual forms are comparable in that they perpetuate traditional views of femininity that demand either the complete denial of the sexual body or its exclusive use for reproduction. I also want to show that the popularity of these nonfigurative or disfigurative visual forms might have been due to the imaginative possibilities they released in whatever realm they appeared—in the circus, on the movie screen, in the myth of Icarus, and in the world of fashion. Whereas the link between flying and fashion rests on the theme of reinventing the self, by imaginative possibilities I mean a sort of metaphorical resonance that is strong enough to become a historical legacy for today. Finally, I associate this metaphorical resonance to a premodern/postmodern or even antimodern imagery of flying. The last engages in a dialectic with another model of historical change, one based on linear progress and a strictly metonymic understanding of modernity as serialization, mass production, and segmentation.

Femininity in Flight

Flying through Clothes:
Androgyny and Cross-Dressing

In comparison to their European colleagues, Italian women climbed more slowly into the cockpit. It was not until the 1930s that the airplane was truly accessible to many of them. Even then, women fliers were usually aristocrats, intellectuals, or artists. For the record, the first Italian woman to earn a license as a civil pilot was Rosina Ferrario in 1913. Yet her achievement was so isolated that in 1928 the *Almanacco della donna italiana* forgot to mention Ferrario, and mistakenly assigned the record to Clelia Ferla, who flew fifteen years after Ferrario. In the wake of these two pioneers, a few years later Princess Miriam Potenziani, Contessa Bonmartini, Contessa Di Sanbuy, and the Marchesa Carina Negroe di Cambiaso went up into the air, whether alone or with a male partner is not clear.[14]

Moving from the historical record to the cinematic screen, we encounter the Baroness Troixmonde, or Filibus, the female air pirate played by a little-known actress, Cristina Ruspoli, in the film *Filibus* (1915), directed by Mario Roncoroni. She is a rocambolesque criminal who lives in a dirigible filled with silent, faceless male assistants in tight black skin-suits. At ease with all kinds of technological gadgets, including a heliograph (a sort of solar-powered telegraph), Filibus engages in four major activities: observing the whereabouts of her enemy, Detective Hardy, scheming against her on the earth below; traveling between the ground and the sky inside an elevator that looks like a moving can; operating ground technology to keep in touch with the dirigible hidden among the clouds; and swiftly assuming new identities by putting on different sets of clothing. Whenever she is not wearing one of her disguises such as the sober tuxedo of "the dandy Count de La Brieve," Filibus appears with all the feminine accoutrements of her aristocratic class, including a large brimmed hat. This accessory not only quivers in the wind, but also is ornately trimmed with feathers, an elegant reminder of her avian "underground" activities. Even though this female pirate is competent on land and in the sky, and at home in the worlds of fashion and technology, she never manages to drive her Zeppelin household to a destination that belongs only to her. In a sense Filibus enjoys Daedalus's technological ingenuity, but she never lands in Sicily.

If an airplane was not easily available, any kind of reference to flying, even through fashion, was a statement of emancipation for the Italian woman. In Alberto Degli Abbati's *La memoria dell'altro* (Gloria Films, 1913 or 1914), Lyda Borelli is a famous aviatrix whose flight is an endless source of fasci-

69. The dirigible in *Filibus* (Corona, dir. Roncoroni, 1915). Courtesy of the Netherlands Film Museum, Amsterdam.

nation for the camera. With her short but supple acting style, wavy blonde hair, and liquid hand gestures, Borelli was considered by critics and fan alike the most D'Annunzian of all divas, the ultimate embodiment of the art nouveau arabesque.[15]

In *La memoria dell'altro,* the first part of the narrative deals with the success and courage of Lyda as a female pilot. Later on, this positive persona is set against another portrait of Lyda—a woman suffering and in isolation because she loves a married man, Mario. It is as if the diva were interpreting two different characters through one role: no better example could be found of how the new woman of modernity could live next to the mater dolorosa of Catholic iconography. To be sure, Lyda's commitment to Mario is "everlasting," so that it comes to resemble a blood pact, a mother's attachment to her son.

La memoria opens with a sequence at an airfield. As soon as she lands, a group of admiring men surrounds the beautiful Lyda, who is wearing pants and a pilot's beret. Lyda's outfit recalls Pierrot's jupe-culotte, the first kind of loose pants available to city women for daily wear. According to the historian Michela De Giorgio, the very first Italian woman to wear pants in public appeared in Piazza San Carlo, Turin, in 1911. Of course she caused an amazing stir. Apparently a few men addressed the woman so rudely that she was obliged to leave the street.[16]

A few days later, in Florence, Lyda Borelli was also photographed in

Femininity in Flight

a jupe-culotte; her choice of garment turned a social transgression into a trendsetting gesture.[17] This was, indeed, the power of the diva: in *La memoria dell'altro*, her character also named Lyda chooses self-annihilation after her beloved Mario's death. This means that her love is so total, so all-consuming, that it coincides with a sort of self-imposed martyrdom comparable to a step toward sainthood—another synonym for total love according to Catholic doctrine. In real life, however, the actress Lyda Borelli could get away with all sorts of eccentricities. The aviatrix's jupe-culotte also required a thin figure; therefore, for the first time, thousands of Italian women went on diets. The matronly look of Italia Almirante Manzini, a diva starring as Sophonisba in Giovanni Pastrone's *Cabiria* (1915), did not fit with the fast heartbeat of modernity, urbanization, and technology. Clothes and nutrition were just two aspects of women's cult of Borelli, a true divinity worth all sorts of changes and sacrifices, within the unique formula of "borelleggiare."[18]

It is as if the cinema needed Borelli's special aura of celebrity to justify women's association not only with pants and thinness, but also with flying. Nevertheless the diva's aerial identity is characterized by some major limitations. The aviatrix, for instance, becomes visible only when she has her feet on the earth. This unrepresentability of the woman pilot at the controls is not exclusively attributable to technological limitations. It is true that in 1913 the film technology necessary to shoot someone flying from another vehicle also in flight was not readily available. Cameras were still heavy and awkward to handle. This is also why Roncoroni's *Filibus* depends on miniature models to depict landscape overviews, dirigibles, and hot-air balloons. But this approach in *Filibus*, a fantasy-adventure film, undermines the realism of the sequence. Such a loss of verisimilitude was not an option in *La memoria dell'altro*, where the idea was to document the daily routine in the life of a celebrity woman pilot. Besides these technological constraints, Borelli's grounding contains a hidden agenda: to delineate a woman's proper place, namely, either in front of a mirror or in the passenger's seat. This approach is not only inflected by gender, but also by class. When the aviatrix arrives at the airfield, she sits in the back of a car driven by a chauffeur.

It is only before her flight that the camera dwells on Lyda's dressing up. She carefully positions a pilot's beret on her head. The actress's precise, little movements suggest her concern to continue to look feminine despite her unusual headgear. Thus, the new woman can be born only through male clothing, whereas the way to construct her image from a female point of view remains as vague as a breath of fresh air.

Despite the ideological limitations built into the character of Borelli's aviatrix, the partnership of airplanes and women in film is too anticonformist to stop at just one episode. Here is a second example where the costuming for an aerial dance about the cinema suggests that freedom thrives inside the metaphors of women's imagination, even though they may not have access to the technology itself. My description of Giannina Censi's dance costume that contains allusions to the cinematic apparatus as well as to airplanes is based on several black-and-white photographs published by Claudia Salaris in her volume on aviation and futurism.[19] In 1917 Marinetti wrote directions for a performance titled *Danza dell'aviatrice* (*The Aviatrix's Dance*). In line with Marinetti's original approach, Giannina Censi danced on a brightly colored map of the world; on her bosom she wore a huge celluloid propeller, supposedly shaped like a flower to signify her gender, but also resembling a reel of film mounted on her projector-like body. On her head, Censi wore a white hat shaped like a monoplane. No photographic record exists of Censi performing Marinetti's 1917 choreography. In Salaris's book, however, the photographs of Censi dancing a comparable piece in 1931 suggest fluidity, especially when the dancer stretches her arm outward in a straight but nonaggressive line—a line that wants to be a wing instead of an arrow. The 1931 photographs indicate that Censi emphasized shape-shifting and plasticity, rather than virile penetration of soft clouds at sunset, which was the way Marinetti imagined the 1917 piece. Furthermore, in Censi's performance of 1931, the wing motif replaces Marinetti's airplane with its belly full of bombs of 1917. This last example illustrates a woman dancer's power to move beyond Marinetti's view of aviation as a masculine monopoly, an expression of virility and violence.

Yet another telling anecdote concerns Diana Karenne, a diva of Slavic origin, who seeks D'Annunzio's cooperation in order to take off into the sky of fantasy.[20] In 1918, as the representative of the Lega Aerea Nazionale, an organization interested in producing a film about the heroism of Italian pilots, Karenne traveled to D'Annunzio's residence at the Cargnacco, in Gardone Riviera, to plan such a project. Around that time, the poet was approaching the climax of his involvement with the airplane. Karenne's arrival is preceded by a suggestive telegram:

> My soul is dreaming of becoming one of your women through the mystery of art STOP shall arrive on Sunday. From the living breath of your spirit I hope one of your creatures can be born in me STOP shall arrive in Desenzano at 10.[21]

Here Karenne wishes to be reborn as a D'Annunzian heroine for a tale of wings, technology, and erotic mystery. More important are the larger questions raised by this episode: What happens when a woman, the diva Diana Karenne, identifies with the sky diva of the movies and aspires to become an aviatrix in a new film? Will she function as a fantasy icon for men, for women, or for both? Karenne's telegram seems to declare that her crossing over into the new woman of modernity depends on the way the dandy D'Annunzio creates ambiguous images of femininity in his literary work. It is as if Karenne, in real life, was stepping into the "clothes" of the historical spectators mesmerized by the D'Annunzian features of the film diva Borelli in *La memoria dell'altro.* Put another way, in order to find alternative avenues of expression for her desire, a woman (Karenne) identifies with a man (D'Annunzio), who, in turn, is attracted to androgynous heroines in order to reinvent himself as a male artist. Daedalus's labyrinth could hardly be more convoluted than Karenne's romantic connection with flight through D'Annunzio.[22] In a sense he is Daedalus, the architect, and she is Ariadne following the thread toward freedom either via "divismo" or via fashion.

Considering that both Marinetti and D'Annunzio either marginalized or used women to spur male creativity, the question remains: Which of these two artists would have been more tolerable to fly with? Probably D'Annunzio, since Marinetti was more rigid in the matter of gender roles, more concerned with virility and less with androgyny.[23] In *La memoria dell'altro,* Borelli's outfitting herself in men's clothes to pilot a plane does not oblige spectators to give up the heterosexual norm. Yet it enables them to shed the clothing of rigid stereotypes, and perhaps to take on D'Annunzio's outlook on gender roles. Crossing over is not an intolerable transgression, because it immediately becomes an aesthetic choice, an avant-garde position, a fashion statement that receives its seal of approval from highbrow literary culture.

Flying in the Circus:
Gynandry and the Grotesque

Flying was not just an expensive pastime for the jet set of the day, a pack of socialites who crowded the balls and horse races, airfields and art openings. Flying as performing in the air was also a popular form of entertainment in the circus and in silent-film comedy. Borelli in flight was not visible, but she posed, so to speak, in pilot's clothing, before taking off and after landing. By contrast, in silent-film comedy and in the circus, the audience could actually admire women flipping in the air or performing stunts that required them to leap from one roof to the next during a chase scene.

The most famous female athlete in film was Astrea, a Venetian who had formerly been known as Countess Barbieri. A stage name with cosmic implications, Astrea was also an alias for Queen Elizabeth during the English Renaissance.[24] Between 1910 and 1920 many Italian aristocrats were involved in the movies, but they rarely belonged to the world of the circus. This popular, lower-class space of live performance was traditionally reserved for nomadic mountebanks. Among the aristocracy, film was perceived to be a prestigious and lucrative business—a belief reinforced by the fact that the producer Baron Alberto Fassini and the director Count Giuseppe De Liguoro owned palatial homes that either looked like or actually functioned as ready-made sets for the high-culture productions of Film D'Art.[25]

Within the context of an emerging film industry in Italy—owned and run by the aristocratic elite and their immediate associates such as bankers and lawyers—it is all the more striking to think of Countess Barbieri leaving her Venetian palace for the circus ring. Little is known about Barbieri, except that she was so protective of her real name that she narrowed it down to a mysterious "Countess B." Although the title Countess lingered on in her private life, the way Astrea looked onscreen—huge and grotesque—undeniably brought to mind circus freaks. And yet, as a result of an intriguing turn of events, stooping so low in terms of social class for the sake of a professional adventure became Astrea's ticket to cinematic stardom. It is also intriguing, and perhaps just a coincidence, that the word "Astra"—very close to Astrea—an athletic star of the air, also appears conspicuously as a brand name for airplanes in a painting by Robert Delauney titled *L'equipe de Cardiff* (1912–1913). In fact, Astra was the French manufacturer of Wright fliers.

Astrea was first discovered by the French comedian Fernand Guillamme Polidor. With him in the role of Birillo, she starred in four well-known action comedies: *Astrea* (1919), *Justitia* (1919), *The Masks' Counter-Attack* (1919), and *The Last Adventure* (1920). The gigantic Astrea and her small partner, shrewd and goofy, achieved success by playing off each other's sizes and by engaging in picaresque adventures across the world—two traits reminiscent of Don Quixote and Sancho Panza. As a star or queen of the serials in the manner of Pearl White, she emerged as the female counterpart of Maciste, a nonprofessional actor who was a star for a couple of decades, beginning with his first athletic role in Pastrone's *Cabiria*. In contrast to Astrea's noble birth, Maciste (Bartolomeo Pagano) had been a worker in the

Femininity in Flight

70. Astrea. From the author's collection.

Genovese dockyards, with an opposite but also complementary trajectory from poverty to glamour.

It is most interesting that the aerial metaphor at work in Astrea's name can be stretched to include both her gigantic look to the miniature size of Valentina Frascaroli, another star of the comic genre whose screen name was Farfalletta (Little Butterfly). Furthermore, the parallel between Astrea and Farfalletta not only involves airy names, but also includes a similar generic placement in film comedy. Just as the gigantic Astrea paired up with Polidor, the minuscule Farfalletta developed her screen career next to Andrè Deed. The male partners of both actresses are clownish creatures rather than good-looking men. In addition, Farfalletta is so much smaller than the standard Italian woman that she appears childlike, and unable to claim a woman's sexuality. On the contrary, Astrea's ballooning figure suggests the stereotype of the overwhelming mother, one who can never lose weight and therefore become an appealing wife or a seductive mistress.

Besides Astrea, other athletic women started in the circus and went on to star on Italian screens. In the role of Sansonette, Linda Albertini was "an amazon of the air, and a dancer of the prairie." Along with her colleague Emilie Samson, who specialized in airplane stunts, Sansonette excelled in airborne acrobatics involving the trapeze, ropes, horses, and all sorts of flying vehicles. Finally, the aerial motif informed the career of Gisaliana Doria, whose films about war and aviation turned her into an icon of courage, and a female version of the heroic Italian pilot Francesco Baracca.[26] In 1914 the engineer Caproni built the first of eighty-nine bombers to be deployed in World War I. Five years later, Doria starred in the first Italian female war film, *Il pilota del Caproni n.5* (1919).

Arabesque as Abstraction
and Grotesque as Disfiguration

The iconography of physical courage stretching from the muscle-bound female star to the arabesque-like, graceful persona of Borelli seems to indicate that these women of the air wanted to fly away from the confinements of a passive and domestic identity. In this respect, the diva joins ranks with Sansonette and her sisters: they all step outside the conventional roles of obedient wife and timid daughter. It is also true, however, that in comparison to Borelli's androgynous oscillation between nervous but sensual and muscular but fragile, the strong women of Italian silent cinema are by far more statuesque and unidimensional icons of national health. Thus, when placed next to Karenne or Borelli, the airplane endows female desire with wings of self-expression, or at least with the possibility of it. By contrast, in the cases of Sansonette, Farfalletta, and Astrea, flying is more about dexterity, spectacle, and entertainment. Put another way, when Sansonette flies all the way to the top on her trapeze, her trajectory downward is both reassuring and predictable. By contrast, when Borelli disappears in the sky, the camera cannot depict but only wonder about an unknown metamorphosis taking place below the level of clothing or beyond the female body, but definitely behind the clouds.

The semantic asymmetry between the diva and the woman athlete in relation to the theme of flying stems from the fact that the diva belongs to the unconscious, to the boudoir, to an oxymoron of simultaneously futuristic and arcane emotional experiences. In contrast to the diva's backstage location, Astrea and Sansonette happily occupy the facade of family life and national identity. They mobilize and energize the domestic psyche. Unlike these two cartoonlike figures, the diva is a much more contradictory catalyst of repressed desires and an agent of destruction aimed at herself and

Femininity in Flight

at the status quo that surrounds her.[27] Were we to take the comparison of Lyda and Astrea in terms of flying and the issue of class, and narrow its focus to the function of clothing and to the analogy between the art nouveau arabesque and Borelli's protean body, we would gain a much clearer understanding of the changing gender roles at the beginning of the century. Put another way, it is through these limits of representation that it is possible to infer what the audiences of those days imagined behind and beyond the visual forms they saw onscreen.

The comparison of Lyda with Astrea also makes us wonder whether the woman athlete is in any way like the male transvestite.[28] Astrea is not a successful example of transsexuality, for the layering of female clothing on a successful male transvestite is usually meant to tone down the masculine contours of his muscles. Astrea's enlarged size does make her look like a female Maciste. Yet her large hips and beautiful face unmistakably prove that she is a gorgeous, oversize woman. In contrast, Borelli's appearance as a male pilot is an appealing icon, an erotic teaser, as long as her metamorphosis stops at the clothes. If Lyda's female body was changed by her masculine outfit, or, to twist the proverb, if her clothes made the man, the diva's playful androgyny would degenerate into monstrous hermaphroditism—an aberrant mixture deep inside, instead of an intriguing layering on top.

When seen alone, Astrea is a large but striking woman. And yet there is something grotesque about Astrea's muscles towering over little Birillo. There they are: two freaks, two bodies engaged in a comedy of errors made by Mother Nature. She always wears the same male outfit—baggy pants, loose shirt, and a wide-brimmed hat—and there is nothing else she can do: Astrea is just too big for a normal woman. Likewise, her tiny man, Birillo, is no dandy, has lost his male status, and has been reduced to either the child or a dwarf. This is why androgyny is too aristocratic a term for Astrea. By contrast, she is an example of gynandry, a word pointing to the populist reconciliation of high and low social classes. In this respect, Astrea's oversize body is a way of masking divisions that are difficult to bridge in a small, newly born nation.[29]

It is also true that the grotesque, in the history of art, can be a manifestation of weightlessness; thus Astrea's oversize body engages in leaps and bounds and defies the law of gravity that should apply in a naturalistic space.[30] But her victory over the pull of the earth is not an event staged in the utopian and rule-free space of nowhere. Rather, her stunts are a temporary and extreme performance to straighten out a society undergoing radical change.[31] Within this changing world, stable binary oppositions such as male and female, heavy and light, risk turning into stuntlike reversals of values and roles. While she takes one risk after another, Astrea operates within a picture that remains safely figurative—that is, stable and anthropocentric—and does not dissolve into the blank slate of abstraction and revolution.

It is as if the action cinema to which Astrea belongs was made of topsy-turvy pictures where the potential for abstraction begins to show but is nevertheless pulled down by this role of superwoman in charge of maintaining the status quo. It is this sort of denial within the image itself that makes her figure look incongruously large. In other words, the size of her body overbears the architecture shown in the film—namely, the small portions of roofs and chimneys that are set against the open sky—as she chases the evildoers, jumping into the air and sailing from one building to the next. This discrepancy in scale between the protagonist's size and the sets suggests that the fundamental rule of anthropocentric painting, man is the measure of all things, is distorted but not overcome by a woman. On the contrary, Astrea's body bears witness to the deformation of appearance in store for women who dare to leave their social class and domestic space as Countess B. left her Venetian palace. Paradoxically, Astrea's large size is about the relapse into an image of traditional female reproduction combined with the social stigma of monstrosity.

If androgyny means more than one gender to the point of promising a quasi-magic, fluid persona—an arabesque-like body shape—Borelli embodies an androgynous ideal of bipolarity.[32] This ideal could be adopted by men and women alike, as long as they remained within a privileged milieu. In contrast to androgyny's "more than one," gynandry is not about sliding oneself out of one's own mold to become someone else. Rather, it stands for an abnormal male element weighing heavily inside a normative female vessel. When seen as a punitive pregnancy without delivery, gynandry is not only a populist solution rooted within a working-class stereotype but, in a psychoanalytic sense, a sort of *Oedipus interruptus* that defies the metonymic chain between father and son.

Where men and women are concerned, the semiotic transferability of androgyny is broader than the semantic flexibility of aviation. Put another way, it is easier for women to dress like male pilots than to actually fly. Whereas women can translate themselves into the clothing of masculinity, men follow an imperative not to cross-dress, for such a transgression would irreversibly destroy their masculine appearance. Yet, in comparison to women, men have a greater chance to experience flying in the first person, as pilots. It is ironic, however, that androgyny applied to transportation is more transitional—that is, reversible—for women than for men, because women, who are the most transitional in terms of fashion, are also the least mobile in society. And mobility is at the heart of the airplane and the cinema. Yet the slimming down of the androgynous body is closer to an antianthropomorphic abstract mode rather than to the eugenic, procreational expansion of female form achieved through Astrea's gynandry.[33] The latter is a form of reproduction with no production, a reminder of women's ability to give birth by housing another body inside one's own, thus lengthening and reinforcing the oedipal metonymic genealogy that reduces them to procreative agents.

Androgyny is more about suggestions and leaps, layers and hints, and it is the opposite of outright expansion, seriality, and incorporation. As a visual form, androgyny would look odd in a colonial or an industrial narrative or in a family saga, where the emphasis would be on clear-cut sexual, class, and racial roles. In conjunction with flying, androgyny means abandoning one's own heavy shape to the earth in order to experience a metaphysical transition or corporeal transfiguration to the extreme of self-effacement and to the point of veering toward the unrepresentable, the otherworldly. Such a process of self-evacuation is antithetical to gynandry's embodiment. And, in the context of Catholic Italian culture, what could the cultural model of this bodiless, nonsequential, antioedipal leap into abstraction be?

Within the Italian visual culture of the silent period, the strongest term of reference available to the more or less androgynous and arabesque-like film diva was the mystical iconography of the baroque. Put another way, the undulating silhouette-in-jouissance of Bernini's Saint Theresa matched the serpentine line of the art nouveau arabesque as well as the convulsions of the diva's hysterical acting style.[34] It is interesting to note that a religious subtext of self-denial informs Ester Danesi Traversari's account of her first flight over Rome. When she published her impressions on the pages of *La Donna* (1921), the woman journalist wrote:

> Everything seems incredibly small, forsaken, lost during our physical elevation which nearly resembles a spiritual one. This is perhaps what death is like, death which is always near all of us, but we do not feel it, vibrating as we are from this unparalleled joy of flying.[35]

The Virgin Mary's holy body gets to fly because it is "asexual" and hence "angelic." In this case masochism as mysticism wins over the fulfillment of sexual desire; it also defeats the dream of flying that Freud associated with the discovery of sexuality.[36] Traversari's remarks are mostly introspective; and she only briefly touches on why the landscape excites her. Even then, her words are more metaphorical than accurate: the smallness of things down there reminds her how frail mankind is, and her joy, in the end, is like that of a soul traveling toward Paradise. In conclusion, the airplane, within film culture, functioned like a palimpsest-object. The film diva was hidden behind its extremes of freedom and death, and Saint Theresa was hidden behind the diva's extremes of self-destruction and love everlasting.

While it is certainly true that the film diva as a cultural type leans more toward the femme fatale of the nineteenth century, it is also important to remember that crashing during flight could be seen as a demonstration of will-to-power, though one with a negative, masochistic coefficient. And, in some cases the will-to-power stored in the airplane fad was an opportunity for the new woman of modernity to express her enjoyment of life and self-consciousness about agency. This kind of positive voice can be found in Sibilla Aleramo's "Il mio primo viaggio aereo" (1925). Aleramo, one of the most famous and openly feminist writers in early-twentieth-century Italy, described a flight she made in 1920 from Le Bourget airfield, near Paris, to Croydon, borough of London. She writes:

> Only three passengers on board: we were three women. . . . The world. Light areas, dark areas. Subdivisions and quasi-childish, elementary categories. Even time is suspended. Light, a huge light. Behind me the pilot, who knows the invisible way. The ship bounces up and down and has its own jarring song, as if it were giving rhythm to whatever we bring into space, our powers and our frailties. . . . The cruel life, life overflowing with bitterness, where justice and transcendence exist, yes, but too often they are veiled by our tears and by our fatigues, life on that day, up in the sky, a thing made of air, something that a trifle could have blown away, scatter in the happy, azure mists, without regrets, life was something tenuous but imbued with an infinite grace. . . . Thus, if we cannot be sure about anything, if the most beautiful things, which have just happened, can look like ephemeral figments of the imagination, why should we worry about tomorrow's countenance?[37]

In contrast to Traversari's inward gaze and somewhat mournful tone, Aleramo actively enjoys the new scale of landscape and thought. She shuns Traversari's language of finitude and sublimation, and instead celebrates lightness as a form of infinite freedom, seeing as mobile and phantasmagoric, and memory and imagination as sources of self-confidence.

Femininity in Flight

Envisioning the Future through the Past:
Metaphor and Metonymy

Unfortunately, the deployment of mysticism as a model of femininity suggests that Italian women struggled to move forward and dreamt of flying upward. From the point of view of social emancipation, their choice was not much of a choice. In fact, the visual forms available at the time—the grotesque and the arabesque—spelled out two options: either femininity was a nonhuman, almost bestial identity, or it was a flight, a sort of saintly death.[38] Significantly, the film diva's avoidance of gynandry as figurative enlargement, and her choice of androgyny as liminal downsizing, was based on a "negative" economy of metaphorical replacement through loss, absence, and lightness rather than on a "positive" lawful regime of metonymical appropriation through gain, accumulation, and conquest.[39]

To be sure, the oedipal subtext of the Icarus and Daedalus tale, just like the airplane as seen by Marinetti and D'Annunzio, was a metonymical way of mastering time and space and of claiming a masculine monopoly on modernity. Of course, the metonymic chain includes the airplane, which was an extension of the cinematic mobilization of looking. But, owing to her operatic and consequently premodern roots, the diva's iconography of flying is neither compatible with modernist technological metaphors nor applicable to metonymies about twentieth-century industrialization. Borelli's jupe-culotte in *La memoria dell'altro*, for instance, was an extension of the male pilot's outfit brought to the female body, but it became fashionable because it also recalled the traditional Pierrot's costume from the premodern days of the Commedia dell'Arte. Put another way, the jupe-culotte established itself as an acceptable garment for women's daily wear, and not just for female pilots, because it was the most skirtlike-looking pair of pants conceivable at the time. This argument finds confirmation in *L'histoire d'un Pierrot* (1913), a story with a lesbian subtext of the love between Lisette (Leda Gys) and Francesca Bertini in the title role, who elegantly wears the jupe-culotte. Except for the death of Lisette's beloved bird, there is no other avian reference in this pantomime staged in a timeless, arcadian setting.[40] The bird, however, plays a crucial role in the narrative, for his death marks the crisis of Lisette's and Pierrot's marriage. Hence the bird can be seen as a veiled metaphor of sexual flight that bonds the two characters.

On the whole, the theme of femininity in flight amounted to an utterly antitechnological, quasi-therapeutic imagery of veils, feathers, and butterflies, of the winged sphinx and the rising phoenix. Even Gustave Moreau's famous *Salomè* (1876), a major source for the cruel femme fatale, had a pair of little wings attached to her feet when she was dancing on tiptoes at the court of Herodes. The following example about the reinscription of aerial iconography into a premodern register is meant to further demonstrate the continuity of aerial imagery from orientalist fin de siècle painting to silent Italian cinema. Toward the end of Giovanni Pastrone's *Tigre reale* (1916), Countess Natka (Pina Menichelli) lies dead. While her lover mourns the beautiful Russian aristocrat, a huge fire breaks out in the Grand Hotel, where the couple is having their secret and final tryst. The flames invade the screen and for a while everything seems lost; the flames seem to predict their condemnation to hell. And yet a utopian fantasy of romantic love prevails at the end. It becomes clear that, just like Shakespeare's Juliet, the diva only appeared to be dead, owing to the effect of a special drug. More youthful and defiant than ever, she rises again and embraces her mate. Reborn like a phoenix, the bird of eternal youth, Menichelli and her lover leave the burning hotel and are seen against a completely unrealistic background of stars and cherubs. They sail away on a flying vessel, an aerial ship for dreams of never-ending love, while the rest of the world is falling to pieces.

This premodern, fantastic approach, of course, ranges from the arabesque to the grotesque extreme. Pina Menichelli's bizarre owl-like headdress in Pastrone's *Il fuoco* (1915) and Ida Rubinstein's vulturelike motions as Basiliola in Gabriellino D'Annunzio's *La nave* (1921) show how the arabesque of birds flying out into the freedom of an abstract design can turn into the grotesque incorporation of birdlike features expressed by the strikingly elongated body of Basiliola, the ultimately superthin female vamp and killer of men. Likewise, Menichelli, in *Il fuoco,* seems to emerge out of the bushes like a predatory bird. In *La nave*—a monotone and nationalistic tirade directed by D'Annunzio's son, Gabriellino—the dancer Ida Rubinstein, one of D'Annunzio's many lovers, is all beak and bony arms and legs, with a body as angular as the arrows she uses to kill a group of scantily clad, sexy male prisoners, who are trapped inside a pit. Their frenzied gestures are competitive and attention-seeking. Their behavior suggests that they both welcome Basiliola's cruelty and beg her for mercy. The sadomasochistic subtext of this scene in *La nave* echoes Rubinstein's famous performance in the ballet *Saint Sebastian* (1911) by Claude Debussy, a text where the arrow is an instrument of both pleasure and pain.

In the sequential, teleological increase of metonymy, the airplane is only

Femininity in Flight

one element in a long list of new, interrelated inventions, including the cinema. Metaphor, instead, requires the erasure of one image (woman, for example), which is, in turn, replaced by or transformed into another (the butterfly). The butterfly stands for the flight into a new sense of self. Here, the butterfly is an alternative to, or substitute for, the airplane, because the new technology is not easily accessible to women. This is to say that metaphor and metonymy are not unrelated, but the first emphasizes a mental twist conducive to metamorphosis at the expense, if need be, of logical, consecutive development, whereas the second underscores a historically grounded linear movement from one stage to the next. Veils, feathers, butterflies do not mark a logical progression from one stage to the next, but they are only exchangeable and equivalent aerial images. With metaphor, imaginative, analogical associations win over the causal, rational links of metonymy. Premodern iconography fulfills wishes for achievements that are unattainable even in the modern present.

One very complex antimodern or premodern example of aerial imagery used as a metaphor for children's toys occurs in Carmine Gallone's *Maman Poupee* (1920), starring his wife, the diva Soava Gallone. In this film the diva plays an unhappily married woman who draws comfort from her children's miniature world of little houses, streets, rivers, lakes, and villages. But the scale of toys is also the way things look from the pilot's cockpit as the airplane surveys the land below.

As long as the modern technology of flight is linked to childhood and the imaginative power of a children's garden party, Maman Poupee enjoys the aerial point of view. But during the costume party, a sort of eighteenth-century masquerade, the unhappy wife performs as a life-size mechanical doll, gyrating unto herself, expressionless and stiff. Maman Poupee's movements are so rigid and repetitive that they dehumanize her, making her into an oversize toy. In this she is the polar opposite of Evil Maria, a life-size robot in Fritz Lang's *Metropolis* (1927), namely a nonhuman creature that looks and acts utterly human. Not only does she smile lecherously, but she can twist and curve with all the elasticity of human musculature during her seductive snake dance before a crowd of lustful men in tuxedos and monocles. It is intriguing that the curving posture is not available to Maman Poupee, whose movements are either linear or circular. By contrast, Evil Maria's sinuosity suggests that the curve, in and of itself, is evil and anti-industrial, since it is precisely the kind of seductive and pleasurable movement reserved for the wealthy and denied to the faceless workers of *Metropolis*. Their dehumanized behavior makes these workers much closer to the mechanical appearing of Maman Poupee. All this goes to show that, in *Maman Poupee* and in *Metropolis,* the intersections of class and gender literally undermine each other's claim to modernity.

The linear rigid movement is both industrial and antiseductive, but also hypnotic, and, finally, premodern to the extent that it is more about production than consumption; whereas the curve is at once opposed to regimentation, alluring, and a stimulant to consumption, hence fully modern. What the comparison between Evil Maria and Maman Poupee shows is that Lang's android or replicant incites male desire, and, for this very reason, Evil Maria appears as an automaton endowed with an agency, that is, an evil, transgressive mind of her own. Gallone's human, but also brainless, doll simply executes a few tasks over and over again like any other gadget, beyond or below good and evil, because her only will is to move for the sake of doing something. Deprived as Maman Poupee is of any will to please, even at the level of her own appearance, she is nobody and she has no body. Only redundant movement is left, a movement that produces nothing but a spectacle of itself.

In Gallone's *Maman Poupee,* the toylike miniature world is replaced by the real size of people and things when the observer's feet are on the ground. Yet this is exactly when Maman Poupee as moving life-size doll spells out her predicament as an unhappy wife caught in the drudgery of domesticity. An old-fashioned technology often used or depicted by artists from the sixteenth to the eighteenth century—the automaton as a sort of sculpture-in-motion—here becomes the metaphor of overwhelming private despair, whereas the aerial point of view on the miniature world stands for a utopian, but only temporary, space of innocence and play.[41]

Gallone's iconography is doubly misogynist because the airplane is a positive image, but an unviable one for an adult woman, and because the automaton is an outdated technology that discloses the wife's problems in her present life. In either case, in scenes taking the aerial point of view, and in the automaton sequence, Gallone's approach is metaphorical and associational, poetic rather than expository. It is as if the director's choice of iconography, whether it is futuristic or premodern, is at odds with the possibility of linear narration. By virtue of the chiasmus-like structure of her negative associations with technology, Maman Poupee's predicament indicates that both the future and the past are arrayed against the female protagonist in the present.

The diva film's metaphorical rerouting of the future into the past, however, is a two-way street that can also become a bypass around modernity as present history for the sake of a postmodern visionary approach. This is why a scenario of postmodern utopian rebirth through premodern imagery

Femininity in Flight

appears at the end of Nino Oxilia's *Rapsodia satanica* (1915), with Lyda Borelli in the role of Alba D'Oltrevita. Her name means Dawn of the Afterlife. She is an aging aristocrat who temporarily experiences the pleasures of eternal youth thanks to a pact with the Devil. At the end of this film, Borelli wears a long, loose-fitting dress made of gauzylike material with winglike sleeves. Instead of looking like a phoenix, she brings to mind a newly born butterfly emerging out of a constricting cocoon.

A small figure in the distant background, she walks through the huge door of her villa. Framed by the camera from below, Borelli's size gradually increases as she moves forward, toward the beginning of a new day, a new identity beyond history. She has regenerated herself into a third being, an alternative to the previous two stereotypes: the evil seducer who is young, sexual, and dangerous, and the aging diva who is grotesque and full of anger at her inability to defy time. Here Borelli is no longer a stereotype. She is not just "woman" anymore, but has become a person in full—and also a paradox, a person with no body, no weight.

During her exit from the narrative, Borelli's dress and posture resemble the arabesques drawn by the veils of Loie Fuller (1862–1928) and her winglike use of her arms.[42] An American dancer loved by the futurists, Fuller was famous for her choreographies involving veils and electric lights, a veritable mixture of premodern and industrial accessories. Thus she invented a feminine type situated between the cruel Salome and the technologically oriented *donna moderna*. During the electric-light-and-veil dance, Fuller used darkness to hide her body, whereas during the veil dance, her rotund figure would completely disappear in the moving folds of the light fabric attached to long, thin sticks. Wings of light for Fuller and wings of gauze for Borelli: this is how the divas of film and dance kindled the imaginations of men and women who turned to flight and its metaphors to reinvent themselves at the turn of the century.

Wings: Flying out of the Labyrinth

One more element in this discussion needs to be linked to the visual forms of the arabesque as seductive ornament and the grotesque as hysteric convulsion. This is Daedalus's labyrinth, a space overcome only through flight or by Ariadne's thread, a metonymy for fashion. Fashion is such a powerful way of reimagining oneself that it can function as movement without moving, a phrase that can also summarize the cinema. Without Ariadne's thread, however, Daedalus's labyrinth is a space of disorientation. It has

71. Lauretta Vinciarelli, *Wings,* 1998. In 5 panels. 22 × 30.
Courtesy of the San Francisco Museum of Contemporary Art.

been traditionally associated with the female body and the ruling of illogical emotions because either too much change or not enough is taking place. Whereas Borelli's fans once found a way out of the labyrinth through the pilot's jupe-culotte, the question remains as to what has become of this aesthetic solution today. Since it is difficult to prove change in the private perception of gender roles above and beyond public laws and political conquests, I begin to find an answer through just one artistic example: Lauretta Vinciarelli's *Wings* (1998), an elongated winglike painting made of light and sky — sky that could be sea, and light that could be air. These are all formless entities that do justice to the evocative power of reverberations and depths, luminosities and shadows. Like Daedalus, Vinciarelli was trained as an architect; her piece is about a moment or, as critic Diana Agrest has argued, an event, a metaphysical suspension in time outside any recognizable space.[43] Yet we recognize in Vinciarelli's alternation of lighter and darker colors the no-where of abstraction intertwined with the now-here of utopia. Clearly this space is antianthropomorphic: its extension goes beyond the reach of human arms. Yet this space is clearly classical, so centered and stable: it is the image of a timeless yearning that never ends. It is as if out of Vinciarelli's architectural training, the wings of a new kind of imagination had been born. But there is more: with Vinciarelli's *Wings,* Borelli's dance of veils at the end of *Rapsodia satanica* can become a moment of metaphysical concentration and projection when everything stands still, beyond the body and beyond death, while the mystery of the cosmos is temporarily solved. And it is this solution, allegedly a product in suspension or out of sync with history, that makes the space both classical and utopian.

Like Daedalus, the architect who flew out of his own labyrinth and

Femininity in Flight

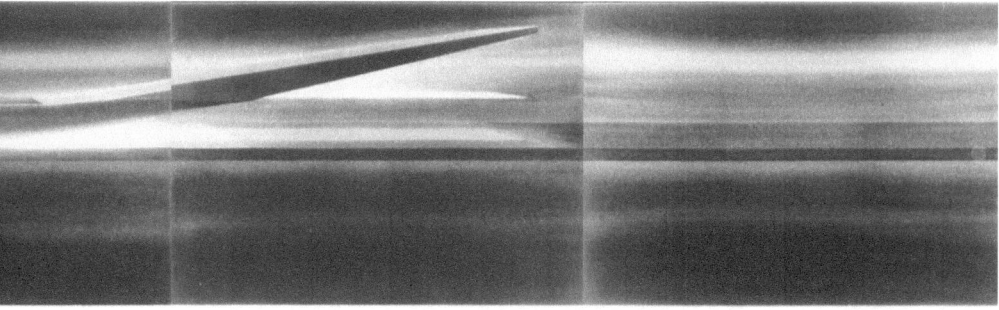

reached a fabled land of eternal youth, Vinciarelli, the architect who paints, wants to take us to Sicily. In *Wings,* the freedom of abstraction defies the labyrinth of the female body, its ties to life and death. Vinciarelli's canvas surrenders to the eye of the viewer's imagination just as the viewer's eye is also consubstantial with a space that moves without moving. And this is why Vinciarelli's eye as an architect and a painter — helpless and extensive, exploratory and vulnerable — posits a viewer's eye that belongs to a cinematic spectator. Looking at *Wings,* we feel we are traveling to the end of time, to the edge of the world, without ever leaving our seat. *Wings,* then, may be about flight, but it is also about the modest trembling of eyelashes, or the horizontalized strip of humble celluloid flickering through the projector. In *Wings,* motion, vision, and light belong only to themselves, and are part of another time, another place, another world.

What can studying the silent film diva in the light of the new woman and the airplane teach us about the history of visual forms such as the arabesque and the grotesque — some of them leaning toward metaphor, others toward metonymy — in relation to processes of historical change? In this essay, the curve of art nouveau, of the airplane, of the diva's acting style is nothing but a form of replacement, an imaginative twist of mind usually called "metaphor," a looping outline of substitutions set against the step-by-step sequence of metonymies, of chronologies, and of stories in search of a final goal for the male hero. The curve as metaphor is the only possible revitalizing and rewriting force of the Icarus myth, for the wing itself curves during flight. A "new" Icarus replaces the young, dead son and the old, wise father, thus enabling the airplane's popular success among men and women at the turn of the century. And this new Icarus, neither father nor son, is also the airborne, secret messenger of women's hopes for the future, for a time of new roles outside the realm of the patriarchal family and oedipal genealogies.

Historical change, when it comes to gender roles, is hardly ever, only, and exclusively linear, generational, or oedipal, and metonymical in a visual sense. That is, it rarely happens as a singular, direct transit from old to new. Rather, linear change is often mixed with transformations and transfigurations, so that the figurative element, or the normative unit of measure, is taken over by abstraction or by some kind of antilinear rerouting to the point that space and time become interchangeable. This rerouting, then, is made of replacement images or metaphors together with development images or metonymies. But the replacement image is more powerful than any other image, for it is about both the disintegration of the labyrinth and the circularity of the sphere. In other words, it is comparable to the metaphysical presence of an absence and, as such, it is like an ephemeral, extracorporeal leap forward into a lingering shadow left behind by the past.

Notes

1. On the cinema, the airplane, and subjectivity, see Paul Virilio, *War and Cinema: The Logistics of Perception,* trans. Patrick Camiller (London: Verso, 1989). On the cinema and the train, see Lynne Kirby, *Parallel Tracks: The Railroad and Silent Cinema* (Durham: Duke University Press, 1997). On airplanes in Italian popular culture, see Piero Botto, "Emilio Salgari e l'aereonautica," in *Emilio Salgari: Documenti e testimonianze* (Predappio: Edizioni Faro, 1939), 154–160. An excellent source on aviation and European culture is Robert Wohl, *A Passion for Wings: Aviation and the Western Imagination* (New Haven: Yale University Press, 1994).
2. The Versailles treaty (1919) prohibited Germany from developing an air force of its own. By contrast, Italy produced the first theoretician of the air, General Giulio Douhet. Born in Caserta in 1869, Douhet began to write in 1909. In his major book, *Il dominio dell'aria,* translated over and over again in several languages, he argued that the air force was so new a weapon that it was best to develop it independently of the army or the navy. This insight proved to be wrong since, during World War II, coordination became the name of the game. In addition, among the armed forces, Douhet maintained that the airplane marked the beginning of total war, where combat was taken, beyond the battlefield and the trenches, in the cities and the factories. He was especially interested in the use of bombing campaigns to break down the morale of the civilian population. Unfortunately, Douhet's second theory was well received by Hermann Goering, who organized the Luftwaffe, and by the American

Femininity in Flight

Curtis Le May, who organized the bombing of Hiroshima. Douhet's name also remains attached to the tragedies of Guernica and Dresden, and, most of all, to Hitler's Battle of Britain.

3 On art nouveau and the arabesque, see Giovanna Massobrio and Paolo Portoghesi, *La Donna Liberty* (Rome: Laterza, 1983); Debora Silverman, *Art Nouveau in Fin-de-Siècle France: Psychology, Politics, and Culture* (Berkeley: University of California Press, 1989). Very useful is the *Journal of Decorative and Propaganda Arts* 13 (summer 1989), a special issue titled "Lo Stile Floreale/The Flowery Style."

4 Filippo Tommaso Marinetti, *Mafarka le futuriste: Romain africain* (Paris: Sansot, 1910). This is not the only work where Marinetti turns to the airplane; the fad exploded in the 1930s with futurist aerial painting and aerial poetry. Other relevant works by Marinetti are *The Monoplane of the Pope* (1911); *The Bombing of Adrianapolis* (1912), written during the Libyan Campaign; and *L'aereopoema del Golfo di la Spezia* (1937). *Canto uomini e macchine della guerra mussoliniana* (1940) was written before Marinetti left for the Russian front and is dedicated to two famous aviators, Italo Balbo and Bruno Mussolini. Finally, shortly before he died, Marinetti wrote one more piece: *L'aereopoema di Cozzarini, primo eroe dell'esercito repubblicano*. On the place of the airplane in futurist iconography, see Enrico Crispolti, *Il mito della macchina ed altri temi del futurismo* (Trapani: Celebes, 1969); and Enrico Falqui, *Bibliografia ed iconografia del futurismo* (Florence: Casa Editrice Le Lettere, 1988).

5 Gabriele D'Annunzio published *Forse che sì, forse che no* in 1910; the novel is about aviation and an erotic quadrangle. See D'Annunzio, *Forse che sì, forse che no*, introduced by Federico Roncoroni (Milan: Arnoldo Mondadori, 1982). Valuable information about D'Annunzio and the airplane can be found in Wohl, *A Passion for Wings;* in Tommaso Antongini, *D'Annunzio*, trans. Tom Antongini (Boston: Little, Brown and Company, 1938); and Massimo Cardillo, *Tra le quinte del cinematografo: Cinema, cultura, e società in Italia, 1900–1937* (Bari: Edizioni Dedalo, 1987), 122–123.

6 Dario Durbè, *Corè: Vita e dannazione della Marchesa Casati* (Florence: Inchiostro Blue/Ritz Saddler, 1986).

7 On Marinetti, metaphors, and women, see Cinzia Sartini-Blum, *The Other Modernism: F. T. Marinetti's Futurist Fiction of Power* (Berkeley: University of California Press, 1996).

8 Edith Hamilton, *Mythology: Timeless Tales of Gods and Heroes* (New York: New American Library, 1969), 139–140.

9 Nino G. Caime, "Personalità femminili della scena italiana: Lyda Borelli," *La Donna*, 5 February 1911, 19.

10 On the diva as arabesque, see Antonio Chiattone, "La Dive Muette," *La Revue du Cinéma*, 13, 18 (May 1948): 68. On the diva in relation to opera and the femme fatale, see Catherine Clement, *Opera, or the Undoing of Women*, trans. Betsy Wing, foreword by Susan McClary (Minneapolis: University of Minnesota Press, 1988); Wayne Kostenbaum, *The Queen's Throat: Opera, Homosexuality, and the Mystery of Desire* (New York: Poseidon Press, 1993); Susan

Leonardi and Rebecca Pope, *The Diva's Mouth: Body, Voice, Prima Donna Politics* (New Brunswick: Rutgers University Press, 1996); Bram Dijkstra, *Idols of Perversity: Fantasies of Feminine Evil in Fin-de-Siècle Culture* (New York: Oxford University Press, 1986).

11 The expert on hysteria in Italy was Cesare Lombroso (1835–1909), the famous criminal anthropologist from Turin. On this topic, see Lombroso, *La donna delinquente, la prostituta e la donna normale* (Turin: Roux, 1893); on Lombroso and criminal anthropology, see Giorgio Colombo, *La scienza infelice: Il Museo di Antropologia Criminale* (Turin: Boringhieri, 1975). An excellent source in English on these issues is Sander Gilman, *Stereotypes of Sexuality, Race, and Madness* (Ithaca: Cornell University Press, 1985). Also see Mary Gibson, *Prostitution and the State in Italy, 1860–1915* (New Brunswick: Rutgers University Press, 1986).

12 For the term "gynandry," see Cynthia Secors, "Androgyny: An Early Reappraisal," *Women's Studies* 2 (1974): 161–169. On androgyny and flying, see Naomi Ritter, "Art and Androgyny: The Aerialist," *Studies in Twentieth-Century Literature* 13, 2 (summer 1989): 173–193. On the grotesque, see Mary Russo, *The Female Grotesque: Risk, Excess, and Modernity* (New York: Routledge, 1994), 17–51; and Wolfgang Kayser, *The Grotesque in Art and Literature*, trans. Ulrich Weisstein (Bloomington: Indiana University Press, 1963).

13 On history and gender in early silent cinema, see Miriam Hansen, *Babel and Babylon: Spectatorship in American Silent Film* (Cambridge: Harvard University Press, 1991); Ben Singer, "Female Power in the Serial-Queen Melodrama: The Etiology of an Anomaly," *Camera Obscura* 22 (1990): 137; Giuliana Bruno, *Streetwalking on a Ruined Map: Cultural Theory and the City-Films of Elvira Notari* (Princeton: Princeton University Press, 1993). For the study of visual forms, illustrious models are Heinrich Wolfflin, *Principles of Art History: The Problem of the Development of Style in Later Art* (New York: Dover, 1950); Henri Focillon, *The Life of Forms,* trans. Charles Beecher Hogan and George Kubler (New Haven: Yale University Press, 1962); Rosalind Krauss and Yves Alain Bois, *Formless: A User's Guide* (New York: Zone Books, 1997).

14 Michela De Giorgio, *Le italiane: Dall'unità ad oggi: Modelli culturali e comportamenti sociali* (Bari: Laterza, 1992), 253–259.

15 Fausto Montesanti, "La parabola della diva," *Bianco e Nero,* 13, 7–8 (July-August 1952): 55–72.

16 De Giorgio, *Le italiane,* 209–253. On fashion and flying, see Karla Jay, "No Bumps, No Excrescences: Amelia Earhart's Failed Flight into Fashions," in *On Fashion,* ed. Shari Benstock and Suzanne Ferris (New Brunswick: Rutgers University Press, 1994), 76–94.

17 De Giorgio, *Le italiane,* 209–253.

18 According to Antonio Baldini, who refers to *Dizionario moderno,* "borelleggiare" means: "exceedingly feminine behavior of young, brainless women, who model themselves on the aesthetically self-conscious and artificial poses performed by Borelli. The latter, in turn, imitated Duse. Feminine graceful gestures and postures which have disappeared as a result of women's increas-

ingly masculine look" ("lo sdilinquere delle femminette, prendendo a modello le pose estetiche e leziose dell'attrice bellissima Lyda Borelli. Questa a sua volta derivò dalla Duse. Grazie femminili scomparse con la mascolinizzazione delle donne"). See "Vent'anni dopo: *Ma l'amor mio non muore (Love Everlasting),*" *Scenario* 2, 2 (January 1933): 7.

19 Claudia Salaris, *Aero—: Futurismo e mito del volo* (Roma: Parole Gelate, 1985), 90.

20 This contact between Karenne and D'Annunzio is documented in the archives of Il Vittoriale—the poet's luxurious villa on Lake Garda in northern Italy. On D'Annunzio's androgynous women and ventriloquist dandies, the best source is Barbara Spackman, *The Rhetoric of Sickness from Baudelaire to D'Annunzio* (Ithaca: Cornell University Press, 1989).

21 (Diana Karenne) "Lega Aerea Nazionale," *Archivio Generale* 65, 4, Il Vittoriale degli Italiani, Gardone Riviera, Italy. All translations are mine.

22 On the labyrinth in architectural theory, see Manfredo Tafuri, *The Sphere and the Labyrinth: Avant-Gardes and Architecture from Piranesi to the 1970s,* trans. Pellegrino D'Acierno and Robert Connolly (Cambridge: MIT Press, 1987).

23 Significant exceptions to this attitude are Valentine de Saint Point's *Manifesto of Futurist Woman* (1912) and *Futurist Manifesto of Lust* (1913). On futurism and feminism, see also Lucia Re, "Futurism and Feminism," *Annali d'Italianistica* 7 (1989): 253–271.

24 Frances A. Yates, *Astraea: The Imperial Theme in the Sixteenth Century* (New York: Penguin, 1977).

25 On aristocrats and divas in Italian silent cinema, see Aldo Bernardini, *Cinema muto italiano: Arte, divismo, mercato, 1910-1914* (Rome: Laterza, 1982); Gian Piero Brunetta, "Il divismo," in *Storia del cinema italiano, 1895-1945* (Rome: Editori Riuniti, 1979), 73–88.

26 Marcello Berti, *Francesco Baracca: Una vita per il volo* (Lugo di Romagna: Walberti, 1991). Readers with a special interest in Astrea and her colleagues should see Alberto Farassino and Tati Sanguineti, "Amazzoni dell'aria e danzatrici della prateria," *Gli uomini forti* (Milan: Mazzotta, 1983). On *Justitia* (1919), Astrea's most important film, see *Bioscope* (London), 4 January 1920; on Farfalletta, see *I comici del muto italiano,* ed. Paolo Cherchi Usai and Livo Jacob (Pordenone: Cineteca del Friuli, 1985), 42–43.

27 Astrea and her sisters fulfill a eugenic ideal. On the popularization of this female type, see the very humorous novelette by Edmondo De Amicis, *Amore e ginnastica* (1892), introduction by Italo Calvino (Turin: Einaudi, 1971).

28 Available for viewing at the Motion Picture Division of the Library of Congress, *L'histoire d'un Pierrot* (1913) with Francesca Bertini and Leda Gys continues to be a little-understood text possibly because the lesbian subtext—articulated across the relations of costume, voice, disguise, and body—has been ignored.

29 On the history of the Italian nation and the belatedness of its constitution in 1860 in comparison to France and England, see Denis Mack Smith, *Italy: A Modern History* (Ann Arbor: University of Michigan Press, 1959).

30 Kayser, *The Grotesque in Art and Literature,* 33, 39.
31 Mary Russo in *The Female Grotesque* is right in associating the grotesque with risk and stunt rather than with utopia and performance, or metamorphosis and freedom. The equivalent of this connection between risk and modernity, but through the "stunt" of gambling reduced to the throw of the dice, is discussed by Mary Ann Doane, "The Erotic Barter: Pandora's Box," in *Femmes Fatales: Feminism, Film Theory, Psychoanalysis* (New York: Routledge, 1991), 142–162.
32 See D. N. Rodowick, *The Difficulty of Difference* (New York: Routledge, 1991).
33 The connection between procreation and eugenic theory is especially strong in the work of Paolo Mantegazza (1831–1910); see *The Sexual Relations of Mankind* (New York: Eugenics Publishing, 1935).
34 Georges Didi-Huberman, *Invention de l'hysterie: Charcot et l'iconographie photographique de la Salpetriere* (Paris: Macula, 1982).
35 De Giorgio, *Le italiane,* 259. De Giorgio's endnote indicates Ester Danesi Traversari, "A volo, su Roma," *La Donna* 17, 5 February 1921 (15 n. 343). Also on a miniature world seen from an aerial point of view, see Susan Stewart, *On Longing: Narratives of the Miniature, the Gigantic, the Souvenir, the Collection* (Durham: Duke University Press, 1993).
36 On dreams and flying with case studies involving male as well as female patients, see A. A. Brill, ed., *The Basic Writings of Sigmund Freud* (New York: Modern Library, 1995), 356–357.
37 Sibilla Aleramo, "Il mio primo viaggio aereo (1925)," in *Gioie d'occasione* (Milan: Mondadori, 1930), 45–53.
38 I have echoed here the title of Peter Greenaway's book, *Flying Out of This World* (Chicago: University of Chicago Press, 1994).
39 Georges Bataille, *Erotism: Death and Sensuality,* trans. Mary Dalwood (San Francisco: City Lights, 1962). On women mystics, see Caroline Walker Bynum, *Holy Feast, Holy Fast: The Religious Significance of Food to Medieval Women* (Berkeley: University of California Press, 1987); Cristina Maria Mazzoni, "Virgin Births and Hysterical Pregnancies: Neurosis and Mysticism in French and Italian Literature at the Turn of the Century" (Ph.D. diss., Yale University, 1991); Angela Dalle Vacche, "Still Life and Feminine Space," in *Cinema and Painting: How Art Is Used in Film* (Austin: University of Texas Press, 1996), 221–245; and Nick Mansfield, *Masochism: The Art of Power* (Westport, Conn.: Praeger, 1997).
40 For an excellent discussion on gender and modernity based on well-circumscribed case studies and on cultural theory mostly relevant to England and France, see Rita Felski, *The Gender of Modernity* (Cambridge: Harvard University Press, 1995).
41 Horst Bredekamp, "The Question of Movement: Sculpture and Machine," in *The Lure of Antiquity and the Cult of the Machine: The Kunstkammer and the Evolution of Nature, Art, and Technology,* trans. Allison Brown (Princeton: Markus Wiener Publishers, 1995), 1–9.
42 Giovanni Lista, *Loie Fuller, danseuse de la belle epoque* (Paris: Stock/ Editions

Femininity in Flight

d'Art Somogy, 1994). In Claude Chabrol's film *The Swindle* (1999), a dance performance with sticks and veils is extremely reminiscent of Loie Fuller's method, in that the body of the dancer completely disappears into waves of movement.

43 Diana Agrest, "Landscapes of Vision," in *Not Architecture But Evidence That It Exists: Lauretta Vinciarelli* (New York: Harvard University Graduate School of Design, Princeton Architectural Press, 1998), 131–137.

LUCY FISCHER

Greta Garbo and Silent Cinema

The Actress as Art Deco Icon

> The stuff [shown at the 1925 Paris International Exhibition of Decorative and Modern Arts] . . . was not the normal output of commerce. It was extreme in its tendencies and not adaptable to the ordinary lives of our people. Actresses may temporarily take some of the stuff into their living quarters as a passing fad, but even they will soon replace it for another sensation. — Arthur Wilcock, "A New York Decorator's Opinion of the Paris Exposition," *Good Furniture Magazine* (1925)

As a teenager, living in Stockholm, a working-class girl named Greta Louisa Gustafson was employed by Bergstrom's — one of the city's major emporia.[1] When the establishment wanted a salesgirl to appear in *How Not to Dress* (1921) — a promotional film for their women's apparel line — they selected the beautiful Gustafson. She also was featured in the store's catalog, modeling hats like those she sold in Bergstrom's millinery department. Years later, she recalled that among all her customers, she most "envied the actresses!"[2]

Greta Louisa Gustafson, of course, eventually realized her dream — leaving Sweden in 1925 to become Greta Garbo at MGM Studios in Hollywood. What is especially intriguing about the early years of her screen career is her continuing association with fashion — a factor that seems presaged in her adolescent job as department store shop girl. For, during the 1920s, Garbo would not only become a leading American actress, but a prominent symbol of the prevalent design style of the era — art deco. Her identification with this trend (and her constitution as one of its pivotal icons) is especially clear in those Garbo films set in the modern period, where her character is seen in a contemporary context.

Greta Garbo and Silent Cinema

For example, in *The Torrent* (dir. Monta Bell, 1925), Garbo's first American film, she plays Leonora Moreno, a Spanish peasant girl with an extraordinary singing voice. As a young woman, she is spurned by Don Rafael Brull (Ricardo Cortez), a rich landowner's son. Though he adores her, Rafael fails to marry her because his betrothal would displease his overbearing mother. Leonora leaves her village and travels to Paris, where she becomes La Brunna—a famous opera singer. In early scenes of the film, when Garbo is playing a simple rural maid, her demeanor is reminiscent of that of Lillian Gish—subdued and quasi-Victorian. But when Leonora appears in Paris, the actress's bearing is totally transformed. Not only does Leonora become La Brunna, but Greta Louisa Gustafson becomes Greta Garbo.

Significantly, the structure of the film moves dramatically between these two poles and stylistic characterizations. When Leonora bids farewell to her village, she sits on the back of a horse cart—a shawl draped over her head, Madonna style. We are told that "a curtain of gray years" intervened, and that "behind it, Leonora Moreno vanished," and "from it emerged a new star—La Brunna, the idol of Paris." We then see Leonora performing on an opera stage. Shortly thereafter, a title introduces us to "The Café American in Paris," a tony nightclub. La Brunna is shown there in a stunning medium close-up, her hair slicked back, wearing a bold white-and-black striped fur collar. The café stage is done in a contemporary mode, with concentric arches and a tiered stairway. After watching the performance, Leonora approaches one of the players to offer him a tip. As she does so, we finally see the entirety of her dazzling outfit: a full-length lamé evening coat completely bordered with fur. Here, in Greta Garbo's first cinematic "glamour shot," she is adorned in chic fashion and inhabits a modernist space. An art deco diva is born.

Throughout *The Torrent,* at heightened moments of the text, she returns to wearing haute deco couture. After being reunited with Rafael in Madrid, the two plan to elope. But, again, Rafael is too cowardly to fulfill his promise. As Leonora futilely awaits him in her apartment, she wears a black-and-white geometrically patterned cape dress, with a stiff, round, ruffled collar. Thus, as she plays the "fool" to Rafael a second time, she looks like a deco harlequin. (Interestingly, in *Vogue* magazine of 15 February 1925, there is a fashion sketch of a woman with a short, manly Garboesque haircut wearing a dress with an almost identical pattern).[3]

But, clearly, it would not be interesting simply to enumerate the scenes in which Garbo appears in a deco-inspired costume or perambulates through a modernist decor. Rather, what I propose is to analyze the semiological role played by the art deco style in her films and the manner in which it fashions her screen image in the 1920s and early 1930s. In so doing, I bring to bear several new perspectives on the study of Garbo and of art deco, a movement that pervades many decades of Hollywood design, but has escaped scholarly attention in the film studies field. Thus I examine the way that art deco reflects a certain gender politics (not only in the cinema, but in the movement's production of sculpture, lamps, jewelry, and objets d'art). I explore how Garbo's iconic persona is created in relation to deco's complicated codes of femininity (in both her costuming and placement in the set by such deco advocates as Adrian and Cedric Gibbons). I also explore this topic in relation to the broad question of modernity and its particular address to the female subject as new woman. Finally, I investigate how the elements of fashion and mise-en-scène can be made excessively prominent in the genre of melodrama, a form that has received little attention for such stylistic tropes (in comparison to, say, the musical).

Of all the decorative arts styles, art deco was perhaps
the most eclectic, drawing as it did on a wide variety
of historical and contemporary sources. — Eva Weber,
Art Deco in America

But first a word about art deco in order to situate our discussion of Garbo and cinema. Deco was a popular international trend that surfaced between 1910 and 1935. In its ubiquity, art deco affected all aspects of world design including fashion, crafts, housewares, jewelry, statuary, architecture, and interior decoration. The term itself was not coined until the 1960s as an abbreviation of the hallmark International Exposition of Decorative and Industrial Modern Arts staged in Paris between April and October 1925. During the 1920s and 1930s, the movement was known as "modernism" or the "style moderne."

In truth, art deco was not monolithic but had many branches and influences. In its insistent modernity, it was identified with the machine age, both in its imagery and graphics. Not only did deco adopt a rhetoric of the mechanical, it also utilized new modes of fabrication. In its industrial orientation, art deco employed synthetic materials like plastic (Bakelite, Lucite, Vitrolite) and metal (chrome, stainless steel, aluminum, and wrought iron). Characteristically, art deco was known for its streamlined, geometric, and symmetrical patterns — traits associated with the industrial age. In keeping with deco's stark high-tech facades, color was often reduced to the basics: black, white, and silver.

Like modernism itself, art deco was tied to the city and was often deemed

72. Garbo in *The Torrent* (dir. Bell, 1925).

the "skyscraper style." In its bonds to urbane modernity, art deco also echoed various avant-garde movements. From constructivism and futurism, it inherited a love of technology; from cubism, a passion for pure form; and from German expressionism, a penchant for distortion.

While beholden to experimental modes, deco was also palatable to the general public. As Mark Winokur observes: "Deco was accessible . . . in a way the various other modernisms were not."[4] With its emphatic consumer orientation, deco imposed itself on all aspects of American culture: "Art Deco romanticized and then sold soap, tires, and train tickets."[5] While deco artifacts at the high end were available at such elegant stores as Tiffany, knockoffs were accessible at low-end stores.

Despite its resolute modernity, however, art deco also entertained an alternate theme—one that contradicted its futurist tendencies. Like many styles of the era, it was influenced by traditional and even primal forms. Specifically, deco evinced a fascination with the "ancient" and the so-called primitive as rendered through a litany of tropes: From Egypt where King Tutankhamen's tomb had been discovered in 1922, deco embraced pharaonic imagery (from sphinx heads and scarabs to cats). From the broader Middle East, deco recycled the Assyrian/Babylonian ziggurat structure—a pyramidal, terraced tower. So popular was this motif (as the base of furniture or objets d'art) that an entire strain of deco came to be known as "zigzag moderne."[6] From pre-Columbian Mexico, deco drew on the sunray image; and from Africa, it took the stylized mask as well as such materials as ivory and animal skins (zebra and tiger).[7]

Beyond deco's attachment to the ancient and primitive, it courted the "exotic." Some designers appropriated contemporary African American forms — especially those associated with jazz — while others looked toward what was termed the Orient. Deco's attraction to the exotic was registered not only in its iconography (images of lotus flowers or cacti), but also in the materials and palettes it employed. Such rare woods as ebony, thuya burl, palmwood, and macassar were routinely utilized, and colors like jade green became popular. In yet another nod to the Orient, deco favored lacquered surfaces.[8] Clearly, art deco's appropriation of the primitive, ancient, and exotic was both contradictory and problematic. How did a cutting-edge mode justify its perhaps retrograde and nostalgic fixation on the past?

In its American incarnation, the discourse around deco evinced a particular fascination with things French, a logical development, given that the 1925 Paris exposition ushered in the popularity of the style. Stores like Bonwit Teller and Bergdorf Goodman named departments with French terminology: the *vingtième* shops, or the *salle moderne*. This attraction to things French also attached to Sergei Diaghilev's Ballets Russes, which opened in Paris in 1909 and was stranded there for many years as a result of World War I and the Russian Revolution. From this famous company, deco borrowed its sense of theatricality — witness one critic's dismissal of the Paris exposition as fostering a "night-club vision of life."[9]

Given this orientation, it is hardly surprising that deco would also become linked to the movies and, from the late 1920s through the mid-1930s, every aspect of film form was affected by the style. To begin with, it clearly influenced set design through the work of a series of art directors associated with particular studios: Van Nest Polglase at RKO, Stephen Gooson at Fox, and Cedric Gibbons at MGM (where Garbo worked). Second, deco also left its stamp on film costuming, especially that of women, with designers like Adrian and Orry-Kelly working at MGM and Warner Brothers respectively. Third, even the physiognomy of actors was used to create deco-inspired designs. As Winokur notes, through blocking, "stars became generic Deco works, [and] sculpturesque pieces."[10] Fourth, a deco aesthetic informed the graphic idiom of many movie posters of the era as well as the font and layout of studio logos (RKO and Twentieth Century Fox, for example). Finally, deco had a tremendous effect on the architectural design of American movie theaters, especially those elegant and luxurious spaces (like New York's Radio City Music Hall) known as picture palaces. As Donald Albrecht has noted, the ubiquity of the art deco mode on movie screens helped popularize contemporary design in America. As he states: "The adoption of architectural modernism by the popular arts had [a] notable effect.... It successfully promoted the modern style to the general public, making it both more accessible and more palatable."[11]

Art deco also evinced a particular fascination with the figure of Woman. In fact, according to Katharine McClinton, deco can be divided into two broad schools that might be imagined along traditional lines of gender. On one hand, there was the "feminine" curvilinear mode that favored such saccharine imagery as "rose[s], ... garlands ... baskets of flowers, fountains, ... doves, female deer ... and nudes." On the other hand, there was the "masculine" geometric pole in which "[c]urves gave way to angularity and motifs of design tended to be ... dynamic."[12]

Clearly, it is from the former strain that art deco's formulation of the female derives. While her representation has its roots in the romanticized, ubiquitous woman of art nouveau (depicted with wild, flowing hair), in deco this archetype becomes more austere and modern. As Winokur remarks, the "Deco shape—a compression and elongation of the Victorian woman's body—would remain a representational norm for at least the next three decades."[13]

The female figure appears in countless deco objects. Consider the translucent works of glass crafted by French designer René Lalique—with their sculpted maidens or etched nymphs. Ponder, as well, the bronze or glass bases for deco lamps, candy dishes, and candlesticks—often shaped to the female form. Regard the metal ashtrays adorned with standing figures of women, or the knobs of glass powder boxes, which were often shaped like female bodies or faces. Contemplate Lalique's car mascot (or hood ornament), "Victoire" (1928), with its polished glass female head—hair outstretched in the wind. Reflect upon the graceful female figures that adorned glass vases by Marcel Groupy or Argy-Rousseau. Consider Alexandre Kelety's sinister bust, "Modern Medusa," fashioned of bronze and poised on a black marble base.[14]

But the craft most associated with the female figure was ornamental sculpture, items typically sold at jewelry stores. As McClinton notes, "Small sculpture figures were in demand as a decorative accessory in the house of the 1890s and they continued to be used into the twentieth century. They were set on mantelpieces, on library shelves, on marble-topped girandoles or wall brackets."[15] Especially interesting were those made with chryselephantine. Such objects were fashioned from African ivory in combination with bronze, onyx, marble, and exotic woods. They came into vogue as early as 1900 and their fabrication consolidated techniques of hand carving and mass production.[16]

According to Victor Arwas, chryselephantine sculptures fell into four categories: hieratic, naturalistic, erotic, and stylized. Hieratic creations (influenced by the Ballets Russes) were "often mysterious queens of the night, dancers wrapped in the metallic folds of rare and costly fabrics and encrusted with jewels at wrist and ankle, their movements frozen into strange theatrical attitudes."[17] The second major source for hieratic deco sculptures was the silent cinema: its costumes, dress, hairstyles, and theatrical mannerisms. Naturalistic statuettes portrayed female athletes, nudes, and dancers. The erotic category was tinged by perversity. Arwas speaks of "kinky, highly sophisticated women dressed in leather trouser suits, insolently smoking cigarettes."[18] The stylized strain of sculpture was the most abstract, reflecting the influence of cubism, Bauhaus, and the Arts and Crafts movement. As Arwas comments, here "features are simplified . . . and the treatment of clothing is increasingly geometric and decorative, without any attempt at realism."[19]

Clearly, it was not only the statuettes that were modern (with their polished onyx or marble ziggurat bases), but the look of the women represented in them. As Arwas remarks, these works generally depicted women who were "slender and boyish in shape [with] hair bobbed."[20] Clearly, their sculptural form was sold as a product in and of itself.

> The habit and the taste for freedom, adventure, and economic independence is becoming generated among millions of women who once merely trod the ancient beaten paths. — Havelock Ellis, *Little Essays of Love and Virtue* (1921)

Clearly, in its staunch modernity, the art deco style was associated with the rise of the new woman, and there is no film star of the late 1920s or early 1930s who so embodies this breed as Greta Garbo. Her biographer, Barry Paris, speaks of how Hollywood had trouble factoring Garbo into its rigid dichotomy of mother versus whore. For she was "neither virgin, vamp, nor flapper, but an entirely new female animal" with "personality enough to make free love sympathetic" to a Puritanical American public.[21] Realizing the uniqueness of her screen persona, Garbo wrote home to Sweden: "They don't have a type like me out here."[22]

Greta Garbo and Silent Cinema

Certainly, the publicity that circulated around Garbo highlighted her sophisticated persona. In a 1935 *Photoplay* article, Ruth Rankin fuels the anxieties of her married female readers in the wording of a caption she places below a photograph of the star: "Maybe you are one of those wholesome-as-bread-and-butter women, and your husband does emotional cartwheels at the mention of the glamorous, languorous-eyed Garbo."[23] Yet another *Photoplay* writer, Ruth Biery, remarks that the "new type" of screen heroine Garbo represents "is an outgrowth of modernity"— the same trend that produced art deco.[24] The specter of the independent woman is apparent in numerous Garbo films of the period in which she plays a female who is unconventional on both the sexual and moral planes. In the words of Garbo's companion, Mercedes de Acosta, the actress played women who "lived gallantly and dangerously."[25]

In *The Torrent*, Leonora abandons her sheltered rustic life to seek fame in a European metropolis. When we first encounter La Brunna in the Café American, other diners stare at her and remark that "she has had many affairs." Similarly, when Rafael flees to Madrid to elope with Leonora, a village elder chastises him for risking his honor "for a woman whose amours are the talk of all Europe."

Garbo enacts a similar character type in other movies of the era. In *Flesh and the Devil* (dir. Clarence Brown, 1926), she plays a seductress who ignites a feud between two lifelong friends. In *Love* (dir. Edmund Goulding, 1927), a version of *Anna Karenina,* she plays a married Russian woman who has a sexual liaison with a military officer. In *The Divine Woman* (dir. Victor Sjöström, 1928), loosely based on the life of Sarah Bernhardt, she plays a country girl who is made a star by a womanizing impresario. In *The Mysterious Lady* (dir. Fred Niblo, 1928), she plays a Russian spy, who, in the process of stealing secrets from Austria, double-crosses her lover. In *A Woman of Affairs* (dir. Clarence Brown, 1928), she plays a lady whose scandalous sexual past destroys her marital future. In *Wild Orchids* (dir. Sidney Franklin, 1928), she plays a wife who allows a flirtatious Javanese prince to court her. In *The Kiss* (dir. Jacques Feyder, 1929), she plays a married woman whose dalliance with a younger man leads to her husband's murder. In *The Single Standard* (dir. John S. Robertson, 1929), she plays a footloose bachelorette who has an affair with an artist/adventurer, accompanying him to the South Seas. Finally, in *Mata Hari* (dir. George Fitzmaurice, 1931), she plays a spy whose erotic charm ruins both men and nations. In all of these films (which are set in the modern period), the license of Garbo's screen character is identified with an art deco aesthetic.

In some works, the connection to art deco is somewhat different. It is sig-

73. Garbo in *Wild Orchids* (dir. Franklin, 1928).

nificant that in *Wild Orchids,* when Lillie Sterling (Garbo) meets up with the roguish Prince de Gace (Nils Asther), she is accompanying her elderly husband, John (Lewis Stone), on an ocean voyage to Java. It is here that the film evinces deco's fascination with the exotic. When the prince romances Lillie on shipboard by moonlight, he compares her to Javanese women: "You are like the orchids of your country—you have the same cold enchantment.... In Java the orchids grow wild—and their perfume fills the air." Later, when the ship docks and she and her husband vacation at the prince's palace, she playfully dons a native costume (which her stuffy husband summarily rejects). Clearly, in the film and in American culture, deco's championing of an orientalist aesthetic (in women's fashions and domestic furnishings) is meant to infuse the staid Western world with the alleged carnality of the East. Though attractive, such sensuality is suspect when attached to the female.

Like Erich von Stroheim's *Foolish Wives* (1921), *Wild Orchids* sees Lillie as somewhat justified in her entertaining adultery, given that her husband completely ignores her and refuses to heed clear warnings about the lascivious prince. In one scene, for example, as Lillie and John retire to bed, she confesses that the prince has tried to kiss her. John, however, does not hear her as he dozes off to sleep. In allowing spectator sympathy for Lillie's conflicted desires, the film reflects progressive changes in society's attitudes toward female eroticism. Advances in contraception had relieved women of continual fears of pregnancy. Furthermore, it was acknowledged that women could experience sexual pleasure. As Samuel D. Schmalhausen noted in 1929, "The happy slogan of the newer generation of feminists, honoring love as radiant passion, is: orgasms for women."[26] Moreover, problems were acknowledged concerning female sexual fulfillment in marriage as greater expectations were placed on the conjugal bond. A newspaper article of 1919 states that "The rock on which most marriages split is the failure of the husband to continue to be the lover."[27] This is, certainly, the situation that confronts Lillie in *Wild Orchids,* as her lust for life is awakened by the seductive Eastern prince. While, on one level, the positive valence associated with exoticism in the film is identified with a deco aesthetic, so is the negative. Ultimately, the narrative validates the latter by having Lillie remain with her repressed Western husband at the film's end.

Nowhere is the theme of orientalism so strong in Garbo's career as in *Mata Hari.* When we first meet our heroine, she is performing an exotic dance in a Parisian nightclub. As turbaned musicians play indigenous instruments and incense burns on the stage, Mata Hari enters garbed in a long silky gown trimmed with sequins and layers of flowing scarves. On her head, she wears a jeweled cap with a hanging pendant, topped off with a multitiered spiked ornament. On her ears dangle huge gems. On the stage is a large Eastern statue (from the "sacred temples in Java"), to which she makes an offering, intoning, "Shiva, I dance for you tonight." To emphasize the scene's exoticism, many shots are framed through the multiple arms of the statue. At one point, her routine becomes decidedly carnal, as she throws off her shawl (as though executing a striptease) and begins to undulate. Throughout the sequence, we cut, repeatedly, to two men watching her perform—General Shubin (John Barrymore), an old lover, and Lieutenant Alexis Rosanoff (Ramon Novarro), a prospective one. The latter gapes and gawks at her, overtaken with desire—making clear the connection between deco exoticism and modern female eroticism.

In later sequences of the film, while Mata Hari's attire remains orientalist, it is toned down as compared to her stage costume. After her dance performance, she meets with General Shubin. Though she wears an exotic headdress, she sports a rather simple, full-length, lamé wraparound dress. Later that evening, as she socializes with casino guests, she wears a jeweled cap with attached earrings and a cutout sequined dress that fits her like snake skin. When Alexis accompanies her home, we glimpse her apartment, which is rendered in deco/oriental style, with arches, stenciled doors, Middle Eastern statuary, and heavy drapery.

In a later scene, Mata Hari wears a deco costume of a more modern kind. Her hair is entirely hidden in a sequin-bordered skull cap. The collar of her coat, her belt, and the off-the-shoulder bodice of her dress are adorned with jewels, as is the outfit's decorative appliqué. Significantly, it is in this deco gown that Mata Hari comes to Alexis's quarters to seduce him and coordinate the theft of his military secrets. In contrast to the contemporary decor of her own apartment, his rooms are adorned with traditional paintings, including portraits of his ancestors. Most prized of these artifacts is a picture of the Madonna, which hangs illuminated by a candle that Alexis has promised his mother would always burn. When Mata Hari arouses him, she orders him to turn off all the lights—including that of the shrine. "Put out that one too!" she commands.

As in *The Torrent,* this scene establishes an opposition between Garbo's character and her suitor's mother. As in the earlier film, where Don Rafael disobeys his mother to pursue Leonora, here, too, Alexis must disregard maternal wishes to find romance. Clearly, by emphasizing this antithesis, the films conceive the modern woman as decidedly *non*maternal. Here we recall Mark Winokur's characterization of the androgynous shape of the streamlined deco female body: "Breasts . . . were reined in so that the feminine would not also mean the maternal."[28]

Two other films of the period cast Garbo as an unconventional female. In *The Single Standard,* based on a novel by Adela Rogers St. Johns, she plays a free spirit named Arden Stuart. As the film opens, an intertitle reads: "For a number of generations men have done as they pleased—and women have done as men pleased." Clearly, this statement makes ironic reference to the film's title and to the fact that there is a double standard in morals and behavior. Arden is introduced to us at a fancy party, set in a grand but traditionally appointed mansion. She is described by other guests as the kind of female to whom "a man would never need to lie." After announcing herself "sick of cards and hypocrites," she leaves the gathering, declaring that she wants "life to be honest [and] exciting." She commands a chauffeur to drive her away at "seventy miles per hour," and he obliges by taking her to a scenic spot. The two become amorous, though he cautions her against it. He asks, "What will people think?" and reminds her that she is a girl who "can't get away with the things a man can." She responds disdainfully: "What difference whether girl or man? Both have the right to—life."

When Arden and the chauffeur return to the party, a scuffle ensues, as the mansion's owner fires the driver for overstepping his bounds. In a shocking development, the chauffeur drives off and purposely crashes his car. An intertitle informs us abruptly: "Thus closed the first chapter in Arden's life. Months later she was still trying to understand it." Certainly, this is a very radical way for a film of 1929 to begin. Not only is the heroine immediately portrayed as promiscuous, but her first lover is dropped entirely from the narrative and his fate is left hanging.

It is significant that, in the sequence that opens the "second chapter" of Arden's life, we see her in her deco-designed home—one adorned with pedestals, modern statuary, geometrically patterned doors, mirrored vanities, boudoir lamps, and platform beds. Furthermore, after she leaves her apartment, she goes to a gallery that advertises (in a deco print font) "Modern Art." It is here that she meets the artist/sailor Packy Cannon (Nils Asther)—an adventurer with whom she becomes enamored. In the portrayal of Packy, there are clear references to Paul Gauguin. One of Packy's paintings portrays exotic, native women, and he is about to set sail for the South Seas—"past pale dreaming islands—in eternal sunlight." On a whim, Arden accompanies him on the voyage, and we see her on board wearing masculine attire. But, after "Weeks...months...strange lands... lonely seas...the blazing Southern Cross...the fiery tropic sun," Packy wants his independence and sends her home.

After Arden returns from her ocean sojourn, people snub her. When one of the town matriarchs invites her to a party, another inquires judgmentally: "You're not going to invite Arden Stuart after that disgraceful scandal?" Displaying a liberal spirit, the matron replies: "You'd be proud to entertain Packy Cannon, right? Well what's sauce for the gander is no longer apple-sauce for the goose." The soiree occurs in a rather traditional home—clearly evidencing how the deco aura is associated, selectively, with Arden. That evening she reencounters Tommy Hewlett (Mack Brown), a young man she had known in earlier days. He declares his love for her and proclaims that he wishes to "take care of" her.

Years pass and we find Arden married to Tommy and the mother of a young boy. Having failed as a wild deco woman, she becomes a respectable parent. As Barry Paris puts it, she is a "girl who demands sexual equality but settles for motherhood."[29] While Arden's new home is decorated in a conventional style, in one scene she wears a deco-inspired lamé coatdress—a signal that trouble lurks. When she learns that Packy has docked in town, she agrees to meet him, and her passion is rekindled. At first, she accedes to run away with him. But then, having second thoughts, she informs him that "One man must always be first in my life—and he is—my son. My life belongs to others now—not myself."

Several aspects of Arden's behavior are interesting. Though she eventually decides to stay with her family, it is fairly radical to have this wife and mother initially ready to abandon them. Even when she decides to remain at home, her vow is to honor her son, not her husband. From this, we might surmise that, had not motherhood intervened, adultery would have been fine. Again the polarity of modern versus maternal woman seems central.

In the final segment of the film, we learn that Tommy has surmised Arden's renewed attraction for Packy. What he does not know is that she has decided to remain at home. Being a noble man, Tommy intends to set her free by staging a hunting "accident" that will release her from her marital bonds. In the scene in which Arden realizes that Tommy's hunting trip is a morbid ruse, she is wearing the most blatantly deco outfit of the film: a black-and-silver knit top with zigzag design. Here, as things are most chaotic and dangerous, she appears again in high deco couture. As in so many American melodramas of the period, the film's conclusion brings a conservative resolution. Tommy is saved from suicide, and repression and responsibility win out; the family unit is preserved.

Garbo's final silent film is *The Kiss,* directed by the Belgian cineast Jacques Feyder who had worked in France in the school of poetic realism. Here she plays Irene Guarry, an independent French wife who is adulterously involved with another man, André Dubail (Conrad Nagel). Like *The Single Standard,* the story opens with Irene meeting her lover. The setting of their tryst—an art museum—seems significant, given the film's engagement of high modernist style. Interestingly, as Irene and André roam through the gallery, they pass paintings with deco overtones: an oriental print and a female nude. Although Irene temporarily terminates her affair with André out of a sense of propriety, another man immediately becomes enamored with her: Pierre Lassalle (Lew Ayres), the young son of her husband's friend. Though Irene is not truly interested in Pierre, she enjoys a flirtation with him and promises to give him her photograph to take back with him to college. One night, he appears at her home, unannounced, while her husband is out. When Pierre requests a farewell kiss, she obliges him. In the heat of passion, he oversteps his bounds and embraces her against her will. Her husband returns unexpectedly at this moment and witnesses the ambiguous scene. A fight ensues between Pierre and Monsieur Guarry and the latter is shot and killed. Since the homicide takes place offscreen, we do not see who has fired the gun. When the police investigate the crime, Irene lies to them—pretending that she was alone that night and asleep when her husband was shot. A trial follows and her former lover, André, a lawyer, defends her. When it is revealed

74. Garbo in *The Kiss* (dir. Feyder, 1929).

that Monsieur Guarry was despondent over financial problems, his death is mistakenly ruled a suicide. After Irene is cleared of culpability, she tells André the truth: that Pierre visited that night and tried to embrace her; that, when her husband attacked the boy, she grabbed a gun and killed him. Despite her confession, she goes free, with André as her companion.

Many aspects of *The Kiss* are quite remarkable, both on a narrative and formal level. Again, the characterization of Irene is bold, with the opening scene showing her in the midst of an affair. Furthermore, she evinces no guilt or regret about her behavior; it is her lover who decides she should no longer "defy convention." We comprehend from the start that Irene's husband is an insensitive bore, and we root for her liberation. (Here, perhaps, we sense the influence on Feyder of the French impressionist film *The Smiling Madame Beudet,* made by Germaine Dulac in 1923). But one illicit relationship does not suffice for Irene or for the drama. When her liaison with André is forestalled, another immediately ignites with Pierre. Again, she skirts the borders of indiscretion, and here her seductive games lead to death. At the end of the story (after telling the jury that she is "indifferent to public opinion"), she literally "gets away with murder" and is allowed to abscond with her paramour. What, for Madame Beudet, is only wishful thinking is reality for the smiling Madame Guarry. A yet more radical note resounds at the end of the film, when a cleaning lady in the court building declares: "I don't blame her! Half us women would shoot our husbands — if we only had the nerve." Clearly, with the institution of the Hays Code a year later, such moral "lapses" would no longer be allowed to taint the popular cinema, especially when centered around female protagonists.

Beyond its plot, the narrative structure of the film is noteworthy for its presentation of Irene's testimony about the facts of the crime. When the shooting first takes place, the camera remains behind the closed door of Monsieur Guarry's study, as the three central characters (he, Irene, and Pierre) battle it out. Hence the spectator does not see what transpires. When, after her husband's murder, the police question Irene, she recounts her story in the form of flashbacks to the night of the crime. Obviously, these scenes are meant to illustrate her deposition and her recollection of the crime.

In one of these shots, we see her on the night of the murder reclining on a sofa, with a clock visible on a table nearby: it reads 9:25. When the police ask her, "What time was it exactly?" we see a close-up of Irene (at the present moment) looking worried, as she replies: "Let me see." We then see the recollected clock with its hands spinning wildly from 8:55 to 9:15 to 9:05 — a trope that signifies she is deceiving the detectives. We return to an image of the murder night, as she crosses the living room and hesitates at the front door. She tells the detectives: "I left the door open — no, I . . ." We then cut back to the murder night and see her closing the door. As she recollects walking into her bedroom, she tells the police: "The windows were open — no, I think they were . . ." At this point, the image depicts the panes of glass magically shutting.

Through these inventive formal strategies, Feyder finds a way to suggest that Irene is waffling about the truth or practicing outright deception (though, at this point, the audience does not have the whole story). If we suspect that she is lying, we assume it is to protect Pierre, and not herself. Whatever the case, the images violate the inherent veracity associated with screen imagery (even of a fictional kind) and instead communicate fraudulence. While many people point to Alfred Hitchcock's *Stage Fright* (1950) for pioneering this dramatic effect, Feyder, in fact, accomplishes a variation of it much earlier. When, after the trial, Irene recounts the true tale to André, we finally see what really happened: in the heat of the fight Monsieur Guarry reached for a blunt object with which to strike Pierre. Afraid he would kill the youth, Irene took a gun from a drawer and shot him. It is crucial that the instability of the text attaches selectively to the figure of Irene—a questionable new woman. But, again, the prime means for signaling her modernity and threat is through her ties to an art deco aesthetic.

As in *The Single Standard,* a few events in *The Kiss* take place in the home of someone other than the heroine. In an early sequence, Irene and her husband dine at the Lassalles—a dignified country estate with all the trappings of tradition. The Lassalle abode is again seen later, when Pierre returns home after his disastrous encounter with Monsieur Guarry. The Lassalle residence contrasts starkly with Irene's, which is decorated in high modernist mode. Irene's is such a complex space that, to comprehend its entirety, the spectator must "stitch" together diverse views offered over numerous sequences. Even then, it is not clear whether the final composite terrain is logistically coherent. In the Guarry living room and entryway are flights of stairs done in zigzag style. A female dancing figure rests on a console in one corner of the salon. The floors are done in polished black, a tone echoed in the outline of an archway. Bold geometric patterns are found on a wall hanging, a sofa, and some curvilinear chairs. A rectangular cabinet sports an exotic ceramic camel. When Pierre comes to visit, he enters through French doors from the garden that are decorated with stained glass panels in the Arts and Crafts mode. Black wall sconces (resembling tiered triangles) adorn the wall. Monsieur Guarry's study has a geometric desk on which is placed a triangular lamp. His bedroom walls are decorated with a linear ceiling border.

But it is Irene's boudoir that is most radically deco—as though the more a room is affiliated with the female body, the more avant-garde the environment becomes. Irene's bed—whose base is done in black striped lacquer—is set on a raised platform. At headboard level is a brash geometric design that is reminiscent of Native American iconography. A wall sconce echoes a similar theme. An abstract black sculpture stands on a pedestal by Irene's bed, and the window panes of the room reveal an Arts and Crafts aesthetic. Some of the curved chairs are covered in a linear fabric. While certain lamp shades reflect a geometric design, others draw on an African motif.

In one bedroom scene (after she and André have parted), the connection of woman and decor is made quite forcefully. A title tells us that Irene has experienced "Weeks of loneliness—of social routine—of striving to forget." We then get an extreme close-up of Irene's face as she adjusts her lipstick with her finger. As the camera pulls back over her shoulders, we realize that we are peering with her into the mirror of a luxurious deco vanity (whose base is, itself, mirrored). On its surface are several modernist objects and, near it, V-shaped wall sconces. Irene, herself, wears a black, metallic, off-the-shoulder dressing gown that lends a modernist touch to her body.

The sets for *The Kiss* were designed under the auspices of Cedric Gibbons—the head of MGM's art department for some thirty-two years. Under his contract with the studio, Gibbons was credited for all films produced in the United States, although he played a prominent role in the creation of only some of those.[30] The man who actually labored day to day on *The Kiss* was Richard Day, a designer who, during his Hollywood career, worked not only for MGM but also for Universal, Paramount, United Artists, Twentieth Century Fox, and RKO.

Although Gibbons did not work on all the projects for which he is credited, his sense of modern aesthetics dictated the "look" of his studio production. As Gary Carey notes, "All [Gibbons's] designs were drawn in accordance with what he called his philosophy of the uncluttered—they were clean, functional and often highly stylized, a look that was to cause a major revolution in movie décor."[31] Significantly, Gibbons was the only major Hollywood set designer to attend the landmark Paris exposition of 1925, and it had a tremendous influence on his career.[32] As a 1937 article in *Theatre Arts Monthly* opined, Gibbons introduced film audiences "to the modernistic settings now so much in vogue."[33] It is interesting that, as Hollywood's deco aesthetic grew stronger, its influence began to supplant that of France. An article in *Photoplay* of April 1934 titled "Hollywood Snubs Paris" states: "[The] movie capital is [now] self-reliant as a style center. Designers no longer look to 'shabby' Paris for ideas."[34]

Cedric Gibbons once said, "In the past the designer of settings has built a notable background for the action of a story. Now he must go one step further; he must design a dramatic background of corresponding value to the theme of the picture. By that I mean a background that augments the drama transpiring before it. *The keynote of this is making the set act with the players.*"[35] Several things are interesting about this statement. First, Gibbons imagines a set as "dramatic" and, furthermore, as reflective of the narrative "theme." Second, he envisions the set as capable of "acting" in a manner commensurate with the players. Hence, if the set must act with the players, the players must act with the set—establishing an equivalence between the two. It is this sense of "parity" (between mise-en-scène and performer) that has been rarely noted in melodrama, a form more apt to be read in terms of pure narrative analysis.

It is precisely this equity that we sense in the dynamics of *The Kiss* and other Garbo films of the 1920s and early 1930s. The art deco sets do not merely provide an artistic backdrop for the actress, nor do they simply fulfill the need for screen realism. Rather, they bear great symbolic force, establishing congruity between decor and heroine, marking her as both avant-garde and perilous. In truth, modernism seems not only to affix to Garbo in these films but also to emanate from her—to constitute itself at the moment she commands narrative space (hence the excessiveness of her home and, especially, of her boudoir). In this regard, such sets fit the category that Charles and Mirella Affron deem "embellishment" in their schematization of filmic mise-en-scène:

> Often opaque, the sets of these films call upon decor for the powerful images that serve either to organize the narrative or as analogies to aspects of the narrative. As a consequence, art direction in these films displays an elevated level of rhetoric, of style.[36]

But a deco aura attends not only to the architecture around Garbo but to her costumes as well. In *The Kiss* (as in *A Woman of Affairs, Love, Mata Hari, The Single Standard,* and *Wild Orchids*), her wardrobe was designed by Adrian (born Adrian Adolph Greenberg). Working in Hollywood between 1925 and 1952, he was the chief costume designer for MGM. Like sets rendered by Gibbons, his costumes were strongly associated with the art deco style. The most modern outfit Garbo wears in *The Kiss* is the dressing gown she sports as she sits at her vanity after breaking up with André. But, in other scenes, she wears more tailored and subdued couture identified with deco's more sedate mode. When she and André have their museum tryst, she wears a simple, formfitting, V-necked dress accompanied by a fur stole. On her head is the requisite cloche hat that hides her hair. Such millinery makes of the female face a simplified, abstract sculpture, and Garbo's stark bone structure is ideal for this fashion. A famous photograph of her by Clarence Sinclair Bull (made to promote *Mata Hari* in 1932) clearly illustrates Garbo's deco physiognomy. According to Michaela Krutzen, her demeanor was highly constructed:

> Photos from 1927 show how Garbo altered her appearance during her first months in the United States to conform to an ideal of beauty which she did not naturally fulfill. Her hairline was evened out, her nose seems to be made narrower and her lips were sloped differently ... Garbo's previously dark and crooked teeth were capped. Garbo was thus brought into line with an existing ideal of beauty."[37]

Krutzen also notes how Garbo generally came to the set hours before the time of filming, since "the creation of Garbo required several hours of work in make-up, hairstyle and wardrobe."[38]

How closely Garbo conformed to the coveted "look" of the era can be seen from perusing women's magazines of the period. One 1928 sketch in *Harper's Bazaar* advertises modern jewelry designed with geometric patterns of lapis lazuli and enamel. The model's hat fits close to her head and her features are reminiscent of those of Garbo.[39] A Lentheric Parfums ad in *House and Garden* of September 1929 sports a sketch of a female head that is shown as though without hair.[40] Again the abstract lines of the face are similar to those of Garbo in Bull's famous photographic portrait.

When Irene meets Pierre at a pet store in *The Kiss,* she wears an elegant black dress and cloche hat. The collar of the outfit is decorated with a black-and-white checked border that flares in a trim that runs down the front of her dress. For an evening at the Lassalles, she wears a simple low-cut sheath, with sequined straps and a jeweled clip. On the fateful night of her husband's murder, she wears a lounging dress whose modernity is registered in its multitoned geometric patches and in the asymmetry of its lapels. Significantly, when Irene stands trial for her crime and a court reporter draws the scene for the newspaper, his sketches look more like fashion prints than they do forensic documents.

Ironically, while within her films Garbo is the height of cutting-edge deco fashion, in her offscreen life she had little patience for haute couture. As Leonard Hall writes in *Photoplay* in 1930, Garbo

> can dress as she darn pleases, and does. If she wants to wear twenty yards of opaque cheese cloth to a formal gathering, it's quite all right with us. In the greatest scene Garbo ever played ... she wore a slouchy old tweed suit and a squashy felt hat. She never looked so mysterious [or] more alluring.[41]

Garbo, herself, confirms her disregard of fashion when she says: "I care nothing about clothes.... When I am off the set I don't want to have to think of clothes at all.... I like to live simply, dress simply."[42]

Also at issue in Garbo's personal attire was the question of its "androgyny." Recall that, at the time, critic Ruth Biery of *Photoplay* observed that "the new cinema heroine can take care of herself, thank you, since she combines, with her mysterious allure, many of the hard-headed attributes and even some of the physical characteristics—the tall, narrow-hipped, broad-shouldered figure—of men."[43] Writing in *Photoplay* of 1935, Adrian touches obliquely on the androgyny of Garbo's attire. As he notes, "Her wardrobe consists of tailored suits, various top coats of the sport variety, sweaters, slacks, berets, sport hats, stocking caps ... and sport shoes. I don't think she has an evening gown and if she has I'm sure she has never worn it."[44] Addressing the issue more directly, Garbo's niece, Gray Reisfeld, denies any "transvestism" in her aunt's apparel. As she states: "She had a great interest in fashion, but it was her *own* fashion.... The pants, the walking suits, the lack of jewelry—all that contributed to what was thought of as 'masculine' but what was really just uniquely *her*. She ran her own train."[45]

At heightened moments of her films (when she is most tempting), Garbo appears in full deco regalia. At times when the drama requires that she pay for her eroticism, her demeanor entirely alters. In *The Kiss,* after Irene has shot her husband and is interrogated by the police, her hair (which has previously been severe and straight) is suddenly frizzy. This gives her face a softer, more Victorian appearance—one appropriate for a long-suffering heroine. When Irene is arrested for murder and awaits trial, she wears a simple black dress. When she takes the stand, she appears in another black outfit, one with a flowing cape and a hat with a trailing veil.

Significantly, when André visits her in prison, two nuns (in long black robes) accompany her. In truth, as the narrative progresses and Irene confronts her crime, she, herself, almost seems to wear religious habits. The same can be said of the closing of *Mata Hari*. When she is tried as a spy, she wears a plain black cape and skull cap. When she is taken to the firing squad (with hair as short as Saint Joan's), she is dressed in black, and escorted by nuns. Interestingly, in describing the simplicity of Adrian's costuming of Garbo, Michaela Krutzen talks of the "monastic severity" of his outfits.[46] The link here between Garbo's screen heroines and holy mothers reminds us of the divide established elsewhere in her films between the deco woman and the maternal female. It is significant that only when the former is stripped of her sexual and modernist charisma can she be associated with any brand of maternity.

Garbo and the screen characters she incarnates are both compelling and troubling—like modernity itself. Her status as art deco icon is telegraphed most clearly in a scene from *The Torrent* in which Rafael surprises Leonora with a visit shortly after she returns to her native village. He comes to her cabin in the midst of a storm, and she gives him one of her deco furs to wear for warmth. Though he is now engaged to a "suitable" woman, he is again overtaken with Leonora's beauty and professes his undying love. She cynically tells him: "I believed in love once and love failed me." She then flaunts her success as a courtesan by showing him a variety of expensive objects that she has received as gifts from her male admirers. One of them is a modern sculpture of a female nude. He peruses it suspiciously, then casts his eyes upon Leonora, as though to compare the two. Nodding affirmatively, she replies: "Why not? A great sculptor made it. He admired my figure." Flashing a hurt, angry glance, Rafael retorts: "Everything they say about you is true," at which point he throws the statue down on her bed. Clearly he is outraged that she has posed for the sculpture, an act that confirms his worst fears about her morality. Stripped of masculinity himself (in transvestite drag, a Venus in Furs), he impotently storms out the door (still wearing her wrap). In this scene, the art deco statue is Leonora—and Leonora is Garbo.

Such self-reflexivity is continually inscribed in the actress's early films. We have already explored the parallels between Leonora and Greta (how La Brunna becomes a star at the moment that Garbo does). But this self-consciousness is evident in other texts. In *The Single Standard,* when Arden Stuart is followed by a masher on the street, she brushes him off by stating: "I walk alone because I want to walk alone." On a similar note, the boat on which she sails with Packy Cannon is called the *All Alone.* Such phrases engage Garbo's reputation for aloofness and independence—qualities that oppose the requirement for women to be ever cordial and social. As Stark Young writes in the *New Republic* of 28 September 1932: "Conceive of someone who stays in when she could go out, who could see people but thinks it a kind of communion, peace, rest or right to be alone sometimes! This has made Miss Garbo almost a national puzzle."[47] Garbo's reputation for reticence and even silence contrasts starkly with her screen image in this era, which speaks loudly and metaphorically through discourses of costuming and mise-en-scène.

Further self-referential elements are found in her films. In *The Kiss,* when detectives question Irene about the murder night, she tells them, "I was all alone." Moreover, the ostensible reason that Pierre Lassalle visits her that night is to obtain a photograph to take back to college. Before he comes, she searches through her desk drawer and unearths a series of portrait prints that resemble actors' professional eight-by-ten glossies. Furthermore, when the murder scandal hits the tabloids, we see a series of newspaper front pages that bear snapshots of and headlines about her. In each case, the newsprint is used by someone for an unseemly purpose: to wrap vegetables or to discard garbage.

One other newsworthy event is significant in *The Kiss*—a real one that had reverberations for the fate of the art deco woman. The reason why Monsieur Guarry is facing economic trouble and seeks a loan from Monsieur Lassalle is because of the world financial crisis. It is referred to directly in the film when Monsieur Lassalle takes the stand and speaks of a "panic on the stock exchange." The opening of *The Kiss* on 15 November 1929 (only seventeen days after the stock market crash) marks an important cultural moment. Lois Banner suggests that, with the economic crisis, many societal gains were lost as the " 'lady-like look' once again became the cynosure of the American woman."[48] Similarly, Robert L. Daniel notes, "The alleged excesses of the flappers and the intrusion of women into the labor market provoked a reaction at the end of the twenties. Women's magazines ... repeatedly reaffirmed traditional views of woman's role as wife and mother."[49] Thus, with the coming of the Depression, not only Irene Guarry but the modern woman stood trial—figures whose "excesses" were linked to the 1920s and a period of perilous social, artistic, and economic change.

Notes

1 Barry Paris, *Garbo: A Biography* (New York: Alfred A. Knopf, 1995), 23.
2 Ibid., 24, 26.
3 "Modernist Art Applied to Painted Fabrics," illustration, *Vogue,* 15 February 1925, 56.
4 Mark Winokur, *American Laughter: Immigrants, Ethnicity, and the 1930s Hollywood Film Comedy* (New York: St. Martin's, 1996), 199.
5 Ibid., 198.
6 Eva Weber, *Art Deco in America* (New York: Exeter, 1985), 12.
7 Ibid., 14, 19.
8 Alastair Duncan, *Art Deco* (London: Thames and Hudson, 1993), 80, 24.
9 Dorothy Todd, "Some Reflections on Modernism: What It Is, Here and Abroad, and What It Is Not," *House Beautiful,* October 1929, 470.
10 Winokur, *American Laughter,* 204.
11 Donald Albrecht, *Designing Dreams: Modern Architecture in the Movies* (New York: Harper and Row, 1986), xii.
12 Katharine Morrison McClinton, *Art Deco: A Guide for Collectors* (New York: Clarkson N. Potter, 1986), 10, 11.
13 Winokur, *American Laughter,* 197–198.
14 Duncan, *Art Deco,* 90; 89, 94; 124.
15 McClinton, *Art Deco,* 185.
16 Victor Arwas, *Art Deco Sculpture: Chryselephantine Statuettes of the Twenties and Thirties* (New York: Academy Editions and St. Martin's, 1975), 5, 7.
17 Ibid., 7.
18 Ibid., 9.
19 Ibid.
20 Ibid., 8.
21 Paris, *Garbo,* 117, 112.
22 Ibid., 111.

23 Ruth Rankin, "Who Is Your Husband's Favorite Actress?" *Photoplay*, February 1935, quoted in *The Talkies*, ed. Richard Griffith (New York: Dover, 1971), 196.
24 Ruth Biery, "The New 'Shady Dames' of the Screen," *Photoplay*, August 1932, quoted in *The Talkies*, ed. Griffith, 197.
25 Paris, *Garbo*, 145.
26 Samuel D. Schmalhausen, "The Sexual Revolution," in *Sex in Civilization*, ed. V. F. Calverton and S. D. Schmalhausen (New York: Macaulay, 1929), 380.
27 "What Makes an Ideal Husband?" *Cumberland Evening Times*, 29 October 1919.
28 Winokur, *American Laughter*, 199.
29 Paris, *Garbo*, 163.
30 Beverly Heisner, *Hollywood Art: Art Direction in the Days of the Great Studios* (Jefferson, N.C.: McFarland, 1990), 341.
31 Gary Carey, quoted in Heisner, *Hollywood Art*, 75.
32 Ibid., 78.
33 Ibid., 39.
34 William Gaines, "Hollywood Snubs Paris," *Photoplay*, April 1934, quoted in *The Talkies*, ed. Griffith, 192.
35 Cedric Gibbons, *New York Telegram*, 9 March 1929.
36 Charles Affron and Mirella Jona Affron, *Sets in Motion: Art Decoration and Film Narrative* (New Brunswick: Rutgers University Press, 1995), 38.
37 Michaela Krutzen, *The Most Beautiful Woman on the Screen: The Fabrication of the Star Greta Garbo* (New York: Peter Lang, 1992), 69.
38 Ibid., 71.
39 "Blue and White," illustration, *Harper's Bazaar*, December 1928, 76.
40 Lentheric Parfums advertisement, *House and Garden*, September 1929, 169.
41 Leonard Hall, "Garbo-Maniacs," *Photoplay*, 1930, quoted in *The Talkies*, ed. Griffith, 270.
42 Paris, *Garbo*, 267.
43 Ruth Biery, quoted in *The Talkies*, ed. Griffith, 218.
44 Adrian, "Adrian Answers 20 Questions on Garbo," *Photoplay*, September 1935, quoted in *The Talkies*, ed. Griffith, 272.
45 Paris, *Garbo*, 268.
46 Krutzen, *The Most Beautiful Woman*, 84.
47 Stark Young, *New Republic*, 28 September 1932, quoted in *Women and Cinema: A Critical Anthology*, ed. Karyn Kay and Gerald Peary (New York: Dutton, 1977), 86.
48 Lois Banner, *Women in Modern America: A Brief History* (New York: Harcourt Brace Jovanovich, 1974), 197.
49 Robert L. Daniel, *American Women in the Twentieth Century: The Festival of Life* (New York: Harcourt Brace Jovanovich, 1987), 87.

The Problem with Periodization **V**

ZHANG ZHEN

An Amorous History of the Silver Screen

The Actress as Vernacular Embodiment in Early Chinese Film Culture

What does it mean to talk about "early cinema" in a Chinese context? How "early"—or how "late"—was early Chinese cinema? Where can we locate it in a broad cultural landscape of modernity, particularly with regard to women's place in it? In the following essay I discuss questions of periodization and historiography in relation to women's roles in Chinese film and modern cultural history. I begin with a historical textual analysis of the silent film quoted in the title, *An Amorous History of the Silver Screen* (dir. Zhang Shichuan, 1931). This self-referential docudrama, which chronicles the rise, fall, and triumphant comeback of a prostitute-turned–film actress in Shanghai, is an exemplary text about the makeup and transformation of early Chinese cinema and its reception. A gender-specific examination of the relationship between body and film technology as evidenced in female screen presence and fan culture allows us to conceive early Chinese cinema as a mass-mediated yet culturally inflected modern experience. Moreover, by inserting and foregrounding woman's place, especially that of the first generation of female stars, in the emerging public sphere represented by the cinema, I reconsider the relationship between cinema and the vernacular movement as well as the interaction of verbal and visual culture within the broader scenario of the democratization of writing and iconography. I argue that the figure of the actress in particular embodies the vernacular experience of modernity in early-twentieth-century China.

"Amorous" Historiography and Early Film Culture

History, for Walter Benjamin, does not unfold in a "homogeneous, empty time." Likewise, historical thinking that attempts to seize in an illuminating flash the image of nonlinear time and heterogeneous experience involves "not only the flow of thoughts, but their arrest as well.... Where thinking suddenly stops in a configuration pregnant with tensions, it gives that configuration a shock, by which it crystallizes into a monad."[1] The year 1931 in early Chinese film history is for me one of those monadic moments when history congeals and implodes, generating as much tension as energy. At that moment, everything seemed possible; all the historical actors found themselves at a masquerade ball that could last forever — but which, of course, did not. Events were taking place at a head-spinning speed as past and present intertwined.

It was a moment when the Chinese film industry, concentrated in Shanghai since the early 1910s, was suddenly seized by an urgency to view self-reflexively its history on the screen, as though propelled by a desire to arrest its own image in a hall of moving mirrors. The craze of the "martial arts magic-spirit" (*wuxia shenguai*) genre was reaching its peak. The advent of sound had triggered a cacophony of public debates as well as a deluge of experiments in various formats, in particular the "dancing and singing" (*gewupian*) genre, to incorporate sound into the silent screen. The film industry was being reconfigured as a result of the establishment of the Lianhua company (which quickly rivaled the veteran Mingxing company) and the campaign to "revive national cinema" (*fuxing guopian*). It was also a time when the Nationalist government took definitive steps to make its legitimacy felt in the film scene by, among other things, instituting a fully fledged censorship organ. The year 1931 was also marked, especially in standard Chinese film historiography, as the turning point at which a more progressive and patriotic cinema began to emerge following the Japanese invasion of Manchuria that same year. That shift was quickened by a new crisis, when, on 28 January 1932, the Japanese also bombarded Shanghai, which brought immense destruction to the film industry.

In the midst of these interconnected changes and on the eve of catastrophe, the Mingxing company, a leading studio in the prewar Shanghai film industry, released an eighteen-reel, two-part feature, called *An Amorous History of the Silver Screen* [*Yinmu yanshi*]. The term "amorous history," or *yanshi* in Chinese, has always denoted deviant history or histories outside or parallel to the official history, often with erotic connotations. Its

An Amorous History of the Silver Screen

usage was particularly prevalent in traditional vernacular literature. *Amorous History,* a product of modern times, stands as the cinematic incarnation of this long tradition. For many decades this film has been ignored, if not purposely omitted, by Chinese film historians. I regard this film, however, as a condensed textual instance that gives expression to the configuration of its particular historical moment. It offers insights into the Shanghai film world poised on a threshold. One of the nine silent films produced by Mingxing in 1931, *Amorous History* is unique in its direct reference, as suggested by the title, to the film world on multiple levels. The film is structured as a backstage drama and showcases the Mingxing studio as a technological wonderland and a simulacrum of the everyday world. It thus also serves as a self-portrait of the Mingxing company and a synecdoche of the broad film world in China in the early 1930s. A docudramatic tale about the vicissitudes in the career of a prostitute-turned–film actress and her troubled personal life, the film presents, more significantly, an ambivalent history about Chinese women's relationship to the cinema—the promise of liberation and social mobility as well as the lure and risks of a new kind of commodification of the body by film technology.

Within this larger frame of reference, the interplay on and off the screen between fiction and reality, between the film world and lived experience, lends important insights to the understanding of *Amorous History* as a self-referential text about film production and spectatorship in China in 1931, a year of historical implosion. It directs our attention to the question of early Chinese cinema in relation to the question of woman and Chinese modernity as a whole. What kind of history could we envisage through the lens of the multiple cameras embedded in the film? Why was the film given the curious generic title "amorous history," and why was it linked to the "silver screen"? Hence, what is the relationship between such an intimate or deviant history to the master narratives of film and national culture of the prewar period as authorized by standard historiography in China? What does this self-referential gesture tell us—beyond the prevalent definition of self-reflexivity often associated with the cerebral modernist obsession with language, interiority, hermeneutic depth, and (masculine) existential angst—about the embodied mass experience of cinematic modernity?[2]

Before I proceed further, a clarification of the term "early cinema" is in order, especially because it has a quite specific reference in film scholarship in the West. More than a period term, "early cinema" functions as a critical category, one that has gained increased attention and weight since the 1978 Annual Conference of the International Federation of Film Archives (FIAF) held at Brighton, England. It refers primarily to the cinema—that is, films as well as media intertexts, industry, and market—between 1895 and 1917. Early cinema has also been alternatively called the "primitive cinema" or the cinema "before Hollywood"—that is, before the emergence of the so-called classical narrative cinema (and the concomitant institutionalization of a particular patriarchal structure of looking) came to be perceived and received as a dominant mode of cinematic storytelling.[3] The conference as well as the annual Giornate del Cinema Muto at Pordenone, Italy, which has made it possible for researchers and the public at large to reexperience early cinema, provided the vital fuel for an archaeological project of rethinking its aesthetic and cultural significance, especially how it contributed to the shaping of a radical new perception of time and space, life and death, subject and object with the onset of modernity.[4]

Scholars of early cinema have arrived at the conclusion that early cinema possessed a set of distinctive aesthetics for (re)presenting the world and lived experience, and that classical narrative cinema, along with the seamless fictional world it created, was not the medium's necessary destiny. This new orientation in historical film scholarship highlights the importance of conjoining theory and practice, critical analysis and archival work, and has opened up many hitherto neglected areas of investigation beyond the films themselves. As early cinema was intimately bound to the practice of exhibition, studies on early audience formation and viewing relations have relocated the experience of early cinema in a wide range of cultural practices such as the vaudeville theater, the amusement park, shopping arcades, and so on. It became possible to envisage the film experience in the broader landscape of modern life, in the street and in the theater, in the city and in the country, and, I hasten to add, in the West as well as in many other parts of the world. In short, the identification and elaboration of early cinema has not only opened new arenas for studying film, but has also offered rewarding conceptual and methodological tools for placing film history in an intermedia and interdisciplinary field.

More recently, a strand of feminist film scholarship has not only contributed to but also critically enriched this new film history by highlighting the aspect of gender, with regard to, among other things, early women film pioneers, and the sexual coding of stardom and spectatorship.[5] This work challenges the prevalent reading of the classical cinema as a seamlessly sutured patriarchal representational system by inserting the conceptual as well as historical female spectator into the picture. At the same time, modes of address such as exhibitionism, heterogeneity, and corresponding patterns of (re)presentation associated with so-called primitive cinema are found to persist in classical cinema. The gender question proves to be of critical importance for understanding the vitality, if not longevity, of not only a particular kind of aesthetic but fundamentally an epistemology and politics.

But how shall we account for early cinema in the Chinese context? And in what ways did women contribute to the formation of the new film culture in early-twentieth-century China? Despite the fecundity of scholarship on early cinema, little has been done about the subject in a cross-cultural field, let alone a consideration of its gender aspects in a non-Western context. In the Chinese context, particularly as used by Chinese film scholars in periodization, the term "early cinema" (*zaoqi dianying*) serves loosely as a common reference to the cinema before 1949, when the Communists drove the Nationalists to the island of Taiwan and founded the People's Republic of China on the mainland. In standard Chinese film historiography, therefore, its connotation has been mainly negative or even pejorative, because early cinema as a whole is not only construed as aesthetically inferior in the evolutionary chain of cultural development (which is also often the case in the Western contexts), but also linked to the "pre-Liberation" and hence feudal and semicolonial political and social system. "Modern," or *modeng*, a term prevalently associated with urban modernity, especially that of Shanghai during the Republican period (1911–1949), conjured up meanings of cultural decadence, sexual promiscuity, social anarchy, and Western imperialism.

More recently, however, with the revival of Chinese cinema and the renewed interest in its historical roots, early Chinese cinema has begun to receive more favorable reassessment, and scholars tend now to make finer periodizations within that long "early" period. Not only have they subtly challenged prevalent ideological assumptions that inform existing historiography of early Chinese cinema, their work as a whole has also tried to delineate the aesthetic and cultural significance of genres such as comedy and martial arts film, which had been largely deemed "vulgar" or "lowbrow."[6] Underlying this diverse, albeit limited, body of scholarly work is the vexed question concerning the political and cultural status of early Chinese cinema, especially in the period before the emergence of the left-wing cinema in the early 1930s.[7] Yet some of these endeavors still betray a one-dimensional historical consciousness and impoverished methodology. *Zhongguo wusheng dianyingshi* [History of Chinese silent film], for example, which was commissioned by the Chinese Film Archive and published on the occasion of the centennial of cinema's arrival in China, is to date the first comprehensive account of early Chinese cinema produced by mainland scholars.[8] The book remains, however, mired in the same evolutionary conception of history, despite its sympathetic revisions of many previously denounced or forgotten filmmakers, producers, actors, and their films.

The unwitting parallel of critical discourses on early cinema in the West and China, despite their divergent circumstances, motivations, and applications, offers an opportune moment to relocate early Chinese cinema in a broader cinematic modernity. The divergent origins of the term in Euro-American and Chinese contexts, and the discrepancies in periodization respectively, alert us to the heterogeneity of the international film scene in the silent period. Rather than trying to find an equivalent—or contemporaneous—period and practice in Chinese film history that squarely fits the category of early cinema in the West, I choose to use the term heuristically for creating a critical space that negotiates its different valences, temporality, and historicity.

The first Chinese film was not made until 1905, and a Chinese film industry as such came into being only in the mid-1920s. The enjoyment and consumption of cinema, however, had already become an integral part of urban modernity with the first public commercial showing in a teahouse in Shanghai on 11 August 1896. The lack of archival holdings of films (actualities, travelogues, educational films, and early short-story films) made before 1922 contributes to the practical difficulty in studying that part of early cinema. Significantly, many features of the extended early cinema in China, in aspects of filmmaking as well as distribution, exhibition, and reception, resonate with similar motifs in the history of early cinema worldwide. The time lag between early Euro-American cinema and early Chinese cinema speaks certainly to the semicolonial nature of Chinese modernity, especially with regard to "belated" technological transfer and implementation. This temporal disparity, ironically, also supplies testimonies to the persistence of early cinema not so much as a rigidly defined aesthetic or period category, but as an emblem of modernity, or rather multiple modernities, on the "non-synchronous synchronous" global horizon of film culture.[9] To disentangle ourselves from the trappings of such a time lag in periodization, a shift in focus from early cinema to early film culture, which includes a wide range of film experiences such as stardom, fan cults, theater architecture, and fashion in addition to what happens onscreen, will allow a more productive interdisciplinary approach to the study of early film history in specific cultural locations. Such a shift will also, more crucially, enable us to expand the horizon of comparative studies of cinematic modernities.

Let me now return to *Amorous History* as a case study to probe the complexity involved in the writing of early Chinese film history, particularly from the perspective of gender. As I indicate in detail below, the film opens onto a geography of film culture, through both its textual inscription and material consumption. As a self-conscious gesture at writing film history on the silver screen, the film and its reception reveal the capacity of the cinematic medium to offer a unique historiographic register in the age of mechanical reproduction of moving images.

According to the synopsis written by publicists of the time, the first part of the film (nonextant) begins with a panoramic view, or establishing montage, as it were, of the rise of Shanghai as a modern metropolis when it was "opened" as an international trading port following China's defeat in the Opium Wars in the mid–nineteenth century.[10] In an urban landscape animated by a prosperous commercial and industrial life, dotted with high-rises and asphalt streets, and crowded with people migrating into the city from all over China and the world, a local film industry is born. One large film company in particular not only boasts a studio with a host of large buildings and a contingent of "bright stars" (*mingxing*—an apparent self-reference to the Mingxing company), but features as well productions that are widely distributed and "popular all over the world" [*fengxing quanqiu*]. One of the bright stars, in the diegesis as well as in real life, rises from the city's pleasure quarters. Wang Fengzhen, played by Xuan Jinglin (1907–1992), is slapped on the face by a client who resents her late arrival. Seeing her tears flowing uncontrollably, the playboy (who is given only a generic name, *Baixiangren*—playboy or hooligan) mocks her: "Since you are so good at crying, why don't you devote yourself to the silver screen to become the oriental Lillian Gish?" He does not, however, expect that his sarcastic joke will prompt Wang to enter the film world.[11] Her dedication and ability to act out the full range of a woman's emotional expression— from the most comic to the most tragic, from that of a young girl to that of an old woman—quickly wins her the title of movie star (*dianying mingxing*). Fang Shaomei, a wealthy dandy, eagerly pursues her by coming to the studio every day and lavishly spending money on her. Wang begins to show signs of negligence in her work. Finally she disappoints the director who has contributed to her stardom by breaching her contract with the studio and becoming Fang's concubine, or according to the fashionable term of the day, entering a relationship of cohabitation (*tongju*).

The extant sequel starts with the demise of Wang's domestic dream and then gravitates toward her comeback to the film world. Despite her desire and effort to become a model housewife, her playboy patron-lover grows increasingly indifferent to her as he begins dallying with a dancing girl (played by Xia Peizhen [1908–?]). One day, after another verbal confronta-

75. Xuan Jinglin in *An Amorous History of the Silver Screen* (Mingxing, dir. Zhang Shichuan, 1931). Courtesy of the China Film Archive.

tion, Wang dozes off and has a daydream in which she sees herself arriving at a dance hall and finding Fang with the dancing girl. After following them to a hotel, she runs into her old director, who is there working on a script. He reveals to her that the reason for her falling out of favor is that she is no longer a film star, and he encourages her to return to the studio. The next day, her dream is fully reenacted, powerfully showcasing the power of cinematic fantasy in conjuring reality. She sets out for the hotel and confronts Fang in front of the dancing girl for the last time, only to be insulted again. She finally makes up her mind: "I will go my way. I won't die hungry for lack of a man!" Arriving at the studio, she tells the overjoyed director to quickly write a script for her so that she can resume her career on the silver screen.

Amorous History begins to take on the look of a mock documentary when the returned star is given a tour of the expanded and technologically updated studio. Forty truckloads of extras arrive for several films being shot simultaneously at different studios of the same company: *The Burning of the Red Lotus Temple* [*Huoshao hongliansi*], a martial arts serial film; *The Red Shadow of Tears* [*Honglei ying*], a melodrama; *Fate in Tears and Laugh-*

ter [*Tixiao yinyuan*], a romance based on Zhang Henshui's popular novel; and *Money Demon* [*Qianmo*].[12] Wang wanders with the director through the sets of both *Money Demon* and *The Burning of the Red Lotus Temple* and is impressed by the sophistication of the new equipment as well as the dedication of the production crews. The organization of the extras is executed in an assembly-line fashion, with a supervisor conducting a collective choreography of makeup within half an hour. Among the extras, Wang recognizes the hooligan who slapped her face back in her former life as a prostitute. Their "reunion" on the set of the film, specially written for Wang's comeback, turns into an act of vengeance with a cinematic license when the plot requires Wang to slap the hooligan character in public. Wang's resolution to return to the silver screen also magically rekindles Fang's love for her. He begins to pursue her again by driving her to and from the studio. The disenchanted dancing girl, realizing the romantic power of being a film actress, decides to try her luck in the film world herself. Along with hundreds of others, she arrives at the studio for an interview, which, without her knowing it, turns out to be a rigorous audition of her acting skill. She is provoked to cry and laugh, to be happy and angry (*xinu aile*). The film ends with her leaving the studio, hoping that she will return and become a film star.

On both thematic and stylistic levels, *Amorous History* not only records a significant segment of Chinese film history but also lends expression to the multilayered experience of those women who in various ways contributed to the making of early Chinese film culture. By infusing the history of Chinese cinema up to the advent of sound into the personal and professional history of an emblematic actress figure (or vice versa) the film chronicles early Chinese film history as characterized by heterogeneous technological practices and spectatorial expectations as well as multiple gender roles available to or imaginable by women. The "amorous" mode thus provides a unique method for understanding and writing women's history and film history as inseparable from each other within the framework of a particular film culture.

Referentiality, Feminine Biography, Film Technology

The particular attraction of *Amorous History* comes from the intertwining of a personal romance and a studio promotional showcase, feminine biography and the history of film technology. Set in the liminal space (as the daydream sequence indicates) between fiction and documentary, the film indulges in cinema's potential for both realism and fantasy—or rather, the magic blending of the two—thereby creating a new perceptual experience of reality. Some Chinese film historians have pointed to the orientation toward referentiality (*zhishixin*) rather than representation, romance (*chuanqi,* or fable) rather than psychological narrative, as the basic features of early Chinese cinema.[13] The elusive referentiality and hyperbolic realism of an "amorous history" (which can also be translated as "romance") inside and outside the film illustrates this observation. The contemporary fans of Mingxing productions, in particular those starring Xuan Jinglin, would readily find Xuan's life story embedded in the film. Born to a poor family (her father was a newspaper vendor) and having had only sporadic schooling, Xuan had become a prostitute when Zhang Shichuan (1889–1953), the director and one of the founders of the Mingxing company, discovered her talent for acting and had her redeemed from the brothel where she worked.[14] Made one year after Xuan's return to the studio, and following the dissolution of her cohabitation relationship with a businessman, the film is in fact a biographical portrait of a cinematic Cinderella, in this case Xuan Jinglin herself.

Xuan's rising stardom paralleled the rising fame and wealth of the Mingxing company.[15] The first (nonextant) part of the film chronicles her bewilderment when she first entered the film world. The Mingxing company, the first fully fledged Chinese film enterprise established by Zhang Shichuan, Zheng Zhengqiu (1888–1935), and others in 1922, was just beginning to outgrow its cottage-industry mode of production and to be transformed into the Mingxing Film Limited Company when Xuan joined the company in May 1925. Mingxing's first glass studio was built while the film in which Xuan played a minor role was being shot. During 1925 and 1928, Xuan portrayed an array of characters, including the country maiden, the poor widow, the dancing girl, and the female gangster. By the time she joined the company for the second time in 1930, Mingxing had just begun another large-scale expansion and modernization following the commercial miracle created by the martial arts film series *The Burning of the Red Lotus Temple.*

The new studio, which the actress in *Amorous History* tours with bewildered eyes, is presented as a magic workshop of virtual reality. When the actress marvels at the grandiose sets, high-tech lighting, numerous other gadgets, and special effects, the love story that dominates the first part of the film recedes. Instead it is taken over by an exhibitionist impulse for display characteristic of early cinema and the showmanship associated with it.[16] The romance between the actress and her unfaithful patron is now replaced by the romance between the female self and cinematic technology. If woman, as Andreas Huyssen remarks, has been prevalently linked to or allegorized as modern technology, as exemplified in Fritz Lang's *Metropolis* (1927), the relationship between the actress and technology in *Amorous History* is organized along a different line that cannot be subsumed under the category of mechanical incorporation or alienation alone.[17] Xuan is not overpowered by the gigantic scale of the new studio and equipment; the latter functions rather as a hyperbolic backdrop for the personal drama in which she redeems her independence. Unlike the dystopic vision of femininity and modern machinery in *Metropolis,* technology here emits a humorous energy—owing to the comic structure of the plot—that facilitates a social transformation embodied in the figure of the actress. Xuan, playing her former self as a prostitute decked out with a huge flower on her chest, is instructed by the director to slap (back) the hooligan in front of the camera. Screen performance and the reenactment of the past facilitates the redemption of her personal history. In front of the camera, Xuan not only literally acts out her ascendance from the lower social depth to the pantheon of movie stars, she is also able to close a painful chapter from the past. "Just as people whom nothing moves or touches any longer are taught to cry again by films," she regains the capacity to feel and emote.[18] The act of revenge made possible by film technology is certainly a utopian representation of women's agency. At the same time, because of the indexical rapport, or fusion, between Xuan's biographical and cinematic life, the slap is not just a make-believe dramatic gesture; it rather serves as the point where the onscreen action unites with its social and experiential referent, and a personal *histoire* with a public spectacle.

Xuan's comeback also coincided with another sea change in film technology that redefined the structure of sensory perception in early Chinese film history. Shortly after the first American talkie was shown in a Shanghai theater in 1929, several Chinese film companies began experimenting with sound, despite the lack of adequate equipment. The Mingxing company once again proved to be a leader in innovation by collaborating with the Pathé recording company of Shanghai to produce the first (partial) sound film, *The Singsong Girl Red Peony* [*Genü hong mudan*], (dir. Zhang Shichuan, 1931), using wax disks. Because sound film demanded the use of *guoyu,* or the standard "national language" based on the Beijing vernacular (as dictated by the Nationalist government, supposedly for universal intelligibility in the Chinese-speaking world), many actors who were not of northern origin suddenly found themselves suffering from a speech handicap. Xuan Jinglin, born and raised in Shanghai, could only speak the

Shanghai vernacular with a Suzhou (her maternal native town) inflection. Determined to catch up with the new technology and surpass her own image as a silent-film star, Xuan took crash lessons in guoyu and singing. By appearing in the first Movietone film while continuing to make silent films, Xuan demonstrated that her comeback was not a mere repetition of her screen image as an icon for the first golden age of Chinese silent film but more of a leap into a new era, embodying coexisting technologies, with their ambivalent relations as well as distinctive possibilities. It is significant that during her tour of the studio, the several films being produced simultaneously are of different genres and appeal, with one of them being a partial sound and color production, *Fate in Tears and Laughter* (dir. Zheng Zhengqiu, 1933). She thus characterizes or personifies early cinema as a critical category—that technological change does not easily translate into a shift in aesthetic modes and spectatorial address but can expose the very contradictions of technology and its multiple appropriations.

Besides the main plot surrounding the actress's double-edged amorous history, the film, with its numerous references to both production and reception contexts, points to the breadth and depth of a film culture far beyond the silver screen and exhibition space. In fact, *Amorous History* virtually inventories a cluster of interconnected practices that sustain and feed back on the film industry: money, stardom, fan culture, as well as the broader urban landscape. In this landscape, film experience is interwoven with other contiguous forms of the urban experience—such as ballroom dancing and window shopping—which underscores the constant transaction and contagion between them. The emphasis on the commercial nature of the film industry is clearly seen in a crucial scene inside the studio. At the moment when the actress is led to see, as a spectator, the set for *Money Demon* and is taken aback by the gigantic mask of the money demon descending from above and crushing a circle of dancing young women and men, the film is at its most self-reflexive about the commodity nature of the cinema, as well as women's ambivalent place within the film world.

Throughout the film, the figure of the actress embodies not so much the glamour of stardom as the multiple and concrete social roles available to women at the time, in both the domestic and public spheres. This multiplicity manifests itself in Xuan's repertoire of characters of different ages and classes as well as in her own life experience. To be sure, women's presence in the film world remained largely confined to the performing sector. Their visibility as public figures and their heightened social status were nevertheless considerable, especially at the threshold of the 1930s when the film industry had secured its legitimate place in everyday life, if not quite yet on the altar of art.

The cinema created not only a new vocation for women but also a significant social position and public image. Because many of them contributed substantially to early film ventures in capacities that went beyond acting, it is not too far-fetched to consider them pioneers of Chinese cinema and builders of film culture as well. Traditionally Chinese women had been largely excluded from the public arena, let alone regarded as public models for emulation. (That was only reserved for the few very chaste or filial who sacrificed themselves for patriarchy.) Before the advent of the cinema, only women from poor or marginal social groups worked as actors, mainly in all-women traveling opera troupes catering to the rural population or town residents of lower classes. Women and men were not supposed to appear on the same stage, and, as audience members, women either were not allowed in respectable theaters or had to be seated separately. While cinema as a mass attraction drastically changed the gender makeup of audiences, and women quickly became avid spectators, the earliest Chinese films featured only male actors coming mainly from theatrical backgrounds. In 1913, Yan Shanshan became the first Chinese woman to appear on the silver screen in a short-story film, *Zhuang Zi Tests His Wife* [*Zhuang Zi shiqi*], directed by her husband Li Minwei. Ironically, Yan played the minor role of the maid while Li played Zhuang Zi's wife.[19] At the time, it was inconceivable for women to appear in film, let alone play leading roles. Before becoming the first film actress in Chinese film history, Yan was known as a member of the female bombing squadron during the Republican Revolution in 1911. Afterward no women played female roles until 1921, when Wang Caiyun, a theater actress–turned–singsong girl, was asked to play the leading female role (a prostitute) in *Yan Ruisheng* (dir. Ren Pengnian), a feature-length docudrama based on a sensational murder case in Shanghai. The filmmakers wanted to achieve as much authenticity as possible and chose her not only because no other ordinary woman would play such a role but also because of her close relationship with the prostitute before the murder.[20]

The cinema boom and especially the proliferation of long narrative films, along with a growing popular "taste for reality" and melodrama, in the early 1920s created a demand for actresses not just to fill the scenes but also to play leading roles.[21] The profession of screen acting thus provided an unprecedented opportunity for many women of diverse backgrounds, including the new-style female students who defied family and societal prejudice to embrace the screen life, as well as courtesans or singsong girls who saw in cinema a chance for changing their social standing. With the help of the print media, including early trade journals and fan magazines, a proto–star system was born. Actresses like Wang Hanlun (1903–1978), Yin Mingzhu (1904–?), Yang Naimei (1904–1960), Zhang Zhiyun (1905–?), and Hu Die (1908–1989) displayed their courage in embracing a modern mass medium that was still shunned by the elite society.[22] Their stardom partly derived from their image as champions of the modern lifestyle in many aspects — in fashion, hairstyle, car driving, and an unconventional sexual life (such as having boyfriends or choosing cohabitation over marriage).[23] They were in fact the first generation of Chinese "modern girls."

Among them, Yin Mingzhu and Yang Naimei were probably the most prominent. Yin, born to a gentry family, studied at a Western-style women's college in Shanghai. At school Yin excelled in dancing, singing, horseback riding, biking, and car driving. Because she always dressed in the manner of foreign movie stars, she came to be called Miss F. F. (Foreign Fashion).[24] Together with Dan Duyu, an artist-turned–self-made director, they created the Shanghai Shadowplay Company, one of the early cottage-industry style ventures. In addition to her involvement in the operation of the company, Yin was the leading star of their popular productions. Yang Naimei, in contrast, was famous for her romantic lifestyle and her penchant for "strange clothes." The only daughter of a successful Cantonese businessman, Yang went to a girls' school and indulged in performances. After a small role in a Mingxing box-office hit, *The Soul of Yu Li* [*Yu Li hun*] (dir. Sun-fung Lee, 1923), she quickly became a major star and character actor, specializing in playing "wayward" or "amorous" women like herself. Her hobbies included high-speed driving through the main thoroughfare in central Shanghai. Yang's fame (or infamy) outraged her father, who considered acting as nothing less than prostitution and consequently disowned her. In 1926, Yang sensationalized the film world by appearing in tableaux vivant fashion during the screening of *The Resurrection of Conscience* [*Liangxinde fuhuo*] (dir. Bu Wancang, 1926), lip-synching the song she "sang" in the film. Unsatisfied with being dictated to by male directors, she founded her own company, the Naimei Film Company, and produced a film about a legendary modern woman in 1928; none other than she herself played the protagonist.[25]

In light of the history of women's contribution to early Chinese film culture, the referentiality of *Amorous History* appears all the more significant. The film did more than record the prime of Xuan Jinglin and the Mingxing company, both at a moment of crucial transformation. In weaving together

76. Yang Naimei, from *Yinxing* [*The movie guide*], no. 12 (1927).

the personal and institutional histories in a docudramatic romance, the film offers a compelling glimpse into prewar Chinese cinema from both an insider's and a woman's point of view. Xuan's career as represented on the screen is thus indexical of the collective career of women pioneers of the Chinese film industry.

The history of film technology as presented in the film is involved, yet not without a critical distance. The self-reflexive impulse is never steeped in psychological absorption but rather inscribed on the social skin of the cinematic experience. Instead of abstracting that experience for moral didacticism or formal indulgence, it motivates in the viewer a heightened awareness of its significance as part of the larger sensorial economy of modernity. Indeed, this referentiality and self-reflexivity should be viewed more as a combination of a residual aesthetic of display or monstration, with a direct address to the "(in)credulous" audience that characterizes early cinema and at the same time the impulse to narrativize or update this early history more than three decades after the advent of the cinema.[26]

More importantly, the impact of the film also vibrated on the reflexive horizon of reception. The film came into contact with an audience unrestrained by geographical location and educational level, thereby becoming a vehicle for the expansion of knowledge and the sharing of experience beyond the limits of Shanghai. After seeing the film, one viewer wrote a long letter from the remote Jilin province in Manchuria to the editors of *Movie Weekly* [*Yingxi shenghuo,* literally "Shadowplay Life"] in Shanghai. In the letter, he expressed his enthusiasm for the film and gratitude to the Mingxing company for generously sharing the secrets behind the scenes and imparting to the audience basic knowledge about film production. He lamented the fact that, because of the remote location of his native town from metropolitan Shanghai, it usually took months before a new film reached Jilin, where the only theater was the auditorium of the local YMCA, which held screenings mainly for the purpose of education. However, as an avid fan he watched everything shown there. *Amorous History,* unlike anything else he had seen, opened his eyes to what was behind the world of illusion on the screen. He was particularly impressed by the tour sequence in the film when the actress visits the sets of several films, encountering famous actors, directors, and cameramen. What astonished him most was how film technology was capable of manufacturing a different kind of reality, or a second nature:

> What a big electric fan! It makes us realize the origin of torrential rain or snow in a movie. What a big mountain and what a fast train! Now we know how a mountain is made and a train is manufactured.
>
> We know now that a skeleton is painted; a pavilion is but a miniature; a lavish living room is a backdrop; and a bustling street is artificial! Flying and leaping in the air—what impressive martial arts! But it's made possible by a hanging rope! Tears flowing—what a profusion of emotion! Do you know, though, that he is just using fake tears?!
>
> Furthermore, [we see] the way the director works, how the camera runs, and operations in the makeup room and on the sets—all the things we have never seen or heard of![27]

The sense of bewilderment as well as the exhilarating enlightenment about the "true nature" of the cinema, "the magic metamorphosis rather than a seamless reproduction of reality," as Tom Gunning underscores, "reveal not a childlike belief, but an undisguised awareness of (and delight in) film's illusionistic capabilities."[28] Moreover, the revelation, or surfacing, of the cinematic magic paradoxically only intensified the provincial viewer's passion for the cinema. Beyond the gadgets and special effects, he was gripped by the vivid presence of the people who produced the magic: "the models draped in gauzy dress, the country women who cry and laugh hyperbolically, the directors who shout in panic through their loudspeakers, and the stars with a cocky aura."[29] Seeing these people vicariously through Xuan

Jinglin's eyes, the viewer experiences the film as a three-dimensional virtual space in which the flatness of images on the silver screen materializes into a tangible reality. The crowded and simultaneous presence of extras, the hidden masters of illusion (in other words the directors and cameramen), and the sheer size of sets and equipment endow the film with an overwhelming visibility and physicality, as well as a democratic appeal. Nothing is withheld from the viewer; every person and every object comes to the foreground, even though they are governed by a certain hierarchical organization. This experience puts the audience of a remote provincial town in direct touch with the pulse of metropolitan modernity, which the film world both fashions and represents.

Woman as Embodiment of Vernacular Modernity

If *Amorous History* offered a rare occasion for the provincial spectator to travel to Shanghai's film scene without riding a real train and crossing mountain ranges from Jilin province, it has provided me with an entry point from which to begin to make sense of a film world that existed decades ago. When I watched the film for the first time on a small video screen at the Beijing Film Archive in August 1995, around the centennial of the cinema, the astonishment and enlightenment I experienced then was perhaps not much less than the viewer seated in the YMCA auditorium in northeast China more than sixty years ago, even though I had the advantage of a historical hindsight mediated through a new kind of screen practice. Just as *Amorous History* offered an introductory lesson on the ABC's of the cinema to the provincial viewer, it proved to be an eye-opening phantom ride that transported me to the Shanghai film world. That world suddenly came to life. At that moment, I was overcome by the power of embodiment the film transmitted. I was moved not so much by the rare visual encounter with an extant silent film and the story it presented as by the sensation aroused by the virtual tour of the film world of 1931, by being in the company of Xuan Jinglin as well as her contemporary moviegoers. I realized that here I had not simply a precious primary source but also a methodological guide for conceptualizing the relationship among women, cinema, and modernity. In the amorous history of early film culture in China, as well as elsewhere, women were never simply flat images or representations but were active agents and makers of this history.

By further locating early Chinese film culture and women's presence in the historical landscape of early-twentieth-century China, it is possible to challenge existing views of Chinese cultural modernity, the origin of which has been habitually associated with the May Fourth movement and the related vernacular movement in the late 1910s and well into the 1920s. Shifting away from the supremacy accorded language and literature in the discourse on Chinese modernity, I argue that early Chinese film culture, particularly women's amorous and ambivalent relations to the silver screen, embodies modernity as a constellation of interconnected vernacular experiences that defy any rigid boundaries between high and low culture, the visual and verbal, and the aesthetic and the political.[30]

My theoretical investment in the term "vernacular" is not simply motivated by a desire to get away from the much contested and delimiting categories of the "popular" or "mass culture" deployed in current discourses on marginality vis-à-vis hegemony, or subversion vis-à-vis domination. Rather, it is propelled by an urge to reestablish the historical connection, or dialogue, between film culture and modernity, and to rescue the vernacular from the exclusive claim of linguists and literary historians. At the same time, as a historical experience arising from the particular juncture of the vernacular movement and the attendant cultural nationalism, early Chinese cinema does share the ambivalence toward a global vernacular represented by Western cinemas, in particular that of classical Hollywood. The emergence and survival of the Chinese film industry and film market is thus a tension-ridden process of negotiating between cosmopolitanism and nationalism, between film as a utopian "universal language" on one hand, and local vernacular(s) on the other.[31] In that sense, the vernacular experience from which the early Chinese film culture emerged, and which it in turn refashioned, is inherently plastic and polyvalent. It was constantly being experimented with, lived out, and redefined. The formation and reception of modern imagery were informed by a host of old and new technologies and related cultural practices. Simultaneously, the emergence of a film culture in the cosmopolitan setting of Shanghai drastically transformed gender relations and perceptions of the body as configured in a modernizing urban space with the impact of mass media and commodity culture.

Standard Chinese film historiography has consistently regarded the film practice of early Chinese cinema, in particular that of the 1920s, as part of the nonprogressive popular culture outside the May Fourth movement proper.[32] In an influential but rather biased essay, the veteran screenwriter and film critic Ke Lin asks rhetorically: "Why didn't the strong shock waves of the May Fourth movement reach the film circle?"[33] According to Ke Lin, it was only after the Japanese bombing of Shanghai on 28 January 1932, when the left-wing writers began to enter the film world, that Chinese cinema belatedly connected with the New Culture movement. The May Fourth movement stemmed from a particular political movement, namely, the surge of Chinese nationalism triggered by the students' demonstration in Beijing on 4 May 1919. The students, mostly from Beijing University, joined by Beijing citizens, protested against the imminent signing of the post–World War I Versailles treaty, which allowed the Japanese to take over Shandong province from Germany. The incident was in fact but a pivotal point within a decade-long (1915–1925) cultural movement that was radically antitraditional or even iconoclastic and that has been alternatively labeled the Chinese Enlightenment.[34]

One of the most consequential changes effected by the movement took place in the domain of language, with the promotion and institution of the vernacular language (or Mandarin based on the Beijing dialect) as the standard modern Chinese. The process started during the late Qing reform movement and culminated in the May Fourth period. This vernacular turn had a profound impact on the cultural transformations in China in the twentieth century. It was a massive attempt to reconcile elite and popular culture, orality and literacy, and above all, linguistically to unify China as a modern nation on the ruins of a dynastic past. Countless studies in English on the origin and impact of the vernacular movement have centered around the "literary revolution" (*wenxue gemin*) in the May Fourth movement and the literary corpus it generated. Little effort has, however, been made to locate the question of vernacular writing—modern print culture beyond the confines of literary history—in a broader inquiry on the "technological transformation and implementation of the word," and its interaction with the radically far-reaching form of mass-mediated visual literacy, the cinema.[35]

Hu Shi (1891–1962) is one of the Western-educated intellectuals who spearheaded the Chinese Enlightenment. Hu Shi's status as the "father" of the vernacular movement was established instantly when he published "Some Modest Proposals for the Reform of Literature" in *New Youth* in 1917.[36] The "modest proposals" took the form of a literary and linguistic prescription for a "living literature" (*huo wenxue*) written in the vernacular (*baihua*), so that the latter could take over the canonical status traditionally accorded literature and historiography written in the classical language (*wenyan*). While studying philosophy with John Dewey at Columbia University, Hu Shi also began experimenting with writing poetry in the vernacular Chinese (more than prose and drama, poetry as an art of the educated elite had been composed primarily in the classical language), as a radical act of proving the empirical theory of experience. This experiment to modernize Chinese literary language and sensibility resulted in a book of poetry titled *Collection of Experiments* that became a model text for the vernacular movement.[37]

In the preface for the fourth edition of the collection, Hu articulated writing in the vernacular as visceral. More strikingly, here he compares the vernacular experiment to the physical pain of unbinding feet (*fangjiao*) that many Chinese women were experiencing at the time:

> Now when I look back on the poems I wrote in the past five years, it feels as though *a woman who has unbound her feet* looks back on the changing size of her shoe pattern. Although they have enlarged year after year, each shoe pattern is tinged with the *bloody smell* of the foot binding era....
>
> But women with bound feet can never regain their natural feet. I have once again sorted through my "shoe patterns" over the last five or six years, selected some while omitting those that are totally shapeless and even potentially harmful [to readers]. There remain some "small patterns"; by retaining them, however, I hope people can learn something about the *pain* of foot binding. If that would serve some *historical purpose,* then I would not worry as much. (emphasis added)[38]

The use of foot binding (and unbinding) as a metaphor for cultural renaissance illustrates the point Rey Chow has made about the Chinese male intellectual's masochist identification with (oppressed) women. In assuming the position of the premodern female subject, the male intellectual was able to come to terms with the traumatic encounter with the West and the process of modernization.[39] Rey Chow's psychoanalytical and feminist approach has provoked heated debates on issues concerning gender and national culture in the study of modern Chinese literature. What concerns me here, however, is the sliding, or interchangeability, between writing and body in the production of the vernacular as a cultural practice beyond the limits of language and literature. In other words, the bodily metaphor carries a quite literal or referential weight. The grafting of a linguistic experiment onto the social skin of modernity as a lived, gendered experience — pain as well as liberation — suggests that the cultural ambition of the vernacular movement extends into a larger cultural domain, including the transforming perception of the body and its epistemological status. Rather than being the exclusive property of language or literature, the vernacular is grasped as an affective experience enmeshed in the larger referent of everyday life and social reality (the unbound feet) as well as a discur-

An Amorous History of the Silver Screen

sive formation that demands the creation of a flexible sign system (the shoe pattern).

The production of the vernacular entails, in fact, the production of a historical trope (or purpose) and its attendant forms of expressibility. Language is integral, but by no means the only way this historical trope gets articulated. Hu Shi's effort to anchor the process of vernacularization in the flesh and blood of the female experience of becoming modern remained a literary masquerade. But the historical impulse behind this movement toward recognizing the vernacular as an embodied experience has a heuristic implication for my conception of early Chinese cinema as the quintessential medium of the vernacular. Hu Shi's vernacular poetics emerged largely outside, yet simultaneous with, the early Chinese film culture. The cultural etiology of the bound feet deployed by Hu Shi to convey the pain as well as liberation characterizing the vernacularizing process allows me also to take the word "movement" in the expression "vernacular movement" seriously, and quite literally. The vernacular movement was not a static or pedantic enterprise. It involved the production of a pervasive, if often contradictory, historical force and the emergence and perception of a new social body. This theoretical move resonates with Vivian Sobchack's invocation of Merleau-Ponty's view of language as an "embodied" and "enworlded [sic]" experience for restoring the "sensuous" power of the motion picture to signify. As a new vernacular "language" for perception and expression, the cinematic experience is always already situated (hence the term "*address* of the eye") in the "flesh of the world" and grounded in the embodied existence and material world.[40]

What Hu Shi did not realize, however, was that while he was writing about the pain of unbinding the feet of vernacular literature and trying to resuscitate experience in the endangered poetic form, the first Chinese female film star Wang Hanlun entered the cultural scene with her unbound feet in 1922. Wang became an instant celebrity after she successfully portrayed a widow convinced of the virtue of education in *Orphan Rescues Grandfather* [*Gu'er jiuzu ji*] (dir. Zheng Zhengqiu, 1923), produced by the Mingxing company, which Xuan Jinglin (the actress in *Amorous History*) joined a couple of years later. If the silver screen made her unbound feet, referred to at the time as *wenmingjiao,* or "civilized feet," visible to the public, it was the life story of her unbinding herself from the fetters of an old society that made her an urban legend.[41] Born to a wealthy gentry family, Wang Hanlun was forced to marry a stranger in her late teens. After a hard-won divorce, she supported herself by teaching in an elementary school and later

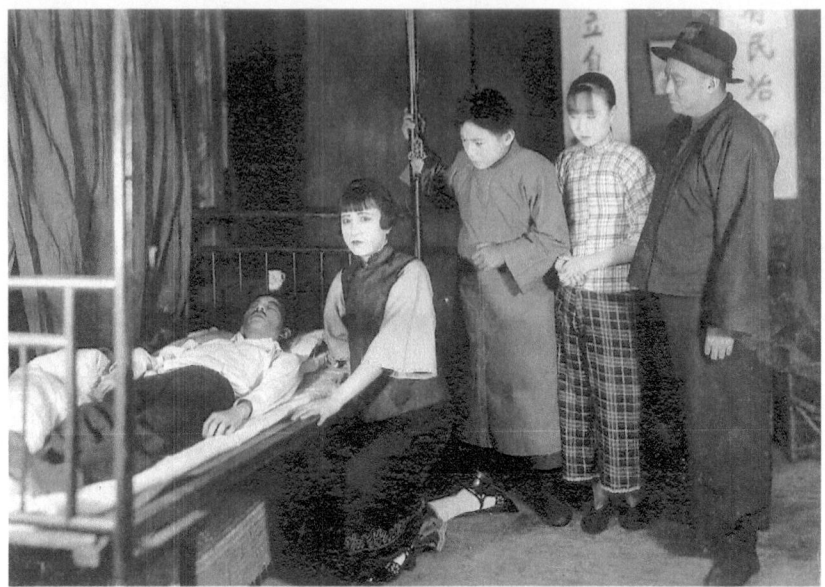

77. Wang Hanlun (center, with her unbound feet), in *Orphan Rescues Grandfather* (China, dir. Zheng Zhengqiu, 1923). Courtesy of the China Film Archive.

working as a typist of English for a foreign company. Her decision to enter the film world was met by her family with both opposition and contempt. Wang Hanlun abandoned her original family name Peng and took Wang as her new name because the Chinese character for "Wang" (which also means king) was part of the unsimplified Chinese character for "tiger" — a fearless creature.[42] Hanlun, on the other hand, was derived from her English name: Helen. The director Zhang Shichuan recalled years later that Wang Hanlun was one of the few rare "modern girls" (*modeng nülang*) of the time; her fashionable dress and makeup deeply impressed him and his colleagues.[43] Her linguistic gift—being able to speak Mandarin and English in addition to the Shanghai dialect—added to her modern flair. Not only did Wang Hanlun boldly show her unbound feet on the screen during the shooting of a film in 1926, she also had her long hair cut in front of the camera. Though required by the plot, this cut (from her past) added another embodied token to her image as a modern girl.

Wang's film career culminated in the opening of a film company under her own name, which in 1929 produced a feature called *Revenge of the Actress* [*Nüling fuchou ji*] (dir. Bu Wancang) in which she starred.[44] It was

An Amorous History of the Silver Screen

78. Wang Hanlun in *The Abandoned Wife* (China, dir. Li Zeyuan and Hou Yao, 1924). Courtesy of the China Film Archive.

practically a one-woman enterprise. She hired a director but had to take care of all other aspects of production, including editing, herself. Because of the negligence of her partners, she eventually bought the shooting script from the director and finished the postproduction by herself. With the aid of a manual projector, she finished editing the film at home. Afterward she traveled with the film all over China, performing live during intermissions. The profit generated by the film enabled her to retire from the screen and establish the Hanlun Beauty Salon, which became a trendy spot in Shanghai.

Both Wang Hanlun and Xuan Jinglin's ascendance as icons of modern women, despite their different social origins, exemplifies the redemptive power of the cinematic medium in the realization of a modern version of the Cinderella fairy tale. The cinema presented both women (and many others) with a chance for a second life both on and off the screen. At the same time, their disparate backgrounds and ways of living out their potential demonstrate the heterogeneous origin of early Chinese cinema as well as the hybrid nature of Shanghai's vernacular culture. While Wang came from a wealthy family and received her education at a missionary school,

523

Xuan belonged to the lower depths of society and was hardly literate when she entered the film world. One escaped from an arranged marriage and cut her ties with a traditional gentry family; the other left the pleasure quarters and later the confines of modern-style concubinage. The film world became their new home as well as the university of life. While the sense of liberation and empowerment felt by Wang and Xuan was certainly never complete and was often ambivalent, the silver screen nevertheless allowed them to experience their changing self-perception through performance or role-playing. It is in the process of blending reality with fiction, their personal histories with the lives of the characters they portrayed on the screen, that the collective experience of Chinese women, poised on the threshold of different worlds and destinies, and deployed by Hu Shi as an allegory for the vernacular movement, began to receive embodied articulation. If the movement toward embodiment in Hu Shi's vernacular poetics remained symbolic and short-lived, the reenactment and transformation of the lived experience of the first generation of film actresses on the silver screen carry the weight of a particular historical indexicality and concreteness.

Notes

I wish to thank Miriam Hansen, Tom Gunning, Harry Harootunian, Judith Zeitlin, Yingjin Zhang, Anna McCarthy, John Crespi, Jennifer Bean, and Magnus Fiskesjö for their helpful comments on this essay at its different stages. I also acknowledge the generous support of a J. P. Getty postdoctoral grant that has allowed me to develop a book-length study from which this essay is drawn.

1. Walter Benjamin, "Theses on the Philosophy of History," in *Illuminations,* ed. Hannah Arendt (New York: Harcourt, Brace and World, 1968), 262, 264.
2. For a study on reflexivity in film and literature, see Robert Stam, *Reflexivity in Film and Literature: From Don Quixote to Jean-Luc Godard* (Ann Arbor: University of Michigan Press, 1985).
3. Some representative works in this trend are Roger Holman, ed., *Cinema, 1900–1906: An Analytical Study* (Brussels: Fédération Internationale des Archives du Film, 1982); John Fell, ed., *Film before Griffith* (Berkeley: University of California Press, 1983); Jay Leyda and Charles Musser, eds., *Before Hollywood* (New York: American Federation of the Arts, 1987); Noël Burch, *Life to Those Shadows,* ed. and trans. Ben Brewster (Berkeley: University of California Press, 1990). The most representative work that maps out the patriarchal structure of looking through the psychoanalytic method is Laura Mulvey's seminal essay "Visual Pleasure and Narrative Cinema," *Screen* 16, 3 (autumn, 1975): 6–18.
4. For a concise sketch of the rise of early cinema as a critical concept, see

An Amorous History of the Silver Screen

Thomas Elsaesser, "General Introduction — Early Cinema: From Linear History to Mass Media Archaeology," in *Early Cinema: Space, Frame, Narrative*, ed. Elsaesser (London: British Film Institute, 1990), 1-8. The volume contains some pioneering studies on early Western cinema from multiple perspectives. However, non-Western early cinemas were not included.

5 See, for example, Giuliana Bruno, *Streetwalking on a Ruined Map: Cultural Theory and the City Films of Elvira Notari* (Princeton: Princeton University Press, 1993); Miriam Hansen, *Babel and Babylon: Spectatorship in American Silent Film* (Cambridge: Harvard University Press, 1991); Anne Friedberg, *Window Shopping: Cinema and the Postmodern* (Berkeley: University of California Press, 1993); Patrice Petro, *Joyless Streets: Women and Melodramatic Representation in Weimar, Germany* (Princeton: Princeton University Press, 1989); Shelley Stamp, *Movie-Struck Girls: Women and Motion Picture Culture after the Nickelodeon* (Princeton: Princeton University Press, 2000); and Antonia Lant and Ingrid Periz, eds., *The Red Velvet Seat: Women's Writings on the Cinema, the First Fifty Years* (New York: Verso, forthcoming). The present volume will no doubt make a significant contribution to this expanding field.

6 For a brief assessment of this emergent scholarship in China, see my article "Teahouse, Shadowplay, Bricolage: *Laborer's Love* and the Question of Early Chinese Cinema," in *Cinema and Urban Culture in Shanghai, 1922-1943*, ed. Zhang Yingjin (Stanford: Stanford University Press, 1999).

7 Recently, some European and Japanese scholars (including Marie-Claire Quiquemelle, Regis Bergeron, Marco Müller, Tadao Sato, and Fumitoshi Karima) have also produced interesting work, mostly in the form of articles that are included in catalogs for retrospectives of Chinese film held in the early 1980s. See for example, Centre de Documentation sur le Cinéma Chinois, ed., *Ombres électriques: Panorama du cinéma chinois, 1925-1982* (Paris: Centre de Documentation sur le Cinéma Chinois, 1982); Centre National d'Art et de Culture Georges Pompidou, *Le cinéma chinois* (Paris, 1985); *Chugoku eiga no kaiko, 1922-1952* [A retrospective of Chinese cinema, 1922-1952] (Tokyo: National Film Center at the Tokyo Kokuritsu Kindai Bijutsukan [National Museum of Modern Art, Tokyo], 1984); *Chugoku eiga no kaiko, 1932-1964* [A retrospective of Chinese cinema, 1932-1964] (Tokyo: National Film Center at the Tokyo Kokuritsu Kindai Bijutsukan, 1988); *Sun Yu kandoku to Shanghai eiga no nakamatachi-Chugoku eiga no kaiko* [Sun Yu and his Shanghai colleagues: Retrospective of Chinese films] (1992). I am grateful to Mitsuyo Wada-Marciano for acquiring the Japanese catalogs.

8 Li Suyuan and Hu Jubin, *Zhongguo wusheng dianyingshi* (Beijing: Zhongguo dianying chubanshe, 1997). The English version of the book was published in 1998 by China Film Press, Beijing.

9 For an early attempt to theorize nonsynchronicity, see Ernst Bloch, "Non-synchronism and the Obligation to Its Dialectics," trans. Mark Ritter, *New German Critique* 11 (1977): 22-38.

10 Printed in the programs of the Afanggong Theater for *Amorous History*, parts 1 and 2, August 1931.

11 The reference to Lillian Gish is an allusion to Xuan Jinglin's real life story. Her original name was Tian Jinlin. While in the brothel she used the nickname Xiao Jinmudan (Little Golden Peony). The veteran director Zheng Zhengqiu helped her adopt a stage name, Xuan Jinglin, obliquely (in Shanghai dialect) alluding to Lillian Gish (*Ganlixu,* in Chinese transliteration). See Tan Chunfa, *Kai yidai xianhe — Zhongguo dianying zhifu Zheng Zhengqiu* [The pioneer — Zheng Zhengqiu, the father of Chinese cinema] (Beijing: Guoji wenhua chuban gongsi, 1992), 308.

12 The first three are actual films produced by the Mingxing company that year.

13 Zhong Dafeng and Shu Xiaomin, *Zhongguo dianyingshi* [History of Chinese film] (Beijing: Zhongguo guangbo dianshi chubanshe, 1995), 14.

14 Xuan Jinglin, "Wode yingmu shenghuo" [My life on the silver screen], *Zhongguo dianying* [Chinese cinema] 3 (1956): 72–74. See also Zhang Shichuan, "Zi wo daoyan yilai" [Since I started directing], *Mingxing banyuekan* [Mingxing bimonthly] 1, 5 (1935). Zhang recalls first seeing Xuan as a little girl with pigtails riding donkeys in the New World Amusement Center where he worked as a manager. Years later, while he was casting for the film *Last Conscience* [*Zuihou de liangxin*] (1925), he managed to find Xuan, who had become a prostitute out of poverty, and asked her to play a minor role. After the successful release of the film, the company paid two thousand Chinese dollars to redeem her from the brothel.

15 The social status of the company in particular and the film world in general was significantly enhanced when Hong Shen (1894–1955), a Harvard-trained professor of English and drama at Fudan University, joined Mingxing as a screenwriter. If the cinema liberated Xuan from prostitution, Hong Shen's decision to enter the nascent film industry (which at the time was still regarded as a low entertainment form rather than art) and to place himself in the company of an ex-prostitute like Xuan aroused shocked reactions in the intellectual circle, including his family and friends. His action was labeled by a Fudan colleague as "prostitution of art." Hong Shen was nevertheless resolute about his commitment. See Hong Shen, "Wo de dagu shiqi yijing guo le ma?" [Has the time of my drumming passed already?], in *Hong Shen quanji* [Collected works of Hong Shen], vol. 4 (Beijing: Zhongguo xiju chubanshe, 1957), 517. Xuan starred in *The Mistress's Fan* [*Shao nainai de shanzi*] (1926), scripted and directed by Hong Shen.

16 For a groundbreaking study on the exhibitionist mode of presentation of early cinema, which challenges the prevalent voyeurist paradigm used in studies of classical Hollywood cinema, see Tom Gunning, "The Cinema of Attractions: Early Film, Its Spectator, and the Avant-Garde," *Wide Angle* 8, 3–4 (1986), 63–70. Miriam Hansen has described such a presentational practice in terms of "excess of appeal," "diversity and display," and "public performance." See "A Cinema in Search of a Spectator: Film-Viewer Relations before Hollywood," in *Babel and Babylon,* 23–59.

17 Andreas Huyssen, "The Vamp and the Machine," in *The Great Divide: Mod-*

ernism, Mass Culture, Postmodernism (Bloomington: Indiana University Press, 1986), 65–81.
18 Walter Benjamin, "One Way Street," in *Walter Benjamin: Selected Writings,* vol. 1, *1913–1926,* ed. Marcus Bullock and Michael W. Jennings (Cambridge: Harvard University Press, 1996), 476.
19 It remains a common practice for men to impersonate women in the Peking opera. At the turn of the twentieth century, this practice was carried over to the modern spoken drama and subsequently cinema for some time.
20 The film became a huge box-office success, which helped stimulate the popular taste for the new medium. For a synopsis of the film, see *Zhongguo wusheng dianying juben* [Chinese silent film scripts], ed. Zheng Peiwei and Liu Guiqing (Beijing: Zhongguo dianying chubanshe, 1996), 4–5.
21 The term "taste for reality" is adapted from Vanessa R. Schwartz, "Cinema Spectatorship before the Apparatus: The Public Taste for Reality in Fin-de-Siècle Paris," in *Viewing Positions: Ways of Seeing Film,* ed. Linda Williams (New Brunswick: Rutgers University Press, 1994), 87–113.
22 For an instructive account of the relationship between early movie actresses and public discourse in China, see Michael Chang, "The Good, the Bad, and the Beautiful: Movie Actresses and Public Discourse in Shanghai, 1920s–1930s," in *Cinema and Urban Culture in Shanghai, 1922–1943,* ed. Zhang Yingjin, 128–159.
23 Gongsun Lu, *Zhongguo dianying shihua* [Historical accounts of Chinese cinema] (Hong Kong: Guangjiaojing chubanshe, 1976), 39–41, 53–54.
24 There were two other famous modern girls known also by their "foreign" names—Miss A. A. (Ace Ace) and Miss S. S. (Shanghai Style). Miss A. A.'s real name is Fu Wenhao, and she also appeared in films. She was allegedly the first Chinese woman to earn a driver's license in the International Settlement of Shanghai. See Cheng Bugao, *Yingtan yijiu* [Reminiscences of the film world] (Beijing: Zhongguo dianying chubanshe, 1983), 57.
25 Gong Jianong, *Gong Jianong congying huiyilu* [Robert Kung's memoirs of his silver-screen life], vol. 1 (Taipei: Wenxing shudian, 1966–1967), 123.
26 Tom Gunning, "An Aesthetic of Astonishment: Early Film and the (In)Credulous Spectator," *Art and Text* 34 (spring 1989): 31–45.
27 Zhong Yuan, "Guan 'Yingmu yanshi' hou" [After watching *An Amorous History of the Silver Screen*], *Yingxi shenghuo* [Movie weekly] 1, 34 (1931): 15–17.
28 Gunning, "Aesthetic of Astonishment," 43.
29 Zhong Yuan, "Guan 'Yingmu yanshi' hou," 16–17.
30 For a perceptive study on female stardom and vernacular modernism in Chinese silent film of the 1930s, see Miriam Hansen, "Fallen Women, Rising Stars, New Horizons: Shanghai Silent Film as Vernacular Modernism," *Film Quarterly* 54, 1 (fall 2000): 10–22.
31 The discourse on film as a potential universal language or visual Esperanto was intimately linked to the emergence of the cinema as a social and cultural institution in America in the 1910s. See Hansen, *Babel and Babylon,* 76–

89. Hansen argues that "the celebration of film as a new universal language ultimately coincided in substance and ideology with the shift from primitive to classical modes of narration and address that occurred, roughly, between 1909–1916" (79). In other words, the creation of a cinematic universal language went hand in hand with the cultivation of a uniform code of narration and the concomitant abstraction (or textual inscription) of a spectatorship. A similar process occurred in Chinese film, but lasted well into the mid-1920s, when feature-length narrative cinema finally began to dominate the film scene (though never completely so).

32 The most established text that holds this orthodox view is Cheng Jihua, Li Shaobai, and Xing Zuwen, *Zhongguo dianying fazhan shi* [History of the development of Chinese cinema], 2 vols. (Beijing: Zhongguo dianying chubanshe, 1981).

33 Ke Lin, "Shi wei 'Wusi' yu dianying hua yi lunkuo" [An attempt at drawing a contour for the May Fourth movement and the cinema], in *Ke Lin dianying wencun* [Selected extant writings of Ke Lin], ed. Chen Wei (Beijing: Zhongguo dianying chubanshe, 1992), 286–302. Ke Lin entered the Shanghai film world as a left-wing writer in the early 1930s.

34 See Vera Schwarcz, *The Chinese Enlightenment: Intellectuals and the Legacy of the May Fourth Movement of 1919* (Berkeley: University of California Press, 1986).

35 Walter Ong, *Interfaces of the Word: Studies in the Evolution of Consciousness and Culture* (Ithaca: Cornell University Press, 1977).

36 Hu Shi, "Wenxue gailiang chuyi" [Some modest proposals for the reform of literature], *Xin qingnian* 2, 5 (1917), reprinted in *Modern Chinese Literary Thought: Writings on Literature, 1893–1945*, ed. and trans. Kirk Denton (Stanford: Stanford University Press, 1996), 123–139. *New Youth* published the first piece of fiction written in the vernacular by Lu Xun in January 1918. Hu Shi first experimented with vernacular writing and publishing when he studied in new-style schools in Shanghai as a teenager from 1904 to 1910 before he left for America. See Hu Shi, "Sishi zishu" [An autobiography written at the age of forty], in *Hu Shi zizhuan* [Hu Shi's autobiographical writings], ed. Cao Boyuan (Hefei: Huangshan shushe, 1986), 54–62. "Sishi zishu" was originally published in booklet form by the Yadong Library in Shanghai in 1935.

37 Hu Shi, *Changshiji* [Collection of experiments] (1920; Shanghai: Yadong tushuguan, 1922).

38 Ibid., 2–3. According to this preface, the first three editions sold about ten thousand copies within two years, a phenomenal number for a poetry collection.

39 See Rey Chow, *Woman and Chinese Modernity: The Politics of Reading between West and East* (Minneapolis: University of Minnesota Press, 1991), especially chapter 4, "Loving Women: Masochism, Fantasy, and the Idealization of the Mother." Bound feet did, however, play a concrete role in Hu Shi's personal experience. Before he went to America, he was engaged to a woman with bound

feet whom his mother chose for him in his native Anhui province. When he was studying at Columbia, he fell in love with an American woman. Unable to absolve his feeling of moral obligation, he married the Chinese woman on returning to China.

40 Vivian Sobchack, "Phenomenology and the Film Experience," in *Viewing Positions: Ways of Seeing Film,* ed. Linda Williams (New Brunswick: Rutgers University Press, 1997), 36–58.
41 Gongsun Lu, *Zhongguo dianying shihua,* 50–52.
42 Wang Hanlun, "Wode congying jingguo" [My experience with the cinema], in *Zhongguo wusheng dianying* [Chinese silent film], ed. Zhongguo dianying zi liaoguan (Beijing: Zhongguo dianying chubanshe, 1997), 1471–1475.
43 Zhang Shichuan, "Zi wo daoyan yilai," *Mingxing banyuekan* [Mingxing bi-monthly] 1, 4 (1935): 16.
44 Wang Hanlun, "Wode congying jingguo," 1476–1477. The original English title for the film is *Blind Love.* For a synopsis of the film, see *Zhongguo wusheng dianying juben,* 1849–1850.

MARY ANN DOANE

Technology's Body

Cinematic Vision in Modernity

Two historical anecdotes seem to me to circumscribe the limits of the woman's position in the discursive construction of cinema as a technology of modernity. The first is an outgrowth of the somewhat nostalgic conceptualization/mythification of the "first spectator's" response to the filmic image. The more familiar version of this scenario stipulates that the spectator is male or, at the very least, sexually nonspecific (a member of a crowd). This is the spectator who, overly susceptible to the filmic illusion of the real, flees in terror at the sight of Lumière's advancing train, and in doing so seems to fully accept the technological premises of the apparatus (that it can "capture" the real in a way heretofore impossible). Another, less familiar, conceptualization of the original naive spectator is presented by Michael Chanan, who relays a story told by an early inventor and entrepreneur, William Friese-Greene, "about a woman at one of the earliest demonstrations who went and poked her fingers at the image on the screen of a girl's face, convinced that the whole thing was an impossible illusion, and that there were holes in the screen for the eyes of a real girl standing behind it."[1]

The two types of stories (the spectator fleeing from the image of a train on one hand, and the woman doubting the image's very claim to be an image on the other) have different implications. The first concerns the illusion of reality, the second the reality of the illusion. The woman is no less wrong but her suspicion represents a higher level of sophistication—her suspicion is that the image is only pretending to be an image. What is at issue is not the authenticity of the relation between sign and referent but the authenticity of the sign's claim to be a sign. The conceptualization of the "first" spectator as a skeptical woman poking and testing the screen raises different questions, which nevertheless return to the issue of the cinema's relation to the real. For the woman doubts the viability of the apparatus itself as an apparatus. Her gesture constitutes a fundamental denial of cinematic technology in favor of the belief that there must be a real body there somewhere.

Technology's Body

The second historical anecdote I would like to cite is derived from a 1915 farce titled "A Photographer's Troubles." The play is structured by the problems of recognition and misrecognition associated with bodily images as they are played out in the context of a photographer's studio. A series of characters typified primarily by their desire to be other or different from themselves raise issues of photographic realism in relation to a finite and deficient body. A stout woman wants to look thin, a thin woman more fully rounded, and so forth. The question of photographic realism is thus suspended between the poles of referential truth and technical manipulation of the image. But beyond the rather banal logic of the plot, the most telling moment of the play perhaps is incarnated in dialogue attributed to a woman represented as singularly uneducated, unsophisticated, and lower class. Presenting her ugly children to be photographed, the woman insists, "I don't want my picture took. I had a tooth pulled onct and it hurt orful and I bet it hurts worse to hev your picture took."[2] The farcical nature of this comment, its absurdity, is a function of the immediate, unquestioned notion that photography is a technology that does not "touch" the body. The idea that "taking a picture" implies corporeal loss or diminishment can only provoke laughter.[3] The innocuousness of photographic technology (and this applies to any technology), its instrumentality, and hence its rationality are in a sense predicated on its separability from the human body which it strives to represent in all its contingency. Nevertheless, alongside this doubt, this assertion of a nonrelation between photography and the body, there continues to exist a certain fascination with the possibility of an imbrication of technology and the body.

The two historical anecdotes situate the woman as deviant spectator (poking the screen to find a pair of real eyes) or recalcitrant object (misreading technology's relation to the body as one of pain) of imaging processes. In other words, the figure of the woman is here defined as *excentric* to the real drama of the body being staged by and through the cinema. Such discourses indicate her marginal status in the male's epistemological confrontation with the technologies of modernity. For what is at stake in the early stages of development of the cinema is very much the body, but it is a body that is preeminently masculine, a body threatened and haunted by the specter of flaw or failure and by an anxiety generated by a conception of modernity as an assault on the body and its perceptual powers. My intention in this essay is to trace some of the consequences of the language of failure and compensatory prosthetic power that surrounds early speculation about the cinema.

The suspicion that lingers about the relation between technology and the body is that there may indeed be a connection between the two and that this connection can only be thought as a form of compensation. This is the idea of technology as prosthesis—an addition to or supplementation of a body that is inherently lacking, subject to failure, ontologically frail. Photography, as a technology of representation, would compensate for a perceived deficiency of the eye. This deficiency has to do with time and movement and, hence, what is often referred to as a "blurring" of discrete images associated with persistence of vision. In an 1888 issue of the *British Journal of Photography,* a writer claims that

> the light rays [in photography], if of sufficient energy, can, as we know, produce their due effect in a time which, to human appreciation, seems infinitely small. Thus, photography can observe and record the successive positions of a rapidly moving object; whereas, to the eye, the successive movements are, by the persistence of human vision, blended into a sort of general average, as in the case of a galloping horse; or lost in confusion, as in that of a rapidly spinning wheel.[4]

In 1881 J. D. B. Stillman, who was hired by Leland Stanford to analyze Muybridge's famous sequential photographs of horses in motion, made a similar point, arguing that the human eye is unable to discern a "distinct image of an object in an almost unconceivably short space of time."[5] The concept of the persistence of vision presupposes that a delayed image (an afterimage) blurs empirical distinctions between imperceptible stages of movement in time. Hence, the afterimage is the symptom of a failure in human vision for which photography, as a technology of images, compensates (unlike the cinema, which reinscribes this failure). The afterimage points to a flawed temporality.

As Jonathan Crary has compellingly demonstrated, the retinal afterimage became a central concept in the investigation of vision from the early years of the nineteenth century, when such investigations shifted from a focus on optics and the physics of the transmission of light to the physiological properties of human vision. He links the idea of persistence of vision to two different types of studies: one based on self-observation (associated with Goethe, Plateau, and others); the other the result of "accidental observation of new forms of movement, in particular mechanized wheels moving at high speeds."[6] For Goethe, the afterimage and other aberrations in human vision could not be contrasted to a "true" or "real" perception—instead, they begin to "constitute an irreducible component of human vision."[7] From this point of view, photography and the cinema were not the modern inheritors of the logic of the camera obscura (which resulted in the disembodiment of vision—its rationalization) but, rather, the consequences of the philosophical and scientific tendencies to conceptualize vision as a physiological function of the human body.[8] Crary traces a reorganization of the understanding of the observer during the nineteenth century that points to an increasing embodiment and subjectivization of vision.

In Crary's argument, the rupture that separated thinking about vision as a function of a perfectly operating camera obscura from thinking about vision as a physiological phenomenon linked to the body and temporality is the historical rupture that pinpoints the emergence of modernity. Interestingly, he claims that the increasing embodiment and subjectivization of vision lead to its increasing abstraction. As an attribute of the subject, vision becomes divorced from the realm of the referential and open to specific social manipulations. This is the project of modernity—to make the subject adequate to the construction of a new reality of fleeting images, exchangeability, flow. Modernity is here defined by the mobility of signs and commodities, the circulation of "vast new amounts of visual imagery and information."[9] Ultimately, for Crary, both modernity and modernism (as an aesthetic movement) are antireferential.

But I think the situation with respect to the cinema and its role in modernity as well as its relation to the body is more complex. Referentiality and the realist imperative certainly do not disappear in its dominant forms or from claims made for the apparatus and its relation to human vision. And unlike Goethe, figures more immediately linked to the advent of the cinema such as Etienne-Jules Marey and Eadweard Muybridge did indeed conceive of persistence of vision and the afterimage as a failure of adequation to the real and hence a flaw in human vision. The function of sequential photography, in their view, was to rectify this failing in the service of science and its project of understanding the reality of movement in time. Subjectivity constituted a hurdle to be overcome.

Although recent investigations have undermined the alleged scientific validity of the concepts of persistence of vision and the afterimage, at the turn of the century in the work of such figures as Marey, Muybridge, and Frank B. Gilbreth, the afterimage was embraced for its explanatory value and was understood as the scientific-philosophical concept underpinning the emergence of the cinema. Marey and Muybridge, who photographed animals in various stages of movement, are frequently cited as the predecessors of the cinema despite the fact that Marey, in particular, decried cinema and precinematic devices as "unscientific." The cinema, as Jean-Louis Comolli has pointed out, would seem to reinscribe the deficiency of the human eye, to exploit the notion of the afterimage in order to transform a series of still photographs into an illusion of movement.[10] Hence, we are faced with the strange consequence that the cinema, as a technology of images, acts both as a prosthetic device, enhancing or expanding vision, and as a collaborator with the body's own deficiencies.

When the woman in the 1915 farce implies that photography "hurts," the humor generated acts as a safeguard to protect the body from the dehumanization of the machine—and a machine that, in this case, "takes" bodily images. Pain signals the indisputable presence of the human body, its irrefutability as well as a certain resistance and inaccessibility to rationalization. If photography does not hurt, neither does the cinema; but it is interesting to note the extent to which proponents of the early cinema feel the need to demonstrate this over and over again—assuring the viewer that the spectatorial body is safe. This is done partially through the hypothesis discussed earlier of the unsophisticated spectator who runs away in terror from the image of the oncoming train, a myth of cinematic origins that is not entirely mythical, as Tom Gunning has provocatively demonstrated.[11] It is also partially accomplished through a certain self-reflexive tendency within the early cinema—a tendency to narrativize spectatorial dilemmas in relation to an unresponsive image. The most widely discussed instance of this is Edwin S. Porter's short 1902 film, *Uncle Josh at the Moving Picture Show,* in which the country rube, Uncle Josh, misrecognizes the film image as the real and attempts to interact in some way with the three films shown, hopping on the stage to dance with the Parisian dancer, fleeing in terror from an approaching locomotive, and jealously interfering with relations between a represented couple in the only way he can: by tearing down the screen. *Uncle Josh* dramatizes an unabatable surprise that vision could be dissociated from the body and mechanized in a way that left the body of the spectator untouched, unaffected. By inscribing the credulous spectator as comic, like the woman in the 1915 farce about photography, the film disavows any real relation between the cinema and the spectatorial body, the body figuring only as imaginary content.

This strategy acts as a form of buffer against the conceptualization of the cinema as an assault on the spectator. Indeed, the most recent theorization of the primitive cinema conceives of it in Benjaminian fashion as a series of visual shocks that are consistent with the disruption, rapid change, and sensory assault associated with modernity. But it is also the case that the cinema works to diminish this potential aggressivity by repetitively demonstrating the principle of spectatorial distance. Perhaps the most useful way of conceptualizing this attempt on the part of the early cinema to simul-

Technology's Body

taneously involve and yet safely bracket the body lies in Tom Gunning's analysis of the notion of the "thrill." Gunning aligns the aesthetic of what he calls the cinema of attractions (an early form of cinema organized around single events) with popular art's discourse of "sensations" and "thrills." He refers to "the particularly modern entertainment form of the *thrill*, embodied elsewhere in the recently appearing attractions of the amusement parks (such as the roller coaster) which combined sensations of acceleration and falling with a security guaranteed by modern industrial technology."[12] The very terms "sensation" or "sensational" hinge on the notion of an agitation of the body and its sensory apparatus. The thrill promises an excitation of the body without the accompanying threat of breaching its integrity. The early cinema seems to play out the extremely intricate imbrication of anxiety and reassurance associated with modern technology.

One particularly effective way of titillating the spectatorial body while guaranteeing its safety is to displace the potential aggressivity of the relation between film and spectator onto the register of the signified. Hence, there is a fascination in many early silent films with a surprisingly frank and unmediated sadism. In *Execution of a Spy* (Mutoscope/Biograph, 1902), a coffin is carried into the frame, a firing squad takes position, and the spy is shot. The event here, or in Gunning's terms, the "attraction," is quite simply the moment of death. A film titled *Reading the Death Sentence* (Mutoscope/Biograph, 1903) dwells on the moments before death when the female prisoner is formally presented with her death sentence, taken from her cell and led offscreen, presumably to her death. The continuation of this one-shot film, *An Execution by Hanging* (Mutoscope/Biograph, 1905), is more direct, its tableau presenting the preparation of the same female prisoner for a hanging, the draping of her body and head in a black sack, and the subsequent opening of the trap door and confirmation of death.[13] This fascination with death or the brink of death is also sustained in films like *Beheading the Chinese Prisoner* (Lubin, 1900), where the prisoner's head is displayed directly to the spectator, and *Electrocuting an Elephant* (Edison, 1903), in which smoke rising from the elephant's feet and the elephant's collapse assure the spectator of the authenticity of this depiction of death. As Miriam Hansen has pointed out, these films often effectively blur the usual distinctions between fiction and documentary: "The sensationalist appeal of such films cuts across documentary and fictional modes of representation and overtly caters to sadistic impulses; later films could do this only in the guise of narrative motivation and truth."[14] The predilection for death by execution is explicable by virtue of the fact that execution constitutes the only form of death that can be timed (as a public event) and hence "captured" by the camera. Whether the films are documentary or fictional their fascination is reliant on the cinema's capacity to provide the indexicality of an actual record.

Unlike live television, however, the filmic record is not instantaneous and films aspiring to be more overtly documentary often had to settle for an investigation of the traces of death. Two films made in 1900 that document the aftermath of a hurricane — *Searching Ruins on Broadway, Galveston for Dead Bodies* (Vitagraph) and *Scenes of the Wreckage from the Waterfront* (Lubin) — evince an obsessional return to the themes of death, disaster, and catastrophe. Even within the genre of comedy the humor is usually derived from a rather sadistic infliction of pain, often associated with a wife's beating of a husband who has proven to be unfaithful (*Appointment by Telephone* [Edison, dir. Porter, 1902]). In other comic shorts, as Noël Burch has demonstrated, closure can be conceived of only in terms of catastrophe.[15] And, finally, the influential genre of the magic film promoted by Georges Méliès and others was often structured around the sudden appearance and disappearance of bodies. These films seem to suggest that early cinema quickly made the body that which was most prominently at stake.

The spectatorial body the cinema addresses and the body its representations inscribe is a body continually put at risk by modernity. Indeed, modernity has been consistently theorized as an assault on the body and its sensory capacities. Georg Simmel wrote, in "The Metropolis and Mental Life," that "the psychological basis of the metropolitan type of individuality consists in the *intensification of nervous stimulation* which results from the swift and uninterrupted change of outer and inner stimuli."[16] Modernity is fundamentally an urban phenomenon — hence the relentless sarcasm directed at the "country rube" in early cinema. Inspired by Simmel, Walter Benjamin also analyzed modernity as a series of sensory shocks provided by new technologies and congested urban settings, contributing to an already widespread understanding of what Allan Sekula has referred to as "the essentially *pathological* character of metropolitan life."[17] In much of the philosophy and literature of the early years of modernity, this nervous overstimulation is linked to an accelerated temporality — to an almost unassimilable speed and series of rapid changes. Although such an image of modernity was certainly transnational it is most fully associated with the United States. Robert Musil, in *The Man without Qualities,* refers to the "social *idée fixe*" of "a kind of super-American city where everyone rushes about, or stands still, with a stop-watch in his hand."[18] Later in his novel, Musil draws a parallel between anxiety about temporality and anxiety about one's body image.

> For the looking-glass, originally created for delight—so it was expounded—had become an instrument of anxiety like the clock, which is a compensation for the failure of our activities to follow each other in a natural way.[19]

Furthermore, modernity is perceived as invasive in its relation to the body—reaching within the corporeal envelope to shock and shatter the nerves and sensory apparatus.

Another threat of modernity lies in its homogenization of bodies. The persistent return to the theme of the crowd in nineteenth-century literature reveals a fear of the anonymity and destabilization of identity associated with the city's throng of bodies. The monstrosity of Edgar Allan Poe's "The Man of the Crowd" resides in the fact that he fully accedes to this logic of anonymity, actively striving to lose himself in the crowd.[20] The protagonist of the story, catching a glimpse of this man from his chair at a London coffeehouse window, follows him in a wild attempt to know more about an individual he cannot categorize, ultimately discovering that the man can be characterized only negatively, through his absolute dread of being left alone. What is at stake is a fear of unreadability as a function of urban space. Walter Benjamin labels Poe's story "the X-ray picture of a detective story," invoking it in order to refine his analysis of Baudelaire's flâneur.[21] I am more interested in the question of knowledge and its relation to the body and identity as it is played out in this story. The protagonist spends his time in the opening moments of "The Man of the Crowd" visually cataloging the passersby outside his window—they are immediately typed by him as clerks, pickpockets, gamblers, merchants, and so on. But the face of the man of the crowd presents itself to him as an avatar of unreadability—in its uniqueness, it refuses all recognition and categorization and thus prompts the protagonist's voyeuristic pursuit. Significantly, the story is bracketed by references to an unreadability that is yoked to the phenomenon of crime. The first sentence presents a German saying (that is reiterated at the end): "It was well said of a certain German book that *'es lässt sich nicht lesen'*—it does not permit itself to be read."[22] Modern urban space presents itself to the subject as a dilemma of reading, of recognition, of identification. In the context of the fears about loss of identity, various technologies for stabilizing identity—including photography—are invoked. The popularity of physiognomy and phrenology (the science of reading one's inner character from the structure of the skull) indicate the extreme stress of anonymity. As Allan Sekula has pointed out, "Here was a method for quickly assessing the character of strangers in the dangerous and congested spaces of the nineteenth-century city."[23]

The body as the support of both identity and subjective perception is assaulted by a modernity understood as disruption, speed, and anonymity. In order to buttress the failing notion of identity, there arose an entire psychology of identity based on a certain relation to temporality that demands both duration and continuity. The French sociologist Gabriel Tarde argued in 1890 that "Identity is the permanence of the person, it is the personality looked at from the point of view of its duration."[24] The terms of this psychology of identity are remarkably similar to those used to provide the psychoscientific justification of the perception of motion in the cinema—in other words, the vocabulary of persistence of vision and the afterimage. The afterimage, as a lasting impression underpinning the perception of movement where there is none, guarantees the psychological stability of the image for the subject—it is the means by which a potentially disruptive movement is stabilized. When Simmel describes the excessive stimulation of the metropolis he opposes it to a form of psychological continuity defined in terms that quite precisely suggest the theory of the afterimage.

> Lasting impressions, impressions which differ only slightly from one another, impressions which take a regular and habitual course and show regular and habitual constraints—all these use up, so to speak, less consciousness than does the rapid crowding of changing images, the sharp discontinuity in the grasp of a single glance, and the unexpectedness of onrushing impressions. These are the psychological conditions which the metropolis creates.[25]

From this point of view, the psychoscientific designation of the afterimage as the technical raison d'être of the cinema provides a form of defense against modernity's assault on the body. Despite Benjamin's particular appropriation of Simmel in an argument about film as the inscription of shock and disruption, such a notion of continuity through time would act as an antidote to the discontinuities of modernity.

Ironically, such a continuity is based on a failure or flaw specific to human vision. The theory of the afterimage presupposes a temporal aberration, an incessant invasion of the present moment by the past, the inability of the eye to relinquish an impression once it is made and the consequent superimposition of two images. Paralleling the psychoscientific dominance of the afterimage in the period presaging and coinciding with the emergence of the cinema is a philosophical obsession with a nonlinear temporality as the mark of human subjectivity par excellence. This can be seen as in some respects a response to the conceptualization of modernity as accelerated temporality. But it takes the form of a new understanding of psychical history, of memory, and of a nonlinear temporality—particularly in the work of two thinkers who are in other respects quite diverse and even opposed: Henri Bergson and Sigmund Freud. In the work of both Freud and Bergson, the specificity of the human is linked to a temporal gap.

Bergson asserts, in *Matter and Memory,* the importance of duration, of waiting—of the gap between stimulus (sensation) and response. Perception is not in its essence subjective but resides in things; it is external rather than internal; it is lodged within the real. However, it is important to point out that this perception exists only in theory because it is continually invaded by memory.

> This perception, which coincides with its object, exists rather in theory than in fact: it could only happen if we were shut up within the present moment. In concrete perception, memory intervenes, and the subjectivity of sensible qualities is due precisely to the fact that our consciousness, which begins by being only memory, prolongs a plurality of moments into each other, contracting them into a single intuition.[26]

Perception, from this point of view, is only an "occasion for remembering" and "there is for us nothing that is instantaneous. In all that goes by that name there is already some work of our memory."[27]

The human experience of perception hence pivots on a temporal lag, a superimposition of images, an inextricability of past and present. To that extent it is a perverse temporality, a nonlinear temporality that cannot be defined as a succession of instants. According to Gilles Deleuze, "Bergsonian duration is defined less by succession than by coexistence."[28] And it is this peculiar temporality that for Bergson is the mark of the human—which is encapsulated in his theory in the term "spirit." In a Darwinian gesture, Bergson describes the development of various stages and intensities of "spirit" as a function of lower and higher "tensions of duration."

> We can conceive an infinite number of degrees between matter and fully developed spirit—a spirit capable of action which is not only undetermined, but also reasonable and reflective. Each of these successive degrees, which measures a growing intensity of life, corresponds to a higher tension of duration and is made manifest externally by a greater development of the sensori-motor system. But let us consider this nervous system itself: we note that its increasing complexity appears to allow an ever greater latitude to the activity of the living being, the faculty of waiting before reacting.[29]

Bergson goes on to insist that this more complex organization of the nervous system is in fact only a symbol of the human being's greater independence from matter, its freedom, hence its memory. In the interval between perception and action, an interval crowded with memories, lies the Bergsonian spirit, that is, human freedom.

For Freud, the specificity of the human psyche, as opposed to spirit, is also a function of a particular relation to temporality. Psychoanalysis is predicated on the notion that the human being is born *too soon,* that its organic immaturity forces an immediate dependence on the other that instigates the delays productive of desire, and that sexuality emerges long before the possibility of reproductive "use-value." Freud consistently appeals to the "specific prematurity of birth" of humans, particularly in comparison with other species. Furthermore, one of the most important concepts in the psychoanalytic theory of determination is a temporal one — that of deferred action (*après coup, Nachträglichkeit*). Again, as in Bergson, it is a question of a temporal gap — not between perception and action but between two different temporal moments that, although separate in time, collide in the psyche, the second occasioning a rereading of the first. Sexuality, for Freud, is the perfect field for the operations of deferred action because of its slow and uneven development in the human subject. An older child, more fully positioned within sexuality, rereads an earlier sexualized scene that was not understood in its sexual dimension at the time of its occurrence. This rereading is provoked by a second scene, which resembles the first only superficially and may be, in fact, completely desexualized. Psychical determination is hence not compatible with the concept of linear time and is, instead, a function of the reverberation between two events. According to Laplanche and Pontalis, it is not lived experience or the actual event that is subject to a later rewriting but rather "whatever it has been impossible in the first instance to incorporate fully into a meaningful context. The traumatic event is the epitome of such unassimilated experience."[30] The trauma would be the raw material that is never really accessible as such, outside meaning, its effectivity fundamentally dependent on its future readability.

Hence, for both Bergson and Freud, temporality is not measurable as the sum of discrete instants in linear formation. There is a certain failure of separation (between present and past; for Bergson, between matter and memory; for Freud, between readability and unreadability). For both, this aberrant or disorderly temporality is the mark of the human. Human temporality is defined as an uneven superimposition of moments. On one hand, this superimposition could be understood as failure in relation to "real" linear time or the "real" separability of past and present, or failure in relation to other species, that in comparison are not born prematurely in such a formative dependence on the other. On the other hand, this superimposition of temporal moments could be seen (and is by both Freud and

Technology's Body

Bergson) as the specificity of the "highest" species, the human. The polarity of possibilities is deceptive for there is a sense in which the specificity of the "highest" species *is* its failure. It is arguable that for Bergson this failure exists in the service of a higher continuity (of spirit), but for Freud the failure and discontinuity are more fundamental. Failure is constitutive of the human psyche in Freud — the inevitable failure of delay, the noncoincidence between desire and its object, the uneven development of sexuality. There are other significant differences between Freud and Bergson as well. For Bergson, memory is the mark of human freedom, of indetermination. For Freud, memory is the mark of the overdetermination of subjectivity.

Whether the failure or flaw exists in the service of a higher continuity of spirit or is a fundamental fact of the psyche, for both theorists the failure is not rectifiable through access to a pure present that would constitute the real. But from the point of view of the positivist science embraced by people like Marey, Muybridge, and the author of the article in the *British Journal of Photography,* the failure is an error that is rectifiable through the machine, the photographic apparatus that can capture a real not given to human vision. Bergson's perception equivalent to matter and Freud's unreadable raw trauma are not accessible to the human subject. Yet, for Muybridge, the moment of the real could be said to be the moment when the horse's hooves all leave the ground, a moment accessible only via the machine. It is in this sense that the cinema constituted for Marey and Muybridge the antireal — an illusion predicated on a failure of the human optical system.

For Marey and Muybridge, the afterimage is the biotechnical support of an illusory continuity. The reason why the cinema "works" — its ability to provide an illusion of movement — is conceptualized as a basic failure or weakness in human vision. Yet, this argument would seem to problematize the conceptualization of the cinema as a technology that would serve as a prosthesis in extending the capacities of the human body. For, as discussed earlier, from the scientific point of view, the afterimage marks a deficiency, a failure in human perception. The suggestion that the cinema operates by virtue of its inscription of such a failure or flaw indicates an attempt on the theoretico-philosophical plane to humanize the cinematic machine, to deny its status as a technology. The cinema's constant return to the body is symptomatic of a troubled confrontation with the dehumanization of the machine.

To perceive the cinema as collaborating in this way with the body's own deficiencies is not to rule out the possibility of a simultaneous imagination of the cinema as a prosthetic device that would improve on the human body. But what is the failure of the body that the early cinema, as prosthesis, responds to? I would suggest that there is another flaw at stake here and that we might call this flaw contingency. Contingency has to do with the very embodiment of vision, that which constitutes its finitude. In its propensity for the travelogue or the attraction that might otherwise go unseen, the cinema *makes up for* the contingency of human vision, its embodiment in a particular and limited time and place. What makes the suggestion that photography and by extension the cinema hurts laughable is the disembodiment of vision presupposed by the two technologies. From this point of view, the early cinema would incarnate a double and contradictory desire addressed to modernity—the desire to humanize the machine (by inscribing what are perceived to be flaws of the human body in an apparatus) and yet to simultaneously appeal to it as a supplement of the body, as a prosthesis that makes up for a lack. One could isolate two impulses in tension at the turn of the century—the impulse to rectify the discontinuity of modernity, its traumatic disruption, through the provision of an illusion of continuity (to resist modernity), and the impulse to embody (literally give body to) discontinuity as a fundamental human condition (to embrace modernity). The cinema, in effect, does both.

The body at issue in these discourses is a sexually and racially unspecified body. Such a configuration always suggests that what one is dealing with is, in fact, the white male body. And indeed, the language of failure or flaw and prosthetic power are those of a masculine scenario in which it is the male body that is put at risk by modernity. Furthermore, both Bergson and Freud make appeal to a theory of evolution that opposes the more advanced, civilized, and neurotic exemplar of the human species to a primitive—that is, racial other—defined in terms of an immediacy of the body and unrestricted sexuality. In Freud, a metonymic chain is constructed that links infantile sexuality, female sexuality, and racial otherness. Woman is the "dark continent" and the adjective "dark" here signifies not only unknowability but blackness in its racial connotations. Similarly, movements in the arts in modernism define themselves in terms of a complex and ambivalent relation to the concept of the "primitive."

Modernity's assault on the white male body is consistently theorized through the concepts of shock and trauma, which indicate a reverberation via the body to the psyche as a whole. There is a great deal of speculation in the late nineteenth and early twentieth centuries about the malleability of the human body in the face of technological and industrial changes associated with urban life. The body is seen more and more frequently as a complicated machine and less and less as a finite limit, grounding in an ahistorical nature the possibilities of human perception. In 1915, the Italian

Technology's Body

futurist Marinetti describes the superhuman of the future as a *man* "built to withstand an omnipresent speed. . . . He will be endowed with unexpected organs adapted to the exigencies of continuous shocks."[31] As discussed earlier, the notions of speed and the faster pace of urban life consistently recur in discourses on the restructuration of perception in modernity. Subjectivity seems particularly permeable to the effects of a revised organization of temporality. And such a temporality is perceived as having direct consequences for the body. The concept of shock, as deployed by Marinetti, Simmel, and Benjamin, is transformed into *the* theoretical concept capable of measuring the impact of a changing temporality. Shock, which originally referred to a physical blow and was part of a military-medical vocabulary, gradually came to indicate, in the context of the nineteenth-century technological accident, the disequilibrium of the entire organism, and, from there, a purely psychical malady that was legally recognized as such.[32] Similarly, the term "trauma," as Jean Laplanche demonstrates, was originally—and still is—operative as a medical term denoting a physical wound. But it gradually became psychologized as well and came to designate a purely psychical shock or penetration. Laplanche describes one of the semantic dimensions of the term "trauma" as "a breaking into the organism, entailing the rupture or opening of a protective envelope."[33]

Modernity is hence conceptualized in terms—shock, trauma—that suggest a penetration or breach of an otherwise seamless body. One way of dealing with the ensuing anxiety would be to envisage, as Marinetti does, a superhuman body endowed with new organs. Another way, which may ultimately come to the same thing, would be to construct a discourse that effectively constitutes itself as a denial of the body through the projection of contingency and embodiment onto the white woman or the racial other. This is in effect accomplished in the cinema through the progressive despatialization and disembodiment of the spectatorial position. The spectator is increasingly detached and dissociated from the space of perception. Such a position is most conducive to the reception of a technologically supported spectacle—a spectacle whose principal content is female embodiment.

The implicit alliance between the spectacular deployment of the female body in the cinema and the activation of technology as a compensatory prosthesis manifests itself in a specular organization that is present in the earliest films. From the one-shot films made in Thomas Edison's studio, which are only seconds long (the "Annabelle" dance series, 1895), to the early cinema's fascination with peeping Tom scenarios (e.g., *The Bride Retires* [France, ca. 1902], *Pull Down the Curtains, Suzie* [Mutoscope/Biograph, 1904]), the female body has been situated as the content of a cinematic dem-

543

onstration of technological prowess. While that prowess is incarnated as a somewhat rudimentary stare in these films, it is gradually elaborated to the level of a technically intricate manipulation of space. By the 1930s, the logic of this specular organization is fully in place and finds an exemplary instanciation in the work of Busby Berkeley.

I want to briefly consider Berkeley's work here as a kind of coda to the above discussion of the dialectic of failure and compensatory prosthetic power in early speculation about the cinema. His work is particularly appropriate to such a consideration because, simultaneous with the strong inscription of classical cinematic strategies in his films, there is a certain flirtation with modernism as well as a confrontation with modernity as dilemma and potential assault on human perception. His films also could be said to constitute a veritable celebration of the disembodied spectator or, in the words of Michel de Certeau, "the lust to be a viewpoint and nothing more."[34] Berkeley's spectacular regimentation of female bodies and his deployment of them as ornaments in a larger design have been extensively discussed. Berkeley himself situates "girls" as the pure content of spectacle.

> I love beautiful girls and I love to gather and show many beautiful girls with regular features and well-made bodies. It is the idea of spectacle which is expressed in "What do you go for?" What do you come to do, why do you go to a spectacle? It is not the story, it is not the stars, nor the music. What people want to see are beautiful girls.[35]

The spectacular presentation of the female body is buttressed in his films by the sheer technological prowess of elaborate crane shots and his famous (or infamous) through-the-legs tracking shots.

I would like to isolate three scenes from Berkeley's *Golddiggers of 1935* (Warner/First National) as exemplary dramas of the anxiety about modernity and the body I have tried to delineate here. The plot of the film is a fairly banal one about the courtship between a young and impoverished medical student working as a desk clerk in a posh summer resort and the overprotected daughter of a wealthy matron who is a guest at the resort. The wealthy woman's unenthusiastic financial backing of a charitable "milk fund" show is the rationalization for the inclusion of two characteristically Berkeleyesque spectacular numbers. The first of these is introduced by the opening of the curtains on the stage. From this point on, there is no pretense that the space of the production number is that of an outdoor stage with all its implicit limitations. To the contrary, the camera proceeds to mark out a series of impossible spaces. The camera initially cranes down from an image of the moon to a pastoral scene of Dick Powell singing to

Technology's Body

Gloria Stewart underneath a tree. After a series of closer shots including some shot/reverse-shot configurations, it tracks back to a long shot of the couple. There is subsequently a dissolve from this shot to that of a model of the couple beneath the tree resting on a large white piano played by one woman who is accompanied by two others who continue Powell's song. After a cut to a close-up of hands playing the piano, the camera pulls out to reveal an impressive multiplication of pianos with women in white playing them. The pianos are arranged on a kind of modernist stairway against a black background. The bulk of the sequence is a demonstration of the technical prowess of the camera in capturing a complex choreography of identical women playing identical pianos that seem to glide in and out of various designs. At one point there is a typical Berkeley overhead shot of two lines of pianos swinging together and apart in synchronization—neither the women nor the pianos are recognizable or distinguishable. Toward the end of the sequence, the camera tracks back from one woman dancing on the combined piano tops through a grillwork soon recognizable as that of a piano to some large artificial keys. A cut brings us back to a close-up on the woman's hands playing the first piano as the two other women accompany her. The camera tracks back as the woman blows out a candle on the piano top and the three ascend some stairs. From a close-up of a clock striking midnight, the camera tracks back to the miniature model of the couple under the tree, which is still resting on the piano. After a track into the model, there is a cut to the initial scene of Dick Powell and Gloria Stewart under the tree. A final cut to the audience applauding reestablishes the space of the diegesis.

What is most striking about the scene is the way in which it obliges the spectator to occupy a series of impossible places—inside a model or a piano or high above, looking down on the spectacle. There is no attempt whatsoever to rationalize the space, either in terms of the framing narrative or in its own right, as a tangible material space that might be occupied by a finite human body. The ensuing radical disembodiment of the spectatorial gaze mimics de Certeau's "lust to be a viewpoint and nothing more." In contrast to this bodi-less male gaze is the woman's relegation to the role of pure body, even if this body is abstracted in the service of sheer design. Going further than the traditional conventions of musical spectacle, the sequence inscribes this dialectic between disembodiment and embodiment as a crucial point of its very process.

Beyond the fairly weak supporting reference to the romantic relationship between Powell and Stewart, this musical sequence is completely disengaged from the overall narrative of the film. At first glance, this might seem to be even more true of the second musical sequence in the milk fund show, the more famous "Lullaby of Broadway" number. Unlike the piano number, however, this sequence contains a mininarrative whose structure and oppositions are reminiscent of those of the framing narrative. It also begins with the opening of the stage curtains but the space revealed is even less legible than that of the previous number. A singing female head, surrounded by blackness, is gradually brought closer until it is in full close-up. The head turns, brings a cigarette to its mouth, and is transformed into an aerial view of a cityscape. The camera tracks into this representation of the urban and the sequence proceeds to chronicle the temporal progression of a workday—the delivery of milk, the ringing of alarm clocks, women pulling on stockings, a ride in the subway, and various forms of labor. The female protagonist of the mininarrative, however, violates the normal and regularized progression of the workday by returning home from a night on the town to sleep just as everyone else leaves for work. She sleeps through the entire workday, rising only in order to prepare for another night on the town. The rest of the sequence traces her nighttime activities—drinking, dining, and dancing. The gay exuberance of this lifestyle is celebrated in the penultimate scene where she and Dick Powell, perched high above the dance floor at their own solitary table, witness a Busby Berkeley spectacle of regimented dancing bodies. However, the sequence takes a surprising turn when the female protagonist is coaxed to come down and dance with the others. Powell follows and she flees both the crowd of dancers and Powell to take refuge outside on a balcony behind a pair of glass doors. She and Powell kiss through the glass doors and then the crowd and Powell surge forward and open the doors. The female protagonist is pushed by the opening doors off the ledge and falls to her death. Her death is represented as a revolving point-of-view shot on the city street below, which gradually turns into a revolving shot of the clock outside her apartment window reading 3:30 A.M. The camera travels through her open window to reveal her empty bed and then to the door and her hungry cat, waiting to be fed. The sequence then returns to the cityscape, which is transformed back into the head of the woman smoking her cigarette. She completes the song "Lullaby of Broadway" as her head once again recedes into the distance.

The oppressive and pessimistic tone of this sequence seems radically out of place in the context of a musical show. It confronts many of the thematic motifs of modernity that are absent from the framing narrative—issues of work versus leisure time, the anonymity and regimentation associated with city crowds, the standardization of labor processes and the rationalization of temporality, the unrestricted sexuality associated with the modern

Technology's Body

woman. The female face merging into the cityscape indicates the collapsing together of two threats to the male body emerging from the scenario of modernity. The woman's perverse relation to temporality, her overturning of the hierarchy of work over leisure, leads inevitably to her death, represented as a revolving point of view of urban space brought back to the question of time and its rationalization through the image of the clock. Yet, in Busby Berkeley's work, an unconscious optics ensures that the opposition between work and leisure is destabilized and ultimately collapses. Leisure is no escape from work, for the Taylorist logic of the body that informs the workplace infiltrates the scene of entertainment through the regimentation and exact synchronization of the choreography. The dance numbers evoke Siegfried Kracauer's theory of the mass ornament, which he associates with such phenomena as the Tiller Girls, a dance troupe that performed in Busby Berkeley-like configurations. The mass ornament was "the aesthetic reflex of the rationality aspired to by the prevailing economic system" and it was a reflection of Taylorism insofar as "the hands in the factory correspond to the legs of the Tiller Girls."[36]

The "Lullaby of Broadway" number, seemingly completely disengaged from the narrative proper, is in reality a lyrical expansion of a basic premise of the narrative structure, briefly alluded to at the beginning of the film. The film's narrative is set in an upper-class resort hotel for the rich and the elite and while its emphasis on "golddigging" in the formation of couples mobilizes certain aspects of class difference and class conflict, for the most part the economic infrastructure of the resort is effectively repressed. However, a brief sequence at the beginning of the film delineates the role of the worker as the condition of possibility of the narrative itself. The film begins when a policeman interrupts a tramp reading a copy of *Saddle and Spur* on a park bench. After the tramp leaves, the policeman's glance is caught by an open page containing an ad for the Wentworth Plaza. A track in to the sign for the hotel dissolves to the actual sign being polished by a black worker. The camera pulls back to reveal a series of black "bellboys" sweeping the sidewalk in exact synchronization with the music. The rest of the sequence traces the various forms of work — gardeners clipping bushes, maids folding sheets, tables being unstacked and arranged — necessary for the preparation of the resort's summer season. All these activities are presented as part of a musical number, with regimented bodies moving in an exactly synchronized choreography that mimics that of the later staged numbers. But what is most striking about the sequence is the way in which its initiating shot centers black workers who subsequently disappear altogether from the narrative. The rest of the film effectively effaces any references to racial difference. Although hotel workers are intermittently worked into the plot, all of them are white. The black is situated outside the discourse of class conflict and social mobility characteristic of the motif of golddigging.

It is as though the inscription of blackness were a necessary prelude to the spectacular deployment of the white female body. Such a juxtaposition of the black male body and the staging of white femininity is even more strikingly evident in the work of German artists of the Weimar period who share an obsessive fascination with America and Americanism. One of John Heartfield's collages of 1927, for example, produces a mixture of typical American motifs and includes images of the Ku Klux Klan and a lynched man as well as lineups of beauty queens and dancers.[37] A 1924 woodcut by Gerd Arntz, titled *Things American,* conjoins three basic elements—a row of identical automobiles, and a lynched man and line of chorus girls sharing the same stage.[38] All the bodies are schematized and faceless but the lynched man is clearly black whereas the chorus girls are white. Under the shadow of Fordism and serialization, both are produced as the spectacular effects of a dialectic of embodiment and disembodiment. Lynching was a drama played out in relation to white male fears about black sexuality and the idea of the essential purity and perfection of the white woman. In *Things American,* a broken black male body is juxtaposed with the predictable, serialized perfection of the white female body—its abstraction and deployment within spectacle. It is the white male whose bodily absence from the representation is marked. The black female is totally excluded from the paradigm.

In *Golddiggers of 1935,* the figure of the black does not return, or returns only as the textual trace of exclusion. In the "Lullaby of Broadway" sequence, a strikingly white female face emerges from and gradually dominates a background of blackness. In the piano number, the whiteness of the women, of their costumes, and of the pianos is marked. In what seems reminiscent of a form of "white panic," the sequence constitutes a hysterical reassertion of the perfection of the body and of the fundamental inviolability of white femininity, regardless of the unleashed sexuality of the new woman.

A particular relation to spectacle thus emerges as the effect of a theoretico-philosophical dilemma concerning the body. Through their obsessive embodiment, the black male and the white female take on what modernity has specified as the burdens of contingency and embodiment. The threats associated with shock and trauma, with modernity's assault on the body and its perceptual powers, can be ameliorated through a certain logic of the spectacle supported by a vast technology. Berkeley's flamboyant crane shots implicate the female body in a representational process at the same time that they deimplicate the male body, producing it as a pure despatialized gaze. If the cinema is perceived in technical-philosophical discourse as a technological inscription of the optical deficiency evidenced by the afterimage, its practice can and does attempt to compensate for this flaw or failure through an emphasis on the prosthetic powers of the machine. Its *represented* vision is not flawed but, on the contrary, signals a superhuman mastery of space. To the extent that this is predicated on the refusal of contingency and embodiment, it shelters the white male body from the various shocks of modernity.

Ultimately, however, I think it is perhaps more interesting to underline the contradiction harbored in this discourse of technology and embodiment/disembodiment. A visual failure or confusion (understood as "persistence of vision") is technologically inscribed within the cinematic apparatus, producing a form of technical verification of what is perceived as a specifically human visual deficiency. This is one way of humanizing the cinematic machine — hence the diatribes of investigators like Marey who decry the cinema's "unscientific" nature, its destiny as a pleasure machine. But the cinema also and in contrast disembodies and mechanizes vision, countering its alliance with contingency. As such it functions as a prosthesis, extending and enhancing perceptual capabilities and, in the process, disengaging them from a finite and deficient body. Through the cinema, technology's relation to the body becomes one of both analogy and extension. Perhaps some of the continuing social ambivalence about the cinema's status as good object or bad object can be traced to the formulation of such a problematic in the early years of speculation about the new technology of representation.

Notes

1 Michael Chanan, *The Dream That Kicks: The Prehistory and Early Years of Cinema in Britain* (London: Routledge, 1980), 15.
2 Jessie A. Kelley, *A Photographer's Troubles: A Farce in One Act* (New York: French, 1915), 5.
3 I am referring here to a modern Western tradition of representation. The perception of a relationship between photography (or any production of an iconic likeness) and corporeal loss varies in different cultural and historical contexts.
4 H. Trueman Wood, "Some of the Applications of Photography to Scientific Purposes," *British Journal of Photography* (16 March 1888): 166.
5 J. D. B. Stillman, *The Horse in Motion* (Boston: Osgood, 1882), 12.

6   Jonathan Crary, *Techniques of the Observer: On Vision and Modernity in the Nineteenth Century* (Cambridge: MIT Press, 1990), 111.
7   Ibid., 97.
8   The logic of the camera obscura leads to the mechanization of vision in an apparatus that dissociates that vision from the human body, transforming it into a function of geometrical optics. Because the camera obscura is based on the principles of Renaissance perspective, it assumes a unified and centered subject. However, it represents that subject not as a body but as a position in space. See Jean-Louis Comolli, "Technique and Ideology: Camera, Perspective, Depth of Field," *Film Reader* 2 (1977): 135–137 for further discussion of the camera obscura.
9   Crary, *Techniques*, 96.
10 See Comolli, "Technique and Ideology."
11 Tom Gunning, "An Aesthetic of Astonishment: Early Film and the (In)Credulous Spectator," *Art and Text* 34 (spring 1989): 33.
12 Ibid., 37.
13 It was a common practice in the early days of the silent cinema to distribute multiple-shot films as separate one-shot products and to allow the exhibitor freedom to determine whether the shots would be shown singly or together.
14 Miriam Hansen, *Babel and Babylon: Spectatorship in American Silent Film* (Cambridge: Harvard University Press, 1991), 31.
15 Noël Burch, *Correction Please or How We Got into Pictures* (London: Optichrome, 1979), 20.
16 Georg Simmel, "The Metropolis and Mental Life," in *The Sociology of Georg Simmel,* trans. and ed. Kurt H. Wolff (London: Collier-MacMillan, 1950), 409–410.
17 Allan Sekula, "The Body and the Archive," *October* 39 (1986): 21.
18 Robert Musil, *The Man without Qualities,* trans. Eithne Wilkins and Ernest Kaiser (London: Secker, 1979), 30.
19 Ibid., 207.
20 Tom Gunning has a very provocative discussion of this story as a kind of parable of film spectatorship. See "The Book That Refuses to Be Read: Images of the City in the Early Cinema" (unpublished manuscript).
21 See Walter Benjamin, *Charles Baudelaire: A Lyric Poet in the Era of High Capitalism,* trans. Harry Zohn (London: New Left Press, 1973), 48.
22 Edgar Allan Poe, "The Man of the Crowd," in *Edgar Allan Poe,* ed. Philip Van Doren Stern (New York: Viking Press, 1945), 107.
23 Sekula, "The Body and the Archive," 12.
24 Ibid., 25.
25 Simmel, "The Metropolis and Mental Life," 410.
26 Henri Bergson, *Matter and Memory,* trans. N. M. Paul and W. S. Palmer (New York: Zone Books, 1988), 218–219.
27 Ibid., 66, 69.
28 Gilles Deleuze, *Bergsonism,* trans. Hugh Tomlinson and Barbara Habberjam (New York: Zone Books, 1988), 60.

29 Bergson, *Matter and Memory*, 221–222.
30 Jean Laplanche and J. B. Pontalis, *The Language of Psychoanalysis*, trans. Donald Nicholson-Smith (New York: Norton, 1973), 112.
31 Cited in Stephen Kern, *The Culture of Time and Space, 1880–1918* (Cambridge: Harvard University Press, 1983), 122.
32 See Wolfgang Schivelbush, *The Railway Journey: Trains and Travel in the Nineteenth Century*, trans. Anselm Hollo (New York: Urizen, 1979), 145–151.
33 Jean Laplanche, *Life and Death in Psychoanalysis*, trans. Jeffrey Mehlman (Baltimore: Johns Hopkins University Press, 1976), 129.
34 Cited in Constance Balides, "Scenarios of Exposure in the Practice of Everyday Life: Women in the Cinema of Attractions," *Screen* 34, 1 (spring 1993): 27.
35 Cited in Lucy Fischer, "The Image of Woman as Image: The Optical Politics of *Dames*," in *Genre: The Musical*, ed. Rick Altman (London: Routledge, 1981), 71.
36 Siegfried Kracauer, "The Mass Ornament," trans. Barbara Correll and Jack Zipes, *New German Critique* 5 (1975): 70.
37 The collage was produced as endpapers for J. Dorfmann, "Im Lande der Rekordzahlen" (Vienna/Berlin, 1927), reprinted in Beeke Sell Tower, *Envisioning America: Prints, Drawings, and Photographs by George Grosz and his Contemporaries 1915–1933* (Cambridge: Harvard University Art Museums, 1990), 52.
38 Collection Kees Broos (Arnhem, 1924), reprinted as figure 43 in Tower.

CATHERINE RUSSELL

Parallax Historiography

The Flâneuse as Cyberfeminist

> Cyborg imagery can suggest a way out of the maze of dualisms in which we have explained our bodies and our tools to ourselves. This is a dream not of a common language, but of a powerful infidel heteroglossia.
> —Donna Haraway

Haraway's cyborg manifesto may seem an odd choice of theoretical paradigms for developing insight into silent cinema; and yet I would like to suggest that new media technologies have created new theoretical "passages" back to the first decades of film history. The flâneuse, an imaginary construction of female subjectivity who is our guide in this journey, is herself a cyborg. She figures the relationship between women and technology as a mobile, fluid, and productive means of, in Haraway's words, "building and destroying machines, identities, categories, relationships, spaces, stories."[1] Recent developments in film historiography by feminist theorists have shifted the emphasis from textual analysis of the woman onscreen to the invisible history of the spectator-subject. As Patrice Petro puts it, "In contrast to formalist film historians, who seek to recover what is increasingly becoming a lost object, feminists have been primarily concerned to unearth the history of the (found) female subject."[2] This is a discovery that calls for discourse drawn from the utopian genres of technofeminism.

That this "discovery" of female subjectivity has been motivated by the parallels between early cinema and new imaging technologies is, I believe, a fundamental aspect of the new feminist film historiography. The term "parallax" is useful to describe this historiography, because it is a term that invokes a shift in perspective as well as a sense of parallelism. In this article I explore the parallels between visual culture at the beginning and end of the twentieth century, and also the historical effects of this parallax historiography: what does it say about history alongside what it says about cinema? I suggest that it constitutes a real challenge to the hegemony of

Parallax Historiography

classicism and all that it entails within the discourse of film studies. I argue that parallax historiography is a discursive formation premised on the archival function of new technologies that enable us to rewrite film history; and also that this rewriting constitutes a valuable revision of the modernity of cinema as a site of shifting identities and viewing positions.

In the early 1990s three books appeared on silent cinema that, taken together, articulate a new perspective on the first decades of film, a perspective very much formed by the transformations of visual culture at the end of the century. Miriam Hansen's *Babel and Babylon* (1991), Anne Friedberg's *Window Shopping* (1993), and Giuliana Bruno's *Streetwalking on a Ruined Map* (1993) share a very specific historical perspective on cinema spectatorship.[3] Although they appear to be somewhat conversant with each other's projects, these three writers seem to have worked through a similar set of problematics more or less independently. For each of them, the parallels between early cinema and late-twentieth-century visual culture constitute a bracketing of "classical cinema" as an intermediary period. The most important link between pre- and postclassical cinema, and what motivates this parallax historiography, is a construction of spectatorship that challenges the unitary, transcendental spectator position of the classical period. Before and after classical cinema, spectatorship is conceived as more fluid, mobile, unstable, and heterogeneous than the limited position of "mastery" that has been theorized as both masculinist and bourgeois.

The parallels between the avant-garde cinema of the 1960s and 1970s with early cinema were instrumental in the rethinking of preclassical cinema as an integrated, autonomous practice deserving of close study when film scholars turned their attention to it in the late 1970s. And yet, the implied "eclipse" of the classical period, the reduction of classical cinema to a historical blip in the middle of the twentieth century, is an important consequence of this most recent incarnation of parallax film historiography. Hansen has herself posed a series of questions regarding the parallels between early and what she calls "late" cinema. She asks, "What is the point of such a comparison? How can we make it productive beyond formalist analogy, beyond nostalgia or cultural pessimism? How can we align those two moments without obliterating their historical difference?"[4]

Hansen's own response is to think about larger transitions in the development of the public sphere that occur at either end of the century. The potential of the cinema to produce an "alternative public sphere" is manifest in the specific forms of reception and exhibition of the two periods. In other words, unlike the earlier parallelism between the avant-garde and so-called primitive cinema, there is no real formal analogy between the two periods in this parallax historiography. That is to say, the works of the two periods may not look the same, but they have similar functions in the public sphere. Hansen focuses on the interactivity of audience-film relations in both periods, and the ways that "marginalized and diverse constituencies" are addressed. Early and late cinemas do not, she argues, have a homogenizing effect on the diversity of spectators, but enable subcultural formations of reception. The historical interlude of classical cinema also marks the brevity of "mass culture," which may have dominated visual culture from the 1920s into the 1960s but, Hansen argues, has given way to "the diversifications of global electronic media."[5]

Thus, for Hansen, "late cinema" refers specifically to shifts in the public sphere, brought about by new technologies of distribution and exhibition of visual culture. The term invokes the equally indeterminate categories of "postclassical" and "postmodern" cinemas, which imply corresponding shifts in industry practices and aesthetics. If postclassical cinema refers to the stylistic and institutional changes in Hollywood films since the 1960s dissolution of the "classical" system of studio production, postmodern cinema refers to the shifts in spectatorship entailed by that dissolution.[6] Timothy Corrigan argues that "in the contemporary cinema without walls, audiences remove images from their own authentic and authoritative place within culture and disperse the significance across the heterogeneous activity that now defines them."[7] "Late cinema" denotes the historical significance of these shifts as being on a threshold. And it is this sense of a cusp between "the decline of classical humanism" and the "possibility for multiple and polymorphous re-embodiments" engendered by new imaging technologies that is encompassed by the term "late cinema." For Rosi Braidotti, postmodernity is most importantly a "threshold of new re-locations for cultural practice," which includes a shift toward more imaginative styles of theorizing.[8] The parallax historiography of early and late cinemas, featuring the flâneuse as the mobile, virtual spectator, is precisely such an instance of postmodern feminist historiography.

Equally uncertain is the designation "early cinema" in Hansen's analysis of the parallels between the two periods. While "early cinema" often refers to the cinema before 1905, in Thomas Elsaesser's influential anthology *Early Cinema* it refers to the cinema before 1917.[9] Hansen's theorization of the public sphere of silent film in *Babel and Babylon,* however, covers the entire silent period, to the end of the 1920s. Without losing sight of the immense changes in institutions and aesthetics that took place over the first thirty-five years of the cinema, we can also point to the continuity of woman's contradictory role throughout this period. During the

Parallax Historiography

slow transformation of "the cinema of attractions" into classical cinema, women were at once fetishized, terrorized, and stereotyped onscreen, while being courted as potential consumers and spectators offscreen.[10] To the extent that this constellation of effects was sustained throughout the silent period—until women got their voices—for the purposes of this essay I would like to designate early cinema as more or less synonymous with silent cinema. This is in keeping with Hansen's call for an alternative view of film history that would include all the extrainstitutional aspects of the cinematic experience that enabled female spectators to construct imaginative responses to onscreen images, by extending the "space" of the film into public life.[11]

Architectures of Reception

The model of spectatorship that Bruno, Friedberg, and Hansen coincidentally describe is best thought of as a counterapparatus theory. By locating early cinema within a complex cultural space of architecture, theater, journalism, and diverse popular entertainments, the activity of film viewing is conceived as a function of everyday life. Moreover, the mobility of the spectator through the diversity of spectacles, along with the role of intertextuality in early cinema, renders the viewer's participation highly interactive. If the spectator position of apparatus theory aligns viewing with transcendental forms of consciousness and the illusions of visual mastery, the spectator of early and late cinema is an embodied, socially configured, and heterogeneous construction. Classical cinema becomes aligned with apparatus theory, and designates a period in which the cinema acquired a certain autonomy from other mediums of representation.

Although parallax historiography may have evolved along with real changes in cinematic production, exhibition, and spectatorship, it also implies a critique of the discursive alignment of classical cinema and apparatus theory. We should be suspicious of the conflation of a historical period with a theory of spectatorship. None of the authors actually goes so far as to make such a critique; indeed late cinema is defined by Hansen and Friedberg as constituting a break with classicism. And yet in advocating and developing an alternative theory of spectatorship, these theorists are also impinging on the very framework of the classical period. In her discussion of Rudolph Valentino and female spectatorship in the 1920s, Hansen promotes the identification of spectators who read "against the grain" of the classical text, and encourages an appreciation of the diversity within classical cinema.[12] The most radical effect of parallax historiography may be an ultimate denial of the existence of classical cinema and its constitutive forms of spectatorship. Perhaps classical cinema was only a mode of viewing and theorizing film; perhaps Laura Mulvey's call for "passionate detachment" has always been an option for viewing that is only fully realized in early and late cinemas, precisely because of their architectures of reception.[13]

By noting the dispersed and fragmented modes of spectatorship common to early and late cinemas, we can perhaps understand how important architecture is to notions of spectator "positioning." The ideal of classical narrative cinema, theorized by Christian Metz, fixes the gaze of the spectator onto the projector/camera's line of sight. In retrospect, this constitutes a denial of the gaze that looks "nearby," the sideways glance, and the possibilities of assuming alternative viewing positions.[14] Such assumptions of classicism as a monolithic apparatus tended to collapse important distinctions between genres and modes of film practice that, in fact, solicit very different forms of spectatorship.[15] Why should we deny the potential for distracted, resistant, and differently gendered viewers seated in the thousands of film theaters all over the world?[16] Parallax historiography suggests that apparatus theory was itself an ideological production of mass culture, a construction that reproduced, in theory, a specific architecture of reception.

The importance of architecture as a context of film viewing is one of the central contributions of Giuliana Bruno's work on early cinema. The central figure of her book is Elvira Notari, a prolific Neapolitan filmmaker whose work had been largely overlooked by historians of Italian cinema. Notari's films, many of them filmed on the streets of Naples, were screened in theaters incorporated into the huge gallerias, glass-covered shopping malls that became important social centers in late-nineteenth-century Europe. Bruno describes the Neapolitan version of a phenomenon that existed in many metropolitan centers:

> the Galleria extended the function of the piazza (forum), the Italian urban site of meeting and promenade, social events, and transitory activities. It represented the coalescence and transformation of public life, typically and traditionally set in the urban piazza, into modern terms. Cinema, housed in the arcade, was thus grounded in a locus of spectacle and circulation of people and goods, in a metropolitan site of diverse social configurations—from those of a social elite and intelligentsia to that of the underworld.[17]

These arcades are of course the focus of Walter Benjamin's great unfinished key work of cultural studies. It is important to keep in mind that

Parallax Historiography

he describes these structures as the allegorical ruins of the nineteenth century lingering into the twentieth. He perceived them as "passages" through time as well as through space. Bruno and Friedberg both take this as a cue for their own work on early cinema, as a means of framing their investigations from the perspective of a much later date. Cinema in the passages, or arcades, is seen as the emblem of a version of modernity that aims to challenge the different modernity of classical cinema. Theirs is an inverted modernism, one that looks "back to the future" as a means of locating a different formation of the modern subject. All three writers quote Benjamin's words from "The Work of Art in the Age of Mechanical Reproduction":

> Our taverns and our metropolitan streets, our offices and furnished rooms, our railroad stations and our factories appeared to have us locked up hopelessly. Then came the film and burst this prison-world asunder by the dynamite of the tenth of a second, so that now, in the midst of its far-flung debris, we calmly and adventurously go travelling.[18]

As we know, it is not only the implantation of cinema in the shopping arcades of the turn of the century that preoccupied Benjamin, but its role in urban, metropolitan culture. He linked cinematic effects of montage and spatial construction to the psychological experience of big city life. The stimulus and shock of traffic, of the crowd, of the dense fragmentation of space, have been recognized as determining factors of the first two decades of film culture.[19] Benjamin's notion of "shock" is at once a means of describing the aesthetics of early cinema and the spectator's experience of everyday life, in which the cinema is implicitly implicated.

Benjamin's theorization of cinema and modernity in fact informs the parallax historiography of early and late cinema on several different levels. The loss of "aura" that he attributes to mechanically reproduced art is the basis of this historiography insofar as electronic media represent another stage in the transformation of the public sphere. The loss of aura does not refer to an attitude of nostalgia toward that which is vanishing, but to a perspective of historical transformation that is fundamentally utopian in nature. In contrast to a teleological or evolutionary historiography of "progress," Benjamin advocates a dialectical historiography. Within the context of the arcades project, Benjamin wrote:

> The dialectical image is an image that emerges suddenly, in a flash. What has been is to be held fast—as an image flashing up in the now of its recognizability. The rescue that is carried out by these means—and only by these—

can operate solely for the sake of what in the next moment is already irretrievably lost.[20]

The correspondence between early and late cinema is constructed as a dialectical relation in which the electronic age plays the role that photographic technologies played in the early decades of the century. If in the cinema Benjamin recognized the traces of earlier forms of experience sustained allegorically in what he called "the land of technology," we need to ask if there is a parallel redemptive effect in this second stage, this corresponding shift in the technologies of representation at the end of the century. Insofar as electronic imaging technologies are themselves a means of retrieving the past in visual form, the redemptive effect lies precisely in the production of a historically mobile spectatorship.

Bruno mentions "airplane cinema" as a recent incarnation of the implantation of cinema in architectures of transit. She claims that "embodying the dynamics of journey, cinema maps a heterotopic topography," "a site whose system of opening and closing both isolates it and makes it impenetrable, as it forms a type of elsewhere/nowhere," a description that seems to fit nothing as well as it does the Internet, although she is referring to the cinema of the first decades of the century.[21] In a more recent article, Bruno has developed her observations on the architectures of early cinema into a larger theorization of the cinematic experience as a haptic, transitory inhabitation of space. She writes:

> Locked within a fixed gaze, the film spectator was turned into a *voyeur*. Speaking of siteseeing implies that, because of film's spatio-corporeal kinetics, the spectator is a *voyageur* rather than a *voyeur*. Through this shift to *voy(ag)eur*, my aim is to reclaim female mobility, arguing, from the position of a (film) *voyageuse*, that film is a modern cartography. It is a mobile map.[22]

Implicit in Bruno's rethinking of cinema spectatorship is an alliance between the implantation of silent cinema in the metropolis, and the traveling afforded by the Internet and channel surfing. The dethronement of the eye as the key instrument of visual culture constitutes her feminist challenge to theories of cinema as voyeurism and mastery.

Hansen, for her part, claims that it is the video market that has made "the classical spectator an object of nostalgic contemplation."[23] It is within the specific framework of the disintegrating aura that the alternative public sphere, as a "heterogenous, and at times unpredictable horizon of experience," is made possible. The plurality of spectatorship is inscribed within the sites and conditions of reception—besides forms of textual address,

Parallax Historiography

which conceptions of classical cinema struggled to unify and universalize. The most important effect of parallax historiography on contemporary visual practice is to consider it as an opening up of new forms of spectatorship, ones that may have some parallels in the visual culture of a hundred years ago, but more significantly, transform the public sphere of classical cinema into a vanishing form of experience. In fact the eclipse of the "subject" of classical film narrative may not be an occasion for nostalgia at all, because this unitary (male) subject may not even have existed outside the theoretical discourses of mass media and psychoanalytic semiotics.

Of the three writers, Friedberg comes closest to erasing classicism, although even she does not make such a claim, perhaps because she is interested in the changes brought about by postmodern modes of viewing. She goes much further than either Hansen or Bruno in describing the changes in visual culture effected by electronic media. Televisual spectatorship constitutes a fundamentally different form of subjectivity, one that is distinguished above all by its temporal dislocations. For Friedberg VCR time shifting—the ability to record TV shows, and the ability to interfere with a film's narrative temporality during playback—is the most significant shift in the public sphere of electronic media. She further links this temporal mobility to the spatial mobility of multiplex film exhibition located in shopping malls. The idea is that spectators "shop" for movies in the video store, in the shopping mall, via channel surfing, or eventually, on the Internet (although Friedberg does not include the Net in this 1993 book).

Friedberg also maps the parallels between early cinema and postmodernism most thoroughly. Her model of "the mobile, virtual gaze" links these two periods, and differentiates them from classical cinema. The temporal and spatial mobility of the gaze is developed in nineteenth-century forms of tourism and travel before it is inscribed in cinematic representation; the virtual aspect of the gaze precedes the cinema in the array of dioramas, panoramas, wax museums, and photography. The mobile, virtual gaze refers to the consumer-as-subject in visual culture; Friedberg argues that the spectator-shopper "tries on identities" and time travels through film and cultural history. If Internet chat rooms are the apotheosis of this "trying on of identities," classical cinema is a throwback to a static novelistic form, a discursive trap that prevented the medium from realizing its true heritage as a phenomenon of urban, global culture.

Friedberg argues that "Postmodernity is marked by the increasing centralization of features implicit (from the start) in cinema spectatorship." She goes on to say that "The subjectivity of the 'postmodern condition' appears to be a product of the industrialized acceleration of spatial and temporal fluidities" dynamics that were commodified in the mid-nineteenth century.[24] The implication is that electronic imaging technologies are the realization of various effects of modernity that were originally inscribed in cinema, but were unrecognizable until the late twentieth century. The cinema in this reading is a passage through or across time that enables us to understand modernity differently. The parallax historiography of early and late cinema is thus not really about cinema at all, but about modernity. Film studies' preoccupation with formalism and narratology has masked the modernity of the public sphere that the cinema continues to construct and reconstruct.

If new electronic media and digital forms of representation do represent a loss of cinematic aura, it is referentiality itself that is lost. The "secondariness" of Benjaminian allegory has become a more radical detachment of signification in an era of digital image processing, so that images themselves become the substance of a materialist culture. The surfaces, styles, and textures of the past become a phantasmagoria of history. Benjamin's theory of representation is, however, one that is already built on a temporality of displacement and loss; if parallax historiography encourages us to understand contemporary image culture differently, I would argue that it foregrounds the archival function of postmodern recycling practices. The American Library of Congress has made part of its collection of early cinema available on the Internet; and one can "travel" on the Internet to the Web site of the American Mutoscope and Bioscope Company, where one can virtually visit its New York studios of the 1890s, and buy an array of merchandise, including screen savers and videos.[25] Not only is the marketing of early cinema in the late 1990s made possible by the Internet, but new media has made early cinema into a consumable product. Teaching silent cinema becomes easier every year, as more resources become available in electronic form. What is lost in terms of auratic experience is gained in terms of the expanding repertoire of image culture, a repertoire in which the loss of experience is unambiguously inscribed.

Digital imaging technologies enable a redemption of media culture in their archival function, but for feminist film historians, it is most definitely not nostalgia that informs the backward view into history. In the gendered world of silent cinema, parallax historiography scans the texts for clues to the women who watched them, without fixing our gaze on the images of women that those women were offered. The critic's gaze, like the spectators of silent cinema, is a mobile, virtual gaze that is both spatially and temporally discontinuous. I would argue that this form of spectatorship is

Parallax Historiography

a key element in the conception of late cinema developed within parallax film historiography. When we shop for films on video, we can shop for historical moments; and we can perform a kind of rescue of the female gaze, if not save the emblematic woman tied to the tracks.

The Flâneuse

The different kind of modernity developed in parallax historiography finds its most sustained model in the flâneur who was introduced by Charles Baudelaire as a "passionate spectator" of "the flickering grace of all the elements of life."[26] The man in the crowd who transforms urban space into a kaleidoscope of imagery, who is at once detached and himself part of the spectacle, becomes, for Benjamin, the aura of heroism in modern life, an essentially melancholy figure.[27] Flânerie constitutes the activity of living in public, of moving through city streets, a form of subjectivity in transit. For the nomadic flâneur, the street becomes a home, while the buildings and the cityscape provide the contours of the rooms in which he dwells. Thus the cinema, as an extension of flânerie, inverts this spatial mobility, rendering the interior of the theater an exterior space in which to wander. But flânerie equally refers to a specifically modernist temporality. If the Benjaminian flâneur sees the traces of experience, of previous times within the fashions of commodity culture, the film spectator likewise sees "reality" as an allegorical, secondary representation—as a virtuality. The flâneur thus brings together all the key themes of parallax historiography: spatial and temporal dislocation, and mobile spectatorship within a public sphere of visual culture that includes the cinema within a larger field of technologies, mediums, and architectures of reception.

For both Baudelaire and Benjamin, the flâneur was indisputably male. Chief among the sights of the city through which he wandered was the prostitute, herself a streetwalker, as the title of Bruno's book reminds us. In mid-nineteenth-century Paris, as Baudelaire's discourse of modernity unfolded, women were part of the phantasmagoria of commodity culture, evoking in the male poet a complex desire for the mass-produced modern object. She functioned as an emblem of the intersubjectivity of flânerie, the object that "looks back" in a distanced, allegorical way. One of the things that Benjamin is particularly drawn to in Baudelaire's poetry of modernity is the frozen gaze of the women. Their eyes are "polished"; they are "illuminated like shop windows." The woman's glance figures prominently in Baudelaire's poetry, but it is a dangerous, fleeting look that causes the flâneur no end of anxiety.[28] The woman on the street provokes a specific form of modern subjectivity, but she herself is denied subjectivity.

Contemporary feminism has grappled with the notion of the flâneuse, a female incarnation of the flâneur. Janet Wolff has argued that the flâneuse is an impossible concept because of the engendering of modernity that could not account for the presence of women in the public sphere.[29] It was impossible for women who were "on the streets" to gain the invisibility of the flâneur. While men could observe the parade of modernity from the cloak of anonymity, women needed to go in drag to achieve such freedom. Wolff quotes George Sand, who had to adopt the dress and manner of the male flâneur to move about Paris freely.[30] It is well established that women of many classes and occupations were a visible presence on the metropolitan streets of Europe and North America since the mid-nineteenth century, although, as Anke Gleber puts it, "they didn't own the streets."[31] Insofar as the predominant image of the woman on the street was the prostitute, for whom the street was her workplace, the visibility of women was closely linked to a sexual threat. For the male flâneur this produced a paranoid fear of losing himself in the erotic charge of city streets.[32] The sight of unaccompanied single women was a catalyst for the eroticization of femininity in public life, such that the modernity of urban space was explicitly feminized by many writers of the early twentieth century.[33] Writing about the display of women in the cinema of attractions, Constance Balides argues that "in rehearsing the boundaries of space, the films point to the way the scandal of prostitution — its everyday visibility — could attach itself to women more generally."[34]

As a conceptual paradigm, the flâneuse is a means of prefiguring the sexualized, fetishized inhabitant of the city as an agent of spectatorial activity, whose power rests not only in her eye, but in her mobility as well. Gleber has suggested that the "discovery" of the female flâneur "would offer an alternative to woman's status as an image," inscribing a model of resistance for woman.[35] Friedberg and Bruno have both revised the notion of the flâneuse to recover some of the power that is latent in the female look described by Baudelaire. What he saw only as a "glance" or a "stare" was in fact developed as a "gaze" by an emergent consumer culture. Friedberg argues that the female consumer was addressed directly as a flâneuse by the department stores and arcades of the nineteenth century. Moreover, the relation between looking and buying that was configured in the increased emphasis on display and shop windows constructed the flâneuse as a mobile spectator. The mobile, virtual gaze that is institutionalized in the cinema thus had its origins in a consumer culture and its coextensive production of female subjectivity. Bruno further develops this version of the flâneuse into the psychological space of fantasy opened up by the cinema:

> Cinema provided a form of access to public space, an occasion to socialize and get out of the house. Going to the cinema triggered a liberation of the woman's gaze, enabling her to renegotiate, on a new terrain of intersubjectivity, the configuration of private/public.[36]

Female spectatorship, theorized on the model of the flâneuse, is a function of shopping and consuming. To the extent that cinema is inscribed within consumer culture, it realizes the potential of image culture to provide an alternative public sphere for women. It is a model that tends to negate narrative forms of identity formation and subject positioning, in favor of the activity of moviegoing as one among many urban pleasures. Miriam Hansen does not invoke the figure of the flâneuse herself, but describes the alternative public sphere of early cinema as a space where the "conditions of possibility" of a "tradition of female spectatorship" can be traced.[37] She concedes that this function may not be measurable "in any empirical sense," and yet textual and extratextual evidence suggests that "a commercially fostered threat to the male monopoly of the gaze" circulated within the public sphere of early cinema.[38]

Among the many films popular among women were the white-slavery films of the 1910s, a cycle that was indisputably stimulated by the anxiety provoked by the visibility of women on metropolitan streets.[39] This small "genre" of white-slavery films was spawned by *Traffic in Souls* (1913), a film that, Tom Gunning has suggested, initiated the "urban thriller" genre that we now associate with film noir. Gunning argues that the city in *Traffic in Souls* prefigures the omniscient underground systems that Fritz Lang would develop in the 1920s. He describes these networks as "impersonal systems of entrapment, both legal and illegal, a traffic which pulses beneath the city's surface, determining direction and circulation beyond our will or even our knowledge." In the narrative logic of the film, this system "has its origins in the contradictory relation of the figure of the prostitute to the categories of visuality and urban space."[40]

If these decentralized systems described by Gunning evoke the hidden web of communications technology that has begun to replace urban space in the twenty-first century, the flâneuse assumes her place as the cyberfeminist who has displaced the voyeur. In Sadie Plant's technofeminism, the triumph of technology is a triumph over "man" and his dualistic categories of "humanity." "With the development of self-regulating systems, man has finally made nature work, but now it no longer works for him. It is as though humanity was simply the means by which the global system, the matrix, built itself; as if history was merely the prehistory of cyberfeminism."[41] Thus the flâneuse is a figure who may well be fictional, who may even be a parodic figure, but is above all a projection of feminism onto a history of oppression. Parody, argues Braidotti, is an important strategy for "opening up, through successive repetitions and mimetic strategies, spaces where forms of feminist agency can be engendered."[42]

Parallax Historiography

Shopping and other forms of entertainment and spectacle flank early cinema in much the same way as contemporary theater and TV advertising contextualize film viewing at the end of the century. Indeed channel surfing and Internet browsing again suggest themselves as parallel models of spectatorship. However, we don't tend to think of these modes of spectatorship as particularly or necessarily relevant to female viewers. It may only be through the parallax effect of this historiography that they become the terrain of the flâneuse. In fact the parallels between contemporary forms of spectatorship and those of early cinema are only partial. To the extent that we are witnessing a proliferation of new modes of viewing film at home, a domestication of visual culture, we are in the midst of a devolution of the urban setting of the cinema. The cinematic public sphere is being reconfigured as an "emergency geography" of disparate moments, locations, and viewers.[43] Numerous theorists have described the different temporality of video culture as nonlinear and instantaneous—a state of perpetual catastrophe in which the fragmentation effect of image culture has moved onto a fundamentally different level than the fragmentation provoked by the metropolitan culture of the early twentieth century.[44]

If cities contain the traces and ruins of previous generations layered over each other, digital technologies produce new structures of memorialization in which fragments are recombined and recontextualized in new architectures of reception, including the classroom, the compilation film, and the digital image banks of electronic storage. Relocated in the archive, early cinema is remade and rethought along the lines of the invisible, impossible flâneuse; modernity itself is thus engendered differently as the cultures of shopping and image consumption are seen to collide. It is an invented, fantastic, even literary form of historiography based more on contemporary desires for new models of female spectatorship than on empirical evidence

Parallax Historiography

or historical documentation. And yet, the mobile, virtual gaze is also a gaze into history, invoking cinema as a time machine that can always take us back, but we will always go back differently, as different women.

The utopian discourse of cyberfeminism is stimulated by a breaking down of received categories of thought, including the dualities of nature/culture, subject/object and male/female.[45] The posthumanism of the electronic age points to the incorporation of technology into daily life, an incorporation that cinema spectatorship was instrumental in inaugurating in its first decades. If we can imagine the flâneuse as a cyborg, we can historicize the role of women in this virtual world of urban space. Moreover, the category of the flâneuse enables us to think beyond the structures of voyeurism and visibility that have hitherto kept women as the objects of the gaze.

The recognition of the past as coming to legibility now, in a Benjaminian configuration of the lightning flash or the "waking" of the dialectical image, is a fundamentally different historiography than that evoked by a critic such as Jean Baudrillard, who argues that after the linearity of modernist "progress," sometime in the 1980s, history took a turn in another direction: "In our non-Euclidian space of the end of the century, a malevolent curvature invincibly reroutes all trajectories. . . . Every noticeable movement of history brings us imperceptibly closer to its antipode, indeed to its point of departure."[46] The multiple international celebrations of the centenary of cinema do indeed seem to qualify as what Baudrillard describes as "a misdirected or misfired labour of mourning that wants to review, re-write, restore and facelift everything." He wonders whether "the movement of modernity is reversible, and is the reversibility, in turn irreversible? How far can this retrospective activity, this dream of the end of the millennium go?"

I would respond that the parallax historiography of early and late cinema does not simply involve a rewriting or reversibility of history. Instead, it conceives of history as a panorama that shifts according to the gaze of the observer. Other gazes besides those of the flâneuse have been projected onto early cinema. Fatimah Tobing Rony, for example, has cast what she calls a "third eye" on early ethnographic experiments in racial representation.[47] If Baudrillard advocates an "alternative temporal orbit" that would "take an elliptic short-cut and go beyond the end by not allowing it to take place," this is precisely the effect of parallax film historiography. The new modes of spectatorship that have been "discovered" in early cinema have not yet actually been experienced. The flâneuse did not exist, because she could not be recognized within the construction of the modernist gaze.

Now that we know who she is, we can go on to locate her in the new media of the twenty-first century. The institutional form of classical cinema is potentially disappearing along with the analogue technologies that held spectatorship in place. Thus, the parallax historiography of early and late cinema is a fundamentally utopian feminist projection within the postmodern public sphere.

Benjamin's dialectical historiography has itself come into perspective at the end of the century, as his observations on the phantasmagoria of consumer culture seem to have increasing relevance to the expanding technologies of commerce and communications. At the same time, his warnings about the "aestheticization of politics" need to be heeded in a climate of increasing consolidation of media ownership. What redemptive effect of electronic imaging can be harnessed for resistance to the power formations of new technologies? I would locate the redemptive effect in the revisioning potential of the expanded archive, which, among other things, enables us to dismantle the monolith of "classical cinema" into a heterogeneity of fragments. The bodies of stars, the textures of landscapes and cityscapes, and the vocabularies of fashion and objects take on new referential and evidential (documentary) value in the dismantling of narrative space that is enabled by the digitization of cinema. Since the dismantling of apparatus theory, new methods of film analysis that review cinema as the site of cultural performance have revitalized feminist film scholarship in important ways.[48]

The transformation of classical cinema into a cultural museum is a function of architectures of reception that Paul Virilio argues have in fact been in place since cinema's inception: "Since the beginning of the twentieth century, the classical depth of field has been revitalized by the depth of time of advanced technologies."[49] Virilio's claim that with the Lumières' first projections, "the screen abruptly became the city square, the crossroads of all mass media," is, of course, an observation that can only be made from the perspective of the end of the twentieth century.[50] And yet, once we overcome the duality of classical cinema and its "others" of preclassical and postclassical cinemas, we are better able to understand the role of cinema in the twentieth century as a continuously evolving site of public negotiation of the appearances and values of social life.

Parallax historiography entails a wholesale rethinking of the modernity of cinema. For feminist film historiography the eclipse of classicism enables a rereading of gender as a function of the public sphere of cinema, legible in textual discourses of excess alongside the detail of everyday life. Melodrama as it has been theorized by Thomas Elsaesser and Peter Brooks may be a means of mapping this continuous, unbroken, but ever-evolving history of narrative cinema as a language of popular desires, fears, and values.[51] The modernity of melodrama, as it intersects with technologies of "mechanical reproduction," produces not a single spectator, but a plural and heterogeneous spectatorship that becomes even more fragmented through the historical distances produced in the archive. The mobility of the flâneuse as cyberfeminist is precisely a temporal mobility, produced through the archival function of digital imaging technologies.

The modernity of cinema, reconceptualized through the discourse of parallax historiography, eclipses classicism and the hold of what Benjamin described as "the novelistic" on our discourse on cinema. Apparatus theory was premised on the identity of the viewing subject as a singular consciousness. The specificity of the cinematic apparatus insisted on a production of the subject "cut off" from social processes, in the half-light of the imaginary. "Storytelling," in contrast, which Benjamin saw as giving way to "information" in the media culture of the twentieth century, is grounded in the realities of social life and intercommunication.[52] If he saw the information society as replacing the wisdom and counsel of storytelling, perhaps the archiving of narrative cinema constitutes a redemption of storytelling in allegorical form. Peter Brooks likewise has suggested that the modernity of melodrama lies in its relevance to the struggles of everyday life in the absence of moral absolutes.[53] The parallels between early and late cinemas point to the way that the forms and institutions of moving pictures are deeply implicated in social space. As we have seen, the public sphere of cinema, since its origins in the metropolis, was specifically gendered, populated, and marked by the feminine. The modernity of cinema is thus the extent to which it has always been, and continues to be, the expression of a "new society" in which gender roles, chief among social relations, are endowed with continuously evolving forms, textures, and moral values. For feminist film historiography, this constitutes a reclaiming of all cinema as women's cinema, a "breaking out of the cave" (as Bruno puts it), and an inscription of the body into the modernity of cinema's public sphere.[54]

Cinema may not be "over," and yet as it becomes increasingly enmeshed with video and digital technologies, its autonomy may well be giving way. Parallax historiography encourages us to rethink film history in terms of the different forms of spectatorship engendered by the spatial and social inscriptions of visual culture in everyday life. Late cinema is modeled on the notion of archival cinema, in which film is remade electronically and viewed in a diversity of architectures. "Late cinema" may in fact be a more useful term than "postmodern cinema," because it suggests transition rather than termination, cycles rather than breaks, and designates the curious isomorphism of cinema and the twentieth century as the basis for an alternative view of cinema's modernity.

Notes

1. Donna Haraway, "A Manifesto for Cyborgs: Science, Technology, and Socialist Feminism in the 1980s," in *Feminisms,* ed. Sandra Kemp and Judith Squires (New York: Oxford University Press, 1997), 482.
2. Patrice Petro, "Feminism and Film History," *Camera Obscura* 22 (1990): 11.
3. Miriam Hansen, *Babel and Babylon: Spectatorship in American Silent Film* (Cambridge: Harvard University Press, 1991); Anne Friedberg, *Window Shopping: Cinema and the Postmodern* (Berkeley: University of California Press, 1993); Giuliana Bruno, *Streetwalking on a Ruined Map: Cultural Theory and the City Films of Elvira Notari* (Princeton: Princeton University Press, 1993).
4. Miriam Hansen, "Early Cinema, Late Cinema: Transformations of the Public Sphere," in *Viewing Positions: Ways of Seeing Film,* ed. Linda Williams (New Brunswick: Rutgers University Press, 1994), 140.
5. Ibid., 136, 138.
6. Peter Kramer, "Post-Classical Hollywood," in *The Oxford Guide to Film Studies,* ed. John Hill and Pamela Church Gibson (Oxford: Oxford University Press, 1998), 289.
7. Timothy Corrigan, *A Cinema without Walls: Movies and Culture after Vietnam* (New Brunswick: Rutgers University Press, 1991), 6.
8. Rosi Braidotti, "Cyberfeminism with a Difference," in *Feminisms,* ed. Kemp and Squires, 521, 525.
9. Thomas Elsaesser, ed., *Early Cinema: Space, Frame, Narrative* (London: British Film Institute, 1991).
10. Gaylyn Studlar, "The Perils of Pleasure? Fan Magazine Discourse as Women's Commodified Culture in the 1920s," in *Silent Film,* ed. Richard Abel (New Brunswick: Rutgers University Press, 1996); Ben Singer, "Female Power in the Serial-Queen Melodrama: The Etiology of an Anomaly," *Camera Obscura* 22 (1990): 91–130.
11. Miriam Hansen, "Adventures of Goldilocks: Spectatorship, Consumerism, and Public Life," *Camera Obscura* 22 (1990): 66.
12. Hansen, *Babel and Babylon,* 245–268.
13. Laura Mulvey, "Visual Pleasure and Narrative Cinema," *Screen* 16:3 (autumn, 1975): 6–18.
14. Christian Metz, *The Imaginary Signifier: Psychoanalysis and the Cinema,* trans. Celia Britton et al. (Bloomington: Indiana University Press, 1982). See Trinh T. Minh-ha, *Framer Framed* (London: Routledge, 1992), 96.
15. Williams, ed., *Viewing Positions.*
16. In a scene from the novel *The God of Small Things* by Arundhati Roy (1997), set in India, a family drives a great distance to see *The Sound of Music* in a

town called Kerala. The story is set in 1969, and this outing is a regular family ritual. Once inside the theater, the little boy in the family is so excited by the songs that he sings along very loudly and his mother asks him to go and sing in the lobby because he's embarrassing her. He is then molested by the Refreshments Counter Man, although the boy is so entranced by the filmgoing experience that he hardly knows what is happening to him behind the refreshments counter. I cite this fictional example of spectatorship because it is so suggestive of how even so-called classical cinema can become the site of a complex set of relationships, activities, and cultural contestations, and how it produces a public sphere that extends far beyond the text of the film itself, even if it is also very much produced by that textuality.

17 Bruno, *Streetwalking*, 43.
18 Walter Benjamin, "The Work of Art in the Age of Mechanical Reproduction," in *Illuminations,* trans. Harry Zohn, ed. Hannah Arendt (New York: Schocken, 1969), 236.
19 Ben Singer, "Modernity, Hyperstimulation, and the Rise of Popular Sensationalism," in *Cinema and the Invention of Modern Life,* ed. Leo Charney and Vanessa R. Schwartz (Berkeley: University of California Press, 1995).
20 Walter Benjamin, *The Arcades Project* (1927–1939), trans. Howard Eiland and Kevin McLaughlin (Cambridge: Belknap Press of Harvard University Press, 1999), 473.
21 Bruno, *Streetwalking,* 57.
22 Giuliana Bruno, "Site-Seeing: Architecture and the Moving Image," *Wide Angle* 19, 4 (1997): 10.
23 Hansen, *Babel and Babylon,* 3.
24 Friedberg, *Window Shopping,* 179.
25 American Library of Congress. The Life of a City: Early Films of New York, 1898–1906 http://memory.loc.gov/ammem/papr/nychome.html (2000). American Mutoscope and Bioscope Co. http://www.muto1895.com/main page (2000).
26 Charles Baudelaire, *The Painter of Modern Life and Other Essays,* trans. Jonathan Mayne (New York: Garland, 1978), 9.
27 Walter Benjamin, *Charles Baudelaire: A Lyric Poet in the Era of High Capitalism* (1929–1940), trans. Harry Zohn (London: Verso, 1983), 66.
28 Benjamin, *Charles Baudelaire,* 149–50, 124–125.
29 Janet Wolff, *Feminine Sentences: Essays on Women and Culture* (Berkeley: University of California Press, 1990), 47.
30 Ibid., 148; Anke Gleber, "Women on the Screens and Streets of Modernity: In Search of the Female Flâneur," in *The Image in Dispute: Art and Cinema in the Age of Photography,* ed. Dudley Andrew (Austin: University of Texas Press, 1997), 59.
31 Gleber, "Women," 61.
32 Katharina von Ankum, "Gendered Urban Spaces in Irmgard Keun's Das kunstseidene Mädchen," in *Women in the Metropolis: Gender and Modernity in Weimar Culture,* ed. von Ankum (Berkeley: University of California Press, 1997), 164–165.

33 Patrice Petro, "Perceptions of Difference: Woman as Spectator and Spectacle," in *Women in the Metropolis,* ed. von Ankum, 41–66.
34 Constance Balides, "Scenarios of Exposure in the Practice of Everyday Life: Women in the Cinema of Attractions," in *Screen Histories: A Screen Reader,* ed. Annette Kuhn and Jackie Stacey (Oxford: Clarendon Press, 1998), 75.
35 Gleber, "Women," 78–79.
36 Bruno, *Streetwalking,* 51.
37 Hansen, *Babel and Babylon,* 125.
38 Ibid., 121.
39 Shelley Stamp Lindsey, "Wages and Sin: Traffic in Souls and the White Slavery Scare," *Persistence of Vision* 9 (1991): 90–102; Tom Gunning, "From the Kaleidoscope to the X-ray: Urban Spectatorship, Poe, Benjamin, and *Traffic in Souls* (1913)," *Wide Angle* 19, 4 (1997): 25–61.
40 Gunning, "From the Kaleidoscope," 52.
41 Sadie Plant, "Beyond the Screens: Film, Cyberpunk, and Cyberfeminism," in *Feminisms,* ed. Kemp and Squires, 508.
42 Braidotti, "Cyberfeminism," in *Feminisms,* 526.
43 Timothy Corrigan, "Immediate History: Video Tape Interventions and Narrative Film," in *The Image in Dispute,* ed. Andrew, 309–327.
44 Corrigan, "Immediate History"; Mary Anne Doane, "Information, Crisis, Catastrophe," in *Logics of Television: Essays in Cultural Criticism,* ed. Patricia Mellencamp (Bloomington: Indiana University Press, 1996), 222–239; Doane, "Temporality, Storage, Legibility: Freud, Marey, and the Cinema," *Critical Inquiry* 22 (winter 1996): 313–343.
45 Haraway, "Manifesto," in *Feminisms,* ed. Kemp and Squires, 482.
46 Benjamin, *The Arcades Project,* 461; Jean Baudrillard, "Reversion of History," trans. Charles Dudas, *Ctheory* (1992) http://www.ctheory.com/a-reversion_of_history.html. Feb. 2, 1999.
47 Fatimah Tobing Rony, *The Third Eye: Race, Cinema, and Ethnographic Spectacle* (Durham: Duke University Press, 1996).
48 Pamela Robertson, *Guilty Pleasures: Feminist Camp from Mae West to Madonna* (Durham: Duke University Press, 1996); Sarah Berry, *Screen Style: Fashion and Femininity in 1930s Hollywood* (Minneapolis: University of Minnesota Press, 2000); Stella Bruzzi, *Undressing Cinema: Clothing and Identity in the Movies* (London: Routledge, 1997).
49 Paul Virilio, "The Overexposed City," in *Rethinking Architecture: A Reader in Cultural Theory,* ed. Neil Leach (London: Routledge, 1997), 389.
50 Ibid.
51 Thomas Elsaesser, "Tales of Sound and Fury: Observations on the Family Melodrama," *Monogram* 4 (1972): 2–15; Peter Brooks, *The Melodramatic Imagination: Balzac, Henry James, and the Mode of Excess* (New York: Columbia University Press, 1984).
52 Benjamin, "The Storyteller," in *Illuminations,* 87.
53 Brooks, *The Melodramatic Imagination,* 205.
54 Bruno, *Streetwalking,* 56.

Contributors

CONSTANCE BALIDES is Associate Professor in the Department of Communication at Tulane University. She has published articles in *Screen, Camera Obscura,* and various anthologies, and is completing a book on women and silent cinema titled *Making Dust in the Archives: Archaeologies of Vice, Thrift, and Management in U.S. Silent Film.*

JENNIFER M. BEAN is Assistant Professor of Cinema Studies at the University of Washington, Seattle. She is an advisory board member for the Women Film Pioneers Project, and is coeditor, with Diane Negra, of a *Camera Obscura* special issue on early women stars. She is currently working on her book *Bodies in Shock: Gender, Genre, and the Cinema of Modernity.*

KRISTINE J. BUTLER is Assistant Professor of French at the University of Wisconsin, River Falls. She is currently working on a book-length manuscript on the aural flâneur in late-nineteenth-century French literature and early film. She has published on Caribbean women's literature, and on the films of Chantal Akerman, Pedro Almodóvar, and Jean-Luc Godard.

ANGELA DALLE VACCHE is Visiting Assistant Professor at the Georgia Institute of Technology. She is author of *The Body in the Mirror: Shapes of History in Italian Cinema* and *Cinema and Painting: How Art Is Used in Film.* She is currently working on two projects: a book on the diva of silent Italian cinema and an anthology on classical film theory and the history of art.

MARY ANN DOANE is George Hazard Crooker Professor of Modern Culture and Media and of English at Brown University. She is the author of *The Desire to Desire: The Woman's Film of the 1940s* and *Femmes Fatales: Feminism, Film Theory, Psychoanalysis.* She has also published a wide range of articles on feminist film theory, sound in the cinema, psychoanalytic theory, and sexual and racial difference in film, melodrama, and television. Doane is currently completing a book on technologies of representation and temporality at the turn of the century, tentatively titled *Technologies of Temporality in Modernity.*

LUCY FISCHER is Professor of Film Studies and English at the University of Pittsburgh, where she directs the film studies program. She is the author of *Jacques Tati, Shot/Countershot: Film Tradition and Women's Cinema, Imitation of Life, Cinematernity: Film, Motherhood, Genre,* and *Sunrise.* She is currently at work on a sixth book, *Designing Women: Art Deco, Cinema, and the Female Form.*

CONTRIBUTORS

JANE M. GAINES is Professor of English and Director of the Program in Film and Video at Duke University. She recently completed *Fire and Desire: Mixed Race Movies in the Silent Era* and coedited *Collecting Visible Evidence*. Her book on early women in the film industry, *Fictions and Histories,* is forthcoming.

AMELIE HASTIE is an Assistant Professor in the Film and Digital Media Department at the University of California, Santa Cruz. She is currently at work on a historiographical consideration of writings by women who worked in the silent-film industry as directors or stars. Her other research interests concern fashion, television, Hong Kong film, and independent women's production. Her work has appeared in *Afterimage, Cinema Journal, Post Script, Enterprise Zones: Critical Positions on Star Trek,* and *Camera Obscura*.

SUMIKO HIGASHI is Professor Emerita at the State University of New York, Brockport. She is the author of *Cecil B. DeMille and American Culture: The Silent Era* and numerous works on women in silent film, film history, and film as history.

LORI LANDAY is Assistant Professor of General Education at Berklee College of Music in Boston. Her publications include *Madcaps, Screwballs, and Con Women: The Female Trickster in American Culture* and essays on cultural history and digital narrative. She is currently working on an interactive CD-ROM on Jazz Age America, animated music videos for the Web, and a book on American film comedy.

ANNE MOREY teaches at Texas A & M University in the English and Performance Studies departments. Her book *Outside In: Self-Commodification and the Hollywood Outsider, 1914-1934* is forthcoming.

DIANE NEGRA is Lecturer in Film and Television studies at the University of East Anglia. Along with Jennifer Bean, she is coeditor of a *Camera Obscura* special issue on early women stars. Her publications include *Off-White Hollywood: American Culture and Ethnic Female Stardom* and a number of articles in anthologies and journals. She is currently preparing an edited collection titled *The Irish in Us: Irishness, Performativity, and Popular Culture*.

CATHERINE RUSSELL is Associate Professor of Film Studies at Concordia University, Montreal. She is the author of *Narrative Mortality: Death, Closure, and New Wave Cinemas* and *Experimental Ethnography* (Duke, 1999).

SIOBHAN B. SOMERVILLE is Associate Professor of English and Women's Studies at Purdue University. Her publications include *Queering the Color Line: Race and the Invention of Homosexuality in American Culture* (Duke, 2000) and articles in journals such as *American Literature* and the *Journal of the History of Sexuality*.

SHELLEY STAMP is the author of *Movie-Struck Girls: Women and Motion Picture Culture after the Nickelodeon,* named to *Choice Magazine*'s list of Outstanding Academic Titles in 2000. She is Associate Professor of Film and Digital Media at the University of California, Santa Cruz.

CONTRIBUTORS

GAYLYN STUDLAR is Rudolf Arnheim Collegiate Professor of Film Studies at the University of Michigan, where she directs the program in film and video studies. She is the author of *This Mad Masquerade: Masculinity and Stardom in the Jazz Age* and *In the Realm of Pleasure: Von Sternberg, Dietrich, and the Masochist Aesthetic.* She has coauthored four anthologies, most recently *Titanic: Anatomy of a Blockbuster* and *John Ford Made Westerns.* She is currently working on a social history of women and Hollywood film culture.

RADHA VATSAL is a filmmaker and graduate student at Duke University. She lives and works in New York.

KRISTEN WHISSEL is Assistant Professor in the Program in Film and Video at the University of Michigan, Ann Arbor. She is currently completing a book titled *Picturing the Nation: Moving Pictures and American Modernity.*

PATRICIA WHITE is Associate Professor and Chair of Film and Media Studies at Swarthmore College. She is a member of the editorial collective of *Camera Obscura* and author of *Uninvited: Classical Hollywood Cinema and Lesbian Representability.*

ZHANG ZHEN is Assistant Professor of Cinema Studies at New York University. Her critical and creative writings have appeared in numerous journals and anthologies, including *Public Culture, Asian Cinema, Cinema and Urban Culture in China, 1922–1943,* and *Spaces of Their Own.* She is currently completing a book on early Chinese film culture and vernacular modernity.

Index

Abel, Richard, 5, 195, 217
Acker, Jean, 65
Addams, Jane, 185
Adrian, 478, 480, 494
Adventurous Sex, The, 240
Affairs of Anatol, The, 315, 318, 321
Affron, Charles, 493
Affron, Mirella, 493
Agrest, Diana, 468
Albrecht, Donald, 481
Aleramo, Sibilla, 462
Allan, Maud, 74, 80
American Federation of Labor, 178
American Museum of the Moving Image, 1
Amorous History of the Silver Screen, An, 21, 501–503, 506–511, 512, 516, 517, 521
Anger, Kenneth, 67, 68–69, 71
Arbuckle, Fatty, 66
Armatage, Kay, 92
Art deco, 477–497
Arwas, Victor, 482
Arzner, Dorothy, 88, 89, 91–93, 98, 99
Astrea, 20, 445, 450, 456–457, 458–461
Astrea, 456
Auerbach, Nina, 382

Badger, Clarence, 237–238
Baker, Josephine, 232
Balides, Constance, 152, 153, 562
Ballets Russes, 79, 405, 480, 482
Banner, Lois, 497
Bara, Theda, 77, 79, 202–203, 374, 379, 385, 386–387, 393, 404, 414. *See also* Goodman, Theodosia
Barriscale, Bessie, 423
Battery B Arriving at Camp, 151
Baudelaire, Charles, 537, 561–562
Baudrillard, Jean, 565

Baudry, Jean-Louis, 12, 97, 99, 100, 101, 107, 109, 111, 433
Bauhaus, 482
Bear, A Boy, and A Dog, A, 123
Beard, George Miller, 144
Beardsley, Aubrey, 68, 72, 79–80, 81
Bederman, Gail, 144, 145, 155
Beheading the Chinese Prisoner, 535
Bellamy, Madge, 224
Bellour, Raymond, 12, 433
Benjamin, Walter, 9, 34, 47, 408, 425, 429, 431–432, 435–436, 502, 534, 536, 537, 538, 543, 556–558, 560–561, 565, 566–567
Bennett, Tony, 241
Benstock, Shari, 37
Berger, John, 221
Bergman, Ingrid, 376
Bergson, Henri, 47, 230, 539–542
Bergstrom, Janet, 12, 13
Berkeley, Busby, 22, 544–549
Bernardi, Daniel, 156
Bernhardt, Sarah, 78–79, 413, 483
Bertsch, Marguerite, 256, 257
Billing, Noel Pemberton, 80
Biograph films, 170
Birth Control, 270, 271, 284–292
Birth of a Nation, 37, 263, 271, 272
Blaché, Herbert, 34, 47, 48–49, 50. *See* Guy-Blaché, Alice
Blaché, Simone, 106. *See* Guy-Blaché, Alice
Black Oxen, 240
Blackton, J. Stuart, 257
Blade Runner, 119
Blood and Sand, 98
Bluebird Film Company, 169
Blumer, Herbert, 221, 235
Blumin, Stuart M., 299
Boardman, Eleanor, 299

Bordwell, David, 8, 9, 68
Borelli, Lyda, 20, 445, 448, 450, 451–453, 455, 457–459, 463, 467
Bow, Clara, 17, 224, 227, 232, 233, 234, 237–243, 299, 339, 400
Boyer, Paul, 183
Brady, Alice, 423–424
Braidotti, Rosi, 554, 564
Brandeis, Madeline, 16, 122, 127–136
Brennan, Timothy, 388
Bride Retires, The, 543
Brooks, Louise, 224, 232, 233
Brooks, Peter, 566–567
Brownlow, Kevin, 169
Bruno, Giuliana, 10, 13, 14, 22, 91, 100, 105, 167, 553, 555–556, 558–559, 562–563, 567
Bruno, Michael, 376, 395
Bryant, Charles, 64, 65
Buck-Morss, Susan, 431
Burch, Noel, 536
Burning of the Red Lotus Temple, The, 508, 510
Burstein, Jessica, 429
Butler, Alison, 9, 10, 11

Cabbage Fairy, The, 15, 101, 103–104, 106–109, 111, 116 n. 54
Cabinet of Dr. Caligari, The, 66
Cahiers du Cinema, 103
Callahan, Vicki, 7, 200, 206, 216, 436
Camille (1921), 65, 71, 77, 78
Camille (1927), 99
Carey, Gary, 492
Carroll, Noel, 228
Castle, Irene, 232, 406, 417–418, 426
Castle, Vernon, 232
Cazals, Patrick, 202
Censi, Giannina, 454
Chalupec, Apolonia, 375. See also Negri, Pola
Chanan, Michael, 530
Chaplin, Charles, 124, 230, 385, 396–397
Charcot, Jean-Marie, 427
Charney, Leo, 7
Cheat, The, 306, 310, 334
Children of all Lands, 128, 129, 132
Chosen People, The, 63

Chow, Rey, 520
Civic Repertory, 64
Cleo Madison Stock Company, 90
Cody, Lew, 335
Cohl, Emil, 103
Colette's Minne ou L'ingenue libertine, 216
Colored Troops Disembarking, 156, 157
Commedia dell'Arte, 463
Comolli, Jean-Louis, 411, 533–534
Comstock Laws, 271, 292
Cook, Burr C., 409
Cooper, Mark, 154
Corbin, Virginia Lee, 224
Corner in Wheat, A, 169
Corrigan, Timothy, 554
Courtney, William Basil, 258
Courtot, Marguerite, 406
Covered Wagon, The, 99
Cowie, Elizabeth, 109
Crary, Jonathan, 418, 532–533
Crawford, Joan, 17, 221–224, 231–237, 243, 299, 338, 339
Cripps, Thomas, 252, 263
Crofts, Stephen, 89
Cross-dressing, 258–261
Crowther, Bosley, 68
Cuban Refugees Waiting for Rations, 157, 158
Cultural studies, 12, 13
Cunard, Grace, 122, 406, 415, 417, 426
Cup of Life, The, 16, 167, 169, 170, 172, 174, 180, 181, 183–185
Curse of Eve, The, 291

Daddy-Long-Legs, 352, 364
Damaged Goods, 274
Dancing Mothers, 233
Daniel, Robert L., 497
D'Annunzio, Gabriele, 445–447, 456–457, 463, 464
Danza dell'aviatrice, 454
Darmond, Grace, 406
Daughter of the Gods, 414
Davies, Marion, 344
Day, Richard, 492
De Acosta, Mercedes, 64, 483
De Certeau, Michel, 544, 545
DeCordova, Richard, 366–367

INDEX

Deleuze, Gilles, 539
Delsarteanism, 231, 233, 234
D'Emilio, John, 380–381
DeMille, Cecil B., 243, 334; sex comedies of, 298–322
Denig, Linda, 280–281
De Putti, Lya, 379
Deren, Maya, 70
Diaghilev, Sergei, 480
Dietrich, Marlene, 63, 64, 67, 376
Digital Imaging Technologies, 10, 552–568
Dijkstra, Bram, 360, 398
Dillaye Family, 44
Divine Woman, The, 483
Doane, Mary Ann, 4, 203, 210, 221, 223, 423, 430–431
Dodge, Grace H., 176
Doll's House, A, 64, 77
DOMITOR (International Society for the Study of Early Cinema), 25 n. 23
Don't Change Your Husband, 300–314, 316–317, 321
Doria, Gisaliana, 20, 458
Dorothy Vernon of Hadden Hall, 354, 363
Douglas, Ann, 40, 379
Dracula, 381
Dressler, Marie, 406, 422, 425
Drew, Sidney, 255
Drunkard's Reformation, A, 170
Dulac, Germaine, 89, 122, 489
Dumb Girl of Portici, 277
Duncan, Isadora, 231, 233, 234
Dyer, Richard, 76, 88, 98, 154, 389

Eakin, Paul, 37
Early Cinema: and archival research, 3; and authorship, 88–111; birth control films in, 270–293; and Chinese film culture, 501–524; in cross-cultural context, 11; and ethnicity, 11, 61, 63, 374–401; and female directors, 90, 119–136; husband/wife teams in, 118 n. 72; and immigration, 374–401; Italian divas in, 444–470; and masculinity, 141–160; meanings and reconceptualization of, 6–12, 504; memoirs of female figures in, 55 n. 26; and modernity, 5, 14, 21–22, 530–549; and race, 2, 141, 155–160, 261–266; reception studies in, 233; white slave films in, 271, 275
Eastman, Max, 233
Eco, Umberto, 14
Edison, Thomas, 262, 543
Edison Manufacturing Company, 16, 126, 141–160
Eiffel, Gustave, 42
Eisenstein, Sergei, 48
Electrocuting an Elephant, 535
Ella Cinders, 227, 228–230
Elsaesser, Thomas, 5, 554, 566–567
Enemies of Women, 240
Enlighten Thy Daughter, 284
Erens, Patricia, 3
Eugenics, 275–276
Ewen, Elizabeth, 318
Execution By Hanging, An, 535
Execution of a Spy, 535
Exploits of Elaine, The, 405, 414
Extra Girl, The, 420

Fairbanks, Douglas, 99, 366–367, 413
Fan magazines, 334–345
Fantomas, 195, 199
Farfalletta (Valentina Frascaroli), 457, 458
Fass, Paula, 338, 361
Fatal Ring, The, 405, 414
Fate in Tears and Laughter, 508–509, 512
Fazenda, Louise, 344
Feature Players, 90, 122
Federation Internationale des Archives du Film (FIAF), 1, 25 n. 23; annual conference of, 503
Feminism: crisis in, 2
Femme fatale, 75, 77, 78, 79
Fetterley, Judith, 40
Feuillade, Louis, 17, 195, 199, 206, 216, 217
Filibus, 451, 452, 453
Fitzgerald, F. Scott, 299
Fitzgerald, Zelda, 299
Flaming Youth, 227
Flanerie, 167, 203–208, 211, 213, 214, 217, 537, 552–568
Flapper, The, 299

577

Flappers, 17–18, 299, 339–341; and film, 221–243
Flesh and the Devil, 483
Fletcher, Adele Whitely, 78, 81
Florida Enchantment, A, 18, 251–266
Folies-Bergere, 201
Foolish Wives, 484
Fool There Was, A, 202–203, 374, 393
Ford, Francis, 122
Forster, Annette, 2
Foster, Gwendolyn Audrey, 126, 130
Foster, Hal, 430
Foucault, Michel, 168, 300, 322
Foundling, The, 351
Freedman, Estelle, 380–381
Freeman, Mark, 35
Freeman, Paul, 31
Freud, Sigmund, 4–5, 43, 45, 47, 300, 420, 435, 539, 540, 542
Friedberg, Anne, 10, 22, 553, 555, 557, 559–560, 562
Friese-Greene, William, 530
Fuller, Kathryn, 334
Fuller, Loie, 467
Fuller, Mary, 195, 419–420
Fuoco, Il, 464

Gaines, Jane, 1, 121
Gallone, Carmine, 465–466
Gallone, Soava, 465
Garbo, Greta, 20, 21, 63, 64, 376, 476–496
Gardner, Helen, 1, 90
Gaumont, Leon, 34, 104, 105, 106, 107, 120, 199
Gaumont Studio (House of Gaumont), 42, 46, 50, 90, 104–105, 195, 217
Gauntier, Gene, 90, 122. *See also* Feature Players
Gautier, Theophile, 202
Gay Shoe Clerk, The, 152
"Gaze" theory, 4
Gibbons, Cedric, 478, 480, 492
Gibson, Helen, 406, 414, 418
Gibson girl, 299
Gilbreath, Frank B., 533
Gilman, Charlotte Perkins, 300
Gilman, Sander, 79
Gilmore, Leigh, 31, 44, 49

Giornate del Cinema Muto, 25 n. 23, 504
Girl with the Jazz Heart, The, 233
Gish, Lillian, 37, 404, 477, 507
Glaum, Louise, 423
Gleber, Anke, 204, 562
Glickman, Lawrence, 178–189
Glyn, Elinor, 243
Goethe, Johann Wolfgang, 532–533
Golddiggers of 1935, 21, 544–549
Goldman, Emma, 280
Gompers, Samuel, 179–180
Goodman, Theodosia. *See* Bara, Theda
Gooson, Stephen, 480
Graduate, The, 235
Graham, Martha, 231, 233, 234
Grapevine Video, 126, 127, 128, 129, 130, 132
Grauman, Sid, 317
Grieveson, Lee, 272
Griffith, D.W., 5, 37, 103, 136, 170, 263, 271, 362, 363, 367, 400, 404, 414
Griffith, Richard, 389
Guinan, Texas, 406, 425
Gunning, Tom, 5, 24 n. 12, 170, 204, 210, 254, 422, 516, 534; and cinema of attractions, 159, 262, 535, 563
Gustafson, Greta Louise. *See* Garbo, Greta
Guy-Blaché, Alice, 3, 14, 29–50, 89, 90, 94–95, 101–108, 120, 122, 123, 136; disappearance from history of, 29–30; memoirs of, 33–50, 90; as mother of cinema, 56 n. 35. *See also The Lost Garden: The Life and Cinema of Alice Guy-Blaché*
Gypsy Blood, 387–388, 391, 396

Hales, Peter Bacon, 185
Hall, G. Stanley, 144
Hall, Gladys, 78, 81
Hall, Stuart, 252
Hand That Rocks the Cradle, The, 18, 270, 271, 284–292
Hansen, Juanita, 406, 420, 421–422
Hansen, Miriam, 9, 10, 22, 61, 71–72, 81, 333, 431, 535, 553–555, 558–559
Haraway, Donna, 552
Harrison, Louis Reeves, 169, 182

INDEX

Hart, Lynda, 215
Hastie, Amelie, 2, 102, 103
Hawks, Howard, 89
Hays, Will, 66
Hazards of Helen, The, 414
Heart of Nora Flynn, The, 306
Heath, Stephen, 98
Henry, Gale, 90
Here Lies the Heart, 64. See also De Acosta, Mercedes
Hidden Hand, The, 423
Higashi, Sumiko, 3
His Forgotten Wife, 302
Hitchcock, Alfred, 490
Hoganson, Kristin, 155
Holland, Vyvyan, 68
Hollywood Babylon, 69
Holmes, Helen, 407, 432, 434, 436
Horak, Jan-Christopher, 69
Hotel Imperial, 377–378
How Not to Dress, 476
How to Educate a Wife, 302
Hu, Die, 514
Hu, Shi, 519–520, 521, 524
Huyssen, Andreas, 511
Hypocrites, 273

Imperialism (imperial ideologies), 16, 141–160, 376–401
Ince, Thomas, 169
Internet Movie Database, 129
Irma Vep, 17, 195
Iron Claw, The, 405, 416
It, 237–243

Jay, Martin, 418
Jazz Singer, The, 263
Joan the Woman, 316
Jolson, Al, 263
Joyce, Alice, 406
Judex, 201, 216
Justitia, 456

Kaplan, Amy, 143, 158, 376
Karenne, Diana, 454–455, 458
Ke, Lin, 518–519
Kellerman, Annette, 406, 414–415
Kelley, Mary, 39–41, 43
Kendall, Elizabeth, 74, 232
Kenyon, Doris, 406, 423, 425

King, Anita, 406, 415, 416, 417
King, Mollie, 406, 423
Kirby, Lynne, 150, 422, 436–437
Kiss, The, 20, 483, 488–494, 495, 496–497
Kracauer, Siegfried, 547
Krutzen, Michaela, 493, 495
Kuhn, Annette, 9
Kuntzel, Thierry, 12

LaBadie, Florence, 406
Lacan, Jacques, 433
Lacassin, Francis, 29, 108
Lambert, Gavin, 60, 63, 65
Lang, Fritz, 465–466, 511, 563
Laplanche, Jean, 543
Lasky, Jesse L., 301, 310, 315, 321
"Lasky" lighting, 334
Last Adventure, The, 456
Lauritzen, Einar, 120, 123, 129
Leab, Daniel, 252
Le Gallienne, Eva, 64
LeGoff, Jacques, 36
Lejeune, C.A., 70, 73
Leventon, Mariam, 63. See also Nazimova, Alla
Leys, Ruth, 435
Lightning Raider, The, 405–406
Lindsey, Vachel, 360, 368, 369
Lippman, Walter, 321
Little, Anna, 406
Little Annie Rooney, 352, 355, 356, 363, 364
Little Lord Fauntleroy, 352, 354
Little Princess, A, 351, 352
Lloyd, Harold, 413
Lois Weber Productions, 90
Lonely Villa, The, 362
Loos, Anita, 3, 225
Lost Garden: The Life and Cinema of Alice Guy-Blaché, 30, 32, 35, 39
Lost in the Jungle, 421
Lot in Sodom, 71
Love, 483, 493
Love Dodger, The, 340–342
Love Everlasting, 448
Love Light, The, 354
Loves of an Actress, 398
Lubitsch, Ernst, 375, 382, 385, 387, 391

Lucille Love, the Girl of Mystery, 415
Lumière Brothers, 30, 530, 566
Lundquist, Gunnar, 120, 123, 129
Lupino, Ida, 89
Lynd, Helen, 337
Lynd, Robert, 337

Mabel Normand Feature Film Film Company, 90. *See also* Normand, Mabel
Mabel's Married Life, 120
Macpherson, Jeanie, 303–304, 307, 308, 311
Madison, Cleo, 406, 429
Mahan, Alfred Thayer, 143
Making Both Ends Meet: The Income and Outlay of New York Working Girls, 166–167, 173, 174, 175–177, 186
Male and Female, 304, 310
Maman Poupee, 465
Mandarin Film Company, 90
Manning, Susan, 234
Marcus, Jane, 80
Marey, Etienne-Jules, 533, 541, 549
Marinetti, F.T., 430, 445–447, 455, 463, 543
Marion, Frances, 3, 354
Mark of Zorro, The, 99
Marks, Elaine, 64
Marple, Albert, 412
Marsh, Mae, 414
Marshall, Glesca, 64
Masks' Counter-Attack, The, 456
Mata Hari, 483, 485–486, 493, 495
Maternity (The Cry of the Unborn), 291–292, 424
Mathis, June, 99
May, Lary, 256
May Fourth Movement, 518–519
Mayne, Judith, 6, 92
McClinton, Katharine, 481
McMahan, Alison, 1, 90, 102, 103
Melies, Georges, 30, 103, 228, 411, 536
Melville, G. W., 143
Memoirs of a Star, 375
Memoria dell'altro, La, 451–453, 455, 463
Menichelli, Pina, 464
Merton of the Movies, 99, 335

Metro (later MGM), 63, 64, 65, 476
Metropolis, 465–466, 511
Metz, Christian, 12, 38, 39, 433, 556
Michelena, Beatrice, 413
Mimesis, 432–437
Miracle of Life, The, 272
Mix, Tom, 413
M'Liss, 350
Money Demon, 509, 512
Moon, Michael, 79
Moore, Colleen, 17, 224, 226–230, 232, 233, 234, 237, 243, 400
Moore, Owen, 366
Moreau, Gustave, 464
Motion Picture Classic, 316–317, 384, 398
Motion Picture Magazine, 63, 78, 81, 319, 321, 409, 410, 427
Motion Picture News, 316, 317, 318, 350
Motion Picture Patents Company, 254
Motion Picture World, 77, 278
Motography, 183
Moving Picture Weekly, 282
Moving Picture World, 50, 123, 125, 131, 169, 182, 280, 288, 290, 416
Mugnier-Serand, Yvonne, 108, 109
Mulvey, Laura, 22, 556
Munsterberg, Hugo, 409
Musidora, 197, 199, 200–202, 206, 216–217, 436
Musil, Robert, 536
Musser, Charles, 5, 107, 124, 126, 158, 159
Muybridge, Eadweard, 152, 153, 532, 533, 541
Mysteres de New York, Les, 199
Mysterious Lady, The, 483

Naldi, Nita, 376, 379
National Consumers League, 166, 177
Naughty But Nice, 228
Nazimova, Alla, 11, 15, 60–83, 99, 344; exotic ethnicity of, 76–77; Jewishness of, 67, 77, 78–79; and lesbian representational history, 60. *See also* Leventon, Mariam; Winters, Peter M.
Nazimova Productions, 90
Nederlands Filmmuseum, 127
Negra, Diane, 203, 208–209

INDEX

Negri, Ada, 375
Negri, Pola, 11, 20, 63, 374–401. *See also* Chalupec, Apolonia
Nell Shipman Company, 90. *See also* Shipman, Nell
"New Woman," 9, 14, 16, 19, 80, 142; and consumer culture, 298–322; Ibsen's version of, 76–77
New York Dramatic Mirror, 183, 260, 280, 288
New York Hat, The, 362–363, 364
Niblo, Fred, 99
Ninth Infantry Boys Morning Wash, 151
Nora, Pierre, 32, 35
Normand, Mabel, 1, 123–124, 406, 420
Notari, Elvira, 13, 92, 100, 105, 556
Novarro, Ramon, 335, 485

Odem, Mary E., 174
Olcott, Sidney, 122
Old Ironsides, 99
Old Wives for New, 300–314, 315, 316, 319
Olney, Martha, 322
Orchids and Ermine, 227
Orientalism, 61, 310
Orphan Rescues Grandfather, 521
Orry-Kelly, 480
Our Dancing Daughters, 221–224, 226, 234–236, 299, 338

Parallax historiography, 10, 22, 552–568
Paramount Studios, 375, 382–383, 384, 387, 388, 391, 398, 415, 416
Parchesky, Jennifer, 121
Paris, Barry, 482
Park, Ida May, 95, 136
Passion, 387, 390–394, 396
Pathe Exchange, 199
Patten, Simon N., 175
Pavlova, Anna, 277
Payne Fund Study, 221–223, 225, 235, 238
Pearl of the Army, 405
Peary, Gerald, 29, 30
Pease, Donald, 376
Peiss, Kathy, 318
Perfect Flapper, The, 227
Perils of Pauline, The, 199, 405, 414, 419

Perkins, David, 12
Petro, Patrice, 552
Phillips, David Graham, 303
Photoplay, 19, 62, 78, 283, 319, 384, 386, 417, 483, 492, 494; fiction of Adela Rogers St. Johns in, 333–345
Pickford, Mary, 19, 63, 122, 126, 301, 349–369, 404. *See also* Smith, Gladys
Pietrovskij, Adrian, 415
Plant, Sadie, 563
Plastic Age, The, 299
Polglase, Van Nes, 480
Polidor, Fernand Guillaume, 456
Pollyanna, 352, 365
Polo, Eddie, 413
Poor Little Rich Girl, 351
Porter, Edwin S., 103, 534
Port of Missing Girls, The, 342–343
Positivism, 14
"Postfeminism," 2. *See also* Feminism (crisis in)
Powell, Dick, 544–546
Price, Steven, 81
Production Code, 232
Progressive era, 166–187, 197
Pull Down the Curtains, 543

Question, The, 272–273, 274

Rabinovitz, Lauren, 240
Race, The, 416–417
Rags, 350
Rambova, Natacha, 64, 65, 71, 72, 74, 78, 79, 376. *See also* Shaughnessey, Winifred
Rapsodia Satanica, 467, 468
Reading the Death Sentence, 535
Reagan, Nancy, 67
Rebecca of Sunnybrook Farm, 351, 357–359, 364, 365
Rebel Without a Cause, 235
Red Shadow of Tears, The, 508
Reformers, The, 169
Reid, Dorothy Davenport, 90
Reisfeld, Gray, 494–495
Resurrection of Conscience, The, 514
Revenge of the Actress, 522–523
Rich Men's Wives, 302
Riis, Jacob, 185

Riviere, Joan, 356
Rohauer, Raymond, 68
Roland, Ruth, 406, 407, 428
Rony, Fatimah, 157, 565
Roosevelt, Teddy, 144; and the Rough Riders, 155
Rosen, Marjorie, 3
Rosita, 354
Ross, Andrew, 69
Rotundo, Anthony, 144
Rubinstein, Ida, 79, 464
Rudman, Lisa, 381
Ruggles of Red Gap, 99
Russo, Vito, 251
Ryan, Mary P., 225–226, 299, 338

Sadoul, Georges, 42, 103
Sage-femme de Premiere Classe, 103–104, 116 n. 53
Said, Edward, 158
Sais, Marin, 406
Saladin, Linda, 75
Salome, 15; Gustave Moreau's version of, 464; and queer historiography, 60. *See also* Nazimova, Alla
Samson, Emilie, 20, 458
Sanger, Dorothy, 18
Sanger, Margaret, 270, 271, 275, 280, 283, 284–286, 290–291, 292, 299–300
Sansonette (Linda Albertini), 20, 457–458
Sartre, Jean-Paul, 424
Saturday Evening Post, 303, 318
Schmalhausen, Samuel D., 485
Schmidt, Christel, 126
Schnapp, Jeffrey, 431
Schwartz, Hillel, 224, 234
Schwartz, Vanessa, 7
Secret of the Submarine, 422
Sekula, Allan, 536, 537
Serial-queen melodramas, 195, 404–437
Shapiro, Ann-Louise, 198
Shaughnessey, Winifred, 64. *See also* Rambova, Natacha
Sherwood, Robert E., 62
Shining Adventure, The, 128, 129, 132
Shipman, Nell, 1, 90, 92, 123, 406
Shoes, 16, 127, 167, 169, 170–172, 174, 175, 176, 177, 178, 181–182, 184–185

Showalter, Elaine, 80
Shub, Esfir, 3, 122
Shuffle Along, 232
Sigsbee, Charles, 145–146
Simmel, Georg, 427–428, 536, 538, 543
Singer, Ben, 413, 427
Single Standard, The, 20, 483, 486–488, 489, 491, 493, 496
Singsong Girl Red Peony, The, 511
Sklar, Kathryn Kish, 177
Slide, Anthony, 3, 90, 125, 129, 130, 133
Sloan, Kay, 169
Smiling Madame Beudet, The, 489–490
Smith, Albert E., 256, 257
Smith, Gladys, 349. *See also* Pickford, Mary
Smith-Rosenberg, Carroll, 299, 300
Smuts, Robert, 391
Sobchack, Vivian, 521
Social Darwinism, 141
Solax, 32, 34, 45, 46, 48, 50, 90, 123. *See* Guy-Blaché, Alice
Sontag, Susan, 68
Soul of Yu Li, The, 514
Spanish-American War: actualities of, 16, 141–160
Spanish Dancer, The, 396
Sparrows, 352, 363, 364–365
Springer, John Parris, 342
Squaw Man, The, 301
St. Denis, Ruth, 231, 233
St. Johns, Adela Rogers, 19, 333–345, 486
Stacey, Jackie, 9
Stage Fright, 490
Staiger, Janet, 8, 9, 107, 202, 208, 333
Stamp, Shelley, 2, 71
Star Prince, The, 128, 129, 130, 131–132
Stella Maris, 364
Stewart, Gloria, 545
Stillman, J.D.B., 532
Storey, Edith, 251, 253, 259–260
Strachey, James, 43
Studlar, Gaylyn, 71, 74, 75, 79, 142, 223, 334, 335
Style Moderne, 21
Suds, 364
Sumurun, 375
Sunset Boulevard, 63

INDEX

Susman, Warren, 303
Swanson, Gloria, 301, 302, 307, 311–313, 319, 320–321, 387, 399
Sweet, Blanche, 344

Tarde, Gabriel, 538
Temple, Shirley, 367
Tenth U.S. Infantry, Second Battalion, Leaving Cars, 153, 154, 156
Tenth U.S. Infantry Disembarking from Cars, 153
Tentler, Leslie, 390
Tess of the Storm Country, 350, 352
Theweleit, Klaus, 430
Thiberville, Anatole, 101, 106
Third Republic, 196–197, 203
Thompson, Kristen, 8, 9, 70, 71
Through the Back Door, 352, 354
Tillie Wakes Up, 422
Too Much Wife, 302
Torrent, The, 20, 477, 478, 483, 486, 495
Traffic in Souls, 274, 275, 563
Traversari, Ester Danesi, 461, 462
Travis, Jennifer, 80
Treloar, Al, 153
Trust Your Wife, 302
Turner Classic Movies, 1, 23 no. 4
Turner, Florence, 90
Tydeman, William, 81

Ullman, Sharon, 258
Uncle Josh at the Moving Picture Show, 534
United Artists, 61, 66, 352
U.S. Battleship Indiana, The, 148
U.S. Cavalry Supplies Unloading at Tampa, Florida, 149

Valentino, Rudolph, 65, 98, 335, 343, 396, 555
Valley of Decision, The, 284
Vamp, The, 202
Vampires, 379–383
Vampires, Les, 17, 195–197, 201, 205–216
"Vamps," 14, 61, 74, 77, 202–203, 338, 339–341, 374–401. *See also* Femme Fatale
Van Enger, Charles, 65
Van Tuyle, Bert, 123
Variety, 75, 78, 131, 260, 316, 317, 351

Vicinus, Martha, 361
Vinciarelli, Lauretta, 468–469
Virilio, Paul, 566
Vitagraph, 18, 74, 251, 254–258
Von Stroheim, Eric, 484

Walcamp, Marie, 420–421, 428
Wang, Hanlun, 514, 521–524
Ward, Fannie, 334
Warhol, Andy, 71
Warrenton, Lule, 90
Watson, James, 71
Webber, Melville, 71
Weber, Lois, 3, 18, 45, 46, 48, 63, 95, 102, 122, 127, 169, 270, 273, 275, 281, 282, 283, 284, 285, 290, 292. *See also* Lois Weber Productions
Wee Scotch Piper, The, 129, 133
"Welfare" films, 166–187
West, Mae, 232
What Happened on Twenty-third Street, New York City, 152
Where Are My Children?, 18, 270, 272–292
Which One Shall It Be?, 131, 132–133
White, Pearl, 195, 199, 404–407, 413–414, 415, 416–417, 419, 434, 456
Why Change Your Wife?, 300–301, 303–315, 315, 316, 317–318, 319
Wiegman, Robyn, 11
Wilde, Oscar, 15, 60–62, 65, 67, 68, 69, 72, 74, 79, 80, 81, 82
Wild Orchids, 20, 483, 484–485, 493
Williams, Kathlyn, 195, 406, 420–421, 426, 428
Williams, Linda, 4, 152
Wilson, Elizabeth, 213–215
Windy Day on the Roof, 152
Wine of Youth, 299
Wings, 468–470
Winokur, Mark, 479, 480, 486
Winters, Peter M., 65. *See also* Nazimova, Alla
Wolff, Janet, 233, 562
Wollen, Peter, 79
Woman of Affairs, A, 483, 493
Woman of the World, A, 398
Women Film Pioneers (Project), 1, 23 n. 4, 121

583

Xuan, Jinglin, 507–508, 510, 511–512, 514, 516–517, 521, 523–524

Yang, Naimei, 514
Yates, Frances, 47
Yin, Mingzhu, 514
Young, Clara Kimball, 414

Zecca, Ferdinand, 103
Zeeman, E.D., 424
Zhang, Zhiyun, 514
Zhuang Zi Tests His Wife, 513
Ziegfeld Follies, 74
Zukor, Adolph, 301, 315, 318, 382, 383

LIBRARY OF CONGRESS CATALOGING-IN-PUBLICATION DATA

A feminist reader in early cinema / edited by Jennifer M. Bean and Diane Negra.

p. cm.— (A Camera Obscura book)

Includes index.

ISBN 0-8223-3025-3 (cloth : alk. paper) —

ISBN 0-8223-2999-9 (pbk. : alk. paper)

1. Women in motion pictures.   2. Women in the motion picture industry.   3. Feminism and motion pictures.   4. Feminist film criticism.   I. Bean, Jennifer M.   II. Negra, Diane.

PN1995.9.W6 F467   2002

791.43′652042—dc21   2002007087

www.ingramcontent.com/pod-product-compliance
Lightning Source LLC
Chambersburg PA
CBHW022132300426
44115CB00006B/148